Prophets of the Revolution

❧❧❧

By Robert J. Alexander

    The Peron Era (1951)

    Communism in Latin America (1957)

    The Bolivian National Revolution (1958)

    The Struggle for Democracy in Latin America (1961)
       (co-author with Charles O. Porter)

    Prophets of the Revolution (1962)

Prophets of the Revolution

Profiles of Latin American Leaders

Robert J. Alexander

The Macmillan Company

Fourth Printing 1969

The Macmillan Company
Collier-Macmillan Canada Ltd., Toronto, Ontario

Printed in the United States of America

Library of Congress catalog card number: 62-7363

To Margaret Alexander Rado

Preface

This volume is the product of two decades of research in Latin American affairs. My interest in the other twenty American republics was first aroused while I was a student at Columbia University in the late 1930's and was fortunate enough to take several courses with Dr. Frank Tannenbaum. At that time Dr. Tannenbaum was intimately connected with the events transpiring in Mexico under the leadership of President Lázaro Cárdenas, and had a vast knowledge of affairs in the other Latin American nations as well. Because of his personal contacts and sympathy with the changes taking place throughout Latin America, Dr. Tannenbaum was able to arouse a lasting interest in the area not only in me but in scores of other students who were lucky enough to come under his influence. Many of the younger generation of Latin American scholars in this country owe him a lasting debt of gratitude.

My first field of research in Latin American affairs was the trade-union and Socialist movements of the area. However, investigations in these fields inevitably led to a wide interest in the economic, social, and political problems of Latin America. They led, too, to a realization that Latin American social reform was not following any guidelines laid down in Europe or anywhere else but rather was opening new paths of its own. It became clear to me that in their attempt to modernize their countries, raise the productivity and the levels of living of their peoples, and develop new political institutions, many Latin American political leaders were learning by doing rather than by trying to pattern their ideas and policies on those first adopted elsewhere. Indeed, the Latin Americans have frequently been pioneers in the fields of economic development, social legislation, and modern constitutional law.

Although there is a great deal of variation in the approaches which individual Latin American political leaders have taken to the task of bringing their nations into the twentieth century, it seemed to me that the areas of agreement among many of them were broader than their divergences. This fact is the basic inspiration of the present volume. I hope that in its pages I have been able to present more or less adequately the main guidelines which have been followed by the outstanding figures in what I have chosen to call the "Latin American Revolution."

I have been fortunate to know a number of the people whose careers I have traced in the following pages. I consider José Figueres, Rómulo Betancourt and Victor Raúl Haya de la Torre among my best Latin American friends. I have had the chance to converse at greater or less length with Arturo Alessandri, Víctor Paz Estenssoro, Hernán Siles, Juan Perón, and Luis Muñoz Marín. I have heard Fidel Castro speak on several occasions. Unfortunately, I was never able to meet Getulio Vargas or Lázaro Cárdenas, and José Batlle y Ordóñez died while I was still too young to be interested in him or in Latin America. However, I have long been a student of the careers of these last three and hope that I have been able to understand what it was they were trying to accomplish, and how they have gone about carrying out their objectives.

I am indebted to many people who have helped to make this book possible. Eight of the men here discussed have submitted to my questioning, and I must here thank them for their patience. Mrs. Frances Mastroianni, of Rutgers University, has spent long hours in typing this manuscript, and Robert De Maria of The Macmillan Company, has spent even more time in editing the book. I am also grateful to Clarence Senior for his extensive and excellent criticisms of the manuscript. And as always, my wife, Joan Alexander, has helped to develop it from the stage of a nebulous idea to printed volume by listening patiently to long discussions of the work, and by contributing insights of her own, drawn from her personal contacts with some of the people treated in it and from her general observations on things Latin American. Much of what is good in this work is due to the people I have mentioned; all of the errors are my own.

Rutgers University
New Brunswick, N.J.
July, 1961

Contents

Introduction

"Revolution" is a respectable word in Latin America. Leading public figures pledge their loyalty to one revolution or another. The word is used in the names of political parties in a dozen countries. The "Party of Revolutionary Institutions" rules Mexico, the "National Revolutionary Movement" has been governing Bolivia for nearly a decade.

The average United States citizen is not unacquainted with what he believes to be the Latin American proclivity for revolutions. About the only time he reads about the other American republics in his newspapers is when the government of one or another of them is overthrown. "Revolutions," therefore, seem to him to be endemic in the area.

However, the word "revolution" is used very differently in the two hemispheres. What the North American reads about in his press as "revolutions" in Latin America are more often than not mere *coups d'état* or military uprisings by discontented colonels or generals. In contrast, when the Latin American uses the word he means a fundamental alteration of the political, social, and economic life of his country. It is this type of revolution that we are talking about in the present volume.

The men discussed in these pages have all sought to lead their countries through a process of basic transformation, to bring them into the twentieth century, if you will. They have sought to destroy old institutions and to put new ones in their place. They have attempted to break old and rigid traditions in politics and in social and economic organization. They have sought to make agrarian reform, modernized agriculture, manufacturing industry, labor unions, social insurance, and other innovations a part of the life of their nations.

Furthermore, these men have all been indigenous social re-

1

formers. Although they have not been unaware of events taking place elsewhere in the world, and have occasionally borrowed ideas from outside the hemisphere, they have sought to bring about a revolution cut to the cloth of their own particular nations. They have been nationalists in politics and in intellectual inspiration. A few of them have interpreted nationalism as loyalty to a concept of Latin America as a single nation. Though several of them aligned themselves with political currents from outside the hemisphere, they have not been subservient to the dictates or the ideas of any extra-Latin American power or political movement.

Of course, the Latin American Revolution is part of a worldwide movement. In recent years virtually all the "underdeveloped" countries of the world have sought to catch up with the nations of Western Europe and North America which preceded them in the path of industrialization, and to adapt their economic, social, and political institutions to this change. However, in many ways the Latin American countries were pioneers in this movement. They were already independent while most of the countries of Africa and Asia were still colonies, and thus were able to strike out on original paths while their counterparts in these continents were still struggling against imperial rule. The reforms of José Batlle in Uruguay and the reforms of the early years of the Mexican Revolution preceded the Bolsheviks' coming to power in Russia by at least half a decade. Most Latin American nations had experimented with social security and labor legislation and were attempting to industrialize while the present leaders of Asian and African nations were still languishing in colonial jails.

The men whose lives and work are sketched in this volume have varied greatly in personal characteristics. Physically, some, like Arturo Alessandri and Getulio Vargas, were short men who seemed driven by a kind of Napoleonic determination to make people forget this fact. Others, like Perón, were large men whose physical attraction was a factor in their success. Intellectually, some of these men have been remarkable thinkers and philosophers, as is Haya de la Torre, while others have been relatively unconcerned with ideas.

In social backgrounds, too, these men differ profoundly. Two of them, José Batlle y Ordóñez and Hernán Siles, were sons of former presidents and were men of influence from their youth. Others, like Lázaro Cárdenas and Rómulo Betancourt, came up from very humble beginnings.

However, all the "Prophets of the Revolution" have some characteristics in common. They are all men of action, and have spent a large part of their lives in the rough-and-tumble of politics. All are men of strong character with an ability to influence and lead others. And all have played key roles in changing the direction of their countries' history.

It has long been the author's contention that the best guarantee against the triumph of fascist or communist totalitarianism in Latin America is the growth of indigenous movements of social reform which can carry out the changes long overdue in the region, and direct the process of economic development and industrialization which will make possible the improvement in the standards of living of the people of the area. Political democracy can be solidly established in most of these countries only if the social and economic revolution becomes an accomplished fact.

However, the pages which follow indicate that democracy is not an inevitable result of social revolution. Although most of the men we discuss were convinced democrats, three were not: Vargas, Perón, and Castro. Furthermore, Vargas and Castro showed themselves willing to throw in their lot with the particular brand of totalitarianism which was in the ascendant at the time they were in power—Nazi-Fascism in the case of Vargas, Communism in the case of Castro.

Indeed, the essence of the revolutionary drama being acted out in Latin America today is contained in these contrasting attitudes of Vargas, Perón, and Castro on the one hand and the other revolutionary leaders on the other. The major question facing Latin America today is whether the necessary social and economic changes can be brought about through the instruments of political democracy and without alliance with totalitarianism on a world scale. Perón and Vargas posed this question ten to twenty years ago, Fidel Castro poses it today.

It is within the foregoing frame of reference that we have chosen the twelve men who are discussed in the present volume. There is, we believe, a certain logic both in selection of the men for discussion and in the order in which they are presented in the pages that follow. José Batlle y Ordóñez was chronologically the first of the Prophets of the Revolution. He was an initiator of labor reform and social security even before World War I, and an experimenter with the use of government institutions for the development of the nation's economy during the same period. He was also a pioneer in attempting to deal with the age-old problem of dictatorship in Latin America and in seeking a formula which would establish a healthy system of political democracy. He set up the framework for his country's development during his own generation and the one that came after him. He is undoubtedly the father of modern Uruguay.

Lázaro Cárdenas, although he did not become president of Mexico until 1934, represents the culmination of a great movement for reform, the Mexican Revolution. He finished the work of transforming the institutional structure of Mexico and laid the basis for the remarkable economic expansion of that country during the past two decades.

Arturo Alessandri belongs to a generation younger than that of Batlle but older than that of most of the other men discussed in this volume. His most significant contributions to the recasting of Chilean economic, social, and political life were made during the 1920's, though he continued to be a powerful force in his country's civic affairs until his death in 1950.

Víctor Raúl Haya de la Torre has been the philosopher of the whole movement for social revolution in Latin America. The parties headed by Rómulo Betancourt in Venezuela, José Figueres in Costa Rica, and Víctor Paz Estenssoro and Hernán Siles in Bolivia freely acknowledge their intellectual debt to Haya de la Torre and the Peruvian Aprista movement. Perón adopted many of the ideas of Aprismo without bothering to credit their origin. Within Peru, his native country, Haya de la Torre has been the most important political figure for more than a generation.

Rómulo Betancourt, José Figueres, and Luis Muñoz Marín, of Venezuela, Costa Rica, and Puerto Rico respectively, have been contemporaries and close friends. Each in his own country has headed a political movement which has pushed forward social and economic change within a framework of political democracy. Each

has been by all odds the outstanding political figure of his generation in his native country, and each has had the qualities of a thinker
and a philosopher as well as those of an expert politician.

Víctor Paz Estenssoro and Hernán Siles have headed a political
group whose program and policies have borrowed much from both
the Mexican Revolution and the Aprista movement. They have
given leadership to a movement for social change in Bolivia which
is the most fundamental alteration in the *status quo* to occur in
any Latin American country since the Mexican Revolution.

Finally, Getulio Vargas, Juan Domingo Perón and Fidel Castro,
though included among those who have led in the process of recasting the fundamental economic, social, and political institutions of
their respective nations, have differed profoundly from all the rest
in one essential respect. Unlike all the others, they have not been
convinced democrats. Each was at one time dictator of his nation,
though Vargas in the last phases of his career governed in a democratic manner. However, both Perón and Vargas were responsible
for transferring power from the rural aristocracy to the urban middle
and working classes and made labor organization, labor legislation,
and social security integral parts of their governments' policies.
They both adopted for the first time in their respective nations an
avowed policy of government support for industrialization. Fidel
Castro's impact on the economy, society and political life of his
country can certainly not be gainsaid.

There may be other men whose importance in transforming
their individual Latin American countries has been equal to that
of those whom we are discussing, but we do not believe so. However,
it is perhaps only right that we explain why some leading figures in
recent Latin American political history have not been included in
this volume.

We have not discussed any leader of the Mexican Revolution
other than Lázaro Cárdenas because at best their contribution to
that movement was a partial one. It was Cárdenas who brought
the great movements of agrarian reform, labor and social legislation, and economic nationalism to fruition and who launched the
process of industrialization on a large scale.

Several Central American figures other than José Figueres might
conceivably have a claim for recognition in these pages. José Arevalo,

ex-President of Guatemala, and President Ramón Villeda Morales of Honduras come immediately to mind. Yet Arevalo bears much of the responsibility for the abortion of the very promising Guatemalan Revolution because of his inability to form a political party of defined Latin American social revolutionary ideology which might have been able to prevent the Guatemalan movement from being made captive and ultimately being sacrificed by the Communists. Villeda Morales is too newly arrived on the scene for us to know whether or not he will measure up to the opportunities presented to him in the most underdeveloped of the Central American republics.

There is no one in Colombia who really rates discussion in the present book. The Liberal Party presidents of the 1930's began a certain process of social change, but they failed to attack the country's fundamental problems. Jorge Eliecer Gaitán, had he lived, might have developed into the type of leader we are discussing here, but he was assassinated at a time when it was difficult to say whether he was going to lead a real revolution or was merely a popular demagogue. It is too early to say whether Alberto Lleras Camargo will bring about these changes.

Arturo Frondizi, elected president of Argentina in 1958, may in time develop into the type of man we are discussing. If he can mend the damage which Perón did to the economy of Argentina, he may well be able to build a solid foundation for political democracy and a strong national economy on the basis of the social and political changes which Perón himself left as his heritage, as well as pushing these changes still further. However, Frondizi's achievements in this regard remain to be accomplished and are not a matter for historical analysis.

Two dictators, Somoza of Nicaragua and Trujillo of the Dominican Republic, have brought about some of the changes which constitute the binding theme of this book. They both started the process of economic development, and both established social institutions which under democratic regimes may yet be of benefit in the fulfillment of the Latin American Revolution. Yet both these men treated their country so much like a personal plantation that they really belong in the ranks of the old-fashioned military *caudillos* rather than in those of the modern social revolutionaries of

Latin America. Furthermore, Trujillo, at least, maintained such an absolute tyranny that it is doubtful if the Dominican Republic can learn the ways of democracy within the next generation.

Finally, one might mention Luiz Carlos Prestes of Brazil and Vicente Lombardo Toledano of Mexico. Prestes achieved almost legendary fame as a precursor and missionary of social change in Brazil in the 1920's. Lombardo Toledano presided over the first successful hemispheric confederation of organized workers, and undoubtedly contributed for a while to the strengthening of one of the strongest forces working for social revolution in Latin America, the labor movement. However, both these men are excluded from the pages of our book because they are not indigenous social reformers. Rather, they are part of the international communist movement. Their success would not mean further progress in the Latin American Revolution, but would mean rather that that revolution would be warped so as to fit the mold established by international communism.

We hope that the pages which follow will give the reader a better understanding of the basic forces now at work in the Latin American nations. The problems with which the twelve men here discussed have had to deal are of importance not only to their respective countries but to the hemisphere as a whole. If relations between their nations and the United States are to be established on a firm basis of friendship and cooperation, the first prerequisite is that North Americans have some comprehension of the problems which face the Latin American countries and the various ways by which Latin American political leaders have sought to solve these problems.

José Batlle y Ordóñez,
the Pioneer

Seldom has a nation been as much influenced by the career of one man as was the Republic of Uruguay by the lifework of José Batlle y Ordóñez. Largely through his inspiration and leadership, this little nation on the northern side of the Rio de la Plata estuary was converted from one of the most turbulent and backward of the Latin American nations into the model state of the hemisphere. Batlle's imprint was so great that the lessons learned during his long tutelage were still the most powerful single force in the country's political life a generation after he had passed from the scene.

However, Batlle's influence was not limited to his native country. The social and economic experiments which he launched there were closely watched throughout Latin America. He was the pioneer in the ideas of economic nationalism, social reform, and effective political democracy which became the widely accepted program of political groups and leaders throughout the hemisphere.

Throughout the colonial period Uruguay had been the scene of a long struggle between the Portuguese and Spanish empires in America. Lying, as it did, on the borderline between these dominions, it passed back and forth between them throughout the three centuries of Iberian domination of that part of the world. These struggles continued even after the South American nations had broken away from their European mother countries, and Uruguay became the battleground in the clash between the new Empire of Brazil and the Confederation of the Rio de la Plata, which was in time to become the Republic of Argentina.

It was not until 1833 that the formal independence of the Republic of Uruguay was recognized by Brazil and Argentina, and the new nation became in effect a buffer state between its two more powerful neighbors. However, even this recognition did not bring

9

peace to the country. The struggles which had formerly been carried on between two alien powers were now continued between rival political factions within the new republic. The whole history of Uruguay during the nineteenth century is the story of an intense struggle for power between the Colorado Party, which came to be representative of the city of Montevideo and a few of the provincial towns, and the Blanco Party, which was dominant in the countryside.

This internecine struggle frequently broke out in open violence in revolutions and even civil wars. Seldom did a president come into office legally and give up his post to an elected successor. The typical successful politician of the time was a man who was as capable of leading an army in a civil war as he was of making a speech from a party platform. Attempts at compromise between the rival factions were frequent, but, even when they succeeded, the agreements arrived at were seldom kept for long.

This constant internal warfare was fed by foreign influences. Both the Argentines and the Brazilians were constantly meddling in the country's affairs, backing one party or the other. In the 1860's the famous Paraguayan dictator Francisco Solano López did the same thing, with the result that Uruguay was dragged into the famous and debilitating War of the Triple Alliance as an ally of Argentina and Brazil against Paraguay.

Several times the country suffered under severe personal dictatorships. The atmosphere was not conducive to the development of a normal democratic political life, and the overthrow of one tyrant was not infrequently followed by the installation of another.

It was in this atmosphere that José Batlle y Ordóñez was born and brought up. He was the son of a famous Colorado *caudillo,* General Lorenzo Batlle, who was one of the principal leaders of his party in the civil wars and served as president of the republic in the 1860's. Young José Batlle, born in 1856, was well aware of the nature of his country's political life, and very early declared his belief in the necessity of putting an end to the constant quarreling and to the use of force and in the need for establishing sound foundations for a democratic regime.

José Batlle's first love was philosophy. As a very young man in 1879 he formed part of a group of university students and recent graduates who established the Philosophical Section of the Ateneo, a debating society in which all the then fashionable streams of philosophical thought were continually and passionately discussed. He and his associates were highly critical of the popular positivist philosophy, and published a short-lived periodical, *El Espíritu Nuevo,* which defended a deistic "spiritual rationalism" opposed both to positivism and Catholicism.

It was during these early philosophical discussions that José Batlle hammered out the personal philosophy which was to guide him throughout his political career. His firm belief in political democracy and in civil peace became cornerstones of his long career.

Batlle's philosophical studies and disputations were interrupted in November, 1879, when he went to Europe for two years. In the Old World he became acquainted with the political ideas which were then gaining force there, particularly nationalism and socialism. Although his nationalism always remained reasonable and constructive and he never became an avowed advocate of socialism, Batlle was undoubtedly deeply influenced in his thinking by his studies and experiences during these two years in Europe. Upon his return in 1881 Batlle turned to political problems rather than to philosophy.

Meanwhile slow but fundamental changes were coming about in the economic life of his native country. The end of the Corn Laws in Great Britain in 1846 had thrown open the gates of that nation to foodstuffs and raw materials from all over the world. The Rio de la Plata area was particularly influenced by this development, and both Uruguay and its neighbor Argentina soon became important suppliers of these products to the British market.

Uruguay became one of the most important sources of wool for the British textile industry as well as a supplier of meat for the British family table. The grazing industry, which had existed in a somewhat desultory fashion ever since colonial times, received new impetus by the end of the nineteenth century. As the raising of cattle and sheep grew more profitable it became necessary to have facilities to get these products to the port of Montevideo, whence they could be shipped to their markets overseas. Hence, with the help of British investors the development of the railroads began, thus ending the isolation of large parts of the country from the outside world and bringing civilizing and tranquilizing influences to these sections of the nation. By the turn of the century a packinghouse industry had begun to develop in Montevideo, Salta, and one or two other towns.

The economic developments had their inevitable political repercussions. The metropolis began to overshadow the culturally and politically backward hinterland. The urban middle class was strengthened, and a small wage-earning working class developed in the capital and other towns. Immigrant workers from Spain and Italy brought with them the new doctrines of anarchism, socialism, and trade-unionism which were by then gaining ground in their native lands.

The Colorado Party, as the traditional political spokesman for the metropolis, stood to gain from these developments. However, it could do so only if it found a leadership that could make it a spokesman for the new social and economic groups which were coming more and more to dominate Montevideo. José Batlle y Ordóñez provided such leadership.

In 1886 Batlle established a newspaper, *El Día,* which became his personal vehicle and the voice of the younger and more progressive wing of the Colorado Party. Although the newspaper faced a very precarious financial situation during its first years and was subjected to hostile treatment from various governments which Batlle very strongly criticized, it soon became recognized as one of the best journals published in the republic.

Batlle became increasingly involved in practical political activity. As the son of Lorenzo Batlle he had a ready-made position in the councils of the Colorado Party if he wanted to assume it. However, he very soon created a position of his own through his consistent opposition to President Idiarte Borda's dictatorship in the middle 1890's and through his criticism of the role of the military in the country's political life.

In 1897 Juan Lindolfo Cuestos became president. He had pledged himself to the elimination of the military from politics and to the respect for the rights of the opposition. An agreement had been reached in 1896 to put an end, for the time being at least, to the bitter quarrels between the Colorados and the Blancos by giving the latter control of six provinces (departments), while the Colorados remained in charge of the other provinces and of the national government in Montevideo. Local private armies of various Blanco *caudillos* were supposed to be disbanded, though this in fact did not happen.

Batlle played an important role in the administration of President Cuestos. He served as a member of the Council of State and as president of the Senate. In the latter capacity he was for a while Acting President of the Republic when the chief executive was out of the country. His reputation as the leading figure among the younger generation of Colorado leaders rose steadily during the 1890's and early years of the present century.

José Batlle was one of the leading candidates in the presidential election of 1903. He had widespread support from the rank and file of the Colorado Party, but in those days the president was elected by Congress, not by the people. In order to obtain the presidency, therefore, it was necessary to get the adherence of a majority of the members of the legislative branch. During the negotiations which preceded the actual casting of ballots Batlle himself stayed in the background. However, through the skillful maneuvering of his faithful lieutenant Domingo Arenas, Batlle finally was successful. He lined up a majority of the Colorado members of Congress as well as a significant minority of the opposition Blanco Party who were opposed to the leadership of that party's *caudillo* Aparicio Saravia.

One of the first problems that faced Batlle as president was the traditional quarrel of his party with the Blancos. Saravia, the principal Blanco leader and a Gaucho *caudillo* of the old style, a veteran of many military uprisings and civil wars, was restive under the continued control of the Colorados over the central government. For his part, Batlle was anxious to put an end to the arrangement whereby several of the most important provinces were ruled by Blanco officials and constituted virtually a separate nation.

These conflicting attitudes of the traditional parties flared into civil war again shortly after Batlle's inauguration. Although he was anxious to halt the unending series of *coups d'état* and rebellions which had been Uruguay's fate since independence, and hoped to do so through establishing a democratic atmosphere in which the opposition could express itself freely and bid for power through the electoral process, he had no alternative but to fight back once Saravia had raised the Blanco forces in outright military insurrection against his government. Indeed, his own son joined the national army which went out to meet the Blancos, and was wounded on the field of battle. After a short campaign the forces of the government were victorious. This was the last civil war Uruguay was to suffer and one of the last armed movements against the government. Under Batlle a new and more peaceful pattern was to be set.

The first four-year term of Batlle was taken up largely with a consolidation of the democratic regime which he had guaranteed to provide. There was the greatest freedom for friends and enemies of the government alike. They could express their opinions in the press and from the tribune, and carry on political agitation, so long as it did not degenerate into overt rebellion against the constituted government.

At the same time the Batlle government began openly to encourage the growth of the labor movement. Since his early days as publisher of *El Día*, Batlle had defended the right of the workers to organize and to bargain with their employers. He had argued that the workers were in the weaker position, and if it was they who appeared to be the aggressive party through launching strikes, this was only because all the employers had to do to win out against the workers' demands was to sit tight and refuse to meet them. It took no positive action on the employers' part to defend their interests, whereas to obtain justice the workers frequently had to withhold their labor from the employers.

As president, Batlle reiterated his belief in the right of the workers to defend their interests. In his first instructions to the police in 1904 Batlle started with the phrase: "The workers have the right to declare themselves on strike." [1] He defended this right so long as he remained president.

The labor movement at this time was largely controlled by anarchosyndicalists who, in theory at least, were strongly opposed to any kind of government. However, Batlle succeeded in winning the confidence and support of many of them, and during his second term in office was able to draw into his administration a number of men who had started out as anarchist labor leaders.

Aside from his sympathetic attitude toward the labor movement, Batlle gave some other indications during his first term of office of the path toward social reform which he would ultimately take. In the field of education he sponsored the establishment of a women's university in Montevideo, a very advanced move at a time when few women were even daring to think of the possibility of receiving an advanced education. He also started a program for extending primary education to all parts of the country, particularly the rural areas, a program which was to have its fruits a couple of generations later when Uruguay came to enjoy one of the highest literacy rates in Latin America.

In December, 1906, three months before the expiration of his first term, Batlle sent to Congress a proposal for a law limiting the working day. It would have established the nine-hour day immediately and the eight-hour day within a year for manual workers, and a limit of eleven hours the first year and ten the second for white-collar employees. The law was not passed at that time, and, in fact, it was ten years before the eight-hour day finally became the law of the land.[2] However, Uruguay, under Batlle's inspiration, was the first country in America to adopt this measure.

Although he failed during his first presidential term to get Congress to adopt the eight-hour day, Batlle did succeed in one important step on behalf of labor. Before his exit from the presidency a new Ministry of Labor and Industry was established for the first time. In this, too, Uruguay was a pioneer in America.

By the end of Batlle's first four-year term the country was quieter and more orderly than it had been in many decades. The question of the presidential succession, which in previous years had caused so much dissension and had frequently even been the cause for revolts, was peaceably solved by the election of Claudio Williman, a Colorado Party member who had served in Batlle's cabinet.

In order not to embarrass his successor Batlle left Uruguay soon after giving up the presidency and spent the next three years in Europe. He traveled widely in the major countries of that continent as well as in Switzerland. His was a study tour, and he sought as much information as possible about various reform movements which were then gaining influence in the Old World.

Perhaps his principal preoccupation was to find in the Old

World an answer to the perennial Latin American problem of preventing the chief executive from absorbing the powers of all three branches of government. In this connection he was particularly impressed with the success of the collegiate government of Switzerland, with its nine-man executive council in place of a president, and the system of having one of the nine serve each year as presiding officer and titular head of state. In the years that followed, Batlle was to spend much time and energy in trying to convince his fellow countrymen of the virtues of this type of government.

Meanwhile the administration of President Williman had been decidedly unpopular with the urban masses, who constituted the chief electoral force of the Colorado Party. The workers and many of the Colorado political leaders as well looked back with considerable yearning to the days when Batlle had been president. Upon his return from Europe in 1910 he was the virtually unanimous choice of his party for another term, to run from 1911 until 1915.

It was during this second period as president that José Batlle began to carry out the program of reform which was continued by his immediate successors and upon which his fame is based. This was an exceedingly varied program, extending into many fields.

During Batlle's second administration he proposed a series of labor and social laws. Not all of these were passed during the four years of his presidency, though all owe their origin directly or indirectly to Batlle. To understand the pioneering nature of Batlle's proposals, one must remember that they were made several years before the leaders of the Mexican Revolution assembled in the Constitutional Convention of Querétaro and directed the country's legislature to enact an extensive body of labor laws, a decade before Chile adopted the hemisphere's first labor code, and two decades before the labor and social security legislation of the New Deal in the United States.

Batlle's proposals included a comprehensive workmen's compensation scheme, which was enacted into law in July, 1914; a law providing for an obligatory day of rest each week; legislation providing leave with pay for women workers for a month before and a month after giving birth; and the famous "law of the chair," which provided that employers must have available chairs upon which their women workers could sit while working. A year after

Batlle left the presidency his suggestion of a limitation of the work day for all workers in industry and commerce to eight hours was finally passed into law.

An extensive social security system was established. This included the enactment of workmen's compensation for workers who were injured or fell sick on the job. It also included a series of retirement funds for different groups of workers, which came to include under their coverage virtually everyone working for wages in the republic.

In his social security legislation Batlle set a bad precedent which was followed by a number of other Latin American nations. Instead of establishing a single over-all system to cover all employed workers the government set up the social security system on the basis of numerous separate funds, each covering a specific group of workers. This resulted in an excessively large bureaucracy and a situation in which entirely too much of the money collected was spent upon costs of administration. However, it proved easier from a political point of view to establish the social security system on this piecemeal basis.

Throughout his administration Batlle continued his policy of friendship toward the trade unions. He refused to allow the police to be used as allies of the employers in their conflicts with their workers, and he used his influence to get employers to deal justly with their employees' organizations.

Typical of his attitude toward the labor movement was an incident which occurred soon after he took office for the second time. The trolley-car workers of Montevideo had been on strike for some time, and the principal central labor group of the time, the Federación Obrera Regional Uruguaya, decided to call a three-day general strike in solidarity with them. In connection with this general walkout the FORU organized a demonstration in the Plaza Independencia and invited Batlle to address the meeting. The Socialist newspaper *El Socialista* reported that "Citizen Batlle y Ordóñez acceded to the request and told the workers that they had been right to unite and organize and that they would be supported by the public authorities in the exercise of their rights so long as they acted legally. The demonstration then broke up in the midst of great enthusiasm." [3]

However, it is worthy of note that Batlle, though favorable to labor, did not enact any legislation designed to tie the trade-union movement to the government's apron strings. He did not adopt the system which subsequently became popular in the Latin American countries of providing for legal registration of the unions and of forcing the employers to deal with registered workers' organizations. Apparently Batlle believed that it was not the government's business to determine who did and who did not represent the workers, or to meddle in the internal affairs of the labor organizations. As a result of this attitude the Uruguayan trade-union movement has remained one of the few in Latin America which are not enmeshed in laws which can be used to put them under the thumb of government labor officials.

Like many Latin American politicians of the succeeding generation, Batlle was a nationalist as well as being aware of social problems. His nationalism was expressed principally in the field of economic policy, where he favored establishment of a more diversified and independent economy.

With the development of the grazing and meat-packing industries the Uruguayan economy had flourished, but at the same time it had become much more unstable than it had been previously, and large segments of it came under the control of foreign investors. The country's prosperity came to depend upon the prices of meat and wool, which tended to fluctuate widely and violently. When these prices rose, the country's economy boomed; when they fell, the nation was thrown into a tailspin. At the same time the packing houses, railroads, public utilities, and much of the insurance and banking business was in the hands of companies with their headquarters in Europe or North America.

Batlle did not want to do anything to undermine the grazing industry, but he felt that it should be supplemented by more extensive agriculture and manufacturing. He also felt that the fundamental institutions of the economy should be placed in the hands of Uruguayans as quickly as possible.

Batlle undertook energetic measures to encourage agriculture. Agricultural experiment stations were established in various parts of the country. Reforestation was undertaken. The importation of agricultural machinery was encouraged by the removal of all tariff duties upon them. Finally, a law was passed allowing the president to expropriate a number of large haciendas and to raise by means of bonds a sum to be used for purchasing them from their owners. The law provided that the haciendas thus acquired were to be subdivided and sold to small farmers, who could finance their purchases through the newly nationalized Mortgage Bank.

Batlle undertook to encourage the growth of manufacturing. One step in this direction was the extension of tariff protection. Among those receiving this protection were manufacturers of shoes, glass, wine, cement, and dairy products. At the same time raw materials needed for Uruguayan industries were freed from all import duties, and other raw materials which were imported for the purpose of processing and reexport were given the benefit of a "drawback"; that is, the duties paid were given back to the importer when the processed products were exported.

The Batlle administration established several research organizations to help new industries. One of these was the Industrial Chemicals Institute, which, according to the law that created it, was "to perfect the technical procedures of our industrial establishments, promote the organization of new industries, and provide information related to improvements in technology." Another was the Fishing Institute, which had much the same purposes.[4]

During Batlle's second administration and in ensuing periods when the government remained largely in the hands of people under his influence, a wide program of nationalization was carried out. The ports were placed under a special government administration, and their operation was reorganized. The telephone and electric-light system was put in the hands of a government-owned corporation. A government insurance company was established which operated in various fields and was given a monopoly in several, notably workmen's compensation insurance.

The banking system was reorganized, with the government taking full ownership of the Central Bank and using its influence to encourage the growth of Uruguayan-owned industries. The old Mortgage Bank was nationalized, and its operations were greatly extended to aid and encourage agriculture. Government firms were established to monopolize the tobacco industry and to set up and operate cement, chemical, and petroleum-refining industries. Much later, in the 1940's, the railroads were almost completely nationalized. A government-owned National Packing House was established in competition with the private firms, thus applying what Franklin D. Roosevelt a generation later called the "yardstick principle" to the country's basic industry.

Batlle thus was also a pioneer in a development which after his death was to become general throughout Latin America, that is, the use of the economic power of the government to encourage the diversification of the national economy and the development of manufacturing. This program of Batlle's was not inspired by any ideological bias in favor of socialism. After his death, however, even the Uruguayan Socialists admitted that it was a program with which they had no basic disagreement. Batlle's inspiration was nationalist. He sought to develop and broaden the economy of Uruguay, and realized that the only institution which was able to undertake this task with some chance of success was the government. The example which he gave was followed during and after the Great Depression by most of the countries of Latin America, and, indeed, was followed after World War II by leaders of the underdeveloped countries in all parts of the world.

Luis Hierro Gambardella has underlined the nationalist objectives of Batlle's program of establishing state-owned industries. He says:

> The State organizes as an instrument of the nation to impede the escape of public wealth, produced by the installation of foreign companies. This, then, is another of the fundamental lines of Batllista doctrine: The public services under the control of the State are the maximum assurance of their control by the nation. Where monopolies are controlled by foreign capital this is reason enough for the State to intervene and nationalize them.[5]

Batlle himself explained in his newspaper *El Día* his philosophy concerning the nationalized industries. Writing on June 30, 1923, he said:

> The industrial activities of the State must not be a source of profit, but rather of low prices, of welfare. In those activities which tend towards human degeneration, such as alcohol and tobacco, one can demand a profit, but not so in public services of credit, social security, consumption, transport, etc., the best return of which consists in the

quality and cheapness of their services once they have been financially consolidated—that is their contribution to general welfare. To make expensive the consumption of alcoholic drinks and tobacco is to reduce their consumption and therefore to improve health, but we seek to reduce the price and increase the facilities of other public services rather than trying to restrict them. The enemies of State industrialism well know that the funds they try to take from the autonomous agencies are now being used for the consolidation, the progress and the rapid growth of the institutions which now possess them.[6]

Later in the same year, on November 10, Batlle wrote in *El Día:*

The tendency for the industrial enterprises of the State to increase is characteristic of the present epoch. It obeys, fundamentally, three causes. First, a fiscal cause, which is the need for new resources to cover the constantly increasing costs of national progress. Second, a social cause, that of limiting the profits of capitalism, the dividends of which come from the money of the people. Finally, a political cause, which consists of the unquestionable need in democratic society to tie as closely as possible the social activity of the State to the masses of the nation of which the State is the juridical expression.[7]

Education was another fundamental aspect of Batlle's government program. His approach has been followed in only a few Latin American countries to this day. He took education to the countryside instead of concentrating all efforts in the urban areas. He also sponsored a program for developing vocational education, thus attempting to adapt the educational system to the new needs of an expanding economy.

Batlle looked upon education not only as a weapon against ignorance and misery but also as a means of social and economic reform. It was his principal arm in the struggle against one of the greatest evils of Uruguay's traditional society—the large landholdings, or latifundia. Most rural areas were in the hands of a relatively small number of proprietors of huge cattle and sheep *estancias* whose employees were miserably paid and lived in a kind of semifeudal dependence on their employers.

Batlle never made an all-out attack on the problem of latifundia. Perhaps this was part of the price for getting the Blanco Party, the spokesman for the large landholders, to give up its belief in revolution and to accept democratic agitation and the ballot box as the legitimate methods of changing governments. However, Batlle did push through labor legislation favorable to rural workers, including a minimum-wage law covering them.

Perhaps Batlle hoped in time to undermine the latifundia system through the extension of education. Through his program of building schools in the countryside there were soon primary schools in virtually every village and small town in the interior and at least one secondary institution in every province. He felt that if the children of the workers learned to read, write, and cipher and became familiar with their country's history and their duties as citizens, they would be less willing to continue to live under the traditional latifundia system.

Batlle also attempted to reform the relations between State and Church. He himself had never been a practicing Catholic since childhood, and although he believed in a deity he was not an active member of any religious organization. In principle he was in favor of separation of Church and State, which was finally established in the Constitution of 1917. During his period in the presidency he greatly reduced the government's financial contributions to the Church and ended the custom of having Church dignitaries participate in all official ceremonial occasions.

He also supported the passage of laws legalizing divorce when rerequested by either marriage partner. He likewise sponsored legislation protecting the rights of illegitimate children.

Batlle's most important contribution to Uruguayan life was the establishment of a pattern of democratic government which has been followed with only a few exceptions by all his successors. In both his first and second administrations Batlle acted as a convinced democrat. He sponsored legislation for a secret ballot, proportional representation, municipal autonomy, and other democratic safeguards. Even more important, however, was the fact that he gave the greatest possible freedom to people of all political colors to express their points of view and to present them to the public. By his administration the press was untrammeled, the parliamentary tribune was unfettered, and the freedom of assembly was respected.

This was an innovation in Uruguayan politics. However, even more startling was the spectacle of a Uruguayan president seriously suggesting not only that the powers of his office be curtailed but also that the office itself be abolished. During the third year of his second administration Batlle formally proposed that the constitution be amended to abolish the presidency and to put in its place a council of government on the Swiss model.

Batlle's original idea was that the powers of the president should be shared by members of the council. These members should consist of representatives of the largest party and of the principal opposition party. Batlle believed that this arrangement would serve to let the opposition know the details of what was going on in the government, and thus would put them in a position to check any arbitrary actions which might be contemplated by the majority group. At the same time it would give a certain degree of participation and responsibility to the opposition party and thus dissuade it from attempting to change the government by force. Undoubtedly he looked upon this measure, in part, as a means of bringing the still restless Blanco Party into full participation in the kind of democratic regime which he was trying to establish and make secure.

Batlle believed passionately in this solution for the problem of dictatorship in Uruguay and in Latin America in general. He put forward the suggestion while he was still president in spite of the fact that it aroused the most intense opposition among his own supporters and led to a split in his party. A number of his ministers resigned because of their disagreement with Batlle's proposal, which came to be known as the *colegiado,* and several of his closest collaborators were turned into violent political opponents.

Those who opposed Batlle on the collegiate-presidency issue broke away from the main branch of the Partido Colorado and formed rival groups under different leaders. Batlle's followers meanwhile reorganized as the Partido Colorado Batllista, which during most of the following half-century remained the largest single political party in the country.

The Partido Colorado Batllista during most of this period was the principal spokesman for the urban masses of Montevideo and some of the interior towns. Its program might be compared with that of a European social democratic party, and, indeed, its existence is the principal reason why the Socialist Party of Uruguay, which was organized in 1910, never became more than a minor factor in the nation's politics. The Partido Colorado Batllista left little room for parties further to the left. The Socialists were never able to win the support of more than 10 per cent of the national electorate. After the appearance of the Communist Party in the early 1920's the Socialists and Communists tended to divide between themselves the backing of a minority of the Montevideo working class. When the Socialist vote rose, that of the Communists fell, and vice versa. However, neither of them was ever able to make serious inroads in the labor following of the Batllista Party.

Batlle proposed a constitutional convention for the purpose of making the changes which he suggested. However, he was unable to get this approved during his term in the presidency. It was not until 1917 that a constitutional convention finally met to deliberate on the *colegiado* and other suggestions which had been made to modify the country's basic document.

Although Batlle was a delegate to the 1917 constitutional convention, he stayed in the background during its deliberations. He felt that the issue had become such a personal one with many of the opponents of the *colegiado* that his appearance on the floor to advocate the abolition of the presidency would only serve to secure its defeat.

The opposition to the suggestion was very strong in the convention. Other proposals backed by Batlle, such as separation of Church and State, were readily accepted, but the *colegiado* had very hard sledding among the delegates. However, through a series of complicated negotiations with the anti-Batllistas, Batlle was able to get at least part of what he had advocated. He accepted a compromise as better than nothing and as a first step toward the achievement of the kind of regime which he wished.

The final arrangement was to maintain the presidency but to supplement it with a council of government. The powers which had formerly been held solely by the president were to be divided between him and the council. Some cabinet members were to report to the chief executive, others to the council. However, control of finances, defense, and foreign affairs was kept in the hands of the president.

Although Batlle had been only partially successful in gaining ac-

ceptance for his project f a collegiate form of government, he felt
that it was one of the principal achievements of his career. Ironically
enough, it resulted in his bitter political enemies, the Blancos, coming closer to national political power than they had been in seventy-
five years. Although the presidency continued to be held by the
Partido Colorado Batllista during the rest of Batlle's life, the Council
of Government was controlled during most of the 1920's by the
Blancos. However, Batlle did not complain, but merely insisted on
the necessity for his party to reinforce and amplify the program
which he had laid down for it during the years of his presidency.

The *colegiado* lasted until 1933, five years after Batlle's death.
At that time, when Uruguay was suffering from the effects of the
world depression and the economic situation was exceedingly grave,
President Gabriel Terra, a member of the Colorado Batllista Party
and a former close associate of Batlle, engineered a *coup d'état* in
which he abolished the *colegiado* and proclaimed himself dictator.
Terra made his coup in alliance with the Blanco Party, and a new
constitution drawn up subsequently not only reinstated a one-man
presidency but also provided for equal representation of the two
major parties in the Senate, thus giving the Blancos an absolute veto
over virtually all measures proposed by Terra or his successors.
After five years of troubled rule Terra gave way to General Alfredo
Baldomir in 1938, and three years later Baldomir made a coup of his
own, changing the constitution so as to eliminate the provision for
parity in the senate.

In the 1942 election the Colorado Batllistas again returned to
power, and four years later a second experiment with the *colegiado*
was undertaken. This new attempt to work out Batlle's old idea had
the support of both the Colorado and Blanco parties. It provided
for the abolition of the presidency and the substitution of a nine-
man council of government. Six of the members of this council would
be chosen from the majority party, three from the opposition. The
proposal, adopted in a referendum held simultaneously with the
presidential election of 1946, provided that the man elected as president in 1946 would serve as chairman of the council of government
during the balance of his term, but that in subsequent four-year
periods the chairmanship would rotate among four of the six majority members of the council.

The leader of the opposition to this second *colegiado* experiment was Luis Batlle Berres, nephew of José Batlle y Ordóñez. He was elected vice president in 1946 and succeeded to the presidency in the following year upon the death of his running mate Tomás Berreta. Although he served loyally as a member of the council of government from 1946 until 1958, Batlle Berres maintained a constant stream of criticism against the system. However, in a referendum held in 1958 on the subject of abolishing the *colegiado*, he was defeated by the voters. As this is being written Uruguay continues to be governed by the multiple presidency, José Batlle's old dream. It is the only country in the New World to adopt this idea.

With the exception of the Terra dictatorship between 1933 and 1938 the presidency of Uruguay remained in the hands of the Partido Colorado Batllista for thirty years after Batlle's death in 1928. His party continued to be the principal representative of the middle and working classes of Montevideo and the smaller cities and towns of the interior. During most of this period the Batllistas were the strongest party in congress, when they did not constitute an absolute majority of that body.

During the years in which they remained in control of the country the Batllistas continued to add to the basic structure which José Batlle had laid down during the period of his leadership. The social security system was gradually enlarged, as was the body of labor legislation. During the late 1940's, under the leadership of José Batlle's nephew, Luis Batlle Berres, the Batllista policy of using the power of the State for diversifying the national economy found expression in two programs. One of these was a policy of exceedingly high tariffs to protect manufacturing industries which had developed during World War II. The second was a program for stimulating and protecting agriculture, particularly the growing of wheat. Uruguay had always been a grazing rather than an agricultural nation. However, under threats of the Perón regime to cut off Argentine wheat in reprisal for Uruguay's hospitality to refugees from the Argentine dictatorship, Luis Batlle Berres pushed large-scale wheat growing in his country.

Although they thus continued in the path laid down by José Batlle, the latter-day Batllistas failed to recognize the crisis in the country's affairs which developed after World War II. They failed to realize that they had blindly followed Batlle's program without taking into consideration the basic economy which had to bear its cost.

To an outside observer this crisis seemed to have several facets. First, many of the industries which had grown up during the crisis of World War II were highly uneconomic and supplied Uruguay with their products only at an exceedingly high cost. Second, the agricultural protection program of Batlle Berres also went to extremes. The wheat produced was higher in cost than that grown across the Rio de la Plata, which in itself might not be an argument against its protection. However, the prices offered by the Uruguayan government for grain grown within the country were so high that they encouraged the production of more wheat than the country itself could consume, and there was little chance of shipping the product abroad in competition with grain from Argentina, the United States, and other major producers. The government thus found itself caught in a vicious circle of subsidizing the growth of wheat which it could not dispose of. Furthermore, much land which had been devoted to grazing was turned into wheat production, bringing about a crisis in the grazing industry.

Meanwhile the social security system had become larger than the nation's economy could support. It became possible in a number of industries for workers to retire in their forties, and an excessively large part of the population was found on the rolls of the pension receivers though most of them continued to work in other jobs. At the same time few, even among those who really had to live on their pensions, received amounts large enough to make it possible for them to live at a minimum level of decency.

Government employment rolls had grown excessively large, while hourly pay remained frugal in the extreme. The result was that most government employees held two or more jobs, working at their government employment only part of the day and often not doing a very efficient job while in the government office.

Throughout the 1950's this crisis continued to grow worse. It called for drastic reorganization of the nation's economy, through reasonable reduction of subsidies to industry and agriculture, establishment of reasonable retirement age in the social security system and the raising of pensions to the level of decency, and a rationalization of government employment to provide full-time jobs at full-time pay.

However, no political leader of the Partido Colorado Batllista had the kind of courage and vision which the founder of their party had shown a generation earlier. Rather than urging the kind of program which would cope with the crisis, they continued to rely on the prestige which their party and its founder had among the urban middle and working classes and to promise to do more of what Batlle had made popular when they were still children.

Rather than seeking solutions to the country's pressing problems, the Batllista leaders fell to quarreling among themselves. The result was that in the late 1940's they split into two groups. One, the so-called Partido Colorado Batllista List No. 14, was led by José Batlle's son, César Batlle Pacheco. The other, the Partido Colorado Batllista List No. 15, was under the leadership of the older Batlle's nephew, Luis Batlle Berres.*

The upshot of this was growing discontent against the Colorado Batllista government, which culminated in November, 1958, in the defeat of the Colorados at the polls for the first time in almost a century. The election of that month was won by the Partido Blanco, in alliance with a new political figure, Benito Nardone, a radio commentator who had become immensely popular among the lower classes in the countryside because of his acid attacks on the government.

However, this very defeat of the Partido Colorado Batllista was a tribute to José Batlle y Ordóñez. In spite of the tremendous shock experienced by the Batllista leaders in learning that they had been defeated by the voters, there was never any question about their willingness to turn power over to the victors. They had learned well Batlle's lesson in political democracy. Uruguay, in spite of its eco-

---

* Both of these parties, as well as the anti-Batllista Colorados, officially remained only factions of the Partido Colorado. Under Uruguay's peculiar electoral system all factions of each party could run separate lists of candidates, and the votes cast for all these lists were added together to determine whether the Colorados or the Blancos had won. The presidency or majority in the Council of Government then was given to that faction within the majority party which had gotten the most votes. However, all factions of both major parties were represented in Congress in proportion to the vote each individual group had received.

nomic and social difficulties, remained one of the few secure political democracies in Latin America—thanks largely to the heritage of José Batlle y Ordóñez.

Batlle's influence over his countrymen was certainly due not only to his ideas but to his personality as well. He was a man of exceptionally strong character and of devotion to his ideas and ideals. He was capable of arousing both the most profound loyalty and the most passionate dislike.

Batlle's long-time political associate, elected president of Uruguay with Batlle's support in the 1920's, José Serrato, has given a thumbnail sketch of his old friend. He has written:

. . . I always saw Batlle y Ordóñez in the same moral line: honesty in the extreme . . . just to the point of obsession, patriot to the depths of his spirit, exemplary democrat.

No circumstance, no promise, no ambition ever made him falter in his duty or in his respect for himself.

He had the natural habit of command; he possessed good manners which were never violated even in moments of greatest frustration and anger (I think no one ever heard him utter a crude word); and he had for his collaborators, his friends, and even his enemies the same scrupulous consideration and courtesy which he demanded for himself.

No one ever gave more prestige to his ministers, or stimulated with more fervor the projects which he considered good, no matter where they came from, or defended with such jealousy the prestige of republican dignity. Neither the peddler of influence, the crafty but mediocre, the audacious ignoramus, the self-inflated "leader," the electoral manipulator, nor the blowhard ever occupied under the influence of Batlle y Ordóñez the posts which only capable, meritorious, and worthy citizens should obtain.

He liked loyalty, not submission.

Those are mistaken who attempt to present him as sharp, intolerant, and authoritarian. He neither repelled nor refused to hear arguments opposed to his position, nor did he attempt to impose his way by means of coercion or violence. He did not exclude from his consideration and friendship those who didn't think as he did.[8]

Batlle was a figure of importance for all of Latin America. Largely through his efforts his country was converted from a backward, chaotic, and relatively unimportant nation into a land studied and admired by political thinkers and leaders from all over the hemisphere. He was a pioneer advocate of programs of social reform, government encouragement of rapid economic growth, and nationalism which were to become common among the political leaders of all of the nations of Latin America during the generation after his death.

Above all, Batlle was a convinced and fervent democrat. He never was one who believed that democracy should or must be sacrificed in order to attain social and economic progress. Quite the contrary, he gave ample demonstration of the fact that it is possible to carry out the broadest program of social and economic change while strengthening and extending political democracy, even in a country which had had little experience with effective democratic government.

Lázaro Cárdenas
and the Fulfillment
of the Mexican Revolution

৪৩৯৪৩

Very early in the morning of a day in the late 1930's the members of the village band of a small Mexican pueblo planted themselves self-consciously and importantly under a window of one of the better houses in town. All duly arranged in their customary positions, they suddenly began to play, loud enough to awaken the whole town and the countryside for miles around. Shortly after they began, a long-faced man stepped out onto the balcony just above where the band was playing and waved to the musicians.

He stayed there watching them until the music ceased, whereupon the leader of the band, taking off his wide-brimmed sombrero and shuffling from one foot to the other, made a short speech. The gist of his words was that the band had come to honor "el señor Presidente," and they hoped that he would be kind enough to notice that many of their instruments were very much worn out, which caused some of the musicians occasionally to hit a sour note, and that they would be very grateful if "el señor Presidente" could see his way clear to making funds available to replace the worn-out instruments.

The man to whom this little speech was addressed thanked the bandleader and his instrumentalists, and assured them that he would do his best to see to it that they received the new pieces they needed. Stepping back into his bedroom, he called one of his aides and gave instructions that the proper authorities be notified to make funds available for reequipping this village band.

The man standing in the balcony was General Lázaro Cárdenas, President of Mexico, and the incident is characteristic of the close

31

contact which General Cárdenas maintained with the people of Mexico before and during his presidency. It also symbolizes the reasons for his tremendous popularity with the humble folk of his country and explains in part why he was able to do more to fulfill the promise of the Mexican Revolution than had all his predecessors combined. Lázaro Cárdenas was undoubtedly the outstanding figure of the Mexican Revolution. His career spanned the three periods of that great upheaval: the destruction of old institutions, the establishment of foundations for new ones, and the building of a new institutional framework on these foundations. Like most of the leaders of the movement, he had risen to high rank through participation in the almost continuous warfare of the first decade of the Revolution, when the institutions and individuals of the old regime were swept from the face of Mexico. He had held important posts in the revolutionary regime, including a state governorship and cabinet positions in the Federal administration, during the succeeding fifteen years, in which the painful job was begun of building the bases of new institutions to replace those which the holocaust of 1910–20 had destroyed.

During his own presidency, from 1934 to 1940, Cárdenas stamped out the last remnants of the chaotic violence of the first part of the Revolution. At the same time he completed the task of building solid foundations for a new way of things which characterized its second phase. Finally, he began the process of economic development and political maturation which has characterized the Mexican Revolution during the last two decades. Since leaving the presidency he has been the veritable watchdog of the revolutionary institutions and morale, and has remained the single strongest private citizen in the nation, though appearing only infrequently before the public.

The Mexican Revolution began in 1910 as a purely political movement to bring to an end the long personal dictatorship of Porfirio Díaz, who had ruled the country since 1876. It was led in the beginning by Francisco Madero, a liberal-minded large landowner from the northern part of the country, who had little vision that the movement he began would go farther than to carry into practice his slogan "Effective Suffrage! No Reelection!" However, the Revolution soon slipped from the grasp of Madero. There had rallied to his banner large groups of peasant soldiers who wanted to convert the political movement into a process of fundamental social change. They demanded land for the landless peasants and an end to the age-old peonage system. They demanded that the Indian and mestizo masses be given real participation in the government of the country. Some of these peasant soldiers refused to lay down their arms even after Madero had won and had been inaugurated as president of Mexico early in 1911. Under the leadership of such people as Emiliano Zapata, in the State of Morelos southwest of Mexico City, and Pancho Villa, in the northern State of Chihuahua, they continued the struggle to transform the Revolution into a movement to right the age-old wrongs from which the Mexican people had suffered since the coming of the Spaniards four centuries before.

With the assassination of President Madero in February, 1913, and the seizure of power by the ruthless and reactionary Victoriano Huerta, the peasant rebels were joined by the supporters of the murdered president, and the Revolution began to take the form which its more radical leaders had advocated. The armies of Zapata, Villa, and General Venustiano Carranza, who had raised the banner of "constitutionalism" against Huerta, marched toward the capital, from which they drove the usurper during the last days of 1914.

However, the victory of the constitutionalist forces did not end this struggle. It was impossible to compromise the personal and ideological differences among the Zapata, Villa, and Carranza forces. As a result Villa remained for some time in control of Mexico City, Zapata withdrew to his stronghold in the State of Morelos, and Carranza was forced into a defensive position along the Gulf coast, in the State of Vera Cruz.

Out of Carranza's desperation came the first legal steps to transform the Mexican Revolution into a basic movement for social change. Forced to bid for the support of the peasants and the city workers against Villa and Zapata, Carranza, under the prodding of his principal field commander, Alvaro Obregón, issued a series of fundamental decrees early in 1915. One of these constituted the first timid approach to the agrarian reform and authorized the restoration to peasant villages of land which had been illegally seized from them during the Díaz period and subsequently. A second recognized the legitimacy of the trade-union movement and authorized the workers' organizations to function freely behind the lines of the constitutional army, in return for which the trade-union movement agreed to raise military forces to help Carranza.

The military victory of the Carranza forces gave legal validity to these decrees. They were confirmed and broadened by the Constitution of 1917. Thus the aspirations of the social revolutionaries became part of the basic law of the land.

The constitutional convention which met in Querétaro in December, 1916, was composed of two principal groups: the self-made soldiers who had been carrying on the battles of the Revolution on many fronts, and the civilian lawyers. It was the revolutionary soldiers who were the more radical of these two elements. They insisted on writing into the new constitution provisions for the division of the great landed estates which had come down from colonial times and had grown to include most of the country's arable land during the Díaz regime. They added to the new document a long list of labor reforms, providing Mexico with one of the most advanced codes of social legislation then to be found in the world. It was these same soldiers who insisted on asserting the rights of the Mexican nation to the subsoil resources to the exclusion of both national and foreign individuals.

Carranza survived the writing of this constitution by only three years. When early in 1920 he attempted to impose a hand-picked successor, he was deserted by most of the army under its old leader Alvaro Obregón. After a short provisional regime of Adolfo de la Huerta, Obregón was elected president. With his inauguration the second phase of the Mexican Revolution got under way.

During the next two administrations, those of Obregón and Plutarco Elías Calles, the bases of some of the fundamental institutions of the new regime were established. These administrations protected and fostered the growth of the labor movement, subsidizing the workers' organizations and giving important political posts to their leaders. A legal procedure for redistribution of the land was established, and institutions were founded to make this procedure effective. A large irrigation program was gotten under way. The national banking system, which had been virtually destroyed during the ten years of armed conflict, was reorganized, and at its pinnacle was established the Banco de Mexico, S.A.

In 1928 the threat of revolutionary chaos again arose suddenly.

The constitution had been changed in the previous year to allow the reelection of Alvaro Obregón to the presidency after he had been out of office only one term. However, he never took office, since he was assassinated by a fanatical young Catholic student who was outraged by the anticlerical policies of the Obregón and Calles regimes. General Calles took immediate charge of the situation, and for the next six years remained the strong man of the Mexican regime, though he never again assumed the presidency. Three men served during this period, the lawyer Emilio Portes Gil, and Generals Ortíz Rubio and Abelardo L. Rodríguez.

As the election of 1934 approached, General Calles selected General Lázaro Cárdenas to be the candidate of the government party, the Partido Nacional Revolucionario, for the presidency of the republic. This assured his election. But Calles little knew the changes which Cárdenas would bring about during his six years in the presidential palace.

The period 1928-34 had been chaotic. Not only were there three chief executives in this short span, but there was one serious attempt at military revolt, and government policies changed abruptly with the installation of each new president. Portes Gil had pushed the program of agrarian reform and other revolutionary measures energetically. His successor, Ortíz Rubio, virtually brought the agrarian program to a halt. General Abelardo Rodríguez renewed the land reform, but on a more modest basis than it had been carried out in the 1920's.

The fact was that the group around General Calles had become conservative. They felt that the time had come to halt the progress of the Revolution. They themselves had become rich and had private interests to protect and so were opposed to any further radical measures on the part of the government. The Revolution had reached a dead end with them.

However, although he had been a part of the same group, General Lázaro Cárdenas felt differently. He believed that the promises of the Revolution to the peasants and urban workers were still largely unfulfilled, and that it was necessary for the government once again to adopt an active policy of carrying out the principal reforms gotten under way during the early years of the movement.

General Cárdenas was a Zapotec Indian from the State of

Michoacán. He had had only three years of formal schooling, and at the age of twelve had had to go to work to provide for a widowed mother and younger brothers and sisters. At the age of sixteen he had joined the ranks of the revolutionaries, walking halfway across Mexico to join the army of General Calles during the Carranza days. He had been a good soldier and a strong leader of his men, and had risen rapidly in the ranks. During the 1920's he had been governor of the State of Michoacán and had served in the president's cabinet.

Unlike many of the "Socialist millionaires" of the Calles group, Cárdenas had not lost contact with the people and had not forgotten the real aims of the Mexican Revolution. He remembered too well his own experiences and the poverty and injustice surrounding his boyhood days, and, unlike many of his contemporaries, he had apparently evolved a philosophy of his own and a conception of what were the basic purposes of the Revolution.

Cárdenas was not a talkative man and had kept his own counsel. There are those who argue that during the years before he came to the presidency he labored under an inferiority complex and felt that his own merits had not received sufficient recognition. These people say that therefore, when he came to the presidency, he was determined to make a record which would be long remembered.

It is certain that ex-President Calles did not expect that Cárdenas would be the kind of chief executive that he turned out to be. Had he had such suspicions, Calles would certainly not have placed Cárdenas in the presidential post. However, Cárdenas had given some evidence during the long campaign preceding his formal election that he was a man of a rather different stripe from his recent predecessors. He took the campaigning for office seriously, though there was absolutely no doubt about his victory. He used the campaign as a means of establishing contacts with the people throughout the country and of explaining in some detail what it was that he planned to do once he was in the president's office.

The first thing the new chief executive had to do was to free himself from the control of ex-President Calles. This meant that he had to get complete control of the Army, which hitherto had been in the hands of the ex-president, and he had to build up counterweights to the Army upon which he could call if he had difficulties with Calles' followers there. Cárdenas took two measures in this direction. First, he followed a policy of quietly and unspectacularly shifting army commands. He placed in the lower ranks of key garrisons junior officers on whose loyalty he could completely count. When this process had been accomplished, he did the same thing with the middle ranks of officers, and when the backing of this group was assured, it was a relatively easy matter to remove the generals and colonels who still felt more loyalty to the past president than to the incumbent.

At the same time that he was quietly shifting army commands Cárdenas was building up auxiliary armed forces. During his interminable tours around the country after taking office Cárdenas met with local peasant and trade-union leaders, outlined to them his program and his difficulties, and provided them with small arms to be used in support of the government in case of a clash with the Army.

Once the Federal Army was well in hand, Cárdenas had to suppress the last remnants of the "private armies" which were under the control of various self-made generals of the Revolution. During the military phase of the Revolution each general had gathered around him a larger or smaller force which was personally loyal to him rather than to the government or the Revolution. During the 1920's it was customary that when a general was shifted from one command to another, his troops went along with him. It was a long time before the control of the President over the armed forces was sufficient that the military commander could be thought of as distinct from the force which was under his command.

By the time Cárdenas came to power most of these personal armies had been eliminated. However, a handful of them still remained, and they constituted a threat of some importance to his control of the country. He dealt with different military leaders in different ways. A few he sent abroad on honorary diplomatic missions which were, in fact, equivalent to exile. Others he gave cabinet posts or other positions.

It was not until 1938 that he was able to eliminate the last of these figures, Saturnino Cedillo, the absolute boss of the State of San Luis Potosí and the commander of a personal army of loyal followers in that state. Cárdenas moved against Cedillo with caution. He kept him in his cabinet as Secretary of Agriculture as long as possible.

Meanwhile he armed large numbers of peasants and trade-unionists in San Luis Potosí who were friendly to the President rather than to the boss of the state. At the same time he quietly moved elements of the regular Federal Army into the state under commanders who were responsible to Mexico City and not to the state capital. Finally, when Cedillo was forced into open rebellion early in 1938, it was a comparatively easy thing for Cárdenas to take the field himself at the head of the Federal troops, aided by the workers' and peasants' militia and to force Cedillo's flight into the hills, where he was soon afterward killed by one of his own men.

However, Cárdenas was not carrying out these actions merely to establish his own personal power or even to establish the power of the Federal government over that of the states or over the Army. Rather, he was acting to assure the success of the social and economic program he had launched soon after taking office. Cárdenas was determined to push toward completion the work of dividing up the land in accordance with the agrarian reform program of the Mexican Revolution. Immediately upon taking power he speeded up the process of expropriating land, and during his six years in office twice as much land was turned over to the peasants as had been given to them in the twenty-four years before he became president.

Some of Cárdenas' applications of the agrarian reform law were spectacular. For instance, he restored lands to the Yaquis, an Indian tribe in the northwestern State of Sonora who had been despoiled over and over again by preceding regimes. Under Díaz the Yaquis had risen in revolt against their oppressors, and after their defeat had been deported en masse to the far-off State of Yucatán in the extreme southeastern part of the republic. In the succeeding decades a sizable proportion of them had drifted back to their original homeland, but they remained without land until President Cárdenas finally restored their traditional holdings to them.

Another case was that of the Laguna region, at the time the country's largest cotton-growing area. There the land of a dried-up lake was very fertile, but it had to be irrigated. Over the years it had come into the hands of a number of large companies and landholding families, many of them foreigners. The workers on these lands lived in great poverty, and the owners, living in Mexico City or abroad, drained virtually all the income from the region.

Early in the Cárdenas administration the agricultural workers in the Laguna area began to organize into peasant unions. They met bitter resistance from the landowners and their straw bosses, and finally the workers went out on strike in 1936. After this walkout had gone on for some time, General Cárdenas suddenly settled the problem by expropriating the land and decreeing that it should be turned over to the farm workers. Shortly afterward he personally visited the region, and in conferences with leaders of the local agricultural laborers worked out the framework for the establishment of a communal agricultural experiment which has been one of the most interesting developments in recent Mexican history.

Cárdenas by no means completed the agrarian reform in Mexico. Indeed, it is still going on. However, by the end of his administration approximately a third of the population of Mexico had received land under the program. About 51 per cent of the rural population consisted of members of the *ejidos* established by the agrarian reform, and they had approximately 47 per cent of all land used for crops in all of Mexico.

Not only did Cárdenas greatly speed up the process of distributing land, but he made two fundamental alterations in the program. First, in 1935 he decreed that landless villages included within the boundaries of existing plantations which had not previously been eligible to receive land could ask for and be given it.

In the second place, he ended for the time being the somewhat schizophrenic attitude of the agrarian reformers concerning the way in which the land given to the peasants should be organized. One group had favored giving land outright to the peasants as their personal property. Others felt that the land should be given only to the local community and, although granted by the community to individuals for their use, should be inalienable, that is, not subject to sale, barter, or mortgage. Cárdenas sided with the latter group, and virtually all the land distributed by him was given to the communal groups known as *ejidos*. In some cases, as in the Laguna cotton-growing region, Cárdenas encouraged actual cultivation by the community as a group rather than by the individuals who received use title to the land from the *ejido*.

The extensive application of the agrarian reform program by the Cárdenas administration brought foreign conflicts, because much of the land taken by the government had been owned by nationals of other countries, particularly the United States. Cárdenas and the Mexican government maintained that under the Constitution of 1917 and the agrarian reform laws the Mexican government had every right to take over these lands, which in many cases were being held illegally by their foreign owners. This position of Cárdenas was upheld by the Roosevelt administration in the United States, which requested only that the Americans involved be reasonably and justly compensated for the lands which were taken away from them.

Cárdenas also fulfilled his promises to strengthen the organized-labor movement. During the six years before Cárdenas' assumption of power the trade unions had been in a chaotic situation. The Confederación Regional Obrera Mexicana (CROM), which had been exceedingly powerful and had been favored by the administrations of Generals Obregón and Calles, was riven by bitter and violent internecine struggles. When Cárdenas was inaugurated the trade-union movement was divided into at least half a dozen different central labor bodies, each of which was more concerned with fighting its rivals than with dealing with the employers. The administrations preceding Cárdenas had encouraged rather than discouraged this disunity among the organized workers.

Cárdenas took steps to end this situation. He encouraged Vicente Lombardo Toledano, onetime official of the CROM and in 1935 head of his own trade-union group, to take the leadership in the reestablishment of a single large central labor federation. As a result of his efforts and of Cárdenas' support Lombardo Toledano was successful in bringing together most of the existing labor groups to form a new organization, the Confederación de Trabajadores de Mexico (CTM).

The CTM became one of the bulwarks of the Cárdenas regime. Not only did it bring together once again most of the unions in an organization closely associated with the government, it likewise became an integral part of the government political party when President Cárdenas reorganized that group. Finally, the members of the CTM were provided with arms, thus giving an additional military bulwark in case the President had trouble with the official armed forces.

President Cárdenas aided Mexican labor to achieve an important position in the Latin American labor movement, and in the world labor movement. In September, 1938, the CTM played host to a congress of Latin American trade unions which established the Confederación de Trabajadores de America Latina (CTAL), of which Lombardo Toledano became president. The funds for this meeting were undoubtedly supplied by the Cárdenas government, which was anxious at that moment, because of the international crisis over the expropriation of the oil industry, to rally as much hemispheric support for its position as it could muster. In addition to the Latin American delegates attending the meeting there were numerous fraternal representatives, including John L. Lewis of the Congress of Industrial Organizations of the United States, Léon Jouhaux of the French Confédération Général du Travail, and Ramón González Peña of the Spanish Unión General de Trabajadores, as well as observers from the International Federation of Trade Unions and the International Labor Organization.

Although the CTAL became a purely Communist organization during the war and postwar years and the CTM withdrew from it in 1948, it began as a coalition of virtually all labor forces in the hemisphere. Unions under Socialist, Aprista, Liberal, and Communist influence were represented in the Mexico City Congress and became members of the CTAL during its first years. This founding convention of the CTAL was undoubtedly a feather in the caps of both the Mexican labor movement and the Cárdenas government.

The agrarian and labor policies of Cárdenas aroused the strong opposition of ex-President Calles and those closely associated with him. Calles began making speeches and writing articles warning the President of the "danger" of the policy which he was following. Cárdenas bided his time, did nothing until he was sure that the control of the Army and the government was safely in his own hands. Then one day, early in the morning, ex-President Calles and Luis Morones, head of the old CROM and one of Calles' chief political lieutenants, were placed on an airplane and sent off to Los Angeles, California. Calles never returned alive from exile, though Morones came back a few years later to head the CROM once more.

Meanwhile Cárdenas was following a policy of Mexican nationalism. The Revolution from the beginning had had a nationalist tinge. It had sought to make the Indian and mestizo masses effective members of the nation, and it had asserted the rights of Mexico and the Mexicans in relation to foreign residents and foreign interests in Mexico, and in relation to foreign governments.

Cárdenas pushed this aspect of the program of the Revolution with vigor. Not only did he insist on expropriating land which belonged to foreigners, but he also carried out policies which transferred other important parts of the national economy from the hands of aliens to those of Mexicans.

His first move in this direction was the expropriation of the National Railways of Mexico, which had been owned largely by foreign interests. At first he experimented with turning the railway over to the Railroad Workers Union. However, within a few months it became obvious that the leaders of the union were totally unequipped to handle this job, and the government took over the road, establishing an autonomous corporation to run it. The executive body of the corporation contained representatives of the workers but was not controlled by them.

From 1936 to March, 1938, there had been a long-drawn-out labor dispute in the oil industry, which was largely owned by British and United States firms. This dispute had dragged through the Mexican courts, and finally the position of the workers had been upheld by the Supreme Court of Mexico. In paid advertisements in the newspapers the foreign companies then announced that they did not feel themselves bound by this decision and did not intend to carry out its provisions. They reportedly took this position as the result of recommendations of an ex-president of Mexico who was then their lawyer, and obviously neither they nor he expected President Cárdenas' next move.

In the face of the defiance of the foreign oil companies Cárdenas called a meeting in the National Palace of high government officials and Vicente Lombardo Toledano, then head of the Confederación de Trabajadores de Mexico. In the presence of this group President Cárdenas signed a decree expropriating the country's oil industry and turning it over to the workers. He invited the CTM to draw up the details of this labor administration of the industry. Within a few days their plan was ready, and it was soon afterward put into execution. However, the oil workers proved as incapable of conducting the affairs of a major industry as the railroad workers. Before the end of the Cárdenas administration the petroleum industry had been reorganized as an autonomous government corporation, Petróleos Mexicanos, the top officials of which were appointed by the President.

The expropriation of the oil industry caused considerable difficulties for the Mexican government abroad. The British, whose interests in Mexican petroleum had been the largest, broke off diplomatic relations over the issue. The United States government, while recognizing the right of Mexico to expropriate the industry, insisted that the oil companies receive "fair" compensation, and the issue of how much the companies should actually receive was not finally settled until near the end of World War II. Meanwhile the United States and British oil companies were sufficiently powerful to force firms producing oil field and refinery equipment to refuse to sell anything to Petróleos Mexicanos. This boycott ended only with the settlement of the compensation issue in the middle 1940's.

In addition to changing the structure of the country's agriculture and asserting the right of the nation to control its own economic life President Cárdenas took steps toward strengthening and diversifying the economy. The agrarian reform itself put significant amounts of purchasing power in the hands of large numbers of peasants for the first time and thus greatly enlarged the national market.

The Cárdenas administration amplified the nation's banking system. The Banco de Mexico was converted into a true central bank and was given more extensive powers to regulate the private banking institutions. At the same time Cárdenas began the policy of channeling the bank's resources toward economic development.

Besides, he added two significant institutions to the national banking system. One was the Banco Ejidal, designed to meet the credit needs of the agrarian communities created by the agrarian reform. Although it first tried to service virtually all the *ejidos*, in later years it devoted its efforts to offering credit only to the most efficient and economical of the communities. The second new bank was the Nacional Financiera, a government institution set up to encourage industrialization. It undertook to make credit available to those who wished to establish new manufacturing enterprises or to enlarge old ones. It has played an important role in the rapid process of industrialization which has taken place during the past two decades or so.

The Cárdenas government took some important steps toward the democratization of Mexican political life. Under Cárdenas' administration Mexico became the refuge of political exiles from all over the world. There was the widest degree of freedom of speech and a general observance also of the freedom of organization.

At the same time the government party, the Partido Nacional Revolucionario, which had been founded by ex-President Calles in 1928, was reorganized to make it more fully representative of the elements backing the Mexican Revolution. Instead of membership on an individual basis, consisting mainly of government employees and aspiring politicians, the party adopted a collegiate form of organization, with three affiliated groups belonging directly to it. First was the so-called Labor Bloc, which consisted of all those central labor groups and individual unions allied with the government, but of which the CTM was the principal base.

The second group to be a component part of the party, now rechristened the Partido Revolucionario Mexicano (PRM), was the National Peasants Confederation. This organization, made up of federations of the *ejido* communities established by the agrarian reform and of unions of agricultural laborers, was set up with the help and encouragement of President Cárdenas. Its purposes were to give the peasants a more adequate instrument for defense of their rights and to rally the peasantry behind the revolutionary regime.

The third element making up the Partido Revolucionario Mexicano was the so-called "Bloc of Popular Organizations," which consisted of the Government Employees Federation and of groups of business and professional men who were supporters of the administration. It also included a strong women's organization which came to play an increasingly important part. Although in the beginning the popular Bloc was the least effective of the three wings of the PRM, in later years it became the most representative and influential of the three segments of the party, and by the late 1950's was undoubtedly the most powerful of the three groups.

At the time Cárdenas reorganized the party he included the Army as its fourth component part. However, during the administration of his successor, General Avila Camacho, the Army sector was abolished, and since that time the active military men have stayed in the background in Mexican politics.

It was during the Cárdenas administration that the complicated process of give-and-take which constitutes Mexico's essay in democracy took more or less its present shape. Neither Cardenas nor his successors have suppressed parties opposed to that of the government, and there have been several of these with more or less long lives, including the Partido Acción Nacional, a right-wing opponent of the regime; the Communist Party; the Workers and Peasants Party (a dissident Communist group) ; and the semi-Communist Partido Popular, organized by Vicente Lombardo Toledano in 1947. These parties carry on a more or less active day-to-day existence, run candidates in elections, and conduct an active and constant propaganda campaign against the administration.

In addition to these opposition groups there arose in the presidential elections of 1940, 1946, and 1952 dissidents from the government party which, in fact, offered the major opposition to the government's nominees for office. These groups, too, carried on exceedingly violent campaigns against the administration and its party, and upon two occasions, 1940 and 1952, threatened revolutionary action if they were defeated at the polls, but they failed in both cases to make their threats effective.

In spite of the numerous opposition groups there has never been any doubt in any election as to who would win. It is probably true that the government nominee would have won easily, with the possible exception of the 1940 poll, even if the government had done nothing to interfere with the choice of the voters. However, to be doubly sure, the administration in each case has "controlled" the election. Frank Tannenbaum has indicated the nature of this control. He says:

. . . the outcome of the election is never in doubt. The opposition candidates, in spite of an active campaign, have no expectation of being elected. They know that their people will not be permitted to vote; that if they do vote, their votes will not be counted; that if counted and sent into the final test in Congress, they will be disregarded; and, finally, that if elected by some strange accident, they could not govern. . . .[9]

Although this passage is a closer description of the situation in the 1920's and early 1930's than in later periods, it is still near enough to the truth to constitute one side of the picture. It should be noted, however, that beginning in the Cárdenas administration, opposition parties were conceded victories in congressional elections in areas where their strength tended to be overwhelming.

In spite of the assured victories of the government party in Mexican elections, the situation during and since the Cárdenas administration has been considerably more democratic than would at first appear to be the case. The fact is that the important contests, over both issues and officeholders, take place within the government party.

The process of reaching a decision, whether it be a matter of legislation or government policy or the election of a new president, is a complicated one. The initiative may be taken by any of the three elements which constitute the government party—known since the middle 1940's as the Partido Revolucionario Institucional—or by a government official or other important figure in or around the regime. A measure or a candidacy then undergoes wide discussion, and a consensus is usually reached among the various elements which make up the government coalition before the president, whose word is final, makes the decision.

Many elements in the population participate in this process of decision making. They include the country's principal labor organizations, the leading peasant organizations, particularly the National Peasants Confederation, the powerful Government Employees Federation, the Army, the Bloc of Popular Organizations, and the ex-presidents. On important issues concerning economic policy there is usually consultation with the official organizations representing the industrialists, the leading merchants, and professional people. Each of these groups is in a position to make its voice heard and its weight felt. In recent years even the Church has been consulted informally on issues in which it has a vital interest.

Thus there is a wider degree of democracy than might appear at first glance. Since the days of Cárdenas, although the president has had the final word on most matters, the government of Mexico has not been authoritarian nor, in any sense, a one-man regime. The power of the official party and of the various interest groups which make it up—and by the late 1950's these included virtually every important element except the Catholic Church—has grown steadily.

As a result the individual power of the president has diminished.[10]

In December, 1940, when his term of office came to an end, Lázaro Cárdenas retired from the presidency, giving way to his friend and elected successor General Manuel Avila Camacho. However, Cárdenas did not as a result disappear from the national scene. He remained for long the single most important figure in Mexican political life, with probably more actual influence than the president himself.

Cárdenas' continued influence is explained by many factors. First, he was idolized by the peasants, among whom his name was linked with that of Benito Juárez, the great Indian president of Mexico in the middle of the nineteenth century, and Emiliano Zapata, the apostle of the agrarian reform in the early days of the Mexican Revolution. Cárdenas, they felt, was the man responsible for giving them the land.

The workers, too, were dedicated to him, since he had helped to rebuild the labor movement of Mexico. However, with the decline of the influence of Vicente Lombardo Toledano in the trade unions the influence of Cárdenas also tended to decline.

Cárdenas' grip on the loyalty of the officers and men of the Army continued long after he ceased to be president. He had built up a leadership in the Army which owed its position to him, and the officers continued to feel that their destinies were linked to his for a long time after he ceased to be their commander in chief.

Cárdenas' strongest link with the people probably came from his widespread acquaintance with ordinary citizens. Throughout his administration he had continued the practice which he had established during his election campaign of traveling far and wide across the nation. Many a humble peasant had had the honor of sharing his simple meal with the President. Many a minor trade-union official or rank-and-filer had discussed his personal problems and those of his organization with Cárdenas. He had the successful politician's gift for remembering names and faces, and there were men in all ranks of life in all parts of the republic who regarded him as their personal friend or at least as their acquaintance. It was many years before the importance of this personal contact of Cárdenas with the people of Mexico began to diminish.

With the entry of Mexico into World War II, a little more than a year after his exit from the presidency, Cárdenas was summoned back into service by President Avila Camacho as Minister of Defense, a post which he held for the duration of the conflict. Although he was again in the public eye in his new post, Cárdenas tried to remain as much as possible in the background to allow his successor the freest opportunity to exercise his authority.

As Minister of War, Cárdenas improved the caliber of the nation's armed forces. He cooperated fully with the United States and Mexico's other allies, and, with his approval and encouragement, Mexico became the only Latin American country to participate actively in the war in the Pacific. A Mexican air-force group played its part in the Philippine Islands campaign.

After the war Cárdenas resigned as Minister of Defense. Though he did not again hold public office, he continued to be a power behind the scenes in Mexican politics. He issued somewhat oracular statements to the press, and he was consulted by the President concerning matters of great importance.

As the end of the term of President Miguel Alemán approached in the early 1950's the question arose for the first time in several decades of the possible reelection of the President. The old labor leader Luis Morones raised the issue two years before the expiration of Alemán's term, and there were rumors that the chief executive was not entirely unreceptive to the idea.

There is no doubt that Cárdenas was consulted not only about the possibility of reelection but also about the general problem of the succession. There is a story, probably aprocryphal, of a meeting between Cárdenas and President Alemán. The President did most of the talking, explaining to Cárdenas the things which he had accomplished so far in his administration, the things he still had left to do, and the fact that he was afraid that he would not be able to accomplish his whole task before his term was up. He ended by asking Cárdenas what he thought of the idea of his running for reelection. The ex-President is supposed to have replied somewhat along these lines: "Well, Señor Presidente, if we are going to violate the constitution, I think perhaps that I shall run for the presidency again." This comment, the story goes, ended any further discussion of Alemán's reelection. The incumbent knew too well that if there were to be a contest between himself and Cárdenas, the latter would win without any difficulty.

Whether or not this incident actually occurred, it is certain that Cárdenas counseled Alemán about the need for the selection of a successor of a different type from Alemán and from outside his special circle of friends. Although the Alemán administration had accomplished a great deal, particularly in the field of irrigation, electric power production, and public works, it had been particularly marred by scandals and corruption. There was a rising discontent against the administration by the time its term of office was drawing to a close, and there was even some fear of violence if the Alemán group continued in power even without Alemán as the leading figure.

Cárdenas is widely reputed to have personally suggested the choice of Adolfo Ruiz Cortines as Alemán's successor. Ruiz Cortines was a lifelong government official, a man of modest demeanor and unquestioned honesty. It was jocularly said of him that he "had no brothers," a reference to the fact that in past administrations the most outrageous graft had generally been attributed to the closest relatives of the chief executive. Cárdenas and others believed that Ruiz Cortines would be able to limit considerably, even if he could not completely eliminate, the corruption which had become so widespread and was threatening to endanger the Mexican Revolution itself.

Ruiz Cortines' principal opponent was General Heriberto Henríquez, an old comrade-in-arms of Cárdenas and his onetime cabinet minister. Henríquez claimed the backing of the ex-President. However, since Vicente Lombardo Toledano, a third nominee, also claimed the support of Cárdenas, little popular credence was given to either claim. Cárdenas himself said nothing. Ruiz Cortines won the usual easy victory which is reserved for government-backed nominees in Mexico.

During the early part of the Ruiz Cortines administration Lázaro Cádenas became involved in a public controversy over the country's agrarian policy. There were many, including old-time supporters of the agrarian reform, who felt that the country had outgrown the reform, at least on the basis in which it had reached maturity during the Cárdenas administration. According to these people, Mexican agriculture was lagging very much behind the development of industry. The agrarian reform, they argued, had contributed to a division of important agricultural areas into excessively small plots from which their occupants could not draw a sufficiently large income to provide them with adequate purchasing power. This was not only holding down their ability to buy but was also limiting the market for manufacturing industries, thus hampering the growth of the nation's economy.

These people argued that the principal rural problem was no longer the large hacienda but rather increasing the country's productivity. They cited figures to show that the productivity of the *ejido* was far below that of the average small individual landholding. Therefore, they argued, the *ejido*, with its embargo on the sale and mortgaging of land, should give way to the individual peasant landholding. This would permit the more efficient members of the *ejido* to buy out their less efficient neighbors, thus creating larger and more productive units of cultivation. Rural income would be higher, and production would be greater, thus stimulating the urban economy through a larger rural market and through lower agricultural prices and more diversified production. Although they did not feel it likely that the old hacienda destroyed by the agrarian reform would make its reappearance, they urged that, to protect the nation against that eventuality, a top limit should be set to the size of all farms.

There were those who strongly opposed this point of view and who supported the *ejido*. They had various explanations for the lower productivity of the *ejido* but argued that this was not the most important feature of the situation. Rather, they maintained, it was the fact that the *ejido* form gave the peasant protection against possible despoilment at the hands of avaricious moneylenders and land grabbers.

This controversy went on for many months, in scholarly journals, the daily press, and in public lectures and discussions. It was finally brought to a halt, at least for the time being, by a statement from ex-President Cárdenas to the effect that he was unalterably opposed to any move to abolish or reduce the importance of the *ejido*, that it was the core of the agrarian reform program, which itself was the heart of the Mexican Revolution. His words were sufficient to decide the situation for a while at least.

This incident reflects the still decisive influence of Lázaro Cárdenas in Mexican public affairs in the early 1950's. It also reflects his continued adherence to the philosophy and program which he had put into effect a decade and a half before. There are those who argue that it also indicates the general's failure to keep up with the fast-changing pattern of Mexico's economic, social, and political life.

Cárdenas' influence in Mexican public life continued to be great, but there were many among his old followers who were puzzled and disappointed by his attitude toward world affairs. Although during his presidency Cárdenas had given the Mexican Communists full freedom to function, as he had to every other political group, he had by no means been a pro-Communist. He had greatly agitated the Stalinists by giving refuge to Trotsky in 1937. He had clamped down on the Communists when they openly favored the Axis during the first phase of World War II.

Nevertheless, during the late 1940's and thereafter Cárdenas on several occasions allowed his name to be used in campaigns by the Communists. He signed several of the "peace petitions" circulated by the international Communist movement. He figured as a member of the executive of the World Peace Council, which was under their leadership and control. He accepted the Stalin Peace Prize. In 1958 he made an extensive tour of both the Soviet Union and China. Early in 1961 he presided over a Communist-organized "peace" conference held in Mexico City.

Lázaro Cárdenas had certainly not become a Communist. Perhaps only he himself knows why he had been willing to allow himself to be used by the Communist movement on a world scale. One possible explanation is that always, as a Mexican nationalist, he has been fundamentally antagonistic to the predominant influence of the United States in the Western Hemisphere, particularly to its very great influence in his own country's affairs. In his later years, as he retreated further and further from actual exercise of power and responsibility, he perhaps has felt that he can give vent to his antagonism toward the United States by giving at least some aid and comfort to its enemies. Or perhaps, in spite of his wiliness and ability in Mexican politics, he has remained somewhat naïve concerning political trends in the outside world and has really been convinced that the Communists were working for peace and their opponents for war.

Approaching his seventies, Lázaro Cárdenas remains the Grand Old Man of the Mexican Revolution. He played a key role in pushing to fruition the program of fundamental social change which that Revolution stood for. He won the confidence and love of the average Mexican citizen to a degree unmatched by any other leading Mexican political figure in the century. He continues to symbolize the Mexican Revolution.

Arturo Alessandri, the Lion of Tarapacá

The atmosphere in the neoclassical Congress building in Santiago, Chile, on September 8, 1924, was tense. The galleries of both the Senate and the Chamber of Deputies were filled with members of the armed forces. The legislators were faced with a long list of bills which the President had sent to them for immediate action. The urgency of their passage was emphasized by the visitors who were watching Congress at work. There was little discussion of the laws which were passed that day. No sooner was a bill read by the clerk in one house than it was immediately adopted and sent to the other house for approval. Only one legislator, Senator Pedro León Ugalde dared to challenge his colleagues' untoward behavior. He delivered a ringing speech denouncing the military men in the galleries and excoriating with almost equal fervor his fellow legislators who were so busily engaged in doing the soldiers' bidding.

It was in this atmosphere that the legislation which forms the basis of the famous Chilean Labor Code was passed. The man, however, who was most responsible for this legislation was not present in Congress. He waited a few blocks away in the old Spanish mint, which has been the traditional office of Chile's presidents, for news that Congress had acted upon the legislation which he had promised leaders of the Army and Navy as the price for their "returning to the barracks." Congress kept the President's side of the bargain. The military men did not keep theirs. A few days later Arturo Alessandri resigned the presidency.

It was indeed ironic that the labor and social laws which Alessandri had been advocating since he became president almost four years before, but had never been able to get Congress to pass, should have been enacted as a prelude to his ouster from the presidency. However, had it not been for these circumstances, perhaps Arturo

Alessandri would not have figured in Chilean history as the founder of his country's position of leadership in social legislation throughout the hemisphere.

The military men who forced through the basic elements of the Labor Code on September 8, 1924, and a few days later brought about Alessandri's resignation really had little interest in social problems. Their concern was that they were, they considered, underpaid and sometimes not paid at all. They had begun their mutiny a few days before September 8 with a demonstration in the congressional galleries during a discussion of a proposal to raise Congressmen's salaries, a measure the soldiers resented because of their own grievances. When Alessandri sought to rebuke the demonstrators, the chiefs of the Army and Navy expressed their solidarity with them, and the country faced a constitutional crisis.

President Alessandri finally asked the military chiefs what their price was to remove themselves once again from politics. Their reply, much to everyone's surprise, was a long list of proposed laws, including legislation which Alessandri had been urging for years, to which was appended a bill raising the pay of all army and navy personnel. The young officers who drew up the demands felt that it would be indecent to appear to be seeking only the improvement of their own conditions, hence their sudden interest in social problems.

The drama of September 8, 1924, was merely the culmination of a series of crises which the country had faced since the election of Arturo Alessandri as president in 1920. His triumph had meant a veritable revolution in the country's affairs. It meant the transfer of political power from the landed aristocracy to the middle and working classes of the cities. It meant the beginning of a process of transforming Chile from an aristocratic democracy reminiscent of Great Britain before the Reform Bill of 1830 into a modern democracy in which the common people of the urban areas have the last word.

Soon after the achievement of independence, political power in Chile had been consolidated in the hands of the rural aristocracy. Thereafter Chilean politics was marked by a stability virtually unequaled anywhere else in Latin America. The Constitution written in 1833 remained in force for almost a century. Although there were several attempted revolutions between 1833 and 1924, only one succeeded—that against President José Manuel Balmaceda in 1891. Virtually all the presidents, most of the cabinet ministers, and the majority of the members of Congress during this period were drawn from the aristocratic families in whose hands effective power lay.

During the three decades between the revolution against Balmaceda in 1891 and the election of Alessandri in 1920 Chile had experimented with a form of parliamentary government reminiscent of France of the Third and Fourth Republics. Parties became numerous and splintered, cabinets stayed in office for only a few weeks or months at most, coalitions were made and broken rapidly and easily among the contending groups.

Alberto Edwards has written in *La Fronda Aristocrática* that this long period of parliamentary rule was a logical consequence of aristocratic control, that the landed oligarchy feared a strong president because he might do something to disturb the *status quo*. It was this fear which motivated the revolution against Balmaceda and which led to the establishment of the total sovereignty of parliament.

Sharing political power with the landlords were certain political bosses in some of the urban areas. These bosses were particularly strong in the mining areas, where they worked closely with the mineowners to prevent the mine workers from "getting out of line." When the need arose, the local bosses had the help of the national government in the form of extra police and even soldiers.

But there were economic and social forces at work which were undermining the ruling aristocracy and the political system which they supported. As a result of the War of the Pacific of 1879 Chile had seized the nitrate-rich provinces of Antofagasta and Tarapacá from Bolivia and Peru. The intensive exploitation of the nitrate resources in those provinces had quickened the pace of the whole Chilean economy. The country's foreign trade increased, the cities grew rapidly, industry expanded, and the urban working class grew in numbers and militancy.

During the 1880's and 1890's the first serious organized-labor movement began among the artisans of the cities. In the years before World War I the workers of the nitrate and coal fields were partially and sporadically organized, and fought against their employers and the government momentous battles in which hundreds of workers were killed.

World War I stimulated both the country's economic development and the labor movement. Inability to obtain needed manufactured goods from the warring countries of Europe stimulated Chilean industry, particularly the production of textiles, metals, and consumer goods. At the same time, wartime inflation encouraged the labor movement and made it possible for the unions to achieve greater gains than ever before. A militant central labor organization, the Federación Obrera de Chile, including most of the country's organized workers, came into existence. In the maritime trades most workers were brought into a Chilean version of the Industrial Workers of the World.

The Partido Socialista Obrero became the spokesman in politics for part of the labor movement, particularly for the nitrate miners. The older Partido Democrático represented the coal miners and many of the city artisans. The Partido Radical came increasingly to speak for the growing white-collar middle class.

The middle and working classes were becoming increasingly restive against the rule of the rural aristocracy and its city allies, the political bosses. The first showdown between the two occurred in the northern city of Iquique in the province of Tarapacá in a senatorial election in the year 1915. Iquique had long been the personal fief of Senator Arturo del Rio. In 1915 the forces of the left, representing the country's middle- and working-class groups, resolved to defeat Senator del Rio for reelection. They named as their candidate a deputy belonging to a faction of the Liberal Party, Arturo Alessandri. In a hard-fought campaign marked by violence Alessandri was the victor. It was from that campaign that he acquired the nickname "the Lion of Tarapacá," a sobriquet which he did his best to live up to during the rest of his life.

A much more crucial struggle occurred four years later, during the presidential campaign. The lines were sharply drawn. On the one side, behind the candidacy of Luis Barros Burgoño, one of the country's most distinguished political leaders, stood all the forces representing the *ancien régime* united under the banner of the National Union. The aristocracy knew that it was playing for keeps, and all its forces were mustered to elect the National Union candidate.

In the other camp were all the political and social forces which had been coming to the fore during previous decades. These were marshaled in the Liberal Alliance, which consisted of one faction of the Liberals, the Radical and Democratic parties, and several smaller groups. The Alliance had only the tacit support of the Partido Socialista Obrero. The nominee of the Liberal Alliance was Arturo Alessandri.

Alessandri was by this time one of the most spectacular figures in Chilean political life. The grandson of an Italian immigrant who had come to Chile with a group of entertainers but had remained to become the Kingdom of Italy's first accredited diplomatic representative to Chile, and the son of a man who had become a gentleman farmer and had developed connections with the local aristocracy, Alessandri was a man of very complex personality. He was capable of arousing the strongest loyalty and the most violent hatred. He was extremely ambitious and was vain sometimes to the point of absurdity. He was an extraordinary orator, capable of arousing his listeners to frenzied enthusiasm. He also had the reputation of being an extremely shrewd political schemer.

Alberto Edwards has described in *La Fronda Aristocrática* (p. 24) the contradictory nature of Arturo Alessandri's personality and behavior:

. . . No one was more sincerely oligarchical than he while he was enveloped in the atmosphere of the drawing rooms of the Lazcanos and the Fernández Conchas. No one was more "popular" than he, when leaving one environment which was perhaps not the most adequate for his temperament and attitude, and entering another where he found himself surrounded by men of the Left, in the midst of the provincial middle class which was impatient to throw off the yoke, fervently applauded by the workers of the nitrate fields. His sensitive and impulsive soul was engulfed in the spirit which was revolutionary without realizing it; his heated eloquence was nothing more than a reflection of the aspirations and passions which slept beneath the apparent peace of the Republic. A breeze of renovation and of protest then began to blow from the arid pampas of the Northern desert; and the name of the tribune whose words of fire had produced this sudden awakening of a sleeping people became extraordinarily popular throughout the country. . . .

Alessandri was certainly no novice in politics. His initiation had taken place during the Revolution of 1891, when he had participated in street demonstrations and the distribution of subversive leaflets against President Balmaceda, an activity of which he was later ashamed and for which he never tired of apologizing. He was elected to the Chamber of Deputies as a member of the Liberal Party, while in his twenties, and he became the youngest man in the country's history to hold a post in the cabinet. He remained in the Chamber of Deputies until his elevation to the Senate in 1916 and served in several ministries.

The Liberal Alliance candidate brought all his oratorical talents to bear in the 1920 election campaign. He stumped the country, receiving a tumultuous reception from workers and middle-class audiences throughout the nation. In his speeches he put forward suggestions for widespread economic and social reforms.

Alessandri himself summed up the program which he put forward during the election campaign of 1920 under eighteen headings. These added up to a veritable social revolution. They included proposals for revising the constitution to put an end to the system of parliamentary government. They included a revision of the tax system to establish an income tax and "other taxes to improve the financial life of the country. . . ." They demanded protection and assistance for agriculture, mining, industry, and the merchant marine.

The heart of the Alessandri program, according to Don Arturo himself, was "to make the utmost efforts to establish a complete system of social legislation which regulates the relations between capital and labor, recognizing the rights and duties of both elements of production. . . ." Other labor points which Alessandri urged during his campaign included the establishment of "regulations which will provide for the remuneration of labor so as to satisfy the minimum physical and moral needs of the workers and leave a margin for honest recreation," the launching of a government housing program, and the establishment of a Ministry of Labor and Social Security.[1]

Alessandri's enemies have questioned the honesty of his concern for social problems and the welfare of the country's poorer and more defenseless citizens. The famous historian Ricardo Donoso has summed up his assessment of Alessandri's career in the title of his biography of Don Arturo, *Alessandri: Agitador y Demoledor*

(*Alessandri: Agitator and Demolisher*), and gives him little credit for sincerity about anything except his own ambitions. Others have pictured him as a paladin of the humble, dedicating his life to righting wrongs regardless of what it cost him politically. Such a position is represented by another biographer of Alessandri, Luis Duran, in his work *Don Arturo*.

The author feels that the truth lies, as usual, somewhere between these two extremes. It seems to us that he was aware of his role as a man who was to be instrumental in bringing a new, more democratic and more social Chile into existence. He was sincere in his desire to right many of the wrongs which the workers and agricultural laborers were facing. However, he was even more sincere in his belief in his own destiny and in his yearning for power and, in his later years, for a great place in his country's history. Not infrequently his ambition was more important to him than his convictions concerning social and economic problems. He was also a born schemer and political manipulator. As a result, several times during his career he committed acts, some of them truly outrageous, which a man less driven by a belief in his own destiny and his own rectitude would have tried to avoid. We shall note some of these acts later in this chapter.

The election of 1920 was one of the most closely contested in the country's history. The results were so uncertain that a "Tribunal of Honor" was set up by Congress to study the returns and make the final decision. The tribunal finally decided in favor of Arturo Alessandri, and this decision was ratified by Congress. Ever since, a dispute has raged over whether or not Alessandri really had a majority of the popular vote.

The significance of the victory of Arturo Alessandri in 1920 has been summarized by Alberto Edwards in *La Fronda Aristocrática* (p. 240):

. . . The crisis of 1920 was not a simple electoral problem, as many still imagine even today. Something deeper and more fundamental had ceased to exist: the passive obedience of the masses of the country to the old oligarchic circles. As a result, the political form which characterized that sentiment of submission could not continue to exist.

It was not, then, the ambitions or jealousies of this or that politician which brought about what occurred. The Unión Nacional, in submitting the election results to a Tribunal of Honor only recognized that its apparent victory hid a profound defeat: that a regime had come to an end.

Arturo Alessandri was installed as president of Chile in December, 1920. His first cabinet was headed by Pedro Aguirre Cerda, a prominent leader of the Radical Party, the largest group among those which had backed Alessandri for the presidency. This cabinet lasted only a few months because of the stubborn opposition of conservative elements in Congress and the continuance of the parliamentary system. Throughout the nearly four years of Alessandri's first period in office, cabinets followed one another in quick succession.

Although Alessandri was not able to convince Congress to support his program between 1920 and September, 1924, he did present a number of fundamental projects, the most important of which was the proposal for a labor code. Soon after taking office Alessandri had appointed a young lawyer, Dr. Moisés Poblete Troncoso, to draw up such a code, and on June 2, 1921, Alessandri presented a revised version of Poblete Troncoso's draft to Congress. A year later the proposed law was still unpassed, and the President sent a message to Congress defending the bill in the following terms:

It is an error to attribute exclusively to subversive propaganda of agitators the workers' movements which unfortunately have been perturbing the economic production of the country. They are due to deep causes. We need to enact protective laws which support the proletariat in those cases in which it asks and demands justice. We must raise the intellectual and moral culture of the disinherited classes, through the tenacious and persistent diffusion of learning. It is indispensable to combat alcoholism and the socially important diseases which debilitate the spirit, perturb the criterion and destroy the physical vigor of the race, destroying it as a moral and economic factor. We need to support the proletariat by constructing housing, giving it a minimum wage which will meet personal and family needs, and defend it from those material forces which impel it to do debilitating work superior to its capacities.

It is also indispensable to support the proletariat in those hours of misfortune provoked by accidents, unemployment, illness, old age and also at the same time aid women, and help children who are left orphans.

It is necessary to create tribunals of conciliation and arbitration which, with a criterion of high and egalitarian justice, can resolve conflicts produced by the labor contract between the capitalist and the worker. . . .[2]

Alessandri was the second chief of state in the hemisphere to propose such a wide scope of labor legislation. President Batlle of Uruguay had preceded him in this, but in some ways the laws provided by Alessandri were more ample than those enacted in Uruguay.

It is interesting, and important, to know the reasons which impelled Arturo Alessandri to take the lead in establishing a system of labor legislation which was to be a model throughout the hemisphere. Undoubtedly the fact that he had had the support of the organized workers during the 1920 election played a role in inducing the President to suggest legislation on their behalf. But there were other factors that influenced his decision. In a conversation with the author on April 3, 1947, Alessandri gave two reasons for his advocacy of the labor code, reasons which appear also in several of his public documents: the really deplorable conditions under which Chilean workers lived and labored; and the fact that Chile was a member of the new International Labor Organization and duty-bound to pass some of the legislation which the ILO had recommended.

As we have noted, the principal elements of the Labor Code were finally enacted into law during the constitutional crisis of September, 1924, and as a result of that crisis Arturo Alessandri decided to resign from the presidency. He sought refuge abroad soon afterward, going to Italy, where he spent the following months.

A military junta composed of General Luis Altamirano, Admiral Francisco Nef, and General Juan Bennett took over from President Alessandri. Behind them, and with the real power in its hands, stood a junta of young officers who during the months that followed grew increasingly discontented with the administration of the government by their three superior officers. This discontent culminated on January 23, 1925, in a new *coup d'état* led by Lieutenant Colonels Carlos Ibáñez and Marmaduque Grove. The new masters of the situation sent a message to Arturo Alessandri asking him to resume the presidency until the completion of his term in December. This message was seconded by a similar cable from the leaders of the parties which had supported Alessandri. That cable ended with the statement: "Situation entirely favorable."

Arturo Alessandri embarked once more for his native country, arriving in Santiago on March 20. During the next five months the government of Alessandri enacted many projects which profoundly altered the government and influenced the future economy and social system of Chile.

First, Alessandri brought about the establishment of a new national constitution to replace the one which had been in effect since 1833. Soon after his return he named a consultative commission to study the possibility of summoning a constitutional assembly. Subsequently the membership of this commission was considerably enlarged, and Alessandri charged it with drawing up the new constitution. The project prepared by the commission was submitted to a plebiscite on August 30, 1925, and was approved by a majority of 128,381 to 6,040, with less than half the country's registered voters going to the polls.[3]

The new constitution abolished the system of parliamentary government which had existed since the Revolution of 1891, and established instead a system in which the members of the cabinet were responsible to the president, and their removal by congress was made exceedingly difficult. Other changes were made, with the abolition of the Council of State and provision of election of the president directly by popular vote instead of by electoral college, as previously.

There was strong opposition to what was widely regarded as the imposition of a new constitution by a *de facto* government—since Congress, which had been dissolved at the time of Alessandri's overthrow in September, 1924, was not allowed to reconvene after his return. It is worth noting that this constitution remains in force more than thirty-five years later.

Another major political change brought about by Alessandri during his 1925 government was the separation of Church and State. This was achieved through direct negotiations with top Church officials in Chile and the Vatican. It was achieved without bitterness on either side and is generally recognized as having removed the issue of Church-State relations as a major factor in the country's politics.

A very important economic development during the period of Alessandri's restoration was the establishment of a central bank. Although the immediate occasion for this was the visit of a mission headed by Professor Edwin Kemmerer of Princeton University and its recommendation that such an institution be established, Alessandri pointed out that he had been a protagonist of the idea of a central bank for more than a decade and had sent messages to Congress urging its organization during the first four years of his administration.[4]

During the five months of his second period in office Alessandri began to put into effect the legislation passed on September 8, 1924. Unions were organized under the provisions of the law providing for their legal recognition. The social security funds for industrial workers and white-collar workers which were provided for in other laws of September 8 were established. This work was carried out under the direction of the Minister of Health and Social Security, José Santos Salas.

On October 1, 1925, Arturo Alessandri again resigned as president of Chile. The crisis which provoked his second resignation centered in the presidential candidacy of his Minister of War, Colonel Carlos Ibáñez. The nomination of Ibáñez brought about the resignation of the other members of Alessandri's cabinet, and Ibáñez then insisted that Alessandri sign no decree and take no other move which was not countersigned by him as the only remaining member of the cabinet. This demand, which Alessandri felt to be insolent, provoked him to quit the executive mansion and go into exile once again.

The political and personal feud between Arturo Alessandri and Carlos Ibáñez was of classic proportions and became a key factor in the life of the republic throughout the next quarter of a century. The feeling of Alessandri toward his opponent was graphically demonstrated by a picture which hung for many years in the waiting room of Arturo Alessandri's apartment off the Plaza de Armas in Santiago. The picture showed Alessandri and his 1925 cabinet at a social function, and Don Arturo had written across the face of it words more or less to this effect: "This picture was taken at a fiesta at which Colonel Carlos Ibáñez assured Sra. de Alessandri that her husband would be overthrown only over his (Ibáñez') dead body. Two weeks later Colonel Ibáñez overthrew President Alessandri."

Alessandri passed the next six years in exile, principally in Europe. He spent most of his time working for the overthrow of General Ibáñez, who, after a period as Minister of Interior, assumed the presidency in the middle of 1927 and established a dictatorship. Alessandri participated in a number of conspiracies against the Ibáñez regime and helped to raise money for exiled opponents of the dictatorship.

The fall of the dictatorship of Ibáñez in July, 1931, left the country in a state of confusion. It was the middle of the Great Depression, which had had a disastrous impact on Chile. In one year the country's national income had fallen almost 50 per cent as a result of the almost complete cessation of sales of the country's principal exports, nitrates and copper. The dictatorship of Ibáñez had left most of the principal political parties in confusion, and a number of new political groups had arisen, particularly on the left.

Alessandri and all of the other political leaders who had been in exile during the Ibáñez regime returned to Chile and threw themselves into the campaign to elect a successor to Ibáñez. Arturo Alessandri was one of the principal candidates.

Five nominees were finally put forward in the 1931 presidential campaign. Juan Esteban Montero, who had succeeded Ibáñez in the presidency and was very popular for his part in bringing down the dictatorship, was endorsed by the Conservative, Liberal, and Radical parties and by a new group known as Unión Republicana. Manuel Hidalgo was put forward by a group of new Socialist and dissident Communist groups which had appeared in the wake of Ibáñez' downfall, while Elías Laferte was the nominee of the official Communist Party. Augusto Rivera Parga was named by a Conservative group which considered Montero too much to the left.

Finally, there was Arturo Alessandri. He was named by a so-called Convention of the Left. Although he had only the support of one minor political party, the Partido Democrático, Alessandri was immediately regarded as the principal rival of Juan Esteban

Montero. He pictured himself as a champion of the workers and middle-class people who had supported him in his first campaign for the presidency more than a decade before. The most bitter words of the campaign were exchanged between those in the Montero camp and those in the Alessandri ranks.

The result was a victory for Montero. He received some 183,000 votes, while Alessandri got approximately 100,000. The other three nominees trailed far behind the two leaders in the poll.

The administration of President Juan Esteban Montero was short-lived and turbulent. It was marked by a deepening of the economic crisis and by several attempted insurrections. These included a mutiny of the fleet in November, 1931, and an attempt by civilians to seize army barracks at the northern city of Copiapó on Christmas Day. Neither of these attempted insurrections was successful, but the insurrection on June 4, 1932, was successful. The Montero regime was overthrown and was succeeded by a short-lived "Socialist Republic."

The role of Arturo Alessandri in bringing about the downfall of Montero and the installation of a "Socialist" regime has been the cause of bitter controversy ever since June, 1932. Alessandri himself maintained that his role in these events was that of intermediary between President Montero and the rebels. He defended this assertion in his "rectifications" of a biographical sketch published by Ricardo Donoso.

Donoso himself maintained that Alessandri was one of the prime movers in the revolt. The present writer is inclined to agree with this assertion. In an interview with the author in the Senate Building in Santiago on December 26, 1946, Marmaduque Grove, the first head of the Socialist Republic, asserted that the principal figures in planning the uprising were Grove himself, Eugenio Matte, head of Nueva Acción Política, one of the Socialist parties which had appeared after the fall of Ibáñez, and Arturo Alessandri. They made contact with one another through their common membership in the Masons, of which Matte was the Chilean Grand Master. Later, Carlos Dávila, who had been Ibáñez' ambassador to Washington, was also brought into the conspiracy.

Whatever his original connections with the plot against Montero, Alessandri was given no part in the government of the Socialist Republic. A junta was formed, of which Colonel Marmaduque Grove, founder and chief of the Air Force, was the principal figure. It announced a program of nationalization of public utilities, public works, and a variety of other measures, but they had no time to carry out these projects, since Grove was deposed by Carlos Dávila twelve days after the June 4 Revolution. Dávila maintained the Socialist Republic for one hundred days longer, then gave way to a provisional government, which called new elections for president and congress.

Again Arturo Alessandri was a candidate. This time he was supported by his own Liberal Party as well as the Radicals and the Democrats. His principal rival was Marmaduque Grove, who was supported by the various Socialist parties and by most of the organized-labor movement. One faction of the Liberals supported Enrique Zañartu; the Conservative Party named Rodríguez de la Sotta, and Elías Laferte was again named by the Communists. Alessandri was the winner by a strong majority, with Grove coming in second.[5]

The role of Arturo Alessandri during his 1932–38 administration was very different from that in his earlier period in office. Although he had been elected as the nominee of the moderate Left, he swung increasingly to the Right during his administration. The Radicals withdrew from his cabinet, and during most of his government Alessandri relied on the Conservative and Liberal parties for most of his support.

During this administration Alessandri's role was that of the restorer of economic and political stability rather than that of social reformer and advocate of change. He brought about a reorganization of the nitrate industry, encouraged the growth of copper mining, and aided the development of manufacturing. At the same time his administration was faced by serious labor unrest, and although it enacted some new social legislation, the administration's harshness toward the trade-union movement made the second Alessandri government anathema to the workers.

Under Ibáñez the nitrate industry had been organized under a government monopoly. The industry had been in a state of crisis ever since World War I, during which the Germans developed the process of extracting nitrogen from the air. The administration of this monopoly was inefficient and corrupt, and by the time Alessandri took office late in 1932 there was widespread sentiment in favor of abolishing it. The Alessandri government patronized the reorganization of the industry, with the extraction of the nitrates being put in the hands of three private companies—two owned by the Guggenheim interests, the third an Anglo-Chilean enterprise—with the government merely undertaking the work of selling the product abroad through the newly established Nitrate and Iodine Sales Corporation. A considerable degree of prosperity was restored to the nitrate industry after this reorganization, though it never was able to resume the key position in the Chilean economy which it had enjoyed before World War I.

It was during the Alessandri administration of the 1930's that copper mining took the place of nitrates as the principal source of Chile's foreign exchange. The extraction of copper ore was largely in the hands of the Kennecott and Anaconda companies from the United States.

The Alessandri regime generally enjoyed the support of the country's industrialists, and it took a number of steps to encourage the growth of manufacturing. In March, 1933, a law was passed providing for a sizable general increase in tariff duties. The Alessandri administration also continued and developed a policy which had been started before it took office of using "exchange restrictions, import licenses and quotas and the controls authorized by the so-called law of overproduction" as supplements to the tariff as a protection to industry.[6]

Another project of the Alessandri administration presaged the establishment of the Chilean Development Corporation by Alessandri's successor, Pedro Aguirre Cerda, in 1939. This was the organization in the nitrate provinces of Antofagasta and Tarapacá of two Institutos de Fomento Minero e Industrial (Institutes of Mineral and Industrial Development), for the rehabilitation of this area of the republic which was particularly hard hit by the effects of the world depression. These institutes, like the later Development Corporation, were authorized to establish new industries or invest in and lend money to old ones.

Carlos Keller, in discussing the evolution of economic ideas and policy in Chile, calls the Alessandri administration of the 1930's the beginning of "the Socialist Epoch" in Chilean economic history. He notes that in spite of the supposed adherence of the Conservative and Liberal parties to the ideas of free enterprise and economic liberalism, they in fact began the policy of using the resources of the government for aiding and directing the country's economic development and industrialization.[7]

The principal addition to social legislation enacted during the Alessandri administration of the 1930's was the law providing for preventive medicine. This law, which bears the name of its author, Eduardo Cruz Coke, provided for annual health examinations for white-collar workers, and for medical aid and subsidies for any workers found to have any of a number of diseases listed in the law. The law was passed with the blessings of the Alessandri government.

Politically the Alessandri regime of the 1930's restored constitutional government and reestablished the principle that the executive and legislative branches of government are to be chosen at the ballot box and not in the barracks or officers' club. Although Alessandri several times secured "special powers" to deal with political crises, his government was on the balance a democratic one and paved the way, after Alessandri's retirement from the presidency, for a much more rapid evolution of the reform process which Alessandri himself had started in 1920.

Alessandri was faced with a great deal of social and political unrest. There developed during his administration a number of new political groups, at least some of which were to have a very significant impact on the future of the country.

Probably the most important and certainly the most durable political group which appeared during the Alessandri administration was the Socialist Party. This was established by those groups which had supported the Socialist Republic of June 4, 1932, and subsequently had backed Marmaduque Grove as a candidate for the presidency a few months later. From its foundation the Socialist Party was a major force in the country's politics. It controlled the growing trade-union movement and had the support of the majority of the manual workers. By 1938 it was the most important popular party in Chile. The Socialists were bitter enemies of Alessandri during these years.

Another important political party to appear during the Alessandri administration of the 1930's was the Partido Nacista, or Nazi Party of Chile. It was strongest in the southern part of the country, where the largest number of people of German extraction were to be found. Youth groups of the party roamed the streets of Santiago and other cities as the German Nazis had done before them. There were frequent clashes between these Nazi "storm troopers" and the members of the Youth Federation of the Socialist Party.

The Partido Nacista gained additional influence because of the close association with it of the ex-dictator General Carlos Ibáñez. In the presidential election campaign of 1938 the Nacistas formed the principal force in the groups which named Ibáñez as a candidate. Perhaps this close association of the Nacistas with Alessandri's most bitter enemy serves to explain the bloody nature of the suppression of an attempted revolt by the Nacistas on September 5, 1938, in the midst of the presidential campaign.

A group of young Nazis seized the headquarters of the Industrial Workers Social Security Fund, which was located across the street from the presidential palace. They were attacked by the national police and some army units, and all but a handful of those involved in the revolt were killed by the attackers, most of them after they had surrendered. Alessandri's enemies have maintained that he ordered the cold-blooded execution of most of the Nacistas after they had already surrendered. Alessandri himself always maintained that the military officers in charge of the attack were responsible for this outrage.

The incident of September 5 was decisive in determining the results of the election which occurred a few weeks later. General Ibáñez withdrew from the race and ordered his supporters to back Pedro Aguirre Cerda, the nominee of the Popular Front, who won by a narrow majority.

The Popular Front had unified most of the opponents of Alessandri, including the Radical, Socialist, Radical-Socialist, and Communist parties, a faction of the Democratic Party, and the Confederation of Workers of Chile. In a convention of delegates from all of these groups the Popular Front named a leading figure in the Radical Party, Pedro Aguirre Cerda, as its candidate for the presidency. He was a progressive landowner and vintner who was known among his supporters as "Don Tinto" (*tinto* being the Chilean name for good red wine). Aguirre Cerda was a veteran politician who had

gained particular prominence for his work on behalf of public education. Ironically he had been the first Minister of Interior (virtually
prime minister) of Alessandri in 1920–21.

Alessandri did not support Aguirre Cerda. Their paths had drifted
far apart in the intervening eighteen years. Alessandri by 1938 was
the outstanding leader of the Right; Aguirre Cerda was the standard-
bearer of the Left. The influence of the Alessandri administration
was thrown behind Gustavo Ross Santa María, who had been a stal-
wart of Alessandri's administration after 1932 and was the candidate
of the Conservative and Liberal parties.

The closeness of the vote in the 1938 presidential election was
reminiscent of the situation in 1920. Feelings were violent on both
sides. Powerful economic interests feared the results which would
flow from the installation of a Popular Front government. There
was talk about preventing Aguirre Cerda from taking office, but in
a speech before the National Agricultural Society, Alessandri made
the following statement:

I, gentlemen, with honest neutrality, will observe the functioning
of the constitutional processes, and come what may, I will be responsible before the nation for seeing that the presidency is turned over to
whosoever the constitutional processes declare has been elected President of Chile.[8]

Although some of Alessandri's enemies, notably his biographer
Ricardo Donoso, have maintained that Alessandri was maneuvering
to bring about a cancellation of the results of the election and the
extension of his own term of office, the fact remains that Alessandri,
chief spokesman for the groups opposed to Pedro Aguirre Cerda,
turned over the government in due form to him after his November,
1938, election victory.

During the next five and a half years Arturo Alessandri was out
of office, though never out of politics. When Pedro Aguirre Cerda
died early in 1942, prompting a new presidential election, Alessandri
once again played a key role. The candidates in this poll were Juan
Antonio Rios, backed by the parties which had supported the Aguirre
Cerda administration; and General Carlos Ibáñez, backed by the
Conservative Party and a faction of the Liberal Party. Alessandri,

declared enemy of Ibáñez, influenced the majority of the Liberal
Party to support Rios (whom Alessandri didn't like either but
whom he preferred to Ibáñez). Alessandri campaigned actively for
Rios and deserved much of the credit for his victory. Rios won by
260,000 votes to the 204,854 received by Ibáñez.[9]

Alessandri himself became a candidate for public office again in
the middle of 1944. The death of a Communist senator in an area
south of Santiago paved the way for Alessandri's candidacy. He
represented the opposition, running against Radical Party member
Guillermo del Pedregal, nominee of the parties supporting the Rios
government. Alessandri was victorious by a vote of 20,638 to 17,888.
In the following year Alessandri was elected president of the Senate,
a position he held until his death.

By 1945 Arturo Alessandri was the undisputed leader of the
Liberal Party and was the Grand Old Man of Chilean politics. His
influence, particularly among elements of the Right, was very
considerable, and even many of Don Arturo's old enemies of the
Left were tending to look upon him with a rather more tolerant attitude, as was attested in numerous interviews which the author had
with them late in 1946 and early in 1947.

In the middle of 1946 Alessandri again played a crucial role in a
presidential election. Juan Antonio Rios died early in 1946, again
precipitating an election to choose his successor. An attempt was
made to form a united front of the Right-wing parties. A convention
was held for this purpose, but it failed to reach agreement, and the
Conservative Party named Senator Eduardo Cruz Coke, author of
the 1938 Preventive Medicine Law. The Liberals named Arturo
Alessandri's son, Senator Fernando Alessandri, as its candidate.

During this campaign a story circulated in Santiago which epitomized Arturo Alessandri's continuing ambition and high regard
for himself in spite of his advanced age. This tale concerned a meeting of right-wing politicians to discuss the problem of a candidate
for president. One of those present suggested Arturo Alessandri
Rodríguez, old Don Arturo's eldest son, a distinguished lawyer and
long-time head of the Law School of the University of Chile. Another
suggested Senator Fernando Alessandri; a third proposed Arturo
Matte Larain, Don Arturo's son-in-law. Finally someone mentioned
the name of Eduardo Alessandri, a leading member of the Chamber

of Deputies and also a son of old Don Arturo. The old man, who had been listening with some impatience to all this, finally spoke up and asked, "And these sons, have they no father?"

The story is undoubtedly apocryphal, but it indicates the importance which the Alessandri clan occupied in the affairs of the Liberal Party. As a matter of fact, before the Liberals finally named Fernando Alessandri, they tentatively nominated old Don Arturo, who withdrew in favor of his son.

The election was a very close one. In addition to the Conservative and Liberal nominees, Gabriel González Videla, a seasoned Radical politician, was named by the Radicals and Communists, and the Socialist Party nominated the trade-union leader and member of the Chamber of Deputies Bernardo Ibáñez. None of the four candidates got a majority of the popular vote, which meant that the final decision was thrown into the hands of Congress.

Gabriel González Videla had the largest popular vote, but Congress was controlled by the Right. If González was to obtain the presidency, he had to negotiate with elements of the Right. Arturo Alessandri, as spokesman for the Liberals, agreed to throw their votes to González, who in turn agreed to take the Liberals into his cabinet to balance the influence of the Communists, to whom González Videla was also committed to give ministries.

The first cabinet of González Videla lasted from November, 1946, until April, 1947. Early in the latter month municipal elections showed trends which were very disturbing to both the Radical and Liberal parties. The Radicals lost many votes to their Communist partners; the Liberals lost to the Conservatives who were in the opposition.

After the municipal election there was great indecision among the government parties. There were calls from both the Radical and Liberal ranks that their parties withdraw from the cabinet or that the Communists be expelled from it. No decision was made for a week. The deadlock was finally broken by Arturo Alessandri on the Sunday following the election, when he granted a page-long interview in *El Mercurio*, the Liberal daily of Santiago. After a long exposition of the nature of the Chilean Constitution of 1925, Alessandri commented, almost as if it were an afterthought, that he belleved the Liberal Party should withdraw its members from President González Videla's cabinet.

Alessandri's word settled the matter. The next morning the Liberals resigned, followed by the Radicals. Only the Communists refused to quit voluntarily, and President González was forced to ask the Communist ministers for their resignations. A few months later he became their bitterest enemy.

This was Arturo Alessandri's last major intervention in Chilean politics, though he lived four more years, dying on August 24, 1950. With him died an era which had seen a fundamental change in the nature of Chile's economy, society, and politics.

Arturo Alessandri was certainly the outstanding Chilean of the first half of the twentieth century. He was an explosively controversial character whom other politicians either violently supported or bitterly opposed. Perhaps a foreigner is in a better position than most Chileans to assess the impact which Arturo Alessandri made on the life of his country.

Certainly the fundamental significance of Alessandri's career was that he was the instrument through which a social revolution of profound significance was carried out. Through him change in political power from one class to another was achieved.

The forces of which Alessandri was able to seize the leadership in 1920 had been gaining ground in Chile for a long time before the election of that year. Unlike most of the Latin American countries, Chile had built up a sizable public education system that turned out a relatively large white-collar middle class which for a long time found little employment except with the government.

The development of the nitrate industry after 1879 gave an impulse to the growth of manufacturing as well as bringing new prosperity to the country. World War I, by making it difficult for Chile to import manufactured goods from abroad, spurred the process of industrialization. These new industries strengthened the middle class and brought into existence a new wage-earning proletariat.

The growing middle class and the new proletariat was by the second decade of the twentieth century growing increasingly restive at the continued control of Chilean politics by the landowning oligarchy. The middle class found its principal spokesman in the

Radical Party and elements of the badly divided Liberal Party. The miners and industrial workers supported the Democratic and Socialist Labor parties.

Alessandri succeeded in 1920 in channeling behind himself those forces which were tending to undermine the aristocratic structure of early republican Chile. With his victory in the election of that year absolute power over the nation as a whole passed from the hands of the rural oligarchy which had controlled the country since the enactment of the Constitution of 1833. Presidential elections were decided in the cities, though the oligarchy's control of the rural regions of the country was virtually untouched. The land remained in the oligarchs' hands, and they were able to march their peasants to the polls to vote as instructed by the landowners, with the result that until the election of 1952 the rural areas remained the stronghold of the Liberal and Conservative parties, the principal defenders of the rural *status quo*.

The second aspect of great importance in Alessandri's career was his patronage of advanced labor and social legislation. We have noted that he suggested as early as 1921 that Congress enact a labor code, and that the principal elements of this code were actually passed during the crisis of September, 1924. Although some of those critical of Alessandri have sought to deny to him any of the credit for the passage of this legislation in the light of the peculiar circumstances under which it was enacted, the author thinks this criticism is unjust. He was certainly the first chief executive to propose a broad program of labor legislation, and his constant hammering on the subject made the program sufficiently popular that the military men saw fit to use it as a blind for their demand for their own pay increases. The passage of the preventive-medicine law in the Alessandri administration of the 1930's occurred without any pressure from the armed forces.

Alessandri, as the first middle-class president of Chile, as the father of that country's famous labor and social legislation, and as an early exponent of industrialization, has an assured place in his country's history. He is the prophet of the Chilean Revolution, which, though still incomplete, has been largely peaceful, and has been one of the most far-reaching movements for social, economic, and political change in all of Latin America.

Víctor Raúl Haya de la Torre
and "Indo-America"

ॐॐॐॐ

In 1946 a small delegation of Indians from a community in the high valleys of the interior visited the headquarters of the Aprista Party in Lima, Peru. It came to obtain the help of the Aprista leaders to foil an attempt by a neighboring landlord to seize the community's land. The party's Secretary for Indian Affairs spent a long time with the visiting Indian leaders but was unable to obtain from them any proof that the land in question belonged to their group and not to their neighbor. Without such proof the party leaders could extend little help to the Indians.

After several hours of fruitless discussion with his visitors the party secretary turned them over to Víctor Raúl Haya de la Torre, the "Chief" of the Aprista Party. Haya talked quietly with them for a few minutes in their own Quechua language, explaining who he was and what it was that he needed from the Indians. After hearing him out the leader of the group reached down into his Indian pantaloons and pulled out a document signed in the 1760's by King Carlos III of Spain granting to this community the right to hold in perpetuity the land in question.

The Indian leader, addressing Haya de la Torre, said: "Take it, Don Apra. You we trust. This is the most precious possession of our community, except our land. But you may keep it as long as you wish."

Haya assured the Indian that he would need the document only long enough to photograph it, after which it would be returned to the Indians' possession. A few minutes later the document was back in the hands of the Indians, and after a few hours they started their long trek back to the highlands.

This incident epitomizes many things about Haya de la Torre. It is characteristic of his concern for the Indian masses who make up three-fourths of the population of Peru and a significant portion of the whole population of Latin America. It is also indicative of the wide support and respect which Haya and the Apristas have gained among the people of Peru.

Haya de la Torre, who was the founder, remains the most outstanding leader of the Partido Aprista Peruano, the first of the national revolutionary parties that have become such an important element in the political life of Latin America. But Haya de la Torre is much more than that; he is the philosopher of the whole Latin American Revolution. For nearly forty years he has been urging the need for an indigenous movement for the social, economic, and political transformation of the twenty republics which he calls "Indo-America." Over thirty years ago he developed the basic principles for such a movement. These principles, though they have been varied in detail to fit the needs of different countries, have become the backbone of the program of parties throughout the hemisphere.

Haya de la Torre was a close student of the Mexican Revolution, having lived several years in Mexico during the 1920's. He drew many of his ideas from that experience. He also was very much aware of the reform movement launched in Uruguay by José Batlle. Of the other men discussed in the present volume, Betancourt, Figueres, Paz Estenssoro, and Hernán Siles undoubtedly have been deeply influenced by the writings and programs of Haya de la Torre and are glad to acknowledge their intellectual debt to him. One other, Juan Perón, also drew heavily on the ideas of Haya and was personally acquainted with some of the Aprista leaders who were in exile in Argentina in the late 1930's and early 1950's.

Víctor Raúl Haya de la Torre was born in 1895 in the city of Trujillo in northern Peru. He was a member of the provincial aristocracy of that area, and his matronymic indicated his descent from Juan la Torre, one of the lieutenants of Francisco Pizarro in the conquest of Peru. Haya's father was a member of the Peruvian Congress, and an uncle became a candidate in 1920 for vice president of the republic on the ticket headed by Augusto B. Leguía in an election which was not held because Leguía seized power by force.

Haya's parents, particularly his mother, were proud of their "pure Spanish descent." However, Víctor Raúl's physiognomy was a silent witness to the fact that Indian blood as well as that of their

European conquerors ran in his veins. He himself first became aware of this fact when he visited the ruins of an ancient Indian civilization at Chan Chan near Trujillo and saw there carvings of Indian heads which he thought were remarkably like his own profile. Although his mother had no explanation for this strange coincidence, it served to arouse for the first time Víctor Raúl's interest in the Peruvian Indians.[1]

Haya de la Torre's interest in the Indians was heightened during his school days in Trujillo. A number of young intellectuals and students of that city organized a cultural movement during the years before World War I which was "Indianist" in its orientation. Haya joined this movement, though he was still very young. It undoubtedly deepened his interest in and concern for the Indian masses of Peru.[2]

From Trujillo, Haya de la Torre went to the ancient University of San Marcos in his nation's capital, Lima. While attending the University he worked as a clerk in the office of a prominent lawyer, Eliodoro Romero, who was also a leading political figure. In this office Haya got his first on-the-spot acquaintance with politics. He was able to observe firsthand the maneuvers leading up to Augusto B. Leguía's presidential candidacy, since Romero was a leading supporter of Leguía.[3]

Haya became a leader of the Federation of Students of San Marcos University. In that capacity he took an active part in organizing student support for a general strike by the Local Labor Federation of Lima in favor of an eight-hour day, a strike which was successful. Soon thereafter Haya helped organize a congress at which was established the Federation of Textile Workers, the first national union to be set up in Peru.[4]

Víctor Raúl was also active in bringing about the so-called "University Reform." This movement for a reorganization of the traditional structure of Latin American universities had started in 1918 in the University of Córdoba in Argentina and quickly spread to neighboring countries. It had various objectives, including the modernization of the curricula of the universities, which still were excessively humanistic in their orientation. It also sought to establish the autonomy of the universities, freeing them from domination of both Church and State, and putting their control in the hands of the faculty members and students.

In 1920 Haya de la Torre was elected president of the Student Federation, and in that capacity he organized a national student congress, the first in Peru's history. Perhaps the chief result of this congress was a resolution to establish "popular universities" in various cities of Peru. Under Haya's leadership several of these "Universidades Populares González Prada" were set up as adult-education centers in which the university students were the teachers and members of the young trade-union movement made up the bulk of the students.

Still as president of the University Federation, Haya de la Torre signed in 1921 the first Latin American student pact with Gabriel del Mazo, president of the Argentine University Foundation. Fulfilling the terms of this agreement, Haya made a tour the following year in Argentina, Uruguay, and Chile to further the propaganda for the University Reform.

The awakening of the students by the University Reform stimulated their interest in politics. Inevitably they were thrown into conflict with the dictatorship of Augusto B. Leguía. He looked with suspicion on the students "popular universities" as possible foci of political subversion and from time to time interfered with their courses. However, an open conflict between the students and the regime did not occur until May 23, 1923.

President Leguía, in a move designed to ingratiate himself with the Catholic Church, decided to "dedicate Peru to the sacred heart of Jesus" in a colorful ceremony in the streets of Lima. The Student Federation, which was strongly anticlerical, determined to demonstrate against what they considered an "outrage." In cooperation with the Local Labor Federation of Lima they organized a large meeting of protest at which Haya de la Torre was one of the chief speakers.

While the joint labor-student meeting was in progress it was fired upon by police and soldiers, and one worker and one student were killed. Thereafter the government sought the arrest of the principal leaders of both the Student Federation and the Local Labor Federation. Haya de la Torre evaded the police for four and a half months but was finally captured on October 2, 1923.

For eight days Haya was incarcerated in a prison on San Lorenzo island, near Lima. There he engaged in a hunger strike, while both the unions and the Student Federation demonstrated in favor of his release. After eight days, when the doctors reported that Haya's physical condition was worsening and he might well die if his hunger strike continued, the young student leader was spirited out of his prison and was deported, unceremoniously, to the Republic of Panama.

With his deportation Haya began his first period of exile, which lasted almost eight years. During this time, in spite of his youth, he was to develop the fundamentals of his political philosophy and to become a leader of continental significance. For the next eight years Haya wandered back and forth in Central America, Mexico, the United States, and Europe.

While Haya was still in Panama he accepted an invitation from the University of Havana to give a series of lectures there. During his stay in Cuba he was named honorary president of the Federation of Students of Havana University and in this capacity organized a workers' education project similar to the one he had organized in Peru, this time under the name of José Martí Popular University.

By this time Haya's fame was spreading, and he was invited to Mexico by the Minister of Education, José Vasconcelos. In Mexico, Haya first worked as a "missionary teacher" in the rural areas of the republic and then served as Vasconcelos' private secretary. It was during his stay in Mexico that Haya formally established the Alianza Popular Revolucionaria Americana, which was to win continental fame under its initials APRA. The APRA was established in May, 1924.

The next year Haya de la Torre accompanied José Vasconcelos on a visit to the University of Texas. His visit to the United States lasted only a few weeks, after which he embarked on a ship of the Baltic Line for a three months' trip to Russia. There he was an observer at the Fifth Congress of the Communist International and had extensive conversations with a number of the top leaders, including Leon Trotsky, Alexander Lunatcharsky, Minister of Defense General Frunze, and others.

Later Haya de la Torre said that it was during his visit to Moscow that he became convinced that he could not become a Communist and that the program of Moscow was not the correct one for Latin America. He said that the leaders of the Soviet State and of the Communist International showed an abysmal ignorance of conditions in Latin America, not even being able to identify the location of many of the Latin American nations. He reported that Zinoviev, then president of the Comintern, had devoted only a paragraph to all of Latin America in his report to the Fifth Congress of the International. Haya became convinced that the advocates of social revolution and national economic independence in Latin America must establish their own organizations in each country of the area, and that these organizations must be completely independent of any groups from outside the hemisphere.

From the Soviet Union, Haya went back to Western Europe, settling down in Switzerland for the purpose of writing a book on his experience in Russia. While hard at work he was arrested by the Swiss police, all his papers were seized, and Haya was jailed. He escaped and fled across the border into Italy, making his way from there to Great Britain.

In England, Haya became a student at the London School of Economics and from there went to Oxford University, where he completed his studies in economics and sociology. During his stay there Haya de la Torre participated actively in student affairs and represented the Oxford Union in a debate on the Monroe Doctrine with the University of Washington.

In February, 1927, Haya and a group of his fellow Apristas attended the World Anti-Imperialist Congress, organized by the Communists, in Brussels. It was at this meeting that a definitive break occurred between Haya de la Torre and the Communists. Although the latter had been very anxious to get Haya to attend the meeting, they were not happy with his attitude there. He rejected the idea that Communists were the natural leaders of the fight against imperialism. In his book *El Antimperialismo y el Apra* (p. 48) Haya de la Torre describes this incident:

. . . The influence and control of the Communist Party were inescapable in that assembly, which brought together the most illustrious figures in world leftism. In spite of strong Communist pressure and the atmosphere of easy optimism frequent in such assemblies, we maintained our ideological position and the character of APRA as an autonomous political organization tending towards constituting itself into a party. . . . On the key point of the participation of the bourgeoisie and petty bourgeoisie in the anti-imperialist struggle, we opposed the objections of APRA to the Communist slogans. It was then that there occurred the most dramatic polemic of the Congress. The Latin American delegation had to meet apart during five or six hours to convince us. We maintained our reserve. We made note of it when we signed the final conclusions of the Congress; and thus it appeared in the official documents published in all known languages.

Brussels defined the Aprista theoretical line and made very clear our differences with Communism. It was natural that from then on APRA was the target of sharp criticism. For Communism there could not exist another party of the Left which was not the official one of the Third International of Moscow, of Stalinist orthodoxy. Every political organization that Moscow doesn't command must be execrated and combated. After the Brussels Congress of 1927 the APRA was so treated.

In August, 1927, the Peruvian leader returned to the United States, where he remained for three months. He was a speaker at the Institute of Political Science at Williamstown, Massachusetts, and at Columbia University, after which he lectured widely for the League for Industrial Democracy.

Haya de la Torre returned to Mexico in November, 1927, invited to give a series of lectures at the National University. Afterward he made speeches in all the provincial universities as well. Meanwhile his fame brought him invitations to speak at the universities of El Salvador, Guatemala, and Costa Rica in Central America. He subsequently toured that area, but was deported from El Salvador and Guatemala before his full lecture schedule had been completed.

The Aprista leader was regarded as a "dangerous revolutionary" by the dictators of the Central American republics as well as, apparently, by important officials of the United States government. When Haya reached Panama for the purpose of taking ship back to Mexico, he was arrested in the harbor of Panama City by officials of the Canal Zone, although he was not on Zone territory but in that of the Republic of Panama. He was transported across the isthmus and was held in prison until a ship left port—for Germany. Haya was made to pay $90 for his passage and was unceremoniously placed on board this ship.

Once arrived in Germany, Haya was in trouble with the immigration authorities there since he had no visa. Although he received no help from the Peruvian authorities, his case aroused widespread interest among German intellectuals, who were successful in getting Haya's stay in Germany established on a legal basis.

Haya de la Torre remained in Germany for the next four years. Finally, in 1931, a year after the overthrow of the regime of Augusto B. Leguía, Haya returned to Peru to run as candidate of the newly organized Partido Aprista Peruano in elections to choose a successor to Leguía.

During his stay in Europe, Haya de la Torre acted as correspondent for a number of newspapers in Mexico, Argentina, and other Latin American countries. Many of his articles were subsequently collected and published in book form. The most notable of these appeared under the titles *Impresiones de la Inglaterra Imperialista y la Rusia Soviética* (Editorial Claridad, Buenos Aires, 1932), *A Donde Va Indo América?* (Editorial Ercilla, Santiago, Chile, 1934), and *Construyendo el Aprismo* (Editorial Claridad, Buenos Aires, 1933). The first consists of articles written in 1924 and 1925; the second included pieces written between 1927 and 1930, with a final "postscript" sent out by Haya from Peru in 1934; and the third also contained mainly articles of the 1927–30 period.

These books reflect the evolution of Haya's outlook and philosophy. The first part of *Impresiones*, dealing with Great Britain and the Soviet Union, is exceedingly friendly toward the Soviet Union and speaks of the Communists as "comrades" and friends. Haya's discussion of events in Great Britain is written on an orthodox Marxist level. Writing during and after the General Strike of 1926, he sees Britain in the grip of a violent class struggle which is going to destroy completely the country's political democracy. This democracy itself is of dubious value in Haya's eyes.

A Donde Va Indo América? is a quite different sort of book. Its emphasis is completely on the need for Latin America, or "Indo-America" as Haya usually refers to it, to find its own destiny. Although he does not strongly attack the Communists, he virtually ignores them, and puts his emphasis on the program of the APRA, which by that time had branches in various Latin American countries and among Peruvian exiles both in America and Europe. *Construyendo el Aprismo* has a similar focus.

More fundamental than these collections of articles was another book which Haya wrote in 1928 in Mexico but which was not published until six years later. This was *El Antimperialismo y el Apra,* which was a fundamental statement of the Aprista program for Latin America.

In *El Antimperialismo y el Apra,* Haya has moved far from orthodox Marxism. He still considers himself a Marxist but insists that when applying this philosophy to Latin America one must revise it substantially. The immediate problem of the Latin Americans is defeating the advance of imperialism and overthrowing the semifeudal classes which dominate the internal life of the Latin American countries and are, he maintains, the best allies of the imperialists.

From all these writings one can get a clear picture of the Aprista program and philosophy as Haya de la Torre developed it during the 1920's and early 1930's. The original program of the Alianza Popular Revolucionaria Americana, drawn up in 1924, was extremely simple, consisting of five points: [5]

1. Action against imperialism.
2. For the political unity of Latin America.
3. For the nationalization of land and industry.
4. For the internationalization of the Panama Canal.
5. For solidarity with all oppressed peoples and classes of the world.

Haya synthesizes the implications of this program in one paragraph when he writes:

Our historic experience in Latin America, and especially the very important and contemporaneous experience of Mexico, show us that the immense power of Yankee imperialism cannot be confronted without the unity of the Latin American peoples. But since this unity is conspired against jointly by our governing classes and imperialism, and since the former aid the latter, the State, instrument of oppression by one class of another, becomes an arm of our national ruling classes and imperialism to exploit our producing classes and to keep our peoples divided. Consequently, the fight against our governing classes is indispensable; political power must be captured by the producers; production must be socialized, and Latin America must constitute a Federation of States. This is the only road to victory over imperialism, and the political objectives of APRA as the International Revolutionary Anti-Imperialist Party.[6]

In *El Antimperialismo y el Apra,* Haya de la Torre polemizes with the Communists and defends the idea that APRA must become a Latin American political party with branches in every country. It is not enough, he says, merely to protest against United States and other imperialist violations of the national sovereignty of the Latin American nations. Those who oppose these violations must be organized as a political party determined to gain power and so to organize the Latin American nations that they can confront imperialism individually and collectively.

This political party must include within its ranks various class groups. The Communists are utterly wrong, he says, in thinking that a purely workers' party is the answer for Latin America in the immediate future. Rather, the fight against imperialism and the retrograde social systems existing in the Latin American countries must be undertaken by a party which includes the new industrial working class, the peasants, and the middle class.

The middle class has an especially important role to play because it is the first group to feel the full impact of imperialism in these countries. He argues:

. . . the monopoly which imperialism imposes cannot help but bring the destruction and regression of what we call generically the middle class. Thus as industrial capitalism when it appeared in the most economically advanced countries reduced, absorbed, and proletarianized the petty bourgeoisie, only a small part of which became part of the dominant class; so—with the peculiarities of our situation—imperialism subjugates or economically destroys the middle class of the backward countries which it penetrates. The small capitalist, the small industrialist, the small rural and urban proprietor, the little miner, the small merchant, the intellectual, the white-collar worker, etc., form the middle class whose interests are attacked by imperialism. . . . According to the laws of competition and monopoly which are characteristic of capitalism, its imperialist form, which is its culminating

expression, destroys the incipient capitalists and property-owners, sub
jugates them, and encloses them in the tentacles of the great trusts or
under the yoke of credit and mortgages. . . .

In view of all this Haya asks:

Would it be realistic, then, to refuse the alliance of the middle
classes with the working and peasant classes in the anti-imperialist
struggle? Certainly not. Or would it be possible that this alliance be
limited to rhetorical protests, to a mere labor of resistance; or to agita-
tions without any realistic and *political* plan? Obviously no.[8]

The Communists certainly have no answer to the needs of Latin
America, says Haya. He sums up his criticisms of the Third International thus:

Will the Communist party with its headquarters and indelegable
authority in Moscow be the one to conduct Indoamerica to its victory
against Imperialism? Let us reflect on the map of the world, on the
history of our peoples, and on the reality of our situation. The answer,
even of competent Communists—of the few realists, labelled by the
rest as "rightists," "intellectuals," "petty bourgeois," etc.—is in the
negative. The Communist Party in Indoamerica lacks the force and
the authority to lead the anti-imperialist struggle. Neither in the name
of the Third International, nor in the name of its Panamerican Anti-
Imperialist League, which is condemned to failure, can it do anything.
The anti-imperialist current among our peoples is older than the Third
International and more vast than the exclusiveness of their class party.
In order that one social class in Indoamerica could be able by itself to
victoriously lead the anti-imperialist struggle, it would have to achieve
the conditions which Marx set forth for the effective class leadership
of a revolution: "For the emancipation of a people to coincide with
the emancipation of a given class within bourgeois society, it is necessary that that class as such represent all of society." And this exactly
is not the case with our nascent proletarian class, and even less with the
weak Communist Party in Indoamerica, which doesn't even represent
the proletariat. The anti-imperialist movement, which is and must be
a movement of United Front, requires a political organization of the
United Front also. The Anti-Imperialist Leagues are not enough, and the
Communist Party is too much.[9]

The anti-imperialist, multiclass party must seek to gain power as a political party, and once in power must undertake to establish a new kind of state, which Haya calls the "Anti-Imperialist State." He sketches very roughly what the nature of this new type of state will be. He says:

The new organization of the State will evidently have to be something like the so-called "State Capitalism" which was so highly developed during the imperialist war of 1914–18, and which reached a truly extraordinary level of development in Germany. . . . In the Anti-Imperialist State, a State of defensive economic war, it is also indispensable to limit private initiative and control the production and circulation of wealth. The Anti-Imperialist State which must *direct* the national economy will have to deny individual or collective rights in the economic field when the use of these rights implies an imperialist danger.[10]

More specifically, Haya argues that the state must limit the right of the individual or private corporation to enter into contracts with foreign firms for the exploitation of the Latin American countries' natural resources. However, he does not believe that the Latin American nations, even under Aprista leadership, should forbid the importation of foreign capital. On this point he argues:

To the candid thesis of the feudal rulers subject to imperialism who proclaim that "all capital is good," is opposed the antithesis of intense radicals that "We don't need capital." The Aprista synthesis is that so long as the present economic order exists in the world, there is both necessary and good capital and other unnecessary and dangerous capital. We say that it is the State and only it—the Anti-Imperialist State— which must control the investment of capital under strict conditions, which will be met because of the necessity of excess capital of the great industrial centers to emigrate. The capitalist phase, then, must be undergone in our countries under the aegis of the Anti-Imperialist State. . . .[11]

He argues that the foreign investors will submit to controls. On this point he writes:

. . . the foreign capital which comes to our countries needs them as much as our countries need capital. Capital emigrates from the industrial countries to those which are underdeveloped because of an inescapable economic law. To place our countries in a position of inferiority with regard to foreign capital is to be ignorant of this law and to damage our nations. To condition, to limit, to systematize the entry of foreign capital in our countries is not to reject it, as some ingenuously believe. Even among peoples where foreign capital has to support the severest restrictions it enters. Naturally, foreign capital is not going to impose restrictions on itself. This role corresponds to the states which receive the capital. But to condition or restrict investment of foreign capital, it is necessary to have a real plan, economically and financially scientific, laid down by the State of the country which receives capital. A scientific plan presupposes an internal organization of the economy which takes into account national interests, and this is organic economic nationalism.[12]

Haya elaborates still further on the way in which foreign capital should be handled when he says:

. . . What Aprismo considers ruinous for Peru is that in the name of our need for foreign capital, the country is converted into a slave of this capital, and instead of foreign capital serving the progress of the country, the country becomes its servant. But it is impossible to get the country out of its present dependence if parallel to the conditioned and methodical entry of foreign capital, subject to a scientific plan assuring its best use for the country, there is not constructed a national economic system directed towards the greatest possible increase in productivity. A country without its own economy and subject only to dependence on foreign capital is nothing more than a colony. With a nation subordinated to the yoke of foreign capital, which exploits the worker, the merchant, the small proprietor, the taxpayer and the consumer, the State lacks all support to defend its sovereignty and becomes an instrument of foreign capital which directs the economy of the country.[13]

However, there are other problems in addition to that of dealing with the foreign investor with which the Anti-Imperialist State must be concerned, according to Haya. Most of all, it must come to grips with the problem of the land and its ownership. On this point Haya de la Torre writes with respect to Peru:

. . . in the regions of very large landholdings, where the Indian communities are violently oppressed and the worker lives in the most ominous servitude and ignorance, under economic and political tyranny, the State must gradually abolish the large landholdings, support and technically aid the communities, integrally educate the Indian and procure the best use of the riches produced for everyone. The land for him who works it and the maximum exploitation of the land and not of Man are the essential points in an agrarian program which tends to raise production scientifically.[14]

The Anti-Imperialist State must also assure political democracy. In this connection, writing in the early 1930's, Haya protests against the persecution to which the Aprista Party is being subjected. He says:

It would be very interesting to submit the political rulers of Peru to a public controversy over the fundamental problems of the government. Our party has suggested this to all of the men who rule or seek to rule. We do not believe that we are the possessors of absolute truth, but we are ready to discuss on the level of principle with the groups and men who oppose us. This is exactly what we ask: free discussion of the national problems by the Nation itself. We insist and shall insist on this demand now publicly formulated. We don't want to impose Aprismo by force, but we claim the right to discuss without force being used to keep us quiet. And that is what we ask of the people of Peru: that we be allowed to speak freely about the vital problems of the country, that we be permitted to call upon those who govern to debate. What less could the Partido Aprista Peruano demand than effective guarantees for a controversy in which the people will discover what is the best political orientation for Peru? [15]

The Anti-Imperialist State will be organized democratically, on a different basis from that traditional in Peru and most of Latin America, according to Haya de la Torre. He says:

Aprismo advocates the principle of functional democracy as the foundation stone of the life of the State. Functional democracy is associated with economic regionalism. . . . Economic regionalism is for its part a functional form of political and administrative decentralization, economically regionalist and functionally democratic, and must be based on the sovereignty of regional or provincial councils, from which must be chosen the National Parliament or Congress as the unifier and supreme director.[16]

Finally, Haya gives us a quick vision of the Latin America of the future as he sees it after the victory of APRA and the establishment of the Anti-Imperialist State:

With production intensified, organized on the basis of the restoration of the agrarian community, evolved, modernized and provided with all of the elements of modern technology and organized cooperatively, Indoamerica will be the granary and stable of the world. The revindication of the Indian as a man and of his system as a method of production are imperative for economic reasons. The index of production will rise extraordinarily. Adapting the system to the man and the man to the system and extending it to all of the agrarian region of the Andean zone under the form of state cooperatives, the economic transformation of South America will accelerate prodigiously. If we try to extend the system to industry as it develops—especially to mining, adopting all of the most modern production elements and methods—we will add another factor to the vast panorama of total economic transformation, axis of anti-imperialist resistance. The base, as the reader will have noted, is in the millions of indigenous workers of the countryside and of the mines, who still keep as a sacred aspiration for the future the restoration of a social system of the past. Restored in its essence and modernized by contemporary technology, we will have used the past as has no other people to establish favorable conditions for growth in the future.[17]

Haya's first long exile came to an end in 1931. The year before, Augusto B. Leguía, who had exiled Haya de la Torre, was overthrown. However, for almost twelve months the military junta headed by Lieutenant Colonel Sánchez Cerro which took over the government after Leguía's fall, refused to allow Haya to return to Peru. He had to remain in Germany, until he was nominated by the newly formed Partido Aprista Peruano, to run for the presidency against Sánchez Cerro.

Haya's return to Peru was memorable. In spite of his eight years of exile his memory had been kept fresh in the minds of both the students and workers of Peru. Over the years the leadership of the Student Federation continued to be in the hands of disciples of Haya de la Torre, and many of them were sent to jail or were forced by the government to go abroad to share his exile.

As for the organized-labor movement, it too remained under the spell of Haya. Each year the Textile Workers Federation published a special edition of its periodical on the anniversary of his deportation from Peru. He frequently published articles in the same magazine. Union leaders and students continued to cooperate during the first four years in the González Prada Popular Universities, though these were outlawed in 1927 by Leguía, whose government arrested most of the student and workers' leaders, charging them with "communism."

The most important figure in this group during Haya's absence was José Carlos Mariátegui. He had been a contemporary of Haya de la Torre in the university, and after Leguía's seizure of power in 1919 Mariátegui accepted a scholarship offered by the government for travel and study in Europe. There he became a convinced Marxist.

Upon his return from Europe, Mariátegui devoted himself to studying the economic, social, and political conditions of Peru. He published a number of books, the most important of which was entitled *Seven Essays on Peruvian Reality*. He also published a periodical called *Amáuta*. In this magazine Mariátegui published articles by Haya and other Apristas as well as by other Latin American leftist leaders and European Socialists and Communists.

Like Haya, Mariátegui was deeply concerned with the problems of Peru, and though more sympathetic with the Communists than was Haya, felt that communism in Peru must be cut to the national mold. With this in mind he led in the establishment of the so-called Partido Socialista del Peru, which he hoped would be the political expression of the whole leftist movement in Peru. He rejected the idea of naming the party Partido Comunista, though he did agree to its applying for membership in the Communist International.

At the 1929 Congress of Latin American Communist Parties held in Buenos Aires, Mariátegui's Socialist Party was violently attacked by orthodox Communists, and it was ordered by the International to change its name to Partido Comunista and to adopt the orthodox form of organization established by the Comintern for national Communist parties.

Mariátegui did not live long enough to make clear what his reaction to the Comintern's orders would have been. He had been ill with tuberculosis for many years and died before the Partido Socialista had had a chance to decide upon its future. The writer has heard statements from those who participated in the party both to the effect that Mariátegui would have gone along with the Comintern's orders and to the effect that he would have refused to do so. Many of those who ultimately became Apristas felt that had Mariátegui lived long enough to see the formal establishment of the Partido Aprista Peruano on Peruvian soil, he would have been among its founding members.

In any case, Mariátegui did much to hold together the group of students and workers who had first been united under Haya de la Torre's leadership. His memory is honored today equally by members of the Aprista Party, the Peruvian Communist Party, and the Socialist Party of Peru.

Once back in Peru, Haya de la Torre threw himself into the presidential campaign. He barnstormed throughout the country and was met by veritable adulation of workers, students, and Indian peasants. The new Aprista Party gained adherents the length and breadth of the land. Its methods of propaganda were varied and sometimes unique. Carlton Beals has told of seeing dogs whose hair had been trimmed to spell the letters APRA. Enthusiastic members of the party etched its initials in white stone high up on the mountain facing the ancient Inca capital of Cuzco.

Haya himself demonstrated that he had great capacity as an orator as well as a political thinker during this campaign. He held his audiences spellbound whether he was speaking in Spanish or in the ancient Quechua language of the Peruvian Indians. At last he had the opportunity to explain at length to his compatriots the ideas which he and his associates had developed during the long years of exile.

When the votes were counted Haya de la Torre was credited with having received 110,000, while Sánchez Cerro was officially declared the winner with 150,000. Though the Apristas claimed that they had been robbed of victory, they agreed to take the seats which had been credited as having been won by them in the Chamber of Deputies.

For less than a year after the 1931 election Haya and the Apristas were able to continue their legal political activities. However, a few months after the election President Sánchez Cerro, who had promised during his election campaign to "crush the Apristas," outlawed the party. Many of its principal leaders were arrested; others escaped into exile. The Aprista members of Congress were expelled, and many of them were jailed.

Among the Apristas who were incarcerated by the Sánchez Cerro government was Víctor Raúl Haya de la Torre. He was put on trial by the regime for subversive activities, and although his conviction was a foregone conclusion, Haya used the courtroom as a tribune from which to expound his ideas and speak to the people of Peru. The proceedings of the trial were later published by the Apristas.

There was a great deal of violence not only against the Apristas but also by them in retaliation. The most sanguinary incident was a revolt by the Apristas in the northern city of Trujillo in 1932. This was ruthlessly crushed by the Sánchez Cerro regime, and hundreds of Aprista workers, students, and intellectuals were killed, many of them in cold blood after surrendering to the authorities.

This second period of persecution of the Apristas lasted until April 30, 1933, when dictator Sánchez Cerro was assassinated, allegedly by an Aprista, though members of the party denied any connection with his murder. The government was thrown into confusion, but the presidency was soon assumed by General Oscar Benavides, an ex-president and a man whom Haya de la Torre had frequently referred to as "the Peruvian Primo de Rivera."

In the beginning General Benavides sought a truce with the Apristas. Haya de la Torre and other members of his party were freed from prison, and the Aprista members of Congress were restored to their positions. For a short while the Apristas were allowed to carry on legal political activities, but within a few months Benavides followed the actions of his predecessors and once again outlawed the Aprista Party and rounded up all the Apristas upon whom he could lay his hands. This time Haya was not among them. He went into hiding and stayed in Peru during the whole of the next decade of persecution of the Aprista Party by the governments of Benavides and his successor, Manuel Prado. Haya frequently changed his residence, reportedly even spending some time in a convent. His hiding place was usually guarded by a group of young Apristas who were popularly dubbed "the buffaloes."

The unexpired presidential term of the late President Sánchez

Cerro, which was being filled out by General Benavides, expired in 1936. The president called an election to choose his successor. During this campaign the Aprista Party demonstrated that, though it was illegal, it still had the support of a very large part of the population of Peru.

In the beginning it looked as if President Benavides' candidate, Jorge Prado, would win the election without any difficulty. However, quite late in the campaign the miniscule Social Democratic Party of Peru nominated a well known lawyer, Luis Antonio Eguigeren, as its candidate. He was given no chance of success in the beginning, but Haya de la Torre and other underground Aprista leaders spread word among their followers to vote for Eguigeren.

When the counting of the vote began it early became evident that Eguigeren was running far ahead of his rival. In the face of this General Benavides ordered the suspension of all further counting of the ballots and called his puppet congress into session. It obediently agreed to take the unconstitutional step of extending the President's term for three more years. The persecution of the Apristas was intensified.

At the end of this extended term elections were finally held. Outgoing President Benavides threw his support behind Manuel Prado, a prominent banker and one of Peru's richest men. Running against him was Luis A. Flores, nominee of the Unión Nacional, a party which had been organized by Sánchez Cerro to back his 1931 presidential campaign. In the late 1930's the Unión Nacional had decidedly pro-fascist tendencies.

An interesting sidelight on the 1939 election campaign was the alliance between Benavides and Prado on the one hand and the Communist Party of Peru on the other. The Communists backed Prado, and with Benavides' approval Prado accepted the principal Communist trade-union leader, Juan P. Luna, as a candidate for Congress on his ticket.

This was not the first time that the Communists had supported a Peruvian dictatorship. The landholding-mercantile oligarchy and the army leaders who had been the principal forces behind the governments which succeeded Leguía (as behind his as well) were anxious to find some political group which could counter the appeal among the masses which the Partido Aprista Peruano enjoyed from the date of its foundation in 1930. For this purpose they turned almost immediately to the ˙Partido Comunista. This party had been formally established early in 1930 by a number of José Mariátegui's former associates under the leadership of Eudosio Ravines, who had at one time been the head of the group of Aprista students in Paris but had broken with Haya de la Torre in 1928.

During the Sánchez Cerro administration the government-Communist alliance began. Particularly in the trade unions the Communists were given a degree of freedom which was denied to the Apristas. One result of this was that at that time the Communists controlled the largest faction in the organized-labor movement. Although Benavides at first persecuted all factions of the labor movement, he modified this policy after the 1936 election, and the *modus vivendi* between the government and the Communists was renewed.

This alliance continued throughout the administration of President Manuel Prado. He, like his predecessors, was anxious to undermine the popularity of the Apristas. With his approval a Confederation of Workers of Peru was established in 1944 with Communist deputy Juan P. Luna as its secretary general.

The Prado dictatorship was generally more moderate than the two preceding ones. Although Prado did not legalize the Aprista Party, and forced Haya de la Torre and other Aprista leaders to remain underground, in exile, or in jail, the persecution of the Aprista Party was less intense than previously.

During the eleven years of the Benavides and Prado dictatorships the ideology and program of the Aprista Party as expounded by Víctor Raúl Haya de la Torre went through a process of evolution. Although the basic principles of the movement were never abandoned, a fundamental change occurred in the Aprista attitude toward the United States.

Two factors influenced this change. One was the rise of totalitarianism, particularly of the racist Nazi brand, in Europe and its threat to penetrate Latin America. The second factor was the advent of the administration of Franklin D. Roosevelt in the United States, and the Good Neighbor Policy proclaimed and largely followed by Roosevelt and his associates.

Haya himself has summed up the reasons for the modification

of the position of himself and the Aprista Party with regard to the United States. In an open letter written sometime in 1940 to the editor of *Diario de Costa Rica,* who had noted Haya's apparent change from an "adversary" of the United States to a "friend" of the same country, Haya wrote:

. . . the Apristas have not changed their attitude but—fortunately —the government of the United States has. The imperialist policy of the "Big Stick" of the Republicans changed radically with the arrival of President Roosevelt. And we have the right to believe that this change in attitude was much influenced by all of the anti-imperialists of our great Indo American nation: the glorious martyrdom of Sandino in Central America, and the firm policy of some of our States such as Mexico, and Argentina, Bolivia and Chile.

We Apristas have seen with profound sympathy this modification of North American government policy. This turnabout, this change of front, has been beneficial for good relations between both Americas. And even though the phenomenon of imperialism in its roots and its economic phase still exists, it has been profoundly modified by the "good neighbor" policy which has closed the way to all the North American interventionist excesses in our peoples which characterized the Republican policy in Mexico, the Antilles, Central America and Panama.[18]

The importance of the rise of Nazism in influencing the thinking of Haya and the other Apristas is also noted by Haya. In the paragraph following that which we have just cited he says:

Furthermore, in the face of the totalitarian danger which means an imperialism much more aggressive than those hitherto known—because of its frank policy of extermination of weak peoples and its racist philosophy of conquest of mixed peoples—we have no doubts. Our duty is to fight alongside the defenders of democracy and cooperate in its defense, demanding at the same time that the principles of democracy be applied to Inter American relations so that both economically and politically all forms of imperialism will be extinguished.

Thus Haya did not feel that he had fundamentally changed his position concerning imperialism or the basic doctrine of Aprismo. Rather, he had adapted to new circumstances. While accepting the Good Neighbor Policy and the common threat coming from Nazism as a basis for cooperation between the two parts of America, Haya insisted in all of his writings just before and during World War II that this cooperation should be on the basis of equality.

Haya took frequent verbal pot shots at those Latin American politicians who interpreted "cooperation" with the United States as meaning immediate agreement with anything the United States asked and refusal to ask anything in return. He constantly reiterated his old theme of unity among the Latin Americans, so that they could deal on more even terms with the United States. He also suggested once again inter-Americanization of the Panama Canal. He insisted, upon various occasions, that the United States should be more careful in its selection of close friends and associates in Latin America, make more contact with the people and less with the local dictators.[19]

This stage in the evolution of the thinking of Haya and the other Aprista leaders culminated in the publication in 1941 of the Plan Haya de la Torre, otherwise known as the Plan for the Affirmation of Democracy in America. After setting forth the need for unity in America to work against its conquest by the Nazi racialists, it goes on to suggest a number of specific measures for strengthening political democracy on a hemispheric scale and for establishing the basis for economic cooperation between the two parts of the hemisphere.

The Plan called for the establishment of an American Committee for the Defense of Democracy composed of representatives of democratic political parties as well as representatives of the executive, legislative, and judicial powers of government and the universities. This committee was to have subcommittees in every country. The purpose of these organisms was to be to receive complaints concerning violations of the democratic process and civil liberties which are set forth in all of the constitutions of America. Just how it was to function and what its powers were to be were not made clear.

On the economic level the Plan called for the summoning of an economic congress in each of the republics made up of "representatives of all of the live forces of its production, distribution, and consumption: capital and labor, industry, agriculture, and commerce—national and *foreign* in the case of the Indo-American countries." The purpose of these congresses would be to "study the economic reality and formulate a state plan of action with a view to its coordination within an Inter-American program."

Complementary to this would be the establishment of a Great Inter-American Economic Congress "on the basis of resolutions adopted in each country, with a view toward Inter-American coordination." This Inter-American Economic Congress should proceed with the establishment of a single currency for the Indo-American countries, with a value lower than the dollar "but with a stable rate of exchange with it, the guarantee and backing of which would be gold, silver, and raw materials."

The Plan also called for the establishment of export-import banks in all of the American countries "the functions of which would not be confined to isolated loans and credits, but would convert them into directing organs, guaranteeing productive investments, balanced trade and a system of guarantees and assurances which would maintain the stability of exchange, the stimulation and extension of credits, the pushing of trade between the United States and the Indo-American States." It also urged the establishment of an Inter-American Tariff Union, the equalization of transit fees in the Panama Canal for all American states, and other measures.[20]

One notable omission from this Plan is any specific mention of cooperation for the industrialization of the Latin American countries. In contrast, there is specific reference to "the need for a clear delimitation of the great fields or zones of the economy of the New World: that of the United States, preponderantly industrialized and financial, and that of the Indo-American States, preponderantly agricultural, mining and of raw materials." The statement continues, "Both zones complement one another and *each needs the other*," but there is no insistence on the need to develop the Latin American economies away from their exclusive dependence on the production of raw materials and foodstuffs.

This document goes further than any Aprista pronouncement before or since in urging cooperation between the two parts of the hemisphere. It is virtually the only occasion on which Haya de la Torre did not call for unification of the Latin American countries as a necessary prerequisite to their dealing with the United States, but he was urging such a necessity in articles which he was writing about the same time.

With the approaching end of World War II political conditions in Peru began to alter rapidly. As the end of President Manuel Prado's term neared, the problem of choosing a successor became increasingly pressing. Ex-President Benavides, who was then serving as Peruvian ambassador to Argentina, brought his influence to bear on Prado to permit free elections with the participation of the Aprista Party. Prado finally agreed to this.

In May, 1945, a presidential decree legalized the Aprista Party, though it forbade it to use its official name. Soon thereafter the party came out into the open, for the first time in more than a decade, under the name Partido del Pueblo (People's Party). Meanwhile hundreds of exiled leaders of the party streamed back to the country, a general amnesty was proclaimed, political prisoners were released, and those Aprista leaders who had been in hiding left their places of refuge.

The principal Aprista to come out of hiding was Víctor Raúl Haya de la Torre. He was greeted with wild enthusiasm at every meeting at which he spoke amidst a forest of waving white handkerchiefs, the special symbol of the Aprista Party. In the weeks that followed his return to open activity Haya made an extensive tour of the country, rallying the party's supporters, who had not seen their chief for more than ten years.

The legalization of the Aprista Party came too late for it to name a presidential candidate. However, it endorsed José Bustamente y Rivero, a well known jurist and diplomat, a conservative man but pledged to the full restoration of democratic liberties. At the same time the party nominated a full list of candidates for both chambers of parliament.

Bustamente won a smashing triumph, and the Aprista Party enjoyed a strong victory in the congressional elections, winning control of the Senate and falling only a few seats short of a majority in the lower house. With the support of a number of independents the Apristas hoped to be able to carry through the latter body most of the measures which they supported.

When Congress convened it abolished all of the repressive laws of the dictatorship. Meanwhile the Aprista Party set about an almost frantic process of rebuilding its ranks throughout the nation. Schools for training leaders and rank-and-filers were established. The party set up a special Peasant and Indian Bureau to help members of various Indian communities fight off attempts illegally to usurp their land.

Mobile party units consisting of a doctor, a nurse, a teacher, and one or two helpers were dispatched to various parts of the country. These units brought medical help to villages which had seldom, if ever, had the services of a doctor, while the teacher sought out those who had a minimum knowledge of reading and writing and helped them set up schools for teaching their fellow villagers. At the same time contact was established between the villagers and the Aprista Party.

During the three and a half years from 1945 to 1948 in which the Aprista Party was legal Haya de la Torre was the undisputed chief of the party. He sat on all the party's leading committees ex officio, and his word was listened to with great respect and was usually followed. He conferred regularly with the party's parliamentarians and with the Aprista ministers during the eleven months in 1946–47 in which the party had members in the cabinet. He met with the party's trade-union leaders, who had seized control of the Confederation of Workers of Peru from the Communists soon after the legalization of the Partido del Pueblo. He made several speaking and organizing tours in various parts of the country.

Haya also took advantage of his new freedom to make several trips abroad. During one of these, early in 1948, he spent several weeks in the United States renewing acquaintances with old friends, speaking at universities and at public meetings, and bringing the message of the Aprista Party to this country as he had done twenty years before.

However, as time went on, relations between President Bustamante y Rivero and the Aprista Party, to which he owed his election, became increasingly cold. To a considerable degree the responsibility for this was that of the Apristas and of Haya de la Torre himself. An almost impossible relationship existed between Bustamante and the Apristas, particularly between Bustamante and Haya de la Torre. There were, for practical purposes, two presidents of Peru: Bustamante in the Casa del Gobierno and Haya de la Torre in the

Casa del Pueblo, the Aprista Party headquarters. It was virtually inevitable that there would be a clash between them sooner or later.

It is difficult to blame the Apristas for their attitude. They were not only the country's majority party but were virtually the only organized party in Peru. President Bustamante owed his election to the support of the Aprista Party. They felt that he should tailor his administration to suit their wishes. It can also be argued that the Apristas were, after their long period in illegality, too anxious, that they lacked the patience which was needed at that particular moment in Peru's history.

During 1948 the situation between the Apristas and President Bustamante became acute. In January of that year the President sought to frustrate a continental labor congress called at the invitation of the Aprista-controlled Confederation of Workers of Peru to meet in Lima, and out of which came the Inter-American Confederation of Workers (CIT). Later, during the middle months of the year, it proved impossible for congress to meet because the non-Apristas, including Bustamante's personal supporters, refused to attend, thus preventing a quorum.

Finally, on October 3, 1948, the showdown between the President and his erstwhile allies occurred. A naval mutiny led by elements of the Aprista Party took place in the port of Callao. Haya de la Torre and the other top leaders of the party publicly repudiated this uprising, but this did not prevent President Bustamante from blaming the party for it and using it as an excuse to outlaw the Apristas. The government rounded up those Aprista leaders upon whom it could lay its hands.

Haya de la Torre was not among those whom the government arrested. He had gone into hiding once again, before the police could capture him, and he remained out of sight for three months. Meanwhile, late in October, 1948, President Bustamante was overthrown by a military coup led by General Manuel Odría, a declared enemy of the Apristas and, until a few months before his uprising, Minister of Defense in Bustamante's cabinet.

The Odría military dictatorship continued the search for Haya de la Torre and other Aprista leaders. The police were unable to locate Haya, but finally, his health seriously impaired, he found refuge in the Colombian Embassy early in January, 1949. With his entry into the Embassy began one of the most dramatic and historic episodes in the highly colorful life of Víctor Raúl Haya de la Torre.

The Odría regime violated one of the most sacred traditions of Latin American politics in refusing to grant Haya the customary safe-conduct out of the country. The government accused Haya of a long list of common crimes and claimed that he was not in the true sense a political refugee. They continued to insist on this for more than five years, during which Haya remained in the Colombian Embassy, and the Colombians twice took the case to the International Court of Justice at the Hague. That tribunal both times rendered a Solomonic but highly equivocal judgment to the effect that Haya was not guilty of common crimes but the Peruvian government had the right to deny him a safe-conduct.

During all of this period Haya was a virtual prisoner in the Embassy. The Peruvian government had a trench dug around the building, with soldiers stationed in it for twenty-four hours a day. Guns were trained on the Embassy constantly, and everyone who entered or left was searched thoroughly. The Colombian government gave up trying to conduct its business in this building, renting quarters in another part of town and leaving only one official of the Embassy and his family with Haya. There was constant danger of Haya's being shot, and he was unable to approach a window for fear the troops stationed outside would fire upon him. All protests of the Colombians against this outrageous treatment of the official seat of the Embassy went unheeded.

It was not until January, 1954, that this situation was finally resolved. A *modus vivendi* was finally worked out by the government of Peru, the Embassy of Colombia, and Haya de la Torre, whereby the distinguished refugee was finally allowed to leave his Embassy "prison."

During the next two years Haya was once more in exile. He went first to Mexico, where for some months he stayed with the sizable group of Aprista refugees resident there. Then he went to Europe once again, traveling widely from Italy to Scandinavia. A constant student, he was particularly interested in the social system developed in the Scandinavian countries, hoping to find there lessons which might be applicable to his homeland. He also wrote numerous articles for periodicals in both parts of the hemisphere, including a long account of his trials and tribulations in the Colombian Embassy in Lima which appeared in *Life* magazine.

Meanwhile the Odría dictatorship was approaching its end back home in Peru. As the close of Odría's "constitutional" term of office, to which he had had himself "elected" in 1950, approached, the eternal problem of the succession became increasingly acute. Odría first sought support to continue in office beyond his constitutional term, but he found few backers for this idea. Finally he was forced to call elections to choose a successor.

Like all previous regimes of this type in Peru, the Odría government had rested on two groups—the armed forces and the economic oligarchy. During the early years of his regime Odría had had the united backing of the Army and the almost complete support of the large landowners, the big merchants, and the important bankers. As time passed, however, he lost much of the backing of the economic royalists and the Army.

There are probably two basic reasons for the change in the attitude of the big economic interests toward Odría. One of these was the events which occurred in the neighboring republic of Bolivia after April 9, 1952. On that date a revolutionary regime seized power in Bolivia, and proceeded to nationalize the major part of the tin-mining industry, enfranchise and arm the illiterate peasants, and turn over much of the agricultural land of the highlands to the Indians.

Economic and social conditions in rural Peru were very similar to those existing in Bolivia before 1952. The Indians of Peru, who were only vaguely aware of the national boundaries which separated them from their brothers in Bolivia, were very much impressed by the benefits which the Bolivian peasants seemed to be reaping from the revolution there. This situation seemed to presage a fundamental change in Peru sooner or later.

There is little doubt that important elements in the Peruvian oligarchy read the handwriting on the wall and came to the conclusion that changes such as those occurring in Bolivia were inevitable sooner or later in Peru. They also came to the conclusion that it was in their own interest that these changes come about as peaceably and democratically as possible. This meant the old policy of keeping the Aprista Party outside the law ought to be definitively reversed, and that the road should somehow be paved for the ascension of the Apristas to power in a democratic fashion, in the hope that the Apristas would carry out the revolution they preached in a democratic manner and with as little turbulence and bloodshed as possible.

The second factor influencing the attitude of the Peruvian oligarchy was undoubtedly the treatment which many of its members received at the hands of the Odría military regime. That government was a frankly military regime, and it had only slightly more respect for those members of the civil aristocracy who crossed it in one way or another than it had for the persecuted Apristas. Leading members of the ruling economic group were jailed and exiled by Odría because of political differences. Perhaps a number of the Peruvian oligarchs came to the conclusion that even a revolutionary group such as the Apristas was to be preferred to a continuation of an insolent military tyranny.

The election campaign of 1956 resolved itself into a race for the support of the outlawed Apristas. A few months before the election Odría had allowed the return of some Aprista exiles, notably Ramiro Prialé, the party's secretary general. Prialé quickly reorganized the bases of the party in the Lima-Callao area and soon entered into complicated negotiations with the various candidates for the presidency.

Prialé had one basic objective in his negotiations—the legalization of the Aprista Party. This was the *sine qua non* for any candidate to win Aprista backing and with it almost certain victory at the polls.

There were three candidates for president. Odría supported Hernándo Lavalle, an engineer, Haya de la Torre's predecessor as president of the Students Federation back in the period of World War I but by 1956 a very conservative figure. The second candidate was Fernando Belaúnde Terry, an architect and a member of the faculty of the University of San Marcos, a deputy during the 1945–48 period, when he had been an ally of the Apristas. The third nominee was ex-President Manuel Prado, reputedly the richest man in Peru, who was growing old, was not thought to be in very good health, and who had lived abroad during much of the Odría period.

Prialé began his negotiations with Odría and Lavalle. His demand was simple: Cancel the law which made the Aprista Party illegal. Although at first indicating that he might be willing to do this, Odría procrastinated and finally refused to legalize the Apristas before the election, though Lavalle promised to do so right afterward. Prialé did not consider Lavalle's promise sufficient guarantee in view of the equivocal attitude of his patron, Odría.

Prialé passed over Belaúnde Terry in his negotiations in spite of the fact that Belaúnde promised publicly to legalize the Apristas if he should win. There were undoubtedly two reasons for Prialé's attitude. First, he believed that Odría would not turn over power to Belaúnde, who was conducting a violently antigovernment campaign, if he were to win the election. Second, the movement which grew up around Belaúnde during the first months of 1956 represented the first significant popular challenge to the Aprista Party since its foundation more than twenty-five years before. Prialé did not want to inflate the Belaúnde movement unnecessarily.

So, once convinced that negotiations with the government candidate were fruitless, Prialé turned to Manuel Prado. The ex-President was no friend of the Apristas and had kept them illegal during all but a few weeks of his former period in office. Furthermore, he was the epitome of the oligarchy which the Apristas were pledged to remove from power. However, to counterbalance these factors were the solid promise which Prado was willing to give to legalize the Aprista Party as his first act upon taking office and the near certainty that, if Prado was elected, he would be allowed to take over the presidency.

Thus Prialé and the other Aprista leaders inside Peru agreed to throw the Party's support to Prado. However, this decision was taken only ten days before the election, and a heroic effort was needed to get the word out to the Aprista Party people throughout the country. It proved impossible to notify the party supporters in the more remote sections of Peru; in others, particularly in the South, Belaúnde Terry had been claiming Aprista support for himself, and this created considerable confusion. In some cases Aprista members were unwilling to throw their support behind Prado, whom they remembered as the persecutor of their party during his previous administration.

However, generally the word of Aprista support for Prado did get to party members and supporters in the chief centers of Aprista strength. This was shown by the large majority Prado received in the Lima-Callao area and in the northern city of Trujillo, which had always been Aprista strongholds. The party's backing was sufficient to let Prado nose out Belaúnde, who ran second, far ahead of the badly trailing Hernándo Lavalle.

Once in office, Prado proved as good as his word. His first act was to submit to congress a law legalizing the Aprista Party, which was quickly passed and signed by the President. With this law the party returned to full activity. Exiles streamed back home, party headquarters were opened to the public, the party newspaper *La Tribuna* was revived, and the job of organizing local units of the party throughout the country was undertaken with enthusiasm.

Again Víctor Raúl Haya de la Torre returned home in triumph. He first landed in the northern part of the country, and his progress south to Lima was like a Roman triumph. People turned out by the hundreds of thousands to see him, listen to him, and cheer him. In Lima he was met by a crowd of a quarter of a million people in the Plaza San Martín in the center of the city.

Haya returned to his post as "chief" of the Aprista Party. However, this time it was different from the situation in 1945–48. The party had been largely reorganized by Ramiro Prialé and a small group of other leaders without the help of Haya de la Torre. Haya had had no part in the negotiations preceding the elections, negotiations that had revealed an ability for diplomacy and political maneuvering on the part of Prialé which until then had gone virtually unnoticed.

Furthermore, the party was now in a cautious and conciliatory mood, which was a far cry from the romanticism that had been one of its characteristics in the past. Although none of the idealism and willingness to sacrifice which had been such assets in the past had been lost, there was universal agreement among the leaders and rank and file alike that the essential thing was to keep a democratic government in power for the next six years so that the Aprista Party might win the 1962 elections and at last have a chance to carry out its program.

The party had learned to wait. And, although this was a painful process, all agreed that it was a necessary one. Nothing should be done by the Apristas that might be used as an excuse for another military coup. It was necessary for the party to give support to the Prado regime so that it would stay in power, but without participating in it and without becoming responsible for the mistakes which this type of "caretaker" government was almost certain to make.

In this situation the role of Haya de la Torre was fundamentally changed. He had now become the "Grand Old Man" and the philosopher of the party. Although he made several speaking tours around the country and helped in the work of rebuilding the local units of the party, he no longer participated to the degree he had done in the 1945–48 period in the day-to-day activities of the organization. Although his prestige had never been higher and the rank and file had never loved him more, he had ceased to be the effective political leader of the party. There was general agreement, in which he acquiesced, that nothing should be done which would prevent his being elected president of Peru in 1962.

Haya stayed in Peru for a little more than a year. During this period he received innumerable invitations to speak in universities and to political groups throughout Latin America and in the United States as well. In the later part of 1957 he finally decided to accept some of these invitations. He went abroad and gave a number of speeches in neighboring South American countries, after which he returned to Europe. Apparently he was to stay abroad, this time in voluntary exile, until the moment was propitious for his return for what all agreed would be the victorious campaign of 1962.

Meanwhile Haya was busy writing. He published in 1956 the first volume of a study which he entitled *Thirty Years of Aprismo,* in which he reviewed the long history of his party and the evolution of his own ideas. In this volume he insisted on the basic consistency of the line of himself and his party, which, though it had adapted to changes in the world situation and that of the Western Hemisphere, had never varied in its insistence on the assertion of the special personality of "Indo-America." It had never changed in its advocacy for unity of the Indo-American nations and for their control of the foreign capital which came there and which should come only under conditions established by the governments of the region.[21]

Two years later Haya published another book, this time a study of the philosophy of Toynbee. While in the Colombian Embassy in Lima, and subsequently, he had spent much time studying the works of the noted British historian and philosopher, and this work was the fruit of these efforts.[22]

The position of Víctor Raúl Haya de la Torre among our Prophets of the Revolution is unique. He has been the most outstanding philosopher of the whole movement for social, economic, and political change in Latin America during the last half-century. Although not a successful politician by normal standards, he has had an immense influence throughout the Latin American republics. The leaders of many parties in numerous countries of the region acknowledge an intellectual debt to Haya.

Haya de la Torre has been the great preacher of the need for Latin American political life to seek a path of its own. He has urged the necessity for the long overdue changes in Latin American society to come in a specifically Latin American way, the need for these countries to develop political parties and institutions adapted to their own national personalities. He has argued against the too frequent tendency, as expressed in the constitutions and laws and by political leaders of Latin America during its first century of independence, to ape some other part of the world.

At the same time Haya has indicated a middle way in the difficult problems of relating Latin American economic development to the outside world. He has recognized the twin evils of foreign domination of the Latin American economies on the one hand and of utter rejection of foreign investment and aid on the other. He has stressed the need for the Latin American countries to control and direct their own activities and resources and to channel foreign investments so that they would contribute to the most rapid possible general economic development and would strengthen the national sovereignty of the Latin American nations.

Finally, Haya de la Torre has stressed the need for unity among the Latin Americans. He has urged not only spiritual and intellectual solidarity but actual abolition of economic and political frontiers among the nations of the region. Although few politicians outside Peru have gone as far as he has in urging the formation of an "Indo-American nation," there has emerged in recent decades an increasingly strong feeling of group identification among the Latin American countries. And today steps are even being taken toward some kind of economic union among the Latin American nations.

Haya is probably the outstanding spokesman for a generation of political leaders and thinkers which saw the emergence of a strong feeling of Latin American nationalism and an all-but-irresistible drive toward social change and economic development. Others have written in a more orderly fashion, still others have written more realistically, but Haya de la Torre remains the most significant single spokesman for the social revolution in Latin America during the first half of the twentieth century.

Rómulo Betancourt, the Statesman of the Andes

᭤᭥᭙᭥᭤

Venezuela in 1928 was the personal property of Juan Vicente Gómez, infamous "Tyrant of the Andes." His secret police mercilessly tracked down and eliminated every critic of the regime. Gómez, his numerous progeny, and the semi-literate military men who surrounded him, had partitioned among themselves virtually all the country's wealth. The rapidly rising petroleum industry had provided new sources of illicit enrichment for the members of the ruling clique. The Gómez regime had become the classic example of a Latin American dictatorship.

Suddenly the tranquillity of the regime was shattered by a group of young university students, most of them still in their teens, who rose in revolt, seized the presidential palace, and seriously threatened to overthrow the tyranny. For a short while Caracas was in turmoil; the young student orators made inflammatory speeches in the public squares demanding the end of the dictatorship and the establishment of a democratic civilian government.

One of the principal figures in this "generation of '28" was Rómulo Betancourt, a young law student scarcely eighteen years of age. In this short-lived student rebellion the future president of Venezuela got his first political apprenticeship—as did several others whose names were to become famous in Venezuelan public affairs, such as Miguel Otero Silva, Jóvito Villalba, and Raúl Leoni.

After the first shock of the student uprising, the government recovered control of the situation, and most of the student leaders were captured and placed in Gómez' dungeons. For more than a year and a half the students remained in damp, filthy cells, their legs weighted down with ball and chain. They christened their prison "Aramathea," after Joseph of Aramathea, who helped Jesus bear his cross to Calvary.

Finally, in 1930 most of the leaders of the student revolt were allowed to go into exile. Rómulo Betancourt found refuge in the little Central American republic of Costa Rica. There he continued his studies, married a Costa Rican girl, Carmen Valverde, and joined with local students to form the Communist Party of Costa Rica. For some years he was one of the leading figures in that party. In 1935 there was a bitter controversy in the organization as to whether it should become a full-fledged member of the Communist International. Betancourt opposed this move, arguing even at that time that the Latin Americans should find their own way to social change and material progress, and not be subordinated to an international organization whose principal task was to defend the Soviet Union. When the Costa Rican Communists decided against Betancourt's position and joined the Comintern, he withdrew from the party.

There is no doubt that this short experience in the ranks of the Communist movement contributed greatly to Betancourt's political education. It made him intimately acquainted with how the Communists operated, and turned him into a convinced anti-Communist, but one who realized that the Communists are only to be defeated, in Latin American at least, if the ground is cut from under them by a political movement which can appeal to the workers, peasants, and middle class on the basis of profound social and political change and economic progress.

At the end of 1936 Juan Vicente Gómez died quietly in his bed. The presidency passed to his son-in-law and Minister of War General Eleázar López Contreras, who immediately began relaxing Gómez' tyrannical regime. López allowed the exiles to come back and for a short while permitted relative freedom of speech, assembly, and organization. At least six new political groups were formed at this time: Organización Venezolana (which included most of those who later were to form Acción Democrática Party); Partido Republicano Progresista (which included most of those who later formed the Communist Party of Venezuela); Frente Obrero, Frente Nacional de Trabajadores, a regional group in Maracaibo known as Bloque Nacional Democrático, and the Federación de Estudiantes Organización Política.

Within a few months all of these groups merged into the Partido Democrático Nacional, which was soon driven underground, when

López Contreras cracked down on the opposition. Many of its leaders were deported by the regime. In the underground the differences between those of Communist inclination and the anti-Communists became increasingly acute, and in 1938 the Communist element left the Partido Democrático Nacional to form the Partido Comunista de Venezuela. Rómulo Betancourt, who remained in Venezuela in hiding, became the principal leader of the Partido Democrático Nacional.

Betancourt himself has described the significance in the split in the ranks of the Partido Democrático Nacional. Writing in *Cuadernos Americanos* in August, 1949, he said:

The Venezuelan Left was divided into two well-defined groups. One of these based its strategy and tactics not so much on Marxist doctrine as on the successive changes ordered by the Comintern and later by the Cominform, a movement which always had the vagaries of the Kremlin as its Star of Bethlehem. The other, ours, which in the underground was the PDN and later became Acción Democrática, formed by those who, professing a revolutionary concept of the social struggle, thought as Americans and thought of themselves as Americans, did not believe that a transplanted formula or an imported line varying with the international strategy of a certain great power should be the guide to popular action to be carried out with realism and effectiveness.

Hence we advocated and organized a much more amply based party than one based only on the proletariat, since it had within its ranks men and women coming from all of the non-parasitic classes of the population, forming a movement which fought for democracy and sought to adapt it to our own time, with emphasis on social justice and economic redemption. It was a movement, finally, which was not guilty of insularity, but on the contrary, aspired to establish relations with similar groups elsewhere in America, while always refusing to subordinate national interests to the very special objectives of Russian political strategy.[1]

During the next three years the opposition was persecuted by the López Contreras regime and was forced to work underground. The Communists had an advantage over the PDN people in this because they were led by a number of skilled leaders, many of them unknown to the public and to the police, who had been trained in

Moscow by the Comintern in methods of underground organization and agitation. The leadership of the PDN, on the other hand, was limited in experience and numbers, because most of its leaders had been exiled.

Unlike other Venezuelan dictatorial regimes, that of López Contreras kept very few of its opponents in jail. When an opposition leader was arrested, he was promptly deported. In 1940 Rómulo Betancourt suffered this fate; he was sent to Chile. There he was closely associated with the Socialist Party of Chile, which was at the apex of its influence. As a representative of the Partido Democrático Nacional of Venezuela he participated in a Conference of Latin American Socialist and Democratic Parties called by the Chilean Socialists.

In the middle of 1941 the presidential term of General López Contreras expired, and he chose as his successor another general, Isaías Medina Angarita. Although the president of the republic was elected by Congress at that time, and the opposition had no hope of winning against Medina Angarita, the Partido Democrático Nacional nonetheless named as its "symbolic candidate" for the presidency the country's most famous literary figure, the novelist Rómulo Gallegos. He toured the country widely, and his campaign served principally to raise the prestige of the PDN and to make clear its position as the principal opposition party to the regime in power.

With the inauguration of Medina Angarita as president of Venezuela a more democratic regime was installed. Once again the exiles were invited to return, and the opposition was given freedom to agitate and organize. Betancourt returned from his forced residence in Chile, and soon thereafter the Partido Nacional Democrático held a national convention. At this meeting the name of the party was changed to Acción Democrática (Democratic Action), a detailed program for economic, social, and political change was drawn up, and the position of Rómulo Betancourt as principal leader of the party was confirmed.

The next four years were marked by steady progress on the part of Acción Democrática. Its scattering of representatives in Congress put forth fundamental proposals for reorganization of the country's relations with the foreign companies exploiting its oil, for changes in the agrarian sector of the economy, and for a democratization of the regime.

Acción Democrática was without doubt the principal opponent of the Medina regime. The Communists generally supported the administration, although this policy brought a split in that party's ranks. López Contreras first backed Medina but later became increasingly critical; but his influence was in the Army rather than in the general public, and he had no political party behind him.

One of the principal gains of Acción Democrática during the Medina administration was its success in capturing control of the labor movement. Since the death of Gómez the trade-union movement, particularly in the oil fields, had gained increasing strength. From the beginning it was under Communist influence, though there was a sizable Acción Democrática minority in the unions. During the first part of the Medina regime the Communists gained additional ground in the unions because of the benevolence of the administration with which they were allied.

Early in 1944 a congress was held in Caracas for the formation of a national trade-union confederation. When the congress came to discuss the executive committee for the new confederation, one of the Acción Democrática labor leaders proposed that the membership of the committee be divided equally between Communists and members of Acción Democrática. However, a Communist delegate denounced this proposal, saying that since the Communists had a majority in the congress, they should have a majority on the executive committee.

This whole discussion was in defiance of the Venezuelan Labor Law, which strictly forbade partisan political activities on the part of the unions. As a result a crisis occurred and President Medina Angarita suspended the sessions of the labor congress. He also suspended the legal recognition of a large number of unions represented at the meeting, most of them under Communist leadership. In elections which were necessary before these unions could once again get legal recognition the Communists were generally defeated, and Acción Democrática elements succeeded in getting control of a majority of the oil workers' unions and a majority in the general labor movement. From that time until the present AD has continued to control a large majority in the Venezuelan trade-union movement.

As the 1945 presidential election approached, a political crisis developed. Acción Democrática demanded that there be a change in the constitution to provide for direct popular election of the president instead of his being named by Congress, which in effect meant his selection by the outgoing president. Failing in this demand, Acción Democrática then urged upon Medina an agreement between the administration and the opposition on a joint candidate acceptable to both sides. The man they suggested was Aníbal Escalante, Venezuelan ambassador to Washington.

At first Medina Angarita was agreeable to Escalante as a joint nominee, and Escalante himself accepted the nomination, but when he fell sick soon afterward, Medina Angarita selected Angel Biaggini without further consultation with Acción Democrática, and began to put into operation machinery to assure his election by Congress.

Meanwhile there was widespread discontent in the Army. Since the death of Gómez the control of the armed forces had continued to remain in the hands of relatively illiterate generals who had been comrades of Gómez and had helped him seize and hold power. The younger army officers, many of whom had training in the United States and other foreign countries in addition to their training in professional military schools, were restless under the domination of the leftovers of the Gómez regime. They felt that their training and professional competence were not receiving sufficient recognition.

By the middle of 1945 plans were well advanced among the army officers for a *coup d'état* against the Medina regime. Since the army men did not want to have their projected revolt appear to the public as a mere move to gain their own promotions, they looked around for civilian allies. Their logical candidate for a partnership was Acción Democrática, the principal opposition party to the Medina regime and a group which could not be accused of Communist affiliations or sympathies.

At first the Acción Democrática leaders were very hesitant to have anything to do with an army coup, but finally they did agree to listen to the propositions of the young officers. Betancourt and other Acción Democrática leaders urged the military men to hold off until one last effort could be made to get agreement with Medina Angarita on a compromise candidate for the presidency. Further negotiations with Escalante were undertaken. When they finally broke down and Medina Angarita went forward with the candidacy of Biaggini, the Acción Democrática agreed reluctantly to join the proposed military insurrection, under certain conditions. They insisted that the government junta to be established by the rebels would contain a majority of Acción Democrática members and that of its seven members only two would be military men. They also insisted that the new regime be an Acción Democrática Party government and that the military agree not to interfere with its plans for governing the country. The young officers acquiesced on all of these points.

Meanwhile President Medina Angarita had gotten wind of what was afoot, and on October 17, 1945, he ordered the arrest of a number of the military conspirators. As a result, although the uprising had not been planned for that date, it went forward on October 18. In the streets of Caracas there was bitter fighting in which the Acción Democrática civilians joined the rebels and Communists fought for the government forces. After several hours of conflict the uprising was victorious.

At the first meeting of the victorious army men with the Acción Democrática leaders the latter insisted that the conditions under which they had joined the uprising be fulfilled. It was agreed that four Acción Democrática leaders, Rómulo Betancourt, Raúl Leoni, Gonzalo Barrios, and Luis Beltrán Prieto, as well as Edmundo Fernández, a politically independent civilian, would be named to the new Junta Revolucionaria de Gobierno. The military men chose as their representatives on the Junta Major Carlos Delgado Chalbaud, the senior officer in the conspiracy, and Captain Mario Vargas, an officer closely associated with Acción Democrática.

During the next thirty-seven months the government of Venezuela was in the hands of the Acción Democrática Party. Rómulo Betancourt was president of the Revolutionary Junta until it gave way to the country's first popularly elected chief executive early in 1948. During this period he was, in effect, provisional president of Venezuela. The Junta as such existed only in name. After a few weeks of separate meetings the Junta and the Cabinet started meeting jointly, since most of the members of the Junta also held cabinet posts. The individual cabinet members reported to Betancourt as if he were president of the republic.

This procedure did not come about because of any desire on the part of Rómulo Betancourt to monopolize power in the regime. It was a natural consequence of the fact that the revolutionary government was in fact a party government and Betancourt was the acknowledged popular leader of the party.

Rómulo Betancourt had earned his position of leadership. He was not only a consummate public speaker capable of haranguing a crowd, but also a serious student of the problems of his country and his hemisphere capable of providing ideas and inspiration for a group of intellectuals; and he had the respect and affection of all his associates. He possessed great organizing ability and knew how to delegate power and responsibility to others, yet constantly remaining aware of what they were doing or failing to do. He was equally capable of drawing up long-range plans and of making quick decisions in moments of crisis.

If there were any qualities which particularly marked Rómulo Betancourt, they were a tremendous dynamism, a stanch loyalty to his friends and associates, and a firm adherence to the principles in which he believed. Although he was an inveterate pipe smoker, the look of calmness and quiet which this habit frequently gave him was misleading. His personality was vigorous and unconsciously imposed itself upon those around him.

Like most popular leaders, Betancourt had the ability to get along with people of varied backgrounds and conditions, though he often maintained a certain aloofness, which, without annoying or disconcerting those with whom he was dealing, tended to accentuate his position of leadership. This quality was akin to the trait of a good teacher who knows how to be congenial and friendly with his students without ever passing over the line beyond which familiarity breeds contempt.

Betancourt's loyalty to his friends and associates was highlighted during a conversation which the author had with him when he was in exile in Puerto Rico. When Betancourt was asked which of his several periods of exile he had borne most tolerably, he replied,

"The one in 1940 when I was in Chile," and the reason which he gave for this was that during the dictatorship of that period the regime had not jailed, tortured, or persecuted its opponents, and so he was not preoccupied with thoughts of the fate of those friends who remained in Venezuela. His loyalty to friendship and principle was demonstrated too when, during the crisis preceding the fall of the Gallegos government, Betancourt refused to take any steps which might have seemed to place him in opposition to President Gallegos, even though that might have saved the situation for his party.

Betancourt's task was a hard one. He was one of the few civilian presidents in the history of the republic. The Army had always dominated Venezuela, and throughout the Acción Democrática regime there were elements in the armed forces which were jealous of the civilian control of the administration and sought to put full power back once again into the hands of the army officers. So long as he remained at the head of the regime Betancourt was able to handle these military folk. A supremely capable politician, he knew when to concede in minor details, but he also knew how to crack down energetically on military dissidents when a matter of principle was at stake. His successor was not so fortunate.

Once in power, Betancourt and Acción Democrática proceeded to carry out the program which they had been advocating for many years. In its general outlines this program was simple, consisting of three principal points. First, the party wanted to reorganize the political structure of the state to provide the widest possible degree of democracy. Second, it sought a readjustment of the relations with the foreign oil companies so as to provide Venezuela with a larger share of the return from the exploitation of its principal known natural resource. Third, the party advocated the use of this increased return so as to create an economic and social base which would be able to survive if something happened to petroleum.

President Betancourt and his colleagues moved swiftly to fulfill the first part of the Acción Democrática program—the establishment of full political democracy. A new election decree provided for universal adult suffrage, thus giving the vote to illiterates. Voting was to be by lists, each party having its list printed on different colored paper. On election day the voter would choose the list of the party he wished to support and deposit it in the ballot box. There were strict regulations to assure the secrecy of the voting process.

Meanwhile the government was encouraging the formation of political parties representing the nation's various currents of political thought. Until the 1945 Revolution the only well organized parties had been Acción Democrática and the Communists. The Medina Angarita government had an "administration party," the Partido Democrático Venezolano, which owed its existence to its role as patronage dispenser and disappeared with the fall of the Medina regime.

Some thirteen political parties were legally recognized in the months following the October, 1945, Revolution. Most of these were very small and had little impact on the country's politics. Two new parties of major importance then made their appearance. The first was the Comité Popular Electoral Independiente, which came to be known by its initials as the COPEI. This party was organized by Dr. Rafael Caldera, a young Catholic lawyer who had first been named Attorney General by the Revolutionary Junta but soon disagreed with certain actions of the regime and withdrew. The COPEI proclaimed itself a Christian Social or Christian Democratic party, although it came to have within its ranks many of the country's more conservative elements. It was the majority in the mountainous states near the Colombian border, which were strongly Catholic. It was a good deal weaker in the rest of the country.

The second major party to appear was Unión Republicana Democrática. The URD was established under the leadership of Jóvito Villalba, one of the principal figures of the 1928 student movement against Gómez and one of the founders of the predecessor of Acción Democrática, the Partido Democrático Nacional; but he had quit its ranks in 1938. He had remained an independent until after the 1945 Revolution and under the Medina regime had been named a senator with the support of the administration. His party was of the moderate left, professing greater adherence to the principles of free enterprise than did Acción Democrática. Many figures prominent in the Medina regime joined the URD. During most of the AD period it was the most bitter and violent opponent of the administration.

The Communists had split into two groups, known as the Reds and the Blacks from the colors they adopted for electoral purposes. The division between the two groups dated back to the days of the Medina regime. The Black group had favored closer cooperation with Medina than had the Reds, and an informal break had occurred between the two factions at that time. After the October, 1945, uprising there were attempts to unify the two groups, but in the end they failed and two separate parties were established. The Reds took the name Partido Comunista de Venezuela and followed a policy of trying to ingratiate themselves with the Acción Democrática regime; the Blacks became the Partido Revolucionario del Proletariado (Comunista) and were frankly hostile to the AD government.

During the Acción Democrática regime three elections were held. The first, on October 27, 1946, was for members of a constituent assembly called to write a new basic document for the nation. Acción Democrática won a sizable majority, receiving 1,099,601 votes and seating 137 members in the Assembly. COPEI came in second with 185,347 votes and 19 Assemblymen. The URD was third with 53,875 votes and 2 seats. A joint ticket of the two Communist groups received 50,837 votes and also 2 members of the constitutent assembly.

Once the new constitution was written, elections were called to pick the first popularly chosen president and to name members of the Senate and Chamber of Deputies. The Acción Democrática candidate, Rómulo Gallegos, won an overwhelming victory, receiving 871,752 votes. The AD also won 38 seats in the Senate and 83 in the Chamber. Rafael Caldera, running as the COPEI nominee, received 262,204 votes, and the party elected 6 senators and 38 deputies. The URD did not name a presidential candidate but elected 1 senator and 4 deputies. The Communists again put up a joint nominee for president but ran separate tickets for congress. Dr. Gustavo Machado, the Communist presidential candidate, received 36,514 votes; the Red Communists elected 1 senator and 3 members of the Chamber, though the Blacks did not get any congressmen.

Finally, under the administration of President Rómulo Gallegos, elections were held for municipal offices throughout the country.

Once again Acción Democrática had an overwhelming victory, winning control of all state legislatures and most municipalities, except in two states.

Rómulo Betancourt has told the author that the happiest day of his life was on October 27, 1946, the day the people of Venezuela went to the polls under universal suffrage to vote for their representatives to write a new democratic constitution. He felt that this was in many ways the high point of achievement of his career. It repudiated once and for all the idea that the people of Venezuela were "unprepared" to choose their own rulers. It was a justification for democracy in a country which had suffered under military dictatorships for virtually its whole national existence.

In retrospect, however, Betancourt and other AD leaders concluded that they had probably called the citizenry to the polls too often. The constant state of campaigning for most of the three years they were in power kept political temperatures at fever pitch throughout the period, and contributed an element of instability, giving ambitious military men a chance to fish in perturbed civilian political waters, and thus contributing considerably to the ultimate overthrow of the Acción Democrática regime by the Army.

Equally significant as the efforts to establish a democratic regime were the moves of Betancourt and his colleagues in the economic and social fields. One of their first acts was to come to grips with the petroleum problem. Acción Democrática had argued for many years that Venezuela was sharing too meagerly in the exploitation of its own natural resources. So Betancourt and his Minister of Development, Juan P. Pérez Alfonso, entered into negotiations with the oil firms almost immediately after the October, 1945, Revolution.

Out of these negotiations came the famous "50-50" formula which subsequently became standard throughout the oil-producing world. It was agreed that the Venezeulan government would receive 50 per cent of the profits of the Venezuelan oil industry. Part of the government's share would come in the form of the traditional royalty, which was somewhat increased. Another part would come in the form of a new income tax. The rest would be in the form of minor duties levied on the operations of the companies. It was agreed that the oil companies would open their books to the Venezuelan govern-

ment so as to determine what the real profits from the exploitation
of the country's oil were. It was also agreed that the firms would
calculate the sale of crude oil to other firms—even where these were
associated with a common mother company—at such rates that the
profits would not all be passed on to the processing part of the business.

For its part, the Acción Democrática government promised the
oil companies that the petroleum industry would not be expropriated.
The Acción Democrática leaders felt that the country was in no
position at that time to attempt to administer the oil business. Even
twelve years after the agreement with the oil firms Betancourt held
the same opinion. In his monumental study of the Venezuelan oil
industry and its effects on the nation, *Venezuela: Política y Petróleo,*
he wrote (p. 235):

We had always rejected the possibility of applying, in the beginning
of an administration with a revolutionary orientation, a measure similar to that which is the greatest claim to fame of the Mexican regime of
Lázaro Cárdenas, because there are substantial differences between
the situation of Mexico when it nationalized petroleum, and that of
ourselves. Petroleum was and is in the Mexican economy a factor of
importance, but complementing others of considerable size. As a result,
the country did not experience a serious drawback to its normal evolution when the international oil cartel and the governments in agreement
with it decreed the boycott of nationalized oil. In contrast, when we
took over the government, practically all of the Venezuelan economy
and an appreciable part of the fiscal activity of the government depended on petroleum. Of the foreign exchange with which Venezuela
paid for its imports in 1944, the year before the Revolution of October,
92 per cent came from the petroleum industry. Of the $326,000,000
which came into the country in that year, $300,000,000 were obtained
from the exploitation of this mineral. Some 31 per cent of the income
in the Government's Budget came from taxes on hydrocarbons.

Instead of nationalization of the oil industry the Acción Democrática program for petroleum was designed to get the greatest possible contribution to Venezuela itself out of the exploitation of its
subsoil resources. Betancourt outlined this program in the following
terms (p. 236):

1. Increase of taxes to the limit then considered reasonable within the capitalist system and the market economy.

2. Competition by Venezuela, as an autonomous force, in the international petroleum market, selling directly its royalty oil.

3. Cessation of the system of giving concessions to private firms, and planning for a State enterprise to which would be given the power of exploiting, directly or through contracts with third parties, the national reserves.

4. Industrialization of the major part of Venezuelan petroleum within the country; and the organization of a national refinery, with State or mixed capital.

5. Adequate measures for the conservation of petroleum wealth, a typical non-renewable resource; and the utilization of the gas emanating from the wells, which had traditionally been lost.

6. Reinvestment by the companies having concessions of a part of their profits in the development of the agricultural and grazing economy.

7. Substantial improvements in wages, social services and living and working conditions of the workers, white-collar workers and technicians of Venezuelan nationality working in the industry.

8. Investment of a high percentage of the income obtained from the new tax policy on petroleum, in creating a diversified and independent Venezuelan economy.

The effect of this agreement with the oil firms was to increase immensely the government's income from the oil industry. Betancourt says the following on the increase of government revenue during 1947, the last full year that he was in office (p. 247):

The increase of the income of the State for the year 1947, from petroleum was 622.1 per cent greater than the income of 1938. . . . But the increase resulting from increased production of oil was only 130.9 per cent. That is to say that in 1947 an output one and one third greater than that of 1938 represented an increase to the State 5.6 times greater.

With these increased oil revenues the Acción Democrática regime set out to try to transform the economy and social life of the country. They were anxious to build up a more diversified economy, strengthening agriculture and expanding the nation's weak manufacturing industry. Its principal weapon in the field was the Corporación Venezolana de Fomento (Venezuelan Development Corporation), set up by the AD regime on the pattern of the successful Chilean Development Corporation.

According to the statutes of the Corporación, it was to receive at least 10 per cent of the government budget each year. This provision was honored so long as Acción Democrática remained in power. Through it large sums were made available to various projects for diversifying agricultural output. As a result the country subsequently became self-sufficient in sugar and rice, and output of other crops increased considerably.

Through the Corporación de Fomento, funds were provided to the Banco Agrícola y Pecuario for the extension of credits to agriculturists. During the Acción Democrática regime such credits almost doubled. Short-term loans for financing current crops almost tripled in value, and the number of farmers receiving this type of help increased from 14,146 in 1945 to 81,093 in 1948. At the same time the Banco Agrícola y Pecuario established the policy of guaranteeing minimum prices to the agriculturist.

As a result of the policies followed by the Banco Agrícola y Pecuario during the Acción Democrática regime production of basic food products increased significantly. According to Betancourt (p. 328), the increases in certain key products were as follows:

TABLE 1

	Metric Tons	
	1945	*1948*
Sugar cane	1,950,000	2,370,000
Peas	8,000	16,000
Beans	8,000	18,017
Potatoes	9,185	16,000

In addition to augmenting the facilities of the Banco Agrícola y Pecuario, the Acción Democrática regime undertook to encourage mechanization of agriculture and built sizable irrigation projects in various parts of the country. Importation of agricultural machinery by the government increased considerably. The number of tractors brought from the United States, for instance, increased from 519 units in 1945 to 2,105 in 1948.

Rómulo Betancourt has summed up the Acción Democrática government's work in the field of agriculture in the following terms (p. 331):

We do not attempt to claim any extraordinary importance for the things actually achieved during the Government of A.D., insofar as the increase in the physical volume of agricultural production is concerned. These achievements, in terms of tons, were of limited importance, because they were achieved without the fulfillment of a profound agrarian reform, without having extended mechanization to all of the rural zones. They are important, above all, as a decisive argument to refute a thesis which was deeply imbedded in the national consciousness: that agricultural development was impossible in Venezuela, which was condemned to "enjoy the sun while it lasted"; and to feed itself only so long as there was petroleum to pay for imports from abroad of virtually everything which was consumed.

Acción Democrática's government was also firmly committed to a policy of industrialization. Betancourt has stated its objectives in this way (p. 384):

The Development Corporation, charged with fulfilling the industrialization program of the democratic regime, conceived of this process as taking place in four stages. It was not our intention to imitate that which the Government of Perón was undertaking at the same time, that is, to artifically force the process of industrialization for reasons of national prestige and for other less defensible purposes.

The first stage was to stimulate basic industries: electricity, without which development of industry is impossible; and those related to human welfare, such as foodstuffs, clothing, fuel and housing. In this first stage, it was proposed to increase and improve the technology of extractive industries other than petroleum, and stimulate certain industries related to industrial chemistry.

In the second stage were included industries complementary to those already named; in the third stage, medium heavy industries were to be pushed, and in the fourth step, the production of machines, heavy industry. But there was no rigid formula, only a working guide, to be carried out with flexibility.

In carrying out this policy the government gave particular help to the production of edible oils and canned fish, flour mills, and a fertilizer factory. The textile industry was given special attention The Development Corporation advanced credits of 20 million bolivares to this industry, the production of which increased approximately 25 per cent during the three years of AD rule.

A great deal of attention was paid to the electrification of the country. Betancourt notes that the number of installed plants doubled in 1946–47, rising from 322 to 600, and the number of towns served by electricity increased from 319 to 616 (p. 392). A general electrification plan was drawn up with the technical aid of Brus and Roe, Inc., of New York.

Finally, attention was centered on the possibility of establishing an iron and steel industry in Venezuela. Vast iron-ore resources had been discovered in the Orinoco River Valley, and the AD government entered into negotiations with the United States Steel Corporation. The company wanted concessions in the Cerro Bolívar area, and the proposal of the AD regime was to tie these concessions in with the construction of transportation facilities in the region and with the establishment of an iron and steel plant. These negotiations had not been completed when the Acción Democrática government was overthrown. Although its successor granted a concession to United States Steel, it needed seven years more of "study" before an arrangement was made with a European firm to establish a steel company under conditions which were strongly criticized after the fall of the Pérez Jiménez dictatorship in 1958.

Rómulo Betancourt has summed up the results of the Acción Democrática's efforts to diversify the Venezuelan economy and to stimulate industrialization in the following terms (pp. 406–407):

. . . All this has relative importance in the face of a fundamental fact: we had demonstrated with deeds, in agriculture as well as in industry, that it *was* possible to stimulate specifically Venezuelan production. We showed that it was mere speculation of those who were afraid to act and were prophets of defeatism to insist that the country must continue to depend only on petroleum. If the State undertook a creative role of encouraging, orienting and stimulating specifically Venezuelan production, the industrious spirit and the will to work of the people of our land would do the rest. The results obtained in three years in the various fields of economic activity provide an impressive list of achievements to sustain this optimistic thesis.

One of the most interesting projects undertaken by the Betancourt administration was the accord between the Corporación de Fomento and Nelson Rockefeller's International Basic Economy Corporation, which was the result of the Acción Democrática regime's interest in having the oil companies invest some of their profits in the economy of Venezuela. The International Basic Economy Corporation, in which some of the oil companies had an interest, agreed to establish a number of enterprises in Venezuela which would contribute to strengthening the nation's economy. The IBEC would put up 50 per cent of the capital, and the Corporación de Fomento would contribute the other half. It was agreed that within ten years IBEC would sell its interest to Venezuelans, so that the companies would within that time become completely national in ownership.

In addition to trying to stimulate and diversify the nation's economy, the Acción Democrática regime was anxious to build up what Betancourt calls its "social capital," that is, its people. Great emphasis was laid on education and health projects. The number of children in elementary and secondary schools increased in the three years of AD rule from 142,500 to 522,000. During the three years of the AD administration some 5,000 new schoolrooms were opened. Special emphasis was given to teacher training, and enrollment in normal schools rose from 1,200 students in 5 schools to 4,500 students in 12 schools between 1945 and 1948.

Schools were built out in the countryside as well as in the capital cities of the states. For the first time thousands of rural children were given a chance to get an education. Aside from trying to make up for lost time in an area which had been virtually abandoned hitherto, the Betancourt and Gallegos governments were anxious to try to slow down the drift of people to the cities, which was damaging the nation's agriculture and undermining its economy in general. Hence it tried to take education and other social services to the rural areas.

A large hospital building program was undertaken. In 1947 alone, hospitals with 660 beds were completed, and new ones with a capacity of 1,600 beds were started. In addition, the social security system, which had been begun by Medina Angarita and which put most of its emphasis on health insurance, was extended from Caracas, where it had first been established, to several of the interior cities.

The government undertook a large housing program. The Medina regime had started public housing but had concentrated principally on constructing several large apartment projects in Caracas. The AD administration, on the other hand, followed a policy of building housing projects in the interior as well as in Caracas, generally building individual homes rather than apartment blocks.

During 1946–47 the Betancourt administration constructed 5,000 houses, six and a half times the capacity of Medina's El Silencio project in Caracas and twice as many as had been built since the Workers Housing Bank had originally been established in 1929. The work was gaining further momentum during 1948, when the government, through the Workers Housing Bank, invested almost 60 million bolivares in public housing.

In the field of labor relations, too, the Betancourt and Gallegos regimes followed an active policy. Soon after the Revolution the government put its weight behind large-scale wage increases. To modify the impact on prices the government undertook a program to subsidize a number of the basic necessities. As a result, although wage levels rose some 64.7 per cent between 1944 and 1948, the cost of living rose only 29.4 per cent during this period. There was thus a considerable increase in real wages.

The Acción Democrática government gave its blessing to the expansion of the trade-union movement. At the time it took power there were a few more than two hundred recognized unions in Venezuela. By the middle of 1948 there were more than nine hundred. For the first time trade-unionism spread to the countryside, where unions had never been permitted before. There were by the middle of 1948 some three hundred agricultural workers' unions. The total number of union members rose in that period from 20,000 to 125,000.

The great majority of the unions were under the leadership of members of Acción Democrática. Minority elements were controlled by the two Communist groups. Unions in various industries and trades were brought together to form federations, and a regional federation of unions was also established in each state. Finally, late in 1947 the various union groups under Acción Democrática and Red Communist control joined to establish the Confederación de

Trabajadores de Venezuela. The Black Communists remained outside this and had control of only one federation, a minority group in Caracas and vicinity. Early in 1948 the Red Communist oil workers' unions were forced out of the Federation of Petroleum Workers and set up their own federation.

Collective bargaining was encouraged. In February, 1948, the first nation-wide collective agreement was signed between the various oil companies operating in the country and the Federation of Petroleum Workers. It established unprecedentedly high wages in the nation's chief industry and provided various fringe benefits for the workers. It was widely hailed as one of the best collective agreements to be found in the oil industry anywhere in the world.

Perhaps the most important element of the international policy of the Acción Democrática government was the strengthening of economic relations with the neighboring countries of Colombia and Ecuador. The preliminary basis for a customs union of the three countries was laid, and the first step toward joint economic activity was taken with the establishment of a common merchant fleet, the Flota Mercante Gran Colombia.

The perspective which Betancourt had concerning the Flota Gran Colombia and what might come after it was shown in the message which he sent to President Alberto Lleras Camargo of Colombia in April, 1946, upon the occasion of the Colombian government's acceptance of the idea of a joint merchant fleet. Betancourt wrote:

. . . the hour has come to go beyond the old Americanist rhetoric, substituting for it a realistic, positive and creative policy. To exalt common heroes in an historic fraternal endeavor should continue to be an emotional stimulus for Colombia, Venezuela and Ecuador. But along with it we must provide our peoples with those "elements of execution" which Your Excellency mentions, to consolidate in the economic field the political independence achieved by the liberating generation. We have taken a great step in this direction and we must let nothing deter our intention that other steps will follow. After the Gran Colombia fleet must come tariff agreements, the unification of public service charges, joint efforts to see that our mines and other sources of natural wealth will be safeguarded for the use of present and future generations by similar legislation. Isolated and jealous of one another, we will continue to be weak; united we may recover the lost rank which we once had in America. . . .[2]

The Acción Democrática regime accomplished enough during its three years in office to win widespread approbation among the people. Its administration was not besmirched, as were those of some similar popular parties in nearby countries, by any significant degree of graft or corruption.

However, there have been various criticisms leveled against the Acción Democrática administrations, particularly that of Betancourt. Some of these are worthy of investigation. It has been argued that the regime was "demagogic" because it sponsored general wage increases throughout the economy. In reply Betancourt argued that Acción Democrática came to power at a period in which Venezuelan oil was in great demand, the country was quite prosperous, and the economy could well stand such wage increases. Furthermore, he maintained that they served to expand the market inside Venezuela, thus providing a securer base for the economic-development projects which the regime undertook.

Second, the Betancourt administration has been criticized for what is alleged to have been the vengeance it wreaked on members of the regime which it overthrew. It is true that President Medina, ex-President López Contreras, and various members of their administrations were forced into exile. It is also true that special courts were established to investigate and punish alleged graft and corruption which had taken place during the two previous administrations.

However, Betancourt and other members of his government have maintained that many of those who remained abroad during this period did so of their own choice, not because the AD regime forced them to do so. Betancourt has also maintained that Medina, López Contreras, and some others were unwilling to accept the decision of popular suffrage in the various elections held under Acción Democrática and were trying to bring about a change in the regime by conspiracies and force. Furthermore, the AD leaders have argued the mere fact that corruption was not punished under López Contreras and Medina Angarita was no reason why it should not be punished under Betancourt. Acción Democrática, they have maintained, was trying to set an example of honest government, and one part of that attempt was the establishment of severe penalties in the case of corruption.

The AD regime was also accused of roughly handling certain of its political opponents, particularly members of the Unión Republicana Democrática. Certainly various leaders of URD were jailed for short periods under Betancourt. The charges against them were that they were conspiring with military elements against the regime. Subsequently, after the experience with the military dictatorship which followed Acción Democrática, URD leaders were inclined to modify their previous criticisms of the AD regime on the score of supposed undemocratic behavior.

Finally, the AD regime, and Rómulo Betancourt personally, have been strongly attacked for the way in which they came into power in the first place. Many have argued that Acción Democrática betrayed its own democratic professions when it seized power in collaboration with a faction of the Army. The author believes that the AD's actions were justified. The Acción Democrática leaders themselves maintain that the young army officers would have overthrown Medina Angarita in any case and that, had they done so without the alliance with a strong civilian party, the tragic events which followed the November, 1948, *coup d'état* might have occurred three years earlier. Furthermore, their three years in power gave the Acción Democrática leaders a chance to prove in practice not only their professions of faith in democracy but also their belief in a program of drastic but peaceful economic and social change, and their determination to carry out such a policy. Perhaps the final argument to refute these criticisms is the fact that in three years in office they won firm enough support among the people that even after nine years of unprecedented terror against them they were able to return in 1958 as the majority party once again.

In general, the balance of the Acción Democrática tenure in office was an immensely favorable one. Under AD for the first time there existed freedom of speech, press, and assembly, and there were honest elections in which the whole adult population was able to participate. Serious attempts were started to get under way a diversification of the economy using funds made available through new arrangements with the oil companies. The welfare of the humble citizen was the first preoccupation of the regime, and expenditures on education, public health, and housing were increased tremendously, both in absolute amounts and as percentages of total government expenditures. The Acción Democrática, under Betancourt's leadership, gave a good example of what can be done by a government of the Democratic Left to bring about necessary social changes, diversify and strengthen the economy, and build a solid foundation for political democracy.

Perhaps the greatest error of Acción Democrática under Betancourt's leadership was to bring about the election of Rómulo Gallegos as president of Venezuela. Gallegos is a world-famous novelist, an exceedingly fine and humane person, but not a capable politician. In the face of the long history of military rule in Venezuela and the restiveness of the Army under civilian control during the Betancourt regime, the first democratically elected civilian president should have been a man of political talent. He should have been someone who knew when to compromise and when to act.

Unfortunately Rómulo Gallegos was not such a politican. He was named by his party because he was its titular leader during the Betancourt period, because he was a man with a wide international reputation and because he was greatly admired and loved in Venezuela itself. He was not named because of his political experience nor, above all, for his ability to handle the Army.

Rómulo Gallegos was inaugurated early in 1948 in ceremonies attended by distinguished delegations from all of the American countries, the United States delegation being appropriately headed by the poet and essayist Archibald MacLeish. The inauguration was a splendid affair, and democracy in Venezuela seemed secure. However, only a few months later Gallegos was deposed and in exile.

The cause of Gallegos' downfall was a small group of ambitious military men headed by Colonel Marcos Pérez Jiménez. The colonel had been chief of the general staff in the early part of the Betancourt administration, but he had aroused the suspicions of Betancourt as well as of other army chiefs and had been sent off to be military attaché in Argentina. President Gallegos had let him return to Venezuela, and Pérez Jiménez soon began organizing a conspiracy against the regime.

The existence of the conspiracy was rumored during the summer of 1948 and became public knowledge early in November. The group of army officers headed by Pérez Jiménez presented the government an ultimatum demanding that the one-party rule of Acción Democrática be ended by converting it into a party-army administration. They demanded further that "extremists" within the party be curbed.

For more than three weeks President Gallegos did little or nothing to suppress this conspiracy and arrest its principal figures. The leaders of the labor movement urged that he permit them to call a general strike in support of the regime, but this offer was turned down. Elements in the Army loyal to the regime urged him to arrest Pérez Jiménez and other conspirators. Some army people even came to ex-President Betancourt and urged him to take command and arrest Pérez Jiménez and the others, but he refused, since this would have been tantamount to overturning the Gallegos government.

Efforts were made to dissuade Pérez Jiménez and the others from their course of action. Major Mario Vargas, the army leader closest to Acción Democrática and to Betancourt, who was sick in a tuberculosis hospital in Saranac Lake, New York, flew back to Venezuela with this purpose in mind. He failed.

Finally, seeing that the President was not going to take any action against the conspirators, Vargas and Gallegos' Minister of War, Colonel Carlos Delgado Chalbaud, finally joined the movement with the hope of diverting it into less harmful channels. With their adhesion the coup against Gallegos was completed. The President was deposed and sent into exile. Other leaders of the overthrown government were also arrested and deported. The moderating influence of Delgado Chalbaud and Vargas served for little because, a few days after the overthrow of Gallegos, Acción Democrática was declared illegal. In February, 1949, after a strike in the oil fields, the Confederación de Trabajadores de Venezuela and the Federation of Petroleum Workers were outlawed, and the freedom of the labor movement was destroyed.

Meanwhile Rómulo Betancourt, after a short period in hiding, sought refuge in a foreign embassy and, after considerable international pressure was exerted on the military dictatorship, was allowed to go into exile. He went first to Washington, but a few months later moved to Havana, where he stayed until the *coup d'état* of

General Fulgencio Batista in March, 1952, when he moved to Costa Rica. He stayed there until 1955, when, because of growing pressure by the Venezuelan regime on the government of Costa Rica, he moved to Puerto Rico to avoid further embarrassing the administration of José Figueres. He remained in Puerto Rico until a couple of months before the overthrow of the military dictatorship in January, 1958.

These nine years and more were a time of trial and tribulation for Betancourt, Acción Democrática, and the people of Venezuela. The country was ruled by an increasingly tyrannical dictatorship, the party was driven deeply underground, and Betancourt was hounded from one country to another, in constant danger of being assassinated by agents of the dictatorship's secret police.

The military men, after overthrowing President Gallegos, established a three-man Military Junta, composed of Colonel Delgado Chalbaud, Lieutenant Colonel Pérez Jiménez, and Lieutenant Colonel Llovera Páez, to run the country. So long as Delgado Chalbaud remained head of the Junta many of the fundamental policies of the Acción Democrática regime in social and economic matters were kept intact, and the dictatorship itself was relatively mild. However, in November, 1950, Colonel Delgado Chalbaud was kidnaped, taken to a place outside Caracas, and killed. The man who was officially charged with responsibility for this murder, General Rafael Urbina, was shot by the police, so that he did not live to implicate those who were in the conspiracy with him.

As a result of the death of Delgado Chalbaud, Colonel Pérez Jiménez became the dominant member of the Junta. As figurehead president of the Junta a civilian, Dr. Germán Suarez Flamerich, was chosen. With the reorganization of the Junta the regime became increasingly tyrannical. During the next few months one secretary general of the underground Acción Democrática organization, Leonardo Ruiz Pineda, was shot dead in the streets of Caracas. Another, his successor, Alberto Carnevali, was allowed to die in jail without receiving adequate medical treatment. The party was ruthlessly persecuted, and its leaders were jailed by the hundreds.

In December, 1952, the Junta made the mistake of allowing elections for a new constituent assembly. It apparently felt that the people were sufficiently cowed that they could afford the luxury of "constitutionalizing" the regime. However, the Junta was in for a rude shock.

Acción Democrática, of course, was not allowed to participate in the elections, though its supporters were not disqualified from voting. However, there were three parties which did participate— COPEI, Unión Republicana Democrática, and a pro-government group organized for the occasion, the so-called Frente Electoral Independiente. Campaigning was relatively free, and the votes were honestly cast. However, when the results came in it began to be clear that the URD had won a strong victory, the COPEI had shown its traditional strength in the mountain states, and the pro-government FEI had come in a poor third.

The reasons for the URD victory in this election have been widely discussed and disputed since 1952. The URD leaders, naturally, claimed that the victory showed that they had the support of the great majority of the people. Acción Democrática leaders have maintained that the URD victory was due to the fact that AD supported the Unión Republicana Democrática. COPEI leaders have told the writer that in part at least the URD victory was due to the fact that the mass of the people were violently against the government and wanted to show this by voting for the more extreme of the two legal opposition groups.

Whatever the reasons for their victory, the URD leaders were not allowed to enjoy it. Pérez Jiménez executed a coup, announcing that the counting of ballots was "temporarily" suspended, that he was taking over as provisional president. Meanwhile all URD leaders were rounded up and promptly deported. Shortly afterward Pérez Jiménez announced that the FEI had won "an overwhelming victory" and that the new constitutional assembly would meet in January, 1953.

Only the FEI members of the assembly gathered, most of the representatives of the COPEI and URD who had been granted posts by Pérez Jiménez refusing to attend. The body wrote a new constitution which changed the name of the country from Estados Unidos de Venezuela to República de Venezuela and granted the president virtually dictatorial powers. Its last act was to name Colonel Pérez Jiménez as "constitutional" president.

The Pérez Jiménez regime was one of the most scandalous and tyrannical that Latin America has seen in the present century. The oil boom provided the government with vast sums of money, which were spent lavishly in imposing buildings, grand boulevards, and the world's most expensive officers' club in Caracas, and a large road-building program in the interior. Most of the projects for development of agriculture started by the AD and continued with less enthusiasm by the Military Junta under Delgado Chalbaud were brought to a halt, and the Corporación de Fomento's funds were choked off. The programs for education and public health were drastically reduced, while the military budget skyrocketed.

Corruption was rife. Firms could not do business with the government without paying graft. All the leading figures of the regime enriched themselves, and the *New York Times* reported soon after his fall that Pérez Jiménez himself had piled up a fortune estimated at $235,000,000. Graft ran from top to bottom, and it was not unusual for a citizen to be stopped by a traffic policeman with an arbitrary demand for $20 on pain of being brought in "for resisting an officer" if he refused to pay.

The tyranny of the Pérez Jiménez regime matched its corruption. A notorious concentration camp was established at Guasina in the jungles of the Orinoco. The descriptions of conditions there would curdle one's blood. In the jails of San Juan de los Morros and the Penitenciaría Nacional the most barbarous tortures were used. The author has talked to many who suffered them and lived to tell about it. Many other victims were not so lucky.

Members of all the political parties suffered the same treatment, though the Acción Democrática people were by far the most severely and thoroughly persecuted group. Members of all parties were deported by the thousands. By the end of the Pérez Jiménez regime no political party, not even the FEI, was allowed to function openly in Venezuela.

Nor did the Pérez Jiménez dictatorship confine its persecution of the opposition within Venezuela. A young military officer, Lieutenant León Droz Blanco, who had opposed the regime and, after being arrested and tortured, had been deported to Baranquilla, Colombia, was shot dead in the streets there. Several attempts were made on the life of Rómulo Betancourt.

In spite of its unsavory reputation the Pérez Jiménez regime enjoyed the support and acclaim of most other American governments. Late in 1954 President Dwight Eisenhower bestowed upon Pérez Jiménez the Legion of Merit for his actions "before and after becoming President." He received decorations from other governments of the hemisphere. Only Costa Rica, under José Figueres, showed any hesitation about treating Pérez Jiménez as a worthy leader of the "free world." Don Pepe's government refused to send a delegation to the Tenth Inter-American Conference when it met in Caracas in April, 1954, explaining that it could not be a guest of such a tyrant.

It was not until the last months of the regime that Pérez Jiménez began to fall into bad repute with other American rulers. The government of Argentina cut off diplomatic relations because of Pérez Jiménez' friendship for Perón, who had taken up residence in Caracas. The Chilean government broke off relations because it discovered that Pérez Jiménez' government was censoring Chilean diplomatic mail.

Throughout the Pérez Jiménez regime Rómulo Betancourt directed the struggle against it. He remained the undisputed leader of Acción Democrática and coordinated the work of the members of the party in exile with the work of those in the underground organization inside Venezuela. He was in constant correspondence with both the exiles and those remaining in the country.

At the same time Betancourt was active as a journalist and writer. He was a regular contributor to the Cuban magazine *Bohemia*, which circulates throughout Latin Amercia, and wrote for other periodicals as well. He worked for several years on his monumental book on Venezuela called *Venezuela: Política y Petróleo*, in which he drew a detailed picture of the economic, social, and political impact of the rise of the petroleum industry on his country, and gave a detailed history of the position which his party had taken on the problem before, during, and after it had power.

Betancourt did his utmost to tell the rest of America the story of the Venezuelan dictatorship and of the people's struggle against it. He made a trip around South America in 1954, conferring with Acción Democrática exiles, talking with members of various governments, giving press interviews, and writing for the local papers. He several times presented petitions to the Human Rights Commission of the United Nations giving names of those who had been jailed, tortured, and killed by the Pérez Jiménez regime, and asking action against the regime.

During much of his exile Rómulo Betancourt lived in territory of the United States, either on the continent or in the island of Puerto Rico. He always maintained close contacts with the United States labor movement and with the liberals, Socialists, and others interested in Latin America who made up the North American Committee of the Inter-American Association for Democracy and Freedom.

Betancourt was one of the founders of the Inter-American Association, which was established at a conference in Havana in May, 1950. There he stressed his belief in the need for unity of the liberal-minded folk of both parts of the hemisphere. In his speech closing the conference, Betancourt said:

. . . Perhaps for the first time in the history of this part of the world there has met such a numerous group of personalities of the United States and Latin America to seek, apart from the prudent conclaves of diplomacy, the road towards a better tomorrow. This shows how the idea that liberty is indivisible is gaining ground. . . . This conjunction of forces of English- and Spanish-speaking free men is an explicit recognition of the fact that in the United States there coexist and struggle with the advocates of "dollar diplomacy" strong idealistic groups which sincerely support liberty, democracy and progress for all the Americas.[3]

Almost seven years later, at a luncheon given in his honor by the North American Committee of the Inter-American Association, Betancourt returned once again to this theme of the need for unity among liberal forces throughout the hemisphere:

I must recognize, and I do so without difficulty and in an elemental spirit of justice, and to serve the truth loyally, that the United States labor movement together with that of Latin America has given continuous support to our efforts to obtain in Venezuela a regime of law, respectful of public liberties. And I must add more. The way in which qualified representatives of the political, intellectual and trade union world of the United States have spoken confirms a thesis defended and propagated by democratic political movements of Latin America which do not worship at the altars of chauvinistic demagoguery. This is that there is a radical difference between Big Capital in this country, whose investors in our countries do not show belief in the normality of democratic processes and more often than not prefer to get along with and negotiate with irresponsible and venal dictatorships rather than representative governments; and the people, the good people, of the United States. The best spokesmen for this people frequently attack the mistaken foreign policies of their government, and coincide with us sincerely on two basic questions: the right of our nations to self-determination and the adequate enjoyment of our natural resources; and the necessity that there be in them freely elected governments, respectful of human rights and imparters of social justice.[4]

Returning in the same speech to the problem of United States support of Latin American dictators, Betancourt commented:

Those people are mistaken who believe that in Latin America only the Communist minorities are resentful of the foreign policy of the United States in the area. The Communists practice what has been called with justice "strategic hatred" of everything North American. But apart from those minorities, vast political workingclass and intellectual groups of undoubted democratic orientation have felt more than once that they have been defrauded by United States policy. It is not conceivable in Latin America that the same person can call upon peoples to support struggles for liberty in Korea and give medals to dictators. It is not understood why the friendship of the dictators who will disappear is preferred to that of the peoples who will remain. A statesman of this country—Franklin Delano Roosevelt—understood that the path of Inter-American relations must be different from this and that it must be based on the express recognition of the profound democratic conviction of our peoples.

Betancourt also dealt in passing with another theme which he stressed frequently in his years of exile when discussing Inter-American relations, when he commented:

The Latin American peoples also insist that there be a plan for the development and financing of their backward economies. There is not much optimism concerning the results of the coming meeting in Washington of the personal representatives of the Chiefs of State of the continent, and it is feared that the proposed Inter-American Economic Conference of Buenos Aires will end once again with Platonic resolutions instead of concrete and dynamic agreements. But I cannot leave this subject without saying that a large part of the fault for this situation rests with the demonstrated incapacity of the Latin American governments to draw up a common plan and present it for discussion with representatives of the United States. With honorable exceptions, the representatives of those governments come to Inter-American economic meetings to present and defend their small local problem. The lesson of Bandung has not aroused any echo as yet in Hispano America.

During his long period of exile Betancourt had time to restudy his own political history and to decide where he and his party had made mistakes and where they had acted correctly. One conclusion to which he came was that one of the weaknesses of the regime from 1945–48 had been the hostility of the civilian political parties toward one another. Having come to this conclusion Betancourt tried long and earnestly to reach an agreement with the other two principal democratic parties, COPEI and the Unión Republicana Democrática, whereby they would agree, without losing their ideological and political identity, to limit their opposition to one another exclusively to the civilian political field. He felt that they all had to learn that they might win or lose, but they should never either persecute one another or resort to conspiracy with the military in order to upset a constituted democratic regime.

These efforts finally bore fruit in January, 1958, when the leaders of all three parties—Betancourt of AD, Rafael Caldera of the COPEI, and Jóvito Villalba of the URD—were temporarily exiles in New York. There they reached an agreement to work together for the reestablishment of democratic constitutional government and pledged themselves to cooperate to preserve it at all costs once it was achieved.

Rómulo Betancourt remained an optimist throughout the nine years of the dictatorship. Sometimes the author had the feeling that Betancourt's was the forced optimism of the exile, the element which made it possible to continue to live, though on foreign soil, unable to return to a sadly abused and distraught homeland. But Betancourt always maintained his faith that sooner or later the dictatorship would be gotten rid of. He was never one of those who submitted to the easy theory that his country was "unprepared" for democracy. He continued to function always as the leader of the political party which represented the "alternate government" of his country.

Finally, in January, 1958, Betancourt's optimism was justified. After an abortive revolutionary attempt by the Venezuelan Air Force on January 1, an uprising of the people of Caracas and other principal cities finally forced the military men around Pérez Jiménez to order him on January 23 to leave the country and give up the "golden egg" which he had been hatching for so long.

Betancourt remained in New York for about a month after the Revolution of January 23, 1958. When he finally returned, he was greeted at the El Silencio Square in Caracas by a crowd of 40,000 people, the largest number that had met to receive any of the returning exiles. He immediately threw himself into the work of rebuilding Acción Democrática and of getting acquainted once again with the country from which he had been absent for more than nine years. He was accepted once again as the unquestioned leader of Acción Democrática, though he and other returning exiles agreed to leave most of the party machinery for the time being in the hands of the young former underground leaders who had carried on the struggle inside the country during the last months of the Pérez Jiménez regime.

In August, 1958, Acción Democrática held its first open congress in ten years, and Betancourt was confirmed once again as the party's principal spokesman. The party adopted a new political program which took into account the considerable economic and social changes which had occurred in Venezuela since the original party program was adopted in 1941.

Meanwhile the Provisional Government which had taken over upon the fall of Pérez Jiménez moved rapidly toward reestablishing a constitutional regime. In preparation for the election there were prolonged negotiations among the leaders of the three democratic parties seeking agreement on a joint candidate for president. However, when these negotiations finally broke down a few weeks before the election, each group named its own candidate.

As was to be expected, Rómulo Betancourt was the choice of Acción Democrática. In a hard-fought campaign, in which he made an extensive tour throughout the country, Betancourt amply defeated his two rivals, Admiral Wolfgang Larrazabal, backed by URD, and Rafael Caldera of the COPEI. Betancourt received 49 per cent of the total vote, and Acción Democrática received an absolute majority in both houses of Congress.

Upon his inauguration on February 13, 1959, Betancourt organized a coalition administration with cabinet members and other officials drawn from all three democratic parties. The new regime set about the fulfillment of a program which was essentially that of the first Betancourt administration brought up to date and now backed by all three of the nation's major parties. Early in 1960 a thoroughgoing agrarian reform law was passed, and a program for distributing land to all the nation's landless agricultural workers was gotten under way. Meanwhile the government sought to "sow petroleum" through extensive programs for economic development, irrigation, education, public health, and housing. It also began a fundamental change in petroleum policy with the establishment late in 1960 of the government-owned Venezuelan Petroleum Corporation, which took over oil concession lands given up by the international oil companies operating in the country. The ultimate objective of the new firm is to take over all concessions as they expire in the next quarter of a century.

The program of social transformation of the Betancourt regime took on added significance as a result of the Castro Revolution in Cuba. Both the Betancourt and Castro regimes were carrying out generally similar programs of agrarian change, economic development, and social reform. However, the Betancourt government was doing all this while remaining a democratic regime, elected by the people and respectful of the rights of all of the citizens, whereas the Castro regime adopted a Jacobin attitude of increasing disregard for democratic procedures and the rights of those who in any way disagreed with the regime. By the end of 1960 it appeared as if the fate of much of Latin America might well depend upon the relative success of the Betancourt and Castro methods of carrying out a social revolution.

The pro-Castro forces in Venezuela were quite frankly seeking the overthrow of Betancourt by the end of 1960. These forces included the Communists, a dissident group of expelled ADers who organized the so-called Movimiento de la Izquierda Revolutionaria, and part of the URD, which abandoned the coalition government in November 1960.

As during the previous period when Acción Democrática was in power, a major challenge to the regime came from discontented military men. During the first year of the administration several plots were discovered, and in April, 1960, the garrison of San Cristóbal, near the frontier with Colombia, mutinied, but its example was not followed by the military in the rest of the republic. In July, 1960, President Betancourt narrowly escaped assassination, which was officially laid by the government of Venezuela at the door of the government of dictator Rafael Trujillo of the Dominican Republic.

The attitude of the military had changed substantially from the period of the 1940's. Although during the Pérez Jiménez regime Betancourt had been pictured to the army officers as a veritable ogre, upon his return in 1958 he succeeded in winning wide respect among the officers and enlisted men of all the country's military services. The rise of the Castro regime almost simultaneously with the inauguration of Betancourt as president convinced many military men that it was essential for the national security of the nation that his administration succeed.

Rómulo Betancourt's career, though a stormy one, has established him as one of the principal leaders and spokesmen for the Democratic Left in Latin America. His reputation is a continental one, and his words are listened to far beyond the borders of his own country. This is due not merely to the fact that he has been president of one of the richest and fastest-growing nations of the hemisphere. Through the policies he has followed in power and through his written and spoken statements Betancourt has clearly outlined a policy which finds wide echo in Latin America.

Rómulo Betancourt has stood forth as a strong champion of political democracy, both when in opposition and when in power. He has stood for a program of economic development and diversification, and has shown in practice the possibilities of such a program. He has shown concern for the welfare of the humbler part of his country's citizenry by commencing an agrarian reform program and supporting the development of a strong trade-union movement and collective bargaining, as well as by sponsoring the extension of labor and social security legislation. Finally, he has advocated, and when in office has put into effect, a program of moderate yet definite economic nationalism. He has conceived of a Venezuelan nationalist program as not only involving the retention for his country of the largest possible share of benefits from the exploitation of its own natural resources, but as the strengthening of his nation's economy through joint action and possible economic union with his neighbors. He has spoken as a Latin American nationalist almost as much as a Venezuelan one.

The policies and program which Rómulo Betancourt has advocated and sought to put into practice are the basic platform of the forces seeking a democratic social revolution in Latin America.

"Pepe" Figueres:
Dreamer and Man of Action

Radio listeners in San José, capital of Costa Rica, who tuned in their sets at seven o'clock on the evening of July 7, 1942, were surprised to hear an unknown orator, speaking in a flat but intense voice, deliver a violent attack on the government of the day. Halfway through his planned speech the speaker suddenly hesitated, then said these final words:

The police have told me to keep quiet. I shall not be able to say that which I believe should be said. But I can sum it up in a few words: What the Government should do is get out! . . .

His talk suddenly ended, the speaker was seized, dragged from the microphone by the police, and whisked off to jail. The next day he was hurried into exile—a national hero.

This was the first appearance on the political scene of José Figueres, who was to become the principal spokesman in Central America of the Democratic Left. This speech marked the introduction to politics of the man who was twice to become president of Costa Rica and was to put an end to a long-drawn-out crisis in that country's political life, setting in motion new currents which have not yet subsided.

Costa Rica had long been known as the most democratic nation of Central America. It did not have the racial problems which plagued some of its neighbors. Its agricultural life was marked by relatively wide distribution of landownership. For over a quarter of a century two outstandingly democratic figures, Clemente González Víquez and Ricardo Jiménez had alternated in the presidency. A disciple of Jiménez, León Cortés, continued the democratic tradition from 1936 to 1940.

144

However, there was a fatal weakness in Costa Rica's democracy. It was the fact that this was in the finest sense of the phrase an "oligarchical democracy." The political life of the country was dominated by the well-to-do classes. Although the people in each election had a chance to choose between rival candidates selected from among the oligarchical group, they played little part in deciding who should run.

The result was that little attention was paid by the governing classes to the welfare of the workers and peasants of Costa Rica. Meanwhile the younger generation, particularly the young intellectuals, grew increasingly restless with the regime. During the 1930's a number of these youths found an outlet for their discontent in the Communist Party, which had been established by one of them, Manuel Mora, in 1929. However, many other young people were not satisfied with the foreignness of the Communist Party and did not really find their political path until the advent of Figueres.

Figueres' speech of July 7, 1942, brought him from obscurity to national prominence and created a new political figure of first rank in the small Central American republic. It was probably inevitable that the wildest of rumors should spread about who this man was. Some stories circulated that José Figueres was in fact a Spaniard, not a Costa Rican. Others reported that he had fought in the Spanish Civil War, though there was no agreement concerning which side he had served. Other rumors pictured him as a sympathizer with Hitler and Mussolini in the World War then in progress.

There was no truth in any of these stories. José Figueres was a native-born Costa Rican citizen, had spent the 1930's on his *finca* in the hill country south of San José, and had not participated on either side in the Spanish conflict. He was a strong opponent of the Axis and a supporter of the cause of the Allies.

Figueres was born in the Costa Rican town of San Ramón on September 25, 1906, the son of two immigrants from Catalonia, the northeastern province of Spain, Dr. Mariano Figueres Forges and his wife, Paquita Ferrer Minguella de Figueres, an ex-schoolteacher. After going through primary school in his native town, Pepe went to San José, where he studied in the Liceo de Costa Rica and the Seminary College.

Before he came of age Pepe Figueres had shocked his parents by announcing that he was going to the United States to continue his studies. Although his family tried their best to change his mind, he was determined, and before long found himself in Boston. There he took courses at the Massachusetts Institute of Technology and worked as a laborer in a local tea-packing plant. What spare time he had Figueres spent in the Boston Public Library, where he studied particularly economics and sociology. He claims to have learned his very good English by reading Herbert Spencer.

At the age of nineteen Figueres moved to New York, where he earned his living doing translations from English to Spanish and vice versa. He continued his studies in the local libraries during his three years in New York. Then in 1928 he returned home to Costa Rica to begin a career as a farmer and businessman which was to last for fourteen years before he was suddenly launched into the political seas.

In the mountains of Tarrazú, seven hours by horse from San José, there was for sale a run-down hacienda with eroded land and worn-out machinery for processing the hard fibers which had been its principal product. Figueres, with aid from his family, was able to buy this farm cheap, and he set to work to build it into one of the finest agricultural enterprises in all of Costa Rica.

José Figueres applied the most up-to-date methods of scientific agriculture to his plantation. He developed the water resources of his neighborhood and applied the knowledge of electricity and mechanics which he had learned at M.I.T. At the same time he was a model employer, providing his workers with decent housing and with medical care and a small dispensary. He built schools sufficient to guarantee primary education for all his workers' children. All this he did without an attitude of patronage which might undermine the feelings of self-esteem of the workers. As a result, those working for Figueres developed a feeling of friendship and admiration for him which some years later made them exceedingly loyal in time of crisis.

These were years of intense labor for Pepe Figueres. He built a solid reputation among the agricultural and business communities as a hardheaded and efficient businessman. But he gained little attention from the nation at large. Figueres' dedication to his work was symbolized by the name which he gave his plantation, "La Lucha Sin Fin" (The Struggle Without End).

Throughout these years of isolated work in the mountains Fi-

gueres found several occasions to visit the United States on business.
On one of these trips he married a young lady from Alabama, Miss
Henrietta Boggs, and in the years that followed she bore him two
children.

Figueres had no intention of entering politics. However, on July
4, 1942, he was in San José attending an Independence Day celebration at the United States Embassy when a serious riot broke out in
the capital. The excuse for it was the sinking by a Nazi submarine
of the ship "San Pablo" in the Costa Rican port of Limón. The
demonstration of protest, which was generally reported to have been
organized by the Communist Party, degenerated into pilferage of
stores owned by Germans and Italians throughout the city.

There was widespread indignation among the citizenry of San
José over this rioting, which brought unaccustomed violence to the
Costa Rican political scene. The government's halfhearted attempts
to stop it seemed to many to reflect the growing influence of the
Communists in the regime then in power.

Among those who were deeply moved by the rioting was the visiting farmer from the South, José Figueres. Unlike most of those who
were upset by the riot, Figueres decided to do something about it. He
contacted the local radio station and reserved time to make a speech
three days later.

Figueres' talk was a sharp indictment of the administration of
President Rafael Calderón Guardia. He started out:

Rumors preoccupy the President these days. It is said that the
Government has been turned over to the Communist Party. It is said
that the Government has been obliged to throw itself into the arms of
that Party because the ruling classes and other groups have abandoned
it in its political struggle against the party or parties which do not
please it. Perhaps this is true. But the Government has no reason to
play politics instead of governing, particularly in this period of
war. . . .[1]

Figueres then attacked the extravagance and alleged corruption of
the Calderón Guardia regime. He suggested:

Let us look at finances. We all know that the Government is behind in its payments. And they tell us that it is because of the war.
They think we are ingenuous. The truth is that in the two years of

this administration the Government's income has been the highest in our history. . . .

After citing how much the Calderón government had spent, Figueres went on:

That's enough figures—because it is certain that if this government completes its term, it will have cost the country perhaps one hundred million colones outside of the regular budget. But the greatest damage, which cannot be expressed in figures, is the moral damage arising from the corruption of the people through irresponsible management of public funds. . . .

This speech not only made Figueres a political figure of first rank, it converted him into Enemy No. 1 of the Calderón Guardia administration. The government kept Figueres in jail for three days, then deported him to El Salvador. Figueres became the first Costa Rican political exile in almost half a century.

The regime which José Figueres had denounced so vigorously was something new in the country's history. Dr. Calderón Guardia had been a physician whose clientele had been found largely among the poor. He had been a popular candidate, and his administration, which took office in 1940, seemed to promise a new deal for the country. However, before he had been long in office, rumors of large-scale graft, an ill from which Costa Rica had not customarily suffered, began to circulate widely. The regime lost much of its popularity by the time its term of office of four years was half over.

Faced with growing unpopularity, Calderón Guardia had turned to the Communist Party for support and at the same time had begun to enact a considerable body of social legislation. His administration established a social security system and enacted a law for the legal recognition of trade unions. However, it also began to rely more and more heavily on the Communists for arousing popular support for the regime, particularly for organizing street demonstrations, and even for engaging in occasional violence against opponents of the regime.

That it was the corruption and the Communist influence in the Calderón Guardia regime, not its social program, to which he was opposed, José Figueres soon made clear. After a short while in El Salvador and Guatemala he settled in Mexico, where he established a business exporting agricultural implements to Costa Rica. Having been inadvertently launched into a political career, he continued in this role. In 1943 he wrote a pamphlet which was published in Costa Rica under the title *Palabras Gastadas* (Wasted Words). This pamphlet, which was dedicated to ex-President Ricardo Jiménez, was the first published expression of Figueres' political philosophy.

The "wasted words" which the author discussed were "democracy," "socialism," and "liberty." The purpose of the pamphlet was to defend these ideas and to express the author's faith in them. He sums up his defense of democracy thus:

Contrary to what we hear so often, dictatorship is fatally inefficient, because it does without the initiative of its vassals; democracy is essentially efficient, because it is the sum of the free minds of its members. Dictatorship is ephemeral, like the period of lucidity of a man; democracy is stable, as a living organism which is constantly renewed. Dictatorship is pessimistic, because it presupposes the lack of conscience of the masses and it believes in the persistence of ignorance; democracy is optimistic, because it needs the conscious action of each citizen, and it believes in the gradual advance of culture. The one degrades, the other dignifies. Dictatorship looks backwards, and is stagnant, Death. Democracy looks forward, and is evolution, splendor, Life.[2]

In discussing socialism Figueres makes it clear that he does not believe either in unlimited "free enterprise" or in "the class struggle." He states his opposition to the former in the following terms:

. . . What interests us today is this: capitalism or laissez faire, not admitting that the production and use of goods for the consumption of all is . . . an essentially social activity, not a private one, duplicating services without need, destroying goods by speculation and in many other ways; creating an arbitrary division of classes, prejudicial to the group, between directing groups and those engaged in productive activity . . . refining the natural egoism of the human beast, and reducing the field in which the head and heart can develop. . . .[3]

As to orthodox social revolutionary schools Figueres says:

Class struggle? So be it. Let it be the constructive ideas of the employer and the honest workers, against those dictated by short range egoism of the agitator or the bourgeois. Class struggle? So be it. Let it be the struggle of those classes which play the hymn of labor with the spade, the hammer, the brain or the guitar, against the classes of parasites, both above and below. Social revolution? So be it. Let it be the revolution against inefficient methods of work, which are not good enough to cook bread enough for all, and against retrograde methods which are useful to no one. But let the struggle of ideas, the struggle of classes and the social revolution be contests among rational beings, in a democratic battlefield, where each brain is a cannon, where each enemy is a friend. And above all let it never be a fratricidal struggle among the elements necessary to production. . . .[4]

Finally, Figueres summed up his high appreciation for individual liberty when he said:

The vassal of a regime which does not respect his person, in violation of the social contract, or deprives him of the right to participate in the decision concerning the direction of the community, has been defrauded of legitimate right by the very entity which is charged with protecting the purity of contracts. And if he doesn't have within himself an altar where there burns the sacred flame of dignity, the inappeasable thirst for liberty, he may be reduced to a more miserable existence than that of his savage forebears in the untrammeled forest.[5]

Palabras Gastadas, which circulated widely in Costa Rica even before Figueres' return to his native country, served to establish contact between the exiled amateur politician and a group of young men who were seeking the establishment of a new political movement of advanced social ideas and a man to lead it. The group, composed of young university graduates and professional men, had established the Instituto de Estudios Políticos. This organization, which published a periodical called *Surco,* dedicated itself to a serious study of the principal economic, social, and political problems of the country. Its avowed purpose was stated in its first Manifesto thus:

Our ideal is to form a party of political struggle; an authentically democratic doctrinary party, which has always been lacking in Costa Rica. We wish to create an organization which defends principles, not a man. A political party the ideology of which, based on the purest democratic norms, rigorously adequate to the national reality, and thus guaranteeing the progress of our Fatherland, but adjusted to the universal evolution of political, economic, and social ideas as well as to our own particular history.[6]

With the publication of Figueres' *Palabras Gastadas* the young men of the Instituto de Estudios Políticos saw in Figueres a kindred soul, a man who shared their general outlook and their aspirations. Furthermore, he had been proven to be a man of forceful character and decisive action who could well become the leader of a group of intellectuals without any political experience. Upon his return to Costa Rica in 1944 Figueres quickly became the leader of this group, although he was approximately ten years older than most of them.

The presidential election of 1944 intensified the crisis of Costa Rican democracy which José Figueres had highlighted in his radio speech two years earlier. Dr. Calderón Guardia supported Teodoro Picado, who enjoyed the backing of Calderón Guardia's National Republican Party and of the Communist Party, now rechristened Vanguardia Popular. Opposed to Picado was ex-President León Cortés, nominee of the Unión Nacional.

In spite of the widespread popularity of ex-President Cortés, he was defeated, and his supporters insisted that the election had been stolen by Calderón Guardia through his control of the electoral machinery. Two years later the Picado–Calderón Guardia forces were again victorious in congressional elections, which showed a sizable increase in the vote of the Communists, who got 10 per cent of the total.

The opposition to the Picado–Calderón Guardia regime was split into two factions. One group, the Unión Nacional, which was headed by Otilio Ulate, publisher of *El Diario de Costa Rica,* the country's leading newspaper, was composed principally of the country's more conservative elements, who were opposed to the social programs of the Calderón and Picado administrations as well as to their alleged corruption. The other element was the Partido Social Demócrata, led by José Figueres and consisting largely of young intellectuals of democratic left-wing persuasion.

The two opposition groups worked closely together in spite of their ideological differences. Ulate permitted the young people of the

Partido Social Demócrata to publish in his paper articles and studies written by their members. Both groups supported León Cortés in the 1944 elections, and they ran joint tickets in the 1946 congressional campaign.

As the 1948 presidential election approached, opposition protests mounted against what they conceived to be the government's intention of stealing this contest. In July, 1947, the opposition sponsored a political general strike and lockout to back up a demand for the appointment of a nonpartisan body to conduct the elections the following year. A compromise was finally worked out under which a National Election Board, composed of one representative each of the President, Congress, and the Supreme Court was appointed. Although two of these were named by the governmental National Republican–Communist coalition, the opposition apparently had faith in the individuals named to the board.

The election campaign was tense. The two nominees were Otilio Ulate for the opposition and ex-President Rafael Calderón Guardia for the pro-government forces. Campaigning was vigorous. When the votes were finally counted, the National Election Board by a majority of two to one proclaimed that Ulate had won.

The decision of the National Election Board should have resolved the issue. However, there was considerable fear on the part of the opposition that the Picado administration would not honor the certified results of the poll. José Figueres retired to La Lucha Sin Fin, where he gathered together a group of young students, professional men, and workers, and laid plans for a revolt in case Picado would not turn the government over to the president-elect. Ulate himself remained in San José.

The government was undecided what to do about the election results. There is wide difference of opinion among those who claim to know concerning who supported what position. However, it is certain that some of those in the administration were in favor of recognizing the verdict of the National Election Board and that others were opposed to this. The latter group won out.

The National Assembly, controlled by the National Republicans and Communists, was the instrument for canceling the results of the election. According to the constitution then in force the National Assembly was empowered to "certify" the results of elections.

However, until 1948 this had never been interpreted to mean that the Assembly had the power to nullify these results. Nevertheless, this time it did so, proclaiming that Calderón Guardia, not Ulate, was the victor, on the pretext that there had been widespread fraud on behalf of Ulate's candidacy—this in spite of the fact that the administration had been completely in the hands of elements favorable to Calderón.

Soon after the Assembly's decision an attempt was made either to arrest or to assassinate Otilio Ulate, and the owner of the house in which he was staying was killed, though Ulate escaped. Many of his supporters left San José to join the Figueres forces in the hills.

A two-month civil war ensued. Figueres' forces seized several commercial aircraft, and one of these planes was sent to a neighboring nation to obtain arms. His young supporters were given rudimentary military training. Once armed, they began to move toward San José. Meanwhile the forces supporting the Picado-Calderón regime were very much divided among themselves. The national army amounted to only a few hundred men at the command of Picado. The bulk of the pro-government forces consisted of armed civilians divided into three different groups loyal to Picado, to Calderón, or to the Communists. They were almost as much opposed to one another as to the rebels.

There was severe fighting in several battles, at least a thousand people being killed. Finally, early in May the government forces surrendered after a conference between government representatives and Father Benjamín Núñez, chaplain of the rebels, speaking for the Figueres forces. President Teodoro Picado and ex-President Calderón Guardia fled to Nicaragua, and the government was turned over until the end of Picado's term on May 8 to First Vice President Santos León Herrera.

Although the civil war had been fought in order to uphold the sanctity of the March, 1948, election, the rebels did not immediately put President-elect Ulate in office. The forces led by Figueres were eager to use their victory in the conflict to lay the basis for a new, more socially progressive regime.

An accord was signed on May 1 between José Figueres, leader of the rebel army, and Otilio Ulate, recognized in the document as President-elect. The pact stated the following:

1. The Revolutionary Junta will govern the country, without Congress, during a period of 18 months, from May 8. At the end of this period, it can solicit an extension for six months more, if it is considered necessary for its labors.

2. The Revolutionary Junta will convoke elections to choose representatives to a Constituent Assembly. These elections will be held on December 8 of the present year. The Assembly will be convened on the 15th of the same month.

3. The Revolutionary Junta will designate immediately a commission which will draw up a project for the Constitution, to be submitted to the Assembly.

4. The Junta will recognize and immediately will declare that on last February 8 Don Otilio Ulate Blanco was legitimately elected President of the Republic.

5. The Junta will ask the Constitutional Assembly to ratify the election of Otilio Ulate Blanco, so that he will exercise power during the first Constitutional period of the Second Republic, which in this concrete case will not exceed four years.

6. The Junta will name to the National Electoral Tribunal Messrs. Victor Guardia Quirós, Gerardo Guzmán Quirós, and José María Vargas Pacheco. As alternate member will be named Mr. Jaime Solera Benneti.

7. Both parties signing this accord promise formally that they will carry on no electoral political activities during the six months following the signature of this Pact.

The Junta Fundadora de la Segunda República, as the new governing group called itself, was presided over by José Figueres and consisted of members of the group which had first formed the Instituto de Estudios Políticos and then the Partido Social Demócrata. It brought about several important changes in the economic life of the country and laid plans for numerous others.

Two actions of the Junta indicated the direction it intended to take. Soon after taking office it issued a decree nationalizing the four institutions which made up the country's banking system and another decree imposing a 10 per cent capital levy. The first decree was intended to give the government central control over the economy and make possible its plans for expanding farming and industry. Figueres and his associates argued that the private banks had concentrated almost exclusively on financing the export-import trade and that only the largest farmers had been able to get aid from the banks. These had taken little interest in aiding the small cultivator or in helping to stimulate manufacturing.

The second decree was for the purpose of shoring up the severely undermined finances of the government. The leaders of the deposed regime had pilfered the treasury, and had even removed vehicles and taken equipment from many government offices. The Junta promised that the capital levy would be imposed only once.

These moves greatly disappointed and alarmed the conservative elements which had supported Figueres' uprising, in spite of the fact that the Junta also issued decrees outlawing the Communist Party and the labor organization controlled by it, the Confederación de Trabajadores de Costa Rica. However, the new government leaders made it clear that the opposition of the Figueres forces to the regime they had deposed was based on the fallen regime's corruption, not on its advanced social programs.

Another important move of the Junta Fundadora in the economic sphere was the negotiation of a new contract with the United Fruit Company. This firm was the principal producer of bananas in the country and hitherto had paid no taxes except a small impost on each stem of bananas exported. Under the new agreement the company was required to pay an income tax of 15 per cent as well as some other less important taxes.

The Junta Fundadora began a program of planned economic development. The newly nationalized banks were given additional capital and were encouraged to extend their lending operations to small farmers and businessmen. At the same time the Junta Fundadora established the Instituto Nacional de Electricidad as an autonomous government body to develop the country's electricity potential and ultimately to establish a nation-wide electrical grid. The development of power and light was regarded by the Junta as a prerequisite both for industrialization and for the extension of agriculture.

In addition to economic changes the Junta Fundadora sponsored the writing of a new constitution. On December 8, 1949, elections were held for a constituent assembly. However, they were a severe disappointment for the Junta. Opponents of the Junta were largely victorious, and the Partido Social Demócrata received only a handful of seats. A further defeat for the Junta was the Constituent

Assembly's rejection of the Junta's draft of a new constitution. The result was a new basic document which varied only in minor details from the old one which it replaced.

In spite of these defeats the Junta demonstrated its adherence to democracy by refusing to interfere with the results of the elections or with the functioning of the Constituent Assembly. On November 7, 1949, the Junta proclaimed the new constitution to be in effect, and on the following day Otilio Ulate was inaugurated as constitutional president of the republic.

With the end of the government of the Junta Fundadora de la Segunda República, José Figueres retired to private life. Once more he could devote attention to his farm, La Lucha Sin Fin, where he and his family spent much of their time. When not at La Lucha, Don Pepe was at his home in San José or was traveling abroad.

In some ways these were very difficult days for José Figueres. For one thing, he lived under constant fear of attempts at assassination by one or another of the dictators of the Caribbean area, who with some reason looked upon Figueres as a mortal enemy scheming for their overthrow. As a result both his house in San José and La Lucha were heavily guarded, and even when he traveled abroad he was accompanied by a bodyguard. Such constant tension was trying not only to Figueres but also to his wife and two small children.

Family difficulties also occurred during these years. In 1952 Señora de Figueres, the former Henrietta Boggs, obtained a divorce and returned to the United States with her two children. Although the children came for short visits, this was a period of loneliness for Don Pepe which the most frantic activity could not completely overcome.

However, during a trip to the United States early in 1953 Figueres became acquainted with another young American, Miss Karen Olsen. During a visit of Miss Olsen to Costa Rica a few months later they announced their engagement, and they were married soon after Don Pepe's election to the presidency.

Figueres had not retired from public affairs. Soon after leaving office he set to work organizing the forces which had supported the Junta Fundadora. The Partido Social Demócrata was dissolved, and a new party called Partido Liberación Nacional was established.

The avowed objective of the new Partido Liberación Nacional

was to establish an ideological party which would be capable of conducting Costa Rica along the path of modern economic and social development while at the same time conserving and expanding the country's political democracy. Figueres and other party leaders sought to break the tradition whereby political parties were organizations built around specific individuals and established for the purpose of fighting particular election campaigns rather than continuing institutions with well defined programs and policies.

The top leadership of the party consisted of Figueres and the young people who had made up the Instituto de Estudios Políticos and subsequently had played leading roles in his government. They were organized into study group which dealt at length with various problems facing the country—education, agriculture, industrialization, and relations with the United Fruit Company—and sought to work out detailed programs for dealing with each of these problems.

Figueres took an active part in this program making. A man with an exceedingly active and creative imagination as well as considerable experience with the problems which were being discussed, he frequently threw ideas and suggestions into the hopper for consideration and refinement by the group. However, he had another role. In spite of the avowed aversion of Liberación Nacional leaders to their country's traditional "personalism" in politics, they were frankly anxious to use Figueres' personal popularity as a means of gaining power for the party and consolidating its hold on the imagination of the people. So Figueres had an important role to play as the propagandist and agitator of the party's ideas among the general public. Put very simply, it may be said that his campaign for the presidency of the republic began with his retirement as head of the Junta Fundadora de la Segunda República.

However, Figueres' activities were not confined to Costa Rica during these years. Figueres was not an isolationist. He felt that his country's destiny was closely tied to the destinies of the other Latin American nations and to the hemisphere as a whole. He traveled considerably during the interim between his two terms as chief executive.

Figueres made several visits to the United States during this period. In 1951 he made a tour of various colleges under the sponsorship of the Inter-American Association for Democracy and Free-

dom. Being a strong believer in democratic inter-American cooperation, he reestablished old contacts and built new ones with liberal
elements in the United States. He also conferred upon occasion with
State Department officials as well as with representatives of some
of the United States firms doing business in Costa Rica.

One of the purposes of Figueres in his visits to the United States
was to counteract the allegations of communism which were being
made against him by his opponents in Costa Rica and outside. Although he had led a revolution to oust a government which was
closely allied with the Communists, he had alienated powerful
economic interests in the country while president of the Junta
Fundadora, and some of his opponents were doing their utmost to
discredit him in a United States which at that moment was in the
full grip of "McCarthyism."

He was one of the founders of the Inter-American Association for
Democracy and Freedom in Havana, in May, 1950. At this con-
ference Don Pepe delivered a two-hour speech, beginning at two in
the morning, in which he summed up much of his own philosophy.
This speech marked his emergence as a continental leader of the
Democratic Left.

Figueres started out by noting three aspects of Latin America's
basic problems:

The political system adopted by America is full of imperfections
in its functioning. The representative form of government is violated in
many countries, where the rights of man are a dead letter in the constitutional texts. The rest of the countries don't seem to be worried
by this contagious disease in our midst, in spite of the fact they fight
it in the most distant parts of the earth.

The economy of America still presents a contrast between a rich
and opulent minority of the population and a great mass of poverty-
stricken people. The economic middle class is small. The production
of wealth is small.

The culture of America offers a similar appearance: there is a brilliant intelligentsia and a large proportion of illiterates. The average
cultural level is low.

Those three deficiencies of American life, the political deficiency,
the economic deficiency, and the cultural deficiency, are related in
terms of cause and effect, and they present the phenomenon that the
effect reinforces the cause.[7]

Figueres outlined his own economic philosophy and that of the political movement of which he was the principal leader:

The National Liberation Movement of Costa Rica has found that it is possible to have general planning of the economy of the country in its present stage of development, entrusting to autonomous organizations certain general services such as credit, electricity, some principal transport facilities, the scientific control of prices, the stimulation of a balanced economic development and others allowing within these general economic lines the utmost possible activity for private enterprise. Thousands of agriculturalists sow corn for their own account, but the State regulates and protects them through its autonomous agencies and corps of technicians, guaranteeing stability of market and just prices, providing selected seed, financing machinery and costs of production, etc. Such organisms function on the basis of reserves. If there is a national surplus they export without risk of subjecting the internal consumer to a possible increase of price. Such a combination of state agencies and private producers orients the economy towards general efficiency, but subdivides among many enterprisers the job of administration. This job of administration, the desire to see that costs are less than the value of the product, is an element of great importance in economic activity. The more individuals are preoccupied with this, the greater will be the general efficiency of the labor of the community. If this whole job of administration can be given a social orientation through state organisms which provide general services in accordance with a plan, the optimum results can be obtained from the economic efforts of the nation. . . .

In discussing the particular problems of economic development of Latin America he dealt at length with the question of foreign investment in the area. He put forth certain general ideas concerning the limitations within which such investment is possible and advisable. He commented:

In the first place, we believe that we gain no advantage from private investment in firms which have definite characteristics of internal public utilities. This is not because the investors are "foreign," a word which should disappear from our vocabulary, but because we consider incompatible in our environment and given our idiosyncrasies, private profit and general welfare. If it is desired to aid us effectively in this sector of our economy, what is necessary is to give adequate financial aid to our autonomous state organs. These entities have amply demonstrated their ability to manage credit extended to them and to provide public services with general efficiency. . . .

In the second place, we are dubious of the advantage which we can get from firms which come to Latin America exclusively to seek low wages. If our objective is to maintain a lower level of living, our own enterprisers are sufficient. The incentives to establish business in our countries should be others: the convenience of processing locally our raw materials; economy of transport; the possibility of meeting the demand from certain markets from here; the payment of lower taxes during a given period, etc. . . . The policy of the companies must be to explain to the consumer that the prices of products must have relation to the payment of just wages. That is more constructive than the tendency to induce the Latin American countries to maintain low wages so that the public in other richer countries can buy our articles more cheaply. If North American investments are to be useful, their principal aid must consist in their contribution to raising local wages . . . even though to do so it may be necessary to raise somewhat the sales price of articles coming from here. . . .

He attacked the idea that profits of North American companies operating in Latin America have been exorbitant, at least in recent years. He pointed out that they were not much in excess of profits of firms which do all of their business in the United States. Then he added:

. . . The real difference must be found in the fact that the companies which work in the United States (steel, automobiles, etc.) get from the consumer prices which signify adequate dividends for the investors, high taxes for the State, and just wages for the workers. On the other hand, the firms established in Latin America (bananas, rubber, tin, etc.), even though they take good care of the interests of their stockholders or bondholders, contribute little to the governments and see no inconvenience in buying the labor of their workers cheaply. . . .

Thus Figueres put forth three basic ideas concerning economic development and inter-American economic relations which he was to reiterate many times during the next few years: the belief in a mixed economy in which the State has a role as development planner and stabilizer; support of foreign private investment in Latin America under certain specified conditions; and the feeling that many of Latin America's economic problems are due to the inadequate prices which it receives from the big industrial nations for its principal export products.

In passing, Figueres also noted his point of view toward communism. He commented:

Communist fanaticism insists that a total transformation of human society can be carried out in a violent way through a world social revolution. It claims that the cultured people of the Occident can impose upon themselves what the Soviet government has imposed upon the Russian peasant masses. It insists that in order to bring about a renovation of the economic system, we must abandon all moral norms, all the political conquests, all of the human rights which have been established with so much sacrifice. And as if this were not sufficient price, it insists that we must accept a world hegemony of the Soviet Union, probably imposed though a third universal war.

He also attacked the dictatorial regimes of the American hemisphere, arguing that though it might be necessary to maintain formally "friendly" relations with them, it should be made clear that

this equal treatment which the tyrants and caciques receive from the representative governments is a sad emergency, forced upon us by the danger that another tyranny may become general throughout the earth. And it is healthful for the democratic regimes to understand as clearly as possible what a great sacrifice is being imposed on various unhappy peoples of the American Hemisphere.

Relations between José Figueres and his group on the one hand and the administration of Otilio Ulate on the other grew increasingly cool. Although the Ulate government did not undo any of the principal actions of the Junta Fundadora, it showed little enthusiasm for most of them. The stress of Ulate was upon bringing about greater stability in politics and in the finances of the government.

President Ulate's term expired in November, 1953. The first months of that year, therefore, were marked by a presidential election campaign which was vigorously fought and in which the Partido Liberación Nacional candidate, naturally, was José Figueres. He conducted an extremely strenuous campaign, visiting virtually all parts of the country, talking incessantly about the plans of the party to stimulate economic development and extend social services. Liberación Nacional now had an extensive and well-worked-out program.

In the field of agricultural production the program envisaged close cooperation among the government banking system, the Ministry of Agriculture's Technical Assistance Organization, and the Price Stabilization Board. Figueres advocated the establishment in each community of a Farmers' House in which these three groups would have their local headquarters. He envisaged a process in which the costs of production of agricultural output would be driven down by increased technology, aided by the Technical Assistance Organization. At the same time the banking system would supply the farmer with credit needed to cultivate his crop and to purchase farm implements and machinery. The Price Stabilization Board would not only guarantee a good price to the farmer but would also protect localities from the adverse effects of shortages by establishing local community stores of prime food essentials to prevent shortages which might force up local prices.

The Figueres program called for the extension of the services of the nationalized banks. It promised that every local community would have a branch of at least one of the credit institutions. This would have the dual purpose of tapping unused small savings and of encouraging local small enterprisers to expand production.

The Liberación Nacional candidate advocated an effort to industrialize the country and promised to give protection and encouragement to local manufacturing enterprises. At the same time Figueres stressed the importance of the Instituto Nacional de Electricidad, and promised to get under way several large projects and to expand the Instituto's ability to produce electricity at a low price.

In the field of social problems Figueres laid special emphasis on the expansion of public housing. He advocated the establishment of a National Housing Institute to coordinate all the housing activities of the government which hitherto had been carried on by several organisms. He also promised to increase greatly the number of workers' homes to be constructed.

All aspects of the program put forward by Figueres were to be coordinated through a general plan in which the nationalized banks were to play a key role. In his electoral platform Figueres urged the same kind of program which he had put forth two years earlier in Havana.

Two candidates were running against José Figueres. One was Mario Echandi, who had been a member of President Ulate's cabinet and who ran as nominee of Ulate's party, Unión Nacional, though the President himself did not intervene openly in the election. The other nominee was Fernando Castro Cervantes, who had the support of ex-President Calderón Guardia and represented the elements which had been defeated in the 1948 Revolution.

Figueres was an easy victor. He was at the height of his popularity, and his campaign tours throughout the country were more like marches of triumph than like vote-seeking expeditions.

Pepe Figueres was a peculiar type to be a popular hero. Of less than average height even for a Costa Rican, he did not have an imposing presence, although his sharply etched facial features, his piercing eyes, and his determined, almost hard, lips would have attracted attention in any group. He had a physical abhorrence, almost a fear, of the milling crowds that swirled around him whereever he went. He was not a great orator, having a high-pitched and rather rasping voice.

Figueres had remained the intellectual while becoming the man of action. He had the high-flying imagination of the dreamer and the studiousness of the scholar. In private conversation Don Pepe was capable of falling almost into a trance as he talked about his ideas for Costa Rica, America, and even the world in general. In such moods his suggestions for action were not always practical, but when it came to concrete planning for programs and policy his years of successful experience as a farmer and businessman tended to mold his dreams into manageable proportions.

Different sides of Figueres' personality undoubtedly appealed to different groups in the population. Undoubtedly his successful leadership of the 1948 Revolution had created a kind of *mistica* about him which appealed to the man in the street. Figueres was also capable of translating to the masses of his followers some of his own dreams of what the future held in store for his country. On the other hand, the intellectuals among his followers were enthusiastic about his ideas—which he shared with them—of building a left-wing democratic ideological party that would bring to the country many of the social, economic, and political changes which they felt were long overdue. As is usually the case in such situations, his intellectual followers were more critical but less fickle than those who cheered Figueres at election campaign meetings.

In November, 1953, José Figueres was inaugurated as constitutional president in ceremonies attended by representatives of several score countries. The guest of honor, who received only a little less attention than the new president, was Governor Luis Muñoz Marín of Puerto Rico, who received all the honors usually accorded a chief of state.

José Figueres remained president of Costa Rica until May, 1958. During that period his government undertook an extensive program of economic development and social change which considerably altered the face of Costa Rica. Figueres frequently explained the objectives which his administration was following.

As Figueres noted many times, the government was seeking to collect the savings of the people of Costa Rica and to invest them in capitalization, by which he understood both the accumulation of capital equipment and the improvement of the quality—in terms of health, education, etc.—of the population. Before the nationalization of the banks by the Junta Fundadora the government's only means of mobilizing the country's savings had been through taxation. Subsequently the extension of the banking system into all parts of the country made it possible for the first time to gather in small savings which had gone untapped previously, and at the same time made it possible for the banks to use these savings in financing capitalization projects.

While seeking thus to develop and change the country's economy and society the Figueres regime sought also to strengthen political democracy. The establishment of an ideological party was in itself a step in this direction. However, the Figueres regime went further by establishing an impartial system to supervise elections—which in the 1958 presidential poll was strengthened by inviting United Nations representatives to observe the election. During his constitutional regime Figueres continued the work which he had begun with the Junta Fundadora in establishing a civil service law, removing public employees insofar as possible from political pressures.

The concrete program carried out by the Figueres government

can be summed up under six headings: relations with the United
Fruit Company, moves to develop agriculture, the extension of
electric power facilities, sponsoring of industrialization, extension
of social security, and development of public housing.

Several times Don Pepe summed up the philosophy of his government in trying to carry out the economic and social development of
Costa Rica. One instance was an article entitled "We Don't Want
Foreign Investments," which appeared in the *New Leader* on August
31, 1953. He summed up the case against foreign investment as a
means of development thus:

> Foreign ownership of a large segment of a country's economy or
> territory constitutes "economic occupation." This is no wild fancy,
> I know. I am a citizen of a "banana republic." I know how it feels to
> have a state within a state; to play host to a privileged business that
> does not abide by the law of the land, but by the terms of its own
> "concession," by the terms of economic occupation. Please do not offer
> us as a remedy the very grievances of which we complain!
>
> Is it that the company's directors are wicked, or deliberate ex-
> ploiters? Is it that the U.S. Government is imperialistic? Is it that Latin
> Americans are all venal, or stupid, or both? I think not. . . .
>
> Large ownership is . . . a means of limiting local authority, es-
> pecially when it operates under "contract laws" or discriminatory
> "concessions" such as the colonial companies have exacted from the
> weak nations. It would be wise if the U.S. withdrew the economic oc-
> cupation. . . .

If investment capital is not to come from private foreign firms,
where will it come from? Figueres asks this question and answers it
thus:

> . . . Permanent capital should come from their own savings. Tran-
> sient capital could come from temporary investments, or from loans
> granted to the proper development institutions. If some countries, be-
> cause of feudalism or corruption, cannot capitalize a part of their
> income and grow thereby, they cannot grow from foreign investments
> either. . . . Costa Rica, for example, is not thinking of an electronics
> industry or of nuclear reactors. Let the industrial nations, especially
> the U.S., continue to lead. We can contribute our modest part to the
> general effort of supporting mankind by supplying beef. We have the

land, and the rain, and the hands. All this is our own capital. We have only to add an investment of $100, $200, or $300 per worker, and this amount we can save.

In arguing for providing the underdeveloped countries with higher income so that they could save more and invest more Figueres said:

Of course, the capicity to save varies with the national income. And the income of most underdeveloped countries depends, to a great extent on the prices of their exports, of raw materials, minerals, agricultural products. Far more than foreign investments, the underdeveloped countries need stabilization of the world markets. The so-called law of supply and demand is the law of the strong. Economics should be an ethical science. Prices can be stabilized, and they should be in a civilized world. Every nation, like every man, has a right to know how much she is earning, how much she will be paid for the work of her people, when this work is applied to her natural resources, in supplying a part of the world's needs.

Figueres summed up his argument thus:

To summarize the formula for underdeveloped nations: Pay them for their products; tell them how to produce more; tell them how to save, and to grow from earnings; if absolutely essential, grant loans to proper agencies or make temporary investments; but do not try to own them!

Once in office, José Figueres sought to carry out the policy implied in this article. His government consistently offered proposals in international economic conferences for the establishment of "buffer stocks" of the principal mineral and agricultural raw materials and foodstuffs as a means for achieving the stabilization of prices which he advocated. In internal affairs he sought to start the process of converting Costa Rica's principal foreign company, the United Fruit Company, which was running a virtual state within a state, into a mere purchaser of fruit and shipper of it abroad. His administration also sought to increase internal savings and channel them into economic and social development.

Even before he was inaugurated José Figueres entered into negotiations with the United Fruit Company. The company was cooperative, and soon after taking office the Costa Rican government announced a new agreement with the UFCO whereby the company would pay income taxes of 30 per cent of their net profits as well as import duties on goods not essential for the operation of their banana-growing enterprise. At the same time the company agreed that it would give up control of its hospitals and schools whenever the government requested it to do so. This conformed to Figueres' belief that the United Fruit Company should in time reduce its activities in Costa Rica merely to shipping bananas abroad.

This agreement became a standard for the United Fruit Company's operations throughout Central America. The same terms were subsequently offered by the company to Guatemala, Honduras, and Panama and were accepted by those countries.

The Figueres government also undertook to reestablish the banana industry on the east coast of Costa Rica, where it had been abandoned by the United Fruit Company in the late 1920's under the onslaught of the so-called Panama disease. As a result of these efforts the Standard Fruit Company undertook to establish plantations on the Atlantic Coast.

The government's activities in other branches of agriculture have been summed up by Figueres himself in his book *Cartas a Un Ciudadano,* published in 1956. He wrote as follows (p. 92):

Agricultural methods are being improved by technical means and by economic means. In the cultivation of grains, seeds are being used which are selected by the Ministry of Agriculture, the purchase of machinery and fertilizers and the control of plagues are being financed by loans from the State Banks. The propagation of agricultural information has been well accepted by our peasants. The system of price stabilization is being perfected. The resources of the Rural Credit Boards have just been increased by 22,000,000 colones, which will probably be used during 1956.

In coffee and sugar cane, intensive fertilization, irrigation, new varieties, and other recently introduced practices are doubling and even tripling production per acre. The financing of both crops, which requires 80,000,000 colones a year, is being carried out by the National Banking System. . . .

Figueres, himself a scientific farmer of considerable note, was peculiarly interested in the problem of increasing Costa Rica's agricultural output. He undertook personally the work of enlisting the interest in and support of new methods of cultivation among the peasantry. His efforts brought considerable success.

One of the fundamental efforts of the Figueres administration was in the field of electric power. Figueres, in his report to Congress on May 1, 1956, pointed out that between independence and 1953 electric power plants generating a total of 40,000 kilowatts had been established. However, between 1953 and the time he spoke, there had entered into operation or been placed under construction plants with a capacity of 100,000 kilowatts. Most of this program of electrification was being undertaken by the Instituto Nacional de Electricidad and included several large projects to harness the country's hydroelectric resources.

The Figueres government looked upon the extension of the country's electrical resources not only as a means of stimulating agricultural production and the well-being of the citizenry but also as a means for establishing a solid basis for industrialization. It took other steps to encourage the establishment of manufacturing firms. A few months after taking office the administration pushed through the Legislative Assembly a new tariff law raising imposts on a wide range of goods which the government felt could be produced in Costa Rica. This law was the first step in a general revision of the country's tariff structure.

At the same time the resources of the nationalized banks were used to aid new and old industrial firms. According to Figueres' *Cartas a Un Ciudadano* (p. 94) by 1956 the banks had lent some 24,000,000 colones to over four hundred firms for the purchase of machinery. The banking system had received a loan from the International Bank for Reconstruction and Development for the purpose of further amplifying their loans to manufacturing enterprises.

The Figueres government's activities in the field of social security were restricted largely to the construction of several hospitals used by the Social Security Institute. When Figueres came to office the Instituto still was owed a debt by the government, a debt which had been accumulated before 1948, when the administrations had frequently failed to pay sums which the government was obligated to provide to the Instituto. The Figueres regime was forced to spend considerable sums which might have been used for other purposes to repay these debts and thus build up a safe reserve for the Instituto.

Public housing was one of the principal things emphasized by the Figueres regime. Previous to 1953 the government's housing activities had been relatively modest and had been conducted by several dispersed institutions. With President Figueres' support a law was passed in 1954 establishing the National Housing Institute. It carried out a program of constructing individual homes, and in a speech on January 29, 1958, President Figueres announced that the Instituto had built homes for 12,000 citizens, of whom 3,000 had become owners of their own houses. The program had been extended to sixty-four separate municipalities.

Figueres had always emphasized the necessity for general education as a secure base for political democracy. In his report to Congress on May 1, 1957, he summed up his administration's problem in the educational field:

Until now, the number of student teachers graduating each year has been very much inferior to the always increasing needs of our schools. It has been necessary to fill posts with untrained teachers. . . .

We saw that the difficulty must be faced on three fronts: first, bring more students to the normal schools. Second, provide better facilities for qualifying teachers without certificates, particularly in the countryside. Third, to prevent teachers from leaving the profession in search of better-paid jobs.

To achieve the last of these objectives an entirely new pay scale for teachers was adopted providing for increases over a period of five years. At the same time a Professional Institute was established to give special courses for teachers without certificates, thus enabling them to become better teachers as well as to obtain better salaries.

The number of normal-school students was vastly increased. President Figueres reported that there were 2,000 such students in May, 1957, as compared with 6,400 teachers actually in the classrooms.

The Figueres administration also enacted a new basic education law. President Figueres outlined it thus:

The new law, starting with certain philosophic definitions, establishes new teaching programs. It establishes middle schools, and gives emphasis to vocational training. . . . . It proposes a minimum of three years of academic culture for all citizens, so that future workers will have the opportunity of acquiring, before specialization, an acceptable level of general education.

Finally, the administration considerably increased the number of classrooms available. President Figueres commented on this:

. . . It is worth while mentioning certain figures which reveal our rhythm of educational progress, and our future potentialities; never has any administration constructed 350 classrooms. Now, in the year 1956 alone, 450 have been built.

Foreign affairs engaged a good deal of Pepe Figueres' attention. He made no secret of the fact that he and his government were hostile toward the dictatorships which dominated many Latin American countries during much of his term in office. His government gave asylum to refugees from dictatorial regimes in Venezuela, the Dominican Republic, Nicaragua, Guatemala, Cuba, and other countries. Rómulo Betancourt, ex-President of Venezuela, who arrived in Costa Rica some months before Figueres' election and stayed there during the first two years of his administration was one of these.

Figueres made his government's position clear in March, 1955, when he refused to name a delegation to attend the Tenth Inter-American Conference, which met in Caracas, Venezuela. He indicated in doing so that he had no objection to the conference, but objected only to the place in which it was being held and the nature of the host government, that of dictator Pérez Jiménez.

Figueres followed a policy of friendship toward the United States. However, he frequently urged the United States government to change its policy toward Latin America, particularly in terms of its attitude toward dictatorships in the area and in its economic policies. In an article which appeared in the *Journal of International Affairs* (Vol. IX, No. 1, 1955) he set forth his position thus:

a) The Latin American peoples are ripe for democracy. They have heard so much such a long time about representative government, free elections, respect for the dignity of man, division of governmental powers, and all that goes with the democratic creed, that you could no more erase those political aspirations than you could eradicate the Christian faith.

b) You cannot isolate the problems of democracy in Latin America, or elsewhere, from the economic and social struggle, from educational limitations, or even from the world-wide politico-military conflicts.

c) Theoretically, the development of Latin America—economic, social, cultural, political—may take place in two different manners: either as a separate continent and civilization, independent of the United States, or as a part of the general hemispheric effort. In my opinion, the only possible course is the second.

d) A general hemispheric development implies for Latin America the acceptance, nay, the demand of United States' leadership. It also implies the exercise of such leadership by the United States along democratic, Western lines of conduct.

e) The two main contributions of the United States should be precisely its most characteristic national virtues or aptitudes: its political genius, or the ability of its citizens to live together in mutual respect and govern themselves with a common purpose, and its production methods, or the capacity of its economy to produce goods and services at an unprecedented rate.

The principal difficulties in the foreign field which the Figueres regime experienced came from neighboring Nicaragua. That republic's dictator, Anastasio Somoza, was acting as host to ex-Presidents Calderón Guardia and Picado, and two expeditions were organized with his blessing for the purpose of attempting to overthrow the Figueres regime. Both were turned back by the Costa Rican citizens' militia organized after the Revolution of 1948. During the second attack, in January, 1955, the Organization of American States came to the Figueres government's defense, and the United States government sold the Costa Rican government two airplanes for one dollar apiece to help turn back the invading forces.

During his four and a half years in the presidency Pepe Figueres was the best exponent of the policies and actions of his own government. Aside from state papers, such as his annual messages to Congress, Figueres wrote frequent articles for the local press as well as for periodicals in several foreign countries, including the United States. He also found time to write a book entitled *Cartas a Un Ciudadano* (Letters to a Citizen), in which he discoursed at length on his own political philosophy and the policies which were being followed by his government. We have cited passages from this work, which was circulated widely in Costa Rica and abroad.

In spite of the accomplishments of the Figueres regime and the prestige which it enjoyed abroad, Don Pepe and his associates were defeated in the presidential election of 1958. Although the leaders of Liberación Nacional had attempted to form an ideological party, it was personal rivalries that brought about the defeat of the party in this election. Jorge Rossi, who had been Figueres' first Minister of Finance, was anxious for Liberación Nacional's nomination for the presidency. However, the party's convention late in 1957 gave the nomination to Francisco Orlich, the Minister of Public Works and one of Figueres' oldest friends. Figueres took little part in deciding the party's candidate but threw his support to Orlich once he had been chosen.

Rossi refused to accept the party's designation of Orlich and campaigned as an independent. Also in the race was Mario Echandi, who had run unsuccessfully in 1953. He received the backing of ex-Presidents Rafael Calderón Guardia and Otilio Ulate as well as of the Communists. Echandi ran on a platform favoring free enterprise and promising to end the "socialistic" experiments of the Figueres regime and its "alienation" of friendly governments, namely those of the dictatorial regimes.

The split in the Liberación Nacional forces threw the election to Echandi. Although he received less than 50 per cent of the total vote, he did receive more votes than Francisco Orlich, the runner-up, and got more than the constitutional 40 per cent needed for election in a three-cornered race. However, Echandi did not get a majority in the Legislative Assembly. The Liberación Nacional ticket received nineteen seats there, the supporters of Rossi four, and one independent Figuerista was also elected. Dr. Calderón

Guardia's National Republican Party won eleven seats in the Assembly, and Echandi's National Union party received only ten.

With the defeat of his party and the end of his presidential term Pepe Figueres returned once again to private life. However, before doing so he gave his Latin American contemporaries a lesson in democratic procedure. He refused to accede to demands of some of his own followers that he interfere with the results of the presidential election. Rather, he said that he would demonstrate what a good democrat did when he was defeated, and would show how democratic opposition was conducted.

Figueres returned to the leadership of the Liberación Nacional Party. In that post his first job was to rebuild the divided ranks of the organization and to spread a more solid type of party organization throughout the country. In spite of the efforts of the Liberación Nacional leaders the party had remained to too great a degree a personal vehicle for electing Pepe Figueres and his friends. Figueres' job was to build a party organization which could remain active between elections and to train and teach the lower-rank leadership and the rank and file the ideology which was supposed to be the basis of the party.

As leader of the opposition he also had the task of providing constructive criticism of the incumbent and seeing to it that the opposition remained within constitutional bounds so long as the President behaved constitutionally. His role in the opposition may yet do more to spread a true understanding of the meaning of democracy in Latin America than did his tenure in office.

Luis Muñoz Marín
and the "Puerto Rican Miracle"

Early in 1938 a has-been politician who had quarreled with virtually all the powerful figures on the island, and had been thrown out of his party, began scouring Puerto Rico, going from one small town to the next, talking to the common folk, the mountain farmer, the sugar-cane worker, the schoolteacher, and the small shopkeeper. Ten years later this same "has-been" became the first elected governor of Puerto Rico, and ten years later still he had brought about changes in the economic, social, and political status of that island which made it almost unrecognizable.

The politician who was counted "dead" by his colleagues in 1938 was Luis Muñoz Marín, certainly the outstanding Puerto Rican of his generation. He it is who has brought "the revolution" to the island of Puerto Rico, and who has been chiefly responsible not only for a remarkable economic transformation of the country but also for instilling in its people a consciousness of their own dignity and importance which they had never before possessed.

Puerto Rico in the 1930's was an unhappy island. Its principal source of income was the production of sugar cane, almost all of which was sold to the continental United States. Its people were poverty-stricken, and the rapidly growing population was far outstripping any possibilities for employment at home. The island was plagued with large-scale permanent unemployment and underemployment, and the prospects were for the standard of living of the people to continue to go constantly downward.

Although formal political democracy existed, it had little real meaning for the great majority of the people, and vote selling was almost universal. There was widespread discontent with the colonial status of Puerto Rico and resentment against the long series of appointed governors, some of them good, some bad, and some

174

indifferent, but all alien to Puerto Rico and unable really to serve the needs of the people of the island. The government of the "mother country," the United States, had showed little concern for the problems of the island, and the people themselves had little hope that they could rise out of the abyss in which they found themselves and into which they seemed to be constantly sinking more deeply.

The island had come under the control of the United States as a result of the short Spanish-American War of 1898. At the time of the transfer of sovereignty there were about one million Puerto Ricans, and the economy of the island was a rather varied one. Tobacco and coffee were cultivated in the mountains, and sugar along the coasts, although it had not yet preempted the whole of the littoral as it was to do subsequently. Many of the people of the small towns earned their livelihood in artistic needlework, which had a wide market.

The American occupation brought four important changes to the island. First was the rapid growth of the sugar industry. As a possession of the United States, Puerto Rico came within the American tariff wall, and her sugar industry thus obtained a protection which other countries did not enjoy. At the same time the demand in the United States for sugar increased by leaps and bounds after the turn of the century. As a result both United States and Puerto Rican interests began a very rapid expansion of the sugar-growing industry. Although Puerto Rico was not so well endowed by nature for the cultivation of sugar as was Cuba, this product became the principal source of income for the inhabitants of the island. However, Puerto Rico became excessively dependent for its well-being on the market for this product in the United States, and when, as during the Great Depression, United States demand for sugar fell off, the island suffered bitterly.

The second important result of the transfer of Puerto Rico from Spain to the United States was the birth and development of a trade-union movement and a Socialist Party as its political spokesman. Santiago Iglesias, a native of Spain, was the father of trade-unionism in Puerto Rico, and soon after American occupation he established the Federación Libre de Trabajadores, which became affiliated with the American Federation of Labor. Under American rule the trade unions had much more freedom to operate than they had possessed under the Spaniards, and although the movement grew slowly, by World War I it had come to include the workers in the all-important sugar industry.

Along with the Federación Libre, Iglesias formed the Partido Socialista as the political expression of the labor movement. He himself was elected to the insular Senate in 1916 and during the next twenty years was the principal political spokesman for the more humble citizenry of the island. His party and the union movement he organized were of key importance—in spite of themselves—in the rise to power of Luis Muñoz Marín.

United States authorities in Puerto Rico brought about two other very important changes in the island: improvements in health and education. Through the installation of modern public-health methods the death rate of Puerto Rico was drastically reduced during the first years of American occupation, although it remained high compared with continental standards. However, this reduction of the death rate was not an unmixed blessing, since it brought a very rapid increase in the population of Puerto Rico and engendered very serious economic problems, the gravest of which was the unemployment of a large part of the island's adult population.

In addition to public-health programs the United States authorities were also concerned with education. A public-school system was established which slowly extended across the island. At the same time a number of American churches established mission schools which also contributed to the educational effort. However, education also was not completely beneficial to the Puerto Ricans. It was seriously hampered by a long-continued struggle over the question of what language should be used in instructing the students. The result was that during some years teaching was in Spanish, during other periods the attempt was made to instruct the children in English, a language which neither they nor their teachers understood. The result of this confusion is still visible in the Puerto Rican school system, though Spanish has now been firmly established as the language of instruction in the island's primary and secondary schools.

During the first fifty years of United States rule over Puerto Rico the government was in the hands of a governor appointed by the President of the United States. This colonial position of the island rankled with the Puerto Ricans, and "status" was the dominant theme of the island's politics until the emergence of Luis Muñoz Marín in the early 1940's.

Even before United States occupation the Puerto Ricans had struggled for autonomy. In 1868, at the time of the first War of Independence of Cuba, an armed struggle was also attempted in Puerto Rico in the so-called "Grito de Lares." However, the newly proclaimed "Republic of Puerto Rico" was quickly suppressed by Spanish authorities, who, nevertheless, acted more reasonably toward Puerto Rico than they did toward its sister island. The emancipation of the slaves proclaimed by the revolutionaries of 1868 was confirmed shortly afterward by the Spanish authorities, which deprived the independence movement of Puerto Rico of the almost unanimous backing of the Negroes which the Cuban wars of independence enjoyed. Thereafter the struggle of Puerto Rico against the mother country followed a more pacific course.

In 1888 the principal leaders of the struggle for independence were jailed for a short time in Morro Castle in San Juan harbor, and a year later the principal figure in the struggle for self-government, Baldorioty y Castro, died. The new chief of this movement, a young man named Luis Muñoz Rivera, took a different tack from that of his predecessor and tried to reach an agreement with important political elements in Spain itself. In pursuit of this policy a delegation from the Partido Autonomista went to Spain in 1896 and signed with the Spanish Liberal Party an agreement which promised self-government for the island in the eventuality of the Liberals' achieving power. When that came to pass in the following year, the Spanish Liberals were as good as their word, and Puerto Rico was granted an autonomy statute.

Luis Muñoz Rivera became head of the newly autonomous Puerto Rican government in 1897. However, he was in power only a few months when American troops invaded the island, proclaiming as they did so that they had come to "liberate" Puerto Rico. In general, the attitude of the Puerto Ricans at that time was favorable to the transfer of sovereignty, but it meant starting the struggle for autonomy all over again.

Luis Muñoz Rivera was again in the vanguard of the fight. As leader of the Federal Party—a faction of the old Autonomist Party —he fought for greater autonomy for the island. The first Organic

Act, establishing civil government in Puerto Rico after a two-year rule by the Army, was passed in 1900. It provided for a two-house legislature consisting of an upper house appointed by the President and the Governor and an elected lower house. It also provided that virtually all the administrative authorities would either be appointed directly by the President of the United States or indirectly, through the Governor, who was himself named by the United States chief executive. It established the post of Resident Commissioner of Puerto Rico, a member of the United States House of Representatives with a voice but without a vote.

In 1916 Luis Muñoz Rivera, then Resident Commissioner, fought in Washington for a new Organic Act, which was passed a year later, after his death. It granted United States citizenship to Puerto Ricans, and according to *La Nueva Constitución de Puerto Rico* published by the University of Puerto Rico in 1954, it established "a bill of rights with the protection of security, liberty and property guaranteed by the Constitution of the United States; a completely elective legislature, with more control over local matters . . . and a reduction of the number of presidential appointments. . . ."

This second Organic Act, known popularly as the Jones Act, did not by any means completely satisfy most politically vocal Puerto Ricans. These continued as before to be divided between the advocates of United States statehood for the island, who were found in the Republican and Socialist parties, and the supporters of independence, who were largely in Muñoz Rivera's party, which after his death took the name Partido Liberal.

In the 1930's there arose a more extreme group of independence advocates, led by a fanatical visionary, Pedro Albizu Campos, who established and led the Partido Nacionalista. This party, after running candidates in the election of 1932, when it received approximately 10,000 votes, came to the conclusion that it could not win the people to independence by legal electoral action. Instead it opted for "heroic sacrifice," by which it meant terrorism against both United States and Puerto Rican officials in the island. These terroristic methods alienated many of the party's supporters. However, both it and the Liberal Party were subsequently to provide many members for the party of Luis Muñoz Marín.

Luis Munoz Marín was the son of Luis Muñoz Rivera. He was educated in the United States while his father was Resident Commissioner. His first flight into politics startled and shocked many of his father's supporters because he made his debut as a member of Santiago Iglesias' Socialist Party, which at that time definitely represented "the other side of the tracks." This part of Muñoz Marín's political career was not notably successful.

For a number of years in the 1920's Luis Muñoz Marín lived in the United States and was a familiar figure in Greenwich Village and among the radical intelligentsia of New York. He earned a poor living as a free-lance journalist, writing for the *Nation* and other periodicals. It was not until the early 1930's that he returned to Puerto Rico and joined his father's old party, the Partido Liberal.

During the 1930's Muñoz Marín was an important figure in the Partido Liberal, which was the principal opposition party to the ruling coalition of Republican and Socialist parties. This alliance of the Republicans and Socialists was a peculiar phenomenon, since it represented the coalition of the party of the large sugar interests and the party which drew its principal support from the sugar workers. The chief bond of unity between them was the fact that they both favored statehood.

Muñoz Marín, though a supporter of independence, was also strongly in favor of the New Deal and favored Puerto Rico's making the utmost use of the programs which the Roosevelt administration devised for aiding the island. He enthusiastically backed the Puerto Rico Reconstruction Administration, which was the principal New Deal vehicle for Puerto Rico, and became a familiar figure in Washington, where he lobbied extensively with both members of Congress and administrative officials to get more aid for the island. It was undoubtedly during these years that the good contacts which he was to have later with congressional leaders first began to develop, and it was then, too, that the ideas which he was to embody in the program of the Popular Democratic Party first began to take shape.

Muñoz' good relations with the United States government and his frank support of the Roosevelt administration's efforts in Puerto Rico won him the jealousy and enmity of powerful figures in the Liberal Party leadership. The growing conflict between Muñoz and the Liberal chiefs came to a head in 1937 and resulted in his expulsion from the party, although he was one of its principal spokesmen in the insular Senate.

Muñoz Marín was not discouraged by his treatment at the hands of the Liberal Party leaders. Upon being expelled he threw them a challenge that within two years he would have behind him the overwhelming majority of the party's supporters. He more than made good on this promise. In 1938 he established the Partido Popular Democrático (PPD) and set out on a pilgrimage throughout the island to find what it was the people were concerned about and what it was they wanted. It was as the head of this party that he fought the election campaign of 1940.

The 1940 campaign was spectacular. The old coalition parties were discredited. They had dominated the legislature since 1932 and had become soft and removed from contact with the masses. Most serious was the situation of the Socialist Party. Until its election victory of 1932 it had been principally a party of workingmen closely allied with the trade-union movement. After 1932 it was invaded by large numbers of professional people who were anxious to get jobs in the administration. At the same time its principal leaders were removed from direct contact with their supporters, Iglesias going to Washington as Resident Commissioner and lesser leaders going to San Juan as members of the legislature or officials of the administration. By 1940 the Socialist Party was dying.

The first effect of the decline of the Socialist Party was to strengthen the Communist Party, which had been formed early in the 1930's. In the late 1930's it made considerable headway in the labor movement and was on the way to becoming an important force in the island. However, the rise of Muñoz Marín stunted the growth of the Communist Party as it killed the Socialist Party.

The Liberals were not much better off than the parties of the Coalition. They had lost their most outstanding figure in Muñoz Marín, and they were without any real program which could appeal to the people.

The new phenomenon was the Popular Democratic Party. It was different for a number of reasons. First, it refused to discuss the question of the status of the island, an attitude which was unheard of in

Puerto Rican politics. Muñoz and other leaders of the party took the position that the status question could wait, that what was needed immediately was a program for the economic and social rehabilitation of the island to make it possible to sustain whatever kind of status was finally decided upon. The poverty, illness, and ignorance of the people, not the political question, were to be the party's first concern.

Another new angle in the PPD's electoral campaign was its insistence on the necessity for the people to vote honestly. Muñoz and other leaders of the party toured the island urging the *jibaros* (the country folk) and the city workers not to waste their votes by selling them to the highest bidder, as had frequently been done in the past. They urged the people to vote for the candidates who they felt could best represent them, and then to keep track of how those who were elected behaved themselves. This was the first time in many years that any party had seriously challenged the vote buying which was then endemic in Puerto Rican politics.

In the third place, the Populares had a concrete social and economic program to put before the voters. They promised an agrarian reform, an effort for the economic development of the island, the establishment of social security. To fulfill the first promise they said that all that was necessary was to enforce a provision of the first Organic Act of 1900, which had forbidden any corporation to own more than 500 acres of land in Puerto Rico. As for the second point, they urged that the resources of the government of the island be used to establish a basis for economic development by unifying the electric power companies, establishing an island-wide grid, and increasing electrical resources through hydroelectric and other projects.

To the surprise of everyone except the Populares this campaign was highly successful. The PPD in its first try at the polls won a majority in the insular Senate and came only three short of a majority in the House of Representatives. For the next two years the Populares were forced to juggle with the three independents who held the balance of power, but after 1942 the party won a majority which it was to keep for two decades. Indeed, by 1948 the party had almost all members of both houses. As a result, when the 1952 Constitution was written, the Populares, who constituted an overwhelming majority of the delegates, insisted on putting in a provision guaranteeing to minority parties at least one third of the seats in both houses of the legislature.

The advent of the Populares to power in the insular legislature in 1940 coincided with the appointment of New Dealer Rexford Guy Tugwell as governor. He had come to Puerto Rico originally as president of the university and had already established many contacts before he assumed the governorship.

During the next six years Tugwell and Luis Muñoz Marín were to constitute a team which got under way the program of change which has subsequently made the island famous. Tugwell, an experienced administrator and a social reformer himself, was able to guide the first stages of this program and to help the development of the exceedingly efficient corps of technicians and administrators who have been the keystone of the transformation which Puerto Rico has undergone since 1940.

During the war years the program backed by Tugwell and Muñoz was faced with tremendous difficulties. The United States was producing for the war effort and had little to spare to help Puerto Rico. Furthermore, for almost a year, during 1942–43, the sea lanes connecting the island with the mainland were hazardous in the extreme because of German submarine activity in the Caribbean and along the Atlantic Coast.

During this period the government's efforts were perforce confined to a limited range of activities. The promised agrarian reform was gotten under way. Although an attempt was made to have the Supreme Court declare the anti-corporation section of the 1900 Organic Act unconstitutional, this failed, and thereafter numerous sections of land were taken from the corporations which possessed more than the limit. This land was organized into so-called "proportional profit farms," on which the workers were given a share in the profits. It was on some of these farms, too, that experiments got under way for the growing of products other than sugar, the most successful of which was pineapples.

The government also undertook to carry out its promise to consolidate the island's electric power system. Two existing private companies were bought out, and the Water Resources Authority was established to control all electric energy production and distribution

on the island. The authority began a policy, still in effect, of develop
ing resources ahead of actual needs, with a view to possible economic
expansion of the island.

Finally, a beginning was made with an industrialization program.
The Puerto Rican Industrial Development Company (PRIDCO) was
established in 1942, and it undertook to construct a number of plants
which were very much needed during the war emergency. It took
over a cement plant originally built by the Puerto Rican Recovery
Administration and constructed a factory to produce the bottles in
which Puerto Rican rum was shipped to the United States. This was
of particular importance since a large part of the Puerto Rican sugar
crop was shipped to the continent during the war years as rum because of the transportation shortages. The PRIDCO also established
a paper-box factory to make the boxes in which the bottles of rum
were shipped. In addition, a shoe factory was set up by the Industrial
Development Company.

By the time the war was over the program of social and economic
change in Puerto Rico had begun to gain momentum. However, after
the war the basis of the program was changed. Muñoz and other
leaders came to realize that the government did not have resources
sufficient to carry out as large an economic development program as
it wished. Teodoro Moscoso, first president of PRIDCO, has summed
up this attitude of the government officials at that time thus:

The lesson of the first five years of PRIDCO (1942–47) was that
government capital and government know-how were too scarce and too
limited to do a job that could even begin to meet the needs of the
people. . . . We took two basic decisions: first, to use government
funds, not as a principal ingredient, but as a catalyst; and second, to
use tax incentives to attract private capital and the production and
sales know-how that come with it. This took some doing, just to make
the change-over. . . .[1]

The upshot of this change in policy was that PRIDCO sold to
private interests the factories which it had established, and the government set out on an effort to entice private entrepreneurs to build
plants in Puerto Rico. As part of this program the legislature of
Puerto Rico passed a law providing tax exemption for a period of
ten years for firms establishing new industries or expanding old ones

in the island. In addition the PRIDCO—and after 1950 the Economic Development Administration, to which this work was transferred—carried on an active promotion campaign in the United States designed to interest continental industrialists in establishing branch plants in Puerto Rico.

By the late 1950's this program had borne notable fruits. By the middle of 1957 some 579 new manufacturing plants had been established in the island, and 446 of these were still in operation. The new plants were contributing approximately $100,000,000 to the national income by the end of 1957 and were providing approximately 35,000 jobs.[2]

Not only were new industries being established in Puerto Rico but the island's manufacturing was also becoming more diversified. In the beginning most of the firms establishing on the island were in industries employing relatively large numbers of low-cost labor and relatively little capital equipment. By the later 1950's, however, the island had entered the phase of heavier industry, with extensive chemical, metallurgical, and electronics plants being set up. The construction of petroleum refineries was paving the way for a petrochemical industry and many subsidiary manufacturing enterprises.

Along with manufacturing, other phases of the economy were rejuvenated after 1940. After 1955 particular attention was given by the government to the modernization of the island's distribution system, and supermarkets enjoying the advantages of tax exemption began to appear in the major cities and towns.

Throughout the period the government carried on an extensive program of school construction and teacher training with the avowed purpose of having every school-age child in school by 1960. Hospital facilities were extended throughout the country, the effect of which was demonstrated by the fact that by 1958 more than half of the children born in the island were born in a hospital, compared with fewer than 25 per cent some years earlier.

By 1947 the program of economic and social development was well under way, and Muñoz Marín turned his attention once more to the problem of the island's status with regard to the United States. His first move was successfully to urge President Truman to propose to Congress a law whereby Puerto Rico would elect its own governor. As a result of this law the voters of the island went to the polls in

November, 1948, and chose Luis Muñoz Marín as the first elected chief executive of the island.

Muñoz had not as yet definitely retreated from his former position in favor of ultimate independence for Puerto Rico. However, in 1948 there were already evidences that he was changing his mind. This was shown in his attitude toward the avowed advocates of independence. There existed at this time the Congress for Independence, which rallied large segments of popular opinion behind it. The Congress was not a political party, and members of the Partido Popular Democrático were active in it. However, early in 1948 the Popular Party, under Muñoz' leadership, reached the decision that membership in the Congress and in the Party were incompatible with one another, and PPD members were forced to choose.

The upshot of this was the withdrawal of many Populares from the Congress for Independence and the launching by those who remained of a new political party, the Partido Independentista Puertorriqueño. This party differed from its predecessor, the Nationalist Party, in its endorsement of constitutional political action as opposed to violence as the means for achieving independence. Its leaders proclaimed their party's intention of declaring the island's independence as soon as the party achieved a majority in the Puerto Rican Legislature.

In its first try at the polls the Partido Independentista came in third, trailing the Populares and the old Republican Party, which had now modified its name to Partido Estadista Republicano to demonstrate its adherence to statehood for the island. However, in the next election, in 1952, the Independentistas outstripped the Republicans and became the second largest party. They were flushed with victory and enthusiasm, and saw themselves winning control of the country within another couple of elections.

However, in 1956 the Partido Independentista suffered a serious defeat, receiving only a little more than 10 per cent of the total vote and coming in a poor third. This defeat brought a serious internal crisis and threatened the extinction of the PIP as a legally recognized party, since, if it fell below 10 per cent of the popular vote in the next poll, it would no longer have legal recognition. This occurred in the 1960 election, in which the Independentistas received only six per cent of the total vote.

Meanwhile Luis Muñoz Marín had become an advocate of a third position, which was neither independence nor statehood. Upon his urging and with the endorsement of President Truman, the United States Congress on July 3, 1950, passed Law 600, which provided for the reorganization of the Puerto Rican government on a new basis. It granted the people of the island the right to write their own constitution, in the following terms:

> . . . Congress . . . recognizing fully the principle of government by consent of the governed, approves this Law with the character of a compact, so that the People of Puerto Rico may organize a government based on a constitution adopted by themselves.[3]

In conformity with Law 600 a referendum was held to determine whether or not a constitution should be written. Once approved, the constitutional assembly was elected, and during the early weeks of 1952 it drew up the Constitution for the Commonwealth (Estado Libre Asociado) of Puerto Rico.

The Constitution recognized the existence of a "compact" between the Federal government and Puerto Rico. Its first article declared:

> There is constituted the Estado Libre Asociado de Puerto Rico. Its political power emanates from the people and will be exercised in conformity with their will, within the terms of the compact between the people of Puerto Rico and the United States of America.

The spirit which was intended to permeate the new government was set forth in the preamble of the Constitution:

> We consider that the determining factors in our life are citizenship in the United States of America and the aspiration continually to enrich our democracy through the individual and collective use of its rights and prerogatives; loyalty to the postulates of the Federal Constitution; the coexistence in Puerto Rico of the two great cultures of the American hemisphere; the desire for education; the faith in justice; the devotion for a full, laborious and pacific life; loyalty to the values of the human being regardless of social position, racial differences and economic interests; and the hope for a better world based on these principles.

Muñoz and his party thus adopted the position of being opposed both to complete independence and to statehood. They favored the continued association with the United States which, during a controversy over the island's status arising from the admission of Alaska into the Union in 1958, Muñoz Marín declared to be "eternal." At the same time they favored the widest possible degree of autonomy for the island.

Muñoz and others in the leadership of his party frequently expressed their desire to see the commonwealth status "grow." What this growth consists of was seldom publicly stated, but its essence seems to the writer to consist of two things. First, a relatively minor point, Muñoz and his followers wished to see a direct appeal from the Supreme Court of Puerto Rico to that of the United States instead of through the Circuit Court of Appeals of Boston, as has been traditional. Second, Muñoz Marín and his supporters have favored some kind of arrangement which would permit the Legislature of Puerto Rico to declare null and void in the island any law passed by the United States Congress which they did not want to see applied to Puerto Rico.

Independentista critics of Muñoz Marín have centered their attention on the claim that the commonwealth status has not really fundamentally changed the situation of Puerto Rico. They have argued that the relationship between the United States and Puerto Rico is essentially unilateral, that the constitution of the island was written in pursuance of an act of Congress and could theoretically be revoked by another act of Congress. Sovereignty, the independence advocates maintain, has remained in the United States.

Muñoz and his supporters, on the other hand, have based their position on the phrase in Law 600 which says that this law has "the character of a compact," and have insisted that in fact Puerto Rico is "associated" with the United States, not subordinate to it. Luis Muñoz Marín's position was well stated in an article which he wrote for the San Juan newspaper *El Mundo* on July 6, 1958. He said:

. . . Not even I who am its founder can think that the Partido Popular Democrático is so perfect that hundreds of thousands of Puerto Ricans vote in favor of it in spite of being against its principal political contribution to the history of Puerto Rico and of the United

States, the Estado Libre Asociado. I am profoundly proud that Puerto Rico has had the honor of creating a new political form in the American Union. Millions of our fellow citizens of the United States are profoundly proud of this. . . .

The spirit of our people has resisted and will resist the senseless attempt to make us ashamed of ourselves, discrediting the political status which we have chosen. Those who attempt this cite with approval any statement by anyone who knows little or nothing of what the Estado Libre Asociado is, while at the same time ignoring the honorable attitude of those persons who gave the creative vigor of their intelligence, their love for the dignity of the Puerto Rican people and their decision to continue it with increasing prosperity, of those who established the Estado Libre Asociado. I am happy that Alaska has achieved the honorable end which it sought. But I must say with legitimate pride as a Puerto Rican that Puerto Rico has done much more than add a new star to forty-eight others. It has added a new manner and dimension to the United States, while at the same time placing itself in the most favorable position for resolving the great difficulties of its own people.

The Puerto Rican advocates of statehood agree that Muñoz Marín's assertion that association of the island with the United States is "permanent," but allege that any other kind of association than full statehood is "degrading" and "undignified." They also point out that the commonwealth as it existed after 1952 still left the island subject to legislation by the United States Congress, in which Puerto Rico had no voting representation. They therefore have urged the Puerto Ricans to seek to become a state, which would give them two senators and at least half a dozen members in the House of Representatives.

Muñoz' reply to his statehood critics is that, although Puerto Rico wants to be "associated" with the United States, it does not want to be "integrated" with it. The writer heard the governor deliver a speech on July 17, 1958, on the ninety-ninth anniversary of his father's birth, in which he answered his statehood opponents, arguing that Puerto Rico had a cultural tradition and customs which were different from those of their fellow citizens on the continent, and that they had no desire to forego these and become just like other Americans. They wanted to maintain their identity, he said, but at the same time remain United States citizens. They were, he said, participating in a unique experiment in self-government and international association of which both they and continental United States citizens should be proud.

The commonwealth status' greatest asset has been the support of Muñoz Marín. So long as he remains active in politics and throws his weight behind the Estado Libre Asociado it is certain to remain the Puerto Rican form of government, because he has won a degree of ascendancy over the voters of the island seldom equaled in democratic lands. By the early 1950's the most sanguine of Luis Muñoz Marín's opponents had ceased to think in terms of defeating "Don Luis." Plans of all opposition politicians were made in terms of what would happen when he had passed from the political scene.

However, the admission of Hawaii into the Union in the summer of 1959 forced Muñoz and his party to modify their position slightly. Hawaii's admission seemed to answer one of the arguments most frequently offered by opponents of statehood for Puerto Rico: that Congress would never approve the admission of a state lying off the shores of the American continent or one whose inhabitants were not in their majority Caucasian. In September the Popular Party for the first time publicly admitted that Puerto Rico might find it worth while to become a state when its per capita income reached that of the poorest of the fifty states. In an apparent effort to stop further discussion of the issue for a while at least, Muñoz backed a measure passed by the Legislature early in 1960 providing for a referendum on the status question sometime after the 1960 election.

The support for Muñoz Marín comes from the most varied sections of the populace. Certainly the backbone of his supporters has consisted of the *jíbaros,* the simple country folk in the mountains and valleys of the interior of the island. The hill farmer, the small tobacco or coffee grower, and the ubiquitous small merchant supplying the needs of the country man are the people who have come to adore Muñoz.

The support of the *jíbaro* for Muñoz Marín is not something inspired by the governor's actual accomplishments on their behalf. Indeed, it is the more remote country folk who have felt least the impact of the economic and social policies of the Muñoz government that back him most completely. Their support for Don Luis is a kind of personal allegiance, a loyalty not unlike the traditional relationship between master and servant of colonial Spanish America. It is the kind of relationship which explains the persistent strength of personalism in Latin American politics.

Another key source of backing for Muñoz Marín has been the workers in the sugar fields and in the cities and towns who had originally been taught the virtues of organization and political action by Santiago Iglesias. With the decline of the Socialist Party, Muñoz Marín's Popular Democratic Party took over almost *in toto* the rank and file of the former's supporters. The ex-Socialists, particularly those who had some degree of leadership in the old Socialist Party, constitute a considerably less unconditional and more critical kind of supporters than do the unlettered *jíbaros*. Their support has been kept by the government's program of social legislation and by the results of the industrialization program.

Muñoz Marín has also drawn a considerable degree of support from the highly educated professional classes. His backers in this group are nowhere near as numerous as those in the other two categories, but they have been of crucial importance in making it possible to carry out his government's program. It is from their ranks that a large part of the administrative staff for the government's development effort has been drawn. One is likely to find in this group a larger percentage than in the others of people who have both understanding and admiration for the capacity and intelligence of Muñoz. These people, although being more or less critical of certain aspects of Muñoz' behavior or program, have supported him and have been inspired by him.

Luis Muñoz Marín is not a great political philosopher. Although he has a tremendously active mind, which ranges widely over the field of ideas, he is an activist rather than a man of ideas. He has never written long theoretical treatises such as those of Víctor Raúl Haya de la Torre; nor has he attempted to draw together his own basic ideology, as have Pepe Figueres and Rómulo Betancourt; nor has he even gone out of his way, as Perón did, to try to develop a logical justification for his actions in more or less abstract terms.

Muñoz is that rare combination of an idealist and a tremendously successful practical politician. Like Franklin D. Roosevelt, of whom he was a great admirer, Muñoz Marín combines the ability to win the support of the masses with the capacity to listen carefully to the ideas of others and take those which he thinks most useful to carry out the rather broad general aims he is seeking to achieve.

He is a consummate politician. If Muñoz had not had a real genius for politics, his other virtues probably would not have mattered. He has had an ability to get the most diverse kinds of people to work together in harmony, and to get support for himself and his program from the most disparate and unexpected quarters.

Muñoz Marín's personality is his greatest asset. He is a heavy-set man with an "old-shoe" quality of friendliness. In the old days he was known to be very fond of a good time and was notoriously careless about his personal appearance, but in recent years he has become much more the proper gentleman without ever losing the common touch.

Muñoz is an impressive public speaker, and his oratory has a special quality of making his listeners feel that he is talking to each one of them individually. He is as good a listener as he is a talker, and he has a homely touch which puts at ease a *jibaro* from the hills as quickly as a visiting foreign dignitary or member of the United States Congress.

Muñoz Marín is perhaps at his best in personal conversation. His own wide experience with poverty and defeat as well as with success gives him an understanding of the problems of others. His powers of persuasion have become legendary in Puerto Rico, and violent opponents have been known to come away from an interview with Muñoz vastly impressed with his knowledge, his earnestness, and his willingness to listen to their side of the story.

His political ability has undoubtedly been reinforced by his experience as a citizen of two worlds, the United States and Latin America. Muñoz' long residence and schooling in the United States have given him an ability to speak English with virtually no Spanish accent and to understand the ideas and motivations of his continental fellow citizens. But at the same time he has a deep understanding of and a sentimental devotion to the people of his native island.

Muñoz' political prowess is best demonstrated in the nature of his administration. There are few people who could have gotten the two groups which have been the chief elements in his government to work together. He has known how to yoke as a team a group of hard-bitten politicians, interested in the jobs and other emoluments which are the chief preoccupation of professional politicians everywhere, with the group of technically trained, skilled, and idealistic technicians who have been the actual executors of most of the programs of the Puerto Rican government since 1940.

There is no doubt that the Popular Democratic Party has had a highly efficient political machine based on local professional leaders —bosses if you will. These professional politicians, drawn from the ranks of the old Liberal, Socialist, and Nationalist parties, and from among people who had not previously been active in any party, have included people of distinction within the government as well as thousands of local folk whose names are not known outside their own districts. These are the people who have kept the party organization alive, who have gotten out the vote, who have administered such patronage as there was to hand out. They are the people, too, who have filled the seats in the island legislature and in the city councils and mayors' offices throughout the island.

Muñoz' relations with the politicians of his party have been peculiar. During much of the Partido Popular Democrático's tenure in office the hold of any local politician upon his supporters has depended upon his maintaining good relations with Muñoz. The party's followers were more loyal to Don Luis than to any local leader. However, Muñoz has been able to keep his local leaders aware of this fact without making it galling to them. He has kept their loyalty, admiration, and enthusiasm.

At the same time Muñoz has had the enthusiastic cooperation of thousands of technicians in the administration. He has been constantly willing to listen to their advice, though not always accepting it, and has made them feel that they have had a significant part in a really worth-while experiment. He has also protected them from the appetites of the professional politicians. There has been no spoils system in the administrative side of the insular government. The posts in the economic and social departments and in the various agencies of the development program have been filled by the best talent available, and they have never been regarded as political plums available to "worthy Populares."

Muñoz' political acumen has been shown, too, in his handling of groups which were potentially hostile to his regime and in his avoidance of unnecessary controversies and conflicts which might have diverted his program from the essentials and have weakened popular support of it. This is demonstrated in the case of the Catholic Church. Eighty to 85 per cent of the population of Puerto Rico is Catholic, although only a relatively small proportion are very active church members. The hostility of the Church could have hampered Muñoz' program considerably by arousing opposition in Puerto Rico and by engendering hostile forces in the United States which could have seriously interfered with his government's policies.

Muñoz, although he is a divorced man and has a reputation for not being a believing Catholic, succeeded until 1960 in maintaining more or less cordial relations with the Church. The traditional struggle between clerical and anticlerical forces, which is more or less potent in virtually all the Latin American nations, had comparatively little importance in Puerto Rico.

However, in 1960 the Church hierarchy undertook to sponsor the formation of a purely Catholic Party, the Partido Acción Cristiana. It did not receive enough votes to become a legal party in the 1960 election, and its future remains in doubt. Although strongly opposing the new party, Muñoz has made it clear that he has no quarrel with the Church as such.

Finally, Muñoz' political ability has been shown in his relations with the Federal government. Long before becoming governor he made it a policy to get to know key figures in both the legislative and administrative sides of Washington. He is the island's most effective lobbyist when issues concerning Puerto Rico are being discussed in the Federal regime.

There was considerable fear in Puerto Rico of the effects on the island of the victory of the Republican Party in the United States election of 1952. Puerto Rican progress during the previous twenty years had been made under the Democrats, and the Puerto Rican regime itself was generally rated both in the island and on the continent as "New Dealish."

In spite of these fears the Puerto Rican regime suffered no adverse effects from the advent of the Republicans to power. Whether correctly or not, this fact is widely attributed in Puerto Rico to Muñoz Marín's contacts in Washington with Republicans as well as Democrats.

The second great asset of Muñoz Marín has been his unbounded energy. He has kept track of virtually everything which has been going on in the government as well as in political life. Although he has not sought to centralize the administration in his own hands, and has delegated much authority both in the government and in the party to able assistants, he has never lost interest in any aspect of public affairs in Puerto Rico.

The Governor is constantly reviewing and checking on various phases of the widespread program of development, and it is by no means unusual for some administrative branch to receive word that the Governor thinks that such and such a project ought to be tried or that the standard way of doing something should be adjusted in one way or another. At the same time he has never lost contact with the mass of the people to whom he owes his long tenure in power. There are few politicians in the island sanguine enough to think that they can outmaneuver Muñoz Marín, and admiration for his wide knowledge and acquaintanceship as well as for his ability as a political manipulator is widespread even among his strongest opponents. This ability Muñoz maintains because he does not relax his interest in the minutiae of day-to-day politics.

The third great asset of Muñoz Marín has been his ability to listen to the ideas of others and to adapt them to the long-term objectives which he has sought to carry out. In the late 1930's he gathered around himself a remarkable group of young intellectuals who were in many cases very thoughtful men as well as, in some instances, very good administrators. For many years, too, Muñoz maintained close liaison with the university, particularly with the social scientists there.

Over the years Muñoz has shown a remarkable ability to "pick the brains" of these people. Although he has not been especially interested in theories, he has been exceedingly interested in finding new and better ways of fulfilling his basic objectives of fomenting production, raising standards of living, and developing the cultural capacities of his people. Hence he is reputed to have accepted the idea of Operation Bootstrap from one of his closest advisers and to have approved of the commonwealth idea as drawn up by another of his close associates.

His approach is demonstrated by his method of dealing with the problem of developing better methods of distribution in the island.

In the middle 1950's Muñoz became convinced that the old-fashioned small store, with its very small stock of a limited variety of produce, was hampering the further expansion of several sectors of the economy. His recognition of this fact was in itself witness to the way in which he follows closely the island's economic problems. Muñoz was anxious to find a way out of this problem and, in addition, to obtain advice from some of the government technicians who had been studying the problem. He went to Scandinavia in 1955 to make an on-the-spot study of the consumers' cooperative movement there, bringing back with him a Swedish cooperator to act as adviser in this field.

The result was considerable government impetus to the development of consumers' cooperative supermarkets in Puerto Rico, along with encouragement for a number of private firms to come in and establish similar establishments. As a consequence the government is now in a much better position than formerly to encourage the development of local food-growing industries which would have had difficulty under previous conditions in finding adequate stable outlets at reasonable prices. Now with the supermarket chains, cooperative and private, buying in large quantities there is an assured market for several of these food-producing projects.

Muñoz' two great failures, which may in the long run have some effect on the position he holds in Puerto Rican and hemispheric history, have been his inability to sell the idea of the commonwealth to the rank-and-file Puerto Rican and his lack of success in developing a secondary leadership capable of taking over when he is gone. There are those who feel that his failure to convince the people of Puerto Rico that the commonwealth status is a lasting solution to the status problem arises from his own lack of confidence in it. The writer has no way of knowing whether or not this is the case. However, it is obvious that, although most Puerto Ricans are willing to live with the commonwealth so long as Muñoz is for it, relatively few are convinced that it is in any way "permanent." The great bulk of the population is probably still divided between those who would choose independence and those who would opt to become a state in the Federal Union.

It is hard for an outsider to fathom exactly why Muñoz has failed in this regard. Perhaps it is because he has talked about the status as a "growing" one without specifying exactly what it is he wants it to grow into. He leaves the end result of this growth open, so that one is free to presume that it will be one or the other of the classic alternatives. Perhaps Muñoz' failure is due to the fact, as one of his closest associates put it to the author, that the commonwealth status is a "cold" one, that it is not one about which much enthusiasm can be engendered. One can get aroused by patriotic feelings for Puerto Rico concomitant with independence. One can even get enthusiastic about the glories of being part of the United States as a duly admitted state. But the Commonwealth idea is so new and different that it is hard to get passionately attached to it. The arguments in favor of it are largely practical, not sentimental.

Muñoz' second great failure has been to develop anyone to take his place. Perhaps this is an impossible task. Certainly Muñoz' role as a liaison between more or less hard-bitten professional politicians and more or less idealistic intellectuals is a unique one. It would be hard to find anyone else who could fill that role. Muñoz himself has recognized the fact publicly that there is no one who is his logical successor. The fact raises certain doubts as to the ability of Puerto Rico to continue with the same vigor its development program once Muñoz is no longer leading it.

The net effect of the career of Luis Muñoz Marín on Puerto Rico has been threefold: he started a program of economic growth and development which in 1961 seems to have reached the point of self-perpetuation; he has strengthened and given new meaning to political democracy; and he has given Puerto Ricans a self-assurance and hope which they did not before possess. All of this represents a profound revolution in the island's economy, society, and political life. But though changing the old way of life, Muñoz has been concerned with preserving its good things. Material progress has been a means, not an end, for him. His ultimate objective is probably best expressed by his own words uttered in a commencement speech given at Harvard University on June 16, 1955:

A large question arises: Are the attitudes and habits that are associated with modern high productivity inexorably interwoven with the attitudes and manners of relentless material consumption? Can a culture be efficient in production and at the same time wise and modest in consumption? Can it be feverish in output and serene in intake? I say we are getting to the time in which it must—and if it must, it probably can. Economists could tell us that a higher and higher rate of multiple consumption is necessary to a high rate of production, and therefore of employment and of income, and that what I am talking about would bring economies tumbling down on our heads. It need not be so, because of the evident possibility of re-gearing high productivity to higher ends. If it were so, it would most certainly be time to ponder what to do about a situation in which Serenity could bring about catastrophe.

In the Declaration of Independence of the United States the young Republic was dedicated to the rights of life, liberty and the pursuit of happiness. In Puerto Rico we are trying in our modest setting, to bring to a harmonious success, for the good of our souls and bodies and for the observation of our fellow citizens and of such parts of the world as may care to look Operation Bootstrap—the right to life; Operation Commonwealth—the right to liberty; and Operation Serenity—the pursuit of happiness with some hope of really catching up with her.

Víctor Paz Estenssoro and Hernán Siles, and the Bolivian National Revolution

෴

One day late in April, 1952, a festive crowd gathered at the airport high up on the Bolivian Altiplano overlooking the city of La Paz nestled down in its crevice in the three-mile-high plain. Deafening cheers arose as an airplane hove into view, landed, and disgorged its principal passenger, Víctor Paz Estenssoro, Constitutional President of the Republic. The cheering was even more deafening as Hernán Siles, the Vice President, stepped forward and gave the arriving visitor the traditional *abrazo* and welcomed him back to his native soil.

This act marked the culmination of a long struggle and the beginning of one of the most profound social transformations which any Latin American country has experienced in the twentieth century. The two men who embraced below the recently landed airplane were the people most responsible for this transformation and were to guide it through its first turbulent years.

Paz Estenssoro and Siles were the founders and leading figures in the Movimiento Nacionalista Revolucionario, a political party which for a dozen years had been calling for a fundamental change in the economic, social, and political institutions of the Republic of Bolivia. In spite of their different backgrounds they had long worked together to bring about this change and were now to have their opportunity to do so. Perhaps, had either known the difficulties which they were going to face during the next few years, they would not have undertaken the tremendous task which lay before them.

Víctor Paz Estenssoro was born of a middle-class family in the town of Tarija in the southern part of Bolivia, not far from the Argentine frontier. He went to the University of San Andrés in La Paz and ultimately became a professor there. He became a specialist

198

in economic affairs, particularly in the economic problems of his own country, about which he wrote several interesting books.

Hernán Siles, in contrast, was the son of one of the leading politicians of his country who, after being a deputy, senator, and cabinet member, served as president of the republic from 1926 until 1930 and died while ambassador to Peru. Siles, too, had studied at the University and had graduated shortly before the outbreak of the Chaco War between his country and Paraguay.

Both young men served in their nation's armed forces during this war, which went on from 1932 until late in 1935. They, like many of their generation who fought in the war, were tremendously disillusioned by its consequences. They saw their country's army, which had been rated one of the best in Latin America, crumble before the enemy, not because of any lack of valor on the part of the troops but because of the stupid tactics and lack of honesty and patriotism on the part of many of the high officers. They were impressed with the sufferings of the poor Indian troops brought down from the 15,000-foot plateau which had been their whole world to die in the heat and disease-ridden tropics of the barren Chaco.

The Chaco War was the catalyst that started the process of undermining the traditional social system of Bolivia. Arousing the spirit of nationalism and the social consciousness of the youth of the upper and middle classes of the cities, it also had disintegrating effects on the life of the Indians, who were the great majority of the population. For the first time they were taken out of their accustomed milieu and were shown a new and different type of world. Many of them came back unwilling to return to their old way of life and so tended to drift to the cities. Movements began among the largely Indian workers in the tin mines toward organization and defense of their interests against the mineowners.

Soon after the end of the Chaco War the Army overthrew the government of President Tejada Sorzano. The leader of the coup, Colonel David Toro, established what he called a "Socialist Republic," the main innovation of which was to establish for the first time a Ministry of Labor. After a bit more than a year in office Toro was overthrown by another military coup headed by Colonel Germán Busch.

Busch, a hero of the Chaco War, was deeply discontented with the economic and social *status quo* but was not very clear just what he wanted to do about it. With his encouragement, however, the beginnings of a trade-union movement were made among the tin miners. He established for the first time a Ministry of Mines and Petroleum, and signed an order forcing the mining companies to sell most of their foreign exchange to the Central Bank.

One of the economic advisers to Germán Busch was young Víctor Paz Estenssoro, who was already gaining some reputation as a brilliant student of economic affairs. He was principally responsible for the decree of President Busch establishing government control over the foreign exchange earned by the mining companies. He was elected to the Chamber of Deputies during the Busch regime.

President Busch committed suicide—or was murdered (the point is still discussed in Bolivia)—in the middle of 1939, and for four and a half years there was a conservatively oriented administration. It quietly left the foreign exchange decree without effect, and the trade unions made little further progress.

Meanwhile Hernán Siles joined Paz Estenssoro in the Chamber of Deputies in the election of 1940. In the following year Paz Estenssoro, Siles, and three other deputies took the lead in establishing a new political party, the Movimiento Nacionalista Revolucionario (MNR). It was strongly nationalist, as its name implied, and was for some time accused of pro-Nazi sympathies, an allegation which was strongly denied by the party leaders. Part of its interpretation of Bolivian nationalism was emphasis on the importance of the country's Indian heritage. It urged that steps be taken to incorporate the Indians, who lived as virtual pariahs in their own country, into the economic, social, and political life of the nation.

The MNR constituted one of the two principal opposition parties in Congress between its foundation and December, 1943. The other major opposition group was the Partido de la Izquierda Revolucionaria, which proclaimed itself to be an "independent Marxist" organization but out of which the Communist Party of Bolivia emerged some years later. Both groups had some influence in the labor movement.

A few years after the foundation of the Movimiento Nacionalista Revolucionario, Víctor Paz Estenssoro summed up its objectives as follows:

We are the Revolutionary Nationalist Party. . . . We have seen that a country with a semi-colonial structure like Bolivia, in a revolutionary period, and within the present realities, must insofar as possible achieve a socialist regime which will permit the realization of social conquests appropriate to any nationalist policy, the grand objectives of which will be economic liberation and reform of the agrarian system. It is not possible to apply to Bolivia . . . principles applicable or already applied to other people in other countries. Here social phenomena are of a different nature. . . .[1]

During the early 1940's discontent was rising with the government then in power. The miners were particularly aroused against the regime because of a massacre which occurred at the mining camp of Catavi in December, 1942, and they turned to the MNR for support. Paz Estenssoro and other leaders of the party in the Chamber of Deputies bore the burden of interrogating the government upon this occasion, and from this time on a firm alliance was sealed between the miners' organizations and the Movimiento Nacionalista Revolucionario.

In December, 1943, the government of General Enrique Peñaranda was overthrown by a military *coup d'état* supported by the MNR. Víctor Paz Estenssoro became Minister of Finance of the new President, Major Gualberto Villarroel. Although he resigned a few months later, in a maneuver designed to gain recognition of the new regime by the United States and other American countries, the MNR was represented in the government during most of the two and a half years Villarroel was president.

This period, from December, 1943, until July, 1946, was of key importance to the MNR and to the careers of Víctor Paz Estenssoro and Hernán Siles for two reasons. First, it established the party as the principal spokesman for the miners and, to a less degree, for the Indian peasants. In the second place, it paved the way for the downfall of the MNR's principal rival, the Partido de la Izquierda Revolucionaria (PIR).

Under the inspiration of Paz Estenssoro, Siles, and other MNR leaders, the Villarroel government took several measures which were designed to aid the indigenous population. On the one hand, it encouraged the development of a strong labor movement among the tin miners, a movement which was firmly in the hands of the MNR by the end of Villarroel's government. In addition, the Villarroel regime proclaimed the end of the forced labor service which Bolivian Indians had legally been bound to render their landlords. Finally, the government convoked a National Indian Congress, in the process of which President Villarroel, Paz Estenssoro, and other government political leaders discussed at length with the leaders of the Indians the problems which were facing that group.

During most of the period that Villarroel was in office the MNR's rival, the PIR, was one of the main forces of the opposition. Although it had first suggested that it would like to take part in the Villarroel administration, it turned sharply against the regime when the President refused to accept the PIR's conditions for entering the government. It associated closely in the opposition with the principal parties of the landowners and mining interests, the so-called Partido Unión Republicana Socialista and the Partido Liberal. Thus began the discrediting of the PIR in the eyes of the working and peasant masses of Bolivia.

The Villarroel regime came to a sudden tragic end on July 13, 1946, when elements of the population of La Paz revolted, and seized and lynched President Villarroel and several of his close associates. Víctor Paz Estenssoro, Hernán Siles, and other top MNR leaders were able to take refuge in various embassies in La Paz and went into exile in Argentina, Chile, and other countries.

During the next six years the MNR was severely persecuted by the government. Paz Estenssoro spent the period in exile, most of the time in Argentina, but a year in Montevideo, Uruguay, when dictator Juan Perón decided to join the persecution of the MNR leaders. Hernán Siles was in exile in Chile part of the time but returned various times to lead the underground fight of the MNR against the regime.

The six years during which the MNR was out of power were turbulent ones. There were three presidents and a military junta successively governing the country during this period. Labor unrest was constant, and there were two revolutionary strikes and innumerable partial walkouts. Arrests of opponents of the regime occurred almost daily.

In spite of being persecuted, and its leaders being in exile, in jail, or in hiding most of the time, the MNR thrived during the six years.

Its ranks were solidified, and its contacts with the labor movement, especially the miners and factory workers, were reinforced. The party gained considerably from the fact that the PIR continued its policy of cooperating with the Liberals and the Partido Unión Republicana Socialista during most of the six-year period. By the end of this time the PIR had lost virtually all of its influence among the urban workers to the MNR.

The extent of the MNR's popular following was indicated in the presidential election of May, 1951. The MNR named Víctor Paz Estenssoro for president and Hernán Siles for vice president. They were faced with three rival slates, one of which had more or less official blessing of the incumbent government. However, when the votes began to be counted it was clear that Paz Estenssoro and Siles were running far ahead of their opponents.

The government maintained that the MNR candidates had not received the 51 per cent vote demanded by the constitution, and that therefore it should be Congress that selected the new president from the two highest candidates. However, rather than face the tremendous popular disapproval which this move would have entailed, President Mamerto Urriolagoitia preferred to turn the government over to a military junta, which governed until April 9, 1952.

By the beginning of 1952 Hernán Siles was back in Bolivia directing the fight against the junta government. His chief aid in this was Juan Lechin, head of the Mine Workers Federation and one of the principal leaders of the MNR. They entered into negotiations with General Antonio Seleme, Minister of Interior and commander of the Military Police (*carabineros*), who were almost as numerous and well armed as the national army. He was willing to help to overthrow the junta government of which he was a member in return for becoming president himself.

The conspiracy bore fruit on April 9, 1952, when a rebellion commenced in La Paz and the principal mining towns of the republic. The military police, under General Seleme's direction, provided arms for MNR supporters in La Paz, while the miners, armed with weapons they had concealed for years and with dynamite which they were used to handling in their daily work, rapidly overcame the garrisons in the principal mining areas.

By the end of the first day of fighting the struggle in La Paz

204 Prophets of the Revolution

seemed to be going against the rebels. Hernán Siles and Juan Lechín suggested to General Seleme that perhaps he had better take refuge in an embassy, since he would certainly suffer severely if he were to fall into government hands. Siles and Lechín added that they would stay in the streets until all hope had gone. Seleme took their advice.

The next day, when the tide turned in favor of the rebels, General Seleme came out of the embassy once again and sought to assume command of the uprising. However, Siles informed him that, since he had abandoned the struggle, he had no right to take advantage of its approaching victory. Instead of proclaiming Seleme president, as had first been intended, it was decided to make effective the MNR's claim that it had won the 1951 election and call back Víctor Paz Estenssoro from exile.

There is no doubt that what occurred in the period between the victory of the April 9 Revolution and the return of Víctor Paz from Buenos Aires was a tribute to the integrity of Hernán Siles. He in effect had control of the nation in his hands, and it would have been simple—and in good Bolivian tradition—for him to have proclaimed himself provisional president. However, being a man of tremendous loyalty to his comrades and to his own ideals, he refused to take the easy path to power. Rather, he functioned as vice president, temporarily in charge of the government, until Víctor Paz could return from exile. In doing so he gave a lesson which not all of his associates have seen fit to heed.

With the return of Víctor Paz Estenssoro to Bolivia the real work of the Bolivian National Revolution got under way. The MNR, during its years in the political wilderness, had developed an extensive and radical program of government. It had promised to give the Indians full rights of citizenship. It had pledged to nationalize the country's largest tin-mining companies. It had said that it would carry out an agrarian reform, to give the land to the men and women who actually tilled it. Now they began to take steps to carry out this program.

One of Víctor Paz Estenssoro's first decrees extended the right to vote to all adults. Previously only those who were literate in Spanish had the franchise, and fewer than two hundred thousand voters were registered. The new decree increased this number many times over and constituted the first step in making the Indians full-fledged participants in the civic life of the nation.

The next major step was to nationalize the tin mines. This was essential to the MNR government for several reasons. First, they had promised to do so, and not to have fulfilled this promise would have been to put in doubt all the other elements of their program. Second, so long as the existing companies remained in control of the tin mines the MNR leaders could be sure that these companies would use all their very considerable influence to get rid of the MNR regime.

Finally, the MNR leaders felt that as a matter of principle this natural resource should be in the hands of the nation. For many decades the tin companies had taken out the products of their mines while leaving very little in return. They had paid very low taxes, their wage scales had been miserable, and in general the country had benefited relatively little, while the owners of the companies had made stupendous profits. Although this situation had changed somewhat in the years following the Chaco War, it was still felt by the MNR chiefs, as well as by most other Bolivians who had any opinion at all about the problem, that the Big Three mines, those belonging to the Patiño, Aramayo, and Hochschild companies, should be taken over by the State.

President Víctor Paz Estenssoro first appointed a commission to study the problem a couple of months after he assumed office. This commission recommended nationalization. The project was widely debated, and finally, on October 31, 1952, a decree was issued expropriating the properties of the three companies and establishing the Corporación Minera de Bolivia, a government-owned institution, to take over these holdings.

A great deal has been said and written about the "failure" of Bolivian tin nationalization. However, this alleged failure has been grossly exaggerated. Although it would be impossible to deny the considerable decline in both production and productivity occurring since expropriation, this is at most only half the story.

First, let us note some of the bad aspects of what occurred after nationalization. There is no doubt that labor discipline declined notably after the April 9, 1952, Revolution, when the miners felt, with some reason, that they were masters of the mines and of the nation. The mineworkers began to discharge managers instead of the other way round. This situation had only partly improved nine years after the revolution.

In the second place, the mines undoubtedly had excess personnel. A number of miners had been discharged from their jobs for trade-union and political reasons during the six years that the MNR was out of power. All these were ordered restored to their posts as soon as the revolution triumphed, while few other workers were dismissed.

Third, the mines were forced for several years to carry excessively heavy costs ensuing from the management of their company stores. Prices in these were frozen while the general price level was skyrocketing. This resulted in many workers' continuing on the mines' payrolls more for the privilege of buying goods cheaply in the commissaries than for the wages they earned. This problem was partly adjusted with President Hernán Siles' Stabilization Program at the end of 1956.

Fourth, when the mining companies withdrew, they took with them not only virtually all their foreign technicians and engineers but also most of their maps and almost every document of any value in running the mines. As a result it was necessary to promote Bolivians who admittedly were not well qualified for highly technical posts. However, the surprising thing is that these people did as well as they did, not that they did not do as well as their predecessors. In this regard the government of President Víctor Paz Estenssoro might be justly criticized for not seizing the mines provisionally as soon as they came to power, thus preventing the removal of precious documents, including maps of the operating mines and of areas which had been explored for new ones.

Another serious problem facing the nationalized mines was the sagging prices and curtailed demand for their products. Within a year of the revolution the price of tin fell from $1.20 a pound to less than 90¢. By the end of 1957 contracts for the purchase of tungsten and other by-products of the tin mines which had been in effect with the U.S. Government for a number of years expired and were not renewed.

However, the biggest single problem facing the Corporación Minera and the Bolivian Government was the fact that they were not able to settle the question of compensation to the old mining companies. Although a provisional agreement was negotiated in August, 1953, whereby the Corporación paid the old companies a varying amount per pound of tin mined, depending on the cost at which it was sold, no agreement was reached as to the total amount owed. This question was not resolved until the early months of 1961.

Until the question of compensation could be agreed upon, the Corporación Minera was not in a position to go ahead with any program for renovating the mines and exploring extensively for new ones. For a generation relatively little exploration work had been done by the tin-mining companies, and the result was that the percentage of tin in the ore being dug in the existing mines had declined catastrophically by 1952. It continued to fall in subsequent years. In addition, the equipment of most of the mines was very antiquated, and some of it was quite dangerous.

In order for the Corporación Minera to be able to get funds for reequipment of the mines and for extensive exploration and development, it had to be in a position to borrow considerable sums abroad. However, while the issue of compensation was still unsettled and the Corporación did not know just what its debts were, there was little possibility to obtain loans from respectable banking institutions. As a result the future of the mining industry continued to depend on the resolution of the compensation problem, and the productivity of the existing mines continued to fall.

Whatever the pros and cons of the nationalization of the mines in Bolivia, what most critics overlook is that this was only one phase of the total program of the MNR government. Of much more long-run significance for the country were the agrarian reform and the program for diversification of the nation's economy commenced during President Víctor Paz Estenssoro's first administration.

Agrarian reform was the heart of the social reform program of the MNR government. Ever since the coming of the Spaniards to the Altiplano of Bolivia in the sixteenth century there had been a struggle between the Indians and the Spaniards and their descendants for control of the land. The Indian had been the steady loser in this battle. By the middle of the twentieth century most of the land in the Altiplano was in the hands of large landowners of European and mestizo descent and was cultivated by Indians, under conditions reminiscent of those prevailing in Europe during the Middle Ages. The Indians were granted small pieces of land to cultivate for their own account and on which to have a hut, and in return were required to till the land which was cultivated for the account of the landlord. They were also forced periodically to give a week's free personal labor service to the landowner.

As a result of this system Bolivian agriculture was not only socially retrograde but economically backward. With virtually free labor from the Indians the landowners had little or no incentive to adopt modern methods of cultivation or to use machinery.

From the beginning the MNR leaders had been "Indianist" in their orientation and had urged some change in the organization of the nation's rural economy and society. In this perhaps they were influenced by Haya de la Torre and the Aprista movement in neighboring Peru as well as by their own immediate surroundings. However, it was not until the "six years" of experience in the political wilderness that Paz Estenssoro, Siles, and the other MNR leaders finally came out frankly in favor of general redistribution of the land to the Indians.

The MNR government's first move in this direction was to organize the Indians. Peasant unions were established throughout the country, and one of the unions' principal activities was to establish armed militia groups. At the same time the MNR party established local groups in virtually every center of Indian population.

About a year after the revolution a commission was established by President Paz Estenssoro to draw up an agrarian reform law. Vice President Hernán Siles was put in charge, and the commission was composed of university people, trade-unionists, and political leaders. President Paz Estenssoro himself worked closely with the commission. After the submission of its report the cabinet discussed the project thoroughly, and finally on August 2, 1953, the agrarian reform decree was formally signed.

The new law gave outright and immediately to the Indians the small parcels of land which the landowners had allowed them to cultivate for their own benefit. In addition it provided that that part of the haciendas which had been used for the account of the landowner should also be divided among the peasants after a thorough survey and study of each particular hacienda had been made. A National Agrarian Reform Institute was established to carry out the program.

This was the fundamental act of the MNR government. It gave to the Indians a solid economic base for the first time. In effect it liberated them from a kind of semi-serfdom to which they had long been submitted. It gave them a psychological security as small land-owners which they had not possessed for generations. Whatever may happen to the MNR regime in the future, it is unlikely that any future government will be able to undo the agrarian reform law.

Also of very great long-run importance was the MNR government's program for the economic diversification of Bolivia. The MNR leaders had for long argued that this was an absolute necessity for the future growth of the nation's economy, and had insisted that the government take steps to bring it about. Víctor Paz Estenssoro, writing the chapter on Bolivia in a book on Latin American economic thought in 1945, had written about himself and other economic thinkers of his group in Bolivia:

Those who dedicate themselves to economic problems are anti-liberal, to a greater or less degree. In the face of present realities of Bolivia—a country with a semi-colonial economy—it is necessary to oppose "laissez faire, laisser passer" (which provides all the advantages for the large firms) with the intervention of the state, in defense of collective interests. . . . To strengthen the national economy against effects of crises, during which the price of minerals falls almost vertically, it is necesary to diversify Bolivian production. This implies a protectionist policy and industrialization encouraged by the State, in opposition to the thesis of those who wish that Bolivia be exclusively a mining country and import all of its food products and manufactured goods forever. . . .

The program of economic diversification had various aspects. First, it was desired to develop other export goods which could earn foreign exchange for Bolivia to supplement the declining amounts of foreign currency coming from tin and other minerals. Oil provided the best prospects. During the first year of the MNR regime the government spent a considerable amount of its foreign exchange resources to purchase equipment for the government petroleum firm the Yacimientos Petroleros Fiscales Bolivianus. Within three years of the revolution, as a result, the YPFB had reached a production of about five times that of 1951.

However, the administration was not satisfied with this. The government and YPFB did not have the resources sufficient to push the development of the oil industry much further. Therefore the MNR leaders decided to permit international oil companies to seek out and exploit the very large oil reserves which Bolivia is presumed to possess.

The changes in the law which were required to make such international investments possible took place during the last year of the first Paz Estenssoro administration. During the first two years of the succeeding administration of Hernán Siles a dozen or more concessions were granted to foreign companies, particularly United States firms.

In addition to seeking new exports, the MNR government was anxious to develop greater production within the country of both agricultural and industrial products. For this purpose it was necessary vastly to expand the country's transportation facilities, and the government, with a great deal of aid from the United States Point Four Program, undertook a program of building new roads and establishing better maintenance of old ones. First priority was given to the highway into the eastern part of the country from Cochabamba to the city of Santa Cruz. Much of the rest of the government's efforts in this field were devoted to establishing local roads to connect outlying districts with the main trunk highways.

The Paz Estenssoro and Siles governments also sought to encourage the extension and improvement of the country's agricultural output. With the help of Point Four a series of new experiment stations was established, and a system of agricultural extension agents was set up. The government also invested considerable funds in a program of irrigation of a region east of Santa Cruz, where cotton growing was feasible. Textile manufacturing interests in the country cooperated with the government on this last aspect of the agricultural development program.

Several new manufacturing establishments of a fundamental nature were organized by the government. These included a new oil refinery, a sugar refinery near Santa Cruz, and a new cement plant. At the same time the government, again with the help of Point Four, established a big new vocational training school in La Paz to train apprentices and other workers for the country's manufacturing plants.

In general, the industrialists did not cooperate with the government's development program. They resented fundamentally the government's attitude of friendliness toward the trade unions and the relaxation of labor discipline which resulted from this. After December, 1956, the industrialists were also adversely affected by the Stabilization Program which deprived them of the ridiculously low foreign exchange rates which they had been able to use to import their raw materials and surreptitiously to ship some of their profits abroad. The government found it very difficult to enlist the support of local industrialists in the economic development program.

In addition to the economic programs of the MNR government the regime brought about important political changes. Fundamental was the organization of the Indian peasants politically and granting them the right to vote. There was also an attempt to reorganize the armed forces in such a fashion that they would no longer be a danger to civilian control of the government.

The Army, of course, had been defeated in the three-day uprising of April, 1952. Most of the rank-and-file soldiers were sent home, and their officers were generally retired. For more than a year Bolivia had only a skeleton military force. During this period there was a lively controversy concerning whether or not to reconstitute the Army. The decision to do so was finally made a year after the revolution of April, 1952.

Several principles were followed in reorganizing the Army. Officers who had been loyal to the MNR were brought back to provide the officers corps. The military academies were opened largely to sons of workers, peasants, and middle-class people friendly to the MNR. Most of the soldiers were put to work on road building, the construction of sewage and water facilities, the establishing of the basis for a migration program to the eastern forest regions of Bolivia and other economic development projects. A large majority of the armed forces was thus kept a safe distance from the capital, La Paz.

Finally, the government decided to maintain in existence the popular militia which had been established during and after the revolution. Thus, in case the Army leaders should once again seek to follow the traditional role of the military and try to overthrow the government, their influence would be checked by the militia.

The net result of this was positive. The MNR regime had to worry relatively little concerning the possibility that the Army would attempt to oust the government. Since 1952 there has been no serious attempt on the part of the armed forces to oust the civilian administration, an unrivaled record in the history of Bolivia.

The most serious criticism which one can make of the Paz Estenssoro administration was its treatment of the opposition. Paz Estenssoro allowed very little freedom of the press. Many of the leaders of past regimes were forced to stay in exile. Opponents of the MNR were frequently arrested, and some of them were kept in concentration camps.

In order to understand the background of the attitude of the Paz Estenssoro regime toward the opponents of the MNR, one must keep in mind that on several occasions the government issued general amnesties for its opponents. It also should be noted that the opposition continued to believe that governments should be changed in the traditional Bolivian manner, by *coup d'état* or armed revolt. Most of the opposition came to be concentrated behind the Falange Socialista Boliviana, a party patterned frankly on the Spanish Falange of Francisco Franco. Its principal program was a promise to reestablish "order" in the republic, particularly in the countryside. It issued frequent calls to the armed forces and to retired army officers to join with it to overthrow the MNR regime.

During the Paz Estenssoro administration the President was without any doubt the dominant figure in the government. He came to power as the undisputed leader of the MNR with high prestige as an economist and a political leader. He remained the unchallenged top figure in the party and the government.

Hernán Siles, vice president during the first Paz Estenssoro administration, played a leading role in the government and the MNR. He was head of the Agrarian Reform Commission and organized a Planning Commission to project the possibilities of the country's economic expansion. At the same time he came to be regarded as the leader of the more conservative faction of the government party.

Paz Estenssorro's term of office came to an end in July, 1956, and elections were held in June. Four groups of candidates were presented. The Movimiento Nacionalista Revolucionario named Hernán Siles as its candidate for the presidency and a leader of the left wing of the party, Nuflo Chávez, who had been Minister of Peasant Affairs in the Paz Estenssoro government, as its candidate for vice president. The Falange Socialista Boliviana, and the Trotskyite Partido Obrero Revolucionario also named slates for president, vice president, and congress. Finally, the remnants of the old PIR and the new Partido Communista de Bolivia named a joint ticket.

The MNR candidates won handily in a hard-fought campaign. Although they were defeated in Sucre and had only a small majority in some of the other principal cities, the government party had an overwhelming majority in the countryside. Siles was inaugurated early in July, 1956, as the second MNR president of Bolivia.

The new chief executive was faced with exceedingly pressing problems calling for immediate solutions. Although the Paz Estenssoro regime had carried out fundamental reforms in the economic, social, and political structure of the country, it was the task of the Siles government to consolidate these. During the Paz Estenssoro administration the country had been wracked by a severe inflation, which went out of all control during the last months of his rule and the first months of Siles' term. It threatened to undermine and perhaps destroy the whole structure of the MNR regime.

With the aid of the Point Four authorities an economic adviser was brought from the United States to suggest a program for checking the inflation. This expert, George Eder, suggested to Siles the necessity for a severe policy of retrenchment. He urged that all controls be removed over the movement of foreign currencies in and out of the country; that all subsidies be ended to the company stores in the mining camps; that all price controls be abolished; and that a large increase in wages be granted, and then that wages be frozen for some considerable time.

This was a dangerous program for the Siles government to try to carry out. The exchange control system had been a source of quick profits to the country's industrialists, who received a dollar for 150 bolivianos when the general market rate was as high as 15,000. They could thus get their imported raw materials for practically nothing, and as a result production was very cheap and many

Bolivian manufactured goods were being smuggled abroad to Peru, Chile, and Brazil.

The same favored rate of foreign exchange had been given to many trade-union and political leaders on the pretext that they were going to sell the goods imported with these cheap dollars to members of unions and cooperatives, passing on to them the lower prices. However, in fact, many of these leaders had taken advantage of their privilege to get rich and to build up bank accounts abroad. These people, whose power in the MNR was very great, could be expected to oppose any attempt to deprive them of their privileges.

The ending of mining camp commissary subsidies, which resulted in increases of as much as 1000 per cent in the prices of goods sold there, also hurt a group very powerful in the MNR government, which depended to a very large extent on the political backing and the possible military assistance of the armed miners.

However, in spite of these difficulties, Siles determined to go ahead with the program which Eder had recommended to him. In order to backstop the program, he was assured of a fund of $25,000,-000 from the International Monetary Fund, Point Four, and the United States Treasury. The first move was to get Congress to authorize Siles to put such a program into effect. All of the MNR deputies and senators supported it, many of them apparently unaware of what its effects would be. However, once the program got under way, a wave of protest broke out among the trade-union leaders and politicians. This culminated in June, 1957, in a threat of a general strike to begin on July 1.

However, the strike never occurred. The labor movement split violently on this issue, and before the deadline arrived most of the important unions had voted not to support the strike, and had given qualified endorsement to the anti-inflationary program. Only the miners held out.

The mining unions had given trouble from the beginning of the Stabilization Program. When they went on strike in February, 1957, against the end of subsidized prices in their commissaries, President Siles countered by going on a hunger strike, which he did not end until the miners had returned to work. As the deadline of the July 1 strike approached, President Siles went to the principal mining camps, talked personally to the workers there, and got their virtually unanimous support. The strike collapsed completely.

Siles' move in going to the mining camps demonstrated remarkable personal courage. At one point some of the mine union leaders had threatened that he would be lynched if he went near one particular mine. He promptly went there, the union leaders were nowhere to be found, and he won over the rank and file completely.

The rest of President Siles' term was turbulent. Although his victory in the July 1, 1957, strike crisis temporarily gave him complete control of the situation, he failed to push his success to its ultimate conclusions. Instead of seeking to destroy the base of his left-wing opponents within the MNR by bringing about a reorganization of the Mine Workers Federation, as he might well have been able to do at the time, he allowed this powerful organization to remain under the control of Juan Lechín. It continued to provide a focus of opposition to the President.

Opposition to the program of stabilization began to rise again during 1958. Although prices were stable, or relatively so, for the first year and a half of the program, by the middle of 1958 they began to rise again. The situation did not, however, reach the gravity which it had had at the end of 1956, though discontent was nonetheless very widespread in the cities and mining camps.

In general the economy had not yet begun to improve fundamentally by the end of Siles' term of office. The problem of the compensation of the old mining companies had not yet been resolved, and so no major move had been made to refurbish the mining industry. The oil industry had not yet begun to produce appreciable quantities of foreign exchange, and its contributions to the national economy remained largely promises for the future.

The opposition, under the leadership of the Falange Socialista Boliviana, continued to prefer *coups d'état* to steady education of the voters as a means of seizing power. President Siles ended completely the concentration camps which Paz Estenssoro had maintained. He allowed the widest degree of freedom of the press, and by 1958 it was hard to find a paper in Bolivia which supported the government. He urged the exiles to return, and he sought to get them to adopt more peaceful and democratic means of working toward the assumption of power. His efforts largely failed, however.

A crisis occurred early in 1959 when Oscar Unzaga, head of the Falange, died. The government announced that he had committed suicide. Falangistas in Chile and Argentina said that he had been shot by government supporters. President Siles invited a group of distinguished Chilean lawyers to make a thorough study of the claims and counterclaims surrounding Unzaga's death, and they bore out the government's version of the story.

Other problems continued to plague the Siles government. It was faced with a basic lack of skilled personnel capable of carrying out efficiently its development programs and even of running the day-to-day activities of the administration. This lack was intensified because, as a result of the difficult economic situation, many skilled professional people preferred to go abroad to earn their living, where they would be able to get a much larger and more stable income than they could do in Bolivia.

Corruption also continued to be a major worry of the MNR regime. This was nothing that had started in 1952, but it had reached a crescendo during the hyperinflation of the last years of the first Paz Estenssoro regime. Although the Stabilization Program launched in December, 1956, cut off one of the principal sources of corruption—the manipulation of the multiple exchange system—it did not succeed in ending other more orthodox forms of graft and pilfering of the state treasury.

During most of the Siles administration ex-President Víctor Paz Estenssoro served as Bolivian ambassador to London. He came back in 1958 to try to smooth over the differences between Siles and the "miners' wing" of the MNR, headed by Juan Lechin. He had moderate success, and a truce was arranged between the two factions, a truce which did not last more than a few months, however. He returned again a year later, this time to announce his candidacy in the 1960 presidential election. In June, 1960, Paz Estenssoro won the post once again in a four-cornered race in which his principal rival was Walter Guevara Arce, former foreign minister of Siles, who led a dissident MNR group known as the Movimiento Nacionalista Revolucionario Auténtico.

During the years in which Paz Estenssoro and Siles have served as president of Bolivia the country has gone through a profound transformation, a change which no future regime will be able entirely to reverse. The Indians have been made an effective part of the life of the country, though they have not yet learned to adapt themselves completely to this new situation. It would be virtually impossible for any future regime to try to take the land away from the Indians again. It would be difficult to deny them the right to participate in politics. It would be hard to suppress their desire to get education and to learn how to live as equals in Bolivian society.

Víctor Paz Estenssoro and Hernán Siles, the two men who have borne the principal responsibility for this process of revolutionary change in Bolivia, are among the most interesting political figures to appear on the Latin American political scene in recent decades. They are in some ways very different from one another, but each has complemented the other.

Both men are intellectuals. They have studied deeply the problems facing their country, and during long years of political activity have evolved together a program which they feel they must carry out. Both men have been equally loyal to this program once they won control of the nation. However, Paz Estenssoro has been in many ways more logically a man to carry through the "destructive" phases of a great revolution and Siles a man to consolidate the measures which his predecessor had begun.

Víctor Paz Estenssoro is more able than his colleague to arouse passionate loyalty and devotion among the masses of his followers. Although an intellectual and a mestizo, he is able through his oratory to arouse tremendous enthusiasm among the largely Indian masses of the mining areas. He likes to mingle among the workers and peasants of the country, and during his first administration was an inveterate traveler around the country, inspecting various aspects of the government program.

Paz Estenssoro has the tremendous asset as a politician of being able to remember names and faces, and he has built up an almost legendary range of friendships and acquaintances throughout the country. He took a personal part in choosing local officials of the Agrarian Reform Institute and other governmental organizations even in the remotest parts of the country, because he knew personally virtually all the people who might conceivably be qualified for these posts.

He has a decisiveness and a ruthlessness which are lacking in his friend. He also has an ability to engage in intricate political maneuvers without making lasting enemies among those with whom he is maneuvering. Some have accused him, however, of not showing sufficient loyalty to his successor and of not using his vast personal influence sufficiently to help Siles through the almost insoluble problems which he, as Paz Estenssoro's heir, was forced to face.

Whereas the masses of the MNR tended to love and idolize Víctor Paz Estenssoro, they tended greatly to admire Hernán Siles. He was universally respected as a very brave man, not only for his leadership of the MNR underground and the actual fighting of the April, 1952, Revolution, but because of his fearlessness in challenging his opponents among the miners when he was president.

Siles is also respected for his honesty. None of the rumors concerning the president's participation in the corruption of the administration, such as were widespread in Paz Estenssoro's, circulated during Siles' term of office. Siles is extremely modest, reserved, and abstemious almost to the point of asceticism. Nor have his bona fides as a democrat been challenged except by the most extreme enemies of the MNR. His attempt to rebuild the feeling of national unity, which inevitably had to be destroyed during the first period of the revolution, won him wide respect even among the enemies of his party and his government.

Together Paz Estenssoro and Siles have led a revolution which ranks with the Mexican Revolution as one of the most profound social transformations to occur in Latin America in the twentieth century. They have sought to transform the most backward nation in South America into a modern country with a diversified economy and a democratic political life. They have sought to do so in a Bolivian and American way. They have not followed blindly patterns set for them from abroad, though they have borrowed some ideas, have studied events in other countries, particularly in America, and have received help from the United States. The failure or success of Paz Estenssoro's and Siles' efforts in the Bolivian Revolution will go far to determine whether or not other countries of the hemisphere will continue to seek their own indigenous way toward a more productive economy and a more democratic society, or whether they will succumb to the apparently easier method of totalitarian dictatorship.

Getulio Vargas,
"The Father of the Poor"

૪૭કૃ૭ર

On August 4, 1954, Getulio Vargas shot his brains out. He thus put an end to his physical existence but not to his influence on Brazil, his native country. Vargas was undoubtedly the most important Brazilian political figure of the first half of the twentieth century. He was president for nineteen years, dominated the nation's politics for nearly a quarter of a century, and his name remained a potent force in public life even after his death.

Vargas played a decisive role in bringing Brazil from the status of a semicolonial nation suffering under a tremendous psychological inferiority complex to that of a self-confident, booming country fast moving toward the position of a world power. Under his leadership the country began a process of rapid development of its natural resources and of headlong industrialization. At the same time the Brazilian people acquired an appreciation for their own abilities, both past and present, which made them shed once and for all their traditional tendency to pattern their political, economic, and cultural institutions on those of other countries.

Of course, all the changes which occurred between Vargas' accession to power in October, 1930, and his suicide in August, 1954, cannot be attributed solely to Getulio. However, he did guide them and did play an essential part in the direction which the sudden explosion of Brazilian energies took. Some of his influence was certainly negative, but much of it was also positive.

Getulio Vargas was born in Brazil's southernmost state, Rio Grande do Sul. He was proud of his Gaucho background, and perhaps part of his aggressiveness and drive is explained by his upbringing in this state, which has never been characterized by the traditionalism, courtly manners, and slower pace of the older-settled and more northerly states of the Brazilian Union.

219

Yet Vargas was a master of his nation's psychology. One of his greatest gifts as a politician was his appreciation of the deep hold which many generations of plantation society, with its masters and slaves, still has on the thinking and feelings of large numbers of the Brazilian people. His success is to a very considerable degree explained by his ability to picture himself as a kind of supermaster of one big Brazilian plantation. As the "father of the poor," one of his favorite descriptions of himself, he sought to fill the void felt by many humble Brazilians who had torn themselves away from their traditional surroundings and society yet felt lost without the kind of protection and security which the old ways had given them.

Getulio rose through the ranks of Rio Grande do Sul politics until he was governor of his state, in the late 1920's. During his tenure in the governor's mansion he gathered around himself a group of young men of considerable intelligence and with an eagerness to break with at least some of the traditions which had characterized the "first republic."

In 1930 Vargas was the candidate for president of the republic of the Liberal Alliance, a loose coalition of parties in various Brazilian states. Running against him was Julio Prestes, a seasoned politician of the state of São Paulo, and the hand-picked nominee of retiring chief executive Washington Luiz.

The results of the election were a foregone conclusion. According to Brazilian tradition, the candidate of the outgoing president was almost certainly assured success at the polls. The election of 1930 was no exception. Julio Prestes won handily, and Getulio Vargas retired to his native state.

However, Julio Prestes never took office. Times had changed in Brazil, and the traditional system broke down. For one thing, the dominant group of politicians had made a serious mistake. For several terms the custom had been to rotate the presidency between a citizen of São Paulo and a citizen of the state of Minas Gerais. But Prestes, like his predecessor, came from São Paulo. There was serious discontent in Minas as a result.

In the second place, the candidacy of Getulio Vargas had had the sympathy of an important part of the Army, particularly of many of the younger officers. This group, which had come to be called the "Tenentes" (the lieutenants) had been restless for a decade. Upon three different occasions, in 1922, 1924, and 1926, young officer groups had risen in revolt, and although their efforts were crushed, the discontent remained.

The most serious of these three uprisings was that of 1926, when a column of rebels roamed the interior of Brazil for almost two years before they finally crossed over into Bolivia and gave up the struggle. This was the famous Prestes Column, led by Luiz Carlos Prestes (no relation to the 1930 candidate for president), a young army captain, who had seen most of his military service in Rio Grande do Sul. Among the leaders of the Prestes Column were many young men who were to play leading roles in the Vargas government in later years, including João Alberto, Cordeiro de Farias, Juarez Tavora, Eduardo Gomes, and several others.

The Tenentes did not have a very well defined program. However, they attempted to arouse the back-country people against the rule of the landed oligarchy who had dominated the Brazilian government—and those of most of the states—since the declaration of the republic in 1889. They also waved the banner of nationalism and raised their voices in objection to what they thought was the subservience of Brazil to foreign powers and to foreigners resident in the country.

With his defeat for the presidency Vargas began plotting with his friends of the Liberal Alliance and with the Tenentes. Although the frequent voyages of important political and military figures back and forth to Rio Grande do Sul must have aroused the government's suspicions, little was done to try to thwart the revolutionary intentions of Vargas and his associates.

After long discussions it was finally decided not to accept the results of the 1930 election and to attempt a military movement against the Washington Luiz government before Julio Prestes was sworn in as the new president. This uprising began early in October, 1930. At first it moved slowly, at an almost leisurely pace. The rebel army moving up from the South had no major encounters with the Federal troops, which offered only token resistance. At the same time, insurrections occurred in some of the northern states. Finally, the government, for reasons best known to its leaders, decided not to try an all-out struggle with the insurgents. Washington Luiz was packed onto a steamer in Rio harbor and left for Europe, along with

222 Prophets of the Revolution

his victorious presidential nominee, and a few days later Getulio Vargas made a triumphal entry into the capital. He became for the first time provisional president of Brazil.

Vargas soon proved himself to be a very wily politician indeed. He owed much of his victory to the Tenentes, who during the first months really held power in their hands. However, Vargas was able over a period of time to reduce and virtually destroy the influence of the Tenentes as an organized group, and before long it became clear that he was the real master of the new administration.

In some ways this was a tragedy for Brazil. Had the Tenentes been able to organize a political party with a definite program and ideology, with an appeal to moderate nationalism and to the desire for social change, the history of Brazil might have been quite different. The country might have been spared much of the turbulence of the early 1930's and the dictatorship of the latter part of the decade and the first half of the 1940's.

However, Vargas outmaneuvered the Tenentes. They were never able to pool their efforts in a single political organization which might have challenged Vargas' desire to run a one-man show. For one thing, many of the Tenentes chose to stay in the armed forces, where they were somewhat removed from the day-to-day political struggles. In the Army they tended to split, some of them putting loyalty to their early ideals as their first consideration, others feeling that military discipline and adherence to the regime in power was of paramount importance. Those Tenentes who resigned from the armed forces and frankly entered politics were atomized by Vargas' divide-and-rule policies. Like those still in the army they were split between the men who became loyal personal associates of Getulio and those who became disillusioned in his regime and turned against it, only to find that the trump cards in the political game were in the hands of the president.

Vargas came to power at the beginning of the Great Depression. He was faced by tremendous economic problems arising from the collapse of the markets for Brazil's principal exports and the reverberations of this collapse on the nation's internal economy. Getulio would probably have been forced by circumstances to establish extensive government programs to face this situation even if he had been philosophically opposed to doing so. However, Vargas had no compunctions on this score.

The Vargas government engaged in an extensive program of buying up the country's excess production of coffee. It then turned around and dumped much of this excess into the sea or used it for somewhat peculiar purposes—coffee was even burned in Brazilian locomotives for a while.

The government also took drastic measures to bolster up the sugar industry. A Sugar and Alcohol Institute was established, and measures were taken to increase internal consumption of the crop. For instance, for years companies selling gasoline were required to mix a certain amount of sugar-produced alcohol with the fuel which they sold.

At the same time the Vargas government encouraged the growth of manufacturing industries. These would have grown even without government aid, since the country was cut off from its normal sources of supply for manufactured goods as a result of Brazil's inability to sell sufficient coffee to earn the foreign exchange with which to purchase them. However, Vargas intensified this natural trend toward manufacturing by extending protection to new industries and to expanding old ones.

As time went on, other types of encouragement were extended by Vargas to the industrialization of Brazil. There was a chronic shortage of foreign exchange from the time Vargas took office, a shortage which still exists. The government therefore undertook to ration the available foreign currency, and in this rationing it gave a high degree of priority to the importation of capital equipment and raw materials for new industries, while at the same time making it difficult to obtain foreign exchange for goods which would compete with products made by Brazilian manufacturing concerns.

Without necessarily intending to do so, high officials and favorites of the Vargas regime encouraged manufacturing in yet another way. Corruption and the accumulation of fortunes as a result of close association with the government were rife during the Vargas period—though they certainly had not commenced with Getulio's regime. Government contracts, foreign exchange privileges extended by the Banco do Brasil (which was charged with rationing the country's available foreign currency), and pure and simple rifling of the treasuries of government departments were some of the methods used by many of those associated with Getulio in order to enrich themselves. Many of these officials and favorites of the administration who made their fortunes "in the government service" invested at least part of their returns in new industries in Brazil. Thus a group of close associates of Vargas came to be numbered among the country's most important industrialists.

During the first years of his administration Vargas started a policy which was to become a cornerstone of his regime—the enactment of labor and social legislation. One of his first acts was to create a new Ministry of Industry, Commerce and Labor, with a close associate, Lindolfo Color, as the first occupant of the post. Soon afterward Vargas issued a decree-law providing for the first time for legal registration of trade unions. This marked a fundamental change in the attitude of the Brazilian government, which heretofore had been symbolized by the remark of one minister of the interior of the 1920's to the effect that "labor is a problem for the police."

The new law recognizing the legal status of unions did not meet with an enthusiastic response from the existing labor movement. The trade unions were under the leadership of anarchist, socialist, and communist elements. All these opposed the new law, fearing that it meant government interference in the internal affairs of the unions, which it did. Most of the old unions which sought and obtained recognition became markedly less militant thereafter than they had been before getting government authorization.

In spite of the opposition of old trade-union leaders the government-supported labor organizations spread rapidly. By 1935 most Brazilian unions had official authorization. The chief advantage of government recognition was that employers could not legally refuse to bargain with an organization which possessed it, and this was a powerful incentive to the labor groups to seek legal registration.

The foundations for a social security system were also laid by Vargas during the early years of his administration. Funds were established to cover various groups of workers—industrial workers, white-collar employees, seafarers, land transport workers, etc.—and sizable taxes were levied on both workers and employers to help finance these. The government was also supposed to contribute its share to the resources of these funds, but neither under Vargas nor under his successors was the government faithful to its obligations toward the social security system.

During his first four years in office Vargas ruled as a virtual dictator. He was Provisional President, and there was no congress. He appointed "interventors" to run the several states in place of elected governors. Getulio legislated by decree on the Federal level, and his interventors did the same in the states.

A signal of warning against the one-man rule of Vargas was the short-lived São Paulo War in the middle of 1932. Although Vargas had had enthusiastic supporters in São Paulo at the time he took power, the feeling soon became general among the Paulistas that he was slighting their state's interests as well as seeking to perpetuate himself in office. Although the 1932 war was officially an attempt at secession by the state of São Paulo, its principal slogan was a demand for a return to constitutional government.

Soon after the Paulista revolt was suppressed, Vargas took steps toward reestablishing a constitutional regime. Elections were called for a constituent assembly. This group met during several months of 1934 and drew up a constitution along the lines established in the Mexican Constitution of 1917; that is, considerable social and labor legislation was written into it. At the same time a novel experiment in functional representation was provided for when it was decided that some of the republic's senators should be chosen by employers, workers' organizations, and other interest groups rather than by the general electorate. Soon after the convention Vargas was chosen as the first president under the new constitution.

For three years Vargas governed as a more or less democratic chief executive, continuing most of the policies which he had inaugurated during his period as provisional president. However, there was an increasing degree of disillusionment among many of those who had supported him in the 1930 Revolution, particularly among the workers and left-wing politicians.

The discontent against Vargas reached a climax in November, 1935, when an attempt was made to overthrow the Vargas regime violently. Fighting occurred between dissident soldiers and civilians on the one hand and troops loyal to the government on the other, in

Rio de Janeiro, Pernambuco, and a few other cities. This revolt was organized by the National Liberation Alliance, which had been established a year earlier as a species of Popular Front. A heterogeneous group of small labor and socialist parties, some of the old Tenentes, and the Communist Party of Brazil made up the NLA. Its prestige had been greatly increased by the return from Russia—where he had resided for four years—of Luiz Carlos Prestes, leader of the famous Prestes Column of the 1920's and by now a full-fledged Communist. Prestes assumed the leadership of the Communist Party immediately upon his return to Brazil. He was a man with an almost mythical reputation because of his exploits in the Prestes Column and was popularly known as "the Cavalier of Hope." He had refused to support the 1930 Revolution, and after considerable wooing by both Stalinist and Trotskyite Communists, joined the former group. In 1930 he went to Russia, where he worked as an engineer and participated in Communist International planning and direction of the Communist parties of Latin America.

Prestes was the president of the National Liberation Alliance, and the rebels of November, 1935, proclaimed him president of Brazil. However, with the quick defeat of the uprising he went into hiding and was not captured by the police until January, 1936. After a spectacular trial he was sentenced to a long term in jail and remained behind bars for over nine years.

Meanwhile Getulio Vargas continued to be president of Brazil. During the latter months of 1937 an election was in progress to choose a successor to Getulio. Officially he backed one of the candidates, José Americo de Almeida, a well known writer. However, Vargas was unhappy about the prospect of having to give up the presidency. Furthermore, his government was increasingly menaced by a growing fascist organization, with German, Italian, and Portuguese connections, known as Acão Integralista, and led by Plinio Salgado. Although Vargas had accepted Integralista support in the fight against the National Liberation Alliance, the increasingly aggressive attitude of the fascist group was a growing preoccupation of Getulio and his associates.

Finally, in November, 1935, Vargas solved the election question and the Integralista problem by one stroke. He suspended the 1934 constitution, canceled the election, and announced that he was establishing a New State (Estado Novo) patterned after the corporate regimes of fascist Italy and Portugal. At the same time he outlawed the Acão Integralista, arrested most of its leaders, and deported Plinio Salgado to Portugal, where he remained until 1945.

What Vargas' coup of November, 1937, established was his own personal dictatorship. However, he adorned this dictatorship with all the trappings of the fascism which was then so popular and seemed to be "the wave of the future." Getulio was always one to ride the wave which seemed most likely to keep him afloat and at the head of the government.

The Estado Novo provided, on paper at least, for complete reorganization of Brazil's economy and government. All workers and all employers were to be brought under the jurisdiction of *sindicatos*, which were to be authorized by the Ministry of Industry, Commerce and Labor, and which were to conform to an elaborate pattern to be established by the Ministry. Above these *sindicatos*, organized by economic category and municipality, were to be federations, established on a state-wide level, and bringing together municipal *sindicatos* of workers and employers respectively of a similar branch of economic activity. On the national level were to be established a series of confederations to cover the workers and employers respectively in manufacturing, commerce, land transport, sea and river transport, the free professions, and banking and insurance.

Theoretically, at least, these organizations were to have extensive control over the economy and at the same time were to serve as a basis for the political government. However, Getulio never got around to establishing the political side of the Estado Novo framework and was contented with arrogating to himself full executive and legislative powers. On the economic side the Estado Novo framework was only partially established.

The Estado Novo was most effective in its control over the workers. All workers had to pay one day's wage a year (known as the *imposto sindical*, or trade-union tax) to the *sindicato* system. The *sindicatos* and federations were converted into largely social-welfare organizations. In order to gain recognition from the government a labor union had to have an extensive program of medical and dental aid for its members, educational activities on their behalf, and other welfare features. These were paid for by the *imposto sindical*.

What collective bargaining had existed before the installation of the Estado Novo was destroyed. In its place Vargas erected a structure of labor courts. The lowest level of these tribunals, known as the Boards of Conciliation, handled day-to-day grievances of the workers. They were an effective safety valve for workers' protests and problems, and generally tended to give the workers the benefit of the doubt.

The second level of labor courts, the Regional Labor Tribunals, which were established generally on a state-wide jurisdiction, had two basic functions. The first was to handle appeals from the decisions of the local Conciliation Boards. The second was to deal with demands put forward by unions for wage increases and other improvements in working conditions. Although these demands were relatively rare so long as the Estado Novo existed, they tended to centralize the determination of working conditions in the hands of the State instead of leaving them to the free negotiation of workers' and employers' representatives.

The highest body in the labor court system was the Superior Labor Tribunal located in Rio de Janeiro. It handled principally appeals from the Regional Tribunals, which could be made only on points of interpretation of the law and constitution, though it also occasionally dealt with demands made by national labor groups on nation-wide employers' organizations.

This system established under the Estado Novo still exists in Brazil. The great majority of workers' grievances are still handled through the Conciliation Boards, although some of the more independent unions have developed since 1945 a system of processing grievances in direct negotiation with the employers. The majority of demands by unions for wage increases and other improvements are still made to the Regional Labor Tribunals instead of directly to the employers concerned, although here too there has been some modification of the Estado Novo system and some direct collective bargaining.

One major change has occurred in the trade-union situation since the end of the Estado Novo, although it is a mere fulfillment of the system as it was originally outlined in 1937. This has been the creation of four large national labor confederations covering industrial workers, commercial employees, land transport workers, and banking and insurance workers. No such confederations had been set up under the Estado Novo, though they were provided for in the corporate state framework decreed by Vargas.

On the employers' side the Estado Novo framework remained largely incomplete by 1945. The employers were very reluctant to join the *sindicatos* established for them under the Estado Novo because they resented the government interference in these organizations. Generally Vargas did not force them to join.

On a state-wide level the employers' *sindicatos* were brought together on a basis different from that provided for in the laws of the New State. Instead of forming federations of *sindicatos* of specific industries or branches of trade or transportation, the employers' groups generally formed only two state-wide federations in each state—one of industrial employers and the other of commercial employers. In spite of the evident violation of the law involved in this, these organizations were given recognition by the Ministry of Industry, Commerce and Labor.

While reducing the labor movement to harmless proportions Vargas sought eagerly to win the favor of the rank-and-file workers. In constant speeches he drove home the idea that he was the greatest protector of the workers. He adopted the title "Father of the Poor," and took some steps to give concrete expression to his supposed concern for the welfare of the wage- and salary-earning masses.

In 1941 Vargas issued the first minimum-wage decree establishing basic wages in different parts of the country. These wage minima have been raised half a dozen times since they were first enacted, but the system remains. Vargas also further elaborated on the social security system which he had established earlier. Laws for the protection of the workers on their jobs and giving them other benefits were enacted, so that Brazil has today one of the most complicated systems of labor legislation to be found anywhere in the world. Finally Vargas started a modest housing program.

While appealing to the workers on the basis of a social program, he also appealed to their nationalism. He constantly attacked in speeches "foreign interests" which allegedly were hindering the development of the Brazilian economy. More effective than speeches as a nationalist measure was Vargas' move to provide the country with a more diversified economy. The principal aspect of this program was the establishment of a basic iron and steel industry at Volta

Redonda in the State of Rio de Janeiro, about seventy-five miles from the national capital. This plant was built during World War II with the aid of loans from the United States Export-Import Bank, and was opened shortly after the conclusion of the world conflict. It was the first step in providing Brazil with a heavy industry upon which the development of a broad-based economy could be undertaken.

While appealing to the workers and stimulating the diversification of Brazil's economy Getulio Vargas was presiding over a rigid personal dictatorship. All political parties were outlawed with the institution of the Estado Novo. The press was rigidly censored, and Vargas followed the policy of having the government forcibly buy into many of the country's most important newspapers. There were rigid controls on travel within Brazil, and to go from one city to another one needed what amounted to an internal passport. Enemies of the regime were jailed, exiled, or forced into silence between 1937 and 1944.

However, although maintaining a totalitarian-like dictatorship at home, Vargas bent with the international political winds. While in the late 1930's he had expressed great admiration for the fascist powers of Europe and had entered into extensive trade relations—ultimately to Brazil's disadvantage—with Nazi Germany, Vargas was a subtle enough politician to shift his ground when it appeared wise to do so.

At one point Getulio tried to be on both sides of the fence at once. Early in 1942 there occurred an incident which showed a good deal about the opportunism of the man. Getulio delivered a speech on international affairs which was, to put it mildly, not unfriendly to the Axis, who at that time seemed to be dominant in Europe and seemed possibly to be on the road to world supremacy. However, the English version of this speech which was given to the foreign press representatives had a quite different tone and made out the Brazilian President as a strong friend of the anti-Axis powers, particularly of the United States.

However, once the United States entered World War II Vargas shifted definitely to the side of the Allies. A few months after Pearl Harbor, Brazil officially declared war on Germany, Italy, and Japan, using as an excuse the sinking of several Brazilian ships off the country's northeast coast. Subsequently Brazil was the only Latin American country to contribute troops to the fighting in Europe.

At the same time Vargas took energetic measures to curb the dangers represented by the presence of large colonies of Axis nationals, particularly Germans and Japanese, in the southern part of the country. It was forbidden to speak anything but Portuguese on the streets, and all signs had to be in that language. Young men of the German and Japanese parts of the country were drafted into the army and were sent to remote parts of the nation for training, not being released until they could speak, read, and write Portuguese. Attempts were made to colonize Brazilians in the regions which were predominantly Japanese and German.

Meanwhile the participation of Brazil in World War II was widely popular. The activities of the Brazilian troops on the Italian front were spectacularly reported by the press and avidly read by the public. From the Brazilian newspapers it almost appeared as if Brazilian soldiers were driving the Nazis up the Italian boot by their own efforts, unaided by the Americans, British, and other soldiers who were participating in the campaign.

Although it solidified his position in power so long as the war continued, Vargas' decision to take an active part on the side of the Allies brought what were for him unfortunate repercussions. In Brazil, as elsewhere, the struggle against the Nazis was pictured in terms of a fight for democracy against tyranny. As a result the Brazilians began to ask themselves and their ruler with increasing frequency and insistence why, if democracy was being fought for on the battlefields of Europe, it wasn't a good idea for Brazil too.

Pressure for a relaxation of the dictatorship became particularly great in the last half of 1944, when Allied victory in the war had become a certainty. Those opposed to the regime formed a broad organization known as the União Democrática Nacional (UDN) (National Democratic Union), which included people as diverse as old-line pre-Vargas politicians, landholders, intellectuals, and the Communists, and was headed by General Eduardo Gomes. Gomes was one of the old Tenentes who had stayed in the armed forces, had organized the Brazilian Air Force, and had been commander of the Northeastern military region, where the United States had several airfields, during the war.

As a result of the pressure from the UDN and other quarters Vargas slowly began to relax the reins of dictatorship. Late in 1944 he permitted real elections in the trade unions for the first time since 1937. The censorship of the press was reduced. An end was put to the internal-passport system. Finally Vargas promised that presidential elections would be held at the end of 1945, and that he would not be a candidate for reelection.

During the first months of 1945 political activity mounted. In May a general political amnesty was declared, and all political prisoners, some of whom had been in jail for a decade, were released. The UDN put forth General Eduardo Gomes as its candidate for the presidency and reorganized as a political party. Numerous other political groups suddenly made their appearance.

Luiz Carlos Prestes, leader of the Communist Party, was among those released in the May, 1945, amnesty. At his first public appearance after coming out of jail, before 100,000 people in the Vasco da Gama Stadium in Rio de Janeiro, Prestes shocked his listeners by saying that the Communist Party was going to support Vargas, that it thought he should stay in office until after a new constitution had been written, and that there was no hurry about presidential elections. These statements were particularly surprising in view of the fact that Vargas had virtually destroyed the Communist Party, had kept Prestes in jail for nine years, and had turned his German-born wife over to the Nazis. Of course, there was a widely held suspicion that Vargas and Prestes had made a "deal" before Prestes' release from jail, although this was denied by both men. In any case, Vargas gave the Communists a completely free hand for the rest of the time he remained in office.

However, Vargas by no means relied only on the Communists to secure his continued tenure in office. Two political parties were organized under his inspiration, the Partido Social Democrático (PSD) and the Partido Trabalhista Brasileiro (PTB). They remain today two of the country's principal political organizations.

The Partido Social Democratico rallied the more conservative supporters of the Vargas regime, the *tiburoes* or sharks, as they are popularly called. Business elements allied with Getulio formed one segment of the PSD. Another consisted of a series of local political bosses who had enjoyed Vargas' favor for a number of years. The local boss had always been a feature of Brazilian politics, and before the time of Vargas he was likely to be the biggest landholder of a district or someone closely associated with him. Most of these old bosses were swept aside by Getulio, but he put in their place people who were closely dependent upon the Federal government and its patronage and who felt a considerable degree of loyalty to Getulio Vargas. It was these people who formed the backbone of the PSD in the rural and semirural areas.

The Partido Trabalhista Brasileiro, on the other hand, was organized by the top officials of the labor side of the Ministry of Industry, Commerce and Labor, led by José Segadas Vianna, Director General of Labor. Other leading figures were drawn from among the officials of the trade unions which had been established under the Estado Novo. The PTB lacked any very definite ideology, its principal stock in trade being Getulio Vargas, but it soon came to be looked upon by a majority of the country's urban workers as their particular spokesman.

The PTB undoubtedly had two basic purposes. First, it was intended to be a personal vehicle for President Vargas. In the second place, it was intended as a counterweight to the growing influence of the Communists among the workers. The Communists increased by leaps and bounds. Within a year and a half of Prestes' release from prison the party was claiming 150,000 members, whereas in May, 1945, it had consisted of no more than a few hundred. It made considerable inroads into the lower echelons of the trade-union movement and rallied many of those workers who were sick and tired of the Vargas regime. In the 1945–47 period the Communist Party of Brazil was more a pro-Prestes and an anti-Vargas party than it was an orthodox Communist Party, though in subsequent years its degree of orthodoxy considerably increased.

The trade unions had become unusually active as the result of the loosening of the dictatorship. There was a wave of strikes throughout 1945—something which had been unknown for eight years—and many wage increases were won. Congresses of unions were held in several states, and states-wide union organizations were established. Finally a provisional national trade-union group, the Movimento da Unificacão dos Trabalhadores (Movement of Workers Unity) was established. It was largely under Communist leadership, although

Vargas supporters and independent elements were also active in it.

Meanwhile preparations for the December, 1945, presidential election were under way. Officially the PSD nominated General Eurico Dutra, a close military associate of Vargas, as its candidate, against UDN's General Eduardo Gomes. And officially Getulio Vargas supported the candidacy of General Dutra. However, there was considerable doubt as to whether Vargas wanted an election to be held at all. It is certain that the idea of giving up the presidency was unpalatable to Vargas. For almost a year after he promised elections he maneuvered energetically to try to negate this promise. The maneuvers ultimately brought about his first ouster from the presidency.

Early in October, 1945, United States Ambassador Adolf Berle made a speech before a group of United States businessmen in Brazil in which he congratulated Brazil on having taken the democratic road, and expressed his assurance that the election would be held in December as scheduled. Some light was thrown on President Vargas' thinking by his reaction to Berle's speech, which seemed to be one of praise for him and his regime. Vargas denounced Berle's discourse as "interference in the internal affairs of Brazil," and implied that it was none of Berle's or the United States' business whether or not elections were held.

A few weeks later Vargas began one of those shiftings of personnel which were always one of the keys to his manner of conducting the government. Among others, he dismissed João Alberto, old Tenente and long-time associate of Vargas, as Chief of the Federal District Police, and replaced him with his own brother, Benjamin Vargas.

The Army's response to this move by the President was immediate. They felt that the appointment of Benjamin Vargas was intended to pave the way for the cancellation of the scheduled elections and the perpetuation of Getulio in power. Moving quickly, the Army surrounded the presidential palace with tanks and soldiers, and on the early morning of October 25 forced Vargas to resign.

The new provisional government, headed by the Chief Justice of the Supreme Court, immediately announced that the presidential and congressional elections would be held as planned, and that, in addition, those to be elected to congress as senators and deputies would first organize a constituent assembly to draw up a new constitution, after which they would divide into their respective houses. After a few days of suspension of constitutional guarantees, full freedom of press, speech, and assembly were restored, and the electoral campaign began in earnest.

There were by then three candidates. The Communists quickly nominated an engineer who had once been Vargas' public works chief, Yeddo Fiuza, as their candidate. They had no hope of electing him, but they wanted to test their national vote-getting power.

Meanwhile Getulio Vargas retired to his farm in the State of Rio Grande do Sul, where he was left in peace by the new regime. For some time he did not speak out concerning the election. However, he headed the Partido Trabalhista ticket in several states as a candidate for senator. Finally he came out shortly before the election and endorsed the PSD candidate, General Dutra, in spite of the fact that Dutra had been one of those involved in his ouster. Vargas' endorsement was undoubtedly responsible for Dutra's victory.

For more than three years thereafter Getulio Vargas stayed in the background. Although he was senator for his native state, elected on the PTB ticket, he seldom attended meetings of the upper house and did not participate at all in the deliberations of the constituent assembly.

However, in spite of Vargas' reticence his power remained great. The vast majority of the workers were still loyal to him, while most of the rest were followers of Luiz Carlos Prestes. With the eclipse of the Communist Party after its legal banishment early in 1947 the prestige of Vargas rose even higher.

As time for the 1950 election approached there was little doubt that Getulio Vargas would again be a candidate. He had little trouble getting the nomination of the Partido Trabalhista, and the great majority of the country's most important trade-union leaders endorsed his candidacy, even though to do so was to defy the powerful Ministry of Labor. Vargas was backed also by the Communists as the least of the available evils from their point of view.

Against Vargas there were two candidates. The Partido Social Democrático, which had been dominated by Dutra during most of his administration, nominated Christiano Machado, a relative unknown. The União Democrática Nacional once again put up the name of General Eduardo Gomes. The race was a hot one.

During the campaign Vargas played both of his customary themes —his love for the workers and his desire to help them and Brazilian nationalism. He attacked the policies of the United States and implied that the Dutra government had been too subservient to that country. He promised that he would come to grips with the problem of inflation, which was getting increasingly severe and was quickly eating up whatever wage increases the workers were able to achieve. He also promised to reestablish trade-union freedom and to allow new trade-union elections, which had been suspended by the Dutra regime since 1947.

To no one's great surprise, Getulio Vargas was once again elected president of Brazil. He began his second period in office on a wave of popular enthusiasm. Great hopes had been aroused among the workers during the presidential campaign, and his *mistica* (that indefinable Latin quality which is prestige but more than prestige) was higher than it had ever been before or was ever to be again during his lifetime.

However, Vargas' second period in office was at best only a partial success. He was unable to take any real measures against inflation, which became worse rather than better after he assumed office. The corruption which had always characterized his regime reached unprecedented heights. Getulio seemed to give little leadership to the government or to the nation.

Various explanations have been offered for Vargas' behavior during his second administration. Perhaps his weakness came from the fact that he was determined to live down his reputation as a dictator and to preside over a democratic government but really didn't know how to do so. Perhaps it was due to the fact that he was getting old and had lost his grip. Perhaps it was due to the fact that he didn't realize that with a free press and freedom of speech and with a functioning congress, mere demagoguery was not a sufficient program to meet the needs of the nation.

Whatever his weakness during his second period in office, Vargas remained a skillful politician. He succeeded in enticing into his cabinet representatives of the opposition União Democrática Nacional, whose main purpose for existence, presumably, was opposition to Getulio Vargas. He played one politician off against another in a skillful manner. He virtually never held cabinet meetings where problems could be discussed and there could be an exchange of views. Rather he met individually with his ministers, keeping complete control of affairs in his own hands.

There was some indication during this period that Vargas was grooming a successor in the person of João Goulart. From Vargas' home state, this young man had been known by Vargas since childhood. Goulart was suddenly made Minister of Labor early in 1953. The new minister announced his intention of bringing about a complete housecleaning in the trade unions, and it became obvious that he was building up a personal political machine among the leaders of various union groups. Goulart was widely suspected of provoking strikes among various groups of workers so that he could step in and "settle" them to the advantage of labor, and thus win renown and political support. Getulio looked on benignly through all this.

However, the leaders of the armed forces did not take such a patronizing attitude toward the activities of João Goulart. They felt that he was "undermining law and order" and that he was dangerous. They undoubtedly also suspected that Vargas was trying to pass his own mantle on to his young protégé. After something more than a year the leaders of the armed forces brought sufficient pressure upon President Vargas that Goulart was forced to resign.

Meanwhile Brazilian nationalism was growing apace. Vargas had greatly roused nationalistic passions during his 1950 presidential campaign, and the principal question around which these passions swirled during the next few years was that of the exploitation of the country's oil resources. He had suggested that this should be entrusted to a firm owned and controlled by Brazilians and, presumably, by the Brazilian government. Once in office, Vargas was not so insistent upon this, but the campaign to establish such a firm continued anyway. A bill was introduced in congress to establish Petroleos Brasileiros (Petrobras), a firm in which the Brazilian government would have a majority of the stock, though private Brazilians could also be part owners. After a lengthy discussion and an intensive campaign in press and tribune this bill was passed and was approved by Vargas.

The Vargas administration of the 1950's was very active in the general field of economic development. It drew up a long-range development program based on an extensive study of the Brazilian economy and its development problems which had been made in the late 1940's by a mixed Brazilian–United States Commission. It established a National Development Bank for the purpose of giving direction to this program. It negotiated an agreement with the United States government for a line of credit for half a billion dollars to pay some of the foreign exchange costs of the development program. This fund was to be administered through the new Development Bank, and individual projects were to be decided upon by a Mixed Brazilian–United States Commission.

Through no fault of Vargas or the Brazilian government this program was tremendously handicapped in 1953 when the Eisenhower administration in the United States decided unilaterally to cancel the loan fund after only $180,000,000 of it had been allocated. This was done on the excuse that an Export-Import Bank loan of $300,000,000 to clear current commercial debts to United States exporters fulfilled the terms of the original half-billion-dollar line of credit. Quite rightly, Brazilian public officials and the Brazilian press felt that the United States had gone back on its word and had thus torpedoed a very hopeful effort to clear up many of the bottlenecks in transportation, electric power, and other fields which were holding back the process of Brazilian economic development.

Insofar as the workers were concerned, Vargas carried out a number of his campaign promises. As soon as he was inaugurated, he ordered the renewal of regular trade-union elections. He ended government intervention in most of the hundreds of unions in which the Dutra government had appointed receivers. He revised the minimum-wage law in 1953. He began a study of the total reorganization of the social security system.

There are some indications that Getulio Vargas was planning some very fundamental reforms in the Brazilian economy and society shortly before his death. The famous sociologist and writer Gilberto Freyre has written that only a few days before Getulio's death he was summoned to the President's office, where Vargas offered him a new post as director of an institute he was about to establish to undertake a program of agrarian reform and colonization of Brazilians and immigrants on lands to be taken from the country's large landowners. However, death cut short whatever plans Vargas may have had in this direction.

Relations between Vargas and the military leaders had been

delicate throughout his second administration. The leaders of the armed forces had not been particularly pleased with Getulio's election in 1950, though since they regarded themselves as the guarantors of the constitution, they saw to it that he was allowed to take office, since there was no doubt about the fact that he had been elected. However, the military leaders kept a close eye on the President throughout his second term. They were determined that he should not be allowed to establish a new dictatorship—if by any chance he had such an intention.

There were several conflicts between Vargas and the military. One of the most important was that which finally resulted in the resignation of Minister of Labor João Goulart. In July, 1954, a new incident arose between the President and the military leaders. Newspaperman Carlos Lacerda, editor of the fiery anti-Vargas newspaper *Tribuna da Imprensa*, was coming home one evening accompanied by Major Rubens Florentino Vaz of the Air Force. As they approached Lacerda's house they were attacked by armed men, and Major Vaz was killed. This event aroused a tremendous scandal, and it was widely felt that the intended victim of the assassins was Carlos Lacerda, at that time the most bitter opponent of the Vargas administration. However, the armed forces, particularly the Air Force, felt that they had been attacked, and they demanded swift capture and punishment of the murderers.

The complicating factor in this situation was the fact that the first clues in the case seemed to lead to the door of Dr. Luthero Vargas, son of the President. Thus Getulio himself became directly involved in the matter, and there were those who said that Luthero was acting with the connivance of his father. This seems highly unlikely, but it created a very embarrassing situation for the President.

This incident brought relations between Vargas and the military chiefs to crisis stage. They already felt that the lack of direction and the ineffectiveness of the Vargas regime, combined with the continued political maneuvering and corruption, was leading to a situation of political and economic chaos, and their suspicions and fears seemed to be borne out by the murder, which some at least interpreted to be the beginning of a campaign of terrorism against those opposed to the regime.

The upshot of this situation was that late in August the top officers of the armed forces waited upon Vargas and gave him what amounted to an ultimatum. They suggested that he take an "extended vacation" until the end of his term, in effect turning the government over to Vice President João Cafe Filho.

For Vargas this demand meant absolute personal disaster. He was now an old man, over seventy, and if he were to be ousted once again, there was little hope that he would ever be able to regain the presidency. Furthermore, Vice President Cafe Filho, whose nomination had been the result of a political deal between Vargas and one of his most important rivals in 1950, was no friend of Vargas or the administration. He was an old-time opponent of Getulio, had been jailed for some time after the 1935 National Liberation Alliance revolt, and could not be expected to keep in office those who had been closely associated with Vargas.

Since the military leaders' demand meant the end of Vargas' political career, he apparently decided to make his exit as spectacular as possible, and in a way which would assure the continuation of his influence long after his physical disappearance from the scene. He committed suicide, leaving behind him a letter emphasizing once again the themes which had been Getulio's stock in trade throughout most of his political career: love for the workers and concern for their interests, and Brazilian nationalism. The letter, which came to light right after his body was discovered, read as follows:

Once more the forces and interests against the people are newly coordinated and raised against me. They do not accuse me, they insult me; they do not fight me, they slander me and give me no right of defense. They need to drown my voice and halt my actions so that I no longer continue to defend, as I always have defended, the people and principally the humble.

I follow the destiny that is imposed on me. After years of domination and looting by international economic and financial groups, I made myself chief of an unconquerable revolution. I began the work of liberation and I instituted a regime of social liberty. I had to resign. I returned to govern on the arms of the people.

A subterranean campaign of international groups joined with national groups revolting against the regime of workers' guarantees. The law of excess profits was stopped in Congress. Hatreds were unchained against the justice of a revision of minimum wages.

I wished to create national liberty by developing our riches through Petrobras, and a wave of sedition clouded its beginnings. Electrobras was hindered almost to despair. They do not wish the workers to be free. They do not wish the people to be independent.

I assumed the Government during an inflationary spiral that was destroying the value of work. Profits of foreign enterprises reached 500 per cent yearly. In declarations of goods that we import there existed frauds of more than $100,000,000.

I saw the coffee crisis increase the value of our principal product. We attempted to defend its price and the reply was a violent pressure upon our economy to the point of being obliged to surrender.

I have fought month to month, day to day, hour to hour, resisting a constant aggression, unceasingly bearing it all in silence, forgetting all and renouncing myself to defend the people that now fall abandoned. I cannot give you more than my blood. If the birds of prey wish the blood of anybody, they wish to continue sucking that of the Brazilian people.

I offer my life in the holocaust. I choose this means to be with you always. When they humiliate you, you will feel my soul suffering at your side. When hunger beats at your door, you will feel in your chests the energy for the fight for yourselves and your children. When they humiliate you, you will feel in my grief the force for reaction.

My sacrifice will maintain you united, and my name will be your battle flag. Each drop of my blood will be an immortal call to your conscience and will maintain a holy vibration for resistance.

To hatred, I respond with pardon. And to those who think they have defeated me, I reply with my victory. I was the slave of the people and today I free myself for eternal life. But this people to which I was a slave no longer will be a slave to anyone. My sacrifice will remain forever in your soul, and my blood will be the price of your ransom.

I fought against the looting of Brazil, I fought against the looting of the people. I have fought bare-breasted. The hatred, infamy and calumny did not beat down my spirit. I gave you my life. Now I offer my death. Nothing remains. Serenely I take the first step on the road to eternity and I leave life to enter history.

There are those who have argued that this epistle was not actually written by Getulio Vargas. However, it seems highly probable to this writer that he was its author, and whatever strangeness there may have been in its grammar and means of expression—arguments used to "prove" that Getulio did not write it—can be attributed to the emotional state in which Vargas must have been when he was composing it.

It seems to us that Vargas was acting characteristically in leaving a letter such as this as his political testament. The dominating theme in his political career was the love of power, and this, combined with a certain sardonic trait in Getulio's character, make this letter quite understandable. Ousted from power for the last time, Vargas was going to make sure that his influence would continue to be felt even from the tomb. He committed a final act of vengeance against his opponents. By this letter he made sure that though Vargas could rule no longer, Vargasism would continue as a mighty power in the country—and as subsequent events proved, the governing power in the country—long after his death.

With Vargas' death, Vice President João Filho took over immediately, with the support of the armed forces. He carried out a widespread purge of Vargas' adherents and promised to put an end to Vargas' influence on the country's political life. In October, 1955, when Vargas' unexpired term was drawing to an end, Cafe Filho presided over an election to choose his successor.

There were four candidates in the 1955 election. The forces of Vargasism were represented by Juscelino Kubitschek of the Social Democratic Party, who had as his running mate João Goulart, who succeeded Vargas as leader of the Partido Trabalhista Brasileiro. Thus the two parties which Vargas had been instrumental in founding joined hands once again after his death.

The principal rival of Kubitschek was General Juarez Tavora, backed by the União Democratica Nacional, the Brazilian Socialist Party and the Christian Democratic Party. Tavora was an old Tenente who had spent most of his career in the Army (and had to take a leave of absence to run for the presidency). He was noted as a man of high moral character, had long been a critic of the Vargas regime, and promised a clean sweep if he were elected to the presidency.

The other two nominees were Adhemar de Barros, ex-governor of São Paulo, candidate of his own Partido Social Progresista, and Plinio Salgado, nominee of the Integralistas, who had reorganized after the end of the Estado Novo as the Partido da Representacão

Popular. However, the real struggle was between Kubitschek and Tavora.

The campaign was noisy and vituperative. It was clear that it was a struggle between the heirs of Getulio Vargas and his traditional opponents. The atmosphere was electric, and rumors were widespread that Juarez Tavora was the chosen candidate of the armed forces leaders who had provoked Vargas' suicide, and that if he were defeated, Kubitschek would not be allowed to take office.

Kubitschek and Goulart won, nonetheless, by an ample margin. Thereafter rumors continued to circulate that President João Cafe Filho was maneuvering to prevent the inauguration of the victors. The situation was finally cleared up on November 11, when the majority of the armed forces leaders, under the direction of Minister of Defense Henrique Teixeira Lott, deposed President Cafe Filho, announcing that they were doing so to prevent any attempt to thwart the processes of constitutional government. Although the armed forces leadership was far from united behind this move, General Lott's coup was successful, and after some confusion Senate President Neuru Ramos took over for the last two and a half months of the late Getulio Vargas' term.

On January 28, 1956, Kubitschek was inaugurated as president of the republic. His regime was to a considerable degree a continuation of the Vargas administration. Many of the same faces were seen in public offices, and most of the regime's civilian support came from those who had been the adherents of the late president. Kubitschek's tenure in office was assured by the support of the large majority of the leaders of the armed forces.

Thus Vargas continued to be a force to be reckoned with even after he had passed on—as he had foreseen that he would. The Vargas era lasted for another presidential term, until the inauguration of President Janio Quadros at the end of January, 1961. Vargas still remains the idol of a considerable part of the humble folk of the nation, as was shown by the fact that the Getulista candidate for vice president was reelected in 1960, in spite of large majority for anti-Getulio Quadros for the presidency.

There is no doubt about Getulio Vargas' impact on the history of Brazil, the largest of the Latin American nations and the only one which seems destined within the foreseeable future to become one of the world's major powers. Under his leadership political power was transferred once and for all from the landholding aristocracy, which had been dominant from the fall of the empire in 1889 until the Revolution of 1930, to the urban middle and lower classes. During his long period of preponderance in the nation's political life Brazil took giant steps in the direction of industrialization and diversification of its economy with the sympathy and help of the government. Under Vargas the urban working classes, though perhaps many of them were little better off economically than they had been before, became conscious as they had never been before of being citizens and participants in the active life of the republic.

Brazilians in general became aware of their importance as a nation and struck off on original paths not only in matters of constitutional law and government but also in the fields of economics, literature, architecture, music, and general culture. Particularly during the last decade of Vargas' life they lost the feeling of inferiority vis-à-vis the nations of Europe and the United States which had characterized them throughout their history as a politically independent nation.

Certainly all these developments did not conform to any well laid plan which Vargas had followed as a ruler. He was little interested in long-range plans and philosophical problems, and perhaps was not himself fully aware of the tremendous changes over which he was presiding. He was first and foremost a practical politician whose principal preoccupation was maintaining himself in office or regaining it once he had lost power. Nonetheless, Vargas, unwittingly or no, had been instrumental in bringing about a fundamental transformation of his nation, and in the process of doing so had become a *caudilho* and almost a folk hero.

No one seemed more unlikely to be a *caudilho* than Getulio Vargas. He was a very short man who wore glasses and had a professorial countenance. He had a reputation for being a dour man, with little of the gaiety and effervescence characteristic of the average Brazilian. His sense of humor, such as it was, was sardonic. Certainly many better and more persuasive orators than Vargas were active in Brazilian politics during the period in which they were dominated by Getulio. Yet it was he, not they, who captured the imagination of great masses of the Brazilian people.

His strongest points as a politician were certainly his ability to maneuver and his opportunism. Apparently having no very firmly held political convictions himself, he had a remarkable ability to bend with the prevailing winds and almost always to outmaneuver his opponents and rivals. However, the tragic nature of his death would seem to indicate that the methods which he had traditionally used and of which he was a past master no longer served to rule a country of the kind which Brazil had become. Although his talents served him admirably to preside over a period of rapid transition, once this transition had been achieved and the Brazilian economy and government were beginning to take on a new complexity and to require new technical and political skills, Vargas lost control of the situation.

Juan Domingo Perón and "the New Argentina"

Early on the morning of October 16, 1945, an inmate was taken from his cell in the military prison on the island of Martín García, in the middle of the Rio de la Plata estuary. He was carried in a small boat to the outskirts of the Argentine capital city of Buenos Aires to a military hospital. He remained there until the late afternoon, when he was whisked to the Casa Rosada, the presidential palace. A few moments later he stepped out on the balcony of the palace in company of the President. When he appeared, a throaty shout went up from the crowd of 100,000 people in the Plaza de Mayo below. Finally the man raised his hand for silence, and when the crowd had quieted down, his first words were, "I am back! We have won!"

The man was Colonel Juan Domingo Perón. The incident was his return to power after a short period of ostracism and disgrace. It marked the beginning of a ten-year dictatorship of a man who was fundamentally to alter the history of Argentina.

Perón was an accidental social revolutionist. Certainly when he and other top officers of the Argentine Army overthrew President Ramón S. Castillo on June 4, 1943, they had no intention of carrying out any fundamental changes in the Argentine economy and society. Their insurrection was prompted by the prospect of the election of a new president later in 1943 who would be pro-British in World War II then in progress. The top military leaders favored the Axis. However, in spite of their intentions in overthrowing President Castillo, the Argentine Army leaders, Perón among them, paved the way for very far-reaching changes in the institutions of Argentine society.

The basic characteristics of the Argentine society and economy of 1943 had been established during the latter half of the nineteenth century. Even before that, during the ruthless and bloody dictator-

246

ship of Juan Manuel Rosas between 1838 and 1852, most of the arable land of the Argentine pampas had been divided among retainers and friends of the dictator. A large landholding system thus became an integral part of the Argentine economy.

Rosas was overthrown in 1852, and for the next sixty-four years the government of the republic was in the hands of the large landowners. The regimes of this period encouraged the development of grain growing and grazing on the great plains of central Argentina. The pampas were enclosed by barbed wire, the scrawny breed of native cattle, descended from those imported by the Spaniards in colonial days, was crossed with select bulls from Great Britain, until Argentine cattle were rated among the world's best. Similar improvements were made in the corn and wheat growing in the pampas.

Argentina thus developed into one of the principal suppliers of grain and meat to Great Britain and other parts of Western Europe. In order to get these products to the ports of Buenos Aires and Rosario, an extensive rail network was developed by British investors. In order to cultivate the great areas in the center of the country, hundreds of thousands of immigrants entered the country from Spain, Italy, and other nations of Europe. Buenos Aires and Rosario, the nation's principal ports, became large cities, and the beginnings of manufacturing arose to serve some of the needs of the country's consumers, provide some of the metal products needed in the pampas, and some of the equipment for the nation's railroads.

Some of the leaders of the Conservative Party governments which ruled Argentina during this period of more than half a century were statesmen of continental renown. Such a one was President Domingo Fausto Sarmiento, a famous writer, the founder of the nation's system of public education, friend of Horace Mann, and ardent admirer of the United States. Such, too, was President Roque Saenz Pena, who sponsored a law providing for the secret ballot.

The introduction of the secret ballot brought the rule of the landowners' Conservative Party to an end. In 1916 Hipólito Irigoyen, head of the Radical Party, which had the support of the rural and urban middle classes, and of a large part of the urban working class, was elected president. However, in the following fourteen years during which the Radicals were in power the economy and social structure of Argentina changed very little. During Irigoyen's administration he was hamstrung by a congress controlled by the Conservatives. His successor, Marcelo T. de Alvear, though a Radical, was virtually as conservative as the Conservatives and was not sympathetic to any extensive program of reforms.

The period of Radical rule was brought to an abrupt end on September 6, 1930, when Hipólito Irigoyen, who had been reelected in 1928, was overthrown by an Army *coup d'état* supported by the Conservative Party and by small dissident groups of Radicals and Socialists. From 1930 to 1943 Argentina was governed by a series of dictatorships and semidictatorships dominated by the Conservatives and supported by the military. Elections outside the city of Buenos Aires were frequently a farce, and usually when the opposition won control of a province the Federal government found an excuse to "intervene" and oust its elected officials.

The Conservative regimes of 1930–43 were openly favorable to the landowning class and hostile to industrialization and to the interests of the middle and working classes. They signed agreements with the British to keep tariffs low and favored importation of manufactured goods from Great Britain. They refused to enact labor legislation which was being clamored for by the unions. They favored European investors in Argentina, even at the expense of native Argentine capitalist interests. Thus, the rule of the landlord class over the rest of the country was maintained through force and fraud and against the wishes of the great majority of the population. This situation continued until the overthrow of the last of the Conservative presidents, Ramón S. Castillo, on June 4, 1943.

However, the generals and colonels who ousted Castillo soon found that they too were exceedingly unpopular among the civilians. Traditional civilian hostility toward the intervention of the military in politics was intensified by the Army government's dissolution of Congress, its ousting of officials of some of the most important trade unions, and its severe censorship of the press. Virtually all civilians were united against the new regime. This opposition threatened the stability of the military government and made very difficult the process of "legitimatizing" the Army regime.

As a result Colonel Juan Perón, who at that time was secretary to the Minister of War, joined a number of his close associates to seek out civilian backing for the regime. They first turned to the industrialist class, which had been largely in opposition to the Castillo administration. However, the industrialists, who were generally supporters of the Radical Party, felt that as soon as new elections were called, the Radical Party would be certain to return to power, and there was no sense in compromising its prospective victory by a premature agreement with the military men.

Some of Perón's close associates had been put in charge of trade unions when the military regime ousted the elected leadership of some of the principal labor organizations. So Perón and his friends turned to the labor movement when they were rebuffed by the industrialists. After negotiation between some of the military men and those trade-union leaders who were willing to listen, the army officers agreed to try to support some of the aspirations of the labor movement, and the trade-unionists agreed to take a wait-and-see attitude toward the military regime.

Colonel Perón was put in charge of a new Secretariat of Labor and Social Welfare which was given virtually cabinet rank. In this position he spent the next two years seeking to weld the labor movement into a political machine to suport the regime and to back his own personal ambitions. During much of this period Perón also held the positions of Minister of War and Vice President of the Republic as well as Secretary of Labor.

Perón's campaign was carried on on various fronts. He encouraged the workers to organize, giving his personal support to many of these attempts, including that of the packing-house workers and that of the sugar plantation and refinery workers, who had never previously been able successfully to form unions. He also forced employers to accept collective agreements favorable to the unions, granting sizable wage increases and other benefits. Perón also legislated by decree a series of labor and social laws, including the establishment of social security funds for most of the country's wage and salary workers, including those employed in agriculture.

The upshot of all this activity was that Perón won the confidence and support of the majority of the members of the rapidly increasing trade-union movement. This was an extraordinary development in the light of the traditional distrust of the trade-union movement for the military. However, it has various explanations. First, the regime of which Perón was one of the principal members was the first since the Irigoyen administration which had evidenced any concern for the interests of the workers, and the only one in the nation's history which had done anything significant on their behalf. There is no doubt that Perón as Secretary of Labor provided many material benefits for the urban and agricultural workers of Argentina, and there was a feeling of gratefulness on the part of many of those who were thus benefited.

However, an even more fundamental explanation for Perón's ability to win and keep the loyalty of the majority of Argentine workers was the fact that he gave them a feeling of self-esteem and importance which they had never felt before. He made them lose the feeling of inferiority and servility which many workers had felt toward their employers. He made them feel not only that they were important, but that they were the most important group in the community. He made them feel a part of the civic life of the nation in a way which they had never felt before.

Perón's appeal was greatest to those workers who had had least trade-union organization and the lowest social status before his arrival on the scene. Thus Perón's supporters were strongest among packing-house workers, sugar workers, agricultural laborers, and workers in the smaller cities and towns. Perón had least support among printers, maritime workers, railroad engineers, and firemen.

As a result of his success in winning the support of the rank and file of the trade unions he also won the backing of most of the national industrial unions and of the General Confederation of Labor (CGT). From May 1, 1944, on, the CGT was firmly under the influence of Perón.

Throughout most of the 1943–45 period Perón's efforts to build a political machine on the basis of the trade-union movement was aided by the fact that the military dictatorship allowed little civic freedom. Many trade-unionists who opposed Perón's attempts to take over the labor movement were jailed or were forced into hiding or into seeking refuge in exile. Freedom of the press was severely limited, and the workers were allowed to read only Perón's side of the story of what was going on in the labor movement.

Perón's grip on the workers was shown by the events of October, 1945. On October 9 a group of military men opposed to or jealous of

Perón staged a *coup d'état* and forced his resignation from all his posts, and he was made a prisoner on Martín García island. However, President Edelmiro Farrell, a close associate of Perón, was not ousted from his post, and the leaders of the political parties refused to make any attempt to form a government so long as he remained in the Casa Rosada. As a result the country was virtually without a government for a whole week.

The supporters of Perón took advantage of the confusion resulting from the attitude of the anti-Peronista political parties to organize their forces and start a campaign to bring about his return from prison and reestablishment in power. Sparked by the packinghouse workers of Buenos Aires and nearby cities and towns, under Cipriano Reyes, large groups of workers began to march on the capital by whatever means of conveyance they could commandeer. They virtually seized control of the streets of the city, and at the same time a general strike spread throughout the nation.

In the face of these events the Army did little to support the group which had ousted Perón. The troops stayed in the barracks, leaving the control of Buenos Aires in the hands of Perón's supporters. Finally, on October 16, the anti-Perón army and navy men gave up, and Perón was brought back to Buenos Aires and virtually assumed control of the government. Although he did not again resume his posts as Vice President, Minister of War, and Secretary of Labor, his close associates were put in these jobs, and Perón was master of the regime.

A few days after his return to power Perón did two important things. First, he married Eva Duarte, a blond movie actress whom he had known for several years. Second, he announced his candidacy for the presidency and set about to organize political parties to back him in this race.

The principal support of Perón in his first election campaign came from the labor movement. The Partido Laborista was organized for this purpose, and it included among its leaders most of the outstanding trade-union officials of Argentina. Its president was Luis Gay, onetime syndicalist and chief of the Telephone Workers Federation. Its vice president was Cipriano Reyes, principal leader of the packing-house workers unions.

In addition to the Partido Laborista, Perón sought support in the Radical Party. Several second-rank leaders of that group, including Horacio Quijano and Juan Cooke, declared for Perón and established what they called the Renovated Radical Party. Quijano became candidate for vice president on the Perón ticket. Finally a group of "independents" added a third line upon which Perón's name appeared.

All the old parties joined in the Unión Democrática and threw their support to two leaders of the Radical Party, José Tamborini and Enrique Mosca. The Unión Democrática candidates were no match for Perón. They talked about political democracy, going all the way back to the Greeks to get arguments in its favor. Perón, in contrast, toured the country talking of the things which he had done and proposed to do on behalf of the workers. The result, on February 24, 1946, was a victory for Perón and the election of an almost two-thirds Peronista majority in the Chamber of Deputies and the total membership of the Senate except for the two members from the province of Corrientes, whom the Peronistas refused to seat.

Perón was inaugurated as president of the republic on June 4, 1946, the third anniversary of the coup which overthrew the Castillo government. He was reelected in 1951 and remained as chief executive until September 16, 1955.

The fundamental significance of the Perón regime was that it transferred political and economic power in Argentina from the rural landowning class to the lower and middle classes of the cities. The votes which Perón received in successive elections came largely from the agricultural laborer, the urban industrial and transportation worker, and, to a much less degree, from the white-collar workers and other middle-class elements. After he was overthrown, the significance of the change which he had wrought was reflected in the fact that virtually all politicians outdid themselves to win the backing of these same elements in the population, whereas few had been interested before 1943.

Economically, too, Perón dealt severe blows to the rural aristocracy. Although he did nothing significant to bring about an agrarian reform and to shift the control of the land out of the hands of those who had held it for a hundred years, he nonetheless deprived them of the key position which they had hitherto held in the economic life of the nation.

First of all, Perón forced the rural employers to accept the unionization of their workers. Those employed in the great wheat, corn, and cattle growing areas of the pampas were organized into the Federación Argentina de Seccionales Agrarias, which the Perón government authorized to participate with the employers and the government in determining the wages of the agricultural laborers handling these crops. In the wine-growing areas of western Argentina and in the sugar- and quebracho-producing regions of the north there were separate unions, which sat down as equals with the employers at the collective-bargaining table.

Second, Perón enacted extensive social and labor legislation to protect the agricultural workers, and at the expense of the employers. The Statute of the Peon, enacted while Perón was still Secretary of Labor, provided for the eight-hour day and other benefits for these workers. During his last year in office Perón pushed through Congress a law extending social security to the agricultural laborers.

Third, Perón took the sale of the country's basic agricultural export products out of the hands of private interests and centralized it in the hands of the government. The Instituto Argentino de Producción e Intercambio (IAPI) was established in March, 1946, and it was entrusted with the job of purchasing all the country's grain and vegetable-oil crops—and later its meat as well—and arranging for their sale inside and outside Argentina. The landowners were paid prices well below those in the world market throughout the Perón regime, and the profits from this enterprise stayed with the IAPI and the government.

All these measures resulted in undermining the economic and political power of the rural landowning class. However, they also had a disastrous effect on Argentina's agricultural output. According to the January, 1956, issue of the *Boletín Económico de América Latina,* published by the Economic Commission for Latin America, the total amount of land under cultivation in Argentina dropped ·from 21,-814,000 hectares in the 1934–38 period to 17,254,000 in 1955. The amount of land under cultivation in cereals and vegetable oils dropped by 1955 to only 74.4 per cent of what it had been in 1934–38. Some observers have argued that the fall in the amount of land in use was even greater than these figures would show.

Whereas the agricultural landlord was penalized by the Perón government, the urban industrialist was favored. Perón was anxious to build up a more diversified and more balanced economy than the country had hitherto possessed. He saw industrializiation as a means of assuring the future power and greatness of his country. He favored industry in a variety of ways. During the period 1945–49, when Argentina was receiving very high prices for its exports and IAPI was making fabulous profits from this trade, the government siphoned a sizable percentage of the export profit into the purchase of capital goods, particularly for industry. He reversed the tariff policy of his predecessors and established a high protective tariff for industry. Perón also established a government-owned Industrial Bank to make loans to industrialists to expand their plant and equipment.

The social policies which Perón had begun as Secretary of Labor were continued, though on a more modest scale. The work of extending social security to all gainfully employed people was completed by 1955 with the establishment of social security institutions for agricultural workers and self-employed people. The Perón regime had an extensive housing program. A great variety of labor legislation was enacted. Higher education was made gratis and was opened to all who could qualify—though insufficient funds were provided to meet the tremendous wave of students that descended upon the universities as a result. Special educational programs for training workers for industry were established.

Of course there was another side to the Perón regime. It was a dictatorship which became increasingly totalitarian the longer Perón remained in power. The weight of the dictatorship was felt in all spheres of activity and all walks of life.

In the political arena the nature of the regime became obvious very early when Perón's adherents in the Senate refused to seat the only two opposition members elected in 1946. The freedom of opposition parties was increasingly restricted. They were forbidden the use of radio and television, their access to the press was reduced almost to zero, they were submitted to physical terror, leading opponents of the regime were ousted from their seats in Congress, and the constituencies were gerrymandered so as to reduce the opposition to only fourteen members of the Chamber of Deputies by the end of the Perón era.

Freedom of press and speech was increasingly restricted. Typical of the government's action in this field was the suppression of the Socialist Party's weekly paper *La Vanguardia* because its printing shop was found by municipal health inspectors to be "dirty" and "dangerous," in spite of the fact that it was nationally famous for being one of the cleanest and best-run enterprises of the kind in Argentina. Scores of papers were closed down on January 1, 1950, on the grounds that they had violated a decree ordering that all papers bear the legend "Year of the Liberator San Martín" at their masthead—a decree which was divulged only to Peronista papers. Finally, early in 1951 *La Prensa,* the country's largest newspaper and a strong opponent of Perón, was closed down by means of a strike of Peronista-controlled newsdealers, and when it "failed to reopen" it was expropriated by the Peronista congress and was turned over to the General Confederation of Labor.

The universities received the same treatment as the press. One of the principal centers of opposition to Perón consisted of the faculties and student bodies of the country's six universities. Throughout the 1943–45 period there was a running struggle between the government and the students and faculty members. Once in office as president, Perón "reorganized" the universities, putting them completely under the control of the government, thus abolishing the autonomy and faculty-student administration which they had enjoyed since 1918. All anti-Peronista faculty members were dismissed, and no dissent with government policy was permitted to any of the professors of the universities.

The trade-union movement, which was largely responsible for putting Perón in power, received much the same treatment as did the press and the universities, which had been largely opposed to the dictator. Control of trade-union affairs was entrusted by Perón to his wife, Eva Duarte de Perón, as long as she lived. During the years 1948–51 she carried out a thoroughgoing purge of the trade-union leadership, ousting virtually all those union leaders who, without giving up control of their organizations, had supported Perón during the 1943–45 period. The leadership of the CGT and of the national unions became little more than puppets of the First Lady. After her death Perón himself took over the job of strictly supervising the activities of the labor movement.

Collective bargaining became less and less real as the tenure of

Perón in office continued. Increasingly the decisions in important collective-bargaining sessions were actually made by officials of the Ministry of Labor or even by Evita or Juan Perón. Strikes were virtually forbidden unless they were called to bolster some move of the administration.

The government attempted to destroy all independent civic organizations, particularly in the economic field. The attempt was made to establish organizations of all kinds which would be subject to the control of the government. Most famous, perhaps, was the Eva Perón Social Welfare Foundation, which during the life of Evita acquired a virtual monopoly of all charitable enterprises in the country.

The dictatorship of Perón was distinctive in its sources of support. Throughout its existence it rested upon the trade-union movement and the armed forces. Upon several occasions the military turned back attempts to overthrow the Perón regime by force. On these same occasions the trade-union movement was mobilized to come to the defense of the regime and was used frequently to demonstrate against the government's opponents or to embarrass them through strike action.

Perón was certainly well aware of the elements upon which his regime was based. He was able to remind military officers of the events of October, 1945, when they seemed to be wavering in their allegiance toward him. On the other hand, he was able to use the armed forces, as he did upon occasion, when his labor supporters seemed to be getting out of hand.

However, Perón was not just an ordinary Latin American dictator. It is probably true that he was interested principally in maintaining himself in power and was willing to follow any policy which he felt would serve this purpose. However, Perón differed from the general run of Latin American dictators in the effect his regime had upon his country and in his attempt to work out a rationale to justify his regime to himself, his country, and the world in general.

Perón was also different from the ordinary Latin American dictator because of his attempt to have something to say about virtually every field of knowledge. In spite of the fact that his training and background were at best meager in these fields, Perón was not abashed to speak to meetings of actors, philosophers, political scientists, or writers concerning their professions and the ideas with which they dealt. In this, perhaps, he was more like the dictators of the Fascist and Communist states than like those dictatorial regimes with which the Latin Americans are generally familiar.

There is little doubt that Perón had a very strong feeling of his role in the history of Argentina and, he hoped, of Latin America and the world as a whole. He was anxious to be regarded as the founder of a "new Argentina" which would have a much more significant place in world affairs than it had had when he first took control.

Perón and his closest advisers tried to work out a political philosophy to "explain" his movement. Professor George Blanksten has made the most thorough study of *justicialismo*, the Peronista philosophy, which he has analyzed in his book *Perón's Argentina*. Blanksten notes that (p. 283):

Justicialismo maintains that there are not two but rather four basically conflicting forces in society. These are "idealism," "materialism," "individualism," and "collectivism." Two propositions are central to the justicialist interpretation of the four forces. In the first place, each of them has a necessary and desirable role to play in society. Secondly, a constant conflict rages among the four.

Perón and his associates maintained that the domination of one or a combination of two or three of these forces over the others gives rise to some form of tyranny. Thus, the supremacy of idealism results in a technocratic dictatorship; the supremacy of idealism and collectivism was fascist and Nazi tyranny; the combination of materialism and individualism is capitalism; and the alliance of materialism and collectivism is communist tyranny.

The Peronista combination of these four elements is the so-called "Third Position," about which Perón talked at great length throughout most of his time in office. Blanksten sums up Perón's Third Position thus (p. 290):

It is an arrangement which guarantees each of the four basic forces the opportunity to exercise its proper role in society, neutralizes the conflict among the four, and prevents any one—or two—of them from dominating the others. In a sense, *Justicialismo* or the "Third Position" is the "new Argentina's" version of Aristotle's "Golden Mean" in so far as that concept sought the avoidance of extremes. The *Peronista* who knows his doctrine defines it thus: *Justicialismo* is "that doctrine whose objective is the happiness of man in human society achieved through the harmony of materialistic, idealistic, individualistic, and collectivistic forces, each valued in a Christian way." Or thus: "It would be a concordant and balanced combination of the forces that represent the modern state, designed to avoid strife and the annihilation of one of these forces; endeavoring to conciliate them, to unite them, and to put them in parallel motion to be able to form . . . a common destiny with benefit for the . . . forces and without injury to any one of them." *Justicialismo*, then, envisages a temperate social order compounded of "just the right amounts" of idealism, materialism, individualism, and collectivism.

President Perón is quoted by Blanksten as defining the Third Position of the Peronista Party thus (p. 292):

Some say, in grave error, that it is a centrist party. A centrist party, like a rightist or leftist party, is sectarian, and we are totally anti-sectarian. For us there is nothing fixed and nothing to deny. . . . We are anti-Communist because Communists are sectarians, and anti-capitalist because capitalists are also sectarians. Our "Third Position" is not a centrist position. It is an ideological position which is in the center, on the right, or on the left according to specific circumstances.

Perón was very proud of his somewhat vague "Third Position." He is quoted by Blanksten as saying (p. 293):

When I think that we have been the first to announce this solution to men, and when I demonstrate that we have been the first to realize it, I can do no less than affirm my faith in the high destiny which God has seen fit to assign to our country. My soul is filled with emotion when I think that the day cannot be far off when all of humanity, seeking some star in the night, will fix its eyes on the flag of the Argentines.

In addition to his development of a generalized philosophical defense of his regime Perón stressed two principal issues, nationalism and the defense of the workers. A third issue, which he talked about less frequently but which we feel was fundamental to the Perón regime, was his attitude toward the problem of political democracy.

The nationalism of the Perón regime found a number of expressions. It was the motivation of the oft-mentioned desire of Perón and his followers to achieve the "economic independence" of Argentina. Nationalism lay behind the attempt of the Perón administration to exercise leadership throughout South America and even throughout the whole Latin American region. Finally it lay behind the strongly expressed opposition of Perón to the United States, which, though not consistent, was violently and frequently announced.

Throughout his administration Perón laid stress on the theme of achieving economic independence. In July, 1947, he arranged a meeting in Tucumán, where Argentine independence had originally been declared in 1816, to sign a new "Declaration of Economic Independence." This document said in part:

We, the representatives of the people and the government of the Argentine republic, invoking Divine Providence in the name and by the authority of the people we represent, solemnly declare . . . that the peoples and governments of the Argentine provinces and territories break the dominating chains which have bound them to foreign capitalism, and that they recover their right to govern their own sources of national wealth.

Perón is quoted by Blanksten (p. 238) as commenting thus on this Declaration:

Following the course of conduct and the example of San Martín, we have come to Tucumán, we have entered the historical house, we have endeavored to create a similar atmosphere, we have taken the same oath, and we are also ready to die, should it be necessary, to obtain our economic independence.

Perón conceived of many of the measures carried out by his government as being designed to achieve this economic independence. To this end the government used most of the frozen credits Argentina had piled up in Great Britain during World War II to purchase the British-owned railroads. On March 1, 1948, Perón presided over a ceremony marking the official transfer of the railroads to Argentine ownership.

The Peronista government's support of industrialization was also conceived of in terms of achieving the country's economic independence. It was felt by the Peronistas that if Argentina had a more diversified economy, it would be less dependent for its prosperity upon the export of grains and meats to Europe, particularly to Great Britain, a dependence which they maintained served to limit the nation's political independence.

Another expression of Argentine nationalism by the Perón administration was its attempt to assume leadership of the other Latin American countries. On the one hand, Perón sought to bring his closest neighbors into an economic union with Argentina. Treaties to this effect were signed with Chile, Paraguay, and Bolivia, though their effectiveness was quite limited. On the other hand, the Perón government sought to take advantage of various inter-American conferences to form a bloc of the Latin American nations.

The most spectacular attempt of Perón to assume leadership among the Latin American nations occurred during the Ninth Inter-American Conference in Bogotá in April, 1948. At that meeting the Latin American nations pressed the United States to help establish an Inter-American Development Bank. When the United States completely rejected the suggestion, Perón's representatives at the conference announced that Argentina would take the leadership in establishing the bank whether or not the United States agreed to go along with the proposal. Growing economic difficulties reduced this announcement to the proportions of any empty boast, but it was symbolic of the attempt Argentina consistently made under Perón to assume the leadership of the Latin American countries.

Perón did not confine his efforts to gain influence among the other Latin American countries to these activities, however. He used representatives of the two elements upon which his regime was based, the armed forces and the trade unions, in his efforts to seek friends abroad.

The activities of Peronista Military Attachés in the various Latin American countries are, in the nature of the case, difficult to trace directly. However, there is considerable reason for suspecting that representatives of the Argntine military had a considerable hand in *coups d'état* by army elements in Peru and Venezuela in 1948, as well as cultivating specially close relations with such dictators as Generals Anastasio Somoza of Nicaragua, Magloire of Haiti,

Trujillo of the Dominican Republic, Rojas Pinilla of Colombia, and with Colonel Remón of Panama.

Much more obvious were the activities of the Labor Attachés whom Perón attached to every Argentine embassy in the hemisphere. These people, chosen largely from the secondary leadership of the trade-union movement, before they were sent to their respective diplomatic posts, were put through a special course which stressed Peronista ideas and propaganda methods.

The Peronista Labor Attachés sought to infiltrate and influence the trade-union organizations in the countries to which they were assigned. They had lavish funds at their disposal, and part of their job was to arrange all-expense tours for trade-union leaders to Buenos Aires, where they were wined and dined, shown the sights and particularly the accomplishments of the Perón administration, and usually were received by Perón and Evita.

The Labor Attachés succeeded in bringing about the establishment of Peronista trade-union movements in Nicaragua, Uruguay, Colombia, Panama, Costa Rica, as well as establishing organizing committees in Haiti, Chile, Peru, Brazil, Cuba, Paraguay, and Bolivia. They also succeeded in gaining the support of the old Regional Confederation of Workers of Mexico (CROM) and of the Pérez Jiménez dictatorship's pet National Labor Confederation in Venezuela.

With the help of the Labor Attachés, Perón undertook to organize a hemisphere-wide confederation, the so-called Agrupación de Trabajadores Latino Americanos Sindicalizados (ATLAS). For a short while it was a major contestant (with the communist CTAL and the democratic ORIT) for the loyalty and affiliation of the national trade-union movements of the Latin American countries.

Another aspect of the job of the Labor Attachés was their work as agents for the Eva Perón Social Welfare Foundation. Upon various occasions when disaster struck one or another of the Latin American countries the Labor Attachés distributed aid which was rushed to the spot from Buenos Aires by the Foundation. On a more prosaic level, the Labor Attachés undertook to aid various local charities, as well as to distribute gifts to poor children on Christmas and other holidays, all provided by the Welfare Foundation.

The third element of Perón's nationalism was his strong stand against the United States. Starting with his famous "Braden or Perón" campaign during the 1945–46 presidential election, Perón carried on a long and bitter propaganda battle against the United States and all things North American for over eight years. The United States was pictured by the Peronista press and by the President himself as a greedy imperialist nation which was doing its utmost to subjugate the countries of Latin America. The supposed "materialism" of the United States, the more unpleasant aspects of race relations here, and alleged interference by the United States in the internal affairs of various Latin American countries were constant themes of propaganda by the Peronistas.

Perón and his friends had specially selected "devils" among leading North Americans against whom their propaganda was particularly directed. They seldom passed up an opportunity to talk with violent disparagement about Spruille Braden. Only less prominent in the Peronista gallery of North American rogues was Serafino Romualdi, Latin American representative of the American Federation of Labor, who was in the vanguard in the struggle against Peronista penetration of the Latin American labor movements.

There were ebbs and flows in Perón's hostility toward the United States. For a while late in 1950 and early in 1951, when a loan was being negotiated with the Export-Import Bank for $125,000,000, the Peronistas put a damper on their campaign. Soon after, it was renewed with increased intensity. It reached a pitch of particularly shrill fury shortly before the visit of Dr. Milton Eisenhower to Argentina during the summer of 1953. Immediately thereafter the campaign was relaxed and finally virtually disappeared, never again to be renewed so long as Perón remained in power. By 1953 Perón had realized that his economic situation was so serious that he would need a great deal of help from the United States in order to salvage it.

Support for the aims and aspirations of labor was another constant theme sounded by Perón during his nine-year occupancy of the Casa Rosada. He talked frequently of his regime as a "laborist" government and gave long discourses on the Peronista "sindicalist" state. In several crises faced by the government the labor movement was mobilized to support the regime.

It is difficult to tell how much of Perón's protestation of nationalism and of laborism was genuine. One is inclined to feel that he was sincerely an Argentine nationalist, that he stumbled onto the labor issue more or less by accident, but was a clever enough politician to realize its usefulness for maintaining him in power and for building up his prestige as something more than just another Latin American dictator. However, there can be little doubt about one aspect of his philosophy: Perón had little belief in political democracy.

Perón's antagonism to democratic ideals and procedures is clear from his actions. However, it is also clear from some of his public statements. Perón believed in elites. His chosen elite was the military, which he believed had a unique role of leadership to play in modern societies, particularly in Argentina.

It has been maintained that Perón was seeking to establish a corporate state somewhat along the lines of that proposed by Mussolini. There is no doubt that Perón was slowly developing during his presidency a totalitarian state to which all other aspects of society would be subordinated. Whether or not this was "fascist" is perhaps a matter of how one defines fascism. Certainly in many ways the Peronista experience did not conform to the typical facist pattern.

The totalitarian state structure which Perón was constructing was well advanced by the time he was driven from power. Its foundation stones, of course, were the armed forces and the labor movement. The former he sought to hold constantly under his reign by frequent changes in command and occasional purges. The trade-union movement he sought to centralize completely, with the top reins of authority being in his own hands or, so long as she lived, in those of his wife. All power in the national industrial unions was put in their national officers resident in Buenos Aires. The national industrial unions themselves were subjected to the strict control of the General Confederation of Labor, which had power to "intervene" and to oust the elected officers of any one of these organizations upon the slightest show of dissidence or doubt about Perón.

At the same time collective bargaining was centralized in the Ministry of Labor, where increasingly the officials of that organization became the final arbiters of collective contract terms. This process was reinforced by the device of having all collective agreements end on the same day.

With labor firmly in his hands Perón set out to subject other functional groups in the economy to his control. An over-all employers' group, the Confederación General Económica (General Economic Confederation), was established, and shortly before his overthrow Perón sponsored a law passed by Congress which required all employers in the country to pay dues to this organization whether they wanted to do so or not.

Parallel to the CGT and the CGE, Perón sought to establish the Confederación General de Professionales (CGP), or General Confederation of Professional People. The teachers, lawyers, doctors, dentists, architects, and members of all other liberal professions were ultimately to be forced to belong to this organization. Since Perón characteristically used the one-step-at-a-time technique, and since he met his greatest resistance among the professional people, the work of bringing all of them into the CGP had not been completed by the time he was overthrown.

Finally there were to be the Confederación General Universitaria (CGU) and the Unión de Estudiantes Secondarios, which were to have in their ranks all the university and secondary school students. The CGU was a competitor of the older Federación Universitaria Argentina, established in 1918 and traditionally the representative of the university student body in all six of the national universities. It put up strenuous and consistent opposition to Perón, and he had made relatively little progress in getting students into the Peronista group by the time he was ousted, although his success among the secondary school students was markedly greater, since there was no rival group to contend with there.

All these developments seemed to presage a corporative state. Some claimed to see a further step in this direction in a Congress of Productivity held about a year before Perón fell, which met in the Chamber of Deputies and had delegates from the CGT, and the CGP. There were those who felt that this was the first step in the elimination of the politically organized Congress and its substitution by a functionally chosen Corporative Chamber strictly under the control of the Executive.

Be this as it may, the process was left incomplete by the time Perón left office in September, 1955. Whether or not Perón was ultimately seeking to establish a corporative state along fascist lines, it is certainly true that in some other respects Perón's regime had little resemblance to the classic fascist states of Europe.

First of all, Perón came to power in the face of the opposition of the principal elements of the *status quo ante* instead of with their help, as in the cases of Italy and Germany. The large landholders, the industrialists, and most other elements of the Argentine upper classes were violently opposed to Perón, and most of them remained so throughout his tenure in office.

In the second place, Perón, unlike Hitler and Mussolini, had the support on his way to power and after getting there of the organized working class. Whereas the established trade-union movements of Italy and Germany bitterly fought the Fascists and Nazis, the Argentine trade-union movement supported Perón almost from the beginning.

If Perón's was a fascist regime, it was certainly one with a difference. We should prefer to say that it was a totalitarian regime *sui generis* very greatly influenced by the situation in Argentina at the time of its development, which borrowed from other fascist regimes as well as from the Communists and other sources during its tenure in power. However, we do not feel that Perón was consciously patterning his government on that of any other country, and perhaps he himself was not sure exactly where he intended to end up. He was a great one for "playing by ear," and his main preoccupation was keeping intact the fragile and unnatural coalition which had brought him into office, and after that he was interested in carving a place for himself in history as a unique sort of Argentine and Latin American ruler.

There is no doubt about Perón's impact upon the history of his country. He fundamentally changed the balance of power in Argentina, ending forever the control over the nation by the rural landlords who had dominated it for more than a century. He gave a status to the urban and rural working class which no successor regime could take away from them, even if it wanted to. The organized-labor movement became a permanent element of key importance in the power structure of Argentina, and the workingmen had a feeling of having "arrived," which never could be entirely taken away from them.

Perón may well go down in history as a tragic figure. On the one hand, he did much good for his country, bringing about long-overdue changes and making the masses of the people aware of issues which they had not paid attention to before. He confirmed the nation on the path of economic development and industrialization and made both of these elements in the national creed of virtually every Argentinean.

On the other hand, Perón, was unwilling and unable to establish the basis for a solid democracy in Argentina. Although he brought about social and economic changes which might have paved the way for a long period of democratic rule, and indeed might have made possible the withdrawal of the armed forces from the political power which they had usurped in 1930, he made no attempt to do so. Rather to the contrary, he did not want to do so.

In addition, Perón did great damage to the economy of the country, damage which may be of a short-run nature but which nonetheless forced the people of Argentina to go through after his overthrow a period of stringency and suffering for which he was directly responsible. By failing to understand that industralization does not mean the destruction of agriculture and by allowing and encouraging tremendous waste, graft, and corruption Perón greatly weakened the country's economic base. Only heroic measures could salvage the nation from the havoc which he left.

History will have to judge the significance of Juan Domingo Perón. However, there is little doubt that he will emerge as the man who decisively changed the course of Argentine history and as the person responsible for "bringing Argentina into the twentieth century."

Fidel Castro
and Fidelismo

දවිදුව

On October 16, 1953, a young man, tall for a Cuban, stood before a special court in the city of Santiago de Cuba on trial for treason. He had an ascetic face and sad eyes, and as he began to speak to the judges his voice was husky and seemed to come with difficulty. As he continued he appeared to gain confidence from hearing the sound of his own words. His voice, though somewhat high-pitched, was sometimes matter-of-fact, though it rose and fell as he emphasized his points.

The young man went on for four hours, holding his judges spellbound, though he defied them, the government of which they were a part, and the ruling classes of the island. They listened while he promised that he and his young friends would soon rule Cuba and that when they did they would completely reform and reorganize the country's economic, social, and political life.

The young man was Fidel Castro. This speech, which was hardly reported either inside Cuba or abroad at the time, firmly stated his intention to transform his nation. Even those who heard the speech could hardly have guessed the impact which he was soon to have on both his country and the whole of Latin America.

The advent of Fidel Castro to power in Cuba five years later completely transformed the revolutionary struggle in Latin America. Instead of a two-sided conflict between the defenders of the old order and the protagonists of a democratic social revolution this struggle became three-sided. The new contender was a group of revolutionaries who believed that their objectives could be obtained only through the establishment of a totalitarian regime and its alliance with the Communists in world affairs. This group rallied around Fidel Castro inside Cuba and throughout Latin America.

Fidel was not unique in taking this position in favor of totalitarian revolution. Juan Perón, and to a degree Getulio Vargas, had assumed the same posture before him. However, Castro enjoyed a success in rallying a hemisphere-wide movement around his banner which eluded Perón and to which Vargas never aspired.

Fidel Castro was born of a good family of moderately wealthy landowners in the Province of Oriente in the year 1927. He had the customary upbringing of a youth of his social status, being educated at Catholic schools, including the famous Colegio de Dolores secondary school in Santiago de Cuba. During the summers he wandered widely over the hills, woods, and fields of his native Oriente.

From secondary school Fidel went to the University of Havana. There he rapidly became involved in the political life which engaged the attention of so many of the Cuban students in the 1940's. He is reported to have been a member of one of the "revolutionary" groups which then dotted the Cuban political landscape. These groups had been an outgrowth of the struggle against the Machado dictatorship (1924–33). The students who had sparked that struggle had formed several terrorist groups which responded to the force of the dictatorship with a force of their own. Once the fight against Machado had been won, many of these students continued to use the same methods, even after Cuba entered a period of democracy after 1940, frequently turning their terroristic methods against one another.

While at the university Castro developed his talents as an orator. He gave long speeches to his fellow students, who soon found that a discussion with Fidel was likely to be an entirely one-sided affair. He was active in student politics in the Law School.

Two incidents which took place during his university years have been the subject of much discussion and misunderstanding. One of these was his participation in an attempt to organize an invasion of the Dominican Republic by exiles and foreign sympathizers with the fight against the Trujillo dictatorship. This effort, which was to take off from Cayo Confites at the eastern end of Cuba, was finally frustrated when the government of President Grau San Martín prevented the departure of the expedition.

The other incident was Castro's presence in Bogotá, Colombia, in April, 1948, when the people of that city rioted violently for three days following the assassination of the national leader of the

Liberal Party, Jorge Eliecer Gaitán. The presence of Castro in the city during the "Bogotazo" is often cited as "proof" of Castro's long-time membership in a communist underground apparatus. The principal weakness of this argument, however, is the fact that it presumes the Bogotá uprising to have been a communist-engineered and directed event. The writer does not believe that the Communists actually had anything to do with the spontaneous uprising of the Bogoteños in protest against the death of their idol. Had they been its instigators, they would have emerged from the experience in a thoroughly entrenched position, if not in control of the government. Nothing of the sort occurred. Because of the utter lack of organization the Bogotazo served to do little but allow the Bogoteños to work off their frustration and anger.

One other event of importance to Castro occurred during his stay at the university. This was his marriage to a student of the School of Philosophy, Mirtha Díaz Balart, which took place on October 12, 1948. On September 1 of the following year their son "Fidelito" was born.

Once out of the university, Fidel Castro began his career as a lawyer. At the same time he joined the forces of the so-called Ortodoxo (Orthodox) Party. This party was led by an eccentric Senator, Eduardo Chibas, who had broken from the Auténtico Party in 1947, charging it and the government of President Ramón Grau San Martín with vast corruption and betrayal of the promises it had made to the people of Cuba in the years before coming to power. Chibas won particular fame as a radio orator, and it was on one of his own radio programs that he dramatically committed suicide one day in 1951.

Castro became active in Chibas' Ortodoxo Party in Havana. By early 1952 he was head of the party organization in the capital city. He seemed to be on the way to a successful political career, particularly if, as many expected, the Ortodoxos won the election scheduled for June 1, 1952.

However, this election was never held. General Fulgencio Batista, ex-dictator and ex-president and candidate in the June, 1952, election, overthrew the government of President Carlos Prio Socarras on March 10, 1952, less than three months before the election which Batista knew he could not possibly win. After some confusion

Batista took office as "Chief of State," issued a new "Constitutional Statute" to take the place temporarily of the Constitution of 1940, and reestablished the dictatorship which he had voluntarily abandoned a few years before. The people of Cuba were never willing to accept Fulgencio Batista as the legitimate ruler of the island. The organization of the opposition to his regime began the day he seized power. This opposition took many forms and was divided into many groups.

One of the major elements of the opposition to Batista was the Auténtico Party of ex-Presidents Ramón Grau San Martín and Carlos Prio Socarras, which had been ousted from power by Batista's coup of March 10. The Auténticos split into two groups, the one led by Grau trying to oppose Batista "constitutionally," the other, led by Prio, entering immediately into underground plotting against the dictatorship. The Prio Auténtico underground, led by Dr. Aureliano Sánchez Arango, one-time Minister of Education in Prio's government, plotted unceasingly with active and retired military men while bringing in sizable quantities of arms to be used in a coup against the Batista regime.

In 1955 the Auténtico underground split into two groups. One continued to be loyal to Carlos Prio and was known as the Organización Auténtica. The other was led by Dr. Sánchez Arango and took the name "Triple A."

Another major factor in the underground opposition to the Batista dictatorship consisted of the student organizations, particularly that of the University of Havana. The Federación de Estudiantes Universitarios (FEU) reestablished the underground Directorio Revolucionario, which had existed almost a generation before, during the struggle against the Machado dictatorship. In the tradition of the Cuban students' fight against tryanny the Directorio undertook acts of personal violence against officials of the Batista regime. These culminated on March 13, 1957, in an attack on the presidential palace and a near-miss attempt to kill Batista himself.

The final element in the anti-Batista opposition was the movement organized by Fidel Castro. He had begun his activities against the Batista regime virtually the moment the general seized power. Shortly afterward, in his capacity as a lawyer, Fidel entered a plea in the Supreme Court to have the Batista regime declared unconstitutional and illegal and its acts unenforceable. Of course the court refused to do this.

Thereafter Fidel Castro turned his attention to insurrection as a means of getting rid of the tyranny. His first effort in this direction was made on July 26, 1953, when he and a group of followers attempted to seize the Moncada Barracks in Santiago de Cuba. This was the second largest garrison in the island. The plan was to seize it, arouse the garrison, much of which was anti-Batista, and use it as a base for a civil war against the dictatorship.

This effort failed. Many of those participating in the attempt were killed, quite a few of them in cold blood after capture. Others escaped and went into hiding. Still others, including Fidel Castro, were captured and imprisoned. Castro was brought to trial on October 16, 1953, and he served as his own counsel. He delivered a long address to the court which was more in the nature of an indictment of it and the regime it served than a defense of his own actions.

This speech, which has frequently been published under the title "History Will Absolve Me!" was one of the most famous expositions of his philosophy that Fidel Castro ever made. In spite of the situation he was in at the moment, he presumed that revolution was inevitable and that it would be much more than a mere overthrow of the Batista dictatorship. He outlined in some detail the program of extensive change which such a revolution would bring about.

Castro outlined five "revolutionary laws" which the new government would proclaim. Concerning these, he said in part:

The first revolutionary law will return to the people their sovereignty and proclaim the Constitution of 1940 as the true supreme law of the State, until the people decide to modify or change it. For the purpose of reestablishing it and chastising those who have betrayed it, and there existing no popularly elected authorities to carry this out, the revolutionary movement as the momentary embodiment of sovereignty, the only source of legitimate authority, will assume all of the faculties inherent in such authority except the modification of the Constitution: the faculty to legislate, the faculty to execute, and the faculty to judge. . . .
The second revolutionary law will concede the unmortgageable and untransferrable right to the land to all the *colonos*, sub-*colonos*, renters,

sharecroppers who occupy parcels of five *caballerias* of land or less, the State indemnifying the former proprietors on the basis of the income which these lands would produce over an average of ten years.

The third revolutionary law will provide workers the right of sharing 30 per cent of the profits of all industrial, mercantile, and mining enterprises, including sugar mills. Strictly agricultural firms will be excepted from this.

The fourth revolutionary law will concede to all *colonos* the right to 50 per cent of the income from cane, and a minimum quota of 40,000 arrobas to all small *colonos* who have been established for at least three years.

The fifth revolutionary law will order the confiscation of all property obtained corruptly by members of all previous governments. . . .[1]

A bit later in his discourse Castro outlined the longer-range objectives of "the first government due to popular election which would arise immediately afterward." The questions this government would have to deal with were stated thus by Castro:

The problem of the land, the problem of industrialization, the problem of housing, the problem of unemployment, the problem of education, and the problem of the people's health: these are the six points to which our efforts would have been resolutely turned, together with the conquest of the public liberties and political democracy.[2]

He elaborated somewhat on each of these questions, without going into too much detail. The rest of the speech was taken up with indictments of the tyrannical attitudes and actions of the Batista regime. He was particularly harsh in his criticisms of the members of the judiciary.

The judges were uninfluenced by Fidel Castro's oratory insofar as their verdict was concerned. They sentenced Fidel to twenty years in jail, and he was taken to the Isle of Pines National Penitentiary, but he stayed there only until March, 1954, when he was freed in conformity with a general-amnesty law.

After spending a short time in Havana, Castro went into exile. He went first to the United States, where he was very active among the anti-Batista exiles in New York, Miami, and elsewhere. Soon, however, he moved to Mexico, this time with definite plans for mounting an invasion and a civil war against the Batista regime.

The story of the Castro group's preparation in Mexico for armed strife in their homeland has often been told. They rented an estate in an isolated part of the republic where the small group of men who had rallied to Castro's cause were put through a course of training in guerrilla warfare at the hands of General Bayo, Cuban-born onetime officer of the Spanish Republican Army. Meanwhile arms were smuggled in from the United States and elsewhere, in part paid for by a sizable contribution from ex-President Carlos Prio Socarras. A small yacht, the "Gramma" was bought to transport the little Rebel Army from Mexico to Cuba.

In the meantime Castro's supporters inside Cuba were also very active. Forming what they now called "the 26th of July Movement," they began the difficult job of building an underground movement based on small cells in labor unions, professional societies, and neighborhoods. This apparatus became known as the Civic Movement of Resistance.

Finally, on November 25, 1956, the "Gramma" left the Mexican coast with a total of eighty-two men aboard. The boat was seriously overloaded and did not arrive off the coast south of Cuba's Sierra Maestra mountain range until December 2, two days later than had originally been planned. As a result of this delay there was little chance to coordinate the landing with an insurrection which had begun as scheduled in Santiago de Cuba two days before.

After a series of disasters only thirteen of the original eighty-two "invaders" finally reached refuge in the Sierra Maestra Mountains. Batista's propaganda services announced that all the attackers, including Fidel Castro himself, had been killed or captured. More than three months were to pass before the people of Cuba became aware that a civil war had begun in the mountains at the eastern end of the island.

The little band rallied support slowly. For the first few weeks they lived on the meagerest food provided by sympathetic peasants. They began to add to their scanty arsenal—most of their arms had gone astray during the landing—by raiding local police stations.

It was not until March, 1957, that the people of Cuba became aware of what was occurring in the Sierra Maestra. In that month Herbert Mathews, a member of the editorial staff of the *New York Times,* visited Castro in his mountain fastness, interviewed him and his aides, had photographs taken, and then withdrew, returning to New York. His series of three articles was published soon afterward. By one of those freaks of the Batista censorship which occurred from time to time the regime did not prevent the entry of the issues of the *Times* carrying Mathews' articles. As a result word was soon broadcast throughout the republic that Fidel Castro was indeed leading a revolt against the Batista regime.

From then until the final victory of the Rebel Army on January 1, 1959, the battle increased in intensity. The area under the control of the Castro forces increased, until by the middle of 1958 they controlled most of the rural areas of the province of Oriente. Meanwhile a second front was opened in the central province of Las Villas under the direction of the Directorio Revolucionario. This front had been established in the middle of 1957 and had not had any direct connection with the forces of Fidel Castro for over a year. A few months before the final victory over Batista a third front was opened in the westernmost province of Pinar del Rio, led by elements of the Auténtico Party.

Meanwhile the various civilian undergrounds intensified their activities. Castro's 26th of July Movement established five-man cells in most of the trade unions in Havana and in many of the interior cities. It collected millions of dollars to aid the rebel armed forces through the sale of "bonds" in denominations of one peso and up. These bonds were bought by members of all ranks of society from the humblest kind of agricultural and urban worker to some of the richest of the country's industrialists.

Other underground groups were also active. Elements of the Organizacion Auténtica, Triple A, and Directorio Revolucionario were all engaged in organizing the civilian resistance to the tyranny. Instances of sabotage, terrorist attempts against the lives of Batista officials, and other acts of resistance to the regime became widespread.

The Batista regime became increasingly brutal during the last two years it remained in power. No citizen was safe from the depredation of the Military Intelligence Service and the civilian Secret Police. Homes were raided in the dead of night, and householders were taken "for investigation," never to return alive. The most refined tortures were used by the police. It has been estimated that some 20,000 civilians were killed in cold blood by agents of the Batista regime during the two-year civil war.

During most of this period the Communist Party of Cuba stood on the sidelines. The Cuban Communists had been among Batista's closest political associates between 1937 and his first retirement from the presidency in 1944. They continued to be his allies between 1944 and his return to power in 1952.

After Batista's seizure of power on March 10, important Communist leaders suddenly appeared as members of the Batista political party, the Partido Acción Popular. Although the dictator formally outlawed the Communist Party at the end of 1952, most of the important Communist leaders continued to live unmolested in Havana and other cities and towns.

At the beginning of the Castro revolt the Communists made clear their opposition to it. When in August, 1957, and April, 1958, the Castro forces attempted to carry out a revolutionary general strike, the Communists were quite frankly against these moves. However, soon after the failure of the April, 1958, strike attempt, the Partido Socialista Popular (the name of the Cuban Communist party) made its first overtures to the rebel forces. One of the PSP's leaders, Carlos Rafael Rodríguez, was sent to the Sierra Maestra to act as a liaison between the rebel forces and the Communist party apparatus. At the same time the underground trade-union organization, hitherto known as the Frente Obrero Revolucionario, was expanded to include the Communists, and changed its name to Frente Obrero Revolucionario Unido.

Fidel's relations with other opposition groups remained stormy. In his speech to the court in 1953 he had made it clear that he wanted nothing to do with the older generation of political leaders, whom he regarded as universally corrupt. It was not until the latter part of 1958 that an agreement was signed, the so-called Declaration of Caracas, providing for unity of action of all the principal groups opposing the Batista dictatorship, and agreeing on the establishment of a provisional government headed by ex-Judge Manuel Urrutia as soon as Batista was overthrown.

Meanwhile Fidel Castro had become the symbol of the struggle against the dictatorship. Starting in the middle of 1958, his voice became familiar to millions of Cubans as he broadcast regularly from "Radio Rebelde," the station the rebels installed in the heart of the Sierra Maestra country. Tales circulated about his bravery, his magnanimity toward captured Batista soldiers, his plans for the rebuilding of the nation once victory had been achieved. The hopes of a whole nation, particularly of its youth, came to be centered in this young man, who became a sort of combination of David and Robin Hood and José Marti.

In the last months of 1958 the situation moved rapidly toward a victory for the rebels. By August it was impossible to go by railroad or road beyond Las Villas province in the center of the island. The rebels seized most of the rural areas and small towns of the three eastern provinces. As the last days of the year approached, the Rebel Army laid siege to Santa Clara, capital of Las Villas Province. It was the fall of this city on December 31, 1958, that convinced Batista to give up power and flee the country.

On the morning of January 1, 1959, Cuba belonged to Fidel Castro. His underground supporters took over control of Havana and other important cities. The Rebel Army moved into Santiago de Cuba, which it had been besieging for several weeks. The next day a new Provisional Government, under Manuel Urrutia, was established in Santiago, which was proclaimed provisional capital of the republic.

During the next ten days Fidel Castro made a triumphal tour from Santiago to Havana. Accompanied by elements of his Rebel Army, he was greeted by delirious crowds of hundreds of thousands anxious to see the bearded guerrilla warrior, to hear him speak, even to touch his garments. His progress was reminiscent of an ancient Roman triumph.

At that moment Fidel Castro had the enthusiastic support of all but the tiniest fraction of Cuba's seven million people. He was certainly the greatest hero Cuba had seen in the twentieth century. He was looked upon by the people as the savior of the republic, as the slayer of tyrants, as a fabulous hero. He received the kind of unlimited adulation which only someone of the very strongest character could have enjoyed without getting delusions of grandeur.

Meanwhile the new government began its work of reorganizing the life of the nation. The first cabinet of the revolutionary regime represented a coalition of the 26th of July Movement and some of the older opponents of the Batista regime, though none of the other organized anti-Batista groups was officially represented. José Miró Cardona, onetime head of the Havana Bar Association, who had had to flee into exile in 1958, became Prime Minister. Roberto Agramonte, Orthodoxo candidate for president in the 1952 election which was never held, became Minister of State. Dr. López Fresquet, a onetime Auténtico, was named Minister of Finance. Several of the veterans of the Rebel Army also became members of the new government, including Armando Hart, as Minister of Education, Manuel Ray as Minister of Public Works, Humberto Sori Marín as Minister of Agriculture, Luis Orlando Rodríguez as Minister of Interior.

The first job of the new government was to purge the incumbent regime. This involved both punishment for those who had carried out Batista's reign of terror against the Cuban people and cleansing of the public administration of hangers-on and corrupt elements.

While in the mountains Fidel Castro had appealed time and again to the people of Cuba not to take justice into their own hands once the Batista regime had fallen. He promised that the new revolutionary government would punish all those who had murdered and tortured opponents of the dictatorship, and once victory was achieved he moved quickly to make good this promise. Military courts were established, and during the first three months of the new regime over five hundred people were executed in conformity with decisions of these courts. Although the justice was summary, there is little evidence that it was not correctly administered. If one believes in capital punishment, one is forced to agree that those executed deserved to be capitally punished.

Only in two instances were there serious grounds for questioning these trials. One was a case in which the defendant was tried in a public auditorium in an atmosphere which was akin to that of a lynch mob. Fidel Castro ordered this defendant to be tried again, but the retrial did not change the results. The second case involved a number of air force pilots who were freed of charges of bombing open cities when evidence was presented that they had purposely dropped their bombs over unoccupied regions in violation of Batista's orders. In this case Fidel ordered a retrial and dictated the sentences which were to be imposed on the aviators.

While these trials were in progress a wide purge of the public administration was undertaken. Civil service rules were suspended for a period of three months, and during this period thousands of people were removed from the public payroll because their jobs had been mere sinecures or because there were serious charges against them of corruption and malfeasance in office.

Among the more fundamental reforms undertaken by the new regime was the complete reorganization of the tax structure with the more than 150 different taxes being reduced to 21, and the whole system being made more progressive. The social security system was reorganized; the thirty or more different retirement funds were merged into a single Social Security Bank, and a single schedule of contribution and benefits was devised.

The national lottery was also reorganized, with the establishment of a unique system whereby each lottery ticket became a kind of savings bond, paying interest whether or not it contained the lucky number. The funds of the lottery were designated to be used for the construction of low-cost housing.

The trade-union movement was reorganized. On January 1 and 2 the headquarters of all the unions in the island were seized by members of the 26th of July Movement underground. Within two weeks the provisional leaders were confirmed in office by membership of the various unions. Then, between April and June in all the local unions secret elections were held in which 26th of July lists of candidates were elected in the overwhelming majority of cases. In many instances these lists defeated candidates backed by the Communist Party, and during the first six or eight months of the regime relations between the 26th of July and the Communists in the labor movement were markedly hostile. Between June and September congresses of all the national unions were held and confirmed the provisional 26th of July leaders in almost all instances.

During these first months of the new regime Fidel Castro was the heart and soul of the government. In the middle of February he became Prime Minister, in place of Dr. Miró Cardona, and so had the principal responsibility for the conduct of the government's affairs.

Fidel was the wonder of all his associates. He seemed to be working twenty-four hours a day, certainly was awake from eightccn to twenty hours Most of this time he was busy making speeches and supervising one aspect or another of the widespread program of his government. Working in an exceedingly disorganized fashion, he was likely to turn up almost anywhere on the island. Although he had an office in the big building on the new Civic Center at Havana which was to become the headquarters of the National Institute of Agrarian Reform (INRA), he was seldom to be found there.

Castro's role was not only to supervise the wide-flung projects of the regime which he headed but also to explain his government's programs to the people. He did this not only in endless discussions with individual humble citizens throughout the island but also in frequent television appearances. In these sessions, in which he might be interviewed or in which he was the sole performer, he would sometimes go on for three, four, or even six hours at a stretch. He would alternate between earnest explanation of one or another of the government's projects and agitated denunciations of the regime's critics and opponents.

Fidel remained exceedingly popular. Wherever he appeared he would be mobbed. His friendly camaraderie with the humblest citizens and his sense of showmanship and dramatization strengthened his position with the people during these early months of the regime.

During April, 1959, Fidel took three weeks off to make a trip to the United States. Although he came to this country in an "unofficial" capacity, he was received in a generally friendly way. He spoke to large crowds in half a dozen or more cities along the eastern seacoast, including a huge meeting in Central Park in New York. His reception by United States government officials was cautious, though not unfriendly. The Cuban Minister of Finance and President of the National Bank, who accompanied Fidel, had informal discussions with United States authorities concerning possible economic aid to the new regime.

Shortly after his return from the United States, Fidel and the cabinet finally adopted the most fundamental economic change so far undertaken by the new regime, the agrarian reform. This decree, issued the last day of May, 1959, provided a maximum amount of land which any individual or corporation would be allowed to hold, setting this figure in most cases at 990 acres, though making some exceptions in which an acreage of 3,300 would be permitted. It also provided for the division of holdings in excess of these amounts to those holding no land or less than the minimum provided in the law. Such individuals were to be able to receive 66 acres gratis and to be able to purchase 99 additional acres. Expropriated land was to be paid for in the form of government bonds at the value for which it had been assessed for tax purposes.

The National Institute of Agrarian Reform had been established even before the agrarian reform decree was issued, and had been given control of land seized from Batista and his cohorts. It immediately set to work to put the decree into effect.

During the first ten months of the Castro regime there occurred a struggle for power within the government. This struggle centered on several issues: the political policy to be followed by the regime, the nature of the agrarian reform, and the international policy which the new government should follow. One faction sought to have the Revolution continue on the path which it had taken during this early period; the other wanted to take it in a quite different direction.

When Fidel Castro first appeared in Havana he reiterated a promise which he had made frequently in the mountains: that the revolutionary administration would call elections within eighteen months and would thus return the country to a constitutional government. Although as the months wore on he became more vague on this subject, he did not explicitly go back on this promise during the first ten months of the new regime. A strong faction within the government wanted to comply with the pledge to return to a constitutional administration. However, the other group was definitely opposed to this and urged the maintenance and intensification of a revolutionary dictatorship.

The second issue centered on the agrarian reform. The decree as issued at the end of May dealt mainly with the division of land among those who were landless, although it also provided for the formation of voluntary cooperative farms in those cases in which the recipients of land under the reform so desired. Fidel himself had long urged the policy of distributing land in individual parcels to those who desired and needed it. Thus, in his famous speech before the Military Tribunal on October 16, 1953, he had said:

A revolutionary government, after settling as landowners on their own plots those hundred thousand small agriculturalists who today pay rent, would proceed to settle definitively the problem of the land. First, it would establish, as the Constitution demands, a maximum of land to be held by each type of agricultural enterprise, and acquire the excess by means of expropriation, recapturing land which had been stolen from the State, draining marshes, planting meadows and reserving large areas for forest reserves. Second, it would divide the rest of the available land among peasant families, giving preference to those which are largest, encouraging agricultural cooperatives for the common use of costly equipment, packing houses and for common professional technical direction in cultivation and stockraising, and finally providing resources, equipment, protection, and useful information to the peasantry.[3]

However, one element within the revolutionary government had little patience with the idea of establishing a large class of small landholders. Rather, it favored the establishment of large state-directed collective farms more or less on the model of those of the Soviet Union. This was the same faction that favored the maintenance of a revolutionary dictatorship.

Finally, there was controversy within the revolutionary ranks concerning the foreign policy which the new government should follow. One group wanted to align it with the democratic regimes in Venezuela, Colombia, and Honduras, and with revolutionary democratic parties such as Acción Democrática, the Apristas, and the MNR, which in recent years had borne the brunt of the struggle for democracy and social change in Latin America. At the same time, though they favored the establishment of a much wider degree of economic and political independence from the United States than Cuba had enjoyed in the past, they were strongly anti-Communist, both in internal Cuban politics and in international affairs.

The other faction sought to have the Castro government repudiate the links which bound it to the revolutionary democratic parties and progressive democratic regimes in other Latin American countries. They also argued that the government should make an absolute break with the United States and should take a position in world affairs parallel to, if not as part of, the Soviet bloc. They argued that it would be impossible to carry out a meaningful revolution in Cuban economic and social affairs with the blessing of the United States and that it was necessary for the success of the regime to get the full support of the Soviet Union and its bloc.

For several months Fidel Castro did not take a definite position on one side or the other in this dispute as to the future of the regime. He joined in attacks on José Figueres because Figueres took it for granted that the Castro regime would ally itself with the democratic revolutionaries elsewhere in Latin America. He also brought about the dismissal of President Manuel Urrutia because of the latter's strong pronouncements against communism. On the other hand, Castro visited the United States in an evident attempt to win friends there; and he gave the go-ahead to his supporters in the labor movement who wanted to combat the attempts of the Communists to strengthen their influence there.

It was not until the early days of November, 1959, that Castro finally seems to have cast his lot with the faction among his supporters which favored the establishment of a revolutionary dictatorship and alignment with the Soviet bloc. Fidel's decision was symbolized by the disappearance of the two principal leaders of the democratic faction, Hubert Matos and Camilo Cienfuegos.

Matos was commander of the Rebel Army garrison in the city and province of Camaguey and for some time had had disagreements with the policies of Castro and the government. Finally, he officially asked Fidel that he (Matos) be retired from the Army and be given a job as a teacher, which had been his profession before the civil war. Instead of agreeing to this, Fidel ordered Matos arrested and, accompanied by his brother Raúl and by Cienfuegos, went to Camaguey to see that the job was done. A few days later Matos was tried and sentenced to twenty years in the National Penitentiary on the Isle of Pines.

Shortly after the arrest of Matos, Camilo Cienfuegos boarded a small two-motored plane to return to Havana. He was never heard of again. The official story was that this plane had been blown out to sea and had gone down without a trace. Some of his supporters claimed, however, that his plane was later seen in the airdrome of the Camp Columbia military base outside Havana and that Cienfuegos had been done away with by the government.

Whatever happened to Cienfuegos, his disappearance and that of

Matos indicated the final defeat of the democratic element within the regime. The policies advocated by the rival faction were fully adopted by Fidel and the regime.

The government began to clamp down on all opposition groups. By April, 1960, none of the groups which had participated in the struggle against Batista except the 26th of July was functioning. The 26th of July itself had not been organized by Fidel into a real political party, and the only party which was functioning openly in Cuba after the middle of 1960 was the Partido Socialista Popular.

All freedom of the press was ended. The first casualty was the weekly newspaper of the Auténtico Party which was forced to suspend publication by the simple expedient of threatening all advertisers until they stopped advertising in it. Others were "taken over" by their workers' unions. Still others were seized by forcing their publishers and editors into exile. The upshot of this was that by the middle of 1960 there existed no newspaper in Cuba which dared criticize the regime.

The labor movement was completely regimented. Although the national congress of the Confederation of Workers of Cuba (CTC), which met early in November, 1959, refused to go along with Castro's order that it include Communists in its executive committee, a "compromise" was agreed to which permitted David Salvador, the provisional secretary general of the CTC to name the new executive. The principal anti-Communist 26th of July labor leaders did not appear in this new body, and its key posts were given to the few leading 26th of July people who were pro-Communist. The new committee set up a three-man "purge" committee, the alleged purpose of which was to get rid of all those in the leadership of the thirty-four national unions "who had collaborated with Batista." This was a fallacious purpose, since these people had been removed during the first days of the Revolution. The actual function of the purge group was to remove all 26th of July labor leaders who were opposed to Communist participation in the leadership of the labor movement. The leaders of the unions of Tobacco Workers, Maritime Workers, Metal Workers, Agricultural Workers, Musicians, Actors and Artists, Construction Workers, Electrical Workers were among those who were arbitrarily removed by the purgers.

While this was going on, the freedom of the workers was seriously limited. It was decreed that workers could apply for jobs and be employed only through the government's employment service. The right to strike was suspended. All further wage increases were indefinitely postponed. It was provided that the Ministry of Labor would handle all matters which hitherto had been dealt with through collective bargaining.

The agrarian reform also took the definite line of collectivized agriculture. Only a few thousand peasants were actually given individual land grants. The overwhelming majority became members of so-called "cooperative" farms run by managers named by the Institute of Agrarian Reform. At the same time the right of collective bargaining in these cooperatives was abolished, since the farms now "belonged" to the workers, though they continued to work for wages, with the question of what should become of the profits being postponed to an indefinite future.

At the same time, during 1960 the Castro regime expropriated virtually all private firms of any size in Cuba. They were first turned over to the Institute of Agrarian Reform, but early in 1961 were passed to the newly organized Ministry of Industries headed by Castro's leading aide, Major Ernesto Guevara, the Argentine doctor who had become one of the principal spokesmen for the regime.

In international affairs, also, the end of 1959 marked a new departure for Fidel and his regime. In November of that year he began a series of consistent and unmitigated attacks on the United States, using any and every occasion to launch a new blast against his northern neighbor. At the same time he aligned his regime unequivocally with the Soviet bloc, not only extending recognition to all the Communist countries, including Communist China, but also supporting the Soviet position on every major issue in world affairs. Fidel's policies also resulted in making Cuba much more completely dependent economically on the Soviet Union and its allies than it had ever been upon the United States in the past.

This new direction of the policies of the Castro government alienated large numbers of his supporters. Most of those who served in his cabinet during the first ten months of the regime were either in exile, in hiding, or in jail by the end of 1960. Tens of thousands of exiles sought refuge in the United States, Venezuela, and other neighboring countries. By the later months of 1960 most of these exiles, including former close associates of Fidel, were busy trying to overthrow the Castro regime. Guerrillas were again active in various parts of the island.

One can only speculate on the factors which influenced Fidel Castro to take his regime down the path which he finally chose. Certainly the fact that the leaders of the totalitarian faction included his brother Raúl and his close friend Ernesto Guevara was of great importance. Perhaps also Castro interpreted the attitude of friendly neutrality which the United States government adopted after January 1, 1959, as one of hostility, or at least as one which made more difficult the situation of the financially hard-pressed revolutionary regime.

Certainly Castro and his associates had reason to dislike the United States. For over half a century this country had exercised what amounted to a protectorate over Cuba. During the civil war the United States had openly supported Batista, to the extent of arming him during the first fifteen months of the war. However, Castro did not adopt a policy of hostility toward the United States from the first, as might have been expected. In the beginning he apparently sought the friendship of this country.

Another factor in Castro's decision was probably his conception of himself as *the* leader of *the* Latin American revolution. His aspirations to dominate the whole movement for social and economic change in Latin America brought him into inevitable conflict with other leaders of revolutionary movements in Latin America who were not willing to accept his position of primacy. It also brought him into conflict with their policies, including both their attitude toward political democracy and their attitude toward world politics.

Whatever the reasons for his adopting the policies which he did, there can be little doubt about his popularity among wide segments of Latin American public opinion, particularly among the youth of the hemisphere. His violent attacks upon the United States were popular. His flair for showmanship, accentuated by his continuing to wear his wartime beard and uniform, underscored his position as a romantic leader of a struggle against great odds. His denunciations of all Latin American political leaders, whether conservative, liberal, or revolutionary, appealed to the frustrations which by 1959 had become widespread throughout Latin America as a result of the apparent failure of democratic regimes in a number of countries to hasten social reform and economic development.

By the end of 1960 Fidel Castro had unequivocally taken his stand among those who, like Vargas and Perón, felt that necessary social and economic change could not come through political democracy or with the cooperation of the United States. A few months later, on May 1, 1961, Fidel proclaimed Cuba to be a "Socialist People's Republic," thus in effect making it a member of the Communist bloc. At the same time he was proclaiming the Cuban Communists to have been right in 1957–58 in opposing his guerrilla activities in the Sierra Maestra, implying that he had been wrong to undertake these activities.

Meanwhile, "Che" Guevara and other leaders of the Castro regime were promising the formation of a "single party" in Cuba through the merger of the remnants of the guerrilla elements and the Partido Socialista Popular. The establishment of such a party would complete the conversion of the indigenous Cuban revolution and regime into an orthodox Communist government.

Late in April, 1961, the Castro regime succeeded in defeating an attempted invasion of exiles, backed at least unofficially by the United States Government. Nonetheless, the future of the regime remains in doubt. However, Fidel Castro's challenge has raised grave doubts about the future of the hemisphere's democratic and Communist revolutionaries.

Prophets of the Revolution

All the men discussed in this book are leaders of the Latin American Revolution. This Revolution is part of a world-wide phenomenon. It is one aspect of the struggle of the majority of the people of the globe to free themselves from European domination.

Perhaps this struggle really began with the outbreak of the American Revolution in 1775. The thirteen isolated little provinces on the North Atlantic Coast of America were the first colonies to raise successfully the banner of revolt against political control by a European empire. Leaders in many countries have turned in recent years to the fathers of the North American republic for their inspiration.

It is one of the ironies of history that the present day revolt of the peoples of the so-called "underdeveloped" countries is directed as much against the United States as it is against the nations of Western Europe. The United States has remained culturally in close association with Europe, particularly with Great Britain, and its population has been largely of European origin. The growth of the economic power and political influence of the United States has brought it to share rather than challenge the domination of the European nations over much of the rest of the globe.

Thus, though the traditional anticolonialism of this country remains an inspiration, much of its recent history and many of its recent attitudes and actions are the very things against which the revolt of the underdeveloped nations is directed. This is particularly true in Latin America, where the weight of United States power has been felt most directly and for the longest period of time.

Both economic and political factors have brought on the world revolution of our times. The association of the countries of Asia, Africa, and Latin America with the world-wide economy which resulted from the Industrial Revolution in Western Europe and the United States and the wide dissemination of the ideas of popular sovereignty and national self-determination which originated in Europe have both had their profound influence.

As a result of the industrialization of Western Europe and the United States these countries found themselves in great need for raw materials and foodstuffs. Some of them, notably Great Britain, had to import virtually all their raw materials and more than half their food supply. Others, such as the United States and Germany, were more self-sufficient, but also had to bring in from abroad increasingly large amounts of minerals, fibers, "dessert crops," and other products which they did not have or could not grow economically within their own frontiers.

This search for raw materials and food by the industrial powers led to the opening of mines, the establishment of plantations, and the stimulation of production of other agricultural products in scores of countries in Asia, Africa, and Latin America. Copper mines were opened in Chile, Peru, Northern Rhodesia, and other nations; petroleum wells were sunk in Burma, Indonesia, Iran, Iraq, Saudi Arabia, Venezuela, Mexico, and Colombia, to mention but a few; grain haciendas prospered in Argentina; wool growing was stimulated in Argentina, Uruguay, Australia, and South Africa; coffee trees were planted by the hundreds of millions in Brazil and a dozen other Latin American countries as well as in several African nations; sugar production was stimulated in Cuba, Indonesia, Puerto Rico, and various other countries.

These new mines and plantations were virtually the first contact of most of these countries with the industrial ways of Western Europe and the United States. They brought into existence a new wage-earning proletariat, with new skills and education and a new feeling of solidarity. But the secondary effects of the search for raw materials and foodstuffs were even greater. Railroads were built to get the products to market, ports were developed, towns and cities grew. A new stimulus was given to trade, and a larger market developed for the products of the artisans. Even small manufacturing industries were begun to meet the growing needs of the people of the hitherto unindustrialized countries.

For the first time the economies of the countries of Asia, Africa, and Latin America were closely associated with those of Western Europe and the United States. A decrease in economic activity in the industrialized nations meant a decline in the demand for the minerals and agricultural products of the unindustrialized countries. A boom in the manufacturing countries had immediate effects in stimulating economic activity in the mineral and agricultural nations.

The growing susceptibility of the economies of the underdeveloped nations to changes in demand for their export products brought a new instability to these economies. They became subject to violent fluctuations, which in turn gave rise to a growing conviction that something should be done to offset these rapid and extreme changes.

However, in order for this to be possible it was obvious that those nations which were still colonies would have to achieve the right to manage their own economic affairs, and those nations which were politically independent would have to begin to follow policies which would give their nations some protection from the booms and busts exported to them by the highly industrialized parts of the world. A growing conviction became manifest among the people of the underdeveloped nations that they must themselves develop such industries as were within their capacity.

At the same time the underdeveloped nations were deeply influenced by political currents emanating from the highly industrialized nations. Many young men of the intellectual classes received their advanced education in Western Europe or the United States, where they absorbed the ideas of political democracy, the rights of man, and equality before the law, which are probably the finest heritage of present-day so-called "Western civilization." Furthermore, they saw that these principles were more or less operative in the nations of Western Europe and North America.

The young men trained in the ideas of political democracy sought to carry out these ideas in their own nations. In the countries submitted to colonial rule they raised the logical question as to why, if these principles were applicable to Western Europe, they were not equally acceptable for their own nations. Those who came from countries already independent but with regimes which were democratic in form but not in essence sought to give greater real content to democracy in their homelands.

Since World War I the impact of these economic and political currents has been felt with increasing force in the underdeveloped nations. Throughout most of Asia, Africa, and Latin America there has arisen a movement which has sought to destroy the old order which had been dominant during the nineteenth century. This movement, though taking different forms in each country, shared everywhere four fundamental ideas: nationalism, economic development, social change, and political democracy.

The movement against European domination has been essentially nationalist. It has sought to gain political independence in the colonial countries and to fortify this independence in the nations already juridically free. It has sought to use economic development, particularly industrialization, as one weapon in establishing the "economic independence" of the nations of the underdeveloped sections of the world.

The world-wide revolution has also sought to change the social structure of the underdeveloped nations. It has sought to destroy the privileged position of the landed aristocracy, to grant protection to weaker elements in the community, and to transfer power to the middle and working classes of the cities and to the peasantry.

Finally, the revolutionary movement has usually professed belief in political democracy. However, there has been a widespread willingness to sacrifice democracy for the achievement of the other aims of the revolution, or at least to postpone the establishment of democratic institutions until an attack has been made upon the social and economic problems facing the underdeveloped nations.

This is perhaps the weakest point of the world-wide revolution of the underdeveloped countries. And it is the point at which this revolution is attacked by international Communism. There is no doubt that the rapid industrialization of the Soviet Union and the boastful claims of the Chinese Communists about their achievements in the same field have made a tremendous impression on the peoples of the underdeveloped nations. The Communists promise quick economic growth and an end to ancient social injustices, though they do not say what the costs of this rapid development are, nor do they describe the new social injustices which are created by Communist regimes. Finally, they do not point out that a Communist regime is the very negation of political democracy, an ideal which few in the underdeveloped nations repudiate entirely, no matter how much they may postpone its application.

It is against this background of world-wide change that the Latin

American Revolution must be viewed and the role played in it by the men discussed in this book must be judged. The Latin American Revolution has differed from what has gone on in the underdeveloped nations of Asia and Africa in the fact that most of the Latin American nations achieved their juridical independence from Europe more than a century ago, but it is essentially a part of this same world-wide upsurge of the peoples of part of the world which did not share in the Industrial Revolution of the eighteenth and nineteenth centuries.

Although they were juridically independent of Europe, the countries of Latin America throughout most of their first century of independence remained culturally, psychologically, and politically dependent upon the Old World, and grew increasingly dependent economically on Europe and the United States. The elite of the Latin American nations tended to copy slavishly whatever was *à la mode* in intellectual circles in France, Britain, or Spain. There tended to be an inferiority complex among Latin American intellectuals which prevented them from breaking away from the domination of European ideas and trends, and from seeking to find their own peculiar genius. Politically, too, the Latin American nations often seemed to be little more than protectorates of one or another European power or of the United States.

Furthermore, within the various Latin American countries national unity was at best tenuous. In a number of countries, notably Argentina, Brazil, and Mexico, loyalties to regions within the nation were for long stronger than loyalties to the country as a whole. In all of the Latin American nations there was a wide abyss separating the upper-class elite from the great mass of the population, and in some instances, such as Mexico, Guatemala, Peru, Bolivia, and Ecuador, for instance, it was difficult to talk of a nation. The Indian masses of those countries had little feeling of belonging to a modern nation-state, their world being largely circumscribed by the tribe to which they belonged or the plantation on which they lived. The Indian masses spoke no Spanish; they had their own religion; their culture was that of their aboriginal ancestors, not of their Spanish conquerors. To them the concept of "nation" had little meaning.

This lack of a feeling of nationality and of nationalism was reflected in most of the international wars fought among the Latin American countries during the nineteenth century. Some of these were virtually dynastic struggles, provoked by the attempt of a powerful *caudillo* temporarily in command of the resources of one or another of the new states to extend his personal hegemony over other areas. Such were the conflicts arising from the rule of the dictator Juan Manuel Rosas in Argentina, and the War of the Triple Alliance, in which Brazil, Uruguay, and Argentina joined to curb the ambitions of Paraguayan tyrant Francisco Solano López.

Another type of war was that brought about by the attempt of elements of the ruling group in one nation to get control of valuable resources across the frontier. This was the cause of the War of the Pacific in 1879, when Chilean entrepreneurs, goaded and backed by British associates, sought successfully to seize the nitrate deposits of several of the coastal provinces of neighboring Peru and Bolivia. The war between Mexico and the United States from 1846 to 1848 was of the same type, provoked, as it was, by the desire of Southern slave-owners in the United States to extend their hegemony to parts of the neighboring republic.

Some of these conflicts served to arouse a certain feeling of nationalism. They also left behind memories which, with the subsequent development of nationalistic feelings in the various Latin American republics, were cause for irredentism. However, when these wars were actually fought, the great mass of the people in the respective republics were unmoved by the struggle, or if they were involved, it was because of loyalty to a *caudillo* rather than loyalty to a nation.

Throughout the nineteenth century the economy inherited from colonial times underwent little change. The land, principal source of wealth and income, remained in the hands of very small groups. Through their control of the economy the landowners exercised absolute domination over the social and political life of their respective countries. In some parts of America slavery was not abolished until the latter years of the nineteenth century, in others the masses have continued until very recently to live under conditions reminiscent of those of feudal Europe during the Middle Ages.

Education was a monopoly of the upper-class groups. They were European in their orientation and training. The masses of the population had little or no formal education, and their culture was that which they had inherited from their pre-Colombian ancestors or from their forebears who had been brought from Africa.

Politics during the nineteenth century was a game played by the elite. The only role which the masses were called upon to play was that of being common soldiers in the armies of the numerous civil wars which characterized political life during this period. Political loyalties tended to be to individuals rather than to parties or ideas.

The great political struggle during the nineteenth century was that over the relations between church and state. The Catholic Church had come out of the colonial period as one of the two most powerful surviving institutions, the other being the army, which was a product of the wars of independence. The Church was immensely wealthy, and dominated education and such institutions as marriages, charities, and cemeteries. Throughout the nineteenth century the struggle was waged to deprive the Church of the unique position which it had had under Spanish and Portuguese rule. In most countries the victory went to the anticlerical forces, and the lands of the Church were confiscated and were given to the lay landlords, while the State took over control of education and other functions. Here again, the masses played a largely passive role. In all probability, if their opinion had been asked, the victory in the Church-State fight would have lain with the former.

However, the same economic events which so affected the countries of Asia and Africa had their impact on Latin America. The search for minerals and agricultural products by the great industrial powers brought Latin America into the world market, gave rise to a larger internal market, and started the process of economic, social, and political transformation which during the last two or three generations has provoked what we have called the Latin American Revolution.

During the last years of the nineteenth century and the first few decades of the present one, new social and economic classes began to develop. A middle class of more progressive merchants, craftsmen, and small industrialists began to appear, as did an incipient wage-earning laboring class in the mines, on the railroads, in the ports and cities which grew as a result of the entry of these nations into the world market.

These new classes generally came up from the lower social strata rather than down from the old rural and commercial oligarchy. Members of the middle class were often drawn from the people who had

Indian or Negro blood as well as European ancestry. Some few even were of pure Indian or Negro backgrounds. The new urban working class, too, was drawn largely from the countryside, where the incidence of Indian or Negro blood tended to be high. Exceptions to this general rule are found in Argentina and Uruguay, where the middle and working classes both tended to be recruited from European immigrants, and a partial exception is presented in Brazil, where immigrants were very largely represented in both the middle and working classes, but where rural migrants of mixed and Negro ancestry were also of great importance among the workers and of some importance in the new middle classes.

Culturally these new groups were not so closely linked to Europe as had been the old elite. They felt themselves to be Americans, and they had a much greater feeling of belonging to a nation than had either the old elites or the Negro and Indian rural masses. This fact was reflected in a diminution of the tendency to ape Europe and in a growing interest in native American cultural themes and techniques, new and vigorous trends appearing in painting, literature, architecture, and music. Although these new cultural movements still owed much to Europe, they relied even more on the wellsprings of the Indian, Negro, mestizo, and mulatto masses of the population for their inspiration and subject matter.

Politically, too, the scene changed as a result of the impact of the European and North American industrial revolution on Latin America. As the new social classes brought elements of Americanism and nationalism into cultural life, so did they bring them into politics.

What we have called the Latin American Revolution is essentially the eruption of the middle and working classes and, to a lesser degree, the peasantry into the political life of the Latin American countries. They have brought new methods and new ideas to Latin American politics. Elements of the urban middle and working classes have been mainly responsible for the development of meaningful political parties in many of the Latin American countries. In the past most political parties in the area were mere tools of one or another *caudillo* or strong man for the purpose of seizing and holding power. They would come into existence before an election or in the middle of a political crisis and disappear soon after this had passed. The newer type of party is in sharp contrast to this traditional form of political organization. The contemporary parties, in the first place, represent fairly well defined interest groups; that is, they are spokesmen for the middle and working class as well as, in some cases, of the peasantry. Second, they have fairly well defined ideologies or philosophies, varying from democratic socialism to Christian democracy to an indigenous national revolutionary philosophy. Finally, the newer type of political party has generally stood for a program of fundamental economic, social, and political change. Although there is a great variety in the details of this program as a result of philosophical and national differences among them, they all tend to agree on three basic issues, and most agree upon a fourth.

All these newer political parties are nationalist in their orientation. They emphasize the necessity of standing up for the juridical rights of their individual nations against attacks from whatever quarter. In the economic field they seek to have the basic public utilities in the hands of the nation, and to have the government more or less closely supervise the operations of foreign investors within the national boundaries. They assert the right of the Latin American nations to manage their own economies in their own interest.

Closely allied to this nationalism, and perhaps one aspect of it, is the emphasis which all these parties put on the economic development of their respective countries. They all stress the need for diversification of their nation's economies, particularly the necessity for industrialization, within the limits of the respective country's capacity.

These parties challenge the domination of their nations by the traditional rural and commercial oligarchy. Most of them favor an agrarian reform, both as a means of destroying the semifeudal system which has kept large parts of the population in servitude for centuries and as a means of fostering the economic development of their nations. All of them, too, advocate an extensive program of labor and social legislation designed to prevent the industrialization of their nations from resulting in the type of excessive exploitation which characterized the Industrial Revolution in some other lands. Thus they support laws defending the right of the workers—and peasants —to organize to protect their interests. They favor laws guaranteeing the worker a decent minimum income and making available to him such social services as education and medical care.

The great majority of these new parties have fought against two

of the greatest evils of Latin American political life—militarism
and dictatorship. Although the facts of the situation have forced
these parties from time to time to become entangled with the military, even to the extent of plotting with groups of officers, their influence has generally been thrown against the armed forces' meddling
in and domination of politics.

The ultimate objective of most of these parties, which draw their
support mainly from the middle and working classes, has been the
establishment of the widest possible degree of political democracy.
On many occasions they have fought strongly against dictatorial
regimes, and in many countries they have shown a surprising ability
to survive severe persecution at the hands of tyrannical governments.
When they themselves have come to power, these parties have usually
demonstrated a wide degree of appreciation for the fact that democracy means freedom for the opposition as much as or more than
freedom for the members of the ruling party.

The two most important exceptions to the democratic allegiance
of the middle and working-class parties of Latin America have been
the Partido Peronista, founded by Juan Domingo Perón as the principal political vehicle for the maintenance of his dictatorship; and
the movement of Fidel Castro in Cuba. Perón himself is not a believer in democracy, and the party which he founded and of which he
remains the leader was and is totalitarian rather than democratic.
Even in this case, however, it is worthy of note that many of the
rank and file of the Peronista Party accept it as an expression of the
working class of Argentina, while rejecting the anti-democratic pre-
cept of its top leadership. Although Castro failed to organize his followers into a disciplined political party, the movement of which he
is the leader has quite frankly repudiated political democracy and
all of its works.

Getulio Vargas' Partido Trabalhista Brasileiro, which might be
regarded as another exception, was established in the waning months
of the Estado Novo dictatorship. Although it was the principal political implement of Vargas after his overthrow in 1945, it followed the
evolution of its chief and has played an important and loyal role in
the democratic life which Brazil has experienced since 1945.

All the men discussed in this book are representatives and leaders of the Latin American Revolution. All but two of them were important figures in one or another of the political parties of the type we have discussed. José Batlle was the founder of the so-called Partido Colorado Batllista in Uruguay, Víctor Raúl Haya de la Torre established, has been the philosopher of, and still leads the Partido Aprista Peruano. Rómulo Betancourt and José Figueres founded and are still leaders of the Acción Democrática of Venezuela and Liberación Nacional of Costa Rica, respectively.

Víctor Paz Estenssoro and Hernán Siles were among the original leaders of the Bolivian Movimiento Nacionalista Revolucionario, while Luis Muñoz Marín has been the guiding spirit of the Puerto Rican Popular Democratic Party since its foundation more than twenty years ago. Perón and Vargas each established a political party, the Partido Peronista in one case and the Partido Trabalhista in the other, which survived their removal from the political scene in their respective nations. Finally, Lázaro Cárdenas was probably the most outstanding figure to govern Mexico as leader of the party of the Mexican Revolution, which is currently called the Partido Revolucionario Institucional.

Only Arturo Alessandri and Fidel Castro, of all the men discussed in this volume, did not represent one of these new political groups. Although Alessandri was the first great champion in Chile of the emerging middle and working classes, his whole political career was lived within the confines of the traditional Liberal Party. Castro, though leader of an important political current in Cuba and throughout Latin America, has not molded his followers into a coherent political party.

Each of these twelve men has sought to evolve a program of social reform which he thought appropriate to his particular country. Although there is a broad area of agreement among most of them, this arises from the fact that they were all trying to achieve many of the same objectives. They were trying to break the hold of the traditional landed oligarchy on the social, economic, and political life of their nations. They were trying to find some solution to the instability which had been introduced into the economic life of their countries by their nations' association with the world market. They were all anxious to find means of increasing their nations' productivity so as to be able to secure higher levels of living for their people. They were all searching for ways of protecting the weaker elements in the body politic.

However, each of these leaders approached the problems before him with a somewhat different emphasis, depending upon the peculiar conditions of his own country. In Mexico, Bolivia, and Peru, for instance, we find Lázaro Cárdenas, Víctor Paz Estenssoro, Hernán Siles, and Haya de la Torre giving special emphasis to the problem of the Indian and his incorporation into national civic life. Rómulo Betancourt in Venezuela evolved a policy with regard to the petroleum industry which was quite different from that which Cárdenas applied in Mexico because of the different circumstances in the two nations. With Alessandri the problem of social and labor legislation to protect the urban worker seemed of paramount importance, and he was less interested in some of the other elements of a social revolutionary program.

The general approaches of the twelve leaders also varied widely as a result of differences in their personalities and abilities. Vargas and Perón, for example, were political opportunists who stumbled on a program of economic, social, and political reform as a means of getting themselves into positions of power and staying there, though subsequently they may have convinced themselves that this program was their reason for seeking power in the first place. In contrast, Haya de la Torre has always been preeminently the philosopher and idealist, and his chief weakness has been his inability adequately to cope with the small problems of day-to-day political maneuvering. Figueres, too, was perhaps more successful as a thinker and philosopher than as a practical politician. Lázaro Cárdenas, Betancourt, Muñoz Marín and Batlle, on the other hand, combined high idealism with great ability as political strategists.

Many of the leaders we have discussed—notably Haya de la Torre, Paz Estenssoro and Siles, Betancourt, Figueres, and Muñoz Marín—have recognized the existence of political kinship among the movements which they have led, and have been personal friends. However, there has been no "party line" among them. Each of the men has evolved his own ideas and applied his own policies without any direction from outside.

A study of these twelve men highlights the fact that the forces favoring revolutionary change in Latin America are fundamentally split on two key issues: political democracy and the position Latin America should assume in the world at large. The first nine are convinced democrats; Vargas, Perón, and Castro have believed in and worked toward some type of totalitarian society.

Getulio Vargas was an opportunist without democratic convictions. When the "wave of the future" seemed to be fascism, Getulio went with the tide and established a fascist-like corporate state in Brazil. However, when the situation changed, Vargas attempted to change with it, albeit not very successfully. His inability to govern effectively in a democratic fashion finally provoked his suicide.

Juan Perón was a dictator and a totalitarian by choice. Though enjoying a degree of support among the masses of the Argentine people which would have made it possible for him to govern in a democratic fashion, he chose not to do so. He sought to evolve his own form of totalitarianism and to extend his system throughout the hemisphere. He urged his followers to forego the "formalities" of democracy in order to achieve social reform and national fulfillment.

In his efforts to develop a Latin America wide totalitarian movement under his leadership Perón suffered from three major handicaps. In the first place, he was an Argentine. Among some Latin Americans, particularly those situated nearest to the Rio de la Plata, there has always lurked a certain suspicion of the imperialistic motives of Argentine rulers, suspicions rekindled by a militant leader such as Perón.

In the second place, Perón was a general. No matter what else they may be, generals are not usually popular figures in Latin America, and Perón was never quite successful in overcoming this common prejudice against men on horseback. Finally, Perón attempted to establish a totalitarian international in Latin America at a period before the Soviet Union was willing and able to come to the assistance of such a movement which would be willing to challenge the position of the United States in the Western Hemisphere.

Fidel Castro, coming a decade later than Perón, suffered from none of his disadvantages. He was a Cuban, not an Argentine, and no Latin American ever thought of the Cubans as being "imperialistic." Quite to the contrary, there is a tendency on the part of many South Americans to be more or less amused by the Cubans, whom they regard as *"muy tropicales"* (very tropical). This attitude made it possible for them to overlook such peculiarities as Castro's rumpled uniform, beard, and six-hour television performances.

In the second place, Castro was not a general. Rather to the contrary, he defeated a general and, starting with thirteen men, overcame an army of thirty to forty thousand men in a little less than two years. This sole act would have assured him widespread popularity among Latin American civilians, many of whom devoutly wished that they could go and do likewise.

Finally, Castro arrived on the scene at a time when the Soviet Union was willing to move into the American picture on a large scale. It not only signed regular commercial treaties with his government but also promised to take the place of the United States as the island's principal customer and source of supply, and even threatened to use the hydrogen bomb in case of an "attack" by the United States on the Castro regime. For his part, Castro made increasingly clear his growing association, ideologically as well as politically, with Communism and the Soviet Union.

All this means that Fidel Castro constitutes a major challenge to the democratic revolutionary leaders and to the United States as well. By the middle of 1961 the future of the hemisphere depended upon the success of the democratic revolutionaries in bringing about long-needed reforms and carrying out rapid economic development, and upon the willingness of the United States to use the fullness of its influence in behalf of such rapid change and growth.

The security of Latin America against the penetration of totalitarianism, particularly against communism, lies in the success of indigenous democratic social revolutionaries such as those we have discussed in these pages. If they and others like them can succeed in bringing about the long overdue changes which Latin America needs, they can insulate their nations against siren songs coming from Moscow, Peiping, Havana, or any other Communist center. If they can bring about the shift in political power from the traditional oligarchy and the military to the middle and lower classes of city and countryside, if they can successfully pursue policies of economic development which will result in significant increases in the levels of living of the great masses of the people, neither communism nor indigenous Latin American totalitarianism will have much appeal.

The accomplishment of these social and economic objectives will lay the groundwork for a healthy development of political democracy in Latin America. Democracy had relatively little meaning in countries in which the great majority of the people were semi-serfs and had no right to participate in the political life of the nation. It meant little to peasants, whose whole attention was taken up with scratching a miserable living out of the soil. Nor did it mean very much to urban workers who had little right to defend themselves against abuses by their employers, and had levels of wages so low as to permit them to eke out only the barest minimum of livelihood, with no protection against economic catastrophe.

These Latin American political leaders who have been trying to convert their countries into modern democratic twentieth century nations have frequently established institutional arrangements which seem strange and even antipathetical to their fellow Americans to the North. They have asserted the right of the government to expropriate private property for the purpose of redistributing it among the propertyless, as in the land reform programs in various countries. However, such actions are not new in history, nor are they necessarily unjust or wrong. Frequently in the past when a small group has accumulated in its hands most of the tangible wealth of a nation and has reduced the great majority of the people to a type of servitude, reform movements have arisen to reverse this process and to redistribute wealth and income on a more equitable basis. The French Revolution did this with the land. Also, to a certain degree reform movements such as the New Deal in the United States followed similar policies, though on a more moderate basis, because the situation which needed changing was not so extreme as in the case of the Latin American republics.

The democratic leaders of the Latin American Revolution have also undertaken expropriation by the government of foreign-owned firms on several occasions in an effort to secure greater control for the nation over its own economy. This, too, is not something which should be entirely unsympathetic to North American observers. For generations the United States has advocated the right of small nations to order their own affairs, and during the administration of Franklin D. Roosevelt we made it quite clear that we recognized this right among the Latin American nations even when interests of United States citizens were involved.

Finally, the Latin American democratic reformers have tended to give the government a very much wider general role in the economy than it has traditionally had in the United States and, until recently, in Western Europe. However, they have done this because they have felt that only the government has the ability to bring about the social changes which are needed, and because only the government can mobilize the resources necessary for a rapid process of economic development.

There is no doubt that the leaders of the Latin American Revolution have made many mistakes, as have political leaders in all parts of the globe. They have sometimes built up government bureaucracies which have been inefficient and very cumbersome. They have sometimes expanded their nations' social security systems and welfare institutions to a point where these have become serious handicaps to rapid economic growth. They have occasionally submitted to pressures from groups of their followers which have resulted in injustices to other elements in the community.

However, the important fact about the first nine men discussed in this volume has been that they have sought to bring about necessary changes in a way peculiarly adapted to their own countries and to Latin America as a whole. If political leaders who seek such a way out of the problems of class realignment, economic development, and increasing living levels were to fail, the only possible gainers would be the Communists and other totalitarians.

The Communist argument, in the last analysis, is that there is only one way in which the problems of any country can be resolved, and that is through the kind of totalitarian dictatorship which has existed in Russia and China. Although the Communists sometimes seek temporary alliances for tactical reasons with the indigenous democratic social revolutionaries of Latin America, they are well aware that these native elements are their worst enemies. If democratic men of the type discussed in these pages succeed in inspiring hope and loyalty in the people of their countries, the Communists will have little hope of making headway in the Latin American area.

On the other hand, the failure and discrediting of any of the indigenous democratic social revolutionary movements opens the way for the penetration of the Communists and for those like Fidel Castro who are willing to work with the Communists, nationally and internationally. Such failure seems to confirm the argument of the

Communists that only by following the methods so successfully applied (as they maintain) in the Soviet Union and China can an underdeveloped nation rapidly expand its economy and gain its "economic independence" from the United States and the countries of Western Europe.

The Communists and other totalitarians promise many of the same things that the indigenous democratic social revolutionaries have proposed. They argue in favor of agrarian reform, labor and social legislation, and the fight against the military dictators. However, they add to these issues a consistent and bitter denunciation of the United States and all its works, and equally consistent and persevering praise for the Soviet Union and other Communist-controlled countries.

Communist advocacy of long overdue changes in Latin America is merely a tactic in their long-run struggle for power. There is no reason to believe that an agrarian reform program initiated by a totalitarian government in a Latin American country would not be followed rapidly by forced collectivization such as has occurred in the Communist nations of Europe and Asia. There is no reason to believe that totalitarian advocacy of labor and social legislation and of trade-union independence as a means of gaining adherents would in the future prevent a Latin American totalitarian government from brutally exploiting the workers and reducing their trade unions to mere branches of the state. Castro's regime provides ample evidence on these matters.

If North Americans are to understand what is going on in Latin America, they must learn to distinguish between the genuine indigenous democratic social revolutionaries, such as the first nine men described in these pages, and the totalitarians, including the Communists. The former are trying to bring their countries into the twentieth century, and their ultimate objectives are not greatly different from those of liberal and progressive-minded folk in the United States and other democratic nations. The Communists and other totalitarians are the enemies of democracy and social progress not only in the United States but in Latin America as well.

The people of the United States should certainly not give blanket support to any Latin American politician just because he claims to be a social reformer or social revolutionary. Certainly North Ameri-

304 Prophets of the Revolution

can democrats cannot have any sympathy with the dictatorial actions of the Peróns, the Vargases, and the Castros. But neither should the democratic Latin American social reformers be confused with the Communists. Because the social reformers apply in their own countries concepts of property which differ from those in vogue in the United States, and because they have a somewhat different philosophy concerning the role of government in economic affairs than is dominant in this country, these indigenous politicians should not be irresponsibly accused of communism.

If "communism" is really to have meaning, it must have a very specific meaning. A "Communist" is one who belongs to the international political movement led by the Communist parties of the Soviet Union and China and directed from those two centers.

The best hope for continued peace in the American hemisphere and for increasingly friendly relations between the two groups of countries which make up the New World is to be found in the success of the kind of social, economic, and political change which most of the men discussed in these pages have stood for. If the old institutions which have been inherited from colonial times and which have kept the great mass of the people of Latin America in one or another type of servitude can be replaced by modern concepts of the equality of all before the law, the prospect for the development of solid democratic regimes in the twenty Latin American republics will be bright. If these countries can rapidly develop their economies and pass on to their citizens the benefits of this economic growth in the form of higher levels of living, there will be little chance that the people of Latin America will decide that it is necessary to sacrifice the democracy which only a few of them have ever enjoyed in order to obtain social justice and material prosperity.

To reach their objectives democratic leaders of the Latin American Revolution need the sympathy, understanding, and help of the people and government of the United States. In extending such comprehension and aid the North Americans will not only be reinforcing their country's national security but will be giving realistic meaning to their own belief in the dignity of the individual, social justice, and political democracy.

Bibliographical Note

Much of the material in these pages was drawn from personal observation and from conversations with the men who are discussed there as well as with hundreds of other people who have been participants in or observers of their careers. However, the author has also used a wide variety of published material, some of which might be of interest to readers who desire to investigate further the problems which are raised in this book.

In writing about the career of José Batlle y Ordóñez the author has consulted Simon Hansen's *Utopia in Uruguay* (Oxford University Press, New York, 1938) and has also made extensive use of the following volumes:

Francisco Pintos: *Batlle y el Proceso Histórico del Uruguay*, Claudio Garcia y Cia., Montevideo, 1936.

Francisco Pintos: *Historia del Uruguay*, Ediciones Pueblos Unidos, Montevideo, n.d.

Jorge Batlle (editor): *Batlle: Su Vida, Su Obra*, Empresa Editorial Acción, Montevideo, 1956.

Domingo Arena: *Batlle y los Problemas Sociales en el Uruguay*, Claudio Garcia y Cia., Montevideo, 1939.

The career of Don Arturo Alessandri has been widely discussed by Chilean authors, and he wrote extensively about himself, and we have relied principally upon these publications. Among those which we have found most useful are the following:

Alberto Edwards Vives: *La Fronda Aristocrática* (Editorial del Pacifico, S.A., Santiago, Chile, 1945), a study of the evolution of Chilean political life from the time of independence to Alessandri's first administration, with emphasis on the importance of Alessandri's victory in 1920 as a victory for middle and working-class groups of the city over the traditional landed aristocracy.

Ricardo Donoso: *Alessandri: Agitador y Demoledor* (Fondo de Cultura Económica, Mexico, D.F., 1952 and 1954), a two-volume biography of Alessandri by a famous Chilean historian, a violent personal enemy of Alessandri. Although this work is, in the writer's opinion, highly unfair to Alessandri in its interpretations, it is a gold mine of information concerning his career.

Arturo Alessandri: *El Presidente Alessandri y Su Gobierno* (Imprenta Gutenberg, Santiago, Chile, 1926), a compilation of various articles and speeches by Alessandri during his 1920 election campaign and his first presidency.

Arturo Alessandri: *Rectificaciones al Tomo IX* (Imprenta Universitaria, Santiago, Chile, 1941), a justification of his own career by Alessandri, written in answer to attacks upon him by Ricardo Donoso, published in a history of Chile which appeared in Argentina.

Arturo Alessandri: *Recuerdos de Gobierno* (Editorial Universitaria, S.A., Santiago, Chile, 1952), memoirs of Alessandri.

Luis Durand: *Don Arturo* (Zig-Zag, S.A., Santiago, Chile, 1952), an exceedingly sympathetic biography, written almost as if it were a novel.

Finally, mention should be made of Carlos Keller's chapter on Chile in Daniel Cossio Villegas' compilation of essays entitled *El Pensamiento Económico Latinoamericano* (Fondo de Cultura Económica, Mexico, D.F., 1945). This places the attitude and policies of the Alessandri administration of the 1930's in the perspective of Chilean economic history and the evolution of economic thinking in that country.

Of particular interest for a student of the career of Víctor Raúl Haya de La Torre is Harry Kantor's *The Ideology and Program of Peruvian Aprista Movement* (University of California Press, Berkeley and Los Angeles, 1953), a study of the various programs of the Aprista Party and the writings of Haya. The author has relied most heavily on the works of Haya de la Torre himself, none of which, unfortunately, has been translated into English. The most important of Haya's books are the following:

A Donde Va Indoamerica? (Ediciones Ercilla, Santiago, Chile, 1935).

El Antimperialismo y el Apra (Ediciones Ercilla, Santiago, Chile, 1936).

Impresiones de la Inglaterra imperialista y de la Rusia Soviética (Editorial Claridad, Buenos Aires, 1932).

La Defensa Continental (Ediciones Problemas de America, Buenos Aires, 1942).

Y Despues de la Guerra, Que? (Libreria PTCM, Lima, 1946).

Espacio-Tiempo Histórico (Ediciones La Tribuna, Lima, 1948).

Construyendo el Aprismo (Editorial Claridad, Buenos Aires, 1933).

In the case of Rómulo Betancourt we have consulted two collections of his speeches, *Pensamiento y Acción* (Mexico, D.F., 1951) and *Trayectoria Democrática de Una Revolucion* (Imprenta Nacional, Caracas, 1948) as well as his masterly *Venezuela: Política y Petróleo* (Fondo de Cultura Económica, Mexico, D.F., 1956). This last is a detailed study of Venezuelan political and economic history since the early years of the twentieth century, and in it the author expands largely on his philosophy and career. It ranks him as one of the leading Latin American scholars in the field of economic policy.

In writing the chapter on José Figueres we have relied extensively on his own books and speeches. Most important of his books have been the following:

Palabras Gastadas: Democracia, Socialismo, Libertad (San José, Costa Rica, 1955, republished, first edition 1943). This was Figueres' first exposition of his political philosophy written and first published when he was in exile in Mexico.

Cartas a Un Ciudadano (Imprenta Nacional, San José, Costa Rica, 1954), a masterly discussion in simple terms of Figueres' own philosophy and what he considers the role of his political movement to be in Costa Rican and Latin American affairs.

In addition we have referred to the following speeches:

"Mensaje del señor Presidente Constitucional de la República Don José Figueres F., presentado a la Asamblea Legislativa el 1 de Mayo de 1954."

"Mensaje del señor Presidente de la República don José Figueres y Contestación del señor Presidente de la Asamblea Legislativa Lic. don Gonzalo Facio, 1 de Mayo de 1955."

"Mensaje del señor Presidente de la República don José Figueres y Contestación del señor Presidente de la Asamblea Legislativa Lic. don Otto Cortes Fernández, 1 de Mayo de 1956."

"Mensaje del señor Presidente de la República don José Figueres y Contestación del señor Presidente de la Asamblea Legislativa Lic. don Otto Cortés Fernández, 1 de Mayo de 1957."

"Estos Diez Años: Discurso Pronunciado por el Señor Presidente de la República Don José Figueres, el Dia 29 de Enero de 1958."

In all of these speeches Figueres sums up and comments on the progress of his government. The reply of Gonzalo Facio in 1955 contains interesting historical information about the movement led by Figueres, as does Don Pepe's speech of January 29, 1958, in which he sums up what the movement has done within the first ten years after the 1948 Revolution.

A full discussion of the sources used for the chapter on Victor Paz Estenssoro and Hernán Siles can be found at the end of the author's volume *The Bolivian National Revolution* (Rutgers University Press, New Brunswick, N.J., 1958). However, one may mention here the article by Paz Estenssoro on the evolution of Bolivian economic ideas in Daniel Cosio Villegas' book *El Pensamiento Económico Latinoamericano* (Fondo de Cultura Económica, Mexico, 1945), and the collection of Paz Estenssoro's speeches entitled *Discursos Parlamentarios* (La Paz, Bolivia, 1956).

Perhaps the most important source of information on the career of Luis Muñoz Marín is Earl Parker Hansen's *Transformation: The Story of Puerto Rico* (Simon & Schuster, New York, 1955). Although this volume sometimes reads like an apologia for Muñoz, it has valuable insights into his character and information about his early career. Also of importance are two works by ex-Governor Guy Tugwell, *The Stricken Land* (Doubleday & Co., New York, 1947) and *The Art of Politics* (Doubleday, 1958). In the latter Tugwell compares the career of Muñoz Marín with the careers of Franklin D. Roosevelt and Fiorello La Guardia.

The author has also relied for some parts of his chapter on Muñoz Marín on *La Nueva Constitución de Puerto Rico—Informes a la Convención Constituyente preparados por la Escuela de Administración Pública de la Facultad de Ciencias Sociales* (Ediciones de la Universidad de Puerto Rico, 1954), which has much interesting information on the evolution of the political status of Puerto Rico. Of great use, too, have been various of Muñoz Marín's speeches.

The career of Juan Domingo Perón has been written about by many people in the two Americas. The following are of particular use:

George Blanksten: *Perón's Argentina* (University of Chicago Press, 1953), one of the few books which try to develop in a serious way the threads of Perón's political philosophy.

Arthur Whittaker: *The United States and Argentina* (Harvard University Press, Cambridge, Mass., 1954) which traces Perón's international policies against a background of the historical relationship between his country and the United States.

Arthur Whittaker: *Argentine Upheaval: Perón's Fall and the New Regime* (Praeger, 1956), which discusses the causes and events of Perón's fall and the provisional regime which succeeded him.

María Flores: *The Woman with a Whip* (Doubleday & Co., New York, 1952), a serious study of Evita Perón, which gives valuable insights into her relationship with her husband and his regime.

Alejandro Magnet: *Nuestros Vecinos Justicialistas* (Editorial Pacifico, Santiago, Chile, 1954), a perceptive study by a Chilean of the nature of the Argentine dictatorship and its leader.

Perón: *La Fuerza es el Derecho de las Bestias* (Santiago, Chile, 1956).

Lázaro Cárdenas and the role which he has played in the Mexican Revolution have also been widely discussed in print. Among the best books on the subject are two by Frank Tannenbaum, *Peace by Revolution* (Columbia University Press, New York, 1932) and *Mexico: The Struggle for Peace and Bread* (Alfred Knopf, New York, 1951). The first was written before Cárdenas' presidency but remains the best study of the scope and implications of the Mexican Revolution. The second has a great deal of information concerning the Cárdenas regime itself.

Also valuable is a discussion of the agrarian reform, the core of the Mexican Revolution, Eyler Simpson's *The Ejido: Mexico's Way Out* (University of North Carolina Press, Chapel Hill, 1937). A Mexican work which contains a critical assessment of Cárdenas' continued adherence to the *ejido* form is Rodrigo García Treviño's *Precios, Salarios y Mordidas* (Mexico, D.F., 1951).

The meteoric career of Fidel Castro has probably been written about more extensively, at least in English, than any of the others discussed in this volume. Within weeks after he came to power there began a spate of books about him which has not ceased yet. Among those to which we have referred are the following:

C. Wright Mills: *Listen Yankee* (McGraw-Hill, New York, 1960).

R. Hart Phillips: *Cuba: Land of Paradox* (McDowell, Obolensky, New York, 1959).

Ray Brennan: *Castro, Cuba and Justice* (Doubleday & Co., New York, 1959).

Paul Sweezey and Leo Huberman: *Cuba: Anatomy of a Revolution* (Monthly Review Press, New York, 1960).

We have also referred extensively to *Pensamiento Político, Económico y Social de Fidel Castro,* published by Editorial Lex, Havana, in 1959.

Many of the twelve men discussed here have been written about or have themselves contributed articles to periodicals published both in Latin America and the United States. Among those which are of special interest in this connection are:

The New Leader, New York, to which Betancourt and Figueres have contributed.

Journal of International Affairs, Columbia University, New York.

Notes

&⟨❖⟩&

José Batlle y Ordóñez the Pioneer

1. Carlos Rama's chapter on "Batlle y el Movimiento Obrero y Social" in Jorge Batlle (ed.), *Batlle, Su Vida y Su Obra*, Montevideo 1953, p. 43.
2. Rama, *op. cit.*, pp. 48–50.
3. Rama, *op. cit.*, p. 49.
4. E. M. Narancio's "Batlle y la Industria" in Jorge Batlle (ed.), *Batlle, Su Vida y Su Obra* pp. 127–129.
5. Luis Hierro Gambardella's article *"Batlle y los Entes Autónomos"* in Jorge Batlle (ed.), *Batlle, Su Vida y Su Obra*, p. 182.
6. Hierro Gambardella, *op. cit.*, p. 183.
7. Hierro Gambardella, *op. cit.*, p. 183.
8. José Serrato's "Don Jose Batlle y Ordóñez" in Jorge Batlle (ed.), *Batlle, Su Vida y Su Obra*, p. 6.

Lázaro Cárdenas and the Fulfillment of the Mexican Revolution

1. Frank Tannenbaum, *Mexico: The Struggle for Peace and Bread*, Alfred Knopf, New York, 1951, p. 92.
2. Professor Robert Scott studies the process of evolution of the Mexican government party in great detail in his recent book *Mexican Government in Transition*, University of Illinois Press, Urbana, 1959.

Arturo Alessandri, the Lion of Tarapacá

1. Arturo Alessandri, *Recuerdos de Gobierno*, Editorial Universitaria, Santiago, Chile, 1952, p. 38.
2. Arturo Alessandri, *op. cit.*, p. 229.
3. Ricardo Donoso, *Alessandri: Agitador y Demoledor*, Fondo de Cultura Económica, Mexico, D.F., Vol. I, p. 430.
4. Arturo Alessandri, *Rectificaciones al Tomo IX*, Imprenta Universitaria, Santiago, Chile, 1941, pp. 78–87.
5. Ricardo Donoso, *Alessandri: Agitador y Demoledor*, Vol. II, p. 116.
6. George Wythe, *Industry in Latin America*, Columbia University Press, 1945, p. 216.
7. Carlos Keller's chapter on Chile in *El Pensamiento Económico Latinoamericano*, Fondo de Cultura Económica, Mexico, D.F., 1945, pp. 203–216.
8. Ricardo Donoso, *Alessandri: Agitador y Demoledor*, Vol. II, p. 296.
9. Ricardo Donoso, *op. cit.*, Vol. II, pp. 358–360.

Víctor Raúl de la Torre and "Indo-America"

1. Interview with Haya de la Torre.
2. Interview with Antenor Orrego, Aprista leader and onetime leader of Trujillo "Indianist" movement.
3. Víctor Raúl Haya de la Torre, *A Donde Va Indoamerica?* Editorial Ercilla, Santiago, Chile, 1935, p. 15.
4. Interview with Arturo Sabroso, old-time Aprista labor leader, in Lima, Peru.
5. Víctor Raúl Haya de la Torre, *El Antimperialismo y el Apra,* Ediciones Ercilla, Santiago, Chile, 1936, p. 33.
6. Víctor Raúl Haya de la Torre, *op. cit.,* p. 37.
7. Víctor Raúl Haya de la Torre, *op. cit.,* p. 65.
8. Víctor Raúl Haya de la Torre, *op. cit.,* p. 67.
9. Víctor Raúl Haya de la Torre, *op. cit.,* p. 59.
10. Víctor Raúl Haya de la Torre, *op. cit.,* pp. 138–139.
11. Víctor Raúl Haya de la Torre, *op. cit.,* p. 159.
12. Víctor Raúl Haya de la Torre, *Impresiones de la Inglaterra imperialista y de la Rusia Soviética,* Editorial Claridad, Buenos Aires, 1932, p. 149.
13. Víctor Raúl Haya de la Torre, *op. cit.,* pp. 147–148.
14. Víctor Raúl Haya de la Torre, *op. cit.,* p. 146.
15. Víctor Raúl Haya de la Torre, *op. cit.,* p. 143.
16. Víctor Raúl Haya de la Torre, *op. cit.,* p. 151.
17. Víctor Raúl Haya de la Torre, *El Antimperialismo y el Apra,* pp. 180–181.
18. Víctor Raúl Haya de la Torre, *La Defensa Continental,* Editorial Americalee, Buenos Aires, 1946, pp. 93–94.
19. These ideas are expressed in numerous articles republished both in *La Defensa Continental,* Editorial Americalee, Buenos Aires, 1946, and *Y Despues de la Guerra, Que?,* Libreria PTCM, Lima, 1946.
20. Víctor Raúl Haya de la Torre, *La Defensa Continental,* pp. 144–157.

Rómulo Betancourt, Statesman of the Andes

1. Republished in *Rómulo Betancourt: Pensamiento y Acción,* Mexico, D.F., 1951, pp. 141–142.
2. Rómulo Betancourt, *Trayectoria Democrática de una Revolución,* Imprenta Nacional, Caracas, 1948, p. 463.
3. Rómulo Betancourt: *Pensamiento y Acción,* p. 243.
4. Republished in Acción Democrática exile periodical *Venezuela Democrática,* in Mexico, January, 1957.

"Pepe" Figueres: Dreamer and Man of Action

1. Arturo Castro Esquivel, *José Figueres Ferrer: El Hombre y su Obra,* Imprenta Tormo, San José, Costa Rica, 1955, pp. 31–35.
2. José Figueres, *Palabras Gastadas: Democracia, Socialismo, Libertad,* San José, Costa Rica, 1955, p. 18.
3. José Figueres, *op. cit.,* p. 21.

4. José Figueres, *op. cit.*, p. 27.
5. José Figueres, *op. cit.*, pp. 33–34.
6. "Mensaje del Señor Presidente de la República, don José Figueres y la Contestación del Señor Presidente de la Asamblea Legislativa, Licenciado don Gonzalo Facio, 1 de Mayo 1955," Imprenta Nacional, San José, Costa Rica, 1955, pp. 21–22.
7. *Conferencia Interamericana Pro Democracia y Libertad*, record of proceedings of the founding conference of Inter-American Association for Democracy and Freedom, La Habana, 1950.

Luis Muñoz Marín and "The Puerto Rican Miracle"

1. Address by Teodore Moscoso, Administrator of the Economic Development Administration at the International Industrial Development Conference in San Francisco, October 17, 1957, cited by William H. Stead in *Fomento—The Economic Development of Puerto Rico*, National Planning Association, 1958, p. 113.
2. William H. Stead, *Fomento—The Economic Development of Puerto Rico*, p. 70–75.
3. *La Nueva Constitución de Puerto Rico—Informes a la Convención Constituyente preparados por la Escuela de Administración Pública de la Facultad de Ciencias*, Ediciones de la Universidad de Puerto Rico, 1954, p. 573.

Víctor Paz Estenssoro, Hernán Siles and the Bolivian National Revolution

1. Víctor Paz Estenssoro, *Discursos Parlementarios*, La Paz, 1956, p. 208.
2. Article on Bolivia by Paz Estenssoro in *El Pensamiento Económico Latinoamericano*, Fondo de Cultura Económica, Mexico, 1945, p. 67.

Fidel Castro and Fidelismo

1. *Pensamiento Político, Económico y Social de Fidel Castro*, Editorial Lex, Havana, 1959, pp. 29–31.
2. *Ibid.*, p. 31.
3. *Ibid.*, p. 44.

Index

NONVIOLENCE:

A CHRISTIAN INTERPRETATION

William Robert Miller

Nonviolence:

A CHRISTIAN

INTERPRETATION

ASSOCIATION PRESS : NEW YORK

NONVIOLENCE: A CHRISTIAN INTERPRETATION

Library of Congress catalog card number: 64-13197
Publisher's title stock number: 1548

Printed in the United States of America

TO MY WIFE

EDITH LORRAINE MILLER

Contents

Acknowledgments

This book and another, which is to follow it, had their nucleus in an article, "Notes on the Theory of Nonviolence," published in the October 1961 issue of *Gandhi Marg* (New Delhi). By that time the larger study embodied in the present book was well under way. I am first of all indebted to the publisher of this Gandhian quarterly, T. K. Mahadevan, and want to express my appreciation for his tolerance and generosity in giving space to my views, critical as they sometimes were of the orthodox Gandhian outlook.

I am also indebted to Richard B. Gregg, whose book *The Power of Nonviolence* has played such an important part in the United States, India and elsewhere. Although my own thinking has diverged from his, consultations and correspondence with him, especially in connection with the 1959 revision of his book, were extremely stimulating and fruitful. His book itself in its several editions was indispensable as a touchstone and point of departure.

During my years (1956-1962) as managing editor of *Fellowship* and of Fellowship Publications, I was saturated with reading and discussion of nonviolence. I must give thanks first of all to God for this rare opportunity, and secondly to the entire staff of the Fellowship of Reconciliation as well as to the editors of countless periodicals from all parts of the world which contributed immeasurably to my education during this period. I thank my former colleagues Brewster Kneen and the Rev. John C. Heidbrink for their comments and encour-

agement on portions of the manuscript in progress, and also Dr. John M. Swomley Jr., now professor of Christian social ethics at St. Paul's Theological Seminary in Kansas City. For my many talks with the Rev. Glenn E. Smiley, whose work as field secretary carried him into the heart of the nonviolent movement in the South, he deserves my gratitude; and the encouragement of the Rev. John Nevin Sayre of the International Fellowship of Reconciliation has consistently been a special blessing.

Space does not permit an elaborate accounting of the help given by many others who read the entire book or a single chapter, or simply were generous in answering a vital query. Among those who must be mentioned are Robert Brookins Gore of the Congress of Racial Equality, the Rev. Andrew J. Young of the Southern Christian Leadership Conference, Charles Jones of the Student Nonviolent Coordinating Committee, James E. Bristol of the American Friends Service Committee, Gene Sharp, Vincent Harding, Thomas Merton, Prof. A. J. P. Taylor of Cambridge University, Prof. Crane Brinton of Harvard, Prof. Roland H. Bainton of Yale Divinity School, Dr. Elemer Bako of the Library of Congress, Prof. Howard Zinn of Spelman College, Atlanta, Georgia, Prof. Nels F. S. Ferré of Andover Newton Theological School, and Prof. Magne Skodvin of the University of Oslo, Norway. It is hardly necessary to add that none of them can be saddled with blame for any defects the book may display, but in more than one instance their remarks supplemented what was inadequate or corrected what was inaccurate in the original manuscript.

Special thanks are due to Dr. John Oliver Nelson of Yale Divinity School for his long-time encouragement. He read the original draft version, almost wholly different from the final result. With characteristic generosity and Christian spirit, as chairman of Kirkridge, the Protestant retreat center near Bangor, Pennsylvania, he placed at my disposal during the summers of 1961 and 1962 the mountaintop lodge where a

substantial segment of the writing was done. And finally, thanks to my wife, to whom this book is dedicated, for her love and long-suffering perseverence during those long stretches of time when the manuscript was her implacable rival.

WILLIAM ROBERT MILLER

Introduction

Nonviolence is an idea whose time has come. Since its dramatic advent in Mahatma Gandhi's campaigns for India's independence, which began in the 1920s, it has made its mark on the world. Though frequently seen in the struggle for racial justice in the United States in the 1960s, it has seldom been explored in any depth. Most of the studies that exist are imbedded in a context of pacifist propaganda or in the historical matrix of India and Gandhi's specific orientation.

The history of the idea of nonviolence as a religious or philosophical doctrine has been traced by some authors as far back as the Chhandogya Upanishad of ancient Hinduism, the Chinese Tao Te Ching (Sixth Century B.C.) and other ancient texts, not to mention the Bible and the fathers of the early Christian church. It has appeared in many forms, ranging from an exacting monastic discipline to a vague sort of advice, as in Plato, to overcome evil by good deeds. One implication, often erroneous, has been that this philosophy points to a search for quiet and repose. Certainly this bears no resemblance to the activities of such men as Gandhi or Martin Luther King. Nor, in most cases, have these counsels of gentleness served as a basis for movements of social change.

If we turn to the New Testament, we find a close identification between saintly purity and the practice of enduring attack without fighting back. Some individuals have gone so much farther in making what they consider nonviolence a way of life that they forbid killing poisonous insects. The majority of

15

Christians, on the other hand, have tampered with this principle until it has become little more than a caution against striking the first blow in all-out nuclear war. Our purpose is not to issue yet one more edition of the Sermon on the Mount with its hard counsels of perfection, nor to show that it does not mean what it says. Our aim is much more modest and limited: to show how contemporary man, without embracing nonviolence as a way of life, can nevertheless make effective use of it as a method of solving social problems. We shall make no sweeping claims for its efficacy. It is neither a miraculous cure-all nor a crackpot mirage. The choice it offers is not solely between saintliness and wallowing in evil. For those willing to take it seriously, there is a middle dimension and ample historical evidence to show that tangible results can be obtained —not only spiritual but down-to-earth results.

Much of the confusion about nonviolence arises from a tendency to trace its ancestry along an exclusively perfectionist route. One thinks almost automatically of Tolstoy, Thoreau, Francesco d'Assisi, the Friends, the Shakers, the German Baptists and Mennonites. These undoubtedly are important, but they represent only one side of the story. The other side is that of Christian protest and revolt, reflected in such figures as the radical priest, John Ball, who led the English peasants' rebellion; the men of the Boston Tea Party; the Chartists and many others. Often, in such men as Gerard Winstanley and Jan Hus, the two seemingly contradictory principles of nonresistance and revolt have been held together only to be wrenched apart by their followers, as with the two Hussites, Chelčický and Žižka, one a pacifist and the other a revolutionary general. What is relevant, however, is the recurrence of forms of protest which have mobilized masses of unarmed men. Seldom have they even thought about ruling out violence as a matter of principle, and in many cases they have gone on to armed insurrection or turned to conventional political means. Regardless of this they have also had an impact in a more or less nonviolent way. With due allowance for the riots and other dis-

turbances that have punctuated it, the history of the labor movement is clearly in this tradition. Many of the actions led by Gandhi, King and other "apostles of nonviolence" more visibly reflect similarities to an industrial strike than to the traditional ways of religious nonresistance.

‹The fact is that nonviolence can be reduced neither to a moral philosophy nor a pragmatic method. It owes something to each and to the equilibrium that holds the two strands together.›To an incalculable degree this blendedness has escaped the attention of the theorists. We owe much to the example of Gandhi, but it is noteworthy that in his writings he appears to take for granted much of the tactics and strategy adapted from a long tradition of protest and revolt and to place acute stress on his moral discoveries. As he saw it, practical nonviolence was an application of absolute moral truths in the realm of historical action. There is an element of cogency in such a view, but it has its pitfalls. Ultimately it makes the "one perfect act" a virtual substitute for social action. On the other side, however, the thrust of protest, uninformed of the possibilities of nonviolence, can have a destructive effect. How often a righteous cause has become perverted by a desperate resort to strong-arm tactics, rioting and terrorism! When it has worked effectively, both before, during and after the Gandhian era, nonviolence has proved to be an adaptation of the best features of both approaches.

Our intention is not merely to provide an ideological framework to make nonviolence palatable to the Christian mind, nor is it merely to find Christian equivalents for Hindu or other concepts such as those which figure in Gandhi's thinking. Least of all is it to proselytize for Christianity by giving a religious tone to secular ideas. Christianity, after all, is no occult wisdom. Both as a form of conduct and as a strategy of action, nonviolence is not only rooted in the history of the church—a striking fact in itself—but it stems from precisely those realities of human existence with which the Christian faith is vitally concerned. The man of good will who is not a Christian may be

impatient with the theological dimension while still acting in
accordance with an image of man and an ethic distilled from
Christian doctrine. In any case it is not our purpose to promote
the viewpoint of any particular sect. We have felt free to draw
ecumenically from the thinking of Orthodox, Catholic, Protestant and Jewish writers, and to exclude nothing that is relevant.

If there is any narrow bias here, it is a bias of intent, of
commitment to the Christian community of faith. Whatever
this book may do for anyone else, we wish to demonstrate that
contemporary Christians can find within their own tradition
fully adequate resources for nonviolence. They need not, and
in fact would be mistaken to, abandon their faith or their
church—as Tolstoy, for example, argued—in order to use
nonviolence. On the contrary, nonviolence is highly compatible with the church and can contribute to its renewal, making
it more truly itself, while the church by its very nature and
purpose has historically afforded the most congenial setting for
nonviolence.

Although the reader may want to go on to further studies
that would include the important legacy of Gandhi's campaigns
in South Africa and India, we have chosen here to supplement
rather than to rehash that legacy. There are surprisingly few
studies of the many important nonviolent campaigns that have
occurred outside the Gandhian orbit. Those that exist are often
fragmentary or available only by burrowing through many
books for scattered episodes, not all of which are reliable.
Much of what is presented in the CASEBOOK section here is the
product of new research, drawing upon hitherto untapped
sources. Some of it simply makes available well-documented
accounts that would otherwise be hard to find. Examples have
been selected and treated for their instructive rather than their
inspirational value. As much can be learned from representative failures as from successes, and we have attempted to assess
these objectively to show both strengths and weaknesses, scope
and limits. It is not just a matter of conjecture, it is a fact that

"ordinary" Christians and others have been able to make non-violence relevant to their situation. The fact that Christian churches have played a part in these events without abandoning their historic traditions and without thereby becoming perfectionistic, universalistic, pacifist, Gandhian or Hindu, testifies to the undisclosed possibilities of Christian renewal that confront the church as a whole today. One need not be a Christian, however, to appreciate the fact that nonviolence is by no means limited to the special conditions of India or Alabama.

Similar considerations apply to our approach to theory. Insofar as it involves theology, it is a biblical one. We believe this is necessary to a full understanding. Aside from this, the discussion of organization, typology, and psychological and sociological dynamics is religiously neutral, equally compatible with Jewish, Christian or secular types of ethics. To the extent that there is a bias, it is again one of intent. The social structures we have in mind are those of a Western-style urban civilization rather than, say, of medieval serfs or preliterate primitives, and the psychological factors likewise. In short, without denying the essential unity of the human species or the range of application, we recognize the need for cultural adaptation and choose our orientation accordingly. The core of this book may have universal validity, but in its details it is addressed to characteristic Western conditions.

The Dimensions
and Scope of Nonviolence

1

The Meaning of Violence and Nonviolence

What is nonviolence? Many of its critics and protagonists are readier to equate it with some other concept than to define it. Some equate it with love, others with cowardice. The word has been used interchangeably with simple inaction and with "direct action"; with "nonresistance" and with a resistance adorned with such adjectives as "bold" and "daring." It has been identified with "passive resistance" and set in opposition to "passive resistance."

The lack of clear and adequate definitions has not kept nonviolence from occurring and being recognizable in a general way. But if we are to understand how it works and what goes into it, we must have some idea of where it begins and ends, what its limitations and presuppositions are. To do this we shall find it useful to embark on a theoretical inquiry which will bring us into contact with a number of other concepts related to nonviolence but not identical with it. Like any exercise in theory concerning human relations and history, this takes us out of the actual and into the abstract, which is reality of a different order. If we were to search history for an exact model of theoretical nonviolence, we would be disappointed, for history does not work so neatly. It is infinitely more complex than even the most detailed theory could ever be.

At best our definitions can do no more than approximate the actualities they are designed to match—just as, for example, a theory of neurosis will inevitably differ from a psychiatrist's casebook. Yet the two are not unrelated. The actual

cases provide the raw material from which the theory is constructed, and the theory in turn provides a framework on which
the cases can be structured, organized and interpreted. When
we come to examine historic episodes of nonviolence, we shall
see how impossible it would be to make them fit our theory,
but at the same time how valuable it is to have a theory as a
guide to understanding these episodes. Theory does not get
rid of ambiguity; it sheds light on it. Not full daylight, perhaps, but a torch without which we could only grope our way.
    In the case of nonviolence, ideas are not lacking but they
are often vague, imprecise and sentimentalized. A substantial
part of our inquiry as we proceed involves simply a clarifica-
tion of issues that are often confused. What do our central
terms mean? What are they thought to mean but do not and
cannot mean? The first step toward lucid discussion is to separate those ambiguities which are inherent from those imposed
by faulty usage.

Hindu and Biblical Concepts

    One area of confusion clusters around the words "love" and
"nonviolence" and their relation to one another. To some extent the problem is one of translation and to some extent it is
a problem arising from the dialog between Christian and Hindu
ideas with their different emphases and contexts. The term
"nonviolence" itself entered the English language as a translation of the Sanskrit "ahimsa," which Gandhi drew from the
ancient texts of Hinduism to describe the pivotal principle of
his philosophy. But as Pie Régamey has pointed out, in the
French version of Gandhi's From Yeravda Mandir, we can
translate ahimsa as amour (love). Lanza del Vasto identifies
it with charité (charity—from caritas, the word for "love" in
the Latin New Testament).[1] Gandhi himself wrote: "Ahimsa
means love in the sense of St. Paul, and much more."[2]
    Etymologically, however, the meaning of ahimsa is simple

_____
[1] Reference notes appear at the end of each chapter.

enough: "nonharm" or "inoffensiveness." In the Upanishads, in the Yoga Sutra, in the Bhagavad Gita and in other sacred Hindu writings, as well as in the teachings of such recent Hindu sages as Vivekananda and Aurobindo, *ahimsa* is one of several duties or vows of discipline adhered to by anyone seeking saintly perfection. This is what the Mahabharata means when it calls *ahimsa* "the highest duty." But in none of the classic scriptures is it equated with love. In fact, the term has no positive content as such; it connotes only abstention. Although the religious philosophy of *karma yoga* has to do with good works, *ahimsa* figures in it as a purificatory vow, along with such others as celibacy, dietary restrictions and the like rather than as a way of doing good. The concept of love "in the sense of St. Paul" is not present at all.

But Gandhi at least believed that love was implicit in *ahimsa,* and professed to see profound similarities between the Bhagavad Gita and the Sermon on the Mount. In his reinterpretation of the Gita as "the gospel of selfless action" and in his blending of the Hindu concept of Brāhmān as impersonal cosmic truth with the biblical understanding of God as love, Gandhi achieved nothing less than a religious reformation within Hinduism. Thus the *ahimsa* which Gandhi identified with the love spoken of by Paul is no longer the unalloyed "nonharm" of the ancient or the orthodox Hinduism; it is already a Gandhian concept profoundly influenced by the New Testament.

In a later chapter we shall explore the meaning of love in greater depth. Here a basic definition will suffice. The English word "love," like its equivalent in most modern languages, encompasses a wide range of meanings. The Greek of the New Testament affords greater precision. In ordinary usage "love" may mean an emotion of affection, of carnal passion or of platonic affiliation. When we speak of "erotic" love, we are using one of several Greek words for "love"—*eros,* which is generally understood as having to do with sexuality but which in the New Testament means simply that kind of love which

brings self-fulfillment. *Eros* may be expressed sexually or non-sexually. Its object may be a person or it may be the beauty of nature or of a work of art which we love and which thereby elevates us. There is also *philia,* the reciprocal, companionate form of love, as well as *philadelphia* (brotherliness) and *philanthropia* (humaneness or kindliness).

Overarching all of these kinds of love is *agapē,* signifying good *will* rather than good *feeling* toward a person, and carrying the connotation of *"showing* love by action."[3] When we speak of "agapaic" love it is this active, outgoing love that we have in mind, as did Paul. It is the ultimate love from which *eros* and the other kinds are all derived. *Agapē* is the love that "is God" and "is from God" (1 John 4:7-21)—freely given, active, affirming not on the basis of merit or attractiveness but encompassing all for whom God cares: not only self and friend but the stranger, the outsider, the enemy. Such a term as "altruism"—unselfish concern for others—points to *agapē,* but no other concept fully expresses its unique meaning. The theological implications are clear: to love agapaically means to love a person "in God"—to love him with the love that is of God's very essence. It is not something we are spontaneously impelled to do by our own nature; it is an act of faith that goes against the grain of ordinary human nature in a way that is parallel to *ahimsa's* refusal to do harm.

It is not necessary to fuse the two concepts of *agapē* and *ahimsa,* nor to equate them. There are good reasons for keeping them distinct. In all its ramifications, *ahimsa* requires doing no harm at all to any living creature. Blind obedience to this principle has sometimes led, in India, to hordes of monkeys invading Hindu temples and endangering the safety of human worshipers. Gandhi was wise enough to modify the rule out of concern for the people, and in so doing he implicitly bowed to the higher, agapaic law. Although the two concepts may be highly compatible, it is obviously not the same thing to love someone and merely to abstain from harming him. Allowance must be made for those paradoxical cases in which *ahimsa*

may be loveless or in which agapaic love may necessitate doing bodily harm. Granted that the most perfect expression of each includes the other, life nevertheless confronts us with painful dilemmas such as the classic one in which a psychopathic killer is about to shoot an innocent family. Ideally we should show our agapaic love for all by causing him to hand over his gun without hurting him. Or we may volunteer to be his first victim by thrusting ourselves into the line of fire, risking not only our own but the others' lives. Realistically we would have to choose between strict adherence to *ahimsa* toward the killer or a broad enough application of *agapē* to save the family with a minimum of harm to the killer.

The Hindu doctrine of *ahimsa* has its counterpart within Christianity, notably in such ascetics as Francesco d'Assisi and in such heretical sects as the Catharists and Bogomils, forming part of a pattern of bodily self-mortification that was believed to help men in freeing their spirits from the "prison of flesh" as part of a process of salvation. In contrast to this practice, in which *ahimsa* or nonresistance figures as an ascetic discipline for the sake of individual purity, denying the world in pursuit of an otherworldly destination, there is another tradition typified by the Mennonites and Quakers but shared by many other Christians from the earliest times of the apostolic church. In this tradition, the principle of doing no harm is seen as a way of redeeming the world rather than as a ladder for climbing out of it. More accurately, abstention from evil is thus seen as an accompaniment to the doing of good in human, this-worldly terms.

Gandhi may be criticized for failing to achieve the right equilibrium between the ascetic doctrines of ancient Hinduism and the agapaic emphasis of the New Testament. Throughout his life he was absorbed in a rigorous personal asceticism that perhaps had more to do with his own salvation than with the liberation of India. Yet in large measure his impact may be seen as an adaptation of *ahimsa*, modified by his own interpretation of *agapē* and biblical nonresistance, to the social

struggle. Many writers have used "nonviolence" as the equivalent of a term which Gandhi himself coined *satyagraha*. Much more than *ahimsa*, this is a word rich in ambiguities and carrying within it a host of implications. As Frank Moraes observes,

the Mahatma's conception of nonviolence or *ahimsa* was never passive. He certainly never compromised with evil, for he insisted that a wrong should not merely provoke protest but that it should be actively resisted. The practical expression of *ahimsa* was *satyagraha*, which literally means "the power of truth," but is generally described as "soul force." *Satyagraha*, which came to be known in its political form in India as civil disobedience, was described by Gandhi as the weapon of the strong, not the weak, its motive force arising from a feeling of inner strength and its practice calling for self-discipline. For *satyagraha* inflicted physical injury on none but the exponent who by enduring the maximum suffering without thought of counter-violence sought to shame or inspire the wrongdoer into doing right.[4]

— There is much point in the alternative translation of *satyagraha* as "soul force," for "power of truth" alone does not capture the meaning. Behind both there are unsuspected implications. Nikhilananda, in his translation of the Upanishads, defines *"sat"* as "reality, existence." Hence the dual translations "soul" and "truth" involve a single idea around which revolves an elaborate philosophy. Perhaps the most accurate translation of *satyagraha* would have to be something like this: "power which comes through a tenacious devotion to the ultimate reality."

Like *ahimsa*, *satyagraha* is a serviceable enough term so long as we do not subject it to rigorous scrutiny. We are indebted to Gandhi for the general idea it represents, but we must also acknowledge that he never fully succeeded in freeing it from its Hindu context. This is a context that understands the soul or truth—*sat*—as an immutable spiritual principle set off against the instability of the actual world, which is ephemeral or illusory. In it, man's goal is to achieve *moksha* or salvation

by liberating that within him which is likewise real so that it can be absorbed into the cosmic void of ultimate reality. The concepts of being, of the self, of human nature and all the rest that accord with such a philosophy are not very conducive to social action.

There is obvious merit, for example, in the consolation that one's own physical suffering is a small price to pay for the goal of salvation, but the underlying philosophy may be questioned when it also justifies a caste system which rationalizes the same fate for others. It is all too reminiscent of the feudalistic order of medieval Christendom, with its rationalizations of pomp and poverty, and its willingness to countenance physical cruelty on the grounds that it did not damage the soul. Gandhi, who considered himself a *"sanatanist"* Hindu, orthodox by his own standards, attempted to invest the many doctrines of Hinduism with new spiritual content largely derived from the New Testament. As a Hindu religious leader he could not help being preoccupied with such matters as "the service of the cow," the problem of untouchability and many other questions too exotic to warrant our attention. The point is that, whatever its indebtedness to or points of contact with either the gospel of Jesus Christ or Western culture, the warp and woof of Gandhi's thought was that of the Hindu religio-cultural setting. Unless we are Hindu missionaries, it is not our task to transplant these ideas but rather, as Gandhi himself suggested, to find the essential ones in relation to our own understanding of truth and reality. This may prove to be very different from what Gandhi had in mind.

The crux of the matter is that the biblical understanding of life has to do with persons and communities acting in history. The Hindu doctrine of *ahimsa* is based on a belief in the universal oneness of all created beings: the rat, the scorpion and the saint are each bearers of the same immortal soul in successive phases of its earthly migration. The biblical perspective affords scope for a sense of the "reverence for life" which this implies, and we see it vividly in Francesco d'Assisi's sense of

kinship not only with animals but even with "Brother Fire." But it has a different ontological basis, and its primary focus is radically different because it sees man as a *person* in whom historical and biographical features are bound up with the transcendental to form a unique identity. To be sure, there may be inner conflicts and discrepancies, but they occur within an integral whole.

Moreover, as Surjit Singh has observed, "personality is created in relation—in relation between the human I and the divine Thou." [5] For Christians this relation is symbolized in Jesus Christ, but it is observable also in the Old Testament doctrines of creation and covenant, in which God is seen as the divine Person who creates man, breathing his spirit (*ruach* = breath) into him and molding him in his own image, and entering into an agreement with him that respects his freedom and integrity as a person. Interestingly, there is a tangential concept in Hinduism of *prana* as "vital breath" and as an aspect of Brāhmān, the ultimate reality. But in Hindu yoga it is the task of the self to control *prana* in all its forms, thereby subduing the body, while in the biblical view it is the task of the spirit to redeem and direct the self and its body. Through the spirit which makes him a person, biblical man is not given a ladder to climb out of history into the realm of the divine and eternal, but rather a link which binds history to God and gives it a meaning beyond itself.

Just as creation is a paradigm of the interpersonal relation of God and man, it is also a paradigm of the natural relation between human persons. But it must be noted that in each case this relation is flawed by human egotism, man's tendency to use his created freedom to defy God's will and to deny God's love. This is the meaning of sin—not some ineluctable evil implanted in man, but his willful rebellion against God, which is to say, against *agapē,* against spirit, against his own integrity as a person. To speak of sin is to speak of brokenness, both within the person and in relation between persons. And logically it is also to speak of conflict between man and man, and

between groups of men. This is not only logical, it is an observable fact of human life.

Yet it is missing from Hinduism and, for that matter, from numerous forms of purported Christianity which overemphasize ritual, moral rules or other devices that attempt to substitute a method or formula for the "fear and trembling" of faith. These approaches see sin, if at all, as no more than a bad habit to be overcome by earnest tugging at one's own bootstraps or forcing oneself into a prescribed pattern of conduct. It is no argument against ritual or discipline, however, to say that they are not self-sufficient. A lifetime of yogic exercises or of upright "Christian" moral conduct is no substitute for an act of forgiveness or the acceptance of God's freely offered grace.

The biblical view not only recognizes the fact of sin, but shows that man can turn from it and be forgiven and healed, reconciled to God and thereby also enabled to exist in right relation to other men, since all share in the same actual and potential relation to God. The paradigm of this reconciliation is Jesus Christ, whose significance for the dimension of redemption is ably explained by Singh:

Thus the fullness of the measure of the stature of the Son of God is realized through reconciliation with God and then with man and the world. This inner reconciliation results in a coherent outlook by which man no more sees his life piecemeal but as a related whole. . . .

In Christ the primary relation is of person to person, and all other relations . . . follow after it. . . . The primacy of the person-to-person relation does not render it abstract. On the contrary, this relation is at once grounded in the divine-human dimension and the sociocultural dimension.[6]

This understanding of man's nature is both profoundly humanistic in the importance it attaches to man's choices and actions in history, and profoundly spiritual in showing that the measure and value of these historic choices and actions are anchored more deeply than in history—in fact, in the bedrock of ultimate reality.

In existential psychology the "coherent outlook" to which Singh refers is called the "centered self," a condition of existence in which a person's being is authenticated as an integrated whole capable of affirming itself in relation to other persons. It does not presuppose that the persons to whom it relates are centered selves. In fact, the basic principle of psychotherapy in these terms holds that the therapist as a centered self is capable of healing the self that is fragmented. He does so by establishing authentic relation with the patient, in whom he recognizes a potential for growth which can be guided in freedom to overcome the brokenness of neurosis.

The essential content of such authentic relation is agapaic love. In the therapeutic encounter it might be called "concern." In the divine-human dimension it is expressed as communion, and in the social it is experienced as community. Berdyaev uses a single term, *sobornost,* drawn from classical Orthodox theology, to signify the common character of both communion and community in this sense. Unlike the mystical notion of union with God, *sobornost* points to a meeting rather than a merging. Thus communion is an experience of fellowship in which God remains God and man remains man. Community in its truest sense is not something apart from God, for if agapaic love is truly present it is manifested as the Holy Spirit, which is the distinguishing mark of the church in the New Testament sense of *koinonia. Koinonia* means both "sharing" in the human sense of fellowship, bearing one another's burdens, and "having a share in" God's grace.[7] Hence we see how at every level the purposive thrust is the same, toward healing and integrating the solitary man within himself, in relation to God, in relation to another and in groups—all in relation to God and through God's active, unselfish, redeeming love. We shall have more to say about this process in a later chapter.

Force and Violence

What we are interested in at the moment is to note that the above discussion, sketchy as it is, affords some basis for an understanding of the essentials of violence, which we can now provisionally define in two ways: first, as the Oxford Universal Dictionary has it, "the exercise of physical force so as to inflict injury on or damage to persons or property"; and second, as a spiritual violation of the person or his relations. The Oxford definition of the verb "to violate" is also instructive: "to break, infringe or transgress unjustifiably; to fail to keep or observe duly."

Whether physical or spiritual, violence connotes destructiveness, which is intrinsically evil when it affects persons. Several things are left unspecified in the basic definition. Pure, unrestricted violence in its most extreme form is utter chaos—not simply an absolute negative but the negation of order, purpose and creativity: the antithesis of wholeness. If this is so, then in a relative sense we may conceive of a range of attenuation in which some acts are less violent than others. Without attempting to plot such a range in detail, we can distinguish between willful and accidental violence, between that which kills, cripples or mutilates and that which causes injuries that will heal or inflicts pain without damage. Also implicit is a range of psychological effects: some forms of violence may have no physical effects, though they have an impact ranging from momentary panic to severe trauma that produces incurable psychosis, or psychosomatic repercussions leading to death. Spiritually, an act may be called violent if it impairs a person's dignity or integrity, demeaning him or causing him to betray himself or his comrades. Physical violence inflicted on one person may take the form of psychological or spiritual violence in relation to another, either as a real or implied threat or in other ways. For example, self-inflicted violence made conditional upon the behavior of another may be highly violent in spirit.

We are concerned with violence primarily as a mode of conflict. Aside from any moral considerations, Kenneth Boulding has termed it "a chronic disease of society" because in situations of conflict "it frequently inhibits settlement; for it leaves no path to settlement open but conquest, and this may not be possible."[8] Short of complete annihilation, Boulding asserts, violence is able to end conflict by suppressing it, driving it underground, but it can do so only as long as it remains preponderant on the side of the victor. Such resolution as may occur must come from another quarter. Violence cannot effect it.

Physical force is a factor in violence, but not a determining one. There is an area of considerable ambiguity in which questions of proportion and legitimacy arise to distinguish between acts that are clearly violent but morally justified and those that are not justified, and between those that include physical force but not violence. It is clear that all the force present in a given society does not simply add up to a grand total of violence. Some acts of violence cancel each other. Some measures of force curb potential violence or eliminate actual violence, and some exceed their bounds and become violent or provoke violence. As a general observation, we may recognize lawful force as a restricted form of violence, controlled and used for a purpose which is ultimately redemptive. In saying this, we concede that there are circumstances in which a sub-Christian society must avail itself of sub-Christian modes of operation, even as efforts are made to render the latter obsolete. We are referring here to the processes of civilization in which violence yields to force and force to persuasion, not to a terrestrial utopia in which law becomes totally unneeded.

Persons who join together in a commitment of Christian fellowship have no need for sub-Christian means in their relation to one another, and they may choose for themselves a way of responding to violence from the outside which exposes them to harm. But they cannot choose this way for others, for to impose such vulnerability upon others would be to violate

their personal integrity and freedom. Such a committed community, it must be added, will need to pray for grace and repent of lapses into resentment or anger among themselves. It takes more than pluck and grit, no matter how noble the aim.

There is a dilemma here which it is not our present purpose to attempt to resolve. It is sufficient to recognize it and to add that neither of the two choices is wholly satisfactory: the one eschewing any resort to force even at the cost of annihilation; the other seeking equilibrium by a redemptive minimum of force. Both warrant respect and a measure of suspicion. We must remember that we do not approach the question with a clean slate. Force and violence are present in the world as we confront it, and we cannot proceed as if they were absent. That is part of the legacy of sin and the task of redemption. Whatever the lines of demarcation, we cannot claim to be free of involvement in violence. Any attempt to extricate ourselves completely is a deception and a repudiation of history, a surrender rather than a redemption.

One further point must be made concerning the spiritual dimension of violence. Let us imagine that there are two men, one of whom chops his neighbor to bits with an ax in an excess of rage. Afterward, he experiences remorse and, through repentance, accepts his guilt and atones for it. The other man never actually injures anyone, but spends his life gleefully visualizing hideous tortures which he inflicts on persons in his imagination, although he treats those persons civilly when he meets them in actual life. Surely these two men cannot be evaluated solely on the basis of their actions, and surely the fantasy torturer is a worse specimen of mankind than the actual killer who has repented. This is just to suggest some of the many hidden complexities that may be present in a situation that appears very simple on the surface. Moreover, spiritual violence can have harmful results when it connects—possibly more damaging than a bullet wound in some cases.

Nonviolence

Absolute abstention from violence is chimerical, but we can within reasonable limits greatly restrict and control our involvement in violence to a point where we can begin to speak of nonviolence. It is not the general absence of violence which is decisive, however. Just as there is a difference between "unorganized" and "disorganized," or between "unreligious" and "nonreligious," we must introduce a purposive element to distinguish between "unviolent" and "nonviolent" conduct. We may take the former to mean conduct which simply happens to be more or less free of violence, and the latter to mean that which deliberately refrains from using violence or even lawful armed force in circumstances where such expedients could conceivably be applied.

We have insisted on maintaining a distinction between nonviolence and agapaic love. They are not the same, but there is a relation, for even when love may sanction violence it is never violent in spirit. Conversely, since nonviolence at its best is fulfilled by love it is not quite itself when it is loveless. But suppose it is reduced to a bare legalism and then harnessed to ends that are violent in spirit? What about people motivated by hate or ignorance attempting to obstruct justice by "nonviolent" means? An example would be a group of segregationists responding to integration by withdrawing their children from a previously all-white school, leaving it all-Negro. In doing so, they choose deliberately to refrain from overt violence, and therefore we must admit that their action is technically nonviolent.

This is a special case, but it is the kind that tests the rule and serves as a touchstone for the objectivity and ethical neutrality of the term. By saying that nonviolence can be merely technical we open up a wide range of other possible modifications that render it operational. We thus prohibit ourselves from inferring that a given case which meets the technical requirement also necessarily involves the motives and

values we associate with nonviolence. In other words, we can see the difference between "mere" nonviolence and "true" nonviolence and understand that it is agapaic love which makes the difference. We may also see from such an example or others like it how effectively nonviolence may work as sheer technique, and how much it depends on other factors. Analysis in such terms will enable us to inquire, for instance, about the relative strategic importance of a moral purpose and of the means of exerting pressure or coercion in its behalf.

Strictly speaking, then, nonviolence as such "works" by omission, but in so doing it opens the way for forms of positive action of two kinds: personal conduct in relation to the immediate opponent, and tactical or strategic social action designed to coerce or to exert pressure. The positive action which occurs in personal conduct is the "soul force" that activates agapaic love in direct response to actual or threatened violence, but can the same be said of social action as such?

Coercion, Pressure and Persuasion

If we consider violence as essentially destructive, and lawful force as a civilized modification of violence, we may consider coercion as a further refinement of force characterized by virtual absence of any actual violence. In a sense, of course, both violence and force are means of coercion—that is, of securing someone's compliance against his will. A disabling blow or the threat of imprisonment can readily achieve this, but so can other means which, unlike laws that are backed up by the potential force of the state (or extralegal social rules sanctioned by mob violence and the like), are directly coercive without recourse to force or violence of any kind. The social snub, the cold shoulder, the silent treatment are powerful forms of psychological coercion which exploit man's need for social belonging and responsiveness, operating in terms of a simple Pavlovian stimulus-response operation which punishes disapproved behavior with ostracism and rewards approved be-

havior with social acceptance. It may even go on to reinforce approved behavior with tangible signs of acceptance in excess of the norm. Likewise, economic coercion in the form of boycott and other techniques forms a similar pattern. Withdrawal of patronage hurts the merchant's balance sheet and may ultimately force him out of business, while it is left to him to decide whether to let this happen or to regain lost patronage by meeting his customers' demands. Again, good behavior on his part may be reinforced afterward by an increase of patronage above the pre-boycott level. Much the same process occurs in the labor slowdown, strike and other tactics. In addition each of these methods may be used symbolically as a gesture of protest and of solidarity, implying a threat of coercion without actually exerting coercive power.

Coercion may occur without being intended. The early Christians and many later nonresistants did not employ nonviolence as a strategy in any sense, yet simply by witnessing to their faith and abstaining from abhorrent practices they often caused others to re-examine those practices. In some cases their witness may have been only persuasive, but in many others it inevitably took the tangible form of noncooperation which could not help being coercive. Gandhi on repeated occasions underwent fasts which he said were not intended to embarrass or coerce the British, but the circumstances were such that the British were forced to choose between making concessions or letting him die.

In each case, coercion interferes with the freedom of the person or group that is coerced. This poses an ethical problem not unlike that which arises in the case of violence. It would be specious to argue that a tactic which is intrinsically coercive becomes uncoercive when those who use it profess to be nonviolent. The use of such tactics must be acknowledged as inconsistent with an ethic of pure agapaic love. To the perfectionist it is not permissible. But the Christian realist may find in it a sub-Christian means that is relatively more acceptable than violence or force—a means, moreover, which more readily

allows for redemptive modifications. This does not dispose of the ethical problem; it does not mean carte blanche to use coercion indiscriminately. Not only should it be used with a sense of proportion as to the magnitude of the conflict and its issues, but great care should be taken to affirm agapaic love in relation to the person who is the object of coercion. Only when such care is taken can we speak of coercion as "nonviolent." It is never truly nonviolent in itself and can never be fully transformed. It can, however, be conditioned and insulated.

Let us introduce here a somewhat more ambiguous, perhaps intermediate term: pressure. This is a term that seems to bridge both the more moderate forms of coercion and certain kinds of persuasion. It refers to actions that do not actually obstruct the opponent's freedom and yet go beyond the symbolic protest. One way of exerting pressure would be a limited boycott designed not to compel a merchant to change his policies or go bankrupt but only to make him tangibly aware of something amiss. Ethics aside, in many situations in which we seek to coerce, we may be unable to muster enough strength to do more than exert pressure. In others we may have the strength but choose for strategic reasons to exercise restraint. Depending on the circumstances it is of course ethically preferable to achieve as much as possible with the least amount of coercion.

On the other side of the bridge is persuasion, a category of action that is intrinsically more compatible with *agapē* than coercion is. In its purest form it shows a respect for the person which is in fact agapaic, requiring no further conditioning. For to persuade someone is to win him over, to help him to make a change of conduct that is based on an inner change of heart or will. Whether this is accomplished by appeal to reason or to moral sensibilities or religious feeling and conscience, the distinguishing fact is that it effects change from within and does not impose it from outside. Even persuasion, however, has its demonic side. It can be corrupted by auxiliary means that undermine integrity: not only bribery but cajolery, flattery, appeals to prejudice and the like. Even at this apparently far

remove from actual violence there is room for the spirit of vio lence to operate, not in the form of physical injury but in ways that may be even more pernicious. To the extent that this is so, we may speak of "nonviolent" persuasion in a spiritual sense. Perhaps the best kind of persuasion is that exerted by the power of example. Whatever use is made of facts or moral arguments, the agapaic integrity of the nonviolent persuader can be counted on at least as a catalyst and perhaps more.

Complexities of Violence and Nonviolence

One thing emerges clearly from the foregoing. All forms of action that we have examined are relative and imperfect; none of them is intrinsically agapaic. Even those that are generally more open to *agapē* may not be so in specific instances. In addition, the actual situation in which one or another means of action is chosen will have its influence on the fitness of the choice. Moreover, it is clear that the choice of nonviolent means is only part of the process. A campaign of social action could be meticulously nonviolent in every detail but devoid of effective power. We have already noted that agapaic love "is God" and "is of God." It is not a moral principle or an inert abstraction of natural law which we can apply at will. It is power to which we have access not by reason or nature but by our faith and God's grace. It is not neutral but purposive power. We cannot channel it to serve a purpose of our own devising which is alien to it. It is not a power that we can generate. Only God is the generator; our role is that of a dependent transmitter.

Now this must not be interpreted in a moralistic way. God does not deny himself to sinners, and agapaic power is not reserved exclusively for the morally perfect or for those with full understanding of his purposes. When we discuss historic episodes, there is seldom any way in which we can determine how consciously Christian were the motives of the participants. In some cases we may search in vain for evidence of *agapē*. This

does not mean we can afford to bypass God or that it will suffice to feign or fabricate *agapē* in our own nonviolent encounters. But it does evidently mean that history is not the simple product of human actions and that God's grace has its own logic that may baffle the morally upright. Biblical realism is humanistic, but it also relates to a living God who acts in history, sometimes presenting us with moments pregnant with opportunity—moments of potential *kairos,* the fullness of time —and sometimes with moments that are barren of such opportunity, in which we may nevertheless work and witness for God's purposes.

It is possible to compartmentalize the sacred and the secular instead of seeing that they intersect at every point in history. But such compartmentalization is a mistake leading to an arid simple moralism and an equally arid simple amoralism. The one is based on a one-dimensional moral scale in which nonviolence is always categorically right and violence always evil. The other hews to a brittle legalism of static justice. The biblical view is both more transcendental and more existential—it shows love in a fullness and ultimacy undreamed of by either moralist or amoralist, and it shows how relevant such love can be in every aspect of human affairs. But it also shows that man's destiny is not a smooth uphill path, and that God's purpose is worked out in history not solely by the redemptive acts of those who manifest the Holy Spirit, but also in often mysterious ways by the temptations and chastisements that befall them. The latter has frequently been tragically misunderstood and used as a justification by Christians to slaughter their fellow men. The confusion seems to arise from a human penchant for usurping God's prerogatives. "Vengeance is mine, I will repay, saith the Lord" (Romans 12:19) has too often been answered with "Never mind, Lord, I'll do it for you," which completely negates the injunction to leave it to God. To say that even such sin and stupidity somehow fit into God's ultimate purpose is not an endorsement for emulation.

We have to view history, including today and tomorrow,

in perspective. Though doing our utmost to act agapaically through nonviolence, we have to be attuned to the situation in which we find ourselves and not attempt to impose upon it rigid structures of abstraction that do not suit it. To do so is a denial of the dynamic of *agapē*. We must be prepared to retreat as well as to advance, and sometimes to halt and pray for strength and guidance. We must have a finely tempered realism about human nature, gauging how much we can endure and how much our comrades can endure. There is always the possibility of capitulation to violence, especially in the face of provocation, if we overreach our limits; and this can have disastrous consequences.

But it would be moralistic to assert that violence can have no other effects but disaster. As Berdyaev has observed of revolutions, even brutal and widespread violence can, in some situations, clear the air and reshuffle an existing balance of forces so as to open new channels for redemptive work. Ideally, nonviolence attempts to circumvent or forestall the tragic aspect of social change. Its task is never deliberately to provoke it, but there are times when we must accept such tragedy as part of history—and even as a burden of guilt that we must share—and go on with our work as best we can.

Violence does not merely erupt, though it may seem to. The way in which it occurs is important, as is the source from which it comes. The most serious acts of violence are those which are done by persons who are committed to nonviolence. These may indicate the need for increased discipline or better training before moving on. Acts of retaliatory violence by the opponent are, of course, to be expected. But their extent and severity may point to inadequacies in nonviolent conduct or tactics, and in each case it must be decided whether to attempt to overcome such retaliation by means of nonviolence alone or with the aid of police or other agents of lawful force. If the latter are available, only a perfectionist will refuse to call upon them when violence becomes unmanageable, or when it results in injury or death. Unless the entire community is pledged to

vulnerability, those who are nonviolent have a clear responsibility to curb antisocial actions and to see that others are protected from those who commit them. Nonviolence alone can seldom do this. Another source of violence is rivals, allies or undisciplined masses related to the nonviolent movement itself but not actually a part of it. This poses a delicate problem. In a given case it may point up a discrepancy between the objectives of the movement and those of a segment of the community it seeks to represent. A typical example would be a middle-class movement that does not make room for the particular grievances of poorly paid workers or the unemployed against the same general opponent. The frustrations and resentments of these latter groups are likely to be keener and less easily disciplined, flaring up at a stage when those within the movement are able to maintain their own discipline. Maneuvering so as to allow for such factors, and seeking to broaden the social base and strengthen marginal allegiances, are perennial problems of any movement.

At the same time, it is biblical realism as well as sound psychology to observe that marginal outcroppings of violence may serve to underscore the urgency of a given situation and expedite its solution. It may do this or it may stiffen resistance and cause the whole campaign to deteriorate into rioting. Violence is unstable and risky—reason enough to avoid using it if possible. But the point is that its effects cannot be foreseen and provided for in the abstract. The specific lesson is an existential one, to be found in the situation itself. It should in any case be clear that a nonviolent movement has a responsibility to curb such outbursts, never to promote them. As a matter of policy they must be disavowed and should be atoned for by a gesture of penance and restitution within the context of the struggle in which they occur. But this does not preclude private evaluation of their objective historical or strategic effects, nor acting upon this evaluation.

Howard Zinn has argued that there are instances in which the use of a modicum of violence—such as the assassination

of a dictator—can be more effective and actually reduce the sum total of violence that would occur if the outcome were produced in this way rather than through protracted conflict in which nonviolence is outmatched by ruthless armed force. Even in cases where such a simple alternative as a dead Hitler is not available, it is often true that nonviolence precipitates violence. Zinn says:

Nonviolence theorists will insist that the responsibility for the violence rests with those who committed it. But this dodges the question; the fact is that there was more violence in the world *after* the Freedom Riders began their rides than *before*. And for this there is only one justification: that the amount of violence was insignificant compared to the amount of justice won.[9]

The violence that nonviolence produces may not be directed solely at the nonviolent cadres, either. But this is not to say that nonviolence is just the same as other methods of conflict. It is only to caution against viewing it as a panacea or elevating as an absolute the relative truth that violence is evil and its absence is good. For the realist, at least, there are limits of possibility and usefulness within which any method or principle must be regarded, and nonviolence is no exception. Its distinctive merit is not that it keeps the incidence of violence on the level of the status quo, nor that it reduces it below that level; but that in most cases it produces less violence than would be the case if the struggle were waged by violent means. By the very fact of choosing to engage in nonviolent struggle instead of holding to an inert passivity in some quiet nook, we remove nonviolence from the category of the absolute and involve ourselves in existential risk, with all its consequences. It is not possible then to decide in advance what we will take responsibility for, and we must be prepared to share the blame for whatever happens.

The core of nonviolence is imbedded in personal conduct, specifically in the nonviolent person's capacity to absorb violence without retaliating. Without this, there can be no such

thing as nonviolent tactics and strategy, which are only nonviolent to the extent that the leaders, cadres and masses make them so by their conduct. In a given situation, it may happen that suffering is not inflicted at all. What counts, however, is the possibility that it will and the readiness to bear it—and not only to bear it but to do so with dignity and a measure of agapaic resourcefulness. It requires not only courage but faith, and defiance freed of contempt or arrogance. Not every act of nonviolence can be expected to be perfect, but it must at least meet the minimum requirement of nonretaliation—and as much of the rest as the individual is capable of. For the aim is not merely to be a human punching bag but a witness testifying to the power of love by deeds of truth, and thereby fostering his just cause, inviting the opponent both singly and en masse to join him in it.

These in brief are the elements of nonviolence in Christian perspective and the realities with which they have to deal. In later chapters, after further examination of its theoretical scope, we shall describe in some detail how these elements function and what they require in order to do so.

REFERENCES IN CHAPTER 1

1 Pie Régamey: *Non-Violence et Conscience Chrétienne* (Paris: Cerf, 1958), p. 203n.
2 M. K. Gandhi in *Harijan,* March 14, 1936.
3 C. E. B. Cranfield: "Love" in Allan Richardson's *A Theological Word Book of the Bible* (New York: The Macmillan Co., 1958), p. 134.
4 Frank Moraes: "Gandhi Ten Years After" in *Foreign Affairs,* January 1958, p. 259f.
5 Surjit Singh: *Christology and Personality* (Copyright 1961, W. L. Jenkins, and used by permission. Philadelphia: The Westminster Press), p. 20.
6 *Ibid.,* p. 20f.
7 Cranfield: "Fellowship" in Richardson, *op. cit.,* p. 81ff.
8 Kenneth E. Boulding: *Conflict and Defense* (New York: Harper & Brothers, 1962), p. 323.
9 Howard Zinn: "The Force of Nonviolence" in *The Nation,* March 17, 1962, p. 229.

2

Three Types of Generic Nonviolence

When Gandhi began his campaign in South Africa in 1906, he called it "passive resistance." He was never happy about this phrase, however, and near the end of his life some four decades later, he wrote:

Europe mistook the bold and brave resistance full of wisdom by Jesus of Nazareth for passive resistance, as if it was of the weak. . . . Has not the West paid heavily in regarding Jesus as a Passive Resister? [1]

Even the term *satyagraha* came in for qualification: "*satyagraha* of the strong" and "*satyagraha* of the weak." Gandhi was no philologist, no semanticist. He used words loosely and, as the above example shows, he was more concerned with emotive connotations than with objective meanings. He was capable of using the same word in opposite ways because he was content to improvise. He was preoccupied with the immediate and with the ultimate, but little concerned with the historical. He was not the first man of action to leave so hectic a record of his thought—fragmentary, scattered, makeshift and often contradictory. The meanings assigned to the key words he used were often vague as he received them, and his interpreters have done little to correct this.

In the preceding chapter, we worked out a serviceable definition of "nonviolence" that enables us to use the term without requiring that in each case it must be found bold, brave or full of wisdom. Taking "nonviolence" as a generic term for all types of action which purposively abstain from force and vio-

lence in response to conflict, let us now examine the three principal terms which have historically been used to designate specific kinds of conduct that fit the meaning of the generic term. Once we are clear what the terms themselves mean, we can proceed to a further discussion, in the next chapter, of the modes or levels in which nonviolence functions. The three basic types under immediate scrutiny are: 1) nonresistance, 2) passive resistance, and 3) active nonviolent resistance or nonviolent direct action of an affirmative or aggressive kind.

Nonresistance and Resistance

It would be pointless to attempt a definition of any of these terms without first defining "resistance." The Latin components of the word are *re* (back or against) and *sistere,* the causative of *stare* (to stand). As commonly understood, to resist means to withstand, oppose, stand firm against something, to block its movement. All that the word contains in its etymology is "stand against." Whether with bravery or cowardice, armed or unarmed, knowingly or unknowingly are not indicated but remain to be supplied by usage and by adjectival or other explicit modifications. Taken by itself, unmodified, the word "resistance" says nothing about who started the fight, nor even that there is a fight, nor whether that which is resisted is then pushed back, pursued or reversed. All these and many other possible implications are external to the root meaning of the word itself.

By the same token, since the etymology of "nonresistance" simply negates the above, it would be most neatly defined as "not to stand against," hence to yield to something. Such a neat definition, however, would be misleading for our purposes. As is frequently the case with negations, this one comes into the language after the word which it negates has acquired certain connotations through common usage. In this particular case, "nonresistance" is a principle derived from a specific context: the Sermon on the Mount. Jesus says, "But I say unto you, that ye resist not evil: but whosoever shall smite thee on

thy right cheek, turn to him the other also." (Matt. 5:39) So reads the King James text which was in use as the authorized version when the word "nonresistance" entered the English language in 1643. The same verse in the New English Bible (1961) reads: "But what I tell you is this: Do not set yourself against the man who wrongs you. If someone slaps you on the right cheek, turn and offer him your left."

The New Testament passage of which this is a part is called by Robert Graves and Joshua Podro "a *midrash* on Proverbs 20:22 and 24:29, supported by a quotation from Lamentations 3:30. . . . Hillel stated this negatively (*Shabbath* 31a): 'Do not to others as thou wouldst not have them do unto thee.' " [2] The passages which they cite are given in the Revised Standard Version respectively as follows: "Do not say, 'I will repay evil'; wait for the Lord, and he will help you." "Do not say, 'I will do to him as he has done to me; I will pay him back for what he has done.' " "Let him give his cheek to the smiter, and be filled with insults." To these, Graves and Podro add from the Apocrypha, "And what you hate, do not do to anyone" (Tobit 4:15a RSV).

In the Russian version of Matthew 5:39 (influential in the philosophy of Tolstoy, who in turn influenced Gandhi) the words corresponding to "resist not evil" are translatable as the exact equivalent of the King James Version: *"Ne protivsya zlomu."* The Russian root *protiv* functions as a word meaning "against" or "opposite" and also as a suffix corresponding to the English (from Latin) "anti-" and "contra-" as well as "-proof" as in "foolproof." The words for "enemy" and "to oppose" contain the same root. The word which Tolstoy uses for "nonresistance" is *"neprotivleniya."* It is interesting to note that Smirnitsky, the standard Russian-English dictionary, gives the word only with the word for "evil" following it. Thus in Russian, the concept is already narrowed down to "nonresistance to evil" rather than to force, violence or some other term. In actual usage, this is also true of the English word. The con-

tent of the word is suggested by Tolstoy's interpretation of the biblical passage:

> Never resist the evildoer by force, do not meet violence with violence. If they beat you, endure it; if they take your possessions, yield them up; if they compel you to work, work; and if they wish to take from you what you consider to be yours, give it up.[3]

Dietrich Bonhoeffer comments on the same passage:

> The only way to overcome evil is to let it run itself to a standstill because it does not find the resistance it is looking for. Resistance merely creates further evil and adds fuel to the flames. But when evil meets no opposition and encounters no obstacle but only patient endurance, its sting is drawn, and at last it meets an opponent which is more than its match.[4]

From the foregoing it should be clear that what is meant is not a craven acquiescence in evil, but a yielding on one level of conduct which on another level at the same time is some kind of action to overcome the same evil. The Apostle Paul, in his letter to the Roman Christians, recapitulates in his own words the gist of Matthew 5:38ff and adds: "Do not let evil conquer you, but use good to defeat evil." (Rom. 12:21 NEB)

Bonhoeffer comments further:

> We are concerned not with evil in the abstract but with the evil *person*. . . . Patient endurance of evil does not mean a recognition of its rights. That is sheer sentimentality, and Jesus will have nothing to do with it. The shameful assault, the deed of violence and the act of exploitation are still evil.[5]

The point is that Christian conduct, without resisting, is stronger than evil. It should be remembered that nonresistance is only one facet in a many-faceted structure of faith and ethics. By itself it is of no intrinsic value, but it is a way of maintaining righteousness in the face of danger that is not only physical but also moral in that it invites the possibility of evil in the act of resistance. This is clearly a perfectionist view that leaves no room for relativities. But even on its own terms there remains

a degree of ambiguity: does pure nonresistance consist in going about one's business despite persecution or can it also mean engaging in redemptive activity? That is, when confronted with evil does one assume that one's ordinary conduct is sufficient witness for good or does one take the evil as a challenge to extraordinary deeds specifically designed to have a redemptive effect on the evildoer?

André Trocmé makes the point that Jesus rejected not only the temptation of Zealot violence but also that of quietistic withdrawal. He rejects the view of Jesus as

a kind of sublime yogi, a refugee outside the world on the shores of eternity, an ascetic who bade his disciples to follow him into solitude in order to teach them an ideal without relevance to the concrete problems of this world.[6]

This meant, for the early Christians—as for the Jesus who did good deeds on the Sabbath and drove the money-changers out of the temple—carrying out a divinely ordained mission in the world and accepting the consequences in hardship, suffering and death without trying to save themselves by resistance or by flight. Far from being models of sweet reasonableness, however, those who acted in this way more often exhibited scorn than love for their enemies, even while conforming to the rule of nonresistance. Cadoux tells of numerous instances like these from the third century:

One Christian tore down the first edict of persecution posted up by Diocletianus; another fearlessly seized the governor's hand as he was in the act of sacrificing, and exhorted him to abandon his error; another strode forward in open court and rebuked a judge for his ruthless sentences.[7]

At the same time, Cadoux states that "it was quite unusual for Christians to attempt any physical resistance to the violence of the pagans" [8] and

there were those who, stimulated by an extraordinary zeal, exposed themselves on their own initiative to the notice and severity of the government officials, and rushed eagerly to meet the extreme

penalty. In the persecution of Valerianus, three Christians at first avoided martyrdom, but then, repenting, hastened to Caesarea, gave themselves up to the judges, and were sentenced to death.[9]

Throughout history, even during the early centuries of the church's vigor, the Christian witness in all its fullness has been a rarity. Nonresistance has not always been loveless and unkind, but it has often been so, and those who have practiced it have often been emboldened by a bloodthirsty desire for their enemies' destruction, which they have counted upon God to provide.

To summarize briefly the teaching and witness of Jesus on this point, "pure Christianity" consists in doing good for the enemy in a spirit of love and not resisting the enemy but trying to redeem him. If there is any vengeance to be done, that is up to God and it is not for Christians even to wish it. Pure nonresistance remains pure only while it remains part of the context of redemptive activity. In this context, which is perfectionistic, it is validated in terms of the intrinsic goodness of such faith and conduct in immediate relation to God, heedless of worldly consequences. Although the adherent of pure nonresistance shares in the human hope that his actions will be effective here and now, his decision is not conditional upon any expectation of success. Such an absolute commitment promises no tangible results and is not primarily concerned with survival. It offers a way of life that is fundamentally a way to die pure—so far as men can be pure, at any rate— which may in the process purify the world by its meaningful sacrifice. Wrenched from its New Testament setting and erected as a separate principle, it offers the temptation of a way to die with clean hands and a dirty soul.

As we have seen in the preceding chapter, nonresistance figures as a monastic discipline in Hinduism, Buddhism, Catharism and other religions that have as their objective the voluntary annihilation of the self. In each of these and in perfectionist Christianity, nonresistance is seen as a way of ab-

sorbing unearned suffering, which has redemptive effect, and
not as a way of minimizing or averting suffering. As Trocmé
points out above, Christians address themselves to the problems of this world, and it is by virtue of this fact that their
nonresistance is concerned with the world as well as with their
personal purity: through their nonresistant conduct and the
suffering it entails they hope to redeem the evil person, not
merely to use their response to him as a means to their own
salvation.

Entirely absent from the concept of nonresistance is any
notion of its use as a tactic or strategem. By definition it does
not impede the evil person's actions, although of course it may
have a psychological or moral effect of causing him to hesitate,
to halt, to be ashamed of himself and to repent. Only in this
oblique sense can it be at all coercive, and indeed by itself it is
static—a vacuum to be filled with the power of redemptive
love. There is in nonresistance per se a straightforward simplicity that presupposes courage, implying a whole constellation of refusals to obey orders that are sacrilegious or morally
wrong, regardless of whether these refusals are spurred by love
or scorn. The true nonresistant, whatever his motive, will die
sooner than permit the impermissible. He may perhaps not act
to prevent it but offers his life as a sanction. The aggressor may
be deterred by unwillingness to shed innocent blood, or he may
be brutal enough to attain his aim "over the dead body" of the
nonresistant.

Historically, nonresistance has been almost invariably of a
religious character, the expression of a conviction heedless of
cost. There are true martyrs and there is also the "martyr complex," which is in an altogether different category, but always
a temptation. The nonresistant martyr witnesses to his faith
and takes whatever punishment may be meted out to him. It is
the act of witness that counts. The foolhardy pseudo-martyr
is vainly concerned with displaying his suffering, mistaking this
alone for witness and courting it as a good in itself.

On the fringes of authentic nonresistance there is a tendency

to fanaticism that ranges beyond those who court persecution to those who, like the Russian Bezmolitovtsy, set themselves on fire as a means of protest. Somewhere this side of fanaticism are such cases as the Catholic nuns who protected their chastity by disfiguring their faces, or the Hindu women who hurled themselves into a well, committing suicide to escape being raped. It may well be asked whether chastity is so precious as to be equated with life and its redemptive possibilities, and under what circumstances, if any, self-injury is justifiable.

These questions arise on the periphery, but they are latent within the sphere of nonresistance as such. It is impossible to say how much of apparently authentic nonresistance might be motivated by pathological factors such as masochism, for example; and indeed the question need not be an important one for us, except that a sect or movement which embraces nonresistance is likely to attract a certain number of unstable personalities as well as healthy stalwarts.

In the broader context, nonresistance serves as the substance of nonviolent personal conduct. It can also serve as a form of group or mass protest on a temporary and expedient basis, and need not be the expression of a distinct way of life based on permanent commitment, although it is from the latter that it takes its example.

Passive Resistance

If nonresistance is a feature of perfectionism, Christian or otherwise, passive resistance is essentially rooted in a very different tradition, that of pragmatic resistance as conducted by those who were unarmed or poorly armed. We shall later discuss the implications of resistance as a possible prelude to revolution. Here we will only observe that passive resistance has no necessary intrinsic kinship to nonresistance. Historically its appeal has been to justice rather than to love; it has functioned as a means of defending rights and asserting claims rather than of conserving spiritual integrity as such. Sabotage

and the "scorched earth" policy, both destructive, have sometimes been classified under this heading. Hence the term can be used to identify a number of types of direct action—that is, action engaged in directly by the populace rather than through political representatives, military formations or other "indirect" means.

Rioting and assassination are forms of direct action manifesting resistance. A well-disciplined strike is another, and it may come within that sector which we call "passive." Externally, passive resistance differs sharply from nonresistance. If the latter means "going the second mile," passive resistance means refusing to go the first mile. Its characteristic ways of resisting are noncooperation and withdrawal: the walkout, the boycott, which seek to coerce the opponent by a deliberate refusal to fulfill a role which the opponent depends upon the resisters to perform.

The American theorist of nonresistance, Adin Ballou, whose study, *Christian Non-Resistance,* shaped Tolstoy's thinking and through it Gandhi's, asserted the idea of "moral resistance" as an internal link between the two externally dissimilar forms, in effect extending the moral boundary of nonresistance into this new area. In its inception, Gandhi's concept of *satyagraha* is an adaptation of this insight to a Hindu philosophical perspective. We would prefer not to fuse morality with this form of resistance, since it is not innately more moral, but Ballou's essential insight may be preserved in the observation that passive resistance forms an extension of the field of moral possibility embodied in nonresistance—the resolve to avoid bodily injury to the opponent. In other words, we can claim passive resistance as a type of direct action which is more or less clearly nonviolent, and which can be made explicitly so through disciplined nonviolent personal conduct.

Its connotative use as a broad term covering everything from a silent attitudinal protest to the full sweep of defiance verging on revolt has left "passive resistance" often simply a vague synonym for nonviolence, but it has a more precise meaning

that deserves to be reclaimed. Specifically, it has a tactical application in the various forms of nonviolent action that work
by disengagement, refusal to perform, etc. It may indeed form
a whole strategy of withdrawal, or it may serve to implement
a more complex strategy. The point is that technically there
is a range of nonviolent action which is tactically passive, and
this fact has nothing to do with passivity of the will or emotions.

The boycott is a case in point. Withdrawal of patronage is
a passive gesture. It does not actively assert a claim, but makes
the claim known and felt economically through the loss that
results. If the opponent has depended heavily upon the resisters' support, its withdrawal can have a powerful impact.

Nonviolent Direct Action

The basic nonviolent alternative to the boycott is the sit-in
or some other form of action which tactically takes the offensive and moves into the problem area rather than withdrawing
from it. It means inaugurating de facto change rather than
creating pressure to induce change. It places the opponent in
a position in which he must either accept the fact of change
as it confronts him, or resist it. Thus, although in a general
sense this type of nonviolence may be a form of resistance, its
specific characteristics are assertive. It has variously been
called "active nonviolent resistance," "affirmative nonviolence," "positive action" and, perhaps most commonly, "nonviolent direct action." None of these terms is fully satisfactory,
largely because none of them makes clearly explicit the distinction between itself and passive resistance, which as a result
is often lumped with it.

The distinction we wish to observe in this concept is a meaningful one, especially in its implications. For it is usually in
nonviolent direct action that we must confront civil disobedience and the complex of legal and moral problems that it
entails. Also, this form of action places more exacting demands

upon nonviolent personal conduct, since it involves meeting the opponent on his own or disputed territory. Conflict is likely to be more acute here and the threat or reality of force or violence more direct.

In addition to these distinct types of nonviolence there are two categories of action that fit into nonviolent campaigns. First, there are actions which presuppose nonviolence but are mobile in their applicability. The act of standing or sitting as a human obstacle is an example, such as sitting on railroad tracks or on a roadway to block the movement of the opponent's vehicles. Another is the practice of "going limp" when arrested. The nonviolent cadre thus compels the opponent to lift him bodily. Such tactics lend themselves to all three types of nonviolence and defy easy classification, combining elements of passivity and of direct action. This fact raises a problem of interpretation that cannot be resolved theoretically but must be referred to the situation in which such conduct is used. In essence the problem is an ethical one that applies also to the whole spectrum of nonviolence.

It is hard to conceive of any situation in which nonresistance would be ethically prohibited, but the closer we get to direct action the more we have to justify our actions from an ethical perspective and also perhaps from a legal one. As we have already said, extreme measures require extreme compensation by acts and gestures of love. But even granting this, we must ask whether the situation itself justifies the use of direct action at all. We do not arbitrarily move from boycott to sit-in unless the conflict and the issues are so urgent and the boycott so unproductive by itself that a sit-in is ethically defensible. In general, extreme measures are to be reserved until moderate ones have been tried and fail. Given an extreme situation, of course, a type of nonviolence that is equally extreme is justly proportioned and not excessive at all.

But such tactics as bodily obstruction and going limp are psychologically volatile, offering a high level of expressive

gratification that must be judiciously weighed not only against their ethical but their psychological appropriateness. Will they register an effective protest or will they stiffen the opponent's hostility and perhaps offend neutrals? The same questions may be asked of self-imposed suffering in the fast or hunger strike. Although obviously passive as social action, they may be strongly coercive psychologically and interpreted as blackmail of a very reprehensible kind.

Second, there are types of action which form an important part of many nonviolent campaigns but which are outside the scope of nonviolence as such. The poster walk, the march, picketing and other forms of public demonstration can be conducted "unviolently" by persons who are quite unprepared for nonviolence, so long as they occur in a situation where they are accepted as a legitimate form of extralegal protest. Unlike more conventional activities such as voting, petitioning, writing letters to editors and the like, they are nevertheless a form of action which may have to confront force or violence in situations that do not provide the stability of acceptance. And frequently this is the case where social conflict exists on a level that makes any of the types of nonviolence applicable. In such a context these otherwise "unviolent" actions may be entrusted only to those trained and prepared to act nonviolently. They become nonviolent by implication.

Also in this category are certain actions that have historically arisen in the context of nonviolent campaigns and have seldom been used otherwise: the public prayer vigil, both silent and vocal, and the prayer pilgrimage. These have been criticized as a perversion of worship and defended as a religiously purified kind of demonstration that witnesses to explicitly religious motives. Its defenders argue further that, because it is rooted in love, this kind of witness is intrinsically nonviolent. In terms of our analysis and typology, this claim misses the point by confusing love with nonviolence. The two are not identical and from a tactical standpoint these actions resemble

public demonstrations in that they can be performed independently of a nonviolent campaign and, whatever their intrinsic merit, require an effective discipline of nonviolent response to attack if they are to be considered part of a nonviolent campaign. Given the occasion, however, these actions may well play a vital part in such a campaign.

Alternative Classifications

The above classification of types owes much to study and analysis of the work of others who have offered typologies in this area. Gene Sharp arranges nine categories along a "horizontal" spectrum that mixes those we have used above with a separate dimension that we shall consider as levels of conduct, strategy and tactics. Sharp's categories are ranged from conservative to revolutionary in the following order: 1) nonresistance, 2) active reconciliation, 3) moral resistance, 4) selective nonviolence, 5) passive resistance, 6) peaceful resistance, 7) nonviolent direct action, 8) *satyagraha* and 9) nonviolent revolution. One of the difficulties of such a system is the apparent fluidity of its criteria and the consequent arbitrariness of distinctions. *Satyagraha,* for instance, is so generic a term that it encompasses most if not all of the types listed before it, while active reconciliation can be more accurately viewed not as a type of nonviolent action but as a separate process related to any of these types. Also, additional intermediate categories might readily be inserted among those types that do form a consistent spectrum, e.g., "selective nonresistance" or "selective passive resistance." [10]

Along somewhat similar lines, C. J. Cadoux [11] has diagramed a much more elaborate spectrum that is useful in locating conventionally "unviolent" and specifically nonviolent actions within a broad range that includes gradations of these and also of force and violence. This is reproduced on the opposite page with minor modifications:

NONCOERCIVE

Personal example
Intercessory prayer
Conciliatory discussion
Direct acts of love
Nonresistance
Unmerited suffering
Self-imposed penance
Arguments and appeals
Mediation
Arbitration
Promises
Rewards
Bribes

COERCIVE   *Examples*

NONINJURIOUS

Psychological	Noncooperation	Active resistance
	Civil Disobedience	Strike, boycott
	Threats ⎤ show of force	
	Anger ⎦	"War of nerves"

| Physical | Restraint by manual force | |
| | Bodily obstruction | |

INJURIOUS

Temporarily incapacitating action	Judo
Disablement with recoverable damage	Broken bone
Pain without permanent harm	Wrestling hold
Damage to personality (psychological)	Neurosis
Permanent physical disablement	Crippling
Permanent damage to personality	Psychosis
Incidental or accidental homicide	
Willful murder	
Posthumous desecration or mutilation	
Torture	
Mutilation	

As elaborate as it is, this scheme could be elaborated still further as a bare list or refined into comprehensive structural detail. For our purposes it affords an instructive background that is, however, too unwieldy to serve as a tool of analysis.

Closer to our approach is the system devised by the sociologist Clarence Marsh Case, whose pioneer work [12] still commands respect and warrants study. His typology is more

sharply focused along functional lines and is less complicated by moral evaluations than either Cadoux or Sharp:

PERSUASION

1. By argument.
2. By suffering: a) nonresistant martyrdom when suffering is inflicted by the opponent; b) self-inflicted, e.g., a hunger strike.

NONVIOLENT COERCION

1. Indirect action: strike, boycott, noncooperation (withdrawal from voluntary cooperation with opponent).
2. Political action through institutions and culture—combining partisan persuasion and impersonal coercion of law and established traditions. This involves the threat or use of force or "legitimated violence" by police, courts and prisons.
3. Social coercion: a) ostracism, b) collective pressure through passive resistance.

VIOLENT COERCION

1. Threat of violence or force.
2. Use of violence or force.

In general, our departure from Case's system derives from our basic concept of nonviolence as it has developed since Case wrote, and as it is related to our theological and ethical perspective. We would set aside his category of political action as being distinct from nonviolence. Our use of the term "passive resistance" corresponds roughly to his "indirect action" and "nonviolent direct action" to his "social coercion."

As is true of any theoretical formulation, any set of types or definitions must be general enough to withstand contact with the actualities from which it is derived. Those that we have selected are not sacrosanct. It is hoped that they have both sufficient precision and resilience to be serviceable in all cases. But there may well be situations in which the termi-

nology of Case, Sharp, Cadoux or some other theorist can give added guidance. In any event our theoretical equipment is not yet complete until we augment our basic typology of horizontal range with a further typology of vertical levels on which they operate.

REFERENCES IN CHAPTER 2

1 M. K. Gandhi in *Harijan,* December 7, 1947.
2 Graves and Podro: *The Nazarene Gospel Restored* (Garden City, N. Y.: Doubleday & Co., Inc., 1954), p. 238.
3 L. N. Tolstoy: "What I Believe" in *The Tolstoy Centennial Edition* (London: Oxford Univ. Press, 1928-1937), Vol. 11, p. 398.
4 Dietrich Bonhoeffer: *The Cost of Discipleship* (New York: The Macmillan Co., second edition, 1960), p. 127.
5 *Ibid.,* p. 128.
6 André Trocmé: *Jésus-Christ et la Révolution Non Violente* (Geneva: Labor et Fides, 1961), p. 165.
7 C. J. Cadoux: *The Early Church and the World* (Edinburgh: Clark, 1925), p. 531f.
8 *Ibid.,* p. 532.
9 *Ibid.,* p. 529f.
10 See Gene Sharp: "A Study of the Meanings of Nonviolence" in *Gandhi Marg* (New Delhi), October 1959, p. 270.
11 C. J. Cadoux: *Christian Pacifism Re-examined* (Oxford: Basil Blackwell, 1940), p. 45.
12 C. M. Case: *Non-Violent Coercion* (New York: The Century Co., 1923), p. 397, *et seq.*

3

Levels of Generic Nonviolence

In addition to the three basic types of generic nonviolence there are different levels of motivation and organization on which each type can operate. In terms of motivation, the Quaker pamphlet *A Perspective on Nonviolence* [1] distinguishes between: 1) technique adopted as an expedient; 2) policy based on commitment and 3) spiritual discipline as "an act of trust in God and obedience to his will." These three categories may, however, be regarded as basically two: the expedient and the absolutist or holistic, with "policy based on commitment" comprising an area of overlap between these two. Historically the absolutist has usually been typified by nonresistance, though not always; and in more recent times it has often been the absolutists who have taken the lead in developing passive resistance and active nonviolence as a means of achieving relevance without abandoning their absolute commitment.

In a sense, this "absolutism" is of the essence of nonviolence. Nonviolent conduct as such—the act of refraining from violence even under direct provocation or attack—is either completely nonviolent or not so at all, and this fact is decisive in distinguishing between nonviolent action and conventional action. The distinction between expediency and absolutism comes into play in another way, however, in that the former relates nonviolent conduct to a given situation and certain limits, not necessarily excluding armed force or other means in another situation or under conditions that exceed the immediate commitment, while the thoroughgoing absolutist does not con-

62

NONVIOLENCE: A CHRISTIAN INTERPRETATION 63

template any departure from his holistic discipline and is prepared to find his justification outside the realm of historical results.

The levels that are of chief interest to us are accessible to the absolutist, but they are related primarily to the practical structuring of activity as an expedient technique. There are three such levels: 1) the spontaneous or subtactical, 2) the tactical and 3) the strategic. The first of these is in one sense the diametrical opposite of the holistic and in another it may be an expression of it. In the first sense—spontaneous—it is an unstable expression of good will arising from little or no forethought and having no prior, agreed-upon commitment, no idea of developing nonviolence in a systematic or sustained way. A more or less random crowd of unarmed demonstrators which resists provocation but has no plan for further nonviolent action would come under this heading. The other—subtactical—is an action that may be based on a limited commitment of expediency but is more likely to be associated with absolutism. Its chief characteristic is not that it is unplanned but that it is unrelated to a strategy of nonviolence. It is an isolated act or a "witness." It is possible to have a series of such subtactical actions or a variety of them simultaneously without any thought of strategy or of general policy.

This brings us to the all-important levels of tactics and strategy. Cadets of the U.S. Military Academy are taught that strategy is the art and science of developing and using the political, economic, psychological and military forces of a nation, during peace and during war, to afford the maximum support to national policies, in order to increase the probabilities and favorable consequences of victory and to lessen the chances of defeat. Specifically military strategy is the art and science of employing the armed forces of a nation to secure the objectives of national policy by the application of force or the threat of force. The fundamental law of strategy is to be stronger at the decisive point.

Cadets are taught that tactics are the employment of units

in combat, the ordered arrangement and maneuver of units in relation to each other and/or in relation to the enemy.

These definitions sum up the best thinking of military commanders from Sun Tzu and Alexander the Great to modern generals, and perhaps the pithiest definition is Clausewitz's: "Tactics is the art of using troops in battle; strategy is the art of using battles to win the war."

These definitions can be readily adapted from military conflict to social conflict involving nonviolence rather than armed force. Analogous to the West Point definitions we may say that over-all strategy would mean the use of nonviolence along with political action, conventional social action, publicity techniques and other methods in order to achieve an objective and to lessen the chances of defeat. A specifically nonviolent strategy would be an orchestration of a variety of tactics involving strategic leadership analogous to a military general staff. It is the task of the leadership to deploy their units of nonviolent cadres—persons disciplined in nonviolent conduct —in a manner most calculated to exert maximum strength at the decisive point rather than to allow them to undertake uncoordinated or sporadic actions of a subtactical kind.

Pursuing the analogy, nonviolent tactics are those actions undertaken by disciplined nonviolent cadres in direct confrontation with the opponent—in other words, the way in which organized groups of persons trained in nonviolent conduct act within their given sector of action in the furtherance of the larger objectives of nonviolent strategy.

It is the bearing on the objective that is tactical. In the case of a group of nonviolent cadres conducting a sit-in at a store, for example, the act of sitting in is the tactic. It is not all that the cadres are called upon to do; they also have to respond nonviolently to jeering, harassment and the like. These responses form another category as nonviolent conduct. If there are many coordinated sit-in actions, they form a sit-in strategy. But this may not be the case. The strategy may consist largely of economic boycott, and then we would speak of a boycott

strategy supported by sit-in tactics. The distinctions between these levels are flexible and relative, and for greater fluency we might want to refer to minor and major strategies, and to tactics that have a delaying or holding purpose in contrast to those that move toward a strategic objective.

Sit-ins, stand-ins, walk-ins and the like are typical tactics of direct action. Forms of nonresistance such as allowing oneself to be arrested may be used tactically. Walkouts, boycotts and the like are typical passive resistance tactics. In a somewhat distinctive category are a number of bodily obstruction tactics that may be technically passive but carry a strong element of active interference, as exemplified by Indians in the independence struggles who lay down on railroad tracks to prevent trains from moving. Cadres sitting or standing in a doorway or road, singly or in groups interlocking their arms, are likewise using this type of tactic. Perhaps its most common manifestation in the United States has been the practice of "going limp" when arrested, or of pairs of cadres sitting back-to-back and linking arms to make it harder for police to carry them away.

In each specific case, little can be said of the intrinsic merit of any tactic. The questions to be asked are: what purpose does it serve in relation to strategy, what conduct does it demand, what other tactics may be needed to augment it, what further problems does it cause, how effective is it likely to be and is it nonviolent in content and in spirit?

In contrast with the undifferentiated use of nonviolence either holistically or spontaneously, we begin to see a spectrum of consistent levels that begins with nonviolent conduct and discipline as the basic individual resource and advances upward organizationally from subtactical actions by an individual or group to tactical actions by many groups as part of a concerted nonviolent campaign supported by legislative and judicial measures, by radio, television and press appeals, by conventional mass demonstrations and the like, together forming an over-all strategy which expresses a general policy.

Nonviolence in a Supporting Role

Just as troops may be tactically deployed for policing purposes in an internal emergency without a war strategy, nonviolent tactics may be used in the service of a campaign built around conventional political or social action. That is, they may function to support strategies other than nonviolent ones. A sit-in or withdrawal of patronage, for example, may be used tactically to add pressure in a situation where the main effort toward a solution is proceeding through the courts. Such a strategy is judicial rather than nonviolent, even though nonviolent cadres are deployed and may have to withstand harsh treatment just as in a campaign of strategic nonviolence.

Acts of nonviolence, when serving as tactics in a conventional campaign, do not thereby make it a "nonviolent" campaign, though they may give it a nonviolent coloration. There is an understandable tendency among some enthusiasts to claim even ordinary conventional action as nonviolent and to capitalize on the presence of authentically nonviolent elements for propaganda purposes, but as a simple matter of fact it is misleading to describe such campaigns in this way, even if every participant in a conventional action is wholeheartedly committed to nonviolence.

The campaign which has conventional action as its backbone is only one type, perhaps the most prevalent. In others, tactical or subtactical nonviolence may occur as an adjunct to insurrectionary violence. We are not arguing for their compatibility, but historically this has happened: nonviolence in one sector, with sabotage, terrorism and guerrilla warfare in others forming the strategic backbone. Finally, there is a type of campaign in which the strategic burden is carried primarily by nonviolence, supported tactically or subtactically by conventional and even violent actions of some kinds.

There are clear historical examples of social-action campaigns restricted to conventional methods, but every other kind is a mixture involving various proportions of conventional ac-

tion and violence, or conventional action and nonviolence, or all three together. Particularly when resistance occurs on a large scale it becomes a problem to control or coordinate the different kinds of action that may arise—to move people from the conventional to the nonviolent, as well as to curb outbreaks of violence, and to orchestrate the activities of different organizations in the pursuit of the same objective.

As in political or military operations, nonviolent tactics and strategy are arts that require talent and imagination to be effective. The good tactician or strategist not only must understand the principles of nonviolence but also needs a good sense of timing. He must be able to appraise the facts of the situation and decide whether to exercise restraint or daring at the crucial moment. He must be able to conceive the right symbolic act or gesture to dramatize the campaign in a forceful and striking way, and for this he may turn to a number of actions that have no tactical or strategic value as such. Public fasting, silent vigils and the like, though not inherently nonviolent, may serve to underline the spiritual dimension and the nonviolent intent of tactics which are themselves somewhat ambiguous. Poster walks and picketing, though conventional, can be so designed as to point up the nonviolent emphasis. The strategist must know, too, how to sustain reverses and losses and regroup his followers; and, sometimes lacking strategic avenues for their energies, he must devise outlets to enable them to express themselves as much for the sake of releasing charged-up emotions as for communicating with others. Above all, he must be able to coordinate a variety of tactics so that they augment one another.

Broadly speaking, the classic pattern of a nonviolent strategy begins with conventional action: investigating the facts that comprise the issue or grievance; formation of a leadership committee; the building of organized mass support; presentation of the facts to the authorities. (In a later chapter on the dynamics of the campaign, we shall discuss these and subsequent steps in detail.) The committee at this point is presum-

ably able to make a clear case on the basis of the facts and will
be ready with a petition, mass rally or other suitable tactic to
show that it has adequate backing. If the prestige of a number
of distinguished persons or community organizations can be
enlisted in support of the cause, this too may be helpful. In
some few cases where the issue is a clearly moral one, respected by the opponent, the support of a few key persons of
acknowledged moral integrity may be enough to settle the
issue.

Means of Winning Support

If negotiations fail, additional tactical measures may be
employed: publicity through newspapers, magazines, radio and
television in a variety of forms—news releases, advertisements, letters to the editors, etc.—to gain public support beyond the immediate constituency and thus to create additional
leverage. The strategic question will arise now whether to embark on a campaign to secure local or national legislation, to
press for enforcement of existing laws, to carry the struggle
through the courts, to engage in electoral action, etc. A choice
of this kind is most likely of strategic significance and must be
weighed carefully because it will determine the major alloca-
tions of time and effort. A very large campaign may involve
two or more parallel strategies, but even here one or another
is likely to receive primary emphasis throughout the campaign,
or else it may be desirable that the emphasis shift from one to
another strategy. The point here is simply that in considering
political action, for example, a decision must be made whether
to engage in it as a tactical project to which a limited number
of people are assigned, while the main effort is channeled elsewhere; to channel the main effort into political actions; or to
omit it. Once the main lines of strategy are marked out, they
cannot easily be changed without seriously disrupting the
campaign, and while a maximum of flexibility and maneuver-
ability is desirable it is inevitably limited by this fact.

Assuming that circumstances warrant a strategy of non-violence, we may also assume that a number of types of conventional action are simultaneously being used in a tactical capacity. Now we move into a phase of public protest activity: distributing leaflets, picketing, poster-walking, silent vigils. From these tactics on the threshold of nonviolent action, we move into passive resistance focused on the issue, and finally to active nonviolence, likewise focused on the issue.

At no point in the campaign is the door closed on negotiations. They may conceivably be going on throughout, though more likely they are suspended and resumed on the opponent's initiative. At no point does it cease to be vitally important to keep the committee going, to activate interest and rapport with the community, to continue to get wide and favorable publicity. The campaign proceeds by augmenting these tactics with stronger ones, holding the strongest and most difficult tactics in reserve till the final stages, as support for nonviolent direct action.

Circumstances will dictate the departures from the above pattern. It would obviously be foolish to begin with attempts to negotiate if the opponent had already ruled this out. In a police state the would-be negotiators might be shot or imprisoned. Gandhi made it a rule of his strategy that actions were announced in advance, but in such a way that the British were not enabled to nip them in the bud. In this he showed adroitness in managing two things—the act itself and the moral image associated with the manner in which it was performed. Both are important, but sometimes it may be necessary to choose between them. The gesture of openness is an excellent way of enhancing the latter, but it is not the only way and if it forestalls the act itself it had better be foregone. The important thing from the strategic viewpoint is to keep the moral image clear—that is, to make sure that the omission of this or that step is not interpreted as trickery or deviousness. Whatever extenuations there may be for any misconduct, they are not likely to offset the objective outcome. Ways must be found,

not to create an illusion of moral uprightness, but to communicate tangible moral intent without fraud and without surrender.

The general pattern moves by stages from moderate to extreme forms of conventional action and then from moderate to extreme forms of nonviolent action. This movement carries with it a quickening of pace and tempo. As it goes toward the extreme it becomes riskier, harder to sustain. Greater demands are placed upon morale, courage, physical energy and discipline. At the farthest extreme, nonviolent action takes the form of outright breaches of law and if these are on a wide scale we are in the midst of a revolutionary situation in which it may be difficult to maintain order and to curb outbursts of violence. Hence the choice of tactics and their orchestration into a strategy is relatively easy when the means are conventional, but increasingly difficult and delicate as they become more extreme. It is the task of the strategist to map out the campaign as far ahead as possible, to foresee the choices that will be confronted, to devise alternative plans in advance of a rapidly changing situation, and finally to be equipped to make pivotal decisions at crucial moments.

Obviously it would be very unwise to begin a campaign with mass civil disobedience or others forms of direct action. The chances of quick defeat and of riot would be too high. But it is not inconceivable that in certain circumstances, as in a totalitarian state, secret and underground substitutes might be developed in place of what we have called conventional action. In every circumstance, however, the understanding and application of strategy and tactics are essential to the effective use of nonviolence.

REFERENCE IN CHAPTER 3

1   Philadelphia: Friends Peace Committee, 1957.

4

Civil Disobedience

Civil disobedience or civil resistance is a form of nonviolent direct action that involves breaking the law. Because of this fact, it requires detailed consideration by the student of nonviolence.

The term "civil disobedience" is often associated with an essay by Henry David Thoreau, *The Duty of Civil Disobedience*. It is a curious fact, however, that the phrase does not appear in Thoreau's essay at all, which originally appeared in 1849 with the title *Resistance to Civil Government*, as a retort to Paley's *Duty of Submission to Civil Government*.

In law the word "civil" originally pertained to the members of a *civitas* or free political community, and is thus used in modern times to distinguish the rights of the free citizen against the claims of public policy. The term "civil" is also used in contradistinction to "military," "ecclesiastical," "natural" or "foreign." [1]

The question posed by Thoreau is an ancient one. Civil government, whether by democratic or other presumably just means, is a way of maintaining order and justice within a community. Unlike military regulations or church ordinances, which may be arbitrary, and unlike "natural" laws, which are not of man's making, civil law presupposes consent by the whole citizenry for the sake of harmoniously managing their common affairs. Each person tacitly agrees to abide by the will of the civil community even if it does not in every detail correspond to his own will. The same general principle applies in a monarchy, a dictatorship or a democracy. And so does the

counter-principle stated by Thoreau, which is that occasions may arise when a member of the community must withdraw his support. Even in a democracy based on the will of the majority, the minority, whether large or small, Thoreau argues, has rights that it can and must assert whether the majority recognizes them or not.

Lactantius, writing in 304 A.D., addressed this question in terms of Christian civil resistance to the laws of an un-Christian state:

Constancy is a virtue, not in order that we may resist those who injure [us] . . . but that, when [men] bid us act contrary to the Law of God and contrary to justice, we may be frightened away by no threats or punishments from preferring the bidding of God to the bidding of man.[2]

It is worth noting that, like other fathers of the early church, Lactantius here simultaneously affirms nonresistance to the evildoer and stubborn resistance to evil laws. In the third century, according to Cadoux, "Christians reserved to themselves the right of deliberately and avowedly disobeying the laws and orders of the State, whenever those laws and orders came into conflict with what they felt to be the Law of God."[3] In other matters not involving such conflict, they were scrupulously law-abiding.

Thoreau's Application

Thoreau, who was more strongly influenced by William Godwin's libertarian *Political Justice* and by the philosophy of Emerson than by the Christian tradition, appealed to the rights of conscience rather than to the laws of God. The kernel of his political outlook is expressed in the following extracts from his often cited but seldom quoted essay:

Must the citizen ever for a moment, or in the least degree, resign his conscience to the legislator? Why has every man a conscience, then? . . . It is not desirable to cultivate a respect for the law, so

much as for the right. . . . Law never made men a whit more just; and, by means of their respect for it, even the well-disposed are daily made the agents of injustice.[4]

Unjust laws exist: shall we be content to obey them, or shall we endeavor to amend them, and obey them until we have succeeded, or shall we transgress them at once? . . . If the injustice is part of the necessary friction of government, let it go, let it go . . . but if it is of such a nature that it requires you to be the agent of injustice to another, then, I say, break the law. Let your life be a counter friction to stop the machine. What I have to do is to see, at any rate, that I do not lend myself to the wrong which I condemn.[5]

Cast your whole vote, not a strip of paper merely, but your whole influence. A minority is powerless while it conforms to the majority; it is not even a minority then; but it is irresistible when it clogs by its whole weight. If the alternative is to keep all just men in prison or to give up war and slavery, the State will not hesitate to choose. . . . When the subject has refused allegiance, and the officer has resigned his office, then the revolution is accomplished.[6]

There is a discrepancy between civil and moral law, and it is the latter which is of utmost importance. Because men respect the former they are sometimes misled into betraying the latter. If they discover the discrepancy, should they trust to the gradual and orderly processes of the law to resolve it? If it is an incidental sort of injustice, occasioned by the inevitable clumsiness of government, we ought to bear with it. But if, as Thoreau elsewhere states, it is a law such as the Fugitive Slave Law, which was unjust to the fugitive slave, we must break the civil law if we are to obey the moral law which demands justice for the slave. As a matter of individual conscience we must do this, but by so doing our breach of the civil law serves as a vote more powerful than the electoral ballot to repeal that law. If enough men who believe in the moral law will exert their weight in this way, even though they are a numerical minority, they may succeed in clogging the processes of government to such an extent that the government will reconsider its actions. If enough men will break the law and go to jail,

if office-holders will resign in protest, the government will find that the only way to restore order is to accede to their just demands.

In addition to the Fugitive Slave Law, Thoreau protested against the Mexican War and refused to pay taxes for it. His protest was a distinguished one, but it was isolated and ineffective. Although he stated the general principle of disobedience and projected its revolutionary possibility, he offered no strategy for a mass movement.

Thoreau was a man of acute moral righteousness. He was an "individual anarchist" in the sense that he felt that he could live justly without the benefit of the civil law. By obeying the laws of conscience he was sure to obey those of the civil laws that were worth obeying. He was willing to acquiesce in incidental injustices to himself but highly sensitive when the civil law sought to conscript his conscience in behalf of injustice to others. In this his outlook corresponded closely to that of Lactantius. It did also in a further respect: he took it for granted that the just man accepts whatever punishment is meted out to him for his breach of the civil law.

Such a philosophy applied on a social scale must, to be viable, presuppose a society of men who all possess a similar moral righteousness. It is not our concern here to enter into an argument with the proponents of social anarchism on this point. But whether or not an anarchic society is possible on a large and permanent scale, given certain conditions, the historical fact up to the present has been that actual communities of this type have been both small and short-lived. This fact indicates two things—both that it *is* possible for a group of committed and disciplined people to live as Thoreau did (and perhaps better), and that this cannot be expected of the whole population of any community. Even in an emergency when a community makes its best showing there are likely to be individuals who take advantage of the absence of order to commit crimes.

The Churches Take a Stand

Emil Brunner has pointed out the difficulties inherent in the medieval philosophy of "natural law" developed by the Roman Catholic Church, when it entered into competition with the civil law or, as he calls it, "the positive law of the state." The outlook of the men of the Reformation on this question represented a radical departure. "They took their stand clearly on the side of positive law," Brunner says, "granting to the law of nature the function of a criterion." [7] That is, the reformers had the wisdom to acknowledge the existence of a higher moral law to which moral men might aspire and in light of which they might refashion the civil law. But only the civil law could be made to serve as the normative basis for regulating human affairs. Thus an individual has the right and duty to appeal from laws he deems unjust, and to try to change them in accordance with the higher criterion which is the law of God as his conscience sees it. But if there is to be both civil order and liberty of conscience, men must give common allegiance to the civil law and relinquish their pretensions to a monopoly of moral truth.

The point may seem to be a fine one, but it is crucial to an understanding of civil disobedience: the truly conscientious civil resister not only appeals to a higher moral law but he also shows respect for the principle of civil law. Moreover, he recognizes the binding force of the very law which he deems unjust and does not try to evade its consequences. He balances his subjective moral right of disobedience against society's objective legal right to punish him. Though he chooses deliberately to act in defiance of the law, his act is not an act of lawlessness. And this is true, it is important to note, not merely with reference to a higher moral law but precisely with reference to the laws of a society whose basic legitimacy he may question. Thoreau spoke of the rights of a minority, but in many cases in which civil resistance has been invoked it has been a disfranchised *majority* that has done so.

The question of disfranchisement is a pertinent one. Speaking of the resort to nonviolence by Negroes in the Southern
states, Paul Ramsey says:

The duty to observe the law, we have said, has full force only
where people of any race in our society effectively have the vote,
and can participate politically at the state and local levels in the
changing of undesirable local ordinances or discriminatory state
statutes.[8]

Invoking Jean Calvin's doctrine of the right of civil resistance against tyranny or grave injustice in which a "lesser magistrate" may have recourse to the natural law to correct an
erring "higher magistrate," Ramsey continues:

Every man must have political initiative as a "minor magistrate."
His magisterial capacity as a citizen should make it possible for him
to participate democratically in making the laws, applying in his
own right the "criterion" of natural justice to help determine the
legal requirements. Anyone who would cast out the members of
any race from exercising the franchise . . . cannot then with clean
hands and a clean heart insist that they should still be law-abiding
people.[9]

Under the terms of Calvin's doctrine not only civil disobedience but armed resistance is morally permissible, says Ramsey, "where states have become wholly totalitarian, where the
means for changing laws have become clogged and men wholly
frustrated in their search for legal justice."[10] It is prudence
alone, he argues, that dictates nonviolence rather than recourse
to armed revolution.

Which Conscience to Follow?

However conscientious it may be, civil disobedience is a
serious matter that is not justified simply by the willingness
of the civil resister to take the consequences. As Ramsey points
out, the truly conscientious man will respect the conscience of
the law as well as his own. That is, he will consider carefully

whether the issue is of such a nature that he is justified in overriding and thwarting the conscience of his opponents who are upholding the law. Is he challenging a vested minority that has obtained the acquiescence of a misled majority, or is he contesting against a whole society that has had the impudence to disagree with him? Even if it is clear that society is wrong, does he have the moral right to impede its actions when he is free to use methods short of civil disobedience to persuade society to his views?

Alan Lovell has made a useful distinction between the tactical and the strategic significance of civil resistance. In its tactical aspect it serves as a stimulus to a faltering democratic system. "In this case you affect people . . . by an emotional challenge, which eventually affects political parties and eventually governments." Or, like the general strike, it can be seen as "a complete method of politics; that is, if you want to get nuclear disarmament you get it by the fact that so many people refuse to work on armaments that it would be impossible to go on with the arms program." [11]

In the former instance it is a matter of resorting to extralegal tactics in support of a strategy carried on within the legal framework of a democracy, exerting pressure for changes within the system. "If you do an act of civil disobedience, are prepared to go to jail or take some kind of personal risk," Lovell says, "you show that there is something more serious to the business than being just out for your own ends. . . . It adds a quality of seriousness to your action." [12] Here the act of civil disobedience functions as a symbolic gesture; it is not intended to disrupt or thwart the opponent's course of action.

But in the latter case, what is intended is the short-circuiting of democratic processes and the imposition of rule by a self-constituted oligarchy—a strategy with clearly revolutionary implications. We are not here asking whether such a revolutionary step may be warranted or not. It may be that in a specific situation democratic institutions have so decayed or atrophied that revolution by such means is justified. But cer-

tainly it is a grave matter calling for the utmost objectivity in
assessing the situation, lest we find proponents of nonviolence
in the bizarre position of staging a minority *putsch* against a
free society.

In the context of the same campaign for nuclear disarmament in Britain which furnished the context for Lovell's
remarks, Canon L. John Collins discusses the question illu-
minatingly:

First, a distinction must be drawn, I think, between a refusal to
obey a law which is repugnant to conscience and a deliberate breaking of laws, which in themselves cause no offense to conscience, in
order to gain publicity and to bring pressure to bear upon governments. . . . If a citizen is asked by his government to do something
which is repugnant to his conscience then, I believe, he should
refuse—and, of course, accept the consequences.

Secondly, I am not in principle and in all circumstances opposed
to civil disobedience as a technique whether against tyranny or
against a government which, though enjoying the support of the
majority, insists upon policies which are seen as a threat to peace
and justice. . . .

But when and when not to indulge in nonviolent civil disobedience are matters for the most careful consideration. It is a question
of weighing up expedience and consequences. . . .

. . . It is possible [in Britain today] to change policies by legal
methods of persuasion. Some may feel that the democratic processes
are slow, limited and often ineffective . . . but will the technique of
civil disobedience be more likely to produce quick results? . . .

I have much sympathy with those who argue for civil disobedience as a shock treatment to be administered to a lunatic body
politic. . . . But I am inclined to believe that the publicity obtained
by "sit down" and other such demonstrations does not in the long
run prosper our cause but, rather, tends to destroy the effectiveness
of our democratic efforts.[13]

Canon Collins goes on to say that "demonstrations based on
civil disobedience as an expedient technique open the way for
some of the more ugly forms of mob hysteria and violence,"
and cites an instance in which such elements were present.

A technique of what must be described as "blackmail" of a minority against the majority must inevitably strain the police (who are forced to try to uphold the law) and give opportunity for "toughs" and "agents provocateurs" to provoke violence.[14]

Finally he notes the presence of anarchists seeking to make use of the civil-disobedience campaign "to destroy the British Constitution and to bring all administration to a standstill." He believes that if they succeeded the government would be taken over "not by noble devotees of nonviolence but by some ugly and dangerous form of dictatorship." [15]

Gandhi's Views

Gandhi had some idea of the volatility of civil disobedience when he contemplated his first nationwide use of it in 1921. "Those only can take up civil disobedience," he wrote, "who believe in willing obedience even to irksome laws imposed by the state so long as they do not hurt their conscience or religion, and are prepared equally willingly to suffer the penalty of civil disobedience." [16] Twenty-three years later in a speech to congressmen from Maharashtra, June 29, 1944, he reaffirmed this view in even stronger terms: "Civil disobedience is a very potent weapon. But everyone cannot wield it. For that one needs training and inner strength. It requires occasions for its use." [17]

To this we may add that it requires wisdom and restraint on the part of the strategist of nonviolence in choosing the occasions for its use. Maintenance of firm nonviolent discipline and the exclusion of unreliable elements—a difficult task—appear to be of prime importance. As the comments of Ramsey and Collins both suggest, the presence or absence of legal channels for desired change is a key factor in the situation.

Assuming that the situation is one that justifies and demands civil resistance, we must now confront the possibility that if it succeeds it may in some circumstances precipitate a revolutionary situation. We shall turn to this question in the next chapter.

The character of civil disobedience, the manner in which it is asserted and the context in which it arises all hinge on this question, which implies a failure of the existing civil order. So long as the existing order is a stable one, and perhaps even if it is not, certain specific types of purported civil disobedience may be seriously questioned. Is it compatible with the spirit of nonviolence to run from the police, to use bodily force to break through a police cordon, to refuse to obey or resist arrest by physical noncooperation, compelling the police to push or carry the noncooperator? Such actions seem closer to the insurrectionary anarchism of Sorel and Bakunin than to anything envisaged by Thoreau, despite his talk of clogging the machinery of the state. When such methods are invoked in the name of nonviolence without a context of broad popular sympathy as a cushion, the psychological repercussions can be very damaging. Gandhi advised great care and prudence to avoid inciting or needlessly antagonizing the authorities, and for the same reasons such acts can also alienate both moderate sympathizers and the neutral public or, given a revolutionary situation, undermine respect for lawful order in general and promote irresponsible, inflammatory responses leading to chaos. In the case of an isolated individual it may be written off as fanaticism, but when contemplated as part of a campaign, mass civil disobedience is dynamite.

Not every instance of nonviolent direct action constitutes civil disobedience. It may be used, for example, against customs and practices that have no legal basis or expression, or where local and national laws are at variance. Civil disobedience means specifically a breach of the law without recourse to other legality except in a moral sense. We must also bear in mind the important distinctions among selective, symbolic breaches of law to gain publicity or to establish a course of legal action, strategic mass disobedience of one particularly onerous statute, an across-the-board defiance of all unjust laws and, finally, refusal to submit to any laws of an unjust govern-

ment. Within the range of this spectrum are the extremes of moral protest and the verge of revolution.

REFERENCES IN CHAPTER 4

1 See *Black's Law Dictionary* (St. Paul, Minn.: West Publishing Co., third edition, 1933), p. 331.
2 Lactantius: *Divinae Institutiones,* VI, xvii, 24.
3 C. J. Cadoux: *The Early Church and the World* (Edinburgh: Clark, 1925), p. 528.
4 Henry David Thoreau: "Civil Disobedience" in *Walden and Other Writings* (New York: Modern Library, Inc., 1937), p. 636f.
5 *Ibid.,* p. 644.
6 *Ibid.,* p. 647.
7 Emil Brunner: *Justice and the Social Order* (New York: Harper & Brothers, 1945), p. 93.
8 Paul Ramsey: *Christian Ethics and the Sit-In* (New York: Association Press, 1961), p. 96f.
9 *Ibid.,* p. 97.
10 *Ibid.,* p. 92.
11 Alan Lovell: "Direct Action" in *New Left Review* (London), March-April 1961, p. 16.
12 *Ibid.,* p. 18.
13 L. John Collins: "Civil Disobedience" in *Christian Action* (London), Autumn 1961, p. 12ff.
14 *Ibid.,* p. 14.
15 *Ibid.*
16 M. K. Gandhi in *Young India,* November 3, 1921.
17 Quoted in Pyarelal: *Mahatma Gandhi: The Last Phase* (Ahmedabad: Navajivan, 1956), Vol. 1, p. 25.

5

Resistance and Revolution

In Gene Sharp's typology of nonviolence, the final category was "nonviolent revolution." The phrase has an exciting ring and has often been used with oratorical flourish to describe almost any kind of change effected through the use of nonviolence. But properly speaking, in the sense in which Sharp uses it, it means nothing less than the unseating of one political regime in a society and its replacement by another. For the Gandhian it implies much more as well: the establishment of a new, revolutionary type of nonviolent society: *sarvodaya* or nonviolent socialism, a society of federated local units as envisaged by Vinoba Bhave and Jayaprakash Narayan, based on voluntary cooperation and substituting nonviolent sanctions for armed force in the regulation of its affairs.

In this chapter, however, we are not so much concerned with the nature of such a society, nor even necessarily with the question of whether it would be the outcome of revolution. Our primary concern is to inquire how nonviolence can move from active civil resistance that challenges and changes the superstructure of society to full-scale revolution that alters the basic power structure.

The revolutionary potential of nonviolence is already evident in the fact that civil disobedience on a wide and protracted scale is capable of undermining an existing power structure. This may precipitate a crisis that sets the stage for revolution. Is it then possible by nonviolent means to effect a transition to a new society, placing the nonviolent leaders in power and keeping them there?

James M. Lawson Jr., speaking at the 1961 annual meeting of the Southern Christian Leadership Conference, declared: "The emerging nonviolent movement is a revolutionary enterprise moving toward real revolution and total revolution." As a concrete way of effecting this, he proposed the recruitment and training of a nonviolent army of from 2,000 to 8,000 volunteers.

Let us work out with them a private discipline, reconciliation in personal life. Let us establish work camps for training, study, reading, meditation and constructive work in voting, repairing neighborhood slums, community centers.

Let us prepare these people for mass nonviolent action in the Deep South. Let us recruit people who will be willing to go at a given moment and stay in jail indefinitely. . . .

A campaign with such an army would cause world-wide crisis, on a scale unknown in the Western world except for actual war.

The sit-ins and freedom rides won concessions within the existing system. These constitute only "the prelude to revolution"; the nonviolent army would exert such pressure as to cause "structural changes":

There will be no revolution until we see Negro faces in all positions that help to mold public opinion, help to shape policy for America.

Lawson does not go into further detail than this, but it is clear from the above that he envisages the complete wresting of political power from the hands of white supremacists in the states of the Deep South and its transfer to state, county and local governments representing the whole population, including the substantial and largely disfranchised Negro population.

The states in which this would occur have a limited sovereignty within the United States. This fact immediately attenuates the scope of revolution in this context. Granting this reservation, is it conceivable that Lawson's revolution would be wholly nonviolent or would his proposed nonviolent army simply provide leverage to activate the machinery of Federal power, backed up, ultimately, by the legitimate and constitu-

tional use of armed force? In any event, the nonviolent movement in the South has seldom hesitated to invoke the police powers of the Federal Government or to avail itself of Federal justice through the courts. Even if it developed preponderant numerical strength it is apparent not only that it would make maximum use of legal avenues rather than attempt a seizure of power through nonviolent direct action, but that it would appeal to Federal power to aid in opening and safeguarding those avenues.

One student of nonviolence and of revolution, Michael Walzer, has argued that nonviolent methods are inherently defensive, suited to resistance but not to revolution in the proper sense.

The boycott and the strike are forms of resistance, though the passive immobility of the sit-down is perhaps its best symbol. All these were first used in the fight against economic injustice, and socialists once hoped that the worker would carry on from these activities to revolution. But the refusal to work, the refusal to buy, the refusal to move are not, in fact, revolutionary. They are acts of stoppage and withdrawal, expressions of discontent, requiring physical presence, self-control and solidarity. But they do not point to transformation and often enough [they appeal to] threatened standards and ancient liberties, the good society that once had been. The general strike in Budapest in 1956 seems to me an act of resistance: a public and demonstrative repudiation of an oppressive ruling party. But in the absence of any group comparable to the Puritans, Jacobins or Bolsheviks, it would be difficult to argue that there was a Hungarian revolution, in the full sense of that term.[1]

If the Hungarian events did not comprise a revolution in the full sense, however, there is no gainsaying the fact that movement occurred from resistance to active revolt and incipient revolution. And if the presence of a group such as the Puritans, Jacobins or Bolsheviks is the hallmark of a bona fide revolution, is it not a fact that each of these groups had its origins in a tradition of resistance? Turning Walzer's analysis around, it may be said that nonviolent methods are not inher-

ently revolutionary but they can serve as a springboard to revolution, given certain additional factors, of which a revolutionary organization may be one. To the extent that the independence campaigns of India and Ghana may be described as movements of this kind, it may be worth examining the classic pattern of the modern revolution and observing points of similarity with these examples of nonviolent revolutionary change.

Crane Brinton, in his authoritative study, *The Anatomy of Revolution,* has provided us with the basic framework from which we have derived the following outline. Brinton analyzes the stages through which the Cromwellian, French, American and Russian revolutions moved, finding certain uniformities among them that enable us to speak of a classical sequence of events.

Sequence for a Revolution

Revolutions are not begun by people who are starving and miserable; they spring from hope rather than despair. They arise where the antagonisms of social classes are complex rather than simple, and where there are no wide gaps in their stratification. A factor of key importance, illustrated in India by the roots of the independence movement in the Hindu Renaissance, is the intellectuals' desertion of the status quo, inaugurating a revolutionary cultural climate in advance of the political manifestations of revolution. The final factors which Brinton observes are the inefficiency of the government machinery in adjusting to new pressures and the political ineptitude of the ruling class.

What triggers revolution in the classical case is the resistance of the people to the collection of taxes, an act of civil resistance as we have already defined it. In both India and Ghana the initial events were more closely related to the ultimate objective of independence.

Next comes further civil disobedience in the form of overt

illegal acts that challenge constituted authority. A perfect ex
ample is the march of workers in Petrograd in February 1917.
"At the critical moment the soldiers refused to march against
the people, but regiment by regiment came over instead to join
them." [2] Brinton advances the tentative generalization that

no government has ever fallen before revolutionists until it has lost
control over its armed forces or lost the ability to use them effectively; and conversely that no revolutionists have ever succeeded
until they have got a predominance of effective armed force on their
side.[3]

Ghana is an exception in that no armed forces were involved. In India the situation was somewhat complicated by
the fact that both British and Indian troops were in the service
of the British raj; but the defections of the latter into Bose's
Azad Hind Fauz, the naval mutiny of 1948 and the demobili-
zation of some 2,500,000 Indian troops at the end of World
War II all undoubtedly comprise loss of their effective control
by the British. It is not so clear whether they met Brinton's
converse condition, though probably they did in a latent sense,
and if the British had not moved out in time there might have
been military clashes.

We now come to the seizure of power by a broad coalition
of revolutionary forces and the establishment of a moderate
legal government. In India, this was the Congress Party; in
Ghana, the Convention People's Party. The actual accession to
power is relatively easy, so little support does the old regime
have. Brinton calls this the "honeymoon stage" of coexistence
among moderates and radicals who comprise the revolutionary
forces.

After the honeymoon, said the French moderate P. V.
Vergniaud, "the revolution, like Saturn, devours its children." [4]

In all our revolutions there is a tendency for power to go from Right
to Center to Left, from the conservatives of the old regime to the
moderates to the radicals or extremists. As power moves along

this line, it gets more and more concentrated, more and more narrows its base in the country and among the people.[5]

It is perhaps premature to evaluate a development of this kind in India or Ghana, but in each, apparently radical moves have been successfully undercut by a popular chief of state pursuing a left-of-center policy, jettisoning dissident former colleagues and silencing extreme opponents by arbitrary police methods. It is difficult to say whether this represents a bypassing of the subsequent stages of the classical revolution or a kind of encapsulation of them in sublimated form. Or it may be that the fact of nonviolence, though failing to produce a nonviolent society, has indeed produced a new sequence of postrevolutionary developments. But all of this is sheer conjecture.

A key development in the classic pattern that effectuates the drive toward the left is the rise of what Trotsky called *dvoevlastie*—dual power or dual sovereignty. As Brinton puts it,

the legal government finds opposed to it, once the first steps in actual revolution have been taken, not merely hostile individuals and parties—this any government finds—but a rival government, better organized, better staffed, better obeyed. This rival government is of course illegal, but not all of its leaders and followers are from the beginning consciously aiming to supplant the legal government. . . .

Once the first stage in revolution is over, the struggle that arises between moderates and extremists comes to be a struggle between two rival government machines.[6]

In the Russian Revolution, the moderate provisional government faced the more radical and popular soviets, or councils of workers', soldiers' and peasants' deputies. The radical turn of the October Revolution hinged on the cry, "All power to the soviets," and it was through them that the Bolsheviks achieved power. In the French Revolution, Jacobin societies sprang up throughout the country to challenge the authority of the legal

Assembly. In America, deviating from the pattern somewhat, town meetings were controlled by illegalists who developed the Continental Congress parallel to the colonial regimes.

It is interesting to note that although they had precedents in the past the soviets and Jacobin societies arose directly from the revolutionary situation. In the American colonies it was a matter of adapting rooted native institutions to a revolutionary purpose. In India the principle embraced a broad variety of institutions consciously and carefully set up in conjunction with the resistance movement over a period of decades and in large part related to the projected needs of the postrevolutionary society. Hannah Arendt has observed that the springing up of such institutions is a universal feature of revolutions, pointing to a popular instinct for federalism based on the "direct regeneration of democracy" which has consistently been overridden in each revolution by the party system. This is true not only of the four revolutions which Brinton studied, but of the Paris Commune of 1870, the Chinese Revolution, the Cuban Revolution of 1960 and others.[7]

The final phases of the classic revolution are the accession of the extremists, the reign of terror and the Thermidorean reaction. We need not go into great detail here, but let us note that Brinton calls the second of these "the reign of terror and virtue" in which persecution extends not only to counterrevolutionaries but to anyone exhibiting indifference to the revolution. In this situation the extremists set out puritanically to stamp out even minor vices in "heroic attempts to close once for all the gap between human nature and human aspirations."[8] Among the reasons Brinton gives for the terror are the habit of violence, the inexperience of the extremist administrators and the newness of the government machinery, and the recklessness and drive of the leaders. ("They are not formed for compromise, for the dull expedients of politics in unexcited, relatively stable societies.") Arendt would add, as would Martin Buber and others, that this phase also signals the triumph of the state over the federative councils, which now are either

smashed or emasculated and kept as appendages of party government.[9] The reign of terror and "virtue" is imposed by cliques substituting state control for these popular institutions.

In the end there is a reaction against the hectic factionalism and intolerance—or as Brinton puts it, "a convalescence from the fever of revolution"—with the advent of the strong man as ruler: Washington, Cromwell, Napoleon, Lenin. The highest hopes of the revolution recede, revolts by the extreme left (Shays, Winstanley, Babeuf, the Kronstadt garrison) are crushed, the people are tired, and crime, corruption, extravagance and relaxation of discipline all toll the knell of the Republic of Virtue. We shall leave it an open question whether India and Ghana have passed through this stage yet and whether Nehru and Nkrumah fill the role of the strong man. In the French and Russian revolutions the leadership passed from, roughly speaking, Lafayette to Danton to Robespierre to Napoleon, and from Mirsky to Kerensky to Lenin. In the English and American revolutions the shift in the locus of power is not so readily identified with individuals. To the extent that America had a Robespierre it was Samuel Adams or Thomas Paine, but neither of these men decisively held the reins of government at any time. In England, Cromwell himself rode out the transitions much as Nehru did in India.

The Roots of Revolutions

The Russian Revolution was preceded by a century or more of sporadic peasant revolts growing out of direct resistance, which was often bloody. For a time, in some areas, under such leaders as Emilian Pugachov and Stepan Razin, these revolts reached the proportions of protracted guerrilla warfare. When the revolution broke out it reignited these fires of revolt throughout Russia, sweeping the countryside into civil war. This fact brings us back to Walzer's statement about the "unrevolutionary" character of resistance—and to Brinton's observation that the revolutionization of the intellectuals is a

prerequisite to revolution and, indeed, the first real harbinger
of it. Mass discontent may express itself for a long time through
violent or nonviolent acts of resistance without any hope of
producing a revolution. Once the discontent of the intellectuals
has matured to a certain point, however, a chance occurrence
of mass protest offers a kairotic moment for the intellectuals to
step in and provide articulate leadership. In February 1917 all
of the revolutionary parties and leaders, who had long been
advocating revolution, were taken by surprise when one day
they found themselves with a revolution on their hands. As
Trotsky tells us in his *History of the Russian Revolution,* this
did not fit in with the plans of any of the revolutionists, who immediately scrambled to place themselves at the head of the
spontaneous mass movement. Had this not occurred, the February events would have been just one more revolt, not the door-
sill of revolution.

A frustrating fact which the would-be revolutionist usually
cannot face is that revolutions are born, not made. No amount
of revolutionary agitation by a "vanguard" group, be it nonviolent or violently insurrectionary, can produce a revolution.
Such a group would be well advised to invest its efforts in constructive work compatible with the revolutionary goals until
the conditions arise that can produce a revolutionary situation.

The strategic importance of the constructive program of nonviolence will be mentioned in a later chapter. In the context of
revolution we need only to point out its importance in providing a stable, rooted and broad base for the government of dual
power, capable of withstanding attacks both from the old
regime and from internal factions. There must be time for the
instrumentalities of the constructive program to acquire the
status of institutions that transcend political allegiances and
hence command the loyalties of all who in the moment of crisis
may fall prey to factionalism. Probably it is not possible to
avoid factionalism, but it is important to devise ways to moderate it and keep it from breaking out into an overt struggle
for power.

Nonviolence in the Transfer of Power

To return for a moment to the idea of revolution in Lawson's sense—the transfer of power within states having only a limited sovereignty—there is a point at which the constructive program becomes subrevolutionary in relation to the political and social structure. This is evident in the Southern states of the United States, where the objective is not the overthrow of the whites by the Negroes but a change of customs and laws on the basis of equality. Neither Trotsky's nor Gandhi's concept of dual power quite fits the case. Although there is scope for Negro community self-improvement organizations, they would be self-defeating if they only engaged in constructive work within their segregated confines. A distinctive dimension in this struggle is shown precisely in the rise of interracial organizations, both of a semiofficial consultative type such as mayors' committees and of a voluntary character such as the various human-relations councils. In addition, the racial openness of the predominantly Negro civil-rights organizations contributes to the same process, setting a pattern for the racially integrated society toward which these groups are working. In another dimension the effort to increase the Negro vote through lawsuits and voter-education activities has a clearly subrevolutionary function, paving the way for political action to unseat segregationist state and local governments without smashing the machinery but with crucial power changes in view. In the classical pattern of revolution involving a sovereign state, however, such possibilities do not exist.

In both India and Ghana the British withdrew and turned the government over to the indigenous leaders. Had they not done so, could the nonviolent revolution have been consummated in the face of British armed resistance? Bose's success in organizing his Azad Hind Fauz, taken together with the widespread resort to sabotage in the Quit India campaign, suggest the likelihood that the British would have been ousted by armed force. But supposing a much broader movement

firmly committed to nonviolence and geared to a functioning system of dual power, could the British have been forced out by nonviolent methods?

This would have meant appealing directly to each British soldier to recognize and respect the government of independent India and to refuse to obey orders from his superiors to violate India's laws. In principle this is the kind of appeal the workers of Petrograd made to the troops of the tsarist regime with considerable though not complete success. In the Russian Revolution, as in others, the preponderance of the troops of the old regime became troops of the new regime and, augmented by armed civilians, engaged in combat with those troops that remained loyal to the old regime. That is the initial violence of the revolution, which sets in motion the vicious cycle that culminates in the reign of terror.

How is this violence to be averted and the revolution kept on a nonviolent footing? It seems unrealistic to expect that every last soldier can be won over to the side of the new society or even relied upon to remain neutral, so long as his superiors have the power to punish him for failing to obey orders.

Gandhi's solution would have called for a million Indians to let themselves be killed in order gradually to convert the British by the sheer moral weight of their conduct. Maybe this would have worked, and maybe this course would be the only thoroughly nonviolent one, but it presupposes a degree of self-sacrifice far in excess of the human possibilities evident in the history of India or any other country up to now. Nor does this proposal take account of the vast capacities of men to rationalize and divest themselves of guilt. Indeed, such a move might well have inured the British soldier to wanton slaughter of unarmed people by confirming him in his belief that Indian life was cheap. A healthy assertion of the integrity and value of a life risked in the encounter of nonviolence with armed force is part of the dynamic by which such an appeal works. Even if Gandhi's million *satyagrahis* had stepped forward, the sacrifice of their lives would have been a blind gamble.

If the revolution has passed into the stage of dual power, in which the legality of the revolutionary institutions is affirmed and that of the old regime's is denied, then in a juridical sense the latter are outlaws from the viewpoint of the revolution. This fact provides a legal justification for depriving the old regime of its weapons. It would seem to be compatible with the ethics of nonviolence in such a situation to seize and destroy these weapons by nonviolent raids on arsenals and ordnance depots, and to use adequate manual force (not striking but holding so as to render harmless) to restrain would-be attackers, and even to take them into custody.

Some such measures must be devised to meet contingencies of hard-core resistance at this stage, though it would be inadvisable and perhaps disastrous to apply such extreme tactics in any phase of nonviolent strategy short of actual revolution. If such practical measures are not developed and made a part of nonviolent training well in advance of the need for their use, persons who are not committed to nonviolence will almost certainly seize the initiative at this point and resort to arms.

Those who, by engaging in civil disobedience, help to bring about the revolutionary crisis that places this question on the agenda have a moral obligation to face the problems that ensue. If they have assumed leadership in the struggle, they owe it to their followers to see them through and not to hand over their destinies to desperate extremists at a crucial moment that finds them unprepared. The fully nonviolent revolution, triumphing over all obstacles without counting on the prudent withdrawal of the opponent, has yet to be made, and it is not at all certain that it is a historical possibility.

Revolution has a deeply tragic side, nowhere more evident than in the rise and fall of what Brinton called "the reign of virtue" accompanying the extremist terror. Because the revolutionary aims of the holistic believer in nonviolence tend to resemble those of the extremists, it is worth noting what happens to the idealism of the latter when means are (temporarily, it is thought) divorced from ends. As Arendt puts it, "Wher-

ever knowing and doing have parted company, the space of freedom is lost."[10]

The Problem of Means and Ends

Albert Camus says that what so often contaminates revolution is its readiness to substitute abstract virtue for love. When human beings are reduced to statistics as masses to be manipulated, expediency is enthroned and the door is flung open to terrorism. Or as Nikolai Berdyaev expresses it:

Revolution seeks triumph at all costs and whatever may happen. Triumph is achieved by force. This force inevitably turns into violence. There is a fateful mistake of the makers of revolution which is connected with their relation to time. The present is regarded exclusively as a means, the future as an end. . . . But the future in which the exalted end was to be realized never comes. In it there will again be those same repulsive means. Violence never leads to freedom. Hatred never leads to brotherhood.[11]

Yet, possessing destructive power, the utopian visionary is subject to a colossal temptation to use it to eliminate the obstacles he sees standing in the way of the realization of his vision. Robespierre and St.-Just, not bloodthirsty villains but moralists of high purpose, sent to the guillotine those men who, in their judgment, stood in the way of establishing a society in which the death penalty would be abolished forever. If, as they earnestly believed, the hope of such a society rested upon them, did they not have a sacred obligation to remain in power and dispose of anyone who sought to smash this hope? It was only for the immediate present, for the duration of the emergency. Tomorrow, after the storm, they would implement their dream.

"Revolution without honor," wrote Camus, "calculated revolution which, in preferring an abstract concept of man to a man of flesh and blood, denies existence as many times as necessary, puts resentment in the place of love."[12] Brotherhood is not established by destroying the enemies of brotherhood, but only by affirming itself. Resistance may spring from broth-

erhood but it can be corrupted when it acquires power and passes beyond rebellion into revolution. Then, "contaminated by resentment, it denies life, dashes toward destruction" and leads to "rancor, malice and tyranny" which call forth new resistance. Camus' plea is that rebellion set limits for itself, resolving not to sacrifice the present for the future, no matter how great the temptation to think that tomorrow's children can build utopia upon today's injustices.

One solution, of course, would be to avoid the temptation by doing nothing. For many people throughout the world this would mean continuing to endure the unendurable. We live in a revolutionary age and if revolutions are not led by good men they will nevertheless occur. But no man is so good that he can easily resist the temptation either to take the short cut of Robespierre or to retire from the scene, leaving matters to those whom the Robespierres would guillotine. For it is not only a temptation but a dilemma and a challenge. In the end, it must be recognized that the nonviolent method itself is not enough. Its special merit is that it allows scope for love, but it is no substitute for it. In the end, the nonviolent revolutionist must care more about constructive action to build the good society *now,* about effecting a revolution of the spirit *now,* than about attacking evil. The demolition of the old order is necessary but in the end the revolution can only triumph in defense of what is under construction. In Martin Buber's apt phrase, if a revolution is to give birth to a new society there must first be conception and gestation. You don't get a new society from an empty womb. Moreover, the greater likelihood is that nonviolence's major contribution will always be either that of a spur to legal change, as Walzer suggests, or that of a precursor of violent upheaval in which its goals may be sabotaged or perverted.

REFERENCES IN CHAPTER 5

1 Michael Walzer: "The Idea of Resistance" in *Dissent* (New York), Autumn 1960, p. 372f.
2 Crane Brinton: *The Anatomy of Revolution* (New York: Prentice-Hall, Inc., 1952), p. 96.
3 *Ibid.*, p. 98f.
4 Quoted in *ibid.*, p. 134.
5 *Ibid.*, p. 136.
6 *Ibid.*, pp. 147-148.
7 See Hannah Arendt: *On Revolution* (New York: The Viking Press, 1963), p. 265ff.
8 Brinton: *op. cit.*, p. 223.
9 See Arendt, *op. cit.*, p. 269. Also Martin Buber: *Paths in Utopia* (Boston: Beacon Press, Inc., 1958).
10 *Ibid.*, p. 268.
11 Nikolai Berdyaev: *Slavery and Freedom* (New York: Charles Scribner's Sons, 1944), p. 195.
12 Albert Camus: *The Rebel* (original title, *L'Homme Révolté*) (New York: Alfred A. Knopf, 1954), p. 272f.

6

Nonviolent National Defense

George Orwell, whose name has become virtually synonymous with political pessimism, wrote not long before he died: "It seems doubtful whether civilization can stand another major war, and it is at least thinkable that the way out lies through nonviolence." [1]

Orwell wrote these words on the threshold of the nuclear age. Since then, the development of megaton nuclear weapons, supersonic missiles and other devices has increased the catastrophic dimension of modern warfare to an extent that defies comprehension. Estimates vary concerning the possibilities of survival, let alone victory, in a war using such weapons, and it is not the purpose of this book to take a position on this vital issue. There is general agreement, however, that the issue is a grave one, and it is surprising that so little thinking has been done to explore the possibilities of nonviolence as an alternative.

In a discussion of fourteen alternative national policies ranging all the way from a national "act of renunciation" to preventive war, the military analyst Herman Kahn omits any reference to a strategy of nonviolence. After accounting for the distinctive nonresistant witness of the Religious Society of Friends, quoting from their manifesto of 1660 to King Charles, Kahn devotes a paragraph or so to "moral pacifism" and adds the following remarks about "nuclear pacifism":

Many of these nuclear pacifists are willing to use such low levels of force as local guerrilla warfare, or even conventional high explosive military weapons to resist a nuclear attack. Some hope that, by a single dramatic gesture, or a series of them, we can "reform"

the Soviets (and the Chinese?) and then the rest of the world. . . . This argument often concludes that at the worst the United States and Europe, and possibly the world, would suffer a relatively peaceful takeover, and the resultant tyranny would mellow with time.[2]

Kahn does refer vaguely to "volunteer nonviolent groups that could interpose themselves in various situations and risk their lives for the principles of peace and progress," [3] but this and the above are far from a serious discussion of the problem, and it is characteristic of many writers to confuse seventeenth-century Quaker nonresistance with twentieth-century pragmatic nonviolence. Often enough they are encouraged in this by the Quakers and other pacifists, but it is no excuse for responsible thinkers who are capable of detailed and acute analysis to indulge in blurry-eyed fantasy when confronting nonviolence. As a result of this apparent unwillingness to examine the idea seriously and in detail and to speculate about it theoretically, it is relegated to a shadowy and largely propagandistic existence. Slowly, however, the idea has intruded itself into the minds of a few capable nonpacifist thinkers, and it is with their views that we shall be chiefly concerned in this chapter.

The conjunction of thought about nonviolence and nuclear war is largely accidental. India received its independence within a couple of years of the first military use of the atomic bomb. In a broader sense it is also true that the era of Gandhian nonviolence coincides with the era of total war, whether we date the latter from the advent of the Gatling gun, of high explosives or the bombing of civilian populations inaugurated at Guernica, Spain, in 1937. The spread of devastation has a long history that has greatly accelerated the problem of justice in warfare during the past century or more. The advent of the nuclear era has only provided a final, devastating jolt, introducing the possibility of instantaneous annihilation for entire civilizations.

There is no such thing as a nonviolent defense against modern war, and for our present purposes this is as true of the long-

range cannon of World War I as it is of the twenty-megaton nuclear missiles of World War III. There is nothing that passive resistance or civil resistance can do to ward off such an attack if it comes. For that matter, there is little or nothing that can be done by any known available means, military or otherwise, to prevent the damage inflicted by such an attack, and meaningful discussion of the problem usually turns to the question of preventing the attack itself, or of steps to be taken afterward. In speaking of nonviolence in relation to modern war, what Orwell had in mind, in common with others who have thought about it, depends upon face-to-face confrontation with enemy troops equipped for garrison duty: nonviolence as a way of meeting invasion or, more likely, of resisting and repulsing a military occupation force.

A variety of proposals for such action have been advanced. Some of them are rather fanciful and far-fetched, in one case for example presupposing the prior dismantling of the entire military establishment and the virtual conversion of everybody to pacifism. To such views as these we would say, with C. J. Cadoux (himself a distinguished pacifist):

Pacifists would be well advised not to argue as if the State could be expected now in every case to turn the other cheek and to overcome the evil in neighbor-states solely with good. The demand that the State shall act fully up to the highest ethical level which the citizens *as a whole* will approve is perfectly reasonable; the belief that this level can and ought to be progressively raised with the lapse of time is also reasonable: what is not reasonable is to demand, under threat or implication of censure, that the State shall *now* act as if it could share to the full the exacting ethical ideal which is, as a matter of fact, held by only a tiny fraction of its constituents.[4]

Kennan's Approach

The views that we shall consider in this chapter are predicated on the belief that national defense is a necessity of na-

tional existence, that communism is not an enviable political system, that the threat of Soviet aggression is real and not imaginary, and that we do not wish to be ruled by a foreign power or its agents, be it draconically totalitarian or otherwise. Our objective is peace and freedom, by which is meant both civil and international order and a way of life featuring civil rights and liberties for all people, as expressed in our Constitution. We recognize further, with Arne Naess, that the majority of people in our country, as indeed in any country, believe in the present system of defense by military means. "If one takes away the only means of defense a person believes to be truly effective," writes Naess, "he certainly has every reason to feel frustrated. Thus a reduction of reliance on the military must be preceded by the development of increased confidence in and the gradual adoption of alternative means of defense." [5] We are assuming, in other words, that nonviolent means are to be developed to such a point as to warrant public confidence before implementing any significant reduction of armaments. The reader who challenges any of these assumptions may, of course, set them aside in favor of a sunnier view.

George F. Kennan has made an approach to the problem that is worth quoting at length. In 1958 he proposed that Western Europe could be defended not by exclusively nonviolent methods but by means that give wide scope to such methods along with others. His views carry particular weight because of his expert knowledge of international affairs. It was Kennan who, as a member of the policy planning staff on the U.S. State Department, developed the earlier policy of containment which has been credited with holding the USSR's territorial ambitions in check since 1946.

If the armed forces of the United States and Britain were not present on the continent, the problem of defense for the continental nations would be primarily one of the internal health and discipline of the respective national societies and of the manner in which they were organized to prevent the conquest and subjugation of their national life by unscrupulous and foreign-inspired minorities

in their midst. What they need is a strategic doctrine addressed to this reality. Under such a doctrine, armed forces would indeed be needed; but I would suggest that as a general rule these forces might better be paramilitary ones, of a territorial-militia type, somewhat on the Swiss example, rather than regular military units on the World War II pattern. . . . The training of such forces ought to be such as to prepare them not only to offer whatever overt resistance might be possible to a foreign invader but also to constitute the core of a civil resistance movement on any territory that might be overrun by the enemy; and every forethought should be exercised to facilitate their assumption and execution of this role in the case of necessity. For this reason they need not, and should not, be burdened with heavy equipment or elaborate supply requirements, and this means—and it is no small advantage—that they could be maintained at a small fraction of the cost per unit of the present conventional [military] establishments.[6]

The characteristic features of this strategy are such as to localize the structure of defense. For the concept of the ring of steel at the frontier, Kennan substitutes that of the citizen army honeycombing the entire country.

The purpose would be to place the country in a position where it could face the Kremlin and say to it: "Look here, you may be able to overrun us, if you are unwise enough to attempt it, but you will have small profit from it; we are in a position to assure that not a single Communist or other person likely to perform your political business will be available to you for this purpose. . . . Your stay among us will not be a happy one . . ."[7]

Kennan believes that any nation that can say this "will have little need for foreign garrisons to assure its immunity from Soviet attack." Such preparations would serve as a powerful non-nuclear and indeed only partially military deterrent.

We need not concern ourselves here with the paramilitary side of Kennan's proposal. What is of interest to us is his insistence that this citizen army be prepared to function as the core of a civil resistance movement. Need such a movement be headed by citizen-army forces? Might it not equally or better

be built within the primary institutions of society—in local churches, labor unions, public schools, YMCAs and the like? The Federal, state and local governments might aid in coordinating such a movement in its initial stages, but these, together with their armed forces, would bear the initial brunt if invasion actually took place. It would seem wise, therefore, to be sure that other institutions were well seeded for resistance too. In the Basque area of Spain, republican resistance to the Franco regime was carried on through football associations long after the capitulation of the government structures—and this was in a situation in which resistance was improvised only after military defeat.

Loosening the Enemy's Grip

One of the first prerequisites of a nonmilitary defense, according to Arne Naess, is a firm and articulate sense of common purpose. What do we stand for as a nation? What do we have that is worth defending, worth sacrificing for? What are the terms on which we can unite for our common defense? These are questions of vital importance. A decadent, moribund society wallowing in random pleasures with every man out for his own private ends can purchase a nuclear deterrent, but it cannot build a system of defense that requires active community participation.

This does not mean uniformity of thought and certainly not a highly centralized leadership. Diffusion of leadership at the grass-roots level and the habit of making decisions without relying upon commands from "top people"—a maximum of this provides needed resilience for determined action in face-to-face encounters with enemy forces, when normal lines of communication may be broken. This need clearly implies that we will be in a better position to respond to such an emergency (and perhaps more ordinary emergencies as well) if we unglue our eyes from our television screens more often and spend some

time working in a church social-action project or similar small-group activities with linkages to the community.

In Kennan's proposal, civil resistance is characterized as "the united and organized hostility of an entire nation" which will make an invader "pay bitterly for every day" of occupation. Naess, however, argues cogently against anything resembling terrorism or a scorched-earth policy, or even "psychological warfare, which may resort to all types of threats and deception in verbal propaganda." [8] This is not simply a matter of moral puritanism, which could hardly be expected from a large population, but of prudent tactics compatible with a strategy of nonviolence. Consider the situation from the viewpoint of the participants. Our aim is not to make the enemy soldiers trigger-happy, but on the contrary to establish rapport with them as persons and thereby to make them feel incongruous to the situation in which their leaders have placed them. We want to be able to say to each enemy soldier: "What is a nice boy like you doing here? Look at the dirty mess they've got you into, pestering decent folk like your own." Such resistance would manifest hostility not to the man but to the role he has been called upon to play, and we must at all times carefully distinguish between the two in our actions and in the way we verbally and symbolically interpret our actions. Rather than making the actual invader, the person who happens to confront us as a soldier, "pay bitterly," we want to enlist his inner sympathy and move him in the direction of neutrality, ultimately undermining his confidence in his superiors and leading him to mutiny or to desert. As in revolution, so also in war.

Thorough training would be necessary to assure effectiveness. To expect a population of 180,000,000—or a single county for that matter—even to begin to apply such methods spontaneously, without training, would be fatuous indeed. Even after months of the most rigorous training that might be expected, without an imminent threat of war hanging over their heads to impress its seriousness upon them, large numbers of people would still remain unprepared. This is to be expected.

The primary need is not to train every citizen in advance, but first to honeycomb the nation with small groups of trained people capable of organizing and leading resistance in time of crisis, and second to create, as far as possible, a favorable public opinion that would overcome the strangeness of the method.

Great care would have to be taken, of course, to avoid any sentimentalizing. People must not be led to believe that effects will be instantaneous, irreversible or universal. Also, the kind of "fraternizing" with enemy troops envisioned above may lead to a temptation to collaborationism, which must be guarded against. Only full and free discussion during the training period will make it possible to prepare for every imaginable contingency, making full use of the resources of psychologists and social scientists, who will have an important part to play at this stage. Full advantage would also be taken of every available technique of publicity and education by both governmental and voluntary agencies to facilitate the training program. And since it would be impossible to carry this out secretly, it would also be necessary to develop effective means of propaganda to inform the enemy population of our intentions, and especially to counter the enemy's propaganda by which he will try to inoculate his population against our strategy.

The strategy of nonviolent defense does not end with the sole tactic of establishing rapport with the enemy soldiers. Coupled with this would be a variety of measures. It cannot be too strongly stressed, however, that in all of these it is important to maintain rapport with the occupation troops as persons. Our ultimate hope lies in neutralizing those troops or, if possible, activating them against their leaders.

At the same time that we, with manifest personal friendliness, make it clear to the soldier that he is unwelcome as a soldier in our country, we shall be engaging in actions on a social scale that confirm this and make it difficult or impossible for the invader's administration to function. As Johan Galtung

has well said, "a desire for freedom cannot be symbolized by passivity."[9]

Galtung, a colleague of Naess at the Institute for Social Research of the University of Oslo, has made a number of concrete suggestions concerning specific kinds of nonviolent action in such a situation.

Nonviolent resistance must be such that the form of resistance itself clearly indicates the goal which the group has set itself. If one is fighting for democratic rights like freedom of speech, an excellent form of resistance will be to break the prohibitions of the occupying forces on this point, e.g. arrange illegal meetings all over the country . . . and in a speech explain the goals of the resistance. Such a form will make it much clearer to the opponent what the goal is than, for example, a strike of milk delivery men. But the resistance must be made collective, at the same time showing the individual opponent that one is not against him as a person. . . .[10]

Nonviolent resistance operates by refusing cooperation with the opponent in order to prevent him from achieving his goals. How can we prevent the opponent from achieving his goals when we cannot stop him by physical means? . . . We take it for granted that he is interested in exploiting for his own ends the land he has conquered, or in introducing another form of government. . . . In any event he will need a certain amount of cooperation from the inhabitants. . . . Exactly this cooperation or this access to the country's riches can be denied the opponent.[11]

Galtung, who is a pacifist and one who generally adheres closely to Gandhian ideas, considers sabotage to be within the scope of nonviolent action so long as it does not injure persons. For example a train could be wrecked while untended and motionless, but not while manned or in motion. He continues:

The population of the occupied country may choose to lower its standard of living by voluntarily making factories inoperable by removing parts of machines and destroying means of communication rather than cooperate in the opponent's unjust use of them.[12]

Although Galtung also includes an all-industry general

strike, Naess cautions against the use of blanket, all-out resistance:

The weakness of a policy of general nonviolent resistance is that it cannot be upheld at all costs; if repression gradually stiffens it is impossible to continue defending, for instance, the major organizations of a democratic government. Automatic refusal to cooperate in food distribution may result in a famine. Self-inflicted hardships of this sort cannot easily be asked or expected of a populace except in critical periods of very short duration.[13]

Other tactics cited by Galtung are: a concerted boycott against all goods imported from the invader nation, refusal to pay taxes levied by the invader, systematic disobedience of laws promulgated by the invader. (For a classic example of the latter, see page 230.) Preparations will have been made for an "underground government" that will function secretly once the regular government is suppressed or taken over. Depending upon circumstances, government officials might demonstratively resign their posts en masse to inconvenience the enemy administrators. To do this would not be merely a symbolic gesture, however, if it became the signal for a transfer of effective administration to the underground. It would be impossible for the invader to know in detail the names of each person in every neighborhood who held this or that responsibility for education, justice, etc. In a complex society such as ours, important decisions would require the judgment of experts: how, for example, could an underground government maintain control over water supply, electricity and other public utilities and services? Certainly it would be technically feasible for a disciplined underground to inform the people to store water in their homes and then cut off the general water supply for a day or two. Similarly, with adequate and careful planning it might be possible for the people to prepare themselves for a symbolic cut-off of electric power. Numerous tactical strategems of this sort could be devised and planned for. In many cases particular strategems would be one-shot affairs, unrepeatable because of meas-

ures the enemy would take in light of them. In many others undoubtedly the resisters could maintain continuous control.

The resisters would have to expect reprisals and be prepared to endure them nonviolently, avoiding panic that could result in resorting to terroristic methods of resistance. For many of the resisters, terrorism would be a highly prevalent temptation because of its value as a release for pent-up emotional stresses. But the instantaneous satisfactions afforded by stabbing enemy soldiers in the back must be carefully weighed against the long-term strategic emphasis on neutralizing them as enemies. No study has been made—at least this side of the Iron Curtain—of the possibilities of abducting key enemy officials by manual force and attempting, while holding them prisoner, to treat them so kindly as to plant in them seeds of discontent with the regime they uphold. If this idea seems wildly impractical, however, consider the amazing successes of the Chinese Communists in "brainwashing" American prisoners of war during the Korean conflict. If a totalitarian regime can succeed in converting naïve American soldiers into Communist sympathizers, surely there must be ways in which American defenders of democracy could produce real conversions among Communists or other ideologues, even if the latter are well indoctrinated, because of the inner contradictions in their ideology. This is only one of numerous avenues of psycho-social research that would have to be explored.

Problems of Organization

Among the lessons of recent history, however, Naess discusses the successful resistance of Norwegian school teachers against Nazi rule. (See page 253 for a detailed account.) To this he then contrasts the situation in Nazi-occupied Poland, where the pressure on school teachers was in part so heavy that direct resistance at the schools and within the school organizations was impossible. But teaching was conducted "privately" in tiny groups, a form of micro-resistance.[14]

Naess defines micro-resistance as "resistance by individuals and tiny, temporary groups." These would function in a subtactical way, isolated from larger underground organizational structures, and would not be directly affected in the event of the exposure of the latter.

Most of the significant examples of resistance on a national scale which has succeeded in some degree exhibit a number of common characteristics: the resisting country is relatively small and compact and the population is homogeneous in ethnic culture; resistance was improvised after the collapse of military defense and was conducted as an expedient, stopgap measure without long-range strategy; and the invader had a larger population and a sizable occupation force.

In devising a nonviolent defense strategy these facts should be taken into account. A large, ethnically heterogeneous country such as the United States might be handicapped by existing internal divisions. An obvious initial problem in the planning stage would be posed by the prevalence of Negro-white segregation in a large part of the country. This problem must be squarely faced and solved. We are not attempting to prejudge it here on the merits of the case for or against desegregation, but simply to state that it constitutes a problem in relation to foreign invasion. The Norwegians and the Poles did not have this problem.

On the other hand, the size of the country, in both land area and population, would be a distinct advantage. Both China and the USSR combined would find it a vexing problem to deploy the number of troops and administrative personnel to manage a nation as large as the United States, even with a halfhearted program of resistance to cope with. And as we have indicated repeatedly, full-scale advance preparation and planning would introduce an entirely new dimension.

Who would undertake the training of a nonviolent leadership cadre? George Kennan, as we saw, proposed that the members of his paramilitary citizen army would themselves comprise this cadre. For reasons already given, we have indi-

cated the advisability of a separate nonviolent organizational structure. The psychologist Jerome D. Frank, however, has well stated the role the military could perform:

A nonviolent campaign against a Communist occupation would . . . require a tight, highly disciplined organization with diffusion of leadership, carefully worked-out clandestine methods of communication, and other measures very similar to those which would be required to survive a nuclear attack. In fact, if a country ever committed itself to an exclusive policy of nonviolence, it would probably have to rely on the military, as the only group with sufficient knowledge of organization and discipline, to train and lead the civilian population in this type of combat.[15]

While taking advantage of the special skills provided by the military—it is inconceivable that a program of nonviolent defense could be launched without their cooperation—these skills would, in our view, become the property of the churchmen, unionists, school teachers and other civilians after their training. Although liaison with the military and with civil government would be maintained, it would be of such a nature that the nonviolent clandestine groups could carry on independently at a moment's notice if liaison were broken by enemy actions of any kind. Moreover, it is essential that nonviolent organization be predicated on the inner strength of the local community rather than on any overarching authoritarian structure, such as that of even the most democratic of armies. The more inextricably the nonviolent organization is enmeshed in the stable and permanent structures of the society itself, the harder it will be for the enemy to smoke it out and isolate it. The entire congregation of every parish church, for example, must be capable of being suspected as a unit of the nonviolent resistance—though in fact there will exist within it a handful of leaders who have received expert training and, around them, a nucleus of people whom these leaders have trained, with the balance of the congregation informed but not fully trained. This is not a question of holding back training from anyone who wants it, but of realistically facing the fact that it is impossible to expect the

requisite degree of interest and involvement from everyone. Nonetheless, what this adds up to is a church that is organized for nonviolence, and its natural linkages in the over-all scheme will follow the existing contours of ecclesiastical structure and community relationships rather than direct ties with military or governmental districts. By this means, the enemy would have to smash the church as a whole in all its ramifications to get at the agents of resistance. Such a pattern multiplied throughout the fabric of society would make for great resilience.

Given such an organization, asks one Roman Catholic exponent of nonviolence, Kaspar Mayr,

Wouldn't the united action of a people against injustice powerfully heighten their inner defensive strength, build unity and so cause the opposite of what the usurper intends: not submission but life in freedom based on inner strength? Wouldn't nonviolent defense also preserve cultural properties, even if it undoubtedly demanded hard sacrifice . . . ? [16]

That these are more than merely pious hopes founded on a perfectionist ethic is strongly indicated in Frank's observation of the psychology of this "inner strength" when he says that

persons who as individuals might use violence to defend themselves or their families against attack . . . can commit themselves to non-violent methods when they are in the service of a well-worked-out program and have strong group support. Only about 100 of Gandhi's followers were fully committed to his philosophy.[17]

Undoubtedly it would require a widespread sense of imminent crisis to weld together this kind of unity from which to draw inner strength. Contrasting the demands of a nonviolent resistance with those of a military defense policy, Norman K. Gottwald of Andover Newton Theological School observes that "it necessitates a stronger sense of national purpose and a greater willingness on the part of citizens to be informed politically and to subordinate personal interests to state interests." [18] He goes on to weigh the dangers of a "monolithic statism" connected with such a policy as compared with similar dangers

"inherent in our present over-militarized society with its concentration of power and national destiny in the hands of a few political and military leaders." [19] An important difference, as we have already noted, is that a well-constructed movement would be rooted in community institutions outside the power structure of the state as such. But Gottwald's point has relevance if we find government exceeding its role as initiator and coordinator.

The Supranational View

As a cadre-building bulwark of the program, some form of constructive organization has been recommended, oriented in the direction of international relations, to promote cultural contacts and perform work that would strengthen the world image of the resisting nation as peace-loving. Naess lays great stress on such activity.

International service should be undertaken for its own sake, to relieve suffering and meet human needs. It is also important as a means of expressing and implementing our nation's way of life and principles.[20]

In addition to its intrinsic merits, which should form the primary focus rather than any ulterior design simply to *use* such service to undergird our defenses,

international service can contribute to the creation of a more sympathetic attitude toward our country and way of life which would reduce the chances of aggressive action against us. . . . It will help create a positive sense of purpose and mission comparable to that which often accompanies military efforts, but without certain of the disadvantages of such measures, and in giving our citizens experience in working cooperatively in a common altruistic cause it will enhance their ability to practice this cooperation in other tasks in time of crisis.

[Finally,] knowledge of international service conveyed to the troops and population of a potential enemy might reduce their motivation to take aggressive action against us, cause them to carry

out repressive orders inefficiently and increase the chances of their deserting or mutinying in support of freedom.[21]

Gottwald comes to a similar conclusion, though neither had access to the other's writing on the matter. Rather than a strictly national service organization, however, the one Gottwald envisions would be based on the North Atlantic Treaty Organization. Gottwald's "freedom youth corps" would be set up

to carry out cultural and economic projects in all the NATO countries and wherever invited, hopefully, within Communist countries as part of cultural exchange programs. Simultaneously they would be trained in methods of resistance to enemy occupation. They would serve as the cadres for a large-scale civil resistance plan whose aim it would be to make enemy occupation of NATO countries a distinct political and military liability.[22]

The reference to NATO is apt, for the principle of non-violent national defense is relevant to multinational defense as well. Many of the smaller nations might be capable of making a brave gesture of resistance, but this would almost certainly have a negligible impact on a large and powerful conqueror. It is apparent that geographical size and interior diversifications of social organization, technology and other features would be of strategic importance. The invasion of a single small country unaided by any allies poses complex problems that we are not prepared to discuss in any detail here. By "small" here we are thinking of a Denmark, a Latvia or a Belgium. And by "single" we imply that the conqueror is prepared to concentrate his military power on that sole country and rotate his troops sufficiently to forestall any establishment of rapport. Such a case would probably be rare, but we might conjecture that substantial evacuations of refugees and the establishment of resistance bases in adjacent countries might provide a means of using nonviolence for a protracted period. Studies should be made to discover whether some type of nonviolent intervention by countries not under attack would be feasible. If the armed invasion

were countered by a well-prepared nonviolent counterinvasion by international-service cadres of the type suggested by Gottwald, would it result in nipping the armed invasion in the bud, or in the liquidation of the resistance forces of the allies? Such questions as these need to be fully explored by men accustomed to the complexities of military strategy as well as by those in the behavioral sciences.

One highly esteemed military strategist has made a beginning, not on the defense of a single small nation, but of larger nations and of the NATO bloc. Sir Stephen King-Hall, a retired British naval commander with a distinguished war record, is the author of such books as *Imperial Defense* and *Total Victory*. His 1958 book, *Defense in the Nuclear Age,* however, marks Commander King-Hall's entry into a new dimension of strategy. In it, he advances the view that war can no longer be waged by military means. He rejects alike the idea that it can be limited to non-nuclear weapons and that a war with nuclear weapons could result in anything approximating victory.

What is remarkable is that King-Hall emerges as an exponent of nonviolent resistance—on grounds of military necessity! His thorough knowledge of military operations and the fact that he does not regard himself as a convert to pacifism give weight to his assessment of the possibilities of such resistance.

In his discussion of defense plans, King-Hall begins with the assumption that the United States will not go along with his strategy. Hence he speaks of a European Treaty Organization rather than NATO. He proposes that the ETO countries would have no nuclear arms at all, and that their total armed strength would consist of "about ten divisions and corresponding air and sea forces" which "would gradually be reduced to a frontier guard" capable of offering token military resistance.[23]

In the event of attack, after the frontier guards were overcome (their existence would be primarily a safeguard against infiltration of border areas), the ETO nations would resort to

nonviolence. Echoing a caution we have voiced above from various sources, he says:

> To be effective this resistance must be organized in advance and not expected to spring out of the occupation in an *ad hoc* manner, any more than armed forces are expected to be created when military operations begin. A soldier of sorts can be trained in three months; to train a fairly competent nonviolent resister might require three years.[24]

Commander King-Hall examines one pacifist program (outlined in the pamphlet *Pacifism and Invasion* by Jessie Wallace Hughan) and finds its proposals unconvincing. Among his objections are the human impracticability of a nationwide hunger strike or sit-down strike and the limitation of the pacifist vision to "making the occupation difficult for the enemy."

> The object of nonviolent resistance must be to *make the occupation dangerous for the enemy*. It cannot be "dangerous" to him from a military point of view, it must therefore be made dangerous to him from a political warfare angle, for this is the battlefield on which, if victory can be achieved, it will be total.[25]

The primary focus of the struggle, in King-Hall's view, is ideological and psychological rather than military. He discounts as unrealistic the possibility that the Soviet Union (whom he sees as the enemy) would embark on a massacre of the inhabitants, and also regards it as unreasonable to believe the invasion troops would be ready to terrorize the civilian population. On the latter point, he attributes the horrors of the Russian occupation of Berlin in 1945 to the fact that it came as the climax to a long and bitter military struggle—one in which, moreover, the government which the Soviet troops identified with the people of Berlin had been responsible for savage atrocities against the Russians.

> The distinction between an occupation as the climax of a military battle and one as the beginning of a psychological struggle is of the utmost importance.[26]

As a broad outline of resistance conduct, King-Hall offers five suggestions, the first two having to do with the material aspects of the national life of the ETO states and the last three with "ideas and attitudes of mind":

1. The economic life of the country to be maintained, that is to say, transport services, industrial production, agriculture, distribution and all activities concerned with the body-keeping business of the nation should proceed so far as possible in a normal manner or in accordance with directions issued by the occupying power.

2. As regards government, the attitude toward the enemy should be: "We have our well-established administrative arrangements and if you do not like them we await to hear from you what alternatives you have in mind."

3. To refuse *at all costs* to say or write anything contrary to the principles of our way of life or to accept denial of freedom of speech and association.

4. To use every opportunity in personal contact with the occupying forces to expose the fallacies of communism and advantages of democracy.

5. In general to behave *vis-à-vis* the occupying forces with dignity and moral superiority. This is the key rule.[27]

Among the specific applications of the above principles, under point 3 he proposes that the task of a newspaper editor "should be to cause differences of opinion in the enemy administration as to whether or not his paper should be closed down," meanwhile functioning as a "subtle weapon" of resistance. If closed down, "illegal and clandestine news sheets and bulletins and radio transmissions might come into operation." [28]

King-Hall acknowledges the tentative and preliminary character of his proposals. They constitute suggestions rather than a detailed strategy, which would have to be worked out by an authorized body of strategists. A large part of his study is devoted to convincing the reader of the need for rethinking defense policy. The primary need, King-Hall believes, is the establishment in his country of a royal commission ready to

embark on a detailed factual and theoretical exploration of the possibilities.

One of King-Hall's colleagues in the British military establishment, Captain B. H. Liddell Hart, who enjoys a wider reputation than King-Hall as a strategist, has discussed the latter's thinking in his book, *Deterrent or Defense.*

While the practicability of his proposals can be questioned, his argument presents a challenge which deserves the fullest consideration—and cannot be ignored. . . .

Even on practical grounds there is a stronger case for nonviolence than is generally realized. Its power has been demonstrated at various times, and it has achieved some notable successes.[29]

Liddell Hart observes that the sporadic nonviolence against Nazi Germany in Denmark, Norway and the Netherlands impressed Hitler as "contemptible weakness—although there is evidence that it did embarrass many of his generals, brought up in a better code, and baffled them more than the violent resistance movements in occupied countries." [30] Much depends on a fundamental similarity of the moral code of the invaders and the resisters. Nonviolence requires more strict and widespread discipline than an army, and its effectiveness "is undermined if even a small proportion of the community play into the opponent's hand—through weakness, self-interest or pugnacity." [31]

Without closing the door on it, Liddell Hart on balance remains skeptical of the applicability of nonviolence as national policy on two counts. First, he doubts that any government "could be persuaded to embark on such a revolutionary experiment"; and second, he remains unconvinced that it could be practiced effectively on a national scale, for the reasons given above.

His first point is well taken. It is hard to imagine how a government, or any nongovernmental institution of national scope, could have the imagination to allocate funds and personnel to study the question, not to mention embarking on the experi-

ment as a policy. Until this is done, the validity of Liddell Hart's second point will remain obscure. He may be proved right. Meanwhile, the need for competent research and informed speculation on this question will not slacken in its urgency so long as weapons of massive destructiveness continue to be piled up.

REFERENCES IN CHAPTER 6

1 George Orwell: "Reflections on Gandhi" in *Shooting an Elephant and Other Essays* (London: Secker and Warburg, 1950), p. 111.
2 Herman Kahn: *Thinking About the Unthinkable* (New York: Horizon Press, Inc., 1962), p. 236. Reprinted by permission of the publisher.
3 *Ibid.*, p. 237.
4 C. J. Cadoux: *Christian Pacifism Re-examined* (Oxford: Basil Blackwell, 1940), p. 131.
5 Arne Naess: "Non-Military Defense" in a book edited by Quincy Wright, William M. Evan and Morton Deutsch: *How to Prevent World War III* (New York: Simon and Schuster, Inc., 1962), p. 125.
6 George F. Kennan: *Russia, the Atom and the West* (New York: Harper and Brothers, 1958), p. 63.
7 *Ibid.*
8 Naess, *op. cit.*, p. 131.
9 Johan Galtung: *Forsvar Uten Militærwesen* (Oslo: Folkereisning Mot Krig, c. 1959), p. 73. The author is greatly indebted to Mrs. Berit M. Lakey for translating the chapter from which this and the following quotations are taken.
10 *Ibid.*, p. 80f.
11 *Ibid.*, p. 81.
12 *Ibid.*
13 Naess, *op. cit.*, p. 131f.
14 *Ibid.*
15 Jerome D. Frank: *Sanity and World Peace* (Des Moines: World Peace Broadcasting Foundation, 1961. Mimeographed), p. 7.
16 Kaspar Mayr: *Der Andere Weg* (Nürnberg, Germany: Glock und Lutz, 1957), p. 256.
17 Jerome D. Frank: *Sanity and Survival: The Nonviolent Alternative* (Berkeley, Calif.: Acts for Peace, 1960), p. 12.
18 Norman K. Gottwald: "Some Strategies of Nonviolence" in *Worldview* (New York), April 1961, p. 5.
19 *Ibid.*
20 Naess, *op. cit.*, p. 127.
21 *Ibid.*, p. 127f.
22 Gottwald, *op. cit.*
23 Stephen King-Hall: *Defense in the Nuclear Age* (Nyack, N.Y.: Fellowship Publications, 1959), p. 147n.

24 *Ibid.*, p. 192.
25 *Ibid.*, p. 199.
26 *Ibid.*, p. 200.
27 *Ibid.*
28 *Ibid.*, p. 205.
29 B. H. Liddell Hart: *Deterrent or Defense* (New York: Frederick A. Praeger, Inc., 1960), p. 220f.
30 *Ibid.*, p. 221.
31 *Ibid.*

7

An International Nonviolent
Peace Force

In the late 1930s Mahatma Gandhi proposed the idea of a
shanti dal or nonviolent peace brigade to deal with communal
strife between Hindus and Muslims in the struggle for Indian
independence. Of the members of such a locally based organization, Gandhi wrote:

Theirs will be the duty of seeking occasions for bringing warring
communities together, carrying on peace propaganda, engaging in
activities that would bring and keep them in touch with every single
person, male and female, adult and child, in their parish or division.[1]

Gandhi referred to the idea again a few times, but nothing
was ever done during his lifetime to implement it. Who knows
how many lives it might have saved when the hideous massacres began in 1947?

As he conceived it, *shanti dal* was a nonviolent method of
riot control involving individuals or small teams wearing distinctive dress but engaged in constructive work within the local
community until moments of conflict arose, when they would
be ready to do rescue and first-aid work. Later he projected a
similar scheme to deal with international conflict, and shortly
before his assassination he called a conference to discuss it.
When it met without his leadership in 1949 an international
corresponding committee was set up, but it soon lapsed into
silence and inaction.

It remained for his spiritual heir, Vinoba Bhave, and his as-

sociates in the *sarvodaya* movement of the 1950s to revive the concept of *shanti dal* and then later to introduce the idea of *shanti sena,* the nonviolent peace army moving out of the local setting to act on the world scene.

The idea of an international armed force such as the United Nations Emergency Force that was used to resolve the Suez and Congo crises in 1957 and 1961 is a product of fairly recent thinking. It has, in turn, given impetus in pacifist circles to the idea of a nonviolent counterpart or alternative to UNEF. Indeed, to the extent that any thinking has been done it has tended to take the form of a specific adaptation of nonviolence to the situations that UNEF or a more permanent "world army" is designed to deal with. Roy Finch articulates this viewpoint when he observes:

The arms of the UNEF troops in the Near East are only a token; the 2,000-man force could easily be crushed by either side. It is effective only because it is backed up by "world opinion" and by the big powers.[2]

Finch then proceeds to argue from this basis that the United Nations would be ill-advised to expand the "token" arms of UNEF, since its effectiveness lies elsewhere.

Certain aspects of the police-force proposal might make sense— if they were transposed fully into a nonviolent key. A *Peace Service* of unarmed volunteers (men and women also, *not* recruited from regular armies) wearing a special uniform or other symbol and ready to leave at a moment's notice to interpose themselves in conflict situations on behalf of the United Nations might be an effective way of waging peace. . . . It would be an entirely new *kind* of army, as different from the old kinds as the United Nations itself purports to be from old kinds of national sovereignty.[3]

It is fitting that this concept is advanced by an absolute pacifist and that most of the support it has received has also come from pacifists—and no less surprising that, in contrast with the idea of a nonviolent national defense, it has barely begun to receive attention from nonpacifists. For it is precisely here that

the moral scruples and the vision of international peace which
are the twin hallmarks of pacifism compel the pacifist to take
his most principled stand. And conversely it is precisely here
that, from a nonpacifist point of view, the means of implementing this vision without clearly operable moral imperatives are
most nebulous. Novel as the idea of a nonviolent national defense may be, it is basically an adaptation of the techniques of
passive resistance and civil disobedience—which have occurred
in history on a national scale—to ideas of military strategy and
national solidarity that are generally accepted. The idea of the
use of nonviolence in the way Finch suggests, or as a projection from Gandhi's sketch of *shanti dal,* is an adaptation of
nonviolent methods that remain to be developed, to an international ethos which itself has barely begun to take shape.

An International Conference

Consequently there has been little concrete theorizing and
much tentative groping, almost exclusively by persons representing a holistic view of nonviolence, whether of Gandhian or
of Western pacifist origin. In 1960 this groping, however,
began to seek tangible form when the Triennial Conference of
the War Resisters International met in India at Gandhigram.
Chiefly three tributary forces were impelling both *sarvodayists*
and pacifists toward such a step. Two of these we have already
noted: the pressure of international events, with the pacifist desire to convert the United Nations to nonviolence, and Vinoba's
pursuit of the Gandhian concept, which had by now resulted in
the enrollment of 2,000 "peace soldiers" in India. The third
and highly catalytic factor was the rise, during the preceding
few years, of pacifist action groups such as the Committee for
Nonviolent Action in the United States and the Direct Action
Committee Against Nuclear War in England.

Both the American and the English groups (the latter gave
way to the Committee of One Hundred) arose against the
background of larger movements that embraced an ideology of

nonviolence. Although there was nothing that could be called a mass peace movement in the United States, such peace organizations as existed linked themselves with the nonviolent struggle for racial integration, which did have something of the scope of a mass movement. A pacifist direct-actionist could gain experience and whet his morale by joining in a sit-in. And however separate the sit-ins and the peace actions in which he engaged, he had some basis to speculate on the possibilities of mass support for the latter, since the former had already received such support. In England, the mass movement of the Campaign for Nuclear Disarmament provided an even more congenial context for the direct-actionist as a kind of vanguard element of an already pacifist-tinged body. Elsewhere, too, such groups as Action Civique Non Violente in France, though lacking a mass base at home, could find moral support in the British and American movements.

Conditions were such that direct-action groups were able, in this period, to carry out such actions as the boarding of Polaris submarines in both New London and Holy Loch, the sailing of the ketch *Golden Rule* toward the U.S. nuclear test zone in the South Pacific, the San Francisco–Moscow peace march, and other such actions. Although they did not enjoy spectacular growth, these organizations held together, gained experience and began to envision types of action that might have direct and decisive impact on the international scene. Americans and Britons who had engaged in direct action against their own governments made so bold as to hoist banners in Moscow calling for an end to Soviet nuclear tests, and to form a team to invade the French Sahara to protest against a nuclear explosion conducted by the French Government. In 1960 these direct-actionists were very warm to the idea of an international team that would take "the next step" in a direction in which they were already headed.

A Variety of Approaches

As there were diverse origins, so there were diverse conceptions of the route to be taken. One proposal, advanced in a joint statement by the Indian *sarvodaya* leader, Jayaprakash Narayan, and the distinguished Spanish republican, Salvador de Madariaga, pursues the line of reasoning advanced above by Roy Finch. It would call for a body of unarmed World Peace Guards acting under United Nations auspices, to intervene and halt hostilities chiefly by interposing themselves between the armed combat troops of the parties to a given dispute. Following is an extract from the Madariaga-Narayan statement that summarizes this position better than any paraphrase:

The presence of a body of regular Peace Guards intervening with no weapons whatsoever between two forces combating or about to combat might have considerable effect. They would not be there as a fanciful improvisation, but as the positive and practical application of a previously negotiated and ratified Charter binding all UN members. This Charter should insure:

1. Inviolability of the Peace Guards.
2. Their right to go anywhere at any time from the day they had been given an assignment by the UN.
3. Their right to intervene in any conflict of any nature when asked by one or both of the parties involved, or by a third party.

The Peace Guard would be parachutists. They would be able to stop advancing armies by refusing to move from roads, railways or airfields. They would be empowered to act in any capacity their chiefs might think adequate for the situation, though they would never use force. They would be endowed with a complete system for recording and transmitting facts, such as TV cameras and broadcasting material. Their uniform should be simple, clear and appealing.[4]

The authors of this statement recognize the difficulty that would face their proposal before it was even adopted. Their stress, however, is on the recognized international status of their nonviolent peace guard. Given this condition, their tactics

then would be drawn chiefly from the arsenal of Gandhian civil disobedience, with emphasis on bodily obstruction. The condition of legal status under an international charter demarcates this approach from the other two.

A second approach is essentially that of *shanti sena*, projected on an international scale—an autonomous voluntary organization which would not wait for United Nations authorization but would establish itself and make its services available independently, undoubtedly hoping for eventual recognition by all governments. Aside from its unofficial status, its functions resemble closely those of the Madariaga-Narayan peace guard. The following is excerpted from a proposal made by Arlo Tatum, secretary of the War Resisters International:

The World Peace Brigade should aim for becoming an instrument to be used in international agreements and disagreements. In this area would fall:

1. Border patrol and the reporting of violations, as on the Israel-Arab borders and the 38th Parallel in Korea. In such instances there would be a policy of outgoing fraternization, unlike armed patrols. Service to persons in the area would be an integral part of Brigade activities.

2. It should offer volunteers to any nation prepared to disarm.

3. It should be prepared to accept responsibility for inspection and control of any disarmament agreement, as an utterly impartial body.

4. It should stand ready to enter any area where the facts are in dispute as to the cause of disturbances, and report back, but continue to work in the area.

5. The Brigade should develop its own information network, so that such difficulties are discovered when possible *before* a crisis situation develops.[5]

As in the domestic concept of *shanti dal*, Tatum's version of *shanti sena* is coupled with a program of constructive service work, and training in nonviolence would be rooted in domestic depressed areas. "Volunteers would be sought and

trained for Brigade activity in their own community, rather than simply for service in far-off places." [6]

Among the many questions which this proposal suggests are the basic problems of legal status, financing and efficient administration. If, for example, the World Council of Churches and its constituent members, or the International Confederation of Free Trade Unions, were to take so radical a step on their own, it is not difficult to visualize the complex problems of staff and budget that would instantly arise. Assuming that neither of these organizations could be persuaded to take such a step (or, what is the same thing for our purposes, that they could not be persuaded more easily than the United Nations), is it conceivable that the general public in any countries would support a wholly new organizational structure devised expressly to serve as a base for an International Peace Brigade?

This consideration leads us to the third approach to the question of nonviolence on the international scene. It is largely a permutation of the second proposal above. At Brummana, Lebanon, in December 1961, an international conference was held to establish a World Peace Brigade along much the same lines as those Tatum sketches above. The sponsors included a number of distinguished nonpacifists such as Josue de Castro of Brazil, Martin Buber of Israel, Leopold Infeld of Poland, Kenneth Kaunda of Northern Rhodesia, Julius Nyerere of Tanganyika and Alan Paton of South Africa, as well as distinguished pacifists such as Martin Niemöller, Danilo Dolci, Abbé Pierre and others. Very few of the sponsors actually attended the meeting. Virtually without exception the fifty participants are identifiable as Gandhians, Quakers, nuclear disarmers and pacifist direct-actionists.

The final report of the Brummana Conference, written by Bradford Lyttle of the Committee for Nonviolent Action (USA) states: "There has been created an international framework for carrying out and interpreting nonviolent direct-action projects and programs. What is needed now is someone who possesses that strange power of moral and political imagination

and perception which will lead him to see the action which history demands"—in short, a new incarnation of Gandhi. The conference also adopted a Statement of Principles and Aims which leaves the reader in no doubt concerning the nobility of the Brigade's intentions—basically "to bring the liberating and transforming power of nonviolence to bear more effectively on our world." But it says no more about how this is to be done than Arlo Tatum's above-quoted outline.

Practical exigencies made the World Peace Brigade's beginnings much humbler than its envisioned tasks. The first major project was a scheme to stage a march of nonviolent volunteers across the border from Tanganyika into Northern Rhodesia in support of the independence of the latter country, with the encouragement of nationalist leaders Julius Nyerere of Tanganyika and Kenneth Kaunda of Northern Rhodesia and including direct action by Africans in the latter country. In Dar es Salaam, Tanganyika, the World Peace Brigade set up a training center in mid-1962 to train cadres for struggle in nonviolent campaigns for freedom from colonial rule. This idea is interesting as an alternative to the centers operating in the Congo and elsewhere to train saboteurs, assassins and commandos for the freedom movements, but after much fanfare nothing came of this scheme. Another early project of the World Peace Brigade was the sponsoring of a number of small ocean-going vessels on voyages of protest against nuclear weapons. Their impact, however, was negligible.

Both of these ventures are a far cry from the specific purposes envisioned in the idea of *shanti sena,* commendable as they may be as ways of promoting colonial freedom or nuclear disarmament. The World Peace Brigade is little more than an expansion of pacifist direct-action programs from the activities of separate national groups to a coordinated international effort by the same groups, pooling the resources and techniques they formerly used singly. It remains to be seen whether this development can serve as a springboard to a genuine international nonviolent group capable of intervening in disputes be-

tween nations. The latter concept, though only in its infancy, has fired the imagination of a number of people. Among them has been Bertrand Russell, who set up a foundation in 1963 for the express purpose of sending nonviolent cadres on missions in the field of international conflict. It will require further exploration and perhaps relevant experimentation and research by nonpacifists, however, before any meaningful evaluation can be made. Perhaps the key to any further steps must be the chartering of such a group by the United Nations or some other international agency laying claim to both legality and impartiality. The odds against a poorly equipped, underfinanced organization without any recognized credentials except its own avowed good intentions would seem to be overwhelming.

REFERENCES IN CHAPTER 7

1 M. K. Gandhi in *Harijan,* March 26, 1938.
2 Roy Finch: "There Is a Better Way" in *Fellowship,* March 1, 1958, p. 24.
3 *Ibid.*
4 Salvador de Madariaga and Jayaprakash Narayan: "A World Peace Guard" in *Fellowship,* May 1, 1961.
5 Arlo Tatum: "The World Peace Brigade" in *The War Resister* (London), Fourth Quarter 1961, pp. 4-5.
6 *Ibid.,* p. 4.

The Dynamics of
Nonviolence

8

Phases of Action in
a Nonviolent Strategy

How does nonviolence work? Where do we begin and what is required to carry out a campaign based on a nonviolent strategy? So far we have attempted to define nonviolence and to delineate its range of applications, and we have also made some preliminary observations about a possible sequence beginning with conventional action and progressing to the brink of revolution. Not every campaign would begin at the same point, nor would it necessarily go so far. Each campaign, in fact, requires its own strategy based on the distinctive features of the situation it must confront. Tactics that are successful in one situation may or may not be applicable to another. As Kaspar Mayr has well said, "There are no infallibly valid methods applicable to all cases. They must be as various as life itself and at any given time growing out of the situation in which they are to be used." [1]

Mayr's caution is aimed specifically at the temptation to resort to Gandhi's *satyagraha* campaigns as master plans to be imposed on any occasion. So much of the available literature has been based on these campaigns and the Gandhian philosophy on which they were based that the temptation is an understandable one. Nonviolent cadres can benefit greatly from a study of this literature, but it must be placed in proper perspective. By far the best source for this purpose is Joan V. Bondurant's analysis of five *satyagraha* campaigns in her excellent book, *Conquest of Violence* (Princeton University Press

1938, pp. 43-102). Without this and many other studies, our present chapter could not have been written.

Our purpose here, however, is not merely to translate Gandhi's Hindu concepts into Western terminology, and certainly not to offer a master plan of any sort, but to stake out the major considerations that are likely to apply in most campaigns waged in a context of European, American and perhaps some other Western-type society and culture. This will necessitate a degree of simplification which may be overcome through study of actual historical examples, as in the CASE-BOOK of this volume. Also, for the sake of brevity and clarity we shall in this chapter skimp a number of important questions that can be dealt with more fully in the remaining chapters of this section. Taken together, they are intended to enable a group of people to organize and prepare themselves to conduct a nonviolent campaign. As we shall see, the campaign cannot adequately be understood without studying these questions, but they will not become meaningful until we have the broad setting to which they apply.

Preliminary Considerations

The background to any strategy of nonviolence is a recognition of the fact that we are considering nonviolence as a form of social action, and this requires at least an elementary understanding of society as a structure of social forces. Nonviolence on the level of tactics and strategy is not the pure expression of love or good will, not a device for avoiding or patching up conflicts, not a magic remedy for injustice. It is a means of action for waging social conflict, which may or may not achieve its objectives. This is not to say, of course, that it cannot also be seen as a way of life, as we have observed elsewhere.

When we speak of agapaic love in relations between persons, we are dealing with another dimension, relevant to but not identical with social action. In the latter, we must recognize that societies are made up not merely of an aggregate of

individual persons, each a child of God with unique possibilities, nor of a conglomeration of interpersonal encounters, but that in any village, city, state, county or nation there are distinct groupings which function socially. They may be grouped as church members, as golfers, as baseball fans or in many other ways, some of which may be relevant and others less so. The same individual is a part of several social realities, including "the general public," "the electorate," etc. He may be seen as a newspaper reader, a television viewer, a consumer, a worker.

Some of these social roles are more or less random, some are conditioned by habit and custom, and still others are expressed and regulated through institutions. The latter point to the effective centers of social control—broadly speaking, the "power structure" with its leadership or "power elite." This category includes government and its policy-makers, those who wield power through armed force (e.g., a nation's general staff, a city's police commissioner or chief), those who make economic policy (merchants, bankers, industrialists) and those who maintain social norms, class distinctions and the like in a broader sense. Often the same "power elite" members act as a social class.

Admittedly sketchy, some such approach to social structure is indispensable in waging a social struggle. Later on, when we refer to "the opponent," it will not always be possible to specify whether we mean the proprietor of a store, the business community as a whole or perhaps a large segment of the population functioning as a general public, a consumer group or something else. For simplicity, we shall speak of "the opponent" as the ruling group or individual, and any sizable group of non-policy-making people as "the opponent's masses." We may also have occasion to refer to functionaries such as policemen, who form an instrumental part of the power structure below the policy level. Only with such an approach can we begin to distinguish between actions that may be socially relevant and those that are not.

This is only a beginning, and we can do little more than suggest some of the problems that may arise in any social structure. In a given case, is our strategic opponent the whole power elite or only some segment of it? Can we count on the neutrality of some segments of it if we concentrate on others? For example, will pressure directed at merchants have positive or negative repercussions on the business community as a whole? Will it have political effects? Conversely, will pressure directed toward city hall produce desired changes in stores? Again, is the general public reachable through organizations that might be receptive to our point of view? Is it organized in such a way as to facilitate systematic retaliation against us? Is it perhaps unorganized but likely to act as a mob? And if so, is the power structure likely to impede or augment mob action? Finally, are there levels of power such as local and national that are committed to different policies, one of which can aid us against the other? These are a few of the many questions for the nonviolent strategist to consider before launching a campaign, and to keep under review at all times.

Any effort to organize effectively for nonviolent mass action must also confront questions about its own structure that can only be answered fully in relation to its distinctive situation. Basically, however, it will consist of three tiers: the leadership group, disciplined cadres and mass base. These tiers are somewhat analogous to the military categories of staff officers, combat troops and garrison or support troops; but social conflict is not the same as military conflict, and the analogy should not be pressed too closely. There is also a resemblance to the elite-functionary-mass arrangement of the social structure itself, but there are important differences, as there must be between a movement and a stable order. A nonviolent movement has greater fluidity and more overlap. In Gandhian terms, the three tiers consist of fully dedicated *satyagrahis,* constructive workers who are in training to become *satyagrahis,* and masses that may be activated to take part in mass actions led by *satyagrahis.* If we combine the two conceptions it will il-

luminate the distinctive character of nonviolent organization. The leadership functions not only as "general staff" but also takes to the field with the cadres. The cadres who function below the leadership level (as well as those who function at that level) alternate between "combat" and "garrison" duty. And in much of the latter they are engaged in constructive work that involves the masses and provides a maximum of fluidity from top to bottom.

Another important sociological consideration is the innately democratic character of nonviolent organization. This is not to say that it is immune to corruption, that it cannot become petrified in an authoritarian way, but that it usually arises without the existence of a rigid structure and that it depends heavily upon the active support of the masses. Whether the latter formally vote or not, there is little the leaders can do without consulting their wishes; they can be persuaded but not forced.

Overt social conflict, as contrasted with scattered antagonisms, does not spring from abstract principles of injustice or evil. A large number of people may live for a long time in a situation that makes them victims of injustice, and each in his own way feels this injustice as what C. Wright Mills called a "personal trouble." Many may recognize that other people as well as themselves are afflicted by the same trouble, and even recognize that it has the same source, but they still experience it as a "personal trouble" until something happens that reveals it as a social issue. To be sure, there are troubles that remain personal, and not every personal trouble has potential social impact. The point here is that social conflict occurs when a substantial number of people experience a common grievance that is then articulated as a problem which requires not merely individual adjustments but changes in the social structure.

It is out of this process of maturation, which may be very slow or extremely rapid, that the makings of a mass movement are produced—and not by a group of theorists going out to drum up a following. Whether the leaders of such a movement

are already there or come in from the outside, they become the leaders by virtue of the fact that they offer an answer to questions which people in the situation are impelled by their own experience to ask. The nature of the asking is not an intellectual act, however. The masses speak in question marks and exclamation marks, looking for someone to write out the words, which they will then recognize as their own questions and exclamations. The first task of the leader is to serve as a spokesman. Second to this he offers solutions and organizes their implementation. The presence of conflict also brings with it a closing of ranks by the masses. As Lewis Coser has observed,

Conflict with another group leads to the mobilization of the energies of group members and hence to increased cohesion of the group. Whether increase in centralization accompanies this increase in cohesion depends upon both the character of the conflict and the type of group.[2]

If the conflict is an acute one, we may expect that, for the duration of the campaign, community organizations and other institutions of our group will both focus their attention on the conflict and respond favorably to attempts by our leaders to coordinate them, and that with the termination of conflict they will tend to pull apart once more, perhaps even in an exaggerated way. It is the common response to the conflict which initially creates solidarity, not some magical power of nonviolence or of inspired leaders, and a letdown is virtually certain to come if conflict is suspended, unless viable means are devised to assure permanent cooperation in the absence of actual conflict.

The point at which a social conflict recognizably begins is a moment of crisis which may occur dramatically and unexpectedly or may be the result of agitation. Whether spontaneous or induced, however, it is not an artificial event. A social issue has been in the making and it is now precipitated into the consciousness of the masses. The crisis usually comes in

conjunction with some event which otherwise would not call forth a decisive response but which now serves as a pivotal issue, symbolizing the larger social issue. For example, the arrest of Rosa Parks (see page 299) on a bus in Montgomery, Alabama, in itself constituted a minor grievance by comparison with the shooting of a man some time earlier, but it came as a culmination of a series of such "troubles" that added up to an important immediate issue reflecting a social reality: the lack of decent treatment of Negroes on the city buses in a general context of racial discrimination. This issue in turn was expanded from "decent treatment" to "desegregation," and linked with the generic issue of racial equality in other forms of public accommodation. The water was there all the time, but it was the stone marked "Rosa Parks" that made the splash with its circles rippling out from that event.

Given the underlying causes, a group of potential leaders could have been in existence, waiting for such a pivotal event and ready with trained cadres to go into action. They might even take action calculated to cause such an event and thus hasten the process. But it is not the content of the event which makes it pivotal; it is the response of the community to it.

Preparing for the Campaign

It is only with the moment of crisis that leadership becomes effective, social conflict is being waged and a campaign is under way. In many cases there may have been no advance preparation of any kind, and everything has to be quickly improvised, with untrained people getting their basic training in the midst of the conflict itself. There is much that can and should be done well in advance, however, if it is possible to do so. In the following pages we shall discuss the entire course of a campaign, from the preparatory stages through to the farthest-reaching conclusions, even though in many cases the scope of an actual campaign would be less ambitious.

Let us start with the assumption that we are an assortment

of individuals who have decided to meet together in order to discuss what we think is a social issue. We might be a church social-action committee, a ministerial association, a trade-union group or some other such pre-existing body, or we might be individuals who are meeting for the first time. In the former case, we shall have to decide whether we can use our existing organizational apparatus or devise a new one. Here we shall assume that we are starting from scratch.

Our very first task will be to check our several impressions of the situation. Are we all talking about the same problem? Is each of us acquainted with all the relevant facts? What are our respective sources of information? If there are differences of emphasis or interpretation, these should be disposed of and common agreement reached concerning the real issue and the facts that concern it.

Now, granted that we know the facts, one of us must take the responsibility to state them carefully in writing, adding the necessary documentation. It will probably be advisable to set up a file and gather reliable information. Time and facilities will have to be allocated for this purpose. Although each of us should keep informed, one of us should take the responsibility for preparing reports for eventual publication.

Next, how do we propose that the issue be resolved? We discuss the solution and put it into written form, estimating the minimum and maximum demands we are prepared to make, and we decide which of the opponent's representatives may be most effectively approached. When the time comes, we shall have ready a brief and clear statement of grievances and a concise list of maximum demands concerning a tangible issue, supported by documentation—all of this in a form ready to hand to the opponent and to the press and, with abbreviated documentation, to be distributed to the masses we seek to lead. In addition to this, we should draft a detailed statement of the maximum demands we are making, for use in negotiations. We may share this with the opponent, while reserving for our own private use an outline of the minimum we are willing to

settle for. The latter will be disclosed to the opponent in due course if settlement is unobtainable on better terms. It would be poor strategy to make concessions beforehand or to indicate what we are prepared to forego until required to.

Gandhi, despite his insistence on strict, even ascetic discipline for the "true *satyagrahi*," recognized that it was not possible in practice to secure perfect adherence to nonviolence by all members of a mass movement. "It is enough," he said, "for one person only to possess it even as one general is enough to regulate and dispense of the energy of millions of soldiers." [3] Referring to the highly effective and well-organized Salt March, in which thousands took part who were not free of hate or anger in their daily conduct, Gandhi later added: "Their belief in nonviolence was unintelligent. . . . But their belief in their leaders was genuine." [4]

A heavy responsibility therefore rests upon the leadership to be well trained and capable of marshaling the activities and holding the allegiance of masses whom we will be unable to train fully. Recognizing the potentialities and limitations that this implies, we begin to discuss possible strategy and allocate leadership roles. Decisions must be made to bring into the leadership group persons with needed skills or to develop these skills among ourselves. Our group, as it shapes up, should include individuals capable of planning and coordinating a sustained program of action, of interpreting the movement to the opponent and to the public through speaking and writing, of carrying out tactical actions of symbolic significance to illustrate our motives and aims, of administering funds, arranging meetings, handling correspondence, etc. A maximum of versatility is to be cultivated within the limits of individual aptitudes and the needs of the program.

We should begin very early to study and discuss the theory and history of nonviolence and to engage in training sessions among ourselves, not only seeking to adapt historical strategies to our own needs but also to acquire a sufficient knowledge of theory to be able to speak fluently about it to others. It is

part of the leadership's responsibility both to master nonviolence beyond our immediate needs and to equip ourselves not
only to practice it but to teach it to others. This is even more
important in our leadership training and subsequent teaching
of socio-drama, in which we rehearse not only in words but
in actions the various kinds of encounters we expect to have
with our opponents. It is here that we test out our theories
and beliefs and learn how to maintain nonviolent conduct and
discipline under conditions of stress. (See page 165.)

Once our training program is under way, we map out a
suitable constructive program and begin to recruit potential
cadres, joining with them in the constructive work, which
should be intrinsically beneficial and noncontroversial in its
content—ideally, some form of service that is of real benefit
to a segment of our community and that can elicit approval
from our opponent and from neutrals. Some nonviolent campaigns have done without a constructive program or have
relied on normal community activities to balance the strain of
protest action, but they have usually had to pay an unexpected
price later on for this deficiency. A clean-up campaign or a
series of week-end work camps to repair dilapidated buildings
might be particularly well suited to the purposes of a localized
campaign. Proponents of national and international actions
have recommended ongoing service work of the kind done by
the Peace Corps and by such agencies as Ecumenical Voluntary Service, Eirene and Service Civil Internationale.

In the more typical domestic situation of conflict along
racial lines in an American city, let us assume that we are a
Negro leadership group. The immediate issue is not building
maintenance but access to public facilities that are denied to
us, or some such grievance that involves asserting our rights,
making a claim, securing concessions from the dominant white
community which holds effective political power. Nevertheless,
if we mount a constructive effort to repair buildings in the
Negro community we thereby demonstrate our solidarity as
a community and also tangibly undercut charges that we are

only concerned with wresting our rights from the whites, only asking them to do something for us. We also exercise self-respect and heal inner divisions that may exist within our community. This makes possible the interpretation of our protest activity as a basically positive action and identifies the nonviolent cadres as helpful and generous persons. Even more important, this image is not a fake, concocted merely for publicity; it rests on an authentic foundation. This foundation also serves directly to undergird the struggle itself, since we need a healthy cohesion that goes deeper than the immediate issue, while it likewise provides the leaders and cadres with the valuable experience of working together in a common cause under an agreed-upon discipline prior to the onset of direct action.

Through the constructive program, which existing community organizations may be invited to join, an avenue is opened through which such organizations can subsequently link themselves with a campaign of nonviolent action. Meanwhile, their support of the constructive program need not imply anything beyond the immediate work.

Once we have completed our own basic training in theory and practice, we turn to the training of our cadres, with whom we continue working on the constructive program. As their number grows, we select those who are best qualified and assign them to posts of responsibility. The primary organizational unit for both constructive work and protest action is a team ranging in size from eight to sixteen persons, with one team member taking responsibility for the others. Lines of authority should be clarified to avoid confusion and to coordinate the actions of all teams. Ideally, each team of cadres should be a duplicate of the leadership team, capable of interpreting fully the principles of nonviolence and of the campaign, and potentially able to succeed to the leadership if necessary. Definite procedures should be established within each team and within the movement as a whole for making decisions democratically and carrying them out authoritatively.

This means, among other things, that members of the initiating leadership group must eventually be prepared to yield their positions to leaders chosen by the masses. Continuity of symbolic leadership is highly desirable, but there are dangers in its concentration in one person. Flexibility of effective administrative and strategic leadership may be an overriding asset.

The Campaign Begins

We are now ready to initiate the campaign on the level of conventional action and are prepared to follow it up with a nonviolent strategy. Possibly our work in the constructive program has by this time resulted in a change of attitude by the opponent which makes a crisis unlikely. If this is the case, we may find him ready to consider our petition without pressure, and we shall continue to emphasize the constructive work and broaden it. But we shall assume that conditions have shown no sign of improvement.

It is hard to prescribe the next step in general terms. If there has been a series of incidents such as the mistreatment of bus passengers in Montgomery, to which we referred above, the wise course may be simply to wait for the next incident in the series. Or it may be desirable to initiate action through a deliberate act of defiance—not a mass action but an individual or small-group action calculated to precipitate conflict, that is, to bring latent conflict to the surface.

Here we must proceed with caution, selecting as our target a potential issue that can eloquently articulate the mood of the masses and thus bring forth their response—an issue which at the same time can be most readily communicated in simple human terms to the opponent's masses and to neutral or "outside" elements. An example is the sit-in for "a cup of coffee." Another might be defiance of a curfew. The persons chosen to undertake such an action should be well-trained cadres who are able to conduct themselves in an impeccable manner. Par-

ticularly in this event, but also at later stages, it is important that the opponent be deprived of the opportunity to muddy the issue by stigmatizing these cadres in any way. A strong factor in the case of Rosa Parks is that she was known to everyone in Montgomery as a highly respectable person. An injustice to a slovenly person is still an injustice, but the psychological impact is keener when the victim is well-dressed, clean-shaven, clean-cut and well-behaved.

If these cadres are arrested or mistreated, we check the response of the community to which we are offering our leadership. If it is weak, we have miscalculated the situation and had better try another approach. But if it is strong, if people are saying that "something must be done," it is time for us to make our bid for leadership. Depending on the mood of the people and other factors in the situation, we may issue a call for a public rally or mass meeting at which to present our petition to the people, or we may assign our cadres the task of circulating the petition. Or the social structures may be such that we choose to obtain the signatures of key community leaders rather than of the masses. The time element is a factor here, too, and we must choose a course that enables us to move quickly while the issue is hot and before it is taken up by violent elements.

With the petition we are ready to go to the opponent and present our demands. If he refuses to deal with us, we publish our demands and proceed to stage a public demonstration to dramatize the issue, mobilize our masses in support of it and appeal to the opponent's masses to influence their leaders in the desired direction. The appeal to the opponent's masses may take a number of forms such as radio announcements and distribution of leaflets. One of the most difficult but also most promising is door-to-door calling and telephoning by cadres who are prepared to explain our cause and discuss the issues on which the petition is based. A measure of success in direct dialog of this kind can not only open the possibility of early

settlement but if we move on to mass protest action it will enhance the likelihood of a sympathetic response.

We are not using the petition as an ultimatum but as a basis
for negotiations and as an occasion for man-to-man encounter
at the top levels of our respective groups.

Kaspar Mayr has remarked that of the various types of
nonviolence

The most effective form has always been civil disobedience against
users of violence, against usurpers. [But] the goal remains to convince the opponent in his heart that he is in the wrong and that he
is doing wrong.[5]

Much wishful thinking has been devoted to the notion that
nonviolence works chiefly through moral persuasion. Mayr's
emphasis is correct; it would be a mistake to abandon the goal
of converting the opponent just because it is harder and less
likely than the method of compulsion and coercion through
nonviolent pressure. The fact is that the two methods are
complementary, as April Carter has pointed out:

In any nonviolent campaign two broad categories of power are
operative: psychological power and the social power which results
from an alteration of political, social or economic relationships. . . .
A nonviolent campaign involves a blend of psychological power
and social power, the relative emphasis on conversion or coercion
determining the over-all future of the campaign.[6]

An individual's position in the power structure is likely to
decide his responsiveness to a moral appeal if it touches upon
a substantive matter—that is, something his job depends on.
In the bottom strata there may be an unwillingness to risk the
job by responding, but if caught in a conflict of conscience the
individual functionary may look for loopholes to accommodate
us without jeopardizing his position. If there is latent conflict
between him and his superiors, as is often the case, he may
even be capable of rebelling against orders to perpetrate injustice, if the moral appeal is overwhelming. A policeman, for
example, has a certain amount of discretion in dealing with

demonstrators. We may succeed in getting more or less gentle treatment from him, but only in the extreme case can we call upon him to come over and join us, or to take a position of neutrality. As a rule, this is possible only in a revolutionary situation.

The position of the leadership person is different, whether he is an elected official, an appointed executive, a military officer or a management spokesman. Whatever his personal feelings, he holds his position and the power that goes with it as the agent of a constituency, a company, a class or some other entity. Though accustomed to exercising power, his loyalties to the source of that power are usually much firmer than in the case of the functionary. If the group he represents has a vested interest in its side of the issue we are concerned with, it is likely—and he as its agent is likely—to have strong, built-in defenses against a moral appeal. Part of this is the result of compartmentalizing personal and official decisions in the ordinary exercise of his leadership role. Even in the rare case of conversion, such a man is more likely to step out of his leadership role than to take the system with him. Pragmatically, pressure and coercion are more reliable here than persuasion. If he is an elected official, for example, it is more effective to change the mood or composition of the electorate than to try to get him to take a public stand which throws him into opposition with it.

• Nevertheless, it is important in the encounter with the opponent to seek to establish personal rapport. There is the outside chance that the issue at stake hinges on the intrusion of his private attitudes into his official actions, on knowledge or ignorance of the situation, etc. There is also the likelier chance that courtesy, courage and honesty on our part may win us his respect and lead him to curb excesses that are not basic to the system it is his duty to uphold. This is to be desired as affording a better climate in which to wage the struggle. It is also morally sound. But the compelling strategic reason for good conduct on our part is to clear the path for our use of pressure.

It is our task in any encounter with the opponent to strip away his fears and apprehensions and to deprive him of any rationalizations he may be using to distort the facts. It is distinctly to our advantage if we can summon sufficient empathy to see matters from his point of view so that we can help him to see the situation as it actually is.

The fact that we have initiated the conflict is upsetting. It poses a threat of unknown proportions which our opponent is anxious to dispose of. If we confront him with too much meekness, he will be glad to pounce on this as a sign of weakness. If we confront him with overbearing boldness, he will exaggerate the threat we pose to the status quo. Our job is not to wheedle or to bluff, but to show him that we are responsible persons seeking a change of conditions to which the opponent's social structure can adjust, and that we have adequate support for a course of action that will deepen and prolong the conflict. As Martin Luther King has stated, the purpose of direct action is "to create a situation so crisis-packed that it will inevitably open the door to negotiation." [7]

We will reassure him as much as we can, without concealing our ultimate aims and, by indicating our willingness to negotiate, offer some latitude for compromise. In every aspect of our appearance, bearing and conduct, we should avoid provoking the opponent in any way. We should speak distinctly and choose our words with care; and we should remain calm and composed in the face of any provocation he may offer. We do not seek to throw him off balance, though we may permit him to throw himself off balance—a feat which is not so advantageous to us as our gracious act of presently setting him on his feet. We show him by our actions that we are in control of the situation no matter what happens, and that we will not misuse our power. By being honest and fair at all times ourselves, we give him no excuse to be dishonest or unfair to us. In explaining to him our choice of nonviolent means, we not only make a gesture of good will but we also convey the impression that we are secure enough in our strength that we can

confidently set our own limits upon it. Thus our moral position psychologically enhances our coercive power.

The attempt to begin negotiations should be pursued throughout the campaign until they occur and move to a satisfactory conclusion. They may take the form of direct bargaining or of arbitration by an impartial arbitrator. If the opponent contests our facts, we do not hesitate to propose an independent fact-finding commission.

We must recognize that the opponent may consent to negotiations or to other such measures, not to work toward a solution of the conflict but as a delaying tactic to undermine our movement and terminate the conflict on his own terms. He may stipulate that we cease demonstrations or direct action while negotiations are in progress, or for a stated period of time, counting on the resulting inertia to give him a chance to smash the movement. As a general rule, therefore, we should never consent to suspend our activities for longer than a few days and always have new plans in readiness. Exceptions would have to be justified by tangible evidence of the opponent's good faith.

Throughout the campaign, mass demonstrations can serve as a convincing index of numerical strength. To get a maximum turnout, however, they should be wisely spaced, adequately publicized and imaginatively staged with full use of vivid symbols of the movement's purpose and unity as well as devices to amplify the message and boost morale, and to make unmistakably clear the fact that the leadership group and the cadres have the full support of the masses. A mass demonstration is not a specifically nonviolent action. The larger it is, the more vulnerable it will be to provocation by the opponent. Serious risks are involved in staging such demonstrations during periods of acute conflict. The dangers can be reduced if sufficient numbers of cadres are present in the demonstration to keep it under control and head off rioting if it should occur, but provisions should also be made to disperse quickly and calmly in case of disorders. And there will be times when

we shall want to exercise our discretion not to demonstrate en masse but to indicate numerical strength and solidarity in less volatile ways.

In addition to numerical strength, expressed through demonstrations, the readiness of our movement to act can be shown by symbolic acts such as picketing, poster walks and silent vigils carried on by small groups—usually one or more teams of cadres—on a continuous basis: around the clock for several days, once or twice a week for months, etc. In India, fasting was used by cadres, and it has been used by pacifist groups in the West, but in the latter case it has not always communicated. Mass marches and prayer pilgrimages can be very effective symbolic actions if discipline can be maintained. The need for careful planning here is even greater than in stationary mass demonstrations.

All of these actions have value as morale-builders as well as showing the opponent our strength. Other devices should be developed to express our solidarity and purpose. Slogans, emblems, forms of greeting and the like can have strong effect. Winston Churchill's famed World War II "V for Victory" sign, the Communist clenched-fist salute and other such gestures had wide effect and communicated readily. The distinctive white cap of the Indian National Congress, the shout of the word *"mayibuye!"* (freedom) in South Africa and the hymn "We Shall Overcome," adopted by Negro students in the American sit-in movement, are among numerous examples from nonviolent movements. Each is a valuable means of expressing what we stand for in the simplest terms. We shall therefore devise our own and make it a point to display them whenever we can. They should be simple enough for a child to recognize and emulate, clear enough to state the issue at a glance. "Jim Crow Must Go" and "Ban the Bomb" are slogans that meet this specification. They are not only short but have rhythm and ring that make them superior to, let us say, "End Jim Crow" or "Scrap Nuclear Weapons." The same factors should be borne in mind when devising a variety of slogans to be painted

on picket signs or banners. The solidarity symbols have their place among the latter, but there should also be signs that have the more prosaic function of explaining the issue or stating the facts in a rudimentary way, like tabloid newspaper headlines. The lettering should be large and bold enough to be read at a distance and also to be photographed. The publication of a news photo showing our poster walk or our march with banners means free publicity among the opponent's masses and among neutrals and sympathizers. Here again, incidentally, the value of presenting a good appearance through neat attire, erect posture, etc., is obvious.

Initiating Direct Action

Sooner or later, if a date is not set for negotiations, or if negotiations have begun and stalled, we shall announce our intention to launch concerted direct action or to expand those actions which we have already initiated. We work out our timetable and instruct all the cadres, who pass the word to the masses. If we have radio facilities, we may alert listeners to the fact that an important announcement is to be made. In most cases it will be wise not to inform the opponent of the full details of the action that is planned until it is certain that he will be unable to forestall it. We may announce the day and even the hour, but not the content; or we may announce the content of the action but not the time. When we make this announcement, we combine it with an ultimatum, stating that we are prepared to suspend the action or call it off if the opponent meets our demands (for negotiation or for settlement) by a specified time.

The first line of direct action may be symbolic rather than coercive: a symbolic on-the-job work stoppage for fifteen minutes at a prearranged time (with exceptions for certain types of work in which this gesture would be damaging or dangerous) or a one-day stay-at-home strike. At the time the action is about to begin, or as much earlier as we safely can,

we announce to the opponent and to the general public exactly what we are going to do, specifying time, extent, location—all the external details. We also indicate that we are prepared to take further action if this one does not bring results. By announcing in advance just how long the work stoppage is going to last, and then carrying out our plan exactly as stated, we indicate clearly that we are in control. We leave the opponent no loophole to explain the event away or to divorce it from its leadership.

Mass actions such as this should be used sparingly, so as not to deplete the morale of the masses. We must always bear in mind the distinction between the thoroughly trained and disciplined cadre and the more loosely involved masses. If the masses are asked to do too much, they will become tired and the conflict will disintegrate into chaos or apathy. On the other hand, if they are asked to do too little their enthusiasm will wane and the movement will coast to a halt. A wise leadership must have a good sense of timing. We should be able to assess the mood of the masses well enough to know when to call them into action and for how long—and this also means judging when to call a halt so that an action does not end in straggling.

If the symbolic work stoppage does not bring results, we may turn to a number of tactics that do not demand the full participation of the masses and which focus attention on several different teams of cadres, such as picketing beamed at the opponent's masses alternating with a sit-in at one or more offices or stores involved in the issue. Aspects of the constructive program might be given extra emphasis at this stage, along with small-scale prayer vigils, deputations to influential individuals among the opponent's masses (e.g., clergy, professionals and others outside the administrative apparatus) and rallies, prayer meetings and other morale-building events that involve no strain and no struggle.

The next step, which may supplant but more likely will supplement these diverse tactics, is sustained mass noncooperation or passive resistance, focused on the immediate issue. Be-

fore this step is taken, we should consult with our cadres to determine how long this action can be sustained. If it is a selective buying campaign, for example, we may be able to count on the masses to change their shopping habits with relatively minor inconvenience for an unlimited period. But if it is a boycott against a needed commodity we must be prepared to terminate it when the required sacrifice begins to tire the masses, or else take steps to produce substitutes through the constructive program. Gandhi's twin emphases on the boycott of foreign cloth and on hand spinning was a stroke of genius in this respect.

When we begin selective passive resistance of this kind, we should also make plans to expand or intensify it in the event the opponent takes a serious step in reprisal, or as a means of renewing the effort if the initial phase begins to fade. A boycott of certain goods, for example, can be broadened into a complete boycott of the stores which sell those goods. Or it may be extended to another sector—from merchandise to transport and other facilities. In India at one stage, resisters refused to use British law courts to settle civil disputes, but this probably did more to promote the resisters' solidarity than to exert pressure on the British in a direct way.

Although in many situations it may be desirable to hold off from direct action of the assertive type until passive-resistance methods have first been used, there is no intrinsic reason for not using direct action first. Some situations will provide a foothold for the latter and not for the former. Where access to services and facilities is the major issue, there is often little scope for passive tactics except to augment the nonviolent demand for such access through direct action—going and attempting to get service. The two may be phased in sequence or used simultaneously, depending on the situation itself. A key question would be: do we have sufficient purchasing power that its withdrawal could be decisive in altering the policies of a store which bars us from lunch counters, fitting rooms, etc., or must we rely more heavily upon sitting at the lunch counter or entering

the fitting room? Suppose we want admittance to theaters, libraries, public parks or other places where passive resistance would be inapplicable? Here the attempt to enter would be the only alternative to picketing and the like—the only possible form of specifically nonviolent protest.

Before engaging in nonviolent direct action, however, we should examine two factors affecting the context of law and order. First, even if we are only transgressing established customs we may encounter forcible resistance from store owners or employees, hecklers, hoodlums and the like. To what extent can we depend on law-enforcement officers to be on hand to maintain order and protect us from bodily harm, and to what extent are we on our own? What will we do in the latter event? First-aid, rescue and escape preparations will have to be made as well as rigorous selection and training of cadres. In many such cases the police will intervene, often belatedly, and arrest us for "disorderly conduct" or some other specious charge, maintaining both order and the status quo. We shall have to plan to replace the arrested cadres in successive waves as they are removed from the scene, repeat the action after an interval of hours or days, or turn to another tactic.

Second, there is the question of the legality of our action as such, apart from what may happen as a result of it. If we are breaking local ordinances that give police the technical right to arrest us, we may want to initiate court action or we may decide on the basis of higher-court rulings that we have some legal justification for going ahead. Here we must consider the question of civil disobedience as discussed in Chapter 4. With or without a secure legal basis, however, we must also weigh carefully the penalties which the authorities can actually inflict, as well as our own resources to absorb and overcome them. Can we muster enough cadres to fill the jails and "clog the machinery" or at least render ineffectual the opponent's efforts to dispose of our protest in this way? Ideally, we should be able to fill the jails and still have enough cadres left to fill the lunch-counter stools or otherwise carry on the action. If we do resort

to such a tactic our organizational structure should be carefully reviewed and modified to assure continuous leadership, dividing our forces into several strata so that if our top-level leaders are arrested another group can step in and fill their places. For maximum effectiveness it may also be necessary to recruit large numbers of new cadres from among the masses and to bring in cadres from outside the community. By all means, the constructive work should be kept going and stepped up if possible.

Filling the jails is the virtual end of the line for nonviolent strategy, once the point is reached when either all of our forces are behind bars or the authorities are unable or unwilling to put them there. It is not necessarily the end of the campaign, however. The arrested cadres can appeal to their jailers and government officials, who may be moved by the degree of commitment shown in the cadres' willingness to endure imprisonment for the sake of their objectives. In extreme situations that afford no other alternative, those in jail can use the hunger strike as their last weapon of nonviolent coercion, resolving to fast until released. Short of this, efforts to change social policy through appeals to jailers have not been notably successful. Direct appeals to the policy-making officials themselves have a better chance, and psychologically the moral substance of the appeal from jail may not only add to socio-economic pressure such as that created by the boycott or other actions, but it may also provide the officials with a face-saving rationale for meeting the demands: they are giving in to the moral appeal rather than to pressure.

Perhaps the crucial factor at this point, however, is the effect on public opinion. More people can be swayed by the simple fact of suffering than by a righteous cause that does not vitally affect them. Our going to jail may bring the issue to life for them and cause them to exert pressure on those who make policy. Officials who imagined that they were only maintaining law and order may see themselves cast in the role of oppressors and find the image uncomfortable, leading them to rethink their position. Even among the opponent's masses there may be a

change of attitude. Going to jail potentially raises the question whether the offense at issue is so vital to the existence of the opponent's way of life that its whole system of law enforcement must be made to hinge on it.

If this does not bring victory, all is not necessarily lost. Recourse to higher courts, higher governmental intervention and other possibilities may still be open. Or it may be necessary to turn to another strategy for a new campaign.

REFERENCES IN CHAPTER 8

1   Kaspar Mayr: *Der Andere Weg* (Nürnberg, Germany: Glock und Lutz, 1957), p. 260.
2   Lewis Coser: *The Functions of Social Conflict* (Glencoe, Ill.: The Free Press, 1956), p. 95.
3   M. K. Gandhi in *Young India,* September 23, 1926.
4   *Harijan,* February 22, 1942.
5   Mayr, *loc. cit.*
6   April Carter: *Direct Action* (London: Peace News, 1962), p. 30. A pamphlet.
7   Martin Luther King Jr.: *Letter from Birmingham City Jail* (Valley Forge, Pa.: American Baptist Convention, 1963), p. 5.

9

Nonviolent Conduct
and Discipline

Undergirding every tactic of nonviolence is the conduct of the individual cadre. Whether he acts alone or in a team, it is the nonviolence of his individual conduct that gives the tactic its nonviolent character. Although uncoordinated individual acts do not add up to a movement or a strategy, there can be no such thing as a nonviolent movement or a nonviolent strategy without the disciplined nonviolent conduct of its individual cadres. A thorough understanding of this basic fact, leading to study and training to implant it, is a prerequisite for any campaign that chooses nonviolence as its strategy. The ability of each cadre to adhere to a code of strict discipline under stress is a matter that cannot be left to chance, and in some situations where a tinge of violence might spell disaster, the cadre's firmness in nonviolent conduct becomes a strategic imperative.

The essentials of any code of discipline are relatively simple. Its keystone must be: Don't strike the opponent. But this dictum alone will not cover the other contingencies of nonviolent conflict, nor does it explain the why and how of the conduct which discipline is to secure. Let us first outline a basic discipline and then discuss the dynamics of conduct and its effects, together with the basic training that is required. The following is a composite of several codes that have been used:

1. Maintain an attitude of good will at all times.

2. Avoid malicious language, slogans or labels to stigmatize or ridicule the opponent.

3. If force or violence is used against you, your teammates or others, do not retaliate. Never use violence.

4. Do not carry weapons of any kind. Do not carry implements that could be used or interpreted as weapons, such as a pocket knife.

5. Abide by decisions of the group or, when in action, follow orders given by the authorized group leader. Avoid maverick behavior.

6. Without abrogating the above, exercise creative judgment and initiative. Be flexible, willing to experiment.

7. Be ready to assume leadership of the team if required to do so.

8. Submit to arrest promptly and politely unless a policy of noncooperation has been decided upon.

9. Be punctual and precise in carrying out all tasks.

10. Maintain neat appearance and dignified posture at all times, in conformity with the moral image of the cause. This includes speaking simply, clearly and to the point. Avoid tendentiousness and be prepared to give a straightforward reply to relevant questions as well as to ignore with good grace any inflammatory remarks, jeers or other verbal abuse from the opponent.[1]

To these we may add a pertinent point: the team and the movement have a responsibility to give the individual cadre their full support when he acts on their behalf, sharing their available resources to the fullest extent in providing bail if arrested, medical aid if hurt and in general doing whatever is possible and necessary to help him out of any trouble arising from his involvement.[2]

Turning now to the dynamics of nonviolent conduct in face-to-face encounter, let us first examine what Richard B. Gregg, in his book *The Power of Nonviolence,* has called "moral jiu-jitsu":

The nonviolence and good will of the victim act in the same way that the lack of physical opposition by the user of physical jiu-jitsu does, causing the attacker to lose his moral balance.[3]

According to Gregg, the element of surprise is initially the key factor in this process, but it is to be understood in relation to a number of other factors which we may summarize as follows, omitting those portions of Gregg's analysis that are perhaps not central to the process:

1. Lack of physical retaliation disorients the immediate opponent, making him unsure of his ground. The fact that the nonviolent cadre stands his ground without fighting back, manifesting both courage and good will, mobilizes an inner conflict in the opponent between his initial aggressive stance and his latent or habitual tendency to meet good will with good will.

2. At a deeper level, the opponent's "unsureness" is diffuse and undefinable, calling in question a whole configuration of prejudices and value judgments, and making him suggestible. That is, his psychological defense mechanisms are unplugged and he becomes amenable to the well-integrated structure of values which the nonviolent cadre is able to maintain.

3. The juxtaposition of the angry, violent attacker and the calm, unretaliating resister mobilizes spontaneous human sympathy for the latter on the part of any onlookers, and a concomitant censure of the attacker's conduct, which tends to impel him to disengage himself from the immediate conflict.

4. By showing through conduct that he is willing to suffer for his beliefs, the nonviolent cadre wins respect for those beliefs on the part of both opponent and onlooker. This would be the case also if he were to "stand up and fight" with counterviolence, but nonviolent conduct enhances the effect because the cadre thus clearly demonstrates also his respect for the assailant and his steadfast resolve to do him no harm.

5. By controlling the conflict in this way, maintaining his balance while the assailant is thrown off balance by his own unretaliated thrust, the nonviolent cadre is in a position to help the assailant to his feet in a moral sense.

6. Incipiently, at least, by his refusal either to flee or to fight, the nonviolent cadre communicates to the assailant a gesture of

trust which invites reciprocation. This may contribute to conversion, but whether this happens or not it builds an image of the cadre which reflects favorably on his cause and allays the assailant's suspicions.

Gregg acknowledges the difficulties posed by an unusually cruel and insensitive opponent, but counts on "dramatic scenes of prolonged nonviolent resistance" to penetrate eventually. Central to his conception of nonviolence is the belief that the nonviolent individual or group can convert the opponent to an awareness of "essential human unity" in terms of which a common bond is established between the two parties to the conflict.

The French psychoanalyst Maryse Choisy gives a different interpretation of the process:

All the dynamism of nonviolence consists in the fact that it succeeds in totally liquidating the nonviolent person's unconscious guilt feelings, while at the same time in the same degree it activates the opponent's guilt. And it is this bad conscience of the other which renders him more vulnerable. But in the degree that the nonviolent person acts out of love, not only has he brought the other's guilt to consciousness but he has made him *accept* this guilt. It can no longer change into paranoid projection. On the contrary, it inhibits the aggressive *élan*. Because at the instant when it manifests itself, it feels itself already forgiven by the nonviolent one. Thus, in this inner dialog, there is a triple dialectical movement of contradictory relations: the nonviolent one is exalted, the violent one is moved to compassion and the nonviolent one is raised up with him.[4]

Two salient principles are evident in the dynamics of nonviolent conduct: integrity and empathy. Integrity signifies consistency and wholeness, the resolution of contradictory impulses in terms of what is basic to health. Hatred is a disintegrative emotion; it divides and fragments. Evil is the basic principle of disintegration, symbolized in chaos and disorder or equally in an order based on disunity. Gregg's emphasis on "human unity" is one way of stating the essential wholeness and integrity of humanity, but the same principle applies at

every level of existence, authenticating the individual self which becomes integrated as it resolves its inner conflicts, authenticating relations between persons as they resolve interpersonal conflicts and establish common grounds, and likewise authenticating intergroup relations in the same way. This is what Choisy is referring to when she speaks of the nonviolent person having liquidated his guilt feelings. This is also the objective of the Gandhian concept of "self-purification" through fasting and other acts of self-denial. It is all a matter of sweeping out of oneself whatever blocks one's resoluteness of purpose.

There are varieties and degrees of integrity within certain closed orbits. A white supremacist may be a man of honesty and honor in his dealings with white persons, and he may try to act with honor and honesty on a different scale in his dealings with Negroes, but the cleavage between the two orbits with their different concepts of integrity constitutes a flaw in his integrity as a total person—and consequently it is a source of guilt.

We must not suppose that it is impossible to be effective in nonviolent conduct unless we are perfect, nor that adherence to a nonviolent discipline results in perfection. To be operative it is sufficient that outward conduct exhibits integrity, even if it is forced, but it must be undergirded by a certain minimum of inner attitude if it is to be sustained. We run a tremendous risk if we attempt to counterfeit these attitudes or to hold them merely as abstract principles, for ultimately the source of nonviolent power is rooted in love and hinges upon our ability to express that love at a crucial moment in the form of empathy.

Empathy is, quite simply, seeing things from the opponent's point of view. It does not mean feeling sorry for him or merely calculating how we would act if we were in his position. It means understanding him as he understands himself, with all his foibles and prejudices, momentarily setting aside our own standards of value. Only through empathy can we search out and discover the inherent integrity of the opponent's personality which it is our task to enlarge. And we cannot do this

empathically if we have not already developed a degree of integration within ourselves and among one another within our own group.

Romano Guardini has stated this brilliantly in another context:

Everything, to remain human and be spiritually successful, must first pass through the "personal center," that inmost core of the responsible human heart. The true, the good and the right are realizable only if accepted by living poeple with inner, genuine conviction, and to bring this about requires reverence, encouragement, patience. He who would be truly effective with men must respect *their* freedom, stir *their* initiatives, awaken *their* creative centers.

The greater a man's power, the stronger the temptation to take the shortcut of force.[5]

If we take "power" in our context to mean the sheer technique of "moral jiu-jitsu," it is not difficult to imagine the misuse of the latter in an attempt to embarrass the opponent and throw him off balance. A superficial understanding of nonviolence may result in just such tactics, which antagonize the opponent and destroy rather than establish rapport. There is latent in such a view the strong temptation to inflict psychic injury, to damage the opponent's self-esteem while refraining from overt violence against him—in short to use abstention from physical violence as a means of provoking "unwarranted" attack, thus tricking the opponent into a position of moral disadvantage and making him lose countenance. There may be some immediate satisfaction in making a fool of the opponent in this way, but its net effect is to stiffen his opposition and encourage him to engage in further repressions despite the refusal of the "nonviolent" persons to employ violence.

The pressures used in a nonviolent campaign are social and strategic. The object of nonviolent conduct is not to carry them into the realm of interpersonal encounter, but just the opposite. Nonviolent conduct is predicated on the assumption that hostility and moral disintegrity will be manifested by the opponent as part of his response to social conflict, and that these may

take violent forms which we shall then not resist in kind, but on the contrary meet with good will and forgiveness, ready to relieve the opponent of his guilt and establish a new relationship of mutual respect *which we have already unilaterally begun.*

As Maryse Choisy indicates above, nonviolent conduct brings the opponent's guilt to the surface and meets it with forgiveness that inhibits its "aggressive *élan.*" Culbert G. Rutenber gives us a working definition of its implications:

forgiveness must never be interpreted as condoning evil or acting as though its existence really did not make any difference. . . .

Forgiveness, to be morally effective, must satisfy the conscience and moral sense of the one forgiven. . . . [It] must be offered in such a way that the forgiven one is not humiliated and his self-respect is not taken away.[6]

He adds that, to be authentic, forgiveness must be motivated by love, without which it may be nothing more than a gesture of condescension or of contempt which implies that the forgiven one is not worth getting upset about. The occasion for forgiveness should not be glossed over, as if to say "there is nothing to forgive." It should be made clear, verbally or otherwise, that insults and injuries which are forgiven are real insults and real injuries.

The Principle in Action

James Baldwin has written: "I imagine that one of the reasons people cling to their hates so stubbornly is because they sense, once hate is gone, that they will be forced to deal with pain." [7] Hostility is a kind of shield, and in inviting the opponent to dispense with it we are asking him to emulate our vulnerability, which we demonstrate by accepting suffering. In our encounters with individual persons in the opponent's ranks we should consider the extent to which their solidarity is based on conformity to a group standard of hostility. It may be difficult

for an individual opponent to respond overtly with good will toward us because of the pressures exerted upon him by his group, and we should respect his reluctance for this reason. A question to be asked in the situation is whether we seek to pry individuals loose from their group or whether we want to have a more diffuse effect on the group as a whole, prying it loose from its hostilities toward us. In some situations, the two possibilities may work together; in others we may have to choose between them.

We must be careful not to corner our opponent. "Confronted with the impossibility of remaining faithful to one's beliefs, and the equal impossibility of becoming free of them," writes Baldwin, "one can be driven to the most inhuman excesses." [8] Firmness should never become dogmatic rigidity. Although nonviolence places a premium upon the capacity of the nonviolent cadre to endure suffering, each team of cadres should have sufficient tactical flexibility to be able to choose whether to extricate the individual members from a catastrophic situation or, if this alternative is foreclosed, to endure martyrdom with a composure that may cause their attackers to repent afterward.

Charles Walker offers some specific suggestions for nonviolent conduct in direct encounter. First, in response to provocations, cadres should be careful to avoid clever remarks, intemperate statements, name-calling or other inflammatory behavior and should not break ranks or otherwise display disunity. In addition, when actually under attack, he suggests the following procedures:

1. Adhere to group discipline and do not intervene except to help an injured person. Each team member should be prepared to endure attack and not expect it to be warded off by his teammates.

2. Pray for the victim and the attacker. Walker does not state whether to pray aloud or silently, but if sincere prayer is voiced aloud it may communicate moral support to the victim and help to inhibit the attacker's aggressive impulses.

3. If the victim is able to do so, he may try to interrupt the attack by calmly saying to the attacker: "Sir, may I ask you a question?" and transferring the conflict to a verbal level.

4. The group leader gives all instructions and supervises removal of injured persons, assigns cadres to administer first aid or provides for medical attention.

5. Team members may express solidarity by spontaneously singing a hymn or reciting a prayer together. They should generally avoid loud talk, outcries, vigorous gestures or sudden movements. Unless agreed upon in tactical decisions made beforehand to meet the needs of the situation, they should not scatter when attacked but remain close together and maintain uniform bearing, e.g., all standing or all kneeling.

6. Do not appeal to police or bystanders for aid, but be prepared to accept any such aid or intervention with poise and equanimity.

7. Note carefully the attitudes of onlookers, with a view to follow-up as well as to the possibility of their immediate effect on the struggle. Depending on the issue that is involved, they may comprise a source of support for either resisters or attackers, and any shift in their attitudes may be crucial.[9]

If arrested, cadres should comply courteously and promptly with the legitimate orders of police and jailers. There is a school of thought which advises personal noncooperation by "going limp" and compelling the arresting officers to carry the resister, but careful thought should be given to this tactic before using it, since it is likely to exacerbate hostility and may provoke brutality by the police and weaken rapport with neutral onlookers.

If a nonviolent strategy terminates with arrest and a new line of strategy of legal action is begun, cadres may be content to accept bail; but if nonviolent strategy is to be carried into this area the most effective course will be for cadres to refuse bail, to insist on individual trials and thus to fill the jails and glut the court calendar. In jail and in the courtroom, of course, cadres should maintain nonviolent conduct at all times. They

may keep up their morale and enhance their image in relations with the authorities by developing some kind of constructive program inside the jail, rendering service to other prisoners. Those who remain outside should take responsibility for the families and dependents of the imprisoned cadres, as well as for the welfare of the prisoners, in case the latter are subjected to mistreatment of any kind.

Finally, perhaps the severest test of nonviolent conduct occurs outside the situation of direct encounter in team actions. The worst elements among the opponent's masses may inflict brutal reprisals. Homes, churches and other buildings may be bombed or fired upon by anonymous night-riders. Leaders and cadres may receive written or telephoned threats and their children or relatives and friends may be harassed. Individual leaders or cadres may be ambushed or abducted and beaten, tortured, mutilated or killed. They may be fired from their jobs or refused service by merchants. All of these and other reprisals may be taken to break resistance or to provoke retaliatory violence.

There is no panacea for such reprisals. If the situation or the issue is highly charged, some types of vicious action are to be expected, often as a spontaneous response to the conflict. We must entertain no illusions about the depths of human depravity. But by the same token we must look to the creative resources of nonviolent conduct for solution. If individually attacked we must attempt to remain steadfast in our composure and in our manifestation of courageous good will toward the attackers, even if it seems hopeless that we can thereby avert harm to ourselves. Martyrdom is not to be courted, but it may have an indirectly redemptive effect even when it is not directly effective. Scornful defiance or appeals for mercy are likely to destroy this possibility.

In any event it is seldom possible to work through to a conversion of the immediate assailants without appealing to the more responsible elements in their community to quarantine them. Another alternative is to make use of the moral leverage

arising from unretaliated persecution to invoke public censure, pressuring the authorities to act against violence and lawlessness. This of course means mobilizing lawful force against the perpetrators of violence. Any nonviolent movement which on principle rules out this step may find itself confronted at this point with the dilemma of capitulation or extermination.

The Socio-Drama

In order to learn a discipline for nonviolent conduct, it is not enough to memorize a set of rules, even if the theoretical implications of these rules are thoroughly understood. Not only study and discussion but actual training is required. Part of this training will consist of learning teamwork through experience in constructive work and by sharing in spiritual fellowship, meditating together and developing a vocabulary of songs, hymns, slogans and other symbolic devices for building solidarity. But of crucial importance is the socio-drama, in which we actually rehearse nonviolent conduct, putting theory into simulated practice. This is the basic combat training of the nonviolent cadre. It is as vital to him as bayonet drill or target practice is to the recruit in infantry training.

Socio-drama begins with role-playing, in which each cadre becomes a character in an improvised drama without a script. Taking more or less commonplace situations that do not involve conflict, the first sessions aim at articulating empathy by literally trying to understand and act out a given situation from a standpoint not one's own. By doing so in a group setting it is possible afterward to discuss and evaluate one another's performance, not from the standpoint of external details or mannerisms that might be important in the theatrical world, but from the standpoint of inner motivations and impulses. The process may be helpful to many cadres also in understanding themselves, and indeed some of the early role-playing should involve cadres in playing themselves as they would react to given circumstances. It may be as simple as asking a group of

cadres to imagine that they have just been caught in the rain while on their way to a meeting, and improvising conversation and gestures appropriate to such a situation. Later the same cadres may be asked to imagine that they are members of a different group—i.e. with different customs and habits—caught in the same downpour.

After a few such sessions, the cadres will move on into situations of verbal disagreement and eventually to those in which insult and abuse and actual violence are involved. Some of the cadres will assume the roles of antagonists and attackers, hurling abuse and grabbing or shoving other cadres, whose task it will be to respond creatively while adhering to nonviolent discipline. Partly, socio-drama is a psychological and spiritual exercise, but it also includes practice in a number of physical details. Cadres must learn the gymnastics of receiving blows—chewing gum in order to relax tensions and so ease the impact when struck, clasping hands behind the neck and shielding the face with one's arms, drawing the knees up to protect the abdomen when lying down and being kicked, learning how to fall down gracefully when it is impossible to remain sitting or standing. These and other techniques must be both memorized and practiced. Judo or karate training may be an asset in learning them, but in nonviolent conduct only self-protection is permissible. When pulled by an assailant, for example, the nonviolent cadre may attempt to slip his grasp but he must learn how *not* to wrestle, how *not* to cause the assailant to lose his balance, how to avoid any action that could be interpreted as retaliatory.

If the group is serious about its training, those cadres who take the role of the opponent will be sharply criticized if they fail to use the typical language of the actual opponent, obscenities and profanity included. It is not their task to create a mild caricature of the opponent, but to represent him as exactly and as authentically as possible. The purpose is twofold: to accustom the cadres to experiencing such situations with calm and without surprise, and to develop the ability to respond calmly

when an untrained person might understandably panic. Also, of course, by rotating the responsibility for enacting the role of the opponent, each member of the group has a chance to acquire empathy for the latter, as well as to try a wide range of possible situations.

The value of such training can hardly be overstressed. Mere talk about "what you would do if—" is no substitute for the direct sensory experience of being confronted with someone who is shouting at you, calling you dirty names not with a snicker but with menacing conviction, trying to humiliate you, to provoke you to anger, to push you off balance physically or verbally. With prolonged training through socio-drama, nonviolent conduct becomes an easy reflex that can place the cadre in command of a volatile situation. The Congress of Racial Equality has made considerable use of this type of training. Periodically it has held workshops of nonviolence in which, after a series of socio-drama sessions, a seasoned veteran of nonviolent campaigns supervises the trainees in an actual conflict situation of limited scope, in which they can test what they have learned. The presence of an experienced leader is an asset to such training, but his absence does not seriously handicap a group, since imagination and resourcefulness combined with serious study are the chief requirements. There is no elaborate technique to be mastered.

A final consideration in nonviolent conduct is the very ordinary matter of personal appearance and habits. As we have observed elsewhere (see page 146 above), the opponent will seize upon any shortcomings to stigmatize nonviolent cadres as slovenly, undependable, outlandish or crackpot. Cadres must therefore take special care to overcome habits of tardiness, slouching posture and the like, and make it a point to dress neatly, speak clearly, look the opponent directly in the face and in general create an image of self-respect without being overbearing. There is an unfortunate tendency among certain self-styled "radicals" to indulge their personal idiosyn-

cracies under the cover of rationalizations which convince no one but themselves. As Herbert Read has observed:

> To wear "rational" clothes, to eat "rational" foods, to establish "rational" schools—these well-meaning exemplary methods too often tend to create a barrier of suspicion and reserve which makes the communication of any truth impossible. There are, of course, degrees of compromise which are also impossible because they demand participation in evil actions. . . . But perfect love demands not only that we should sup with publicans and sinners, but also that we should not offend them on such occasions by our ineffable superiority.[10]

In a word, nonviolent conduct is designed not only to reduce disorder but also to keep the door open to reconciliation even during the conflict, and to keep the issues in focus. We need not force ourselves to conform to the opponent's whims, but if we want to communicate we owe it both to him and to ourselves not to indulge our own whims, which could become a distracting side issue.

There is a point at which all rules and prescriptions fail and success depends on common sense, timing, imagination, inspiration and the providence of a loving God. In addition, there are human and individual limits. Leaders and cadres should try to extend them but plan their tactics and strategy to allow for them, relieving and rotating frontline activists in alternation with the less strain-provoking tasks of the constructive program. Like any method, nonviolence has its characteristic weakness, which Clarence Marsh Case has called "its tendency to fail from apathy on the one hand or to be betrayed into the use of violence on the other." It demands, he adds, "a stronger self-control, a more enduring solidarity of purpose, a greater capacity for passive suffering, a higher ethical development, than most human beings have thus far attained." [11] Consequently, victory must come swiftly unless great stamina can be mustered to face prolonged adversity.

Partly this may require phasing strategy in such a way as to score a series of minor gains or to secure a single major victory

in the most accessible sector, rather than trying for a cluster of major objectives at the same time. Partly it may mean augmenting nonviolence with other types of action. But in the realm of conduct itself, it also means a further dimension of training.

Gandhi recommended and rigorously practiced a number of bodily disciplines adapted from Hindu asceticism, among them strict vows of celibacy and restricting the diet to bland foods, counting these as prominent among his "experiments with truth" as an important source of power for social struggle. Others, such as Nehru and Subhas Chandra Bose, who diverged from Gandhi's commitment to *ahimsa* as a religious duty, bound themselves to similar vows in order to facilitate the struggle.

In the West, much less attention has been given to such practices except in monastic orders and among adherents of health cults, moralistic abstainers and the like. If we set aside Gandhi's own example and take that of the more pragmatic Nehru, it is still hard to say how much these practices were a feature of the distinctive Hindu background. The Hungarian passive resistance leader, Ferencz Deák, was an habitual cigar smoker. Meat, alcoholic beverages and sex have not proved to be stumbling blocks for other leaders or cadres of nonviolence.

For the Christian, self-denial has no intrinsic merits. It is not a way of salvation, and when it has historically been claimed as one its devotees have been regarded as heretical. Yet it does have a legitimate place in the Christian life. As Dietrich Bonhoeffer has stated the case:

The spirit assents when Jesus bids us to love our enemies, but flesh and blood are too strong and prevent our carrying it out. Therefore we have to practice strictest daily discipline; only so can the flesh learn the painful lesson that it has no rights of its own. Regular daily prayer is a great help here, and so is daily meditation on the Word of God, and every kind of bodily discipline and asceticism.[12]

Some advocates of holistic nonviolence have gone so far as to argue that cadres must rid their lives of music and art, and

sacrifice even personal friendships for the sake of an abstract love of humanity. This chimerical notion has nothing to do with the real issues. Nonviolent conduct does not require the rejection of the normal pleasures of life. But it does mean, as Bonhoeffer suggests, freeing oneself from their domination, ceasing to be possessed by attachments to persons or things, getting rid of unnecessary clutter, disorder and excess.

To achieve this, part of a nonviolent cadre's personal training should involve periods of acute self-deprivation, not to destroy his enjoyments permanently but to purge them of their burdensomeness. A day of solitary contemplation can freshen one's outlook as well as preparing him for the eventuality of solitary confinement in jail. Those who have not tried it will be surprised to find how easily they can endure a three-day fast, and will find the experience of self-control of the will a useful asset in the struggle, in addition to the physiological benefits. To do these things it is not necessary to make vows. Unless a particular habit is decidedly harmful, it is sufficient to interrupt it; it need not be permanently broken. The aim is to develop sufficient inner strength that one can move comfortably from strict solitude to any sort of interpersonal encounter; to be self-contained or self-giving; to eat heartily or go hungry.

Voluntary Suffering

In Chapter 11 we shall return to a fuller discussion of spiritual resources. Now let us consider whether the capacity to withstand suffering has a part to play beyond its function as a necessary ingredient of nonviolent conduct. Does it have any positive tactical significance?

Gandhi set great store by voluntary suffering as a powerful and primary means by which he hoped to touch the hearts of the British rulers in India, and if he did not succeed in influencing their policies thereby he nevertheless demonstrated some such power to sway his own people and to draw sympathy from all parts of the world.

Not all suffering has such an effect. Much of it is in fact useless, though it may produce sympathy. If it is senselessly self-inflicted, it may even provoke scorn and contempt. To have redemptive possibilities, suffering must be meaningful. Where does such meaning come from and how can it have power to work changes either in the sufferer or in the world?

Simone Weil sees the acceptance of evil done to us as a remedy for evil that we have done. The resulting suffering must be unjust, not self-inflicted. The perfect example is the transmutation resulting from the crucifixion of Jesus, the "perfectly pure being," on behalf of a sinful world. "All the criminal violence of the Roman Empire ran up against Christ," she writes, "and in him it became pure suffering." She adds that "redemptive suffering has to have a social origin. It has to be injustice, violence on the part of human beings." [13]

Romano Guardini asserts that "inwardly accepted suffering transforms the sufferer" and "all existential growth depends not on effort alone, but also on freely offered sacrifice." [14] It is not the suffering but the sacrificial act of willing acceptance that makes it spiritually effective, and sacrifice is an act of agapaic love. As Berdyaev has observed, "Psychologically, fear is always the fear of suffering." [15] That is why voluntary suffering is redemptive—because divine love both wills the endurance of suffering and because in this way it casts out fear. As Simone Weil says, "The extreme greatness of Christianity lies in the fact that it does not seek a supernatural remedy for suffering, but a supernatural use for it." [16]

It is no accident that Gandhi considered "fearlessness" indispensable to true *satyagraha* and regarded the capacity to endure suffering as an index of nonviolent power. Commenting on this, however, Régamey reminds us: "The trouble is that the fear of specific danger is frequently contaminated by what Ribot has called 'a primitive, instinctive fear, anterior to all individual experience,' and which is *anxiety*." [17]

Brewster Kneen argues that voluntary suffering has a redemptive effect by terminating a process whereby violence and

involuntary suffering have been passed from person to person. The redemptive sufferer thus "removes any threat to others of having the suffering inflicted upon them. The removal of this threat has the effect of increasing social solidarity . . ."[18]

This may well be true in situations that involve misunderstanding, alienation and tension, though even here the presence of diffuse anxieties may prove to be formidable obstacles, but the matter is greatly complicated if the situation is one of overt social conflict, with the would-be redemptive sufferer actively engaged in creating pressures to coerce the very same persons from whom he seeks to remove the threat of suffering.

In such a setting, says Galtung, much depends upon interpretation:

Even if it is intended to symbolize the willingness to suffer unto death rather than submission or [recourse] to violent means, the interpretation may be as a symbol of innate, cowardly masochism or even as lack of will to resist, since the usual symbols—weapons of violence—are absent.[19]

In a similar vein, Leo Kuper has observed that the active courting of suffering by the nonviolent resister is not effective "where the ruler is a collectivity and responds to the subordinate as a collectivity, and where the suffering is a challenge to the ruler's ideology of domination."[20] Thus what may work in simple interpersonal relations does not necessarily work in relations between two large and well-defined groups. At the same time, Kuper acknowledges that the acceptance of suffering has a liberating spiritual effect among the resisters, creating morale and solidarity within their ranks. Galtung describes this as the expressive rather than instrumental value of the act, and notes that

the gratification from an expressive act is immediate and certain, whereas instrumental acts must be brought from the personal system out into the social system, where the causal chains are uncertain and effects may be positive, but only in the long run. When the expressive need is present, therefore, the temptation will be high to

resort to expressive acts even at considerable cost along the instrumental dimension.[21]

For suffering to be instrumental and lead to reconciliation, it must operate through a nexus of shared values which provide a basis for empathy. Given the opponent's distaste for avoidable pain, and given also an ideology (such as white supremacy or anti-Semitism) which effectively destroys that nexus, voluntary suffering can only tend to confirm the estrangement and justify the opponent in accommodating the resister's seeming appetite for pain. Hence the initial effect of voluntary suffering in such a context is not to bring reconciliation but to exacerbate conflict.

If sadistic tendencies are already present in the opponent, his confrontation with an apparently masochistic resister will be tantamount to an invitation to inflict pain. The use of redemptive suffering therefore demands a maximum effort to establish rapport and to present the opponent with an image that commands respect and can lay a basis for empathy. Kuper suggests, following Georg Simmel,[22] that the resister may appeal to a third party with whom there is an overlap of his own and the opponent's values, and thus set in motion such forces as moral suasion and secondary boycott. A case in point would be the appeal by black Africans to whites who share with them opposition to white supremacy and share with the white supremacists the fact that they are white.

In addition to its expressive value in building interior solidarity, successfully publicized voluntary suffering may focus public attention on the group and thus on its leadership. Even if the act of suffering and by implication the movement that engages in it appear to be despicable, perverse or incomprehensible, they have attained the status of public facts, and the leadership emerges from anonymity and assumes recognizable (even if distorted) personal identity in relation to the opponent. If repressive measures fail, the opponent now knows whom he must deal with.

Kierkegaard writes of the good to be derived by the incurable sufferer who not only accepts but embraces his suffering and invests it with meaning. There is a similar benefit to be derived by the involuntary sufferer of injustice who volunteers to bear a heavier but more meaningful burden of suffering with dignity and group support, perhaps adding to the burden but enduring it knowingly and purposefully with a moral resistance that was formerly lacking. Only the oppressed can fully appreciate Berdyaev's statement that the acceptance of suffering is "an experience of freedom" that can lead to "spiritual victory." [23] Thus by an act of will the sufferer ceases to be an inert object and becomes a freely acting subject. Instead of cringing under the blows and kowtowing to his persecutor, he now stands erect to take the same blows and exercises his power to forgive offenses that he dares to call offensive. In this lies its expressive value.

In addition to voluntarily accepted suffering, there is self-imposed suffering such as the hunger strike and the fast, which may serve to underline the seriousness of a given protest. Such suffering is often coercive rather than redemptive. The hunger strike or prolonged fast (Gandhi's repeated "fast unto death") is an implicit suicide threat which places responsibility for one's life gratuitously in the opponent's hands. Far from being convinced of Gandhi's good will when he undertook such fasts, the British regarded them as an acute form of blackmail. On more than one occasion they were spurred to action by such fasts, not because they were converted but because they feared the repercussions if they were blamed for Gandhi's death. I. N. Steinberg has called the hunger strike "the sharpest weapon in the arsenal of the disarmed" and tells how on several occasions it was used effectively to secure decent treatment for political prisoners under Bolshevik rule in 1919-1920 in Moscow's Butyrki prison.[24] Much depends, however, upon the character of the participants and their demands. If the former are obscure and the latter excessive, the authorities may feel justified in

allowing hunger strikers to perish. It is not a weapon to be used recklessly.

Suffering that is voluntarily accepted rather than self-imposed surely plays an important part in nonviolent conduct, but it is doubtful whether its role is ever more than supportive or that the sufferer himself can derive any earthly benefit from his sacrifice unless it is augmented with tactical and strategic pressures. Although indispensable in maintaining spiritual integrity that has far-reaching implications in the larger context of the struggle, it is no substitute for strategy. Its redemptive value is indirect, through purifying one's own heart in relation to an eternal dimension and liberating oneself from fear and thereby offsetting the demonic element in protest action, but it is the latter that usually must carry the main thrust.

REFERENCES IN CHAPTER 9

1   See Charles C. Walker: *Organizing for Nonviolent Action* (New Delhi: Gandhi Smarak Nidhi, 1962), p. 22. A pamphlet.
2   See *CORE Rules for Action,* a leaflet (New York: Congress of Racial Equality, 1961).
3   Richard B. Gregg: *The Power of Nonviolence* (Nyack, N.Y.: Fellowship Publications, 1959; second revised edition), p. 44.
4   Maryse Choisy: *Yogas et Psychoanalyse* (Geneva: Éditions du Mont Blanc, 1949), p. 240.
5   Romano Guardini: *Power and Responsibility* (Chicago: Henry Regnery Co., 1961), p. 62.
6   Culbert G. Rutenber: *The Reconciling Gospel* (Philadelphia: Judson Press, 1961), p. 51f.
7   James Baldwin: *Notes of a Native Son* (Boston: Beacon Press, Inc., 1955), p. 101.
8   *Ibid.,* p. 171.
9   Compare with Walker, *op. cit.,* p. 31f. The outline given here slightly modifies Walker's presentation, but is the same in its essentials.
10 Herbert Read: *Anarchy and Order* (London: Faber, 1954), p. 31.
11 C. M. Case: *Non-Violent Coercion* (New York: Century Co., 1923), p. 407.
12 Dietrich Bonhoeffer: *The Cost of Discipleship* (New York: The Macmillan Co., 1959), p. 132.
13 Simone Weil: *Gravity and Grace* (New York: G. P. Putnam's Sons, 1952), p. 122.
14 Romano Guardini, *op. cit.,* p. 87f.

15   Nikolai Berdyaev: *The Divine and the Human* (London: Bles, 1949), p. 61.
16   Weil, *op. cit.*, p. 132.
17   Pie Régamey: *Non-Violence et Conscience Chrétienne* (Paris: Cerf, 1958), p. 213.
18   Brewster Kneen: *Voluntary Suffering and Social Change* (New York: Union Theological Seminary, unpublished B.D. thesis, 1961), p. 59.
19   Johan Galtung: "Pacifism from a Sociological Point of View" in *Conflict Resolution,* March 1959, p. 81.
20   Leo Kuper: *Passive Resistance in South Africa* (New Haven: Yale University Press, 1957), p. 91.
21   Galtung, *op. cit.*, p. 70.
22   See Kurt H. Wolff: *The Sociology of Georg Simmel* (Glencoe, Ill.: The Free Press, 1950), pp. 195-197.
23   Nikolai Berdyaev: *Spirit and Reality* (London: Bles, 1939), p. 198.
24   I. N. Steinberg: *In the Workshop of the Revolution* (New York: Rinehart & Co., Inc., 1953), p. 167. See also pages 167-172.

10

Active Love and Reconciliation

Nonviolence, we have said, is not love; nor is it a method for resolving conflict. It is a way of waging social conflict that is compatible with love. It does a minimum of damage and holds the door open to creative, constructive possibilities. But it has no intrinsic power to heal and to build anew. For this we must look beyond nonviolence to active, agapaic love and reconciliation.

This is true in two senses. In the dimension of depth underlying nonviolent conduct it is ultimately love that counts, both as the source of resilient inner strength and as that which authenticates empathy and rapport. Courage based on sheer willpower becomes brittle and will splinter under stress. Likewise, feigned empathy cannot provide true guidance, and ersatz rapport will easily break down. In the dimension of history, of the ongoing interactions of social groups and masses, it is ultimately love that counts in the termination of conflict and the restoration of community between one's own and the opponent's group.

It should not be supposed that nonviolence automatically springs from love or that love automatically follows in the wake of nonviolence. Nor, it is important to note, does the success of a nonviolent campaign necessarily depend upon love. Often in history extraneous events have proved to be decisive. The balance of objective forces such as population and social structures, the presence or absence of the kairotic moment or the charismatic leader—all these and other factors may determine the outcome and compensate for what might otherwise be dis-

astrous defects in conduct, tactics and strategy. There would be no progress if victories in social struggle depended entirely on perfect love. On the other hand, many such victories prove to be hollow, and those purchased cheaply may later reveal a hidden cost.

The kind of love that we are talking about here, obviously, is something more than a natural disposition to treat others fairly or to respond amicably to those we find amiable. It goes beyond the simple moral equation of "live and let live." Nor is it merely an exalted ideal or cosmic absolute. It is not a latent power of human nature, to be activated by discipline and training, nor an overarching principle of human conduct which projects a pattern onto our lives. There is no such thing as love in the abstract—impersonal love, love for humanity. Love is the content of a relationship between persons—between human persons and between the human and the divine. Agapaic love is that kind of love which possesses the power to penetrate barriers. It is love for the stranger, the enemy, the outcast, the ugly, the evildoer. It is love in a different dimension, not only overcoming alienation between oneself and the stranger or enemy, but also deepening and purifying one's natural loves, overcoming residual tensions between friends and resolving inner conflicts within individual persons. It is holy—that is, it contains within itself no mixed motives, no admixture of egotism or pride. Because it is holy, one may agapaically love oneself and one's most dangerous enemy in the same way. But for the same reason, its source and its ultimate focus can only be found in a transcendent God who is a perfect and holy living person.

Romano Guardini has aptly described this love as a "live current" like electricity:

The love Christ means is a live current that comes from God, is transmitted from person to person, and returns to God. It runs a sacred cycle reaching from God to an individual, from the individual to his neighbor, and back through faith to God. He who breaks the circuit at any point breaks the flow of love. He who transmits

purely, however small a part of that love, helps establish the circuit for the whole.[1]

Guardini leaves no room for doubt that this applies to the enemy as well. He quotes in full Luke 6:28-36, which begins: "Love your enemies; do good to those who hate you . . ." (New English Bible).

This is no longer mere justice or even goodness. It is no longer the voice of earthly reason that speaks. Something entirely different is demanded—the positive, heroic act of a bounty that can be acquired only from above, a divine generosity that is its own measure.[2]

Referring specifically to the passage which bids us to turn the other cheek, Guardini observes:

This most certainly does not mean that one must behave like a weakling or surrender oneself to force. Rather, that man should extricate himself from the whole earthly business of defense and aggression, of blow and counterblow, of right and usurpation. . . .

Now we begin to see what Jesus is driving at: a bearing in our relationship to others that is no less than divinely free—not what law and order demand, but what true liberty gives. The measure of that liberty is love, the love of God.[3]

The Role of Faith

It is not possible to achieve this liberty by our own will, nor can we simply decide to appropriate it for our use. We know beforehand that we shall fall short, because we are not holy. At our best we are poor transmitters of divine love. Yet the power is given to us to have faith, to stand with openness toward God and toward the enemy, to allow the redemptive current of divine love to flow through us. "It is God who works in you," wrote Paul, "inspiring both the will and the deed, for his own chosen purpose" (Philippians 2:13, New English Bible). This is the work of no mere principle, but of the living God.

Régamey recognizes this fact as he attempts to come to terms with Gandhi's conception of nonviolence as "truth force" (*satyagraha*). The Sanskrit word *sat*, which here stands for "truth," also means "reality" and connotes "righteousness," all of which are attributes of God as revealed in the Bible. But the biblical understanding of God includes also the facts of "work" and "purpose" which are revealed in God's action in history, definitively and consummatorily in the incarnation of holy love in the man Jesus. The actual existence of Jesus as a man among men provides a humanly authentic anchorage for the revelation of God's love, and points tellingly to the real personhood of holy God in a way that would not be possible if Jesus had been a mythical being or a demigod. To be sure, God is truth, and Jesus incarnated truth in human form: he was "the Word made flesh." But it is the dynamic of action which manifests truth as love. The power of truth is no power at all unless it is manifested as active love. As Régamey says,

. . . this power is nothing but a dream, a wish, finally a trap, if Truth is not all-powerful active Love, bestower of grace and strength. Of course certain unbelievers may have enough confidence in the fundamental goodness of men to hope that it can overcome by itself egotistical interests, wickedness, hatred, violence. And so certain "unbelievers" of good will who believe in man can enlist in the ways of nonviolence themselves. But without being aware of it, their optimism implies a belief in God which alone can justify it, since God is the only one to give it its value and to permit its eventual success.[4]

His latter point is consistent with Paul's statement above, for God is no respecter of ecclesiastical credentials, and the forms of faith are not what makes agapaic love accessible to us. The value of Christianity is not that it provides a direct liturgical pipeline to God, but simply that it offers a correct and articulate understanding of the way God works. It would be naïve to suppose that God does not know those who do not know him. To be truly God his reality must be universally true, whether universally acknowledged or not. God's love is not only for

Christians but for all men who open themselves to receive and transmit it. Indeed, the merely nominal Christian who has no real faith is worse off than the non-Christian whose faith is real but inarticulate.

There is a sense in which love is a natural law. Reinhold Niebuhr explains it in terms that are close to our theme:

Man knows, both by experience and by the demand for coherence in his rational nature, that life ought not to be lived at cross purposes, that conflict within the self, and between the self and others, is an evil. In that sense love is the law of life according to the insights of natural religion and morality.[5]

What biblical revelation does is to show us the source of this love which governs life, and to call us to participate in the relationship which it sets in motion. Niebuhr goes on to affirm that there is no limit to the possibility of agapaic love as an admixture in historical processes. "Even the purest form of *agapē*, the love of the enemy and forgiveness toward the evildoer, do not stand in contradiction to historical possibilities." [6] He goes on, however, to qualify this statement by pointing out (as we have already observed) that it is impossible in social action for this holy love to be completely unadulterated. Agapaic love is not irrelevant but its relevance is conditioned by the sinful and demonic elements that are present in history. Though bidden by divine invitation to open ourselves to the live current of holy love, which is the only kind of love that transcends all contradictions, we must also and beforehand establish the very norms of mutuality and civil order that are thereby transcended. Niebuhr's point, which has often been misinterpreted, is simply that the "leap of faith" implied in our opening ourselves to agapaic possibilities must be predicated on a firm footing of established, operative values which may not be recklessly sacrificed in the act of going beyond them. Each of us as an individual or as members of a community who have expressly agreed on such a course of action may indeed throw caution to the winds and abandon all the safeguards of norma-

tive justice, knowing what it is that we are risking, but we may not legitimately involve others in our risk. That is, we do not have the right to go beyond self-sacrifice; we do not have the right to require that those with whom we ally ourselves in social conflict should engage in self-sacrifice against their will. For this reason we need always to maintain institutional structures that are not dependent for their success upon a higher level of conduct than may safely be foreseen, yet which do not force that level down but are adaptable upward toward the light of the higher level. With reference to criminal law, for example, there is vast opportunity for enlarging the rehabilitative and reducing the punitive elements of this type of justice, and this cannot be done without recourse to holy love; but the prior consideration is the protection of society. We cannot responsibly let every criminal loose unless every member of society voluntarily assents to take the consequences.

In short, and with specific reference to nonviolence in social conflict, we are not entitled wantonly to abandon existing social conventions or laws simply because we think we are prepared to act in accordance with a higher law of love. The approach of Jesus is instructive here, in his statement: "Do you suppose that I have come to abolish the Law and the prophets; I did not come to abolish, but to complete." (Matt. 5:17, New English Bible.) The gospel penetrates to the very heart of the Mosaic Law and renders its meticulous observance unnecessary by going beyond it and doing more than the Law requires. We need not reiterate our earlier discussion of the basis on which we may defy unjust laws. The point is that in social conflict we have no responsible recourse against justice in the name of love. Our concern must be to establish normative, operable justice rooted in actuality and relevant to historical conditions. It cannot be based on purely hypothetical possibilities or absolute demands.

Nonviolence does not require perfect holy love for its success. For nonviolent conduct a strong admixture of it is ultimately needed as a source of enduring strength, but the fact

should not be overlooked that considerations of prudence, of reciprocation and of normative justice are also part of the picture. In all but the rare case of holistic nonviolence, the nonviolent cadre hopes by his exposure to self-sacrifice to gain a realizable historical objective from which he may benefit individually and from which at all events the group he represents will benefit collectively. His prudence consists in a willingness to forego the immediate gratification of violent revenge against injustice for the sake of the higher satisfaction of later enjoying a situation in which injustice has been removed. Further, it is his aim to elicit a reciprocal response from the opponent, leading finally to the establishment of new or altered conventions and laws that are mutually acceptable to both the opponent and himself, terminating the condition of crisis and conflict and allowing him to relax. Indeed, these considerations exert a strong temptation merely to "use" agapaic love as a means to selfish ends.

This, by definition, is impossible. A humanly sinful counterfeit of agapaic love may serve selfish ends, but only authentic love of divine origin can serve God's purposes. Are the aims of our particular social conflict identical with the latter?

Surely it would erroneous to suppose that the alternatives are so starkly opposed—our sinful selfishness versus a perfectionistic conception of discipleship. What introduces relativity and latitude into the picture is the very ambiguity of love. To be sure, we can readily define distinct categories of holy and profane love, and it is true that these operate at different levels of reality. Sometimes, perhaps, they may collide and force us to choose. But they also blend and interact. The mutual love that binds together a man and a woman may be very superficial, undermined by deeper currents of egotism, or it may be undergirded by agapaic depths in which the separate egos are all but lost. In either case, each person at the surface level of mutuality exerts a reciprocal claim against the other. The difference is that in a crisis the latter couple will not be driven apart if the reciprocal relationship is somehow upset or damaged. A mar-

riage may be based solely upon mutual sexual attraction, mutual vocational interests or other forms of reciprocal compatibility, but it will be very precarious unless the couple somehow learn to value one another at a deeper, finally agapaic level.

The function of love in social relationships is naturally more complex and diffuse, and not everything that is said about love between two persons can be true between two groups of many persons on each side. As Howard Thurman has said, "to love means to have an intrinsic interest in another person." [7] When directly confronting an individual opponent, the nonviolent cadre's first task is, through nonviolent conduct, to leave this possibility open by showing a certain minimum of friendliness in response to hostility. This means, in addition to the "moral image" we have mentioned elsewhere, presenting to the opponent what Kenneth Boulding calls a "value image" that is large enough to be accessible to both partisans in a conflict. Martin Luther King has done this by repeatedly stressing the objective of inclusive justice rather than a one-sided aim of securing civil rights for Negroes.

The nonviolent cadre's second task is to communicate the live current of agapaic love, to show authentic concern for the hostile person. This is hard to do, and without faith it is impossible. This is the "leap of faith" in interpersonal encounter. Let us suppose that after several such encounters the opponent's hostility gives way to a friendly response. It is true that this was made possible by *agapē*, but the new relationship now established may well be fairly tenuous. Unless the response is exceptionally strong it is likely to be on a much more mundane, sub-agapaic level on which the opponent is not ready to engage in self-sacrifice for the sake of the nonviolent cadre but is simply willing to refrain from violence and otherwise to accord the cadre elementary respect.

Bridging the Chasm of Estrangement

In the context of the conflict, *agapē* has thus served its purpose and is no longer required in that relationship, which can now stand on its own equilibrium of give-and-take. At this point perhaps we can afford the oversimplification of saying that this process is just a matter of adding up all the encounters between nonviolent cadres and opponents until a certain minimum of community is established between them as sets of persons. But we shall have to bear in mind always the complexities of social structure and the fact that the opponent's leadership group may succeed for a long time in insulating itself against interpersonal contact of this kind. Also the leadership group may exert pressure to induce or force those of its followers who are in interpersonal encounter with the nonviolent cadres to do violence to them against their will. This may severely tax the capacity of the cadres to remain open to *agapē*. Hence the need for a strategy to exert social pressure beyond the possibilities of love.

"The opposite of love is not hate," writes the psychologist Rollo May, "but indifference." [8] Although in many cases overt conflict may bring with it manifestations of hatred, and the precipitating issue may have arisen out of a hostile act, the underlying cause is invariably estrangement between the conflicting groups. The dominant group, often reciprocated negatively by the aggrieved group, has turned its back on the personhood of the latter, imposing restrictions without the latter's consent. It may or may not be doing so with conscious hostility or desire to harm, but what is basic is the withdrawal of human concern, the exclusion of the other, the denial of his real existence as a person—in short, not caring instead of caring. In essence, this is the same as sin, for sin is estrangement from God. The latter may take the form of active rebellion or waywardness, but in any event it implies the statement: "You are unimportant" or "You don't exist." Inasmuch as love of God and of neighbor and enemy are inextricably interrelated, the

indifference that causes conflict is a form of sin, for it implies the same type of statement.

Sin has its consequences, and one of them is that indifference and estrangement provide fertile soil for irrational hostility. Unrepented sin breeds guilt, which in turn creates fear. The next step after denying that God exists is to accuse him of being evil, and the next step after turning one's back on one's neighbor is to fear that the latter will plant a knife in it. In the absence of love the other becomes a blank screen onto which we project our anxieties: the stranger is always potentially a scapegoat for our own unconfessed sins. C. G. Jung confirms this fact:

Anything which disappears from your psychological inventory is apt to turn up in the disguise of a hostile neighbor, where it will inevitably arouse your anger and make you aggressive. It is certainly better to know that your worst adversary is right in your own heart.[9]

The natural human response to indifference is counter-indifference, and to projected hostility, hostility. Man's natural egotism, which is at the root of sin and is, as we have already seen, the antipode of agapaic love, makes him susceptible of rationalizations which place the burden of blame outside himself, whether on a scapegoat or on circumstances or elsewhere. We tend to reason directly from unevaluated experience to what we construe as objective fact: "It is true because I saw it." We do not make allowance for the subjective factor in experience, or if we do we evaluate it invidiously, assigning temperate and benign motives to ourselves and rash, malicious motives to those from whom we are estranged. In the end, a situation develops in which we and our opponent face each other not as we are but as ugly stereotypes which, ironically, tend to confirm each other in fact as well as in fantasy.

Bruno Bettelheim, in his highly perceptive study of the alienated relations between Nazi concentration camp guards and their Jewish prisoners, says that members of both groups

"behaved as if psychological mechanisms comparable to paranoid delusions were at work in them." [10] Each thought of the
other as representatives of a type rather than as individual
personalities, and this had the effect of creating in each group
an illusion of desperately needed emotional security based on
uniform conduct in relation to a uniform, hence predictable,
image of the other. By investing the SS guards with uniformly
bestial, inhuman traits which were often enough actually present, the prisoners were able to retain some measure of self-
respect in submitting to the guards' degrading commands.

In order to understand SS behavior the prisoners had to fall back
on their own experiences. The only way they could explain and
understand the actions of the SS was by imputing to them motives
they were familiar with. Thus they projected into the stereotype
of *the* SS most, if not all, of those undesirable motives and characteristics they knew best, namely, their own. [11]

The real problem, it is easy to see, is not hatred as such but
depersonalization. So long as each party to the conflict stands
behind the defensive armor of stereotype there is an unbridg-
able chasm between them. Somehow the nonviolent cadre must
dispense with this type of armor, bridge the gap and penetrate
the opponent's armor. Only agapaic love can do this, and here
it will be wise to remember that we are speaking of relation,
not emotions. Here, particularly, this calls for more insight
than feeling. Partly this means restructuring one's understanding of the situation and of the opponent, but this involves more
than an exercise of rational intelligence. It involves an act of
faith. Often, by the time conflict has been precipitated, estrangement has reached such a point that the only convincing
clues to the opponent's motives would readily persuade us that
the stereotype is very nearly true. Our task, then, is to take
upon ourselves the risk of attributing to him a basic, underlying
good will for which we cannot expect at first to find much
evidence.

In order to do this, we have to set aside our own defensive

stereotyped behavior, trusting primarily in God's grace and also provisionally in the putative good will of the opponent until the agapaic love that we are thus enabled to transmit establishes elementary respect. The specific nature of a given conflict will of course dictate much of what is required, but the central focus, initially, should be on the common humanity of oneself and the opponent—that is, those features of personality and experience which do not presuppose specific knowledge of the individuals or their groups.

Any exhibition of defiant bravado or undue deference may be misunderstood as a threat or a weakness. We must begin with the fact that, rightly or not, our opponent is suspicious of our motives. The only way we can make clear both our good will and the issue of conflict is by simplicity which avoids extraneous matters—and by God-given courage and love.

The Place of Reconciliation

The whole process of overcoming estrangement is reconciliation, which is the biblical term that stands for the circuit of love as a live current to which Guardini refers. Reconciliation signifies not the bringing together of entities that are intrinsically estranged but the healing of broken communion between persons. It is based on the primal created unity of mankind, which has been disrupted, fractured by sin. Reconciliation is the paramount expression of love as the "law of life" which proclaims that the only ultimate justification of conflict is the achievement of a higher integration of harmony. Reconciliation between God and man occurs when man turns from sin and, with repentant faith, opens himself to receive God's holy and redeeming love. Reconciliation between man and man is part of the same process, in which man turns to his fellow man with trusting openness to transmit this same love and thereby to complete the circuit. The actual process is not instantaneous like plugging in a lamp. It takes time to be con-

summated, and to the extent that our human wiring is defective it is never perfectly consummated in history.

Within the relativities of history, however, we may still speak meaningfully of reconciliation as we speak of agapaic love, in admixture with stable norms of mutuality. Just as we may overlook the manifold fissures within each of two communities that are sundered from each other by a deep cleft of estrangement, so we may consider reconciliation as practically complete when conflict between those communities has ended on a basis of operative harmony. Ultimately the process is endless within historical time: there is always residual estrangement, and when healing has taken place between ourselves and our opponent we may find ourselves allies in facing some new conflict with a third party; or our own internal dissensions, held together by the unity demanded for the conflict that is now resolved, may surprise us from within. In this sense, conflict is never-ending and the need for reconciliation is ever-present.

But within these relativities, each discernible conflict ends sooner or later, whether by reconciliation or in some other way. It may be strategically concluded by conquest or disengagement without being resolved. It may be resolved by compromise, through the adjusting of claims and counter-claims, without reaching any deeper accord, or through arbitration in which a neutral party makes the decision. Only in reconciliation, however, is there a settlement which results in what Kenneth Boulding calls "convergent modifications of the images of the two parties." [12] It is a rapprochement in depth, based not only on a formal adjustment but also affecting attitude and outlook. Boulding sees this as the result of "conversation, argument, discussion or debate," but he makes it clear that something more than talk is involved—something akin to Martin Buber's concept of "meeting" or "dialog." He introduces the useful idea of the "value image" consisting of a vital, irreducible core and a variable outer shell. Representing the constellation of values which a given group lives by, the value

image bears a resemblance to the moral image of the person.
Boulding continues:

> The success of the reconciliation process, then, clearly depends on
> how far the value structures of the parties in the field of conflict
> occupy the core or the shell of the value image. . . . The problem is
> complicated by the fact that the boundary between the core and
> the shell is not fixed but is itself a result of the general value system
> and of the process of communication and argument to which the
> party has been subject in the past. Unskilled argumentation that
> seems to threaten the person of the other party may only serve to
> harden and widen his core of values and so make agreement all
> the more difficult. On the other hand, a dramatic act of renuncia-
> tion symbolizing concern for the person of the rival may produce a
> drastic reorganization of his value structure with a shrinkage of the
> inflexible core and an extension of the malleable shell.[13]

In our present context we may well question the value of a
dramatic act of renunciation as such, since the whole tenor of
a nonviolent campaign would presumably serve the same purpose even more convincingly. Otherwise, what Boulding is
saying accords perfectly with the theological conception of
reconciliation if we take the core of the value image to mean
that which corresponds to the inner integrity of the person
and of a community of persons. In these terms, then, reconciliation is consummated when we and our opponent establish
a common shell within which the two separate cores can
exist side by side. In a formal sense this would mean, for example, agreeing to share equitably in a public facility that our
opponent has denied us the use of. With the support of a certain minimum of mutual respect established in the course of
the campaign by the initiative of active, agapaic love, this
formal agreement would eventually blend into the larger picture of habit and convention in which we and our opponents
virtually obliterate the memory of the situation that created the
conflict.

The process can be exemplified from the experiences of
Irish immigrants and their descendants: 1) mutual hostility

and distrust between Irishmen and non-Irishmen; 2) action to achieve justice; 3) termination of conflict; 4) crumbling of barriers accompanied by discovery of common bonds; 5) celebration of distinctive Irish traits by the non-Irish; 6) lessening of distinctiveness in the awareness of both parties; 7) actual lessening of distinctiveness. In the earlier stages, whether positively or negatively, there is something "special" about being Irish; when Americanization is completed, Irishness is simply part of one's ancestry. Allowing for the factor of color, a somewhat similar pattern may be seen in the history of the Negro, including the occasional exaggerated celebration of acceptance that springs from the effort to assuage guilt.

What we are left with finally is not a stabilization of agapaic love nor even an appreciably heightened articulation of mutual concern, but simply a normalization of relationships with the lines of group conflict removed. Again, this is a temporal process and it may pass through a period of heightened concern, but the end result is nothing more than mutual acceptance, leaving scope for new invitations to transmit God's holy love in completely different patterns of conflict.

There is, to be sure, a certain exuberant type of perfectionist who envisions the coming of the kingdom of God as the result of the infusion of *agapē* and reconciliation into situations of social conflict. Perhaps indeed, amid advances and reverses, this is how the kingdom will eventually bring history to its consummation and conclusion at the end of time, but in the interim we should not scant the very appreciable immediate fact that when reconciliation has run its course at the end of conflict, both we and our opponent unite in a common victory of mutual integrity. Could we ask for any better culmination after that than to return the glory of it to God and go our way together as ordinary men?

REFERENCES IN CHAPTER 10

1   Romano Guardini: *The Lord* (Chicago: Henry Regnery Co., 1954), p. 70.
2   *Ibid.*, p. 74.
3   *Ibid.*
4   Pie Régamey: *Non-Violence et Conscience Chrétienne* (Paris: Cerf, 1958), p. 256.
5   Reinhold Niebuhr: *The Nature and Destiny of Man* (New York: Charles Scribner's Sons, 1953), Vol. 2, p. 82.
6   *Ibid.*, p. 85.
7   Howard Thurman: *Mysticism and the Experience of Love* (Wallingford, Pa.: Pendle Hill Pamphlets, 1961), p. 13.
8   Rollo May: "The Art of True Love" in *United Church Herald* (New York), October 6, 1960, p. 4.
9   C. G. Jung, quoted by Rajendra Prasad in his introduction to Pyarelal: *Mahatma Gandhi: The Last Phase* (Ahmedabad: Navajivan, 1956), Vol. 1, p. ix.
10 Bruno Bettelheim: *The Informed Heart* (Glencoe, Ill.: The Free Press, 1960), p. 221.
11 *Ibid.*, p. 223f. Careful study of pages 218-231 can provide a firm foundation for interpreting many situations involving estranged groups.
12 Kenneth E. Boulding: *Conflict and Defense* (New York: Harper & Brothers, 1962), p. 310.
13 *Ibid.*, p. 312.

11

Sources of Strength

"All nonviolent action that is to any degree broad, vigorous and sustained," writes Régamey, "presupposes the attainment of a fairly high spiritual level." [1] Beyond such techniques and methods as socio-drama, how do we develop the capacity both to withstand violence without retaliating and to maintain openness and rapport to communicate active love under conditions of prolonged or acute stress? Training in technique is invaluable for eliminating the anxiety of uncertainty and surprise, but it cannot produce courage. Likewise, rational understanding of both the situation and the opponent is vital to the initiative of love, but if love itself is lacking in us, if we do not feel the live current passing through us, what are we to do?

In many cases, strategic advantages can go far to make up for serious shortcomings in both personal conduct and teamwork, and of course no level of a nonviolent campaign should be neglected or left to chance. But often the pivotal factor may be precisely the will to sustain nonviolent conduct or to show concern for the immediate opponent as a person, and an otherwise well-prepared campaign may founder on just this point where personal courage and love are demanded. It is at such a moment that we appreciate the truth of Gandhi's statement: "A nonviolent man can do nothing save by the power and grace of God." [2]

Gandhi recognized the importance of prayer as a means of receiving this power: "Prayer is not an old woman's idle amusement. Properly understood and applied, it is the most potent instrument of action." [3] We are referring here, of course,

not merely to the recitation of some fixed form of words in a casual or perfunctory manner. This vitiates the very meaning of prayer, which is ultimately a dialog between man and God or, in Martin Buber's phrase, "the speech of God to man." That is to say, in its depth and fullness, prayer is not only man's quest for God but it is also and paramountly God's response. The highest form of spiritual prayer is a form of acute listening and receptiveness to the Divine Presence. But preceding this stage are a number of preparatory steps.[4]

Prayer is first of all a discipline of mental hygiene, of freeing one's consciousness from distractions and readying one's whole being to respond with "unreserved spontaneity" to this Presence. Jung, in his "Answer to Job," testifies that prayer "reinforces the potential of the unconscious." [5] However stated, the effects are real. Paul E. Johnson refers to the achievement of an awareness of needs and realities, a sharpened perspective, renewal of emotional energy and integration of personality as being among ten discernible psychological effects of prayer,[6] and Walter G. Muelder attributes these benefits to a well-developed life of prayer:

There is a growth in faith and the capacity for faith . . . there is a release of new energies, a purgation of incentives, an overcoming of guilt feelings, and a release of compassion.[7]

Empirically, the externals of a prayer discipline may be nothing more than psychological conditioning, the ordering of consciousness by acts of the will. We begin by making ourselves relax and proceed to focus our thoughts.

Some devout persons find the presence of a cross or crucifix or ikon extremely helpful in focusing their thoughts, while others regard any such object as a distraction. Psychologically, the decisive question must always be which usage is most effective for the individual who is trying to pray. Different temperaments may lean toward different conditions.

Given these conditions to produce a relaxed state of mind, the next step is to concentrate our thoughts. Repetition of a

simple formal prayer such as the Lord's Prayer, the Jesus Prayer or some such form of words can be very helpful in doing this, provided the words are not merely mouthed but are dwelt upon by the mind so that the meaning they embody sinks in.

The essence of this stage of prayer is to organize our thoughts around God—as Nels Ferré says, to recall "who God is. God is sovereign love. He is both ultimate reality and our most intimate friend." [8] Second to this, we should recall that "God loves everyone completely." [9] In prayer we do not simply note these facts and set them aside, nor do we reason about them, but we hold them exclusively in our consciousness and allow them to suffuse our whole being. This is a habit that has particular value in the immediate context of the conflict situation. The further stages of prayer, which Ferré designates as adoration, gratitude and thanksgiving, and finally intercession, should flow easily from this state of recollectedness. Adoration is not a matter of debasing oneself, of bowing and scraping, but of awe, reverence and wonder—not of "praising" God in the human sense of bolstering his ego, but of sensing how one's own inadequacies and weaknesses are overcome by the fullness and grandeur of God's love. Gratitude and thanksgiving might well be called rejoicing in this love, knowing and feeling that it is for us, that every moment of true joy and hope springs from it. Intercession, finally, is our asking God that his love be given, his will be done for persons we think of—for our friends and comrades, for our enemies. In conclusion, we plead for strength and courage, for power and love and faith that we may do God's will ourselves.

Resources for the Mind and Spirit

The whole process can be understood and justified as a form of psychotherapy to purge the mind of rancor and confusion, to restore balance and perspective, and to instill wholesome thoughts and motivations—and indeed that is what it is. The

capacity for nonviolent action has been explained by the French Catholic writer, Hervé Chaigne, as

primarily the result of a whole cluster of psychological and moral forces, the highest state of equilibrium attained by the man who is master of himself and humble before the truth that surpasses him . . . [10]

Many people may be capable of experiencing the therapeutic effects of prayer without conscious reference to God and, indeed, without calling it prayer at all. This may itself be an indication of humility and of candor if they are unable to name the power and presence of divine love as God, if their faith is real but unformed. But for many the absence of an articulated religious sense is a serious handicap. We can better understand the full implications of prayer if we recognize God's part in it.

Nels Ferré takes us a long way toward this kind of understanding in this theological explanation:

Prayer is living with God through the universal love of Christ and in the Spirit. Prayer is talking with God as our Father. Prayer is identifying our lives with the will of God, first for himself and then for all people. Prayer is finding the strength to overcome self, to transcend the battle of the ego and to loose the tensions which hinder seeing, by the power of the Spirit within the reality of our new creaturehood in Christ.

Thus the Holy Spirit, through prayer, gives us the fruit of the Spirit. The world is looking for genuine love and true community. Only as we *are* the truth more than merely speaking it can God utter his truth effectively to us and through us. [11]

Faith, it has been said, can move mountains. The New Testament records an episode in which the disciples of Jesus tried unsuccessfully to cure an epileptic boy (Matthew 17:14-20). Romano Guardini observes: "They had tried to effect a cure by an effort of the will, possibly bordering on magic. He teaches them that the healing of God's disciples is healing in confidence of mission and in faith—pure faith utterly submissive to the will of God." [12] The disciples had good intentions.

Moreover, they had been instructed in right conduct. What they lacked was adequate power, which could come only through trusting God. It was only with the coming of the Holy Spirit at Pentecost that they were imbued with a living faith. Of this event, Guardini says:

It is as if everything Jesus had said and done . . . has sunk into their consciousness only as seed sinks into dumb and passive earth . . . Until now they have been untouched by act and word. But when the Spirit descends, the dormant seed suddenly swells and unfolds, and at last the men who were to be his faithful witnesses spring up, who in turn spread the seed of the Master's sacred word abroad.[13]

The whole process of prayer, then, is first a matter of plowing our consciousness and implanting in it the seed of faith. The harvest is up to God, in his loving response through the Holy Spirit. In this sense, as Ferré says, "prayer is communion." It is consciously entering into relation with God and seeking to elicit his response.

Time should be set aside for regular prayer as a discipline, but we can also learn to pray more and more in every situation in which we find ourselves—to praise God for every joy at the moment we experience it, to ask for guidance and strength at every moment of challenge and, in short, always to keep God close to the edge of consciousness—to be in constant communion, to "pray unceasingly." In periods of crisis and stress especially the nonviolent cadre can find sustenance in this ingrained habit of prayer. Gandhi found it in the ceaseless mental repetition of "Rama," the Hindu name of God. Others have found it in the Lord's Prayer and in other formulas such as the Twenty-third Psalm, portions of the "peace prayer" of Francesco d'Assisi or sentences of their own devising. In each case, the purely psychological effect is to stabilize one's thoughts by providing them with an unshakable center, with the deeper religious effect also of holding open the channel through which agapaic love can flow, overcoming fear and strengthening faith for the immediate task.

In addition to daily devotions it is wise to cultivate the habit of retreat. Gandhi made it a practice to observe strict silence one day a week, but many persons find it adequate to retire into solitude once a month for a few hours or a day, spending this time in silent meditation, perhaps focused on a devotional text, on the love of God or on no specific theme, as a kind of broadened, free-form extended prayer.

During the course of a campaign of nonviolent action, cadres should meet frequently for group meditation. Richard Gregg suggests that they sit together in silence for fifteen to thirty minutes or longer, either simply ridding their minds of all conscious thought and all awareness of sensory perceptions, or focusing their thoughts on an agreed-upon theme such as "an incident in the life of some great exemplar of nonviolence." [14] Gregg asserts that this practice is essential for building a firm sense of unity among members of a team of cadres. The aim is not merely formal unity but a deep sense of shared commitment to the cause, to one another and to God. The dimension of common worship in *koinonia* is perhaps as vital as personal prayer itself and is in fact a communal expression of the same thing.

Annually or more often in a protracted campaign, nonviolent cadres may benefit from a group retreat for a week end, going away to some secluded place and submitting themselves to a regimen of alternating corporate and solitary devotions, manual work, worship and fasting.[15] If jail looms as an imminent possibility, the time in enforced inactivity which this involves may be adapted to serve the purpose of retreat. Certainly jail need not be an occasion for stagnation but can be an opportunity for renewal and spiritual revitalization.

From Praying to Working

Work in the constructive program can also serve as an important source of strength. The tasks which it imposes may be gratifying in the results they produce and enable the construc-

tive workers to experience a sense of satisfaction that binds the group together. Even if results are thwarted or destroyed by the opponent, however, the experience of shared effort and struggle can contribute a bond of unity among the cadres. Not only teamwork but many kinds of team activities can also do this—the use of common symbols and slogans, group singing of songs and hymns, the sharing of inspiring stories of saints and heroes in the nonviolent tradition. These practices build morale or "team spirit." There is always the risk of promoting an exclusive in-group attitude, however, which may be sufficient for endurance but tends to narrow and finally to close off the possibility of rapport and reconciliation with the opponent. For this reason we must take care to introduce into our group meditations and other morale-building activities themes that encompass the opponent as well as our own group.

Even though we may begin with a degree of group solidarity and wish only to heighten it in a nonviolent context, we shall find ourselves enmeshed in a contradiction if we try to go very far in combining nonviolent conduct with an attitude of irreconcilability. Hatred, we must admit, can be a strong motivation to action that involves risks and mobilizes courage. But it is too volatile as an emotion to be successfully repressed for very long. When the lid flies off, there is literally hell to pay. That is one reason why we need prayer that includes as part of its content the affirmation that God's love is for our enemies as well as for ourselves and our friends. That is why, too, in prayer we need to habituate ourselves to deferring our selfish wishes to the wiser will of God.

Prayer might well be preceded by reading 1 Corinthians 13 or 1 John 4, both of which are testimonies to the power of divine love. If we set out to pray with openness toward this power, however little we at first believe in its reality, and with willingness to take the leap of faith that is required, we can become instruments of redemption even as we engage in unremitting conflict. "Not only can we bring about a whole new world through prayer," says Nels Ferré, "but one's own life

can by its means become astonishingly new." [16] The power does not reside in the act of prayer, but in God's love itself which prayer helps to mediate to us. God's love is always there for us. Prayer is the key with which we unlock our ego and open ourselves to receive it.

Public prayer meetings, marches and vigils partake of this same reality if their content and motivation are truly humble and loving. They are a means of communicating with the opponent on a spiritual level. But their authenticity presupposes a high spiritual level in our own lives, without which the public manifestation is likely to smack of hypocrisy and to offend the opponent and observers as an exhibition of spiritual pride. For this reason, too, it is extremely poor strategy to combine such events directly with acts of protest or of pressure. Prayer is not a weapon but a resource. It must be used with fidelity to its intrinsic purpose if it is to yield strength.

REFERENCES IN CHAPTER 11

1   Pie Régamey: *Non-Violence et Conscience Chrétienne* (Paris: Cerf, 1958), p. 294.
2   *Harijan,* June 18, 1938.
3   *Harijan,* June 4, 1946.
4   See Martin Buber: *Eclipse of God* (New York: Harper & Brothers, 1957), p. 126.
5   C. G. Jung: *Collected Works* (New York: Pantheon Books, 1958), Vol. 11, p. 456n.
6   See Paul E. Johnson: *Psychology of Religion* (Nashville: Abingdon, 1945).
7   Walter G. Muelder: "The Efficacy of Prayer" in Simon Doniger, ed.: *Psychological Aspects of Prayer* (Great Neck, N.Y.: Pastoral Psychology Press, 1954), p. 10f.
8   Nels F. S. Ferré: *Strengthening the Spiritual Life* (New York: Harper & Brothers, 1951), p. 29.
9   *Ibid.,* p. 30.
10 Hervé Chaigne: "The Spirit and Techniques of Gandhian Nonviolence" in *Cross Currents,* Spring 1961, p. 125.
11 Nels F. S. Ferré: "Theology and the Devotional Life" in *Theology Today,* April, 1955, p. 9. Used by permission.
12 Romano Guardini: *The Lord* (Chicago: Henry Regnery Co., 1954), p. 63.
13 *Ibid.,* p. 67.

14 Richard B. Gregg: *The Power of Nonviolence* (Nyack, N.Y.: Fellowship Publications, 1959), p. 162.
15 See the following pamphlets: Constance Garrett: *Renewal Through Retreat* (Bernardsville, N.J.: St. Martin's House); Gilbert Kilpack: *The Idea of Retreat* (Wallingford, Pa.: Pendle Hill Pamphlets); John Oliver Nelson: *Retreats for Protestants* (Bangor, Pa.: Kirkridge).
16 Ferré: *Strengthening the Spiritual Life*, p. 26.

12

Christian Nonviolence and the Church

Nonviolence has deep historical roots in the Christian faith and in the church of Jesus Christ, exemplified in its Lord, whom Gandhi once called "the prince of *satyagrahis*." The record of the early church is, among other things, that of a fellowship of nonresistant martyrs. Even after the decline of its original perfectionism in the era of Constantine, currents within the church preserved this witness through monastic orders and such lay movements as the Devotio Moderna, as well as among the early followers of Wycliffe, Waldo, Hus and Wesley. Even Calvin was subjected to its influence in an early version of his *Institutes*, and a vital influence in John Wesley's experience of conversion was the nonresistant Zinzendorf, one of several figures on the radical fringe of Protestantism who have carried this historic witness. Such dissenting Russian sects as the Dukhobors and Bezmolitovtsy have had much in common with the Shakers, Quakers and Inspirationists of the West. Sometimes determinedly biblical, as with the Mennonites, or with admixtures of spiritualism verging on heresy, these many groups have not let the world forget that nonresistance is a Christian teaching.

The main line of church history after Constantine took a different course. Few Christians today can thinkingly rejoice in the savage excesses of violence done in the name of Christ between Catharists and Catholics, Catholics and Protestants, Anabaptists and Lutherans, Christians and Turks or Saracens, to mention only some. Yet even within the main-line churches,

whether Catholic, Orthodox or Protestant, nonresistance has never been wholly repudiated, and hardly a movement for reform or renewal has been able to ignore its claims. Even when ruled out of the sphere of social action, it has been recognized as holding a place in the way of life of the devout, at least in personal affairs.

Nonresistance is a difficult doctrine, and it is not surprising that even the radical sects which officially honor it either dwindle in numbers and disappear or become lax in its observance from generation to generation. For them and for the individual perfectionist within the larger churches, a special problem exists. We are not indifferent to it, but more urgent problems must claim our attention.

Their full dimensions greatly exceed the scope of this book. We can only note some of the elements—the fact that so many Christians today lack vitality of faith; that so many churches have wandered off into pious irrelevance; that we are besieged with the problems of a technological and ideological revolution and divided in our understanding of it. It does not deny the eternal truth of our faith to admit that the era in which we live increasingly predicates its values and standards on new gods of reason or science which are decidedly "post-Christian." Even if a return to the pure nonresistance of the early church should prove to be part of the answer to these problems, it is not an immediate option for the millions of half-believers within the church as it exists, nor can it be offered as such by those committed Christians who have taken it as their task to find answers to the immediate problems.

Thus we find that, of the three kinds of Christians—perfectionist, nominal and realist—it is the third we must be chiefly concerned with. The nominal Christian is content with religion as a commodity; the perfectionist may be content with a verbal semblance of nonresistance, or he may be anxious to make it relevant to the world. The realist has no alternative but to demand relevance.

Christian realism emphasizes responsibility both for the

church, with all its nominal Christians, and for the world which the church is committed to redeem. The realist does not categorically repudiate the nonresistance taught in the Sermon on the Mount, but he is more concerned with acting effectively and is disinclined to increase the risk of failure, which is great enough, by insisting on means which exceed the capacities of those who are called upon to use them. He cannot embrace merely suppositious programs. Experience has taught him to be skeptical about the possibilities of human nature and candid about the obstacles to be confronted by any form of social action.

This does not mean that the realist is unmindful of moral distinctions or the high demands of the gospel, which are most readily conceded in the direct encounter of the individual, but in confronting problems that involve social responsibility he cannot insist on applying them in an absolute way. Even here these distinctions and demands are not discarded, however. But instead of being applied directly to problems they are used as absolute standards against which to assess whatever means are at hand. This involves a high degree of pragmatism, but it is never an unbridled pragmatism. A truly Christian realism never ceases to seek out the most moral of the workable alternatives that present themselves, and to devise and introduce new alternatives that are relevant. It would be a serious mistake to identify this approach with a timid acceptance of the status quo. Realism necessarily involves risk-taking and even sacrifice, but always in a context of responsibility.

Beginning with a commitment to relevance and responsibility, the realist is free to choose from a wide variety of means, including nonviolence. The perfectionist, beginning with a commitment to nonviolent conduct at all times and in all situations, is not free to choose other means, but he is free to enter situations in which nonviolence may be relevant and to work to adapt it effectively. From a realistic viewpoint, this may seem to be sheer realism. For some perfectionists it may in fact be a coincidence, while for others it is a compromise

which means moving out from the pure witness of strict non-resistance to the less clear types of nonviolence that involve pressure and coercion bordering on force.

Restricted to it as he is in principle, the perfectionist has traditionally been eager to imbue nonviolence with his whole outlook. And of course to him the relationship is obvious: nonviolence goes hand in hand with conscientious objection to military service, and it is closely related to other articles of his faith, whatever they may be. If he is a vegetarian, for example, it is for the same underlying reasons that lead him to embrace nonviolence. Within the churches, this circumstance has tended to polarize opinion on the question of nonviolence. It is surely understandable if many realists, habituated to the pragmatic use of force and accustomed to hearing about nonviolence as an adjunct of pacifism, have tended to ignore nonviolence. Having settled the pacifist question, they have unwittingly thrown out the separate question of nonviolence. It has generally required a new and urgent context to force a confrontation with this question, and even in the setting of the nonviolent demonstrations that swept the United States in the 1960s, the burden of old arguments exerted considerable inertia. Virtually all of the pioneering work in developing non-violent methods of struggle was done by pacifists. Gradually, outstanding Negro leaders took it up and some of them also became pacifists. Only then did nonviolence begin to gain currency among realists in the larger community: only after it had proved itself. And even then the movement from grudging to positive support indicated a continuing lag.

Not all realists lagged. A quarter of a century before the Montgomery bus boycott, Reinhold Niebuhr wrote: "There is no problem of political life to which religious imagination can make a larger contribution than this problem of developing nonviolent resistance." [1] For Niebuhr the criterion was that the racial situation is of such a kind that it offers a good chance of success. Events proved his thesis correct. This assessment did not, however, hinder Niebuhr's choice of other means

when considering the aggressions of Hitler and Mussolini. Both nonviolence and military resistance were within the scope of his realism. But, caught up in the debate over pacifism, the majority of Christians who flocked to the banner of Niebuhrian realism in the 1930s and 1940s lost sight of these distinctions.

What once seemed obvious was later to become absurd— the assertion, endorsed by perfectionists and realists alike, that it is impossible to achieve results through nonviolence in one situation unless those who use it are committed to use it in all situations. It has long been a neglected fact of history that most of the major campaigns in which nonviolence has been used effectively have neither required nor resulted in such a sweeping commitment. "The advantages of nonviolent methods are very great," wrote Niebuhr, "but they must be pragmatically considered in the light of circumstances." [2] Those who found themselves in such circumstances were seldom pacifists, and proved their realism by having the imagination to exploit these advantages while, ironically, many who called themselves Niebuhrians were at a loss to do more than issue resolutions.

Sources of Revitalization

How far and how fast the church can move toward regaining the initiative in the understanding and use of nonviolence is a question that is bound up with the larger problem of renewal. The three types of Christians to which we have referred are not, in actual fact, so easily compartmented. Much that passes for perfectionism is nothing but a pious pretense, and much so-called realism is sheer bravado. Granted that there are outstanding individuals, even authentic saints, in both categories, the two groups blend into a total picture that is blurred. This is true even of the background of nominal believers and those estranged from the church. There is flux and movement; there are degrees of commitment even among the largely uncommitted. The church of Jesus Christ, even at its moments of lowest ebb, possesses through the Holy Spirit that

works within it and authenticates it, a resilience and capacity for change exhibited by few if any other institutions. The Reformation came not from external incursions but from monks, priests and theologians nurtured within the Catholic faith, and the great reforms inaugurated by Pope John XXIII were made possible by the selfsame cardinals who had been chosen by predecessors who were unready for these steps—or, more accurately, by the Holy Spirit at work among them.

This is not the place to attempt a survey of the widespread currents of reform and renewal, nor is it relevant here to assess their success or their pace. It would be easy to exaggerate how much is actually happening, and disastrous to minimize the need for vastly increased efforts on all fronts. In every era there have been those to whom the Bible is an honored but purely ornamental object, and those actively engaged in relating its truth to the world. The fact we wish to single out and stress is that nonviolence as a form of Christian action does not go against the grain but points in the same direction as other currents of renewal. It can contribute to the process of transforming the church from what Edwin T. Dahlberg once called "a 'reservation' for people with 'religious' needs" into an authentic community of faith.

One distinguished theologian, Culbert G. Rutenber, has spoken for many proponents of renewal:

The fact of the matter is that much—perhaps most—of what goes on in the local church should be scuttled. Every organization should be forced to justify its existence in the light of the church's mandate from its Lord.

Most of all, the preacher-centered church should be transformed. The church must see itself as primarily a ministering community, not a talked-at congregation. . . . The work and witness of the believing church is inevitably the work and witness of the membership. This is the meaning of the doctrine of the priesthood of all believers.[3]

In contrast with an earlier generation which tended to fragment itself into denominational resolutions, unofficial reform

agencies and congregational complacency, Rutenber's views and others like them are backed by efforts within the churches themselves which seek tangible ways of affecting life at the parish level. Though many of these efforts are faltering and inconclusive, they are being made. One of the forms they take is the establishment of small face-to-face groups to develop new leadership and lay participation, overcoming the audience structure of the congregation. Surely this is one essential step, but when such groups fail it is often for lack of definite tasks to be carried out which can involve their members in both mission and fellowship. They thrive on a well-balanced program of worship, study, discussion and action projects, with the last of these often proving to be the most crucial.

Where Churches Choose Action

While not every house-church group may have occasion to use nonviolence in its community, it is worth noting that nonviolent demonstrations require action by groups of approximately the same size. Christian students who became involved as cadres in the Nashville sit-in movement in 1960 said that their experience of committed fellowship gave them new insight into what the church could be like. The same response was found in the Norwegian church under the Nazi occupation. These were largely nominal, churchgoing Christians, but it is also a fact that more than a few individuals who had turned their backs on the church found their faith rekindled and returned to the fold. In many places where cadres of the Southern Christian Leadership Conference sought to establish a base in the local church, they at first encountered the most apathy in the minister, fearful of jeopardizing his stable position in the community or losing accustomed comforts. Just as often, however, such men became caught up in the atmosphere of commitment and carried forward to leadership in fulfillment of their vocation, surely a testimony to the power of the Holy Spirit.

Even though belated, the response of major denominations to the nonviolent movement for civil rights exhibited a similar spiritual contagion. Many of the official resolutions seem remarkably diffident. The American Baptist Convention, meeting in Detroit on May 17, 1963, stated: "While we regret the need for . . . nonviolent demonstrations, we deplore even more the injustices which provoke and make them necessary." This tepid language, however, was accompanied by the formation of Baptist Action for Racial Brotherhood to spark among local churches "participation in nonviolent demonstrations for civil rights," further specified to include "demonstrations, parades and rallies" and "nonviolent demonstrations of protest" in addition to conventional types of social action. Among the BARB committee's members was Harold E. Stassen, former Governor of Minnesota, who led a Baptist contingent in the massive March on Washington, August 28, 1963.

The United Church of Christ said virtually nothing about nonviolence as such at its Fourth General Synod, but established a Fellowship of the Committed which included these words in its membership pledge: "I commit myself as a Christian to engage now in responsible nonviolent demonstrations when such actions are necessary for racial justice." This body had scarcely been formed before a number of ministers, including some in denominational staff positions, were arrested for carrying out this pledge.

In 1961 the North American Area Council of the World Alliance of Reformed and Presbyterian Churches resolved that "when a law prevails that keeps people from securing justice . . . a Christian, after serious and careful consideration and after sharing his concern with other members of the household of faith, may engage alone or with others in an act of civil disobedience." Two years later Eugene Carson Blake, chief executive officer of the United Presbyterian Church in the USA, was arrested and jailed in a nonviolent demonstration in Baltimore. With him were Msgr. Austin J. Healy, representing the Roman Catholic Archdiocese of Baltimore; the Rt. Rev.

Daniel Corrigan, director of the Home Department of the National Council of the Protestant Episcopal Church; Rabbi Morris Lieberman of the Baltimore Hebrew Congregation; and nearly three hundred others, including numerous Protestant ministers. Undertaken a few weeks before the great March on Washington—itself a tribute to nonviolence, in which more than 200,000 demonstrators maintained model discipline—the Baltimore action was only one of many to come, and not the most challenging.

Other major Protestant bodies, such as the Disciples of Christ, whose United Christian Missionary Society formally approved "direct action," took similar steps to join actively in the broad nonviolent movement for civil rights. Consistently the emphasis was placed on involvement and commitment rather than, as formerly, on paper pronouncements. The United Church's pledge referred not merely to good will but to a "risk-taking witness." A statement of the National Council of Churches not only authorized "the encouragement of negotiations, demonstrations and direct action." It also stated as among "the first actions of a continuing strategy of corporate witness . . . to commit ourselves, as members of the General Board, to engage personally in negotiations, demonstrations and other direct action in particular situations of racial tension." It was in his capacity as a member of the NCC Board that Dr. Blake was jailed, as were others who were to follow.

The Roman Catholic Church, with its distinctive traditions and institutional structure, was slower to articulate a definite program. Nevertheless, individuals from laymen and priests to members of the hierarchy stood shoulder to shoulder with Protestants and Jews. A number of parish priests in the Deep South withstood physical assault in a lonely nonviolent witness to papal and archdiocesan utterances affirming racial equality. One such statement was embodied in these words of Patrick O'Boyle, Archbishop of Washington, as he led the freedom marchers in prayer at the Lincoln Memorial: "May we shun violence, knowing that the meek shall inherit the earth. But may this

meekness of manner be joined with courage and strength."
Various Catholic writers such as Mathew Ahmann, William
J. Kenealy, S.J., and Thomas Merton adumbrated this sentiment in relation to the growing nonviolent movement. Few,
however, within the Protestant or Catholic churches, had begun to develop a theoretical understanding of nonviolence
even in pragmatic terms as they awakened to its relevance.
Like most Christian social action, nonviolence tended to be
viewed either as a direct expression of Christian love or as a
lubricant to secular processes of justice, and little attention
was given to its theological or ecclesiological dimensions. The
following words from a pastoral letter of the Roman Catholic
Archdiocese of New York is not unrepresentative:

Demonstrations and other activities of these [civil rights] organizations, in which the good that is reasonably expected through these
demonstrations outweighs the accidental unfortunate effects, when
they are carried out in a responsible and peaceful manner within
the bounds of Christian charity and justice and finally when they
are undertaken as a last resort in the struggle to overcome the
second-class citizenship of American Negroes, are deserving of the
support and participation of Catholic American citizens.

Other statements have emphasized Christian motivations
more explicitly, but virtually without exception both Protestant and Catholic statements have made it clear that nonviolence is seen as external to the church as such, an incidental,
even regrettable feature of events in the world which, with
proper stipulations, oblige Christians to take part in them. The
note of prudence is legitimate, but while it varies in emphasis
it has tended to be predominant. The situation is urgent; we
must act in it. It is in fact so urgent that we must even go so
far as to take part in, or initiate, public demonstrations. But
they should be peaceful. That is the role of nonviolence.

There is nothing precisely erroneous in this perspective, and
we have already noted some of the vigorous and committed
actions that have stemmed from it. What has been generally
lacking, however, is any conception of nonviolence as a generic

type of social action having special relevance for the church. The conception has been almost uniformly adjectival rather than substantive, a brake rather than an engine.

Yet viewed substantively as a method and a dynamic of action capable of being harnessed to social objectives, nonviolence has a demonstrable contribution to make in the church's encounter with the world. Although many types of community organization—schools, labor unions—can provide a basis and an organizational structure for nonviolent-action teams in the event of a national emergency, nonviolence has a special task to perform in the context of the church. In its fulness, a nonviolent campaign offers a challenge to many aspects of ongoing or sought-for renewal, energizing conventional social-action programs, giving urgency and focus to prayer cells and knitting together the loose strands of church membership into a living fellowship. Even formal worship may gain new vigor.

John Oliver Nelson, who has had long experience both in Protestant retreats and in field work with ministerial students, has indicated how a serious venture into Christian nonviolence might begin in a local church:

It requires patient, prayerful exploration of the meaning of the New Testament, examination of the actions of inspired social leaders in all the years, and lessons in teamwork among a committed group. A minister can raise up within his congregation such a trained nucleus, or any dedicated Christian can draw together a circle of men and women and young people with this aim—if there is directness of purpose and the insight that here is the key answer for our generation amid world tensions.[4]

This is a modest enough beginning. Further steps have been outlined in an earlier chapter (see pp. 131–154). Whether nonviolence is in fact the "key answer," it is certainly a possibility that should be explored. Even if Christians choose realism rather than perfectionism, they should not deny themselves access to Christian nonviolence. Even if they may decide in a given situation that nonviolence is inapplicable, they should be able to do so on the merits of the case and not because they

are unprepared. Being prepared, they will be enabled sometimes to reduce the prevalence of less moral conduct, including
the immorality of inaction. Of all people, Christians should
not allow themselves to be in a position where legal remedies,
conventional social action, brute force and acquiescence are
the only alternatives they know how to handle.

To look honestly and without illusion at the church as it is
today is a sure cure for the temptation to think of nonviolence
as a panacea. We are already getting by with too much easy
verbiage unsupported by risk-taking action. The task is a formidable one, and it would be wild optimism to think that a
sudden transformation, however urgently needed, is anywhere
in sight. The challenge is all the more staggering when we
turn from the encouraging upsurge in the area of civil rights
to consider the twin forces of hedonistic materialism, bourgeois and Communist, that are ranged against us. The only
choice we have, however, is between capitulation and resistance—to let religion become increasingly the irrelevant and
obsolescent commodity of happy robots or Orwellian proles,
or to assert what little understanding and faith we still possess
and pray for more. In a world of increasing depersonalization,
nonviolence has much to recommend it as a safeguard against
too much remote control in the social order and as an aid in
enriching the resources of the human person, not merely to
stand alone in a mass or against it, but to work toward its
transformation and redemption.

If we approach this task with Christian realism, drawing
upon the lessons of the past, we may be enabled to avoid some
of the mistakes of the future. But history is not a blank sheet
on which we are at liberty to write our own destiny, guided
unerringly by experience and theoretical principles, even with
the most effective use of the best means. The God who is love is
also the Lord of history, a living God whose actions condition
all of our historical possibilities. Under his hand seemingly
disconnected events fortuitously combine to produce surprising consequences for good or ill that can be evaluated only

in retrospect. Christian nonviolence is ultimately Christian not simply because it is used by Christians, nor even because its ethic seeks to make Christian love relevant to social conflict, but also theologically in recognizing that its power is not absolute but derivative. Nonviolence shares with all forms of human actions the fact that it can never exhaust the fulfillment of God's will. In his own unfathomable wisdom he may reprieve us from the consequences of our folly or chastise our self-righteous pride. Our actions, our skill in strategy, our steadfastness in conduct are all important, but they are not the whole story. In the end it is faith, hope and love—all in relation to God—that are decisive. Whether we win or lose in history hinges on God's grace and God's judgment. It is always God who has the last word.

REFERENCES IN CHAPTER 12

1 Reinhold Niebuhr: *Moral Man and Immoral Society* (New York: Charles Scribner's Sons, 1932), p. 254.
2 *Ibid.*, p. 252.
3 Culbert G. Rutenber: *The Reconciling Gospel* (Philadelphia: The Judson Press, 1961), p. 127.
4 John Oliver Nelson: "New Testament Power for Social Change" in *The Journal of Religious Thought*, Autumn-Winter 1957-1958, p. 12.

A Casebook of
Nonviolence

13

Purported and Authentic Nonviolence

Since the publication of Adin Ballou's *Christian Non-Resistance* in 1846 there have appeared occasional compilations of brief accounts purporting to show the power of love, kindness, empathy, honest dealing or other virtues to overcome evil. Most often these accounts are very sketchy, carelessly documented (frequently from second-hand sources) and bathed in syrupy sentiment. Some of them are remarkable testimonies to the working of the spirit of Christ in men. But many are plainly trumped up, based on questionable information, faulty reasoning, a misunderstanding of the real situation or a biased and gratuitous interpretation. Such anecdotes may edify the naïve but to a critical mind they can only cast doubt on the whole idea of nonviolence.

The purpose of this chapter is twofold: to puncture these half-true fantasies and to present a picture of actual instances of historical nonviolence, indicating both its strengths and its limitations in practice. Only by such critical study can we equip ourselves to interpret new occurrences of nonviolence or to anticipate problems that theory alone cannot adequately envision.

A large share of these edifying tales are clearly irrelevant to the subject of nonviolence. Although they may be worth telling for other reasons, stories of international mediation, the peaceful settlement of border disputes and the like are in this category, as are tales of the "pacific monarch"—Asoka, Pericles, Queen Jadwiga, "the lost Tsar," etc.—which merely

show that some nations and heads of state are wise enough or prudent enough not to stir up trouble. More characteristic of the genre, however, are stories of individual encounters that hinge upon a battle of wits or a benign misunderstanding by the participants, which are then embroidered in such a way as to inject them with a factor of moral uplift or spiritual power that is quite specious.

One such story is based on the fact that in October 1942 near Stalingrad a wounded German corporal was bandaged by a Soviet medic and then permitted to return to the German lines. This is the factual core of the story. Somewhere between the original report and the second or third retelling, the following embellishments have been added. First, the narrator expresses incredulous amazement that the Russian did not wantonly kill the wounded German. If, as is probable, it was the German soldier who first told the story, it may well be that he *was* amazed because Nazi propaganda had led him to expect nothing but barbarous ruthlessness. The real meaning of the fact might be simply that, in this instance at least, the Nazi stereotype of the Soviet soldier had no basis in fact. The narrator, however, makes no effort to evaluate this amazement or the fear with which it is bound up. It does not serve his edifying purpose to do so.

Second, the author makes the assumption that the Russian was "obeying the moral law" and that he was motivated by simple compassion. This may be so, but it is pure conjecture masquerading as self-evident fact, and it ignores possible alternative explanations. Maybe the Russian was just tired of taking prisoners. Maybe he liked the German's looks and would have shot him if he hadn't. Maybe he reasoned that it would be more patriotic to let the German government hospitalize the man. We have no way of knowing what his motive actually was. The facts are so meager that the field of speculation is wide open. For all its good intentions, such a story shows, among other things, how ambivalent is its author's view of human nature, since in the process of showing that a highly

exceptional Russian soldier could obey the moral law he implies that the average Russian soldier conforms to the Nazi stereotype of Slavic bestiality.

Another example of what often passes for a testimonial to nonviolence is the following episode from *Victories Without Violence* by the English Quaker Anna Ruth Fry. The book repeats almost word for word many of the quaint anecdotes in Ballou's century-old book. This is a more recent one.

In a suburb of Berlin toward the end of World War II there lived a "Mrs. H.," Miss Fry tells us, who "did all she could to help poor Jews when persecuted, hiding them as best she could." One day at the town hall members of the Gestapo warned her and others "not to say a word against the regime."

The impetuous Mrs. H. "lost her temper. 'And I will talk!' she yelled. 'It is a shame what is being done. I don't hate the Jews, no, I don't. And I don't love your Hitler, who is responsible for all this misery.' "

These were bold, heroic words. Having said them, Mrs. H. left the room. The police soon brought her back, "wanting to carry her away." But they let her go. Why? Because they respected her courage or because her compassion for the Jews touched their hearts? Not at all. Some of Mrs. H.'s neighbors interceded for her, explaining that she "hardly knows what she says when she loses her temper." So what we are supposed to believe is a moral issue turns out to be a case of nerves. Apparently Mrs. H. was happy that it worked out that way, since she let it go at that.

We next find the irrepressible Mrs. H. in trouble with the Soviet occupation a few months later. She has been complaining that Russian soldiers are stealing watches. The Soviet commandant calls her in and interrogates her. "Did you protest in the same vigorous way when the Nazis ill-treated the Jews?"

"Certainly I did," she says, and "someone" corroborates her testimony.

The Soviet officer responds warmly to this. He does not say anything about rectifying the injustice that Mrs. H. had been

complaining about, but Anna Ruth Fry and her Mrs. H. are glad to forget about that. "You go home now," says the Russian, "and nothing will happen to you. And try to forget the wrongs you have suffered." Forget about the stolen watches, too!

Perhaps it is belaboring the obvious to say that it is hard to see any "victory" in either of these episodes, which together occupy a little less than one full page in Miss Fry's slender, often-reprinted booklet. The most that can be said is that Mrs. H. made two unheeded protests and got off unharmed. A critical reader is tempted to think that in both cases the authorities wrote her off as a harmless screwball. Yet in the book's introduction Miss Fry claims to give illustrations of a mysterious spiritual power which she identifies as "nonviolent resistance," a "pacifist technique" that can serve as "a possible alternative to the futile crime of war." Mysterious it is indeed; if such an alternative is embedded in the story of Mrs. H., it is hard to fathom.

Most of Mrs. Fry's stories tell of unarmed religious people (usually Quakers) minding their own business when a conflict of some kind arises in which they do not take part, and the outcome of which they do not in any way influence. The "victory" invariably is nothing more than the fact that they manage to scrape through unmolested, or are even taken under the protection of one of the warring groups, as in the case of the Shakers who had Morgan's Raiders as their uninvited protectors during the Civil War. Stories about night-riding bandits and Chinese river pirates always cast the villains as ruthless cutthroats who are touched by the uprightness and Christian courage of their intended victims, as if transformed. But may it not be that their range of responses is wider than Miss Fry gives them credit for? One suspects too that many encounters might be reported in which the good Quakers or missionaries did not live to report victory.

In his book *Shall Our Children Live or Die?* Victor Gollancz tells of a Jewish rabbi tormented by Nazi SS men. On Yom

Kippur, the Day of Atonement, they whipped him, forced him to stand knee-deep in a pile of human excrement and then ordered him to preach. "My friends," the rabbi said to the SS men, "the fundamental principle of the Jewish religion, as of all the other great religions of the world, is: Love thy neighbor as thyself." A cynic might suggest that this was a shrewd way of asking for mercy, but a more generous interpretation—the one intended, which I am inclined to share—sees here evidence of dignity that cannot be defiled, moral nobility and unconquerable good will. The anecdote thus says much about the rabbi. What is missing is the SS men's response to it. Having made his point about the rabbi, Gollancz leaves the story suspended in mid-air. Were the SS men moved to shame, or did they perhaps guffaw and walk away? The story makes no claim to illustrate "nonviolent resistance," but it is one of many that are pacifist favorites and as such often lumped together with accounts that do make such a claim. A book titled *Above All Nations* gives many examples of "enemies" saving the lives of children or other civilians or refusing to shoot wounded soldiers. Such stories remind us that humane responses are possible even in many situations where they are unlikely. They may serve the cause of nonviolence by supplying a source of morale, but their relevance is marginal.

John Lewis, in his provocative book *The Case Against Pacifism,* disposes of many incidents claimed by pacifists as illustrations of nonviolence. In particular he singles out William Penn's honest dealing with the Indians, which understandably won the latter's respect for the Quaker settlers and relieved them of any occasion to choose between armed force and nonviolent resistance since the Indians did not attack them. He also points out that the courageous abstention from violence by Edward Richards and Theodore Pennell in Afghanistan when accosted by "fierce tribesmen" constitutes isolated individual exceptions that have no social validity. Much the same could be said of missionaries and doctors spared by marauders elsewhere. They are exempted because they pose no

threat and perhaps are even respected for their good works—
and above all because they are, in effect, considered either
friends or neutrals. To be sure, there is an element of danger
and risk, but it hinges on the possibility of misunderstanding
rather than conflict. To refrain from the use of arms in such a
situation is, as Lewis points out, only good sense. If it happens
to conincide with a tempcramental aversion to violence or a
principled adherance to nonviolence, as in the case of Richards,
that only provides an additional bulwark to enable one to do
the sensible thing. But basically it is not nonviolence as such
and it is a mistake to extrapolate from such experiences the
possibility of engaging in unarmed conflict with those who in
fact are simply respecting the neutrality of such individuals.
Had Richards, for example, been the leader of a nonviolent
compaign to obtain certain concessions from the Kurds, they
might well have butchered him on the spot. This is Lewis' contention, and whether he is right or not in his estimate of these
specific situations it is clear that there is no warrant but a
partisan and propagandistic one for mixing the category of
individual witness indiscriminately with that of social action.

Once we have set aside the spurious and the marginal, what
are we left with? Historical crises resolved solely by "pure
nonviolence" are virtually nonexistent. Yet there have been
episodes in which a strategy of nonviolence has been the decisive vehicle in waging and winning a campaign. There have
been other episodes in which nonviolence functioned as a
catalyst, precipitating a victory through legal or political channels. There have been episodes of nonviolence within a context
of largely violent struggle, and there have been situations in
which an incipiently nonviolent type of moral appeal has
yielded to armed struggle without any consistent attempt to
test the further possibilities of a systematically nonviolent
struggle. An important borderline area includes the tactics of
strike and boycott in labor struggles and similar kinds of civil
resistance—seldom clearly nonviolent, yet often approximating
nonviolence in a refusal to be provoked to counterviolence

when attacked. Given the actual record of civil resistance, punctuated as it is by departures from its own standards, this is a difficult and problematical category. Barthelemy de Ligt in *The Conquest of Violence* goes so far afield as to call "nonviolent" the action of the German Social Democrats under Bismarck in going underground and deciding against sabotage as a weapon of struggle.

If we set aside Ligt's loose usage of the term and allow for the "impurities" suggested above, the one distinct hallmark of nonviolence in all its authentic varieties is the meeting of actual or threatened violence unarmed and purposely, whether pragmatically or by conviction, making a stand without resorting to physical force against the enemy.

We have had to be selective in choosing the examples that comprise this casebook. Those given range from one case of Christian nonresistance to the incidental, spontaneous nonviolent episodes of the East German and Hungarian revolts of the 1950s. In between are significant cases of major passive resistance and direct-action campaigns. Rather than cram this section with many brief snippets to prove only that nonviolence occurred, we have preferred to devote the available space to a more comprehensive account of fewer cases, giving in each as much detail and historical context as is known and necessary for an adequate appraisal. To do this, we have had to forego the inclusion of Gandhi's campaigns, which in fact pose special problems and deserve detailed study. Perhaps the best source currently available for these is Joan V. Bondurant's *Conquest of Violence* (Princeton 1958). Additional cases from other countries can be found in Mulford Q. Sibley's *The Quiet Battle* (Doubleday Anchor 1963). Both books contain helpful bibliographies.[1]

REFERENCE IN CHAPTER 13

1   See also the extensive bibliography in the book edited by Peter Mayer: *The Nonviolent Tradition* (New York: Orion Press, Inc., 1964).

14

Nonresistance: The Moravian
Indians, 1782

Although Christian nonresistance may sometimes achieve a
socio-political objective, its intrinsic purpose is not this but
a way of faithful obedience. As subsequent chapters will make
clear, nonresistant martyrdom is by no means the only way
Christians have used nonviolence, but it is a way that is close
to the literal teaching of the gospel. Related to the case that
follows is a long history that ranges from the crucifixion of
Jesus to the massacre of Christian Kikuyu tribesmen in Kenya
in the 1950s at the hands of the Mau Mau. Its legacy may be
described as "how to die like a Christian." Our purpose in
including this example is not to recommend it but to provide
a clear illustration of the difference between nonresistance and
strategic nonviolence.

In the mid-eighteenth century Count Nikolaus von Zinzendorf, bishop of the Moravian Church and heir to the nonresistant wing of the Hussite Reformation, founded an Indian
mission at Shekomeko, New York. Within a few decades the
work and witness of his followers had led to the conversion
of considerable numbers of Delaware Indians in Pennsylvania,
of whom Theodore Roosevelt was to write:

The zeal and success of the missionaries were attested by the
marvelous change they had wrought in these converts; for they had
transformed them in one generation from a restless, idle, bloodthirsty people of hunters and fishers, into an orderly, thrifty, industrious folk, believing with all their hearts in the Christian religion in
the form in which their teachers both preached and practiced it.[1]

Chief among the Moravian missionaries was David Zeisberger. Born in Moravia in 1721, he emigrated to Georgia at the age of sixteen and, after a few years there, went north and almost returned to Europe with Zinzendorf. He was already aboard ship when he was moved to jump ashore and join the Shekomeko Mission. By the time he was ordained to the ministry in 1749, he was fluent in the Mohawk and Delaware languages. After a year-long visit to Herrnhut, Zinzendorf's model community in Germany, Zeisberger embarked on an impressive career of evangelism among the Iroquois of New York and Pennsylvania.

In March 1771 Zeisberger went out to the capital of the Delaware Nation in Ohio at the invitation of its grand council. The following year, as a result of his talks with the Delaware chieftains, he returned with an aide, the Rev. John Heckewelder, to found Schoenbrunn, the first of several settlements which he populated with Indian converts to Christianity. The settlements flourished until a few years after the outbreak of the Revolutionary War. Located midway between the American outpost at Fort Pitt and the British at Fort Detroit, the nonresistant Moravians were in fact neutral, but this did not keep them from being an object of suspicion. They earned the hostility of non-Christian Indians, too, by their frequent appeals to them to turn back from the warpath.

In 1781 the warrior Indians, at the instigation of the British, made several raids on the Moravian settlements but failed to deter Zeisberger or his followers. Finally in September, Zeisberger and other missionaries were seized and taken to the Delaware camp, where they found a British captain in charge. Their mission house was sacked, many of the Christian Indians were dispersed and the missionaries were taken to Detroit. For a time, however, they and a large number of the converts were held in a "captives' village" not far from the colonies. The winter was a hard one, and some 150 of the Christian Indians were granted permission to return to the settlements to get food which had been stored there.

One of the settlements was Gnadenhütten, in the Tuscarawas Valley. When they arrived, together with John Martin and five other mission assistants, they learned that only a short time earlier a war party of Sandusky Indians had attacked a farm, butchering a woman and her five children. It was widely rumored that the Christian Indians had committed the crime or had given shelter to the criminals. A man who had been taken captive by the Sanduskys warned them that a party of two hundred frontiersmen was on its way to destroy the settlements.

The Moravians counseled with one another and decided to leave by March 7, counting on their innocence to protect them in the event the frontiersmen arrived earlier. On the morning of March 6 they were busily sacking corn when the latter appeared, headed by Colonel David Williamson. Williamson was very friendly, offering to place the Moravian Indians under his protection, and he set his men to helping them recover goods which they had hidden in the forest when the mission had earlier been sacked. He persuaded the brethren at Salem to set fire to that place, saying that he would soon build them another.

There is some conflict in the precise details of what followed. Probably the best account is that of Bishop Schweinitz:

The white men seemed deeply interested in religion, asked many questions with regard to it, and listened to what they told them of their personal experiences with the profoundest attention. . . . "Truly, you are good Christians!" exclaimed the militia. Meanwhile the Indian boys sported with some half-grown lads of the command, taught them to make bows and arrows, and frolicked gleefully through the forests.

On the bank opposite Gnadenhütten the eyes of the deluded converts were suddenly opened. Coming upon a pool of fresh blood and a bloody canoe, they stopped in mute surprise; but in that moment the militia seized them, bound their hands behind their backs, and hurried them across the river, where they found the rest

of the Indians also prisoners, confined in two houses, and closely guarded.[2]

They were vilified and accused of many crimes in addition to the recent one. The frontiersmen were in a lynching mood. Williamson assembled them in a single row and asked: "Shall the Moravian Indians be taken prisoners to Pittsburgh, or put to death? All those in favor of sparing their lives, advance one step!" Only eighteen stepped forward. Then the frontiersmen debated whether to burn the Indians alive in their houses or to tomahawk and scalp them, finally deciding on the latter.

Although startled to learn of their fate and continuing to protest their innocence, the Indians begged only time to prepare for their death. They were given until the next morning. Through the night, says Schweinitz, "shut up in their two prisons, the converts began to sing and pray, to exhort and comfort one another, to mutually unburden their consciences and acknowledge their sins. . . . As the hours wore away, and the night deepened, and the end drew near, triumphant anticipations of heaven mingled with their hymns and prayers." [3]

The next morning the converts were taken in pairs, men to one "slaughterhouse," women and children to the other. One of the women, Christiana, had once lived in Bethlehem, Pennsylvania, in her youth and spoke fluent German and English. She begged Colonel Williamson to spare her life. "I cannot help you," he said coldly. John Martin's two sons escaped the day before the massacre and were shot down by sentinels. Otherwise all were scalped after being felled by tomahawk, spear or warclub. And all died except two boys who, only stunned, played dead and slipped away. The death toll included twenty-nine men, twenty-seven women and thirty-four children. All but twelve babies and five adults were baptized Christians.

After the massacre, the frontiersmen spent a day securing their plunder before setting fire to Gnadenhütten and moving on to Schoenbrunn to repeat their barbarous act. But mes-

sengers from that place had gone to Gnadenhütten on an errand, returned and gave the alarm.

Zeisberger was deeply saddened by the news when the two boys reached him on March 23. For the rest of his life he continued to shepherd what remained of his Indian flock, leading them from one place to another along Lake Erie and finally settling them at Goshen in the Tuscarawas Valley, where he died in 1808.

The effect of the Gnadenhütten massacre recoiled upon its perpetrators. Theodore Roosevelt tells what happened to a body of 480 Pennsylvania and Virginia militiamen that included "most of those who had taken part in the murderous expedition." In a skirmish with Shawnees and Delawares, seventy of them died of wounds, were killed outright or were captured. The head of the expedition was burned alive. Says Roosevelt:

The Indians were fearfully exasperated by the Moravian massacre; and some of the former Moravians, who had joined their wild tribesmen, told the prisoners that from that time on not a single captive would escape torture.[4]

One man who was condemned but managed to escape saw a number of his comrades tomahawked or tortured to death. And, concludes Roosevelt, "until the close of the year 1782 the settlements along the upper Ohio suffered heavily, a deserved retribution for failing to punish the dastardly deed of Williamson and his associates."[5]

The piety of these "holy innocents" did not save them from death as they had hoped, but it did provoke a terrible and costly vengeance upon their slayers which the Moravians could neither have foreseen nor asked.

REFERENCES IN CHAPTER 14

1   Theodore Roosevelt: *The Winning of the West* (New York: G. P. Put-
    nam's Sons, 1920), p. 6.
2   Edmund de Schweinitz: *The Life and Times of David Zeisberger* (Phil-
    adelphia: J. B. Lippincott Co., 1870), p. 545. See also Eugene F. Bliss,
    editor: *Diary of David Zeisberger* (Cincinnati: Clarke, 1885), Vol. 1,
    pp. 78-82. Also Georg Heinrich Loskiel: *History of the Mission of the
    United Brethren Among the Indians in North America* (London, 1794).
3   Schweinitz, *op. cit.,* p. 548.
4   Roosevelt, *op. cit.,* p. 103.
5   *Ibid.*

15

Passive Resistance in Hungary, 1859-1867

From January to June 1904 the weekly Dublin newspaper *The United Irishman* published a serial by Arthur Griffith titled *The Resurrection of Hungary: A Parallel for Ireland.*[1] Reprinted in booklet form and widely distributed for more than a decade, it has been described as "a milestone on the road to Easter Rising,"[2] the armed rebellion of 1916 which led through protracted guerrilla warfare in 1918-1921 to the founding of the Irish Free State. Its thirty-two-year-old author was the principal organizer of the Sinn Fein movement that began in 1907.

Many things have been forgotten since then—for instance, the fact that Sinn Fein, later known for its terrorism, originated as a movement of passive resistance with hunger strikers as its early heroes. Griffith's record of an earlier Hungarian movement has often been retold in pacifist circles, handed down from one author to the next and becoming ever more abbreviated and cryptic while the sole source, Griffith's booklet, became a rarity. Although most of Griffith's text has recently been reprinted, there are important aspects which it does not cover and which are only now made public beyond the specialized range of the sources. Most striking of these is the crucial role of the Protestant churches. In addition to my own research, I have relied to an incalculable extent on the assistance of Elemer Bako, Hungarian Research Librarian of the Library of Congress, who provided bibliographical data and translated

Magyar sources on the church struggle that forms part of the following account.

The Mounting Storm

Hungary, once an independent kingdom, had been under Austrian rule for more than a century when, in 1828, its people refused to recognize the right of the Habsburg emperor to order a levy of troops. Only a Hungarian Diet, they insisted, had the power to do this. Thus began five years of agitation climaxed by an imperial decree ordering elections to be held which gave Hungary limited autonomy in the conduct of its internal affairs. This concession did not placate the Magyars, however. After 1833 they clamored for more—first for such limited goals as a national education program and later for restoration of Hungary's independence.

In 1847, under the leadership of Lajos Kossuth, the Magyars succeeded in wringing a constitution from the Habsburgs, but the following year was a hectic one. Wallachian, Serbian and Croatian troops attacked the forces of Kossuth but were repulsed. The Austrian viceroy arrived in Budapest to revoke the constitution and was assassinated. A democratic revolution broke out in Vienna and Kossuth sent Hungarian troops to its aid. An Austrian counterinvasion was thrown back by the Hungarians. In April 1849 Kossuth proclaimed Hungary a republic but fled into exile when forces of the Russian Tsar moved in and returned control to the Habsburgs. The Diet was suppressed, the constitution abrogated; even county councils were banned and the nation was carved up into military districts administered by Austrian officers.

Lutheran and Reformed churches bore a heavy brunt for their support of the short-lived Kossuth regime. Following its defeat many pastors and several bishops were imprisoned. Protestants were forbidden the title of bishop and autonomous church organizations were dissolved. Imperial administrators adjusted church districts to correspond to military zones and

sent Austrian officers to watch over church meetings. A decade passed before Hungarian churchmen were able to make any concerted effort to overcome these disabilities, which in any case were for the most part lifted in a year to be reimposed later.

On the political scene, meanwhile, who was to fill the position of leadership vacated by the exiled Kossuth?

One of the men who had been elected to the Diet of 1833 was a twenty-nine-year-old lawyer named Ferencz Deák, a member of the Roman Catholic landed gentry and a descendant of Verboczy, the author of Hungary's ancient Corpus Juris. Not only an able jurist, Deák possessed wide knowledge of the judicial systems of other countries. A monarchist and traditionalist who was once likened to Edmund Burke, he was of such moral caliber that he refused to accept re-election to the Diet in 1843 because of unscrupulous conduct ending in bloodshed by members of both parties. He explained to a friend that he would "always see bloodstains upon the mandate." Nevertheless, it was Deák who drafted the Liberal Program of 1847, and in the following year he accepted the post of minister of justice in Kossuth's government, parting with the latter when the republic was declared.

After the debacle of 1849 the nation looked to Deák for leadership, regardless of class or party, and it was to him that the Austrian minister of justice turned in 1850 to confer on Hungarian affairs. Deák, however, declined, stating that such a conference could have no legal basis unless the constitution was restored. He cautioned his countrymen to be patient and neither concede the right of the Austrians to rule nor seek to repel them by force. "The publication of his letter of refusal," wrote one historian, "made the nation understand that henceforth the watchword of all patriots must be 'passive resistance.' " [3]

At first this was largely a waiting game. When the Austrians in 1850 began to replace the military districts with civil administration, many Magyars grudgingly accepted minor offices, but

most of the educated held aloof from taking posts of responsibility. Except for the abortive Makk conspiracy of 1852, said one of Deák's biographers, the people "refrained with striking unanimity . . . from isolated acts of violence." [4]

The 1850s were a hard period for Hungarian Protestants especially. In 1855 the Habsburgs signed a concordat with the Vatican, giving Catholic bishops authority over the state educational system and attempting to integrate the institutions of Hungarian Catholicism within the structure of the Catholic Church of Austria, a move that provoked opposition from Hungarian Catholic clergy. A similar attempt was made to bring the Hungarian Protestant churches into a unified empire-wide arrangement in which they would forfeit their autonomy.

The Protestants resisted stubbornly. In 1857 a deputation of Hungarian Calvinists went to Vienna to explain their position to the Kaiser and received a polite but deaf hearing. A few months later, at the August session of the Trans-Tisza Church District in Debrecen, Hungary's "Calvinist Rome," it was decided to regard the government order as a mere "proposal," and a plan of educational administration was submitted as an alternative to the official Austrian one. In retaliation, Vienna revoked the right of the University of Debrecen to award diplomas, and added other penalties.

Both sides moved slowly until September 1859, when Vienna began concerted efforts to impose its will in a vigorous eight-month campaign, beginning with the issuance of an Imperial Patent which forbade church autonomy, together with an implementing decree detailing the steps to be taken by the churches.

On October 8, under these laws, Austria prohibited the holding of church district courts and authorized its military forces to disband them if they were held, unless they were reorganized according to the new plan.

At the October session in Debrecen, the Reformed Church's leaders gave their answer. Kálmán Tisza, who was later to become Hungary's first Protestant prime minister, declared the

Austrian move "a grave act, the intentions of which cannot be accepted or promoted without the coercion of our conscience and without contradicting our vows of office and making us renegades to our religious principles." [5] District Superintendent Emeric Révész drew up two detailed memoranda stating the church's case and not only presented them to the government but published them abroad, where their appearance in the *Edinburgh Review,* for example, garnered strong support in Scotland. He also made contact with British, Prussian and Dutch diplomats in Vienna and impressed them with the Hungarian Protestants' plight.

The Austrians countered with raids on the homes of bishops and moderators, many of whom were arrested and brought before magistrates. When these leaders were removed from their positions, the churches refused to fill the vacancies. The situation among the Lutherans was complicated by the fact that many of their congregations were not Magyar. The church historian, Mihály Bucsay, shows the extent of the resistance:

Among the Reformed there were only 25 congregations, i.e. about 1%, ready to let themselves be organized according to the Patent. Of the Lutherans, there were about 226 communities that went along, mostly German and Slovakian, with 333 resisting in spite of promises and threats.[6]

When the Trans-Tisza council, spearheading the struggle, met in Debrecen as scheduled on January 11, 1860, in defiance of the government order, the Kaiser's representative was at a loss to prevent it. Churchmen turned out in full force—500 church officials alone from the nearby parishes, in addition to thousands of laymen. Another church historian tells of the encounter:

Immediately after the opening prayer, the Austrian Imperial Government representative . . . stood up and called upon the meeting to disperse. The chairman [Deputy Bishop Peter Balogh] then asked those present whether they wished to disperse or not, whereupon the huge crowd roared in reply: "We shall hold the meeting;

we will not disperse." Then as the meeting proceeded, fear began to show on the face of the Imperial representative, as he saw thousands of angry eyes turned in scorn upon him. Finally, he could bear the situation no longer, and got up and left; and no one did him harm.[7]

Although he had troops stationed outside, he was evidently reluctant to use them in the face of such determined and unanimous opposition. Attempts were made to persuade a Debrecen delegation to yield to promises of monetary aid for parish administration and teaching personnel, but to no avail.

Turning to another tactic, the government bypassed church officials and ordered pastors directly to accept a slightly modified decree, which they were instructed to read from the pulpit on two successive Sundays. Emeric Révész immediately sent out a message to all churches reiterating the council's position and indicating that the amended decree was to be resisted as firmly as the original one. With the exception of one area which did not receive the message, every minister in Hungary, some 1,500 in all, refused to read the Patent from his pulpit. Many of them were arrested as a result.

Vienna pressed its offensive. During February and March the arrests continued. Not only pastors but bishops were taken to jail. Police broke up church meetings again and again, though sometimes the churchmen succeeded in keeping their meetings going in defiance of the authorities even when government officials were present. "Wherever it was learned that a church leader was to be speaking in defiance of the law," writes Imre Révész, "huge crowds would gather to hear him; the church resistance was thus turning into a national resistance." [8]

Students expressed their solidarity with arrested church leaders by going to the towns where their trials were held and conducting silent demonstrations, dressed in black. In the courtrooms the prisoners rejected any form of legal defense, contending simply that they had acted in accordance with their constitutional rights and liberties. Those who were not arrested proceeded to conduct church affairs as if the hated decree were

nonexistent, and formed committees for the defense of church autonomy. When the Trans-Tisza District held its session on April 20 as scheduled, more than 5,000 laymen were present as a gesture of support.

Meanwhile, support from abroad was beginning to be felt. In January there was a mass meeting in Glasgow, and the British Government queried Vienna about the situation. In February the British prime minister spoke of it in Parliament. Leading newspapers in England, France and Prussia took up the cause of the Hungarian Protestants, and it was rumored that the Roman Catholic Primate of Hungary was preparing to lead a delegation of Hungarian Catholics to consult with the Kaiser and seek a solution. Throughout the struggle, in fact, the beleaguered Protestants received moral support from their Catholic countrymen.

Confronted with its inability to break the resistance of the churches by armed force without running the grave risk of precipitating a new national rebellion and piqued by its faltering prestige abroad, the Austrian Government looked for a way to extricate itself gracefully from the impasse. The Kaiser appointed a new Imperial Governor, the Hungarian Protestant, Field Marshal Lajos Benedek, and on May 15 revoked the decree and substituted a mild alternative which exempted all congregations that did not accept it. The Patent remained formally in effect, but its application to the Protestant churches was nullified and all the arrested ministers were freed.

Compromise, Habsburg Style

This setback for the Habsburg monarchy turned the tide not only for the Protestant churches but for the nation as a whole. The example of resistance was to prove valuable in the near future.

At first it seemed possible that a conciliatory course might yield political concessions in the new atmosphere that seemed to be arising. A few months after its revocation of the church

decree, Vienna instituted a limited form of self-government in Hungary and asked Ferencz Deák to serve in it as Judex Curiae. Deák declined, but he was elected to the Pest County Assembly the following year and persuaded it to enact laws necessary for recruiting soldiers and levying taxes, even though he still considered these measures a concession to an unconstitutional regime. Again he continued to warn his countrymen of the folly of seeking to win their objectives by violence: "You may blow up whole fortresses with gunpowder, but you cannot build the smallest hut with it." [9]

Deák's cautious optimism was betrayed by a new turn of events with the promulgation of a royal rescript creating an Imperial Parliament without Hungary's consent. It now became clear that the crown's intention was to lead the Hungarians toward amalgamation rather than toward autonomy. Deák gave Hungary's reply in an address to the Diet, which approved it unanimously and dispatched it to Vienna:

If it be necessary to suffer, the nation will submit to suffering, in order to preserve and hand down to future generations that constitutional liberty it has inherited from its forebears. It will suffer without losing courage, as its ancestors have endured and suffered, to be able to defend the rights of the country; for what might and power take away, time and favorable circumstances may restore; but the recovery of what a nation renounces of its own accord from fear of suffering is a matter of difficulty and uncertainty. The nation will suffer, hoping for a better future and trusting to the justice of its cause.[10]

Deák made clear the principle that was at stake: "It is sought to transfer to a foreign assembly sitting in the capital of a foreign country the right to make laws for ourselves and our children. Who will acquiesce? No one!" [11] The only legal solution, Deák maintained, was for the Habsburg Kaiser, Franz Josef, to accept the Hungarian Constitution promulgated in 1847 and come to Buda to be crowned Hungary's legitimate sovereign. Unless these conditions were met, the Kaiser was in effect a usurper to the legally vacant Hungarian throne.

238 NONVIOLENCE: A CHRISTIAN INTERPRETATION

Franz Josef's answer came on August 21, 1861. On that day he dissolved the Hungarian Diet. When the Pest County Council protested, it too was ordered dissolved. Defying the Kaiser's authority to do this, the councilmen refused to leave the council chamber until Austrian troops entered and forced them out. Other county councils throughout the nation followed suit, refusing to transfer their services to the Austrians. The constitution, already abrogated, was formally suspended by a royal rescript in November, and the country was placed once again under Austrian military rule.

In calling once more for passive resistance, Deák said: "Let us make ourselves as disagreeable to them [the Austrians] as we can." Clearly he did not conceive of this strategy as a manifestation of Christian love. But he firmly admonished his people to avoid resorting to acts of violence and to adhere to justice and law—Hungarian justice and Hungarian law. For the struggle as he saw it was precisely against Austrian injustice and illegality. "This is the safe ground," he said, "on which, unarmed ourselves, we can hold our own against armed force. If suffering be necessary, suffer with dignity."

The order was obeyed. Griffith tells us how:

When the Austrian tax-collector came to gather the taxes the people did not beat him or hoot him—they declined to pay him, assuring him he was a wholly illegal person. The tax-collector thereupon called in the police, and the police seized the man's goods. Then the Hungarian auctioneer declined to auction them, and an Austrian of his profession had to be brought down. When he arrived he discovered he would have to bring bidders from Austria too. The Austrian Government found in time that it was costing them more to fail to collect the taxes than the taxes if they were collected would realize. In the hope of breaking the spirit of the Hungarians, the Austrians decreed that soldiers should be billeted upon them. The Hungarians did not resist the decree—but the Austrian soldier after a little experience of the misery of living in the house of a man who despises you, very strongly resisted it. And the Hungarians asserted that from their enforced close acquaintance with

the Austrian army they found it to be an institution they could not permit their sons, for their souls' sake, to enter, wherefore they proposed that enlistment in the Austrian army was treason to Hungary, and it was carried unanimously.[12]

When the Imperial Parliament met in Vienna it was boycotted by the Hungarian representatives. Within nine months of the Kaiser's high-handed dissolution of the Hungarian Diet, Austria had become a laughingstock throughout Europe. "Passive resistance," the London *Times* editorialized, "can be so organized as to become more troublesome than armed rebellion."[13]

Although the Diet remained dissolved, its members continued to meet informally under other auspices, not quite "underground"—in agricultural, trade and literary circles: a device practiced by Basque republicans under Franco through soccer teams, and by a later generation of Hungarians in the Petöfi Circle of the 1950s. Hungarian businessmen resolved in their trade meetings of the 1860s, for example, that it was sound economics for Hungarian buyers to choose Hungarian goods rather than Austrian goods. "The results of these discussions," Griffith observed, "had a force as binding as law upon the people."[14]

For a brief period, Austria tried to cope with the Hungarians' economic warfare by issuing an ordinance that declared "exclusive trading" illegal. The Magyars flouted this law with such solidarity that it became unenforceable. "A few months of the jail-filling process," wrote Griffith, "and Austria found herself in another *cul-de-sac*."[15] Nationalism flourished in the Magyar press and "the Hungarian historical novel became a feature of the time." When a minor famine struck the land in 1863 the people's united morale enabled them to endure it.

It was shortly after this, in 1864, that Austria joined with Prussia in a war against Denmark over the question of Schleswig-Holstein. There was talk among some Hungarians of

seizing this occasion for an insurrection, but wiser counsels prevailed, recognizing that to be successful Hungary would need the support of larger powers. To revolt at this time would invite collision with the whole North German Confederation. Deák continued to play his waiting game. Meanwhile Bohemia, after participating in the Imperial Parliament at Vienna for two years, had recalled its deputies in derision, thus further weakening Austria's position.

Franz Josef now took tentative steps to mollify the Hungarians. On December 14 he appeared in Pest in person to reopen the Hungarian Diet, in which Deák was the key figure as "minister, jurist, diplomatist and party leader." [16] The Kaiser's motives were not impeccable. Bismarck, the Prussian chancellor, was maneuvering him toward a showdown that was to come in the *Brüderkrieg* of 1866, a seven-week war that consolidated Prussia's hegemony among the numerous German states and laid the basis for the powerful German Empire that was soon to be established. The decisive battle of the war was lost by Austria at Königgrätz on July 3. Before the outbreak of war the Kaiser had been anxious to placate the Magyars to the extent that they would not resort to insurrection. Not only did he have Deák to contend with, but Bismarck had authorized the exiled Hungarian leader, György Klapka, to form a Hungarian legion equipped with Prussian arms. Now the Kaiser was in desperate straits. A few days after the Königgrätz disaster he summoned Deák to Vienna.

Deák arrived at the imperial palace at midnight. The Kaiser said to him abruptly: "Well, Deák, what shall I do now?"

The Hungarian leader's reply was direct: "Your Majesty must first make peace and then give Hungary her rights."

"Will the Hungarian Diet give me men to carry on the war if I grant it the Constitution at once?" the Kaiser asked.

Deák's answer was "No. I will not make the restoration of my country's freedom a matter of barter." [17]

Deák's waiting game was nearing its end. His refusal to accede to Franz Josef's request sealed Austria's defeat in the war.

In the months ahead, the Kaiser made a number of ostensibly conciliatory overtures, hoping to settle the Hungarian question without meeting Deák's demands. On December 15, a communication from the Hungarian Diet, drafted by Deák, was sent to Franz Josef, making it clear that none of the latter's proposals would even be considered until Deák's demands were conceded.

The Kaiser's ill-considered reply was a decree of compulsory military service which, but for Deák's cool restraint, could have plunged Hungary into a desperate insurrection. Deák persuaded the Diet to send a deputation to Vienna to resolve the crisis as a last-ditch effort before yielding to the clamor for revolt. Both for Hungary and for Austria the situation had become most precarious, and an insurrection might have proved costly to both in the face of Prussia's ambitions.

The Kaiser saw the handwriting on the wall and to Deák's surprise rescinded the odious army law. In another two months events moved rapidly to a climax. Franz Josef reshuffled his cabinet, assigning the post of prime minister to Count Beust, a statesman with whom Deák had already reached an unwritten understanding a few months earlier. Julius Andrassy, a Magyar nobleman who had once had a price on his head for his part in the 1848 revolution, was invited to form a national cabinet for Hungary.

On February 18, 1867, the Kaiser restored the Hungarian Constitution. Deák and Beust signed a compact establishing a dual monarchy and Franz Josef was crowned King of Hungary. Deák's work was done. He had accomplished it by a combination of able statesmanship, patience and passive resistance.

The outcome was not greeted with universal rejoicing in the empire. "The dualist system," as Oszkar Jaszi has pointed out, "maintained the pyramid further on its head with the small correction that they heightened the base from six to twelve million by the addition of five million Magyars and a million Magyar-Germans. This new basis was manifestly unstable against the will of eighteen million people." [18]

In forty years the synthesis came apart at the seams and the empire collapsed. Austria became a small republic and Hungary a small, kingless monarchy. Probably for this reason the name of Ferencz Deák, which shone so brightly for a time, has become obscured.

For our present purposes, however, we are not concerned with debating the stature of Deák or to argue for his perspicacity as a statesman. His importance consists in the fact that he used passive resistance successfully as an integral part of a sustained campaign to achieve an historic goal. As the foregoing account shows, passive resistance alone did not bring the desired result, but it formed a crucial element among other factors, and was the only one over which the Hungarians had complete control. Had they not persevered in this strategy over a period of two decades it is highly likely that they would have failed to make use of the gratuitous leverages (such as those arising from Austria's position vis-a-vis Prussia) that developed during that period.

Unlike the Moravian nonresistants, Deák and his followers were in no sense committed to nonviolence as an article of faith. Their choice of passive resistance was made on wholly pragmatic grounds on a realistic assessment of their situation, although it undoubtedly owed something to Christian motives in the church campaign. Insurrection had been tried once with disastrous results. Although it was kept periodically under review, prudence dictated an alternative course of action which in the end validated itself by its results.

REFERENCES IN CHAPTER 15

1 Arthur Griffith: *The Resurrection of Hungary* (Dublin: James Duffy and Co., 1904). Extracts are reprinted in a book edited by Mulford Q. Sibley: *The Quiet Battle* (Garden City, N.Y.: Doubleday & Co., Anchor Books, 1963), pp. 137-155.
2 Edgar Holt: *Protest in Arms* (New York: Coward-McCann, Inc., 1961), p. 24.

3 C. M. Knatchbull-Hugessen: *The Political Evolution of the Hungarian Nation* (London: National Review Office, 1908), p. 147f.
4 F. M. Arnold-Forster: *Francis Deák* (London: The Macmillan Co., 1880), p. 119.
5 Quoted in Mihály Zsilinszky, ed.: *A Magyarhoni Protestáns Egyhas Története* (Budapest: Athenaeum, 1907), Vol. 4.
6 Mihály Bucsay: *Geschichte des Protestantismus in Ungarn* (Stuttgart: Evangelisches Verlagswerk, 1959), p. 175.
7 Imre Révész: *History of the Hungarian Reformed Church* (Washington: Hungarian Reformed Federation of America, 1956), p. 128.
8 *Ibid.*, p. 132.
9 Quoted in Arnold-Forster, *op. cit.*
10 Quoted in *ibid.*, p. 195.
11 Quoted in A. Fenner Brockway: *Non-Cooperation in Other Lands* (Madras: Tagore and Co., 1921), p. 13.
12 Arthur Griffith, *op. cit.*, p. 57.
13 *Times* (London), August 24, 1861. Quoted in *ibid.*
14 Griffith, *op. cit.*, p. 58.
15 *Ibid.*
16 Arnold-Forster, *op. cit.*, p. 224.
17 Quoted in *ibid.*, p. 237. Compare with Brockway, *op. cit.*, p. 20.
18 Oszkar Jaszi: *The Dissolution of the Habsburg Monarchy* (Chicago: University of Chicago Press, 1929), p. 105.

16

Civil Resistance in Finland, 1898-1905

The situation of Finland under Romanov rule in the Nineteenth Century bears some resemblances to that of Hungary under the Habsburgs, aside from the incidental fact of their common ethnic heritage. Conquered by Sweden in the Twelfth Century, the grand duchy of Finland was ceded to the Russian Empire in 1809. Under Russian rule, Finland was autonomous in its conduct of domestic policy, enacting its own laws through its own parliament, but foreign affairs were conducted on its behalf by the Russian Imperial Court at St. Petersburg, and Russian tsars were monarchs of Finland as well.

For nearly a century this arrangement was largely satisfactory to the population of Finland, and the country prospered culturally and economically, without Russian interference in its internal affairs. But the rise of Pan-Slavism in Russian ruling circles led, in the latter decades of the century, to a series of Russification measures. In 1889 Tsar Aleksandr III annulled certain reforms of the criminal law that had been voted by the Finnish Diet; in 1890 the postal service was brought under Russian control; in 1891 certain officials were required to know the Russian language.

Soon after the coronation of Nikolai II more strenuous moves toward Russification were made, largely at the instigation of Konstantin Pobedonostsev, procurator of the Holy Synod of the Russian Orthodox Church, a man identified both with efforts to raise the spiritual level of the Russian clergy and with draconic persecution of dissenting sects and the Russifica-

tion of minorities throughout the empire. To execute the policy of the new tsar and of Pobedonostsev, General Nikolai I. Bobrikov, who had earned a reputation as a tough Russianizer in the Baltic provinces, was appointed Governor-General of Finland in 1898.

One of Bobrikov's first acts was to call a special session of the Finnish Diet to enact a new army bill. Under an act of 1878 the peacetime strength of the Finnish Army had been set at 5600, with a reserve of 20,000, for the sole purpose of defending Finnish territory. Every adult male was liable to ninety days of compulsory military service, spread over a period of three years. Bobrikov's bill, however, not only raised the term of service to five years but decreed that Finns be conscripted into Russian units, placed Russian officers in command of Finnish regiments, and made the latter an integral part of the Russian armed forces, liable to service anywhere in the empire.

The Diet unanimously rejected the new army bill, whereupon Bobrikov, on February 15, 1899, published an imperial manifesto in which the Tsar arrogated to himself the right to decide what affairs were to be discussed by the Diet and in effect reduced the Diet to a consultative rather than a legislative body.

The Tsar Demurs

Both the Senate and the Diet sent delegations to the Tsar, but neither was received. A constitutional bloc was then formed as a national front representing various political and social groupings. Despite censorship of the press and of the mails, a petition was circulated throughout the nation and 522,931 signatures were secured within two weeks. (The total population of Finland at the time, including children, was about 2,700,000.) Five hundred men from every district of the country made their way to St. Petersburg undetected by Bobrikov's agents, to present the petition to the Tsar. An international deputation bearing a similar petition was also organized. Among its thousand

signatories were Herbert Spencer, Florence Nightingale, Emile Zola, Anatole France, Theodor Mommsen and Henrik Ibsen. The Tsar refused to receive either of these deputations. The army bill was implemented by imperial decree. J. Hampden Jackson gives a concise account of the next steps:

There followed a regime of calculated oppression in Finland. Bobrikov abolished all rights of freedom of speech and assembly. He attempted to enforce the Army Bill by calling up a batch of 25,000 conscripts. Of these 15,000 refused to serve. He could not imprison 15,000 men but he could and did banish seventeen publicists who defended them and dismiss fifteen judges who upheld their case. He replaced the Finnish police, provincial governors and mayors by Russians. He dismissed three hundred civil servants from their posts. He disbanded the Finnish Army and filled the barracks in Helsinki and other towns with Russians. And he made the teaching of Russian compulsory as the principal foreign language in schools.[1]

In response to these measures the Finns resorted to passive resistance. Anatole G. Mazour gives an excellent summary of the form it took during its first phase:

High Finnish authorities refused to attach their signatures to official papers as was required by law; judges paid little attention to recently promulgated legislation or executive orders. . . . Parents were advised to overlook orders requiring their children to be taught Russian. A secret patriotic society was organized for the purpose of drafting petitions and drawing up protests, organizing public demonstrations, rendering legal aid and assisting Finnish emigration or disrupting the enforcement of conscription. All this was carried on while Finnish authorities did little to interfere. Teachers openly advocated passive resistance among their pupils. The Lutheran clergy defiantly preached from the pulpits and appealed for aid for the national cause.[2]

To circumvent press censorship the constitutional bloc launched a publication, *Fria Ord* (Free Words), in Stockholm, which was circulated clandestinely among the Finnish populace. These and other activities from underground and from

exile kept up the morale of the people and provided links of communication among them in the face of ubiquitous Russian power.

For more than five years the struggle continued. The Finns held fast to civil resistance despite increasing repressions by their Russian overlords. Under pressure from one of Bobrikov's most odious tactics, however, a rift was precipitated in the otherwise steadfastly nonviolent resistance. This tactic was the use of agents provocateurs, men hired by the Okhrana, the tsarist secret police, to commit acts of violence against the Russian authorities in order to provide tangible excuses for repressions against the Finns or to provoke the Finns themselves to adopt violent methods. Thus began a round of violent incidents secretly engineered by the Russians against themselves, then savagely revenged upon the Finns by the Tsar's Cossack regiments. These repressions were authorized by a 1903 regulation giving Bobrikov dictatorial powers "for the maintenance of state order and public peace in Finland." At the same time, additional Russification measures were adopted.

Instead of shattering Finnish resistance, Bobrikov's new actions recoiled upon him. He was assassinated on June 16, 1904, by a young Finnish patriot, Eugen Schauman, the son of a former senator, who then committed suicide. Soon afterward a Russian army officer, Lieutenant-Colonel Kramarenko, was assassinated, and an attempt was made on the life of the Russian governor of Viipuri, M. A. Myasoyedov. These and other such violent acts were committed out of desperation by Finns who were in contact with the Russian Social Revolutionary Party. They also collected arms for a possible insurrection.

An Alliance Takes Shape

But passive resistance was not yet over. Its second phase was to come from a new quarter, the fast-growing labor movement. The first Finnish trade union had been founded in 1883, holding its first political congress a decade later. In 1895 the social-

ist newspaper *Työmies* (The Worker) was founded, advocating replacement of the old Diet of four estates with a unicameral legislature based on universal and equal suffrage, in addition to free public schools, an eight-hour work day and other reforms. Much of the support of the Finnish Social Democratic Party which had evolved by 1903 came from agricultural laborers as well as urban workers. Though numerically small (13,500 in 1903), it was well organized. When Russia was defeated in its war against Japan in 1905 the Finnish Social Democrats knew exactly what to do. They called a general strike. Jackson provides the details:

Trains stopped, telegraphs went dead, factories stood empty. This lead was followed spontaneously by the whole nation: shops, offices, schools, restaurants, were shut. The police went on strike and . . . university students formed a corps to maintain order. . . . There was no bloodshed; it was merely passive resistance with a whole nation behind it.[3]

On the sixth day the Tsar's government, which was beleaguered by insurrection in St. Petersburg, came to terms with the Finns, rescinding Bobrikov's innovations and re-establishing constitutional government with a new Diet elected by the votes of every citizen twenty-four years old or more, with no property qualifications or privileges, male and female alike. In the first elections under the new system, held in 1907, the Social Democrats won eighty out of the 200 seats.

If the situation had stabilized at this point we could record a magnificent triumph for nonviolence. But within two years, having consolidated its power after the 1905 upheavals, the tsarist government turned once more to efforts at Russification, this time by clever manipulations of law rather than by the outright illegality of Bobrikov. During this period there was sporadic passive resistance, such as the refusal of twenty-three members of the Viipuri Court to give a dictated judgment on a test case. For this they were tried by a Russian tribunal and imprisoned in a Russian jail. Also, two-thirds of the Finnish

pilot service resigned in protest against control by Russian maritime officials.

Finland retained some of the gains won through passive resistance. Even through World War I, the Finns were exempt from Russian military service. But at the same time, the Russians with impunity doubled the sum which Finland was required to pay in lieu of supplying soldiers, and the Russian War Office built fortifications and moved its troops freely on Finnish soil. Leaders who dared to speak out against Russification, such as the Speaker of the Diet, Per Svinhufvud, were exiled to Siberia.

During the same decade, Finland—or at least Finnish capitalists—enjoyed unprecedented economic prosperity. Fortunes were to be made supplying the inexhaustible Russian war machine. This fact explains much of the inability of the nation to unite as it had done in 1905. In the end, class divisions were to result in civil war at the hour of independence. Twenty-four thousand Finnish lives were lost in 1918 before a republic was established. Social Democratic leaders were imprisoned or exiled by the nationalist forces of Field Marshal Mannerheim.

As in the case of Hungary, we see once again in Finland the great possibilities inherent in a united nonviolent resistance, but also the extent to which these possibilities hinge upon external factors over which the resisters have no control. The dominant role assumed by the general strike of 1905 depended chiefly upon Russia's defeat in the Russo-Japanese War and upon the subsequent crisis of the tsarist regime in the widespread revolts of that year. Granted these facts, however, the Finnish general strike was a decisive event. It did not usher in the millennium. Many of the gains it achieved were lost in a few years, though others endured through independence and after. And in the end the same people who had managed to hold out against the Russians largely without bloodshed were to slay one another with savage ferocity. There is a profound historical irony here and its salient lesson is that the successful use of passive resistance at one moment in history is a means proportionate to

the ends it achieves and not a blank check on future developments.

REFERENCES IN CHAPTER 16

1 J. Hampden Jackson: *Finland* (New York: The Macmillan Co., 1940), p. 68. For further documentation see Mazour, cited below, and the following: Magnus Gottfried Schyberson: *Politische Geschichte Finnlands, 1809-1919* (Stuttgart: Perthes Verlag, 1925); John Henry Wuorinen: *Nationalism in Modern Finland* (New York: Columbia University Press, 1931); and H. Seton-Watson: *The Decline of Imperial Russia, 1855-1914* (New York: Frederick A. Praeger, Inc., 1952).
2 Anatole G. Mazour: *Finland Between East and West* (Princeton, N.J.: D. Van Nostrand Company, Inc., copyright 1956), p. 22.
3 Jackson, *op. cit.*, p. 74.

17

Denmark and Norway, 1940-1943

Nonviolent resistance to the Nazi army of occupation in Denmark and Norway during World War II strongly resembles, in certain respects, the Finnish civil resistance of 1898-1905. The countries invaded were relatively small and ethnically homogeneous, and it was the policy of the German invader not, as in Eastern Europe, to destroy existing political institutions and enslave the population, but to subordinate and manipulate them for the invader's purposes. Although in many ways the Third Reich was more totalitarian than the Romanov Empire, it differed in one point favorable to the Danes and Norwegians. For the Finns were outsiders to the ethnic ideology of Pan-Slavism that figured in tsarist Russia's encroachments, while the Danes and Norwegians, perhaps even purer Nordics than the Germans themselves, were claimed by the Nazis as kinsmen, fellow members of the "master race." Hence, unlike any of the other countries invaded by Nazi Germany, these two nations were given preferential treatment. It is instructive to note, by contrast, that when Germany attacked the USSR many Russians welcomed them as liberators, only to become disillusioned and embittered as a result of the ruthless treatment they received as *Untermenschen* in the Nazi ideology. So rigid were the Nazi racial attitudes that they virtually blotted out any chance of a moral appeal by anyone categorized as racially inferior, such as Jews or Slavs. And by the same token the Danes and Norwegians (and to some extent the Dutch) were punished in a much milder way when they resisted, and not at all when they did not. Hence it is not possible to generalize

from the experience of these countries without also altering the basic given fact of the Nazi race theory and its implications. If this is done, however, there are undoubtedly lessons to be drawn from this segment of history which would apply to situations involving a nonracist type of totalitarianism.

Denmark Under the Nazis

Both Denmark and Norway were invaded in 1940. Of the two, the latter is of greater interest from the standpoint of nonviolence, but the story of Denmark must first be told briefly.[1] This country capitulated without armed resistance, submitting to a one-hour ultimatum to admit German troops. In return, it was assured that Germany would not interfere with constitutional liberties. There was a general coldness toward the invaders, but no serious attempt to make their stay untenable. When the Nazis violated the occupation treaty by hoisting a German flag from a Danish public building, King Christian announced that he would personally remove it if the Nazis did not. They did. Again, the Danish Government repudiated the Anti-Comintern Pact after the Germans had persuaded the Danish prime minister to sign it. In 1942, when the Nazis decreed that Denmark's 8,000 Jews must wear the yellow Star of David, the King made it a point to attend a celebration in a Copenhagen synagogue. His stand was affirmed in protests by the Bishop of Sjaelland and other Lutheran clergy.

Not until August 1943, however, did the Danes resort to determined resistance. Demonstrations flared into a general strike in the major cities. These were quickly crushed by German troops. A military state of emergency was declared on August 28 and reinforcements were sent in. The King was placed under house arrest, the cabinet resigned and the Danish Parliament, which had continued to exist as a democratically elected body, dissolved itself. Thousands of Danes were killed in reprisal for their defiance. A rash plan to destroy Copenhagen by artillery fire was thwarted only by the cleverness of

an anti-Nazi German shipping expert attached to the German legation, Georg Ferdinand Duckwitz. For the rest of the war the Danish underground fought the Germans with sabotage and guerrilla attacks.

One more episode must be reported. In September, Duckwitz told Danish political leaders of a Nazi plan to round up all the Jews on the night of October 1. With lightning speed the Danes spread the report by word of mouth. On September 30 in the Copenhagen synagogue the news was received. When the raid came, only 472 Jews were caught. All the others had gone into hiding—in Protestant churches, in Catholic cloisters, in the homes of friends and strangers, in hotels and on farms. Subsequently, in a remarkably well-organized fashion the Jews were taken by taxi or other means to the seacoast and from there smuggled across the narrow straits of Öre Sound by fishing boat, rowboat and canoe to neutral Sweden, embarking at night to evade German sea patrols. Some 7,500 Jews were thus taken to safety under the noses of the ruthless enemy.[2]

The Norwegian Resistance

The Norwegians responded more vigorously to the invasion, meeting the Germans with armed resistance which lasted for two months. The King and parliamentary leaders escaped to England and formed a government-in-exile. Once the brief but vigorous armed defense ended, the Norwegians quickly adjusted to the mild terms of the occupation forced upon them by the invaders. Attracted by high profits, Norwegian businessmen accepted contracts to furnish the Nazis with military goods. Trade unions were assigned Nazi puppet officials and although resistance quickly developed, the lure of high wages at first had a delaying effect. These were the first steps in a series of moves by which the German occupation authorities sought to transform the nation's democratic institutions into either German agencies or the tools of an indigenous Nazi-type political organization, the Nasjonal Samling. At the top level, this process

was consummated in September 1940 with a series of decrees which abolished all political parties except the Nasjonal Samling.

This puppet government, headed by Vidkun Quisling but under the virtual control of German Reichskommissar Terboven, created a Norwegian equivalent of the Nazi S.A. known as the Hird, which frequently joined with both German and Norwegian political police in combating resistance.

The first real gesture of resistance came when the Norwegian Supreme Court resigned in December in protest against Nazi decrees which violated Norway's democratic laws. During the same period the Nazis dissolved the country's numerous sports clubs and replaced them with new ones, which were so completely boycotted by Norwegian sportsmen that no public games were played throughout the occupation. At the University of Oslo, the student union was abolished, but its Nazi successor was boycotted out of existence, and lecturers appointed to teach Nazi ideology ceased to teach when no one attended their classes.

Regulations were issued which abolished the executive functions of local councilors and appointed new mayors wherever possible, with dictatorial powers. In the dwindling number of communities in which the old mayors remained, they ignored these regulations and continued to consult with their councils in accordance with prewar democratic procedures.

The two most notable sectors of resistance were the churches and the schools. Although teachers bore a harder brunt during this period, it was a time of testing for the church. Bishop Eivind Berggrav wrote in a message to the Swedish Church Assembly in May 1941: "God has led the Norwegian Christians into the great melting pot where everything belonging to us has become small and God has become great." [3] In the midst of hardship there was a great resurgence of faith, symbolized by the return to the church of the noted liberal humanist, Dr. Kristian Schelderup, who was among outspoken and active Christians arrested in 1942. Although the struggle focused on

the established Lutheran state church, other denominations rallied to its cause.

The first encroachment on the church was a decree expunging parliament and the King from the official church prayers. Pastors met this decree by saying this portion of the prayers in silence. A more serious clash occurred when Quisling's ministry of church affairs decreed that pastors must divulge to police on request any information given to them by parishioners in the privacy of the confessional, on penalty of imprisonment. This led first to a protest signed by all seven of the church's bishops and then, in defiance of the state authorities, to a pastoral letter that was read from every Lutheran pulpit in Norway and distributed in printed form. In addition to the interference in church affairs, the church protested the illegalities which had led the Supreme Court to resign, and the terrorist actions of the Hird. No concerted action was taken against the churches at this time, though an abortive attempt was made to recruit pastors into a Nazi-style "Christian Unity Movement." Only twenty pastors in the whole country joined, and they were boycotted by their congregations except for a handful of Quislingites.

Simultaneous with the attack on the church, a series of decrees required Quisling's portrait to be hung in school classrooms, made the teaching of Nazi doctrine compulsory, revised the history curriculum along Nazi lines, and substituted German for English as the second language. Backed up by parents and by the church, both teachers and students showed stiff opposition, in the face of which the authorities withdrew the decrees.

The Nazis renewed their attack on church and school a year later. In the meantime they were slowly consolidating their power, which provoked the trade unions to strike on September 8, 1941. With this as a pretext, a state of emergency was declared and terror reigned for a week under Gestapo auspices. Two strike leaders were shot and journalists and professional men were imprisoned along with hundreds of strikers. A thor-

oughgoing shakeup of the trade unions followed, extinguishing all vestiges of democracy and placing Quisling followers in firm control. Despite this apparent victory, however, throughout the war the industrial workers persistently engaged in slowdowns and in sabotaging machines to hamper war production, under the guidance of underground leaders.

In February 1942 the Quisling government began a new drive to erect a fascist "corporative state," with the Laerersamband, a compulsory teachers' association, and the Ungdomsfylking, a compulsory youth movement, as part of its structure. At the same time that these were set up, the lapsed decrees of 1941 were reinstated and an attack was launched against the church, beginning on February 1 when the dean of Nidaros Cathedral in Trondheim, Arne Fjellbu, was ordered to yield his pulpit to a Nazi pastor. When he defied the order, he was arrested and, after a preliminary hearing, deprived of his office. While this was happening, Quisling promulgated the law requiring children from ten to eighteen years old to join the Ungdomsfylking. On February 14 Norway's seven bishops lodged a protest against this law as abrogating the right of parents to decide about their children's education, and as inculcating the children with ideas that did not have parental approval. This protest was reiterated from the pulpit throughout the nation on February 22 and was followed by an avalanche of letters written by parents to government officials. On February 24 the bishops resigned their administrative posts in the state church, while asserting their spiritual leadership of the church's congregations—in other words, repudiating the authority of an unjust state and disestablishing the church.

The state responded by dismissing the bishops and prohibiting them from exercising any ecclesiastical functions. They arrested Eivind Berggrav, Bishop of Oslo and the titular head of the church, and Bishop Hille of Hamar. For most of the war's duration, Berggrav was kept under guard in his summer house.

The teachers meanwhile were given until March 15 to com-

ply with the order to join the Laerersamband, and in the interval the schools were closed. The deadline passed and the teachers did not give in. On March 20, arrests began and totaled 1,300 by the end of the month. Some were held as long as eight months. In his definitive pamphlet, *Tyranny Could Not Quell Them* (London: Peace News, n.d.), Gene Sharp has told in detail how approximately half of the total number of arrested teachers were turned over to the Gestapo at the Jorstadmoen concentration camp and subjected to "torture gymnastics" and other harsh treatment for a week in an effort to force them to capitulate. Only thirty-two out of 687 gave in. The rest were subsequently sent to Kirkenes, a village in the far north, above the Arctic Circle, and set at hard labor under frugal conditions of clothing and shelter, guarded by Wehrmacht troops. During their imprisonment the underground resistance movement, aided by the government-in-exile in London, sent to the family of each prisoner an allotment equal to the salary he would have been paid as a teacher.

When the schools reopened on April 8, a small number of teachers stayed out, making arrangements to teach privately. The majority returned to their classrooms but remained adamant in their refusal to join the Laerersamband.

Even before this, on Palm Sunday, March 29, a confession of faith titled "The Church's Foundation," drafted by Bishop Berggrav, was surreptitiously distributed throughout the nation and on Easter was read from the pulpit.[4] Congregations were asked to rise as a sign of assent, and only a handful of Nazi sympathizers remained seated. Some ninety-three per cent of all Norway's Lutheran pastors then announced their resignation from the administration of the state church, as the bishops had done earlier. Clergy and church officials were subjected to harassment, placed under house arrest or banished from their homes, and in some cases prosecuted for trumped-up offenses.

Quisling arrogated to himself the position of head of the state church and appointed unqualified laymen and theological students from among his followers to replace the resigned pas-

tors and bishops. The church set up a provisional council to carry on the work of the deposed bishops. Quisling branded it illegal, but parishioners boycotted his pastoral appointees and by the end of the year he was forced to recognize the provisional council and abandon his efforts to control the church.

Likewise, faced with such determined resistance by teachers, students and parents, Quisling abandoned his scheme of nazifying youth and the schools. After a faltering and ludicrous attempt to nazify the trade union movement in similar fashion, Quisling was ordered by Hitler to abandon his attempt to set up a corporative state.

The balance sheet at the close of 1942 showed impressive results for nonviolence, but nothing that could be called victory. The nonviolent movement succeeded in preserving the integrity of the church and of stalemating the corporative state. During the same period, however, a hundred Norwegians were executed, 7,000 were imprisoned in concentration camps and 1,000 were deported to Germany and to Nazi-occupied countries such as Poland. Although as in Denmark the Norwegians made it clear to the German troops that they were unwelcome, no serious attempt was made to persuade them to desert, nor was any effort made to disrupt the economy or the political order so as to make it impossible for the occupation to continue.

In effect, the Norwegian nonviolent resistance was a defensive operation—at best, a holding action which gave way in 1943-1944 to a program of sabotage led by trained guerrillas parachuted from British aircraft, augmented by open clashes between workers and Hird troops and the assassination of SS and Gestapo men.

REFERENCES IN CHAPTER 17

1   For a full account, see David Lampe: *The Danish Resistance* (New York: Ballantine Books, Inc., 1960). Also John Danstrup: *A History of Denmark* (Copenhagen: Wivel, 1948), pp. 173-195.

2   See Harold Flender: *Rescue in Denmark* (New York: Simon and Schuster, Inc., 1963).
3   Quoted in Bjarne Höye's and Trygve M. Ager's *The Fight of the Norwegian Church Against Nazism* (New York: The Macmillan Co., 1943), p. 123. See also a work translated by Laura Wyss: *Norwegische Kirchendokumente aus den Jahren des Kampfes Zwischen Kirche und Weltlicher Macht*, 1941-1943 (Zürich: Evangelischer Verlag, 1943).
4   Full text appears in the appendix to the Höye and Ager work.

18

The South African Struggle
of the 1950s

The basic facts of South Africa are a white population of 3,000,000 divided into two cultural groups, the English-speaking and the Afrikaans-speaking, represented respectively by the United Party and the Nationalist Party in Parliament; and a black population more than three times as large which has no representatives in Parliament and is sharply circumscribed by government policies expressing moderate or virulent forms of white supremacy with concomitant oppression of the blacks. In addition there are some 1,360,000 Coloreds of intermediate status and about half a million Indians.

The beginning of organized resistance by black Africans dates from 1912 with the founding of the African National Congress by a young Oxford-educated African, Dr. P. I. Seme, along conventional lines similar to those of the Indian National Congress before Gandhi. Originating as a result of the virtual exclusion of black Africans from the legislatures of the four South African states and from the parliament of the Union of South Africa which they comprised after 1910, the Congress was set up as a consultative body to present the views of the blacks to the country's white rulers. As a later Congress leader, Albert Luthuli, wryly put it, "to begin with, only the ear was appealed to, until we discovered that it was deaf." [1]

Methods other than appeal to the ear were soon adopted, not always by the Congress, and on a haphazard, uncoordinated basis. A prime object of the protests was the pass system, under which all black men had to carry a police pass at all times

and be prepared to display it on request. Its revocation could mean loss of employment.

There were widespread demonstrations against the newly instituted pass system in 1913 in the Orange Free State, an Afrikaner stronghold, which resulted in numerous arrests. Again in 1919 an anti-pass campaign sponsored by the African National Congress resulted in some seven hundred arrests in the city of Johannesburg alone. Luthuli reports:

In Capetown 400 dockers staged a strike. In 1920, 40,000 African miners came out on strike on the Reef, and in Port Elizabeth twenty-one people were killed by the police. In the following year 163 people were wantonly massacred by the police at Bulhoek, and in 1924 a hundred Hottentots were butchered for refusing to pay an incomprehensible tax on dogs.[2]

In 1928-29 Natal burst into fits of unrest and violence . . . and there was trouble in Durban over taxation. In 1930 there was an outburst in Worcester, and an anti-pass demonstration in Durban. The cost of white supremacy—paid almost entirely in black corpses —rose steadily.[3]

Such was the situation for nearly forty years under the avowedly white-supremacist government of Jan Christiaan Smuts and his associates of the United Party. With the election of a Nationalist government in 1948, bent on an aggressive program of *apartheid* (segregation) even more draconic than that of the Smuts era—which, as the above citations show, was "liberal" only in a narrowly comparative sense—the desultory resistance embodied by the moderate Congress was galvanized into a widely coordinated, massive campaign of nonviolent resistance.

Under the leadership of Dr. James Moroka, its newly elected president-general, the Congress met in 1949 and hammered out a program of action which represented a sharp break with the conservative past.

Representations were done with. Demonstrations on a country-wide scale, strike action and civil disobedience were to replace words. Influenced by the combined action of the Indian community

after the passing of the Ghetto Act [i.e., the Group Areas Act], we agreed to concentrate mainly on nonviolent disobedience.[4]

There are many complexities and details that we have glossed over, and most of these will have to remain obscure for the sake of brevity, but a few must be briefly sketched in at this point. Out of the separate developments of the different states that form the present Republic of South Africa—Natal and Cape Colony, under British rule since 1843 and 1806 respectively, the former having a large population of Indian immigrants and the latter a sizable population of so-called "Cape Coloreds" descended from a mixed parentage of black and English settlers; Transvaal and Orange Free State, strongly Boer or Afrikaner: descendants of the early Dutch settlers—came several of the complexities referred to. In addition to the cleavage in the white-supremacist ranks between the English and the Afrikaner, there is a certain cleavage among the non-whites, who at various times and in different ways have been subjected to victimization by the whites. As Leo Kuper points out, for example, Indians were little affected by the pass laws and Africans little affected by the Group Areas Act, while the Coloreds suffered from neither and possessed certain marginal privileges to boot. However, members of all three groups suffered "more or less equally under discrimination in public services and amenities."[5]

It remains to be added that although the African National Congress was not designed to exclude nonblacks, it was in fact even more a black organization than the Indian National Congress was a Hindu organization. Alongside it were the South African Indian Congress (with which was affiliated the Natal Indian Congress founded by Gandhi, historically the parent of the larger body), the Franchise Action Council and other Colored organizations. Finally, in addition to these, small numbers of whites in the Liberal Party, the Communist Party and the higher circles of the English-speaking Christian churches, as well as in the universities, comprised a tiny and ineffectual bul-

wark against *apartheid* in various degrees and with various motives that cannot be explored here.

A Joining of Forces

This digression helps to set the stage for the events of the 1950s. The "combined action of the Indian community," to which Luthuli refers above, was a passive resistance campaign waged by the Indians in 1946 on an issue that affected their community but not other nonwhites. This was the first use of *satyagraha* since Gandhi's departure from Africa three decades earlier. In this campaign some 2,000 Indians were imprisoned. No doubt its impact was felt among the younger generation of ANC leaders. Certainly it is reflected in the Program of Action adopted in 1949. The program soon bore fruit. Early in 1950 Moroka called a Freedom of Speech Convention in Johannesburg, followed by a May Day demonstration against *apartheid* sponsored by the Communist Party and other groups allied with it, in which blacks, Indians and Coloreds took part. Many children stayed home from school as part of the protest. Demonstrators were attacked and suffered heavy casualties.

A third demonstration occurred on June 26, called by Moroka, as a day of mourning for Africans who had lost their lives in the struggle for freedom, and as a day of protest against the Group Areas Act and the so-called Suppression of Communism Act, of which we shall hear more later. Again there was interracial cooperation among the nonwhites and between them and the white anti-*apartheid* minority, and again school children took an active part.

On May 7, 1951, Coloreds in Port Elizabeth and the Cape Peninsula staged an effective strike against *apartheid* legislation aimed at them, receiving some support from Indians and blacks. Finally in July a conference was held between national executives of the ANC and the SAIC, with representatives of the newly formed Franchise Action Council, and a Joint Planning Council was set up to coordinate the efforts of these three

organizations in a proposed nonviolent "defiance campaign" against the disabilities imposed on each of the groups they represented. According to the Report of the Joint Planning Council, "Defiance of unjust laws should take the form of committing breaches of certain selected laws and regulations which are undemocratic, unjust, racially disciminatory and repugnant to the natural rights of man." [6] A three-stage plan of action was drawn up, the timing of which "would to a large extent depend on the progress, development and outcome of the previous stage." Its three stages were: 1) acts of civil disobedience by "selected and trained persons" in major cities; 2) increase in the number of such volunteers and in the number of cities in which to conduct these acts of defiance; and 3) mass action "on a country-wide scale" embracing people in both urban and rural areas.

The report also includes provisions for the necessary organizational structure. Each of the national organizations was to have its own Volunteer Corps units. Mixed units were to be formed only to defy laws that affected all nonwhites equally. Specific instructions such as the following formed part of the document:

Method of Struggle on the Pass Law. (a) A Unit of Volunteer Corps should be called upon to defy a certain aspect of the pass law, e.g. enter a Location without a permit. The Unit chosen goes into action on the appointed day, enters the location and holds a meeting. If confronted by the authorities, the leader and all the members of the Unit court arrest and bear the penalty of imprisonment; (b) Selected leaders to declare that they will not carry any form of passes . . . and thus be prepared to bear the penalty of the law; (c) Other forms of struggle on the pass laws can also be undertaken depending on the conditions in the different areas throughout the country.[7]

Elsewhere in the report, provision is made for rural action, industrial strike action (to be reserved for the third stage in the plan of action) and a "one-million shillings" fund drive.

Kuper notes, in evaluating the program of action:

The choice of passive resistance as a form of struggle appears to have been governed by considerations of expediency rather than by the ethic of Satyagraha. The planning of the campaign in three stages, culminating in mass action, indicates that we are dealing with a tactical use of passive resistance. A mass movement is clearly aimed at the embarrassment of the rulers, and not their conversion by a change of heart. Moreover, the given historical conditions weighed heavily with the Joint Planning Council, and not the assumed universal efficacy of voluntary suffering.[8]

Accordingly, no provision was made for fasting or other such acts of self-purification or penance which Gandhi, as a Hindu, deemed essential, for the quite simple reason that such practices had no place in the South African context.

To the extent that the South African campaign was governed by religious motives they were chiefly Christian, providing the courage to withstand retaliation but in no sense provoking any more suffering than the situation demanded. Among the principal leaders may be cited such Protestants as Albert Luthuli, who testifies eloquently concerning the relevance of his Congregational faith to his career in the freedom movement, Z. K. Matthews and others. The head of the ANC's Youth League during this period is described by Luthuli as "a forceful and gifted Roman Catholic, Anton Lembede," and undoubtedly there were other Catholics in the movement. By all indications, none of them were influenced by Hindu or other types of mysticism enjoining self-immolation.

The defiance campaign was preceded by a series of mass rallies in Capetown, Port Elizabeth, East London, Pretoria, Durban and elsewhere, involving crowds of as many as 10,000. Letters were sent to the authorities, announcing plans for the defiance campaign. The government's replies were characteristically unconciliatory, threatening "full use of the machinery at its disposal to quell any disturbances, and thereafter deal adequately with those responsible for initiating subversive activities of any nature whatsoever."[9] Also characteristically,

the reply quoted was signed not by the prime minister but by his private secretary.

The African movement, like its counterpart in India, made it scrupulously clear that it was not its aim to "turn the tables" on its oppressors:

The struggle which the national organizations of the non-European people are conducting is not directed against any race or national group, but against unjust laws which keep in perpetual subjection and misery vast sections of the population.[10]

On June 26 the defiance campaign was launched on a nationwide scale, except for Capetown and Natal, which required additional time for preparation. The chief brunt of the campaign was the ubiquitous motto "Europeans Only." Luthuli tells what was planned:

Railway stations, waiting rooms, post offices, public seats, train accommodations, all bear this legend. The volunteers were to abandon the "separate but unequal" facilities set aside for us, and to make challenging use of the alternative white facilities. In addition to this, the flouting of curfew and pass regulations was determined upon. . . . Whenever possible, the authorities were forewarned of the detailed intentions of each batch of volunteers—in some cases full lists of the names of the volunteers were politely handed in.[11]

Although the number of volunteers did not come up to the expectations raised by the size and fervor of the mass meetings, the campaign gathered momentum. The African and Indian congresses of Natal joined the struggle in July and by October, 2,354 resisters were in action. Their discipline, according to Luthuli, was excellent; so much so that the nonviolent volunteers on some occasions took charge of traffic control when the authorities were unable to maintain order. A continuing problem was the prevention of disorderly mob action by African bystanders who were not under the volunteers' discipline. Luthuli tells how he, as head of the Natal branch of the ANC, and Dr. G. M. Naicker, president of the Natal Indian Congress, dispersed a large, truculent crowd of sympathizers after he and

Dr. Naicker had been placed under arrest. The police were unable to do this themselves.

Many of the demonstrations out of which the volunteers came took the form of Christian prayer meetings, and at political gatherings, according to Kuper, "speakers stressed the affinity between nonviolent resistance and the ethic of Christianity" [12] while excoriating the white man's perversion of Christianity as an ideology to sanctify the oppression of the nonwhites. In some instances this went so far as an apparent rejection of Christianity. An African speaker, Moses Kotane, is quoted as saying: "These people are Christians but they eat people. . . . If they represent God then they represent a false God. And if God is like that, then God is no good for Africa." [13] Yet the same speaker used a biblical text as the setting for this remark. The gist of many such statements like this would seem to be simply: "Don't let the white man use Christianity to bamboozle you." No doubt some Africans rejected all outward forms of Christian faith, while clinging to an anonymous ethic derived from it; but many others held fast to a clearly articulated and professed Christian faith in terms of which they, like Kotane, judged the white man's piety as hypocrisy.

The Christian spirit was exemplified in the testimony of volunteers when arraigned in court for the breaking of *apartheid* laws. Following are excerpts from a written statement read to a magistrate in Bloemfontein by S. Mokoena, head of the Volunteer Corps in that city:

It is interesting to speculate, Your Worship, what the reaction of the European would be, were he . . . to discover himself an African just overnight and thus be subjected to the thousand and one irksome discriminatory laws that our people have borne for centuries with Christian-like fortitude. . . .

We do not quarrel with Your Worship when you say you have no alternative but to punish us for deliberately breaking the unjust laws; that is the unenviable duty you are bound to carry out. But, with due respect to Your Worship, we wish to state that punish-

ment, no matter how severe, can be no deterrent to us. We have undertaken this campaign fully expecting such punishment.[14]

Such statements as this were unheard by the white public, for the white newspapers published only terse, impersonal reports of the trials. Indeed, the communication of news through non-white channels was also so poor that it had to be supplemented with mimeographed news sheets and with public demonstrations outside the courts, which were then reported in the press. According to Kuper, for example, prayer demonstrations outside magistrates' courts in Uitenhage and East London were reported in *The Star* on July 23, and in August *Press Digest* reported a gathering of 5,000 praying Africans in Port Elizabeth, welcoming 250 volunteers on their release from prison there. When Dr. Moroka and other leaders went on trial in Johannesburg, *Press Digest* reported that there were white university students among the thousands of non-whites who sang defiance songs and demonstrated all day long at a nearby public square.

At the height of the defiance campaign, on October 18, a series of riots broke out in Port Elizabeth, Kimberley and East London, in which there were bloody clashes between African crowds and the police. The latter did not hesitate to fire into the crowds. A number of Africans and a few whites were killed and others injured. A motion-picture theater was set on fire; a Roman Catholic mission and an Anglican church, among other buildings, were destroyed; a white missionary nun was murdered and her body defiled. In all the disturbances no policemen were killed and few were injured. Both the ANC and the SAIC demanded an impartial commission of inquiry, but the government refused even to conduct routine public investigations. There was reason to believe that the riots were the work of agents provocateurs; the director of the South African Institute of Race Relations was told by Europeans in both Port Elizabeth and Kimberley that "strangers had come into the neighborhood previously to the riots."[15] In East London more

than half of the Africans arrested were juveniles: anti-social *tsotsis* not unlike the teen-age gang boys of American and European cities. By all accounts it is clear that the riots were unrelated to the defiance campaign and very likely were instigated by the government.

The Apartheid Strategy

Whether the government instigated these events or not, it quickly utilized them as a pretext to smear and to smash the defiance campaign. Luthuli sums up the implicit reasoning behind the government's move:

The Defiance Campaign was far too orderly and successful for the Government's liking, and it was growing. The prospect before the white supremacists, if they were going to react to our challenge in a civilized way, was that arrests would continue indefinitely. Behind the thousands already arrested there were more, many more. The challenge of nonviolence was more than they could meet. It robbed them of the initiative. On the other hand, violence by Africans would restore this initiative to them—they would then be able to bring out the guns and the other techniques of intimidation and present themselves as restorers of order.[16]

In a leaflet distributed early in November by the National Action Committee of the ANC and SAIC, the shootings were described as a deliberate attempt to weaken the defiance campaign, and nonwhites were warned not to listen to talk that would divide blacks, Coloreds and Indians among one another. And scarcely three weeks after the first riots, the ANC made so bold as to hold a one-day work stoppage in Port Elizabeth to protest the imposition of a curfew. The strike was estimated to have involved ninety-six per cent of the Africans in the town. Also at this point there was an increase of activity by white sympathizers of the defiance campaign. On December 8 a mixed group of thirty-eight men and women, white, black and Indian, were arrested in the Witwatersrand for entering a "native" location without permits. (The Indian group included

M.K. Gandhi's son Manilal, editor of *Indian Opinion*.) On the following day four white volunteers were arrested for occupying non-European booths at the General Post Office in Capetown, and a week later a white trade-union organizer was charged with the same offense in Johannesburg.

Despite these new steps, however, the campaign was in evident decline, slumping from its October peak of 2,354 volunteers in action to only 280 in November and December. Among the factors accounting for the decline were the jailing of the top leaders and a split in their ranks which occurred when Dr. Moroka broke discipline by choosing to be defended by his own lawyer (instead of jointly with the other nineteen codefendants in his case), and pleading mitigating circumstances instead of being prepared to accept the full penalty of the law. If the president-general of the African National Congress could stoop to currying favor with the whites in this fashion at such a moment, what was the rank-and-file volunteer to think? At the same time, the government issued a proclamation, soon bolstered by legislation in Parliament, which gave it far-reaching powers to suppress and punish any defiance. Under this combination of factors the campaign collapsed.

In December at the national conference of the ANC, Albert Luthuli was elected president-general. So far had the campaign ebbed by now that at a meeting near Johannesburg shortly afterward, when volunteers were called for, only one man responded, "and he was tipsy." The campaign was officially brought to an end on June 26, 1953, the anniversary of its launching, with a message in which Luthuli bade Africans and their allies to light bonfires or lanterns outside their homes "as a symbol of the spark of freedom which we are determined to keep alive in our hearts, and as a sign to freedom-lovers that we are keeping the vigil on that night." [17]

The conclusion of the defiance campaign did not mean merely a return to the status quo ante; it meant a new period of reaction and repression. Although sentences decreed by magistrates in court were seldom severe, prison guards went

out of their way to make life hard for convicted resisters, beating or humiliating them and depriving them of food on the slightest provocation. Clergymen were denied certain privileges, subsidies were withdrawn from schools employing teachers who aligned themselves with the freedom movement, students were refused readmission to school, workers were fired from their jobs, municipal officials canceled the right of black resisters to remain in their location. These and similar tactics were used, or threatened, by the whites.

Under the Riotous Assemblies Act, magistrates were authorized to prohibit specific public meetings in their district and the minister of justice was empowered to bar all public meetings within a specified area for a stated period of time and to prohibit specified individuals from attending public meetings of any kind when the latter were permitted. Additional powers were granted by the Suppression of Communism Act, which made it possible to proscribe organizations and to declare even private gatherings illegal.

Instead of using these powers to the full, however, the government chose to exercise comparative restraint to achieve the same ends, holding the more extreme provisions in reserve. In July 1952 ANC and SAIC and nonwhite trade-union offices were raided, as were the homes of officials of these organizations, and their records were seized—a disruptive tactic that was to be used again after the campaign ended. The planting of police spies in Congress ranks sowed suspicion and distrust. And resistance leaders were often given suspended sentences on condition that they did not commit another offense under the proscriptive acts.

Under the Criminal Law Amendment Act the government authorized flogging for political crimes and provided for confiscation and sale of a resister's property to pay fines levied by the courts. If a banned leader's speech was played on a recording, not only the listeners but the leader was liable to a penalty. Letters could be intercepted and inspected by the government on suspicion of illegality, thus eliminating the privacy

of the mails. Various laws contained overlapping provisions for prosecuting "incitement to civil disobedience."

Luthuli had hardly assumed office when he was banned from entering any of the large population centers of South Africa and forbidden to attend public meetings. Subsequently he was subjected to virtual house arrest, precluding travel outside his home district without express permission for a period of years.

Despite these intimidations and restrictions, however, there were local economic boycotts on a minor scale, as well as other sporadic acts of resistance, and plans were laid for a broad-based Congress of the People, embracing the ANC, the SAIC, the South African Congress of Trade Unions, the South African Colored People's Organization and the Congress of Democrats. The last of these was composed chiefly of whites with a belief in racial equality. The Congress of the People, comprising delegates from every South African ethnic group and from every quarter of the country, met for two days, June 25-26, 1955, at Kliptown, near Johannesburg. This meeting adopted a Freedom Charter which declared that "South Africa belongs to all who live in it, black and white" and that "our people have been robbed of their birthright to land, liberty and peace by a form of government founded on injustice and inequality." The charter set as its goal the establishment of "a democratic state, based on the will of all the people" to "secure to all their birthright without distinction of color, race, sex or belief." [18]

In his book *Inside Africa,* published in 1955, John Gunther concluded his chapter on South Africa with these words: "Is South Africa fascist? Not quite. Not yet." Without venturing a more decisive answer, we may observe that worse was to come. On December 5, 1956, not long after the expiration of his two-year ban, Albert Luthuli was arrested on a charge of high treason, along with 155 other leaders of the freedom movement. Many of them were noted African Christians such as Z. K. Matthews, who lectured at Union Theological Seminary in New York as Visiting Professor of World Christianity

in 1952-1953, as well as a number of Anglican priests and ministers and laymen of the Congregational, Methodist and other churches. Also imprisoned were Dr. G. M. Naicker, president of the Natal Indian Congress, and many other Hindus, Muslims and, of course, persons of no religious affiliation, including Communists.

This is not the place for a detailed account of the celebrated treason trials. After being held in prison for a brief period, Luthuli, Matthews, Naicker and the others were released on bail while the tedious processes of the trials went on, consuming time, money and organizational activity for five years. Much of the money needed to meet the expenses of the trials was raised by the Defense and Aid Fund of Christian Action in London and by the Africa Defense and Aid Fund of the American Committee on Africa in New York, which also placed many distinguished Britons and Americans on public record against the policies of the South African government. Distinguished attorneys placed their services at the disposal of the defendants and such men as Alan Paton, Arthur W. Blaxall and Ambrose Reeves, Anglican Bishop of Johannesburg, publicly stated their opposition to the government's position.

Boycott and the Peaceful "Riot"

What is of more interest, however, is the fact of continuing protest actions by Africans on a local scale during this period, despite the government's success in virtually hamstringing the national resistance organizations. Perhaps the most noteworthy campaign was a bus boycott by Africans in the Alexandra district of Johannesburg, which began on January 7, 1957, in protest against a rise in fares. Significantly, it was not an action against *apartheid* nor was it directed against the government, but againt a privately owned transit company. Nevertheless, mass organized protest action by blacks against a white-owned public facility could not but pose an implied threat to *apartheid* institutions, as government reaction clearly indicated.

Beginning in Alexandra, where Dan Mokonyane organized the People's Transport Action Committee, and spreading to half a dozen other townships, the movement involved some 60,000 Africans who chose to walk rather than pay the higher fares. Some of them walked as much as eighteen miles a day in addition to putting in their hard day's work. According to an American observer, "hundreds of motorists gave daily lifts to weary boycotters; for many Johannesburg whites it was their first human contact with Africans, outside of the master-servant relation." [19]

Although the English-language press viewed the boycott sympathetically, the Minister of Transport, Ben Shoeman, charged on January 16: "The boycott has political motives. It is a trial of strength by the African National Congress. If they want a showdown, they will get it." [20]

The police were given orders to crush the boycott and began a "blitz" against the lift-giving motorists. Cars were stopped and searched and the drivers' names taken down, and as a result many were intimidated into "minding their own business."

Even more harassed, however, were the walkers. One day over a hundred were arrested for crossing an intersection against the light. Some Africans rode bicycles; police deflated their tires and confiscated the valves. African hostels in Johannesburg were raided night after night to catch Africans bunking with friends (without official permission to stay the night) in order to spare themselves two stretches of the grueling hike. In all, during the boycott, there were 14,000 arrests, most of them for violations of the pass laws.

The boycott lasted twelve weeks and was suspended when the Chamber of Commerce negotiated a working compromise, pending an investigation, with the Joint Boycott Committee that had by then been set up with Alfred Nzo as secretary. A final settlement was reached when Shoeman introduced a bill in Parliament doubling the levy on employers to subsidize African transport and thus holding the fares at their previous rate.

The victory for the Africans was implicitly political as well as economic, inasmuch as the government's resort to police measures had given the campaign a political character. Walter Sisulu, a banned ANC leader, said as much afterward: "The bus boycott has raised the political consciousness of the people and has brought about a great solidarity and unity among them." [21] Soon afterward, the ANC launched a wide economic boycott of Nationalist-controlled firms and their products. For a time this tactic enjoyed a certain degree of success and was joined by sympathizers in Great Britain and elsewhere. Efforts to develop economic pressure, internally or on the world market, were not sufficient, however, to cause the government of South Africa to alter its policies. One of the difficulties inherent in a wide-scale boycott, as Luthuli pointed out, is that "it is not easy to avoid injury to the wrong man's pocket, and we have never been callously indiscriminate in our attitudes." [22]

One segment of the long-term, wide-range boycott was a three-month boycott against potatoes grown by convict labor in Eastern Transvaal and elsewhere. Originally conceived as a one-month protest, this gesture struck a responsive chord in the African community. Although it meant hardship for the consumer, since potatoes were the staple of the impoverished Africans' diet, it also meant a vivid rebuke to the whole pass-law system: it was through infractions of the pass laws that labor was obtained for the farm jails where a sizable proportion of the potato crop was grown. At the same time, the act of self-denial served as a gesture of solidarity with the convicts themselves, who had to dig the potatoes with bare fingers, under the lash of an overseer, in bestial conditions of temporary slavery. The "potato boycott" was successful in that it glutted the market with unsold potatoes; and despite the combined efforts of government, merchants and farmers to break it, it held fast until officially called off by Luthuli. It was also successful in that it contributed to the morale of the Africans, giving them a sense of their own moral power. But it did not

bring amelioration in the conditions on the farms, nor did it weaken the pass system.

Indeed the pass system, long applied to African men, was extended to women in 1956. This action brought about a massive demonstration in which black women from every corner of the country took part. Some of them had to travel as far as a thousand miles to reach the capital city, Pretoria, where the demonstration was held. Numbers of white women, organized in the Black Sash Movement, demonstrated in sympathy with their black sisters. In 1957 there were demonstrations in rural areas on this same issue. A South African attorney describes the "riot" in Lichtenburg: "At a meeting there was a disturbance as a result whereof the police fired at the people and killed a number of residents. A number of people were arrested and charged with public violence. They were all acquitted . . . and the magistrate blamed the police publicly for what had transpired." [23] There were subsequent disturbances in Nelspruit and Zeerust, where women either refused to take out pass books or burned them if they already had them, and there were police shootings and arrests.

In 1958 the demonstrations by women reached a high pitch, beyond the organizational powers of the Congress Women's League to control them. This led to mass action in Johannesburg that resulted in more than 2,000 arrests.

In Natal in 1959 a deputation of women from the township of Cato Manor slept in an open field for two nights and planted themselves on the city hall steps in Durban in order to gain an interview with the mayor to protest against injustices in housing. The mayor, says Luthuli, "did try to do something, but it was too little and too late." [24] As demonstrations spread, there were outbreaks of violence, notably the destruction of municipal beer halls and the burning of Bantu Education Schools. The pattern was apparently not unlike that which the government used to dampen the defiance campaign of 1950: destructive acts committed by hooligans or agents provocateurs followed by police brutality directed against the freedom move-

ment or even against innocent bystanders. In Pietermaritzburg, bystanders, including elderly Hindu women, were beaten by police who launched a baton charge against a picket line of African women from the countryside. In nearby Sobantu Village, where schools were burned, the police wantonly shot and killed two African men who had been nowhere near the burning schools. In Camperdown, another rural area near Pietermaritzburg, a group of African women marched with white flags to present their demands to the native commissioner. The police confronted them, ordered them to disperse and then, before waiting for them to obey the order, charged with clubs flying. In another area, Ixopo, when the order to disperse was given, the women fell to their knees and began to pray. The police did not know what to do.

The aftermath of the Cato Manor disturbances was to become an ominous prelude to tragedy. Early in 1960 the police were conducting pass raids at least three times a week there. This fact, coupled with the forced removal of residents to a new "native location" in which they were deprived of certain rights that they had formerly enjoyed, made for a tense situation. Then a trivial incident triggered mob violence that took the lives of nine policemen on a routine raid.

The Pan-African Congress and the Sharpeville Massacre

Throughout its history the African National Congress looked to a multiracial solution within South Africa. Inasmuch as its philosophy has been articulated by Christians such as Luthuli, Matthews and others, it has stressed reconciliation and nonviolence. "As long as our patience can be made to hold out," wrote Luthuli, "we shall not jeopardize the South Africa of tomorrow by precipitating violence today." [25] For some time, however, dating back to the defiance campaign of 1950, there had been developing a so-called "Africanist" wing within the ANC. This faction increasingly identified itself with the ongoing struggle of black Africans throughout the continent

against white colonial rule. In a word, the "Africanists" tended to see themselves as a South African part of a continentwide movement which elsewhere was establishing new independent states. This definition necessarily skimps the complexities of the situation. But broadly speaking it was this emphasis which culminated in the formation of the Pan-African Congress in 1958, under the leadership of thirty-three-year-old Robert Mangaliso Sobukwe.

At a time when the ANC had already begun preparations for a new campaign against the pass laws, Sobukwe seized the initiative and on March 21, 1960, launched a campaign in the name of the Pan-African Congress. The year 1963 was specified as the date by which South Africa was to be free—that is, under black rule. Rejecting cooperation with Indian and other groups, the PAC's manifesto nevertheless called for "absolute nonviolence" and proclaimed as its mission the leading of "the vital, breathing and dynamic youth of our land . . . not to death, but to the life abundant." [26] At the time of its writing, Sobukwe claimed a membership of 30,000, and entire branches of the ANC were said to be seceding to the new movement.

Charging Luthuli with overcautiousness and with being too much under "white influence," Sobukwe said: "We will send our leaders to jail first. That is where our leaders belong—in front." [27] True to his word, on the appointed day Sobukwe led a group of sixty nonviolent resisters to the police station in Orlando township and demanded to be arrested for violating the pass laws. They were. Simultaneously, in Langa and Nyanga locations near Capetown, crowds numbering thousands demanded arrest. "At Langa, Philip Kgosana turned back 30,-000 demonstrators and thus avoided bloodshed, and at Nyanga the whole demonstration degenerated into prolonged riot and arson," wrote Luthuli.[28] Kgosana was a twenty-one-year-old Pan-Africanist, one of the last black students admitted to the University of Capetown before the encroachment of *apartheid* there. This courageous youth was the leader of the procession. Here is his own account of what happened in Langa:

The senior officer in charge of the police refused to arrest me. He wanted to know who would control the demonstrators while I was in jail. I told him that our demonstration was opposed to any form of violence. The police then wanted to know what our plans were. I told them we were marching to the police station where we wanted to be locked up for being without our passes. The senior officer told me that if we went anywhere near the police station he would defend the station to the last bullet and to the last drop of blood.

As I am against violence, I asked my people to disperse. I told the officer I would withhold my labor and I asked him to withhold his bullets. I then picketed the police station, and kept the demonstrators away from the police station.[29]

A police captain later testified that he heard Kgosana say repeatedly to the crowd: "I will not allow the police to be attacked. I will protect them with my life." [30]

Simultaneously in Sharpeville, thirty miles from Johannesburg, on the morning of March 21 a crowd of some 7,000 Africans (nearly half the location's population) massed at the gate as part of the Pan-Africanist nonviolent demonstration. Police were on the scene and tried to disperse the crowd with tear-gas bombs. The orderly, disciplined crowd fell back thirty paces but did not disperse. Armored cars were brought up and military aircraft were used in an attempt to intimidate them.

After several hours of this, a few Africans broke discipline and began to throw stones at the police. Without a word of warning and without firing a warning shot, the police opened fire on the crowd. According to an official report, 476 bullets were fired. Sixty-seven African men, women and children were killed and many others wounded.[31]

Later that day in Langa wild disorder broke out. Police killed three people and that night mobs set fire to schools, churches, a library and administration buildings, all symbolic of white rule. Thousands from both Langa and Nyanga stayed home from work on March 22 and those who did not were approached by Pan-Africanists who told them to quit. According to Norman Phillips of the *Toronto Star,* "Irresponsible

elements joined in, uninvited, and one gang known as 'The Spoilers' was reported in Capetown intimidating Africans still at work." [32]

On March 24 the police invaded Langa and tried to force Africans to go to work, but by noon Capetown was virtually deserted by its black work force. On March 25 Kgosana led a procession of 1,500 pass-less men from Langa to the police station in Capetown and demanded their arrest. The police chief turned them away and they went home in orderly fashion.

On March 30 the government of South Africa decreed a state of emergency, authorizing arrests without warrant or charge. Philip Kgosana hurriedly assembled a protest march of thirty thousand Africans from Langa and Nyanga, and led them, thirty abreast, through the streets of Capetown. As they entered the city, Kgosana halted the crowd and said, "I appeal to you for nonviolence. We must avoid bloodshed at all costs." [33] Then he led the crowd to the police station, demanded the release of the arrested Pan-African leaders and voiced a protest against the police molestations of March 24. He secured a promise from the city's police chief that a small deputation led by Kgosana would be given an opportunity to present their grievances to the minister of justice. Thereupon Kgosana dispersed the marchers—this while truckloads of armed police rolled along the streets and armored cars formed a cordon around Parliament.

That night, under cover of darkness, thousands of troops were sent out to Langa and Nyanga, forming a cordon of steel around the two locations. Kgosana was called in for the promised meeting but was arrested under the Emergency Regulations.

The Africans continued their strike. On April 4 the government unleashed a reign of terror. White bystanders jammed the switchboards of the Capetown newspapers, trying to tell of widespread unprovoked attacks by police on Africans. Clergymen, university professors and others were slapped or beaten with whips. C. F. Regnier, president of the Cape Cham-

ber of Industries, was so disturbed that he went to the chief of police, Colonel I. P. S. Terblanche, and pleaded with him to stop the assaults.

But the situation was even worse in Nyanga. This is Norman Phillips' account:

At 11 A.M. police squads were turned loose inside the location with orders to whip every male African they encountered. They broke into houses to flog men in their beds. Terrified, screaming wives and children watched their husbands being dragged out into the streets.

Whips and batons ruled Nyanga. The hospital clinic was closed down, leaving only one doctor to minister to the wounded. . . . As further punishment, water supplies to the surrounding locations were cut off. . . .

Four Africans were wounded on Monday. At least five, including a seven-year-old child, were injured by police bullets on Tuesday. Fourteen Anglican clergymen appealed to the Government to restrain its use of force. . . .

For sheer sadism, the closest comparison to what happened at Nyanga was when the Gestapo sealed off the Warsaw ghetto and began to annihilate it. Had Nyanga fought back, it too would have been wiped out; but the Africans employed non-aggressive tactics that puzzled the police.[34]

After four days of this the police climaxed their reign of terror by taking 1,525 of Nyanga's people to a police station for screening. Of these they detained 162.

The response of Albert Luthuli and the African National Congress to the Sharpeville massacre was a call for a national day of mourning on March 28, when all people were urged to stay at home and pray. Many Pan-Africanists were among those who honored this appeal. Two days earlier, Luthuli publicly burned his pass and called upon other Africans to do likewise. It was ostensibly in response to this action that the government proclaimed an emergency empowering magistrates and commissioned officers to prohibit public meetings and processions. Under the Emergency Regulations some 1,900

people of all races were arrested without charges or trial and held for three or four months, including two attorneys engaged by the Anglican Bishop of Johannesburg, Ambrose Reeves, to prepare evidence for the Sharpeville Commission of Inquiry. An additional 20,000 Africans were detained on charges of vagrancy. Luthuli was arrested in the home of some white friends, who were also taken into custody, as were a number of Anglican priests. Like many of his countrymen, Luthuli was slapped and reviled by white jailers. After five months in prison he was banned to his home for five years—with a brief suspension in 1961 to permit him to go to Sweden to receive the Nobel Peace Prize for his steadfast adherence to Christian nonviolence.

The Defeat of the Nonviolent Movement

The state of emergency was lifted at the time of Luthuli's release from prison in August 1960, but worse developments were in store. As for the nonviolent movement, its back was broken by Sharpeville and its aftermath. Many of the thousands arrested emerged from the jails convinced that the nonviolent methods of ANC were leading nowhere. A decade of struggle thus ended with heightened tensions and a grim outlook for the future.

It would be easy to say (and it has been said often) that the nonviolent movement was defeated by sheer force and violence. To some extent this is true, but it is nevertheless strange that such a movement, representing seventy-seven per cent of the country's population, could be utterly crushed in a decade. A candid assessment cannot absolve the ANC itself of a share of blame for its defeat.

Although it became a mass organization on the eve of the defiance campaign, the ANC's membership never totaled more than 100,000 by its own estimates—one per cent of the black population. Of this number, only 8,000 volunteers engaged in direct action. And even with this broadening of the member-

ship base, its policies continued to be made by a leadership that had originally constituted itself more as a body speaking to the white power structure than as one arising from the masses.

Add to this a weak and cumbersome organizational structure, based on local branches varying in size from a handful to 15,000 members, virtual absence of any full-time professional staff, and insufficient finances for normal travel, publications and other expenses, and we begin to marvel that the ANC was able to make the impact it did. The simple lack of membership rolls and bookkeeping explains more than the economic poverty of the members (whose dues were less than forty cents a year), since the Congress had no way of knowing who had paid.

Congruent with this pattern was the ANC's general lack of strategy. Edward Feit, in his acute study for the London Institute of Race Relations, has stated it well:

Greater willingness to participate, even to accept losses of wages, might have been developed, had the objects of each campaign been presented simply to African workers and had they been convinced that these objects could be attained. This was not possible, for the leaders themselves were not sure of where they were leading. They knew their destination, but not how to get there. Unanimity existed in the knowledge of the most distant goal . . . but attainable short-term aims were lacking.[35]

The rest is epilogue, consisting mainly of new government repressions countered by sporadic violence from extremists and valiant but ineffectual verbal gestures from ANC leaders. The first outburst was a well-organized regional rebellion in Pondoland in December 1960. In April 1961 Nelson Mandela became the first ANC leader to go underground, and from somewhere in hiding he organized and led a partly successful stay-at-home strike to coincide with the proclamation of the Republic of South Africa in May. It was "partly successful" in that it happened at all, but it had no effect on the government. In December a secret organization, Umkonto We Sizwe—"Spear of the Nation"—derailed trains and set off bomb explosions in

what it described in a leaflet as the beginning of full-scale sabotage, asserting that the patience of black Africans was coming to an end.

The promise of sabotage was not fulfilled, but the government used it as a pretext for the passage of the Sabotage Act in June 1962. This law provided severe punishments, including death, for any form of public protest. Under its drastic provisions even newspapers were prohibited from publishing anything said by any man who had been banned from attending public meetings. A month before it became law, Patrick Baron, Dean of Johannesburg Cathedral, asserted that it would be the duty of every true Christian to disobey it. Black Sash women who demonstrated against it on May 23 were assaulted by Nationalist youths.

With passage of the Sabotage Act, both ANC and Pan-African Congress were outlawed. Hundreds of members of the latter formed themselves into a terrorist organization called Poqo—"We Stand Alone"—which on November 29, 1962, raided the police station in Paarl, near Capetown, killing two white people. Five of the raiders were shot and 346 suspects were arrested. Later raids in the Transkei took a further toll of dead and injured, including both whites and blacks hacked to death. According to testimony before a Commission of Inquiry, one informer was beheaded in his sleep. Other victims were soaked with gasoline and set on fire.

In August 1962 Nelson Mandela and Walter Sisulu, former ANC general secretary, were arrested. Tried under the Sabotage Act, Mandela was sentenced on November 7 to five years in prison. Of those arrested in the Paarl raid, three were executed and 62 others were given prison terms ranging from twelve to twenty-five years. Hundreds of other Poqo suspects were arrested for terrorist activities elsewhere (350 in the Transkei alone), and these were not the only ones nor the last ones. Those arrested ranged from Arthur W. Blaxall, a white minister and former secretary of the Christian Council of South

Africa, to teams of saboteurs intercepted on their return from training abroad.

Despite all efforts, including a United Nations resolution of November 6, 1962, to boycott South Africa, white racism continued to hold its ground. Nelson Mandela, before his arrest, voiced a question that was in the minds of many when he addressed a Pan-African conference in Addis Ababa in February 1962: "Can a government bent on using the utmost force to crush the freedom struggle be forever countered by peaceful and nonviolent means?" The answer given by nearly half of a group of middle-class black Africans sixteen months later, in an opinion poll published by the South African Institute of Race Relations, was an unequivocal "No!" They looked to the banned Pan-African Congress rather than to the ANC for a solution of the problem through the overthrow of the government.

Undisclosed numbers of ANC supporters had long been organized into small underground cells as outlined in what is known as the "M Plan" developed by Mandela during the defiance campaign of 1952. Whether they or the avowedly terrorist organizations would one day act to unseat the rule of white supremacy, no one could say. Possibly aided by the newly independent African nations, almost certainly with armed force, it seemed inevitable to everyone that a major and bloody upheaval lay ahead, though some continued to hope for a miracle. It was clear that nonviolence had tragically failed, and if it had any further part to play on the South African scene it would be only as a tactical prelude to a violent holocaust.

REFERENCES IN CHAPTER 18

1   Albert Luthuli: *Let My People Go* (New York: McGraw-Hill Book Co., 1962), p. 91.
2   *Ibid.*, p. 92.

3   *Ibid.*, p. 93.
4   *Ibid.*, p. 109.
5   Leo Kuper: *Passive Resistance in South Africa* (New Haven: Yale University Press, 1957), p. 101.
6   Full text appears as Appendix C in *ibid., q.v.*, p. 251.
7   *Ibid.*, p. 253f.
8   *Ibid.*, p. 102.
9   Full text appears as Appendix B in *ibid.*, p. 238.
10 Quoted in Luthuli, *op. cit.*, p. 116.
11 Luthuli, *op. cit.*, p. 117.
12 Kuper, *op. cit.*, p. 117.
13 Quoted in *ibid.*
14 Quoted in *ibid.*, pp. 130-131.
15 Quoted in *ibid.*, p. 138.
16 Luthuli, *op. cit.*, p. 127.
17 Quoted in Kuper, p. 145.
18 For full text see Appendix B in Luthuli, *op. cit.*, pp. 239-243.
19 Mary-Louise Hooper: "The Johannesburg Bus Boycott" in *Africa Today* (New York), November-December 1957, p. 14.
20 Quoted in *ibid.*
21 Quoted in *ibid.*, p. 16.
22 Luthuli, *op. cit.*, p. 217.
23 *Christian Action Newsletter* (London), Summer 1961, p. 13.
24 Luthuli, *op. cit.*, p. 217.
25 *Ibid.*, p. 219f.
26 Quoted in Norman Phillips: *The Tragedy of Apartheid* (New York: David McKay Co., Inc., 1960), p. 60.
27 *Ibid.*, p. 61.
28 Luthuli, *op. cit.*, p. 222.
29 Quoted in Phillips, *op. cit.*, p. 163.
30 *Ibid.*
31 For a full account, see Ambrose Reeves: *The Shooting at Sharpeville* (Boston: Houghton Mifflin Co., 1961).
32 Phillips, *op. cit.*, p. 164.
33 Quoted in *ibid.*, p. 165.
34 *Ibid.*, p. 171f.
35 Edward Feit: *South Africa: The Dynamics of the African National Congress* (London: Oxford, 1962), p. 65. Feit's study amply documents the above critique of Congress' shortcomings.

19

Ghana: The Positive Action Campaign of 1950

During the same period when nonwhites in South Africa were embarking upon their defiance campaign, the first in a series of many painful struggles, black Africans in the British crown colony of the Gold Coast were on the eve of a lightning-swift campaign that resulted in complete independence within a very short time.

The Gold Coast on the eve of its independence was strikingly different from South Africa in certain ways. A small, compact country with a population of 4,500,000, all but 0.2 per cent of its people were indigenous black Africans, fifteen to twenty-five per cent literate and thirty per cent Christian. Most of the latter were concentrated in the coastal areas which were also occupied by no more than four thousand British settlers with no appreciable property such as that of the white South Africans. Here the social issues were not complex, if indeed they could be said to exist at all. The struggle for independence turned almost entirely on the question of political administration: how soon and in what manner would the government of the colony be transferred from the hands of the British Colonial Office to those of the Africans themselves? To state the issue so simply is not to suggest that the Africans' own efforts to achieve self-government did no more than to hasten an inevitable eventuality. Without these efforts the British might have procrastinated for decades. The point, rather, is that once this clearly seen goal was realized there were no other considerations that were likely to upset it.

The story of the Gold Coast's road to independence is very largely the story of Kwame Nkrumah and the Convention People's Party. Born in 1909 in a small village, the son of a goldsmith, he received his early education at Roman Catholic mission schools. At the age of twenty-six he came to the United States, where he worked his way through Lincoln University, earning degrees in theology and science as well as a B.A. and M.A. A classmate there described him as a man of set purpose, "sober, reserved and conscientious, as well as brilliant." [1] After serving briefly as an instructor at Lincoln—and experiencing American-style racial discrimination—he went to London, where he lived for a number of years and studied at the London School of Economics.

During Nkrumah's stay in England, a Pan-African Congress (not to be confused with the South African body) was held in Manchester in October 1945, and the thirty-six-year-old graduate student attended and helped to formulate its strategy and tactics. "The delegates," writes George Padmore, "endorsed the doctrine of Pan-African socialism based upon the Gandhian tactics of nonviolent noncooperation." [2] From England Nkrumah kept in close contact with developments in the Gold Coast until two years later, when J. B. Danquah, president of the United Gold Coast Convention, invited him to become secretary of this, the colony's chief political organization.

Nkrumah Assumes Leadership

Nkrumah arrived on December 16, 1947, and set to work immediately. Hardly had his work begun, however, when a national crisis occurred. On February 28, 1948, a peaceful demonstration of unarmed African ex-servicemen set out on a march from Accra to the suburban residence of the British governor to present him with a petition of grievances. Ordered by police to halt, they refused and the police opened fire, killing two and wounding five of the Africans. When news of the incident spread, rioting broke out in several towns and lasted

for days, with twenty-nine deaths and 237 other casualties before it was over.

Prior to the riots there had been a month-long boycott of shopkeepers, which in fact had been terminated on the very day the riots broke out. Neither of these events was the work of the UGCC, which had been engaged in agitation for constitutional reform. Nkrumah, however, had the presence of mind to turn the crisis to the account of the movement. On February 29 in the midst of the rioting he cabled to the Colonial Office in London: "People demand self-government immediately. Send commission supervise formation constituent assembly. Urgent." [3] He also took time to send copies of the cable to *The New York Times,* the Associated Negro Press (a Chicago syndicate serving many Negro newspapers), the Moscow weekly *Novoe Vremya* (which was also published in English, German, French and other editions for world distribution) and eight or nine other key publicity media throughout the world.

To curb the riots the governor assumed emergency powers and on March 13 exiled Danquah, Nkrumah and other UGCC leaders. Nkrumah was sent off to a remote village in the north of the colony, without trial or formal accusation. As a result of an investigation of the underlying causes of the disturbances, however, the governor set up an all-African committee of forty tribal chiefs, conservative politicians and others to draft a new constitution. This body, the so-called Coussey Commission, issued a report which was adopted with some modifications by the Colonial Office as a basis for gradual, guided self-government and for the first general election in Gold Coast history.

Dissatisfied with this solution, Nkrumah, who had meanwhile been released from exile, pressed for a more radical alternative. He precipitated a split within the UGCC, out of which emerged the Convention People's Party on June 12, 1949, with Nkrumah at its head—just eighteen months after his arrival from England. In August, Nkrumah and a team

of nine co-workers embarked on a countrywide tour to present the CPP's program to the people.

They gained wide support quickly and on November 20, 1949, a month after the Coussey Report was issued, the CPP called a constituent assembly such as Nkrumah had earlier demanded of the Colonial Office. The assembly was attended by more than 80,000 representatives of over fifty groups, including cooperatives, labor unions, farm groups, educational, cultural, women's and youth organizations. This body rejected the Coussey Report, specifically its provisions for British cabinet ministers in the key posts of justice, finance, external affairs and defense; its designation of the voting age at twenty-five; and its provision for a number of appointive seats in the legislature in addition to the elective ones. Taking a leaf from India's recent history, the assembly demanded that "the people of the Gold Coast be granted immediate self-government, that is, dominion status," and drew up a memorandum outlining the structure of government, both central and local, which they wanted embodied in the new constitution. Nkrumah also asked for a round-table conference with the British officials, but they remained committed to the Coussey Report and refused to meet with him or with other CPP leaders, or otherwise to recognize the assembly.

Nkrumah gave the British a little more than three weeks to respond and when they did not, says Padmore,

After repeated requests for a round-table conference with British officials, Dr. Nkrumah . . . informed the Governor on December 15, 1949 . . . that the CPP would embark upon a campaign of "Positive Action," based upon Gandhi's philosophy of nonviolent noncooperation, and would continue with it until such time as the British Government conceded the right of the Gold Coast people to convene their Constituent Assembly.[4]

On the same date, in a front-page editorial in the CPP newspaper, the *Accra Evening News*, Nkrumah instructed the nation to prepare. "Remember," he stressed, "the strike is on the basis of perfect nonviolence. There shall be no looting or burn-

ing of houses or rioting or damage or disturbances of any sort. Nonviolence is our creed." [5]

It had not always been Nkrumah's creed, nor was it ever to become a matter of absolute religious conviction for him. In his autobiography Nkrumah indicates how widely eclectic his outlook was. Coming from a Roman Catholic background, as an adult he described himself as a "nondenominational Christian" and a Marxist, while admitting to such widely divergent influences as those of Lenin, Hitler and Gandhi, to mention only a few. Always alert to currents within the struggle for independence throughout the colonial world, Nkrumah was particularly attentive to the developments in India. The final phase of the Indian struggle coincided almost exactly with Nkrumah's own active entry into political life. By all available accounts nonviolence had won a tremendous victory in India at the very time he was taking the helm of the UGCC, and he could well discount the impact of the Hindu-Muslim massacres, since there was no analogous problem in his own country. In his autobiography Nkrumah discloses his thinking on the matter:

At first I could not understand how Gandhi's philosophy of nonviolence could possibly be effective. It seemed to me to be utterly feeble and without hope of success. The solution of the colonial problem, as I saw it at that time, lay in armed rebellion. How is it possible, I asked myself, for a revolution to succeed without arms and ammunition? After months of studying Gandhi's policy and watching the effect it had, I began to see that, when backed by a strong political organization, it could be the solution to the colonial problem. In Jawaharlal Nehru's rise to power I recognized the success of one who, pledged to Socialism, was able to interpret Gandhi's philosophy in practical terms.[6]

We see here no sense of saintly or utopian purpose, no philosophy of redemptive suffering, but a strongly pragmatic evaluation in which the pivotal terms are "effective," "practical," "success"—in the clearly down-to-earth usage of the trained political scientist. Nkrumah made it clear that his con-

ception of nonviolence was entirely expedient and did not imply the abandonment of armed force once the leaders of a nonviolent insurrection obtained a monopoly of such force by taking control of the government. Speaking from the vantage point of experience, he distinguishes two stages in the independence struggle:

First there is the period of "positive action"—a combination of nonviolent methods with effective and disciplined political action. At this stage open conflict with the existing colonial regime is inevitable and this is a test of strength for the organization. Since it is marked by nonviolence and since the forces of might are on the side of the colonial power, there is little chance of complete success in this period.

The second stage is one of "tactical action," a sort of contest of wits.[7]

Already CPP organizers had gone out from the assembly to prepare the people throughout the country for the first stage of civil resistance or "positive action," and now the stage was set for a showdown. The government had earlier tried cracking down on critics of its policies, as if to test the strength of the resistance movement. Three CPP journalists and the secretary of the Ex-Servicemen's Union were imprisoned on charges of sedition and as a result of articles he published Nkrumah was fined £300 for contempt of court. The sum was quickly raised by CPP volunteer women who collected the money in small change from thousands of passersby in the streets. The latter event boosted the morale of the CPP workers and contributed to the massive turnout for the assembly in November.

Now the government apparently yielded. Hoping to forestall the threatened positive action campaign, government officials agreed to a conference with CPP leaders, which began on January 5, 1950. At the meeting, the British told Nkrumah that they were studying his proposals and asked him to postpone positive action. They then announced on the radio that an agreement had been reached. Nkrumah broke off the negotiations when he learned of this and on the same day, January

8, at 5:00 P.M., he called a mass meeting at the West End Arena. "There I declared to the people," he afterward wrote, "that . . . a general strike should begin from midnight. The response of the people was spontaneous. The political and social revolution of Ghana had started." [8] The timing of this sequence of events is sufficient to suggest the efficiency and popular strength of a political organization geared to move into action on so wide a scale on such short notice.

Nkrumah's speech on that occasion reveals a good deal about the personality of the man as well as the dynamics of the movement he led, and is particularly valuable for its immediacy, unadorned by the benefits of hindsight. Here is the working definition of Nkrumah's method as given in verbatim extracts from the speech of January 8:

The term Positive Action has been erroneously and maliciously publicized, no doubt by the imperialists and their concealed agents-provocateurs and stooges. These political renegades, enemies of the Convention People's Party and for that matter of Ghana's freedom, have diabolically publicized that the CPP's program of positive action means riot, looting and disturbances, in a word, violence.

There are two ways to achieve self-government: either by armed revolution and violent overthrow of the existing regime, or by constitutional and legitimate nonviolent methods. In other words: either by armed might or by moral pressure. . . . We believe that we can achieve self-government even now by constitutional means without resort to any violence.

By Positive Action we mean the adoption of all legitimate and constitutional means by which we can cripple the forces of Imperialism in this country. The weapons of Positive Action are: (1) Legitimate political agitation; (2) Newspaper and educational campaigns; and (3) as a last resort, the constitutional application of strikes, boycotts and noncooperation based on the principle of absolute nonviolence.

But as regards the final stage of positive action, namely, nationwide nonviolent sit-down-at-home strikes, boycotts and noncooperation, we shall not call them into play until all the avenues of

our political endeavors of attaining self-government have been closed.[9]

Immediately after the speech, Nkrumah rushed to other key cities—Cape Coast, Sekondi and Tarkwa—formally declaring the onset of positive action in each of them, while CPP organizers spread the word to other areas.

The next morning, from 7:00 A.M., the effectiveness of the strike was greatly in evidence. As Richard Wright describes it,

not a train ran; no one went to work; buses and transportation trucks stood still. The nationalist leaders agreed to the functioning of essential services: water, electricity, health, medical care, etc. For twenty-one days, despite threats of dismissal of workers from jobs, numerous warnings and curfews, and the full evocation of the emergency powers of the Governor, positive action continued.[10]

The Battle of Communications

Although the campaign immediately took hold and held fast, it threatened to falter on the second day as a result of radio broadcasts by the government. Seeking to create division among the strikers, local radio announcers in each section of the country were telling their listeners that people in the other sections had already gone back to work. This bit of psychological warfare might have caused people in Accra, for example, to go back to work, thinking that it was pointless to hold out since the campaign had collapsed everywhere else. And by causing people in Sekondi, Kumasi and Saltpond to act likewise, the fictitious collapse could be made real.

Seeing this, Nkrumah called another mass meeting at the Arena on January 11, where he spoke for two hours to a huge crowd. "At the end of it," Nkrumah reports, "no Government propaganda machine could have succeeded in pacifying them or controlling them. Their blood was fired and they wanted justice." [11]

At 7:00 P.M. on the same day, the governor proclaimed a state of emergency and imposed a curfew. The nonviolent

battle was joined. Nkrumah adds details to the picture already given above:

The whole economic life of the country was at a standstill. Public meetings were forbidden and all party letters were opened and censored. The *Evening News,* the Cape Coast *Daily Mail* and the Sekondi *Morning Telegraph* fanned the flame by exhorting the workers to stand firm and to continue Positive Action. Then the office of the *Evening News* was raided and closed down by the police and the newspaper was banned. The same was the fate of my other two newspapers.[12]

The editors of the newspapers were jailed, as were a score of key CPP leaders, including Nkrumah. There was incidental brutality by the British, who for example took Nkrumah's personal servant and some companions to the police station and beat them, but on the whole they acted with restraint matching that of the Africans. Only one serious incident marred the campaign—an outburst on January 17, at the height of the campaign, when ex-servicemen staged a march to Christiansborg. There was a violent clash in which two policemen were killed. Nkrumah did not halt the campaign on this account and at his trial he disclaimed responsibility for this unauthorized occurrence.

When arrested, Nkrumah offered no resistance and none was made on his behalf. Anticipating this event, he had made it clear to his followers throughout the country that "it was important that they should keep calm and make no demonstration of any kind." [13]

Nkrumah and his colleagues were tried and convicted for "inciting others to take part in an illegal strike," and received prison sentences ranging from six months to two years.

Positive action was over now, but the solidarity it had demonstrated was now channeled to electoral activity within the framework of the elections promised in the Coussey Report. When elections for the town councils took place in Accra, Cape Coast and Kumasi, the condemned CPP won majorities in all three cities. In April 1950 Kimla Agbeli Gbedemah, one

of the jailed CPP leaders, was released from prison. Taking charge of the party as acting chairman, he proceeded to organize it for the forthcoming general elections, receiving directives smuggled out of prison from the other leaders. When the elections were held on February 8, 1951, less than a year after the positive action campaign, the CPP swept the country, winning thirty-five out of thirty-eight seats.

The British, seeing how things stood, were gracious enough to release the CPP leaders who had remained in prison until this time. They literally went from their prison cells into government posts. The governmental structure contained all the defects that they had protested against, but under Nkrumah's leadership these were worked out as the Gold Coast moved by rapid stages toward full self-government and independence, which was proclaimed on March 6, 1957, with Nkrumah as prime minister of the new nation of Ghana. The nonviolent "positive action" campaign was not the sole factor in bringing this result, but it provided strong impetus to hasten the day, and powerful leverage for political action both through the election and in the parliamentary maneuvering that followed. Though not used again, its potential gave substance to CPP moves within the government.

The aftermath of victory, however, saw tragic departures from the spirit of nonviolence. Most of the men who brought Nkrumah to power were purged and either driven into exile or imprisoned under a detention law whereby Nkrumah arrogated to his government the right to hold anyone in jail for as long as twelve years without charges. In September 1961 Kimla Gbedemah, one of Nkrumah's oldest and closest political associates, was ousted as finance minister. He fortunately fled to Togo, for a month later a law was passed which decreed the death penalty for political offenses. Even after amnesties of some 300 political prisoners in May and June 1962, an estimated 200 to 700 remained behind bars, and to their number were added scores of new suspects during a series of attempts to assassinate Nkrumah in August and September of

that year. In one district an estimated 2,000 people were arrested, while homes were looted and pillaged and women raped by Nkrumah's troops. In neighboring Togo there were 3,800 refugees from Ghana, most of them political. Capping the process, the CPP, now clearly Nkrumah's personal instrument, used its overwhelming preponderance of votes successively to install him as prime minister for life, to establish a one-party system of government, and to abolish the ballot in favor of voting by acclamation.

Despite these ominous trends, Nkrumah remained apparently a popular leader and life in Ghana was not unbearable for the average citizen. Yet as Cecil Northcott observed: "In gaining its freedom from imperialists Ghana seems to have lost its independence to an African fascism" in which Nkrumah had become "an astute demagogue-dictator, who is busy creating an image of himself as 'father and founder.'" [14] Nkrumah had tried to mix Gandhi and Hitler. The spirit of the latter had won.

REFERENCES IN CHAPTER 19

1 Quoted in John Gunther, *Inside Africa* (New York: Harper & Brothers, 1955), p. 799.
2 George Padmore: *The Gold Coast Revolution* (London: Dobson, 1953), p. 61f.
3 Quoted in Gunther, *op. cit.*, p. 801.
4 Padmore, *op. cit.*, p. 79.
5 Quoted in Bankole Timothy: *Kwame Nkrumah: His Rise to Power* (London: Allen and Unwin, 1955), p. 97.
6 Kwame Nkrumah: *Ghana: An Autobiography* (New York: Thomas Nelson & Sons, 1957), p. xiv.
7 *Ibid.*, p. xv.
8 *Ibid.*, p. 117.
9 Quoted in Timothy, *op. cit.*, pp. 97-100 passim.
10 Richard Wright: *Black Power* (New York: Harper & Brothers, 1954), p. 95.
11 Nkrumah, *op. cit.*, p. 118.
12 *Ibid.*
13 *Ibid.*, p. 122.
14 Cecil Northcott: "New Gods in Ghana" in *The Christian Century*, November 23, 1960, p. 1367.

20

Nonviolence in the Southern United States Since 1955

A full history of nonviolence in the struggle for racial equality in the United States would probably begin with 1942, when the first component of the Congress of Racial Equality conducted its first sit-in at a Chicago restaurant. It would go on to document the historic Journey of Reconciliation of 1947 in which a group of Negroes and whites led by two secretaries of the Fellowship of Reconciliation, George M. Houser and Bayard Rustin, carried out the first integrated "freedom ride" across the Upper South. But it was not until the Montgomery bus boycott of 1956 and the numerous campaigns following it that nonviolence began to accelerate toward a major, national impact. It is beyond the scope of this book to chronicle each of the proliferating campaigns throughout the country or even in the South, but it is useful to trace the broad outlines and briefly to examine the key events in some detail.

The Montgomery Bus Boycott of 1956

The first sustained mass-scale nonviolent campaign began in December 1955 in Montgomery, Alabama. Earlier the same year five Negro women and two children were arrested and one man was shot to death for disobeying a bus driver's order. It was not unusual for the latter to compel pregnant Negro women to yield their seats to white teenagers, to curse some Negro women and molest others. For many months the Negro community had been smarting under these abuses.

Early in the evening on December 1, a number of white passengers boarded a city bus and, as usual, the driver asked four Negroes to give up their seats. Three did so, but a fourth, Mrs. Rosa Parks, refused. She was arrested and released in bond, with her trial set for the following Monday, December 5.

A mild-mannered seamstress at a department store, this forty-two-year-old woman was well known and highly respected, and news of the incident spread quickly among the city's 50,000 Negro citizens. In the barrooms, hoodlums decided it was time to "beat the hell out of a few bus drivers," and they began sharpening their switchblade knives, readying their pistols and collecting an arsenal of spiked sticks and baseball bats. When word of these preparations reached a number of the community's Negro ministers, they parleyed and decided that some alternative had to be found, and quickly, to avert a riot. A flurry of telephone calls ensued, in the course of which the Women's Political Council hit upon the idea of a boycott. They suggested it to E. D. Nixon, head of the Montgomery local of the Brotherhood of Sleeping Car Porters, the man who had posted Mrs. Parks' bond. Nixon responded enthusiastically. Next morning he phoned two young Baptist ministers, Ralph D. Abernathy and Martin Luther King Jr., who in turn called other ministers and arranged for a meeting at King's church that evening. Nixon and some others began circulating a mimeographed leaflet urging a boycott. By 7:30, when the meeting began, it had already been widely distributed.

In addition to ministers there were physicians, lawyers, schoolteachers, businessmen and union officials at the meeting, representing the leaders of the Negro community. After a brief devotional period the chairman, L. Roy Bennett, president of the Interdenominational Ministerial Alliance, took the floor and proposed a one-day boycott of the buses. After a lively discussion the group agreed to issue a call for both a boycott and a mass meeting to consider further action.

Early the next morning, Saturday, the mimeograph machine

at King's Dexter Avenue Baptist Church was turning out leaflets. By 11:00 A.M. some 7,000 of them were being distributed throughout the Negro community. Meanwhile, the local newspaper, *The Montgomery Advertiser,* had received one of Nixon's leaflets and published it on the front page, unwittingly augmenting the tedious hand-to-hand distribution.

A subcommittee contacted the city's Negro taxicab companies, which agreed to place their 210 taxis at the disposal of the boycott, charging riders the equivalent of their normal bus fare. On Sunday morning the call was sounded from every Negro pulpit. By the afternoon, in one way or another, virtually everyone knew of the boycott scheduled for the next day.

Monday came. Mrs. Parks was tried, found guilty and fined ten dollars plus four dollars costs. She appealed the decision. The boycott took hold with extraordinary effectiveness. Not more than a handful of Negroes rode the buses even during the peak of traffic. Many buses that would normally have been crammed were empty, and many others carried only white passengers. Thousands of Negroes rode in taxis and in car pools. Thousands more walked, a few as far as ten miles. A cautious estimate was that the boycott was eighty per cent effective, a fact that was disquieting to city officials and alarming to Montgomery City Lines, seventy per cent of whose passengers were Negroes.

On Monday evening, some 5,000 Negroes joined in the mass meeting at Holt Street Baptist Church, fired with enthusiasm. Earlier in the day the leadership group had met and founded the Montgomery Improvement Association, with Martin Luther King—to his great surprise—as president. They decided to draft a list of grievances and continue the boycott until they were met. One man later proposed that this decision be reconsidered. The boycott, so successful as a one-day affair, he said, might fizzle out after a few days. "This argument was so convincing," wrote King later, "that we almost resolved to end the protest. But we finally agreed to let the mass meeting . . . be our guide." [1]

The mood of the mass meeting ruled out any hesitation. There was clamor for the boycott to continue. And it not only continued but it grew, holding a level of ninety-five per cent effectiveness for a whole year. Carl T. Rowan, then a reporter for the *Minneapolis Star,* noted other remarkable results: "The Negro ministers . . . had achieved the most unbelievable by pulling the hoodlums out of the crap games and honky-tonks into the churches, where they sang hymns, gave money, shouted amen and wept over the powerful speeches." [2] For months, all classes of people thronged the churches several evenings each week to receive spiritual sustenance and practical instruction for the ongoing struggle. During the day, one might see a Negro doctor's wife offering a ride in her shiny Cadillac to a group of domestic workers, or even an occasional white driver stopping to pick up a Negro. Letters to the editors of local newspapers, written by white people, weighed five to one in sympathy with the boycott.

The campaign was nonviolent throughout. What kept it so? Where did the idea come from? Martin Luther King had heard of Gandhi, but it took some time for the message to penetrate. Even after the boycott was under way, he yielded to his friends' suggestion that he apply for a permit to carry a pistol for self-defense.

The first explicit reference to nonviolence that arose in the context of the campaign came from a white librarian, Juliette Morgan. In a letter published in the segregationist *Montgomery Advertiser* on December 12, 1955, she compared the Negroes' boycott to Gandhi's dramatic salt march of 1930. Unpublicized, however, was the arrival of two men who were to exert an inestimable influence on King's thinking. One was Glenn E. Smiley, a white Methodist minister from Texas, field secretary of the Fellowship of Reconciliation. The other was Bayard Rustin, a Negro Quaker and one of the most courageous men in the annals of nonviolence, who was to serve as a special advisor to King for the next several years.

King was not an immediate success as head of the Mont-

gomery Improvement Association. Failing to achieve an agreement after several meetings with city officials and bus company representatives, the young minister even offered to resign, but was prevented by a unanimous vote of confidence by the MIA's executive board. The vote proved well-founded when the segregationists turned from verbal sparring to rougher tactics.

On January 21 the city commissioners issued a press release for publication the next day, stating that they had reached a settlement and that the boycott was over. In Minneapolis, Carl Rowan saw the advance text when it came in on the Associated Press wire. Incredulous, he phoned King to verify it. As it turned out, the Montgomery officials had duped three Negro ministers, not members of the MIA, into attending a meeting with them and had then issued the statement. King immediately alerted his fellow ministers, and they set out on a Saturday-night tour of the Negro night clubs and taverns to warn the people there. The next morning, from every Negro pulpit came a repudiation of the bogus agreement, effectively countering the newspaper account. The city fathers' scheme fell flat, and the boycott held firm.

Next the segregationists tried intimidation. They arrested drivers in the Negro car pool for minor or trumped-up traffic violations and threatened to arrest waiting riders for vagrancy. King and other leaders were among those taken to jail for "speeding." They also received obscene and insulting, often threatening letters and telephone calls. King alone sometimes got as many as forty a day.

On January 30 a bomb was exploded on the porch of King's home. Hundreds of angry Negroes gathered at the scene, many of them armed and talking of "shooting it out" with the police, who had arrived before them with the mayor and police commissioner. It was the first serious test of nonviolence under provocation. Fortunately no one had been injured in the blast, but King could easily have yielded to the prevailing mood. Silence alone could have triggered a riot.

"Now let's not become panicky," he said, and the crowd

hushed to listen. "If you have weapons, take them home; if you do not have them, please do not seek to get them. We cannot solve this problem through retaliatory violence. . . . We must love our white brothers no matter what they do to us. We must make them know that we love them. Jesus still cries out in words that echo across the centuries: 'Love your enemies; bless them that curse you; pray for them that despitefully use you.' This is what we must live by. We must meet hate with love."

Two nights later a stick of dynamite was exploded on E. D. Nixon's lawn. Again a large crowd gathered but remained nonviolent. A third bombing struck the home of Robert Graetz, white Lutheran pastor of an all-Negro congregation, who was an active MIA member. Miraculously, in all of these explosions no one was hurt, and the terrorists did not succeed in provoking retaliation or breaking the spirit of the boycott. The strain was great, however, and King felt anger welling up in him when he thought of the viciousness of those who might have killed his wife and baby daughter.

On February 22, more than ninety Negroes, including twenty-four ministers, were indicted under an almost forgotten labor law of 1921 outlawing boycotts. They demanded separate trials. No one tried to evade arrest. King's trial was the first, held March 19-22. Though convicted, he appealed and the verdict was eventually reversed.

In May, the MIA asked attorneys of the National Association for the Advancement of Colored People to file a suit on its behalf in the U.S. District Court to overturn the city ordinances which maintained segregation on the buses. The boycott continued for seven months more, as the litigation made its way up to the Supreme Court. Finally, on December 1, 1956, a decree was issued upholding the MIA's plea. The boycott was ended and Negroes resumed riding the buses.

It is widely believed that the year-long boycott resulted in desegregating the Montgomery city buses. Actually it was the court order that did so, to the extent that desegregation oc-

ourred at all. It might also be supposed that the ordeal of passive resistance assured harmony at the end and ushered in a new era in race relations in Montgomery. The facts are less heartening. Long after the court decree, few Negroes actually exercised their right to sit anywhere in the buses. Closer to the event, three white men beat a teenage Negro girl as she got off a bus. A shotgun blast was fired into the front door of King's home. Snipers fired at buses, wounding one Negro woman in the leg. On January 10, 1957, four Negro churches and the homes of two ministers were dynamited. Then violence subsided. But as late as August 1962 the MIA newsletter observed that the buses were "not entirely integrated" and cited instances of continued intimidation of Negro passengers.

The enthusiasm and unity of the nonviolent movement rapidly ebbed. King's stature as a local leader declined. According to his biographer, L. D. Reddick, his colleagues "began to question his judgment, to mention his shortcomings. . . . The people had turned, not *against* King, but to some extent away from him." [3]

The MIA declined, too, playing a modest and restricted role in subsequent years and scoring such gains as the hiring of a few Negro bus drivers on exclusively Negro routes. After the boycott of 1956 it no longer functioned as the leadership group for a mass movement, though it continued to be the chief means of communication with the white power structure of the city.

The real importance of the Montgomery bus boycott does not consist in its purported achievement of a local objective. Though it failed there, it had important repercussions. First, the sheer fact of mass unity shattered the myth that Negroes approved of their inferior status under segregation. It set in motion the concept of the "new Negro" and pricked the slumbering consciences of millions of Americans. Second, it sparked similar boycotts in Birmingham, Tallahassee and elsewhere, bringing out new local organizations patterned on the MIA and a new leadership of ministers such as Fred L. Shuttles-

worth and C. K. Steele. Third, the publicity emanating from Montgomery spurred scores of Southern cities to desegregate their buses even before the court ruling. Fourth, though diminished at home, Martin Luther King's stature was greatly enlarged on the national level, and he became the acknowledged head of a rapidly growing movement led by Negro ministers, the Southern Christian Leadership Conference.

Finally, nobody noticed the fact that the bus boycott had not brought victory. There had been a boycott and then there had been victory. Here was a powerful legend that would inspire others to authentic victories based wholly or largely on nonviolence.

From a purely strategic standpoint, the Montgomery campaign first sought to attain its objective through passive resistance, then shifted to a legal strategy in which such resistance played no part. Even though it continued, it had no discernible effect on the course of events.

Since the outcome was finally the desired one, there is little point in criticizing what was done. But there were possible alternatives. One was to terminate the boycott and endure the experience of segregation until the Supreme Court ruling was issued. Another was to move from passive resistance to nonviolent direct action. This course of action might have been most promising when the U.S. District Court ruled in favor of the MIA, although it could have been undertaken even earlier. It would have meant going to jail for doing what Mrs. Parks had done instead of going to jail for boycotting the buses—in other words, invading segregationist territory and contesting it directly. Many tactics might have been added to either of the strategic alternatives but were not. The next phase was to see a variety of them in use on a wide scale, with direct action forming the strategic backbone.

The Sit-Ins

In January 1960 a freshman at Shaw University in Greensboro, North Carolina, read a "comic book," *The Montgomery Story,* published by the Fellowship of Reconciliation and widely distributed on Negro college campuses in the South. On February 1, he and three classmates decided to try out its principles and went to a local Woolworth store. They sat down at the lunch counter, which was reserved for white customers. Although refused service, they continued to sit. Day after day they returned with increasing numbers and sat at the counter.

Soon they were joined by white students from Greensboro College for Women. Elsewhere, students at Negro colleges throughout the South heard of the Greensboro sit-in and flocked to nearby lunch counters to start their own. Sometimes they too were joined by white allies. Here and there, the growing movement centered around groups that had attended seminars and workshops conducted by Glenn Smiley and others. Copies of Richard Gregg's *The Power of Nonviolence* were sought out and studied. Dozens of these had been given to Negro college libraries by Smiley on his visits there. Thousands of copies of the FOR leaflet, *How to Practice Nonviolence,* and the leaflet, *CORE Rules for Action,* found their way into the students' hands. Many of the students were not primed at all, however, and knew about nonviolence only by word of mouth.

In some places there was disorder. In Portsmouth, Virginia, for example, Negro high-school students rioted in response to provocation from whites, bringing CORE field secretary Gordon Carey in on an emergency mission to instruct them in nonviolence. For a time the FOR had a three-man team at work, together with volunteers, touring communities where sit-ins were in progress. The team included Glenn Smiley and regional secretaries James M. Lawson Jr. and Charles C. Walker. Their work was closed out as local and regional organizations sprang up, while CORE blossomed into a major

nationwide body with many new local chapters and field secretaries in the South, recruited from the student ranks. Under the aegis of the Southern Christian Leadership Conference, sit-in leaders themselves launched a new organization, the Student Nonviolent Coordinating Committee. All of these organizations provided full- or part-time staff to instruct local groups in nonviolent conduct, tactics and strategy, thus curbing or forestalling much of the violence that might otherwise have occurred.

Abundant local leadership was doubtless more crucial to the rapid spread of the nonviolent sit-ins. Typical of many was the situation as it developed in Raleigh, North Carolina, where students from two campuses joined to form the Shaw-St. Augustine's Student Movement during the first week of the demonstrations. One of the leaders, Glenford E. Mitchell, tells how the movement was organized. He points out that, while on some campuses the elected president of the student body readily took charge, in Raleigh and elsewhere the leadership emerged on the spot "by natural selection."

The nine-member Intelligence Committee—five from Shaw and four from St. Augustine's—planned all the strategy with the aid of its subsidiary committees: the Group Movement Committee, which directed the movement of the students on the streets so as to avoid congestion and to effect proper placing of students in or about the stores; the Steering Committee, which studied the day-to-day conditions on the scene and made recommendations such as the best way and the best time to move; the Negotiating Committee, a stand-by committee which consisted of students who represented the schools at Mayor's committee meetings; and the Coordinating Committee, whose members later became representatives to the Student Nonviolent Coordinating Committee. The Intelligence Committee was approved by both student bodies.[4]

At first, says Mitchell, daily mass meetings were held for morale and information, with prayers, speeches and singing, after which the intelligence committee (what would more often be called an executive committee) met to make preparations

for the following day's activities. In doing so, they made it a
practice to keep talking until they were able to arrive at unanimous decisions. "We had learned early in the movement that
to keep the students together we had to be unified as a committee at all times." This in turn made for solidarity among
the mass of students, who "always responded in unison and
with complete acceptance." [5]

At Claflin College in Orangeburg, South Carolina, students
grouped themselves into classes of forty, each spending three
or four days studying and discussing Martin Luther King's
account of the Montgomery bus boycott, *Stride Toward Freedom,* and the *CORE Rules for Action.* "In these sessions,"
wrote a student leader, "we emphasized adherence to nonviolence and discussed various situations which might provoke
violence. Could each of us trust our God and our temper
enough not to strike back even if kicked, slapped or spit
upon?" [6]

From those who felt ready, forty cadres were picked for the
first demonstration in Orangeburg. Action plans were then
charted, taking into consideration every detail: the number
and position of the entrances to the store, the number of lunch-
counter stools, the exact number of minutes required to walk
from the campus to the store by various routes.

The sequence of events in the Orangeburg campaign is
largely representative of the sit-ins as a whole. At 10:45 A.M.
on February 25 the cadres started out in groups of three or
four, each with a designated leader, walking by different routes
timed to arrive simultaneously at the store. The first fifteen
students then entered and seated themselves at the lunch
counter. After fifteen minutes the management posted a sign
there, "Closed in the Interest of Public Safety." The students
left and were replaced by a second wave of twenty, each of
whom sat until the seats were removed.

The next day they returned and stood several rows deep
along the seatless counter. Subsequently the store would not
let more than two Negroes enter the store at one time.

On March 1, a thousand students marched through the streets with placards saying "All Sit or All Stand," "Segregation Is Obsolete" and "Down with Jim Crow." There were no disorders, but the lunch counters were shut down for two weeks. In the interval the students formed a statewide movement and launched a boycott against stores that had lunch counters at which Negroes were not served.

On March 14 the lunch counters reopened. The students planned another mass march to be followed by resumption of the sit-in on the next day. The march began in below-freezing cold. They did not get far before they encountered police with tear-gas bombs and fire hoses, which were used indiscriminately against the young Negroes. Many were knocked down and all were drenched. Over 500 were arrested, of whom 150 were taken to jail. Some 350 others, soaked and shivering, were jammed into an open-air stockade, where they sang hymns and said prayers. After a few hours they were released in ten dollars bond. Trials began the next day, a few students at a time, and all were convicted of disturbing the peace. For some time to come, the Orangeburg campaign was effectively thwarted.

There were variations on this pattern, hinging to some extent on the activities of friendly or hostile whites other than the police. In Tallahassee, white CORE members bought food and passed it to their Negro companions. In Jacksonville, Florida, a mob armed with axe handles and baseball bats descended upon the sit-ins. In Dallas, fifty-eight white students at Southern Methodist University joined two Negro classmates in a sit-in at a drugstore and were sprayed with insecticide.

In North Carolina, where the sit-ins had originated, white and Negro ministerial associations joined in appeals to businessmen. In Raleigh the Catholic Interracial Council issued a statement of support and the local Fellowship of Southern Churchmen circulated a petition among white Christians indicating the signers' support of stores "which decide to reopen their lunch counters on a nondiscriminatory basis." In Durham

the Baptist Student Union of North Carolina College pledged a boycott of stores to "remain in force until unequal policies are terminated." With such responses it is not surprising that victory came quickly in this state. In New Orleans, by contrast, bitter resistance met the sit-ins. Only after two years and more than 300 arrests were negotiations begun, leading to the sudden opening of lunch counters to Negroes at fifteen stores on September 12, 1962. At the other extreme were such communities as Houston and San Antonio, Texas, where variety stores hastened to desegregate their lunch counters before demonstrations even occurred, wishing to avoid the disturbances that had happened elsewhere. In the first two months, sit-ins had spread to fifty Southern cities, with more to come, and some had already yielded.

If Orangeburg offers a good example of planning, probably Nashville is more typical of the characteristic detail. Here, soon after the Montgomery bus boycott, a number of Negro ministers organized the Nashville Christian Leadership Council, one of the strongest local affiliates of SCLC. For years they conducted workshops in nonviolence as well as fruitless negotiations for the desegregation of lunch counters. The organizational instrument was ready for the challenge of Greensboro when it came.

On February 13, students from Fisk and Vanderbilt began their sit-in, harassed by white troublemakers. A Methodist editor on the scene described their conduct:

When called names, they keep quiet. When hit, they do not strike back. Even when hostile white youth pull hair and snuff out burning cigarettes on the backs of Negro girls, the girls do not retaliate. They pray and take what comes, in dignity.[7]

On the first day, seventy-nine students were arrested and convicted of disorderly conduct. For two months thereafter the sit-ins continued, augmented toward the end of March by an economic boycott. On April 12 a mass march encountered white toughs with baseball bats, and a near-riot ensued, where-

upon local merchants agreed to negotiate. On May 10, six lunch counters were opened on a desegregated basis, with others to follow. Three years later, a new campaign was launched to open cafeterias to Negroes, and victory came only after riots in which several persons were injured.

Two predominant facts emerge from an over-all assessment of the sit-ins. First, settlement almost invariably occurred through direct negotiations rather than by court rulings. Second, opponents were seldom if ever won over to the side of justice as a result of voluntary suffering or Christian love on the part of the demonstrators. The key factor was economic leverage, and closely related to this was the merchants' desire for stability and civil order. A marginal factor of varying importance was the basic attitude of the white community: hostile, neutral or sympathetic.

Merrill Proudfoot, a white Presbyterian minister, found himself among the leaders of a six-week sit-in in Knoxville, Tennessee, which he documented in a highly instructive book, *Diary of a Sit-In*. The abuse and mistreatment the demonstrators experienced were similar to those of Nashville and elsewhere. They were pushed, hot coffee was spilled on them and they were sprayed with insecticides. One day white high-school boys were heckling him. They poured Coca-Cola on his head and began striking him in the face. When they started to pull him from his booth, a "neutral" white man intervened and told the youths to get out. A sentimental interpretation would focus solely on this act of decency. But Proudfoot observed that nonviolence had a polarizing effect; it "caused this 'neutral' to declare himself for decency and order" but also "brings out the bully in those who are inclined to be bullies." [8] Moreover, the intervention of a "decent neutral" can no more be considered a token of strategic success than a display of decency by a determined opponent, though certainly these qualities are to be welcomed.

Both Mitchell and Proudfoot agree on the effectiveness of the economic factor. In Raleigh a three-pronged strategy

evolved pragmatically: first, the sit-in; second, picketing as a means of garnering sympathy. The third grew out of the second:

After a week of continuous educational picketing we learned that business at variety stores was suffering a loss of some eighteen per cent. Our new knowledge provided us with a new weapon—the economic boycott. The wording of signs then assumed a new slant. At Easter we appeared with such signs as "Wear last year's Easter bonnets!" [9]

Proudfoot notes that when sit-ins occurred during mealtime they added to the economic drain of the boycott, as did the generally unsettled condition of the shopping district. Many prospective customers refrained from buying, not because they sympathized with the integrationists but because they did not want to get mixed up in what was going on. As a result, the stores "decided they risked greater losses by not desegregating than by desegregating. This is *the one decisive reason* for the speedy success of the movement." [10]

Attitudes do change, but more often they do so as an accommodation to a new situation of order and stability rather than in response to the process of change itself. And they change unevenly. In Proudfoot's Knoxville three years later, as in Nashville and Greensboro, sit-ins had to be waged once again to win new objectives even as an interracial exchange program of children was getting under way. Gang violence may increase at the same time that politicians become more conciliatory.

Although the sit-ins did not go far toward ending racial segregation, they did register tangible gains. More important, they set in motion a large-scale ongoing movement that was to have continuing repercussions. They consolidated the leadership of Martin Luther King and others who were committed to nonviolence. And the nonviolent content of the campaigns added mightily to the stature of the Negro, dramatizing clearly the righteousness of the cause of integration. The calm courage and endurance of the demonstrators contrasted sharply with

the ugly image of their opponents, whose underhanded tactics jolted the public's sense of fair play. Particularly among white students, liberals and churchmen, dormant consciences were stirred.

The Freedom Rides of 1961

As 1960 was pre-eminently the year of the sit-ins, 1961 was the year of freedom rides which "put the sit-ins on the road." Conceived by CORE members along lines similar to the 1947 Journey of Reconciliation, the initial freedom ride set out from Washington, D.C., on May 4, heading for New Orleans. Its participants were six pairs of white and Negro cadres, most of the latter drawn from the student sit-ins. Together with a white CORE observer they were to travel through Virginia, the Carolinas, Georgia, Alabama and Mississippi aboard Greyhound and Trailways interstate buses. At each stop they tested the facilities, entering segregated waiting rooms and seeking service at segregated lunch counters. In some instances both members of a pair entered together, in others the Negro went to the white facility while his white teammate went to the facility marked "colored."

The journey was largely uneventful until the freedom riders reached Rock Hill, South Carolina. Here for more than a year, lunch-counter sit-ins had been held repeatedly both by local students and by cadres of the Student Nonviolent Coordinating Committee from many parts of the South, who were subjected to vicious harassment and jailings. A score of hoodlums were on hand when the freedom riders' bus arrived. When Negro divinity student John Lewis approached the white waiting room he was assaulted by two of them. Three others began pummeling his white teammate, Albert Bigelow, a former U.S. Navy commander. Neither of them offered any resistance. Only when another CORE member, Genevieve Hughes, was pushed to the ground did police intervene.

Most of the stops en route to Atlanta were without incident,

but the next leg of the trip was a harrowing one. When the Greyhound bus arrived at Anniston, Alabama, it was attacked by an angry mob armed with iron bars. They smashed windows, punctured tires and set fire to the bus with an incendiary bomb. Some of the freedom riders were beaten as they emerged from the smoke-filled bus before police arrived and tardily dispersed the mob. After the injured were treated at the hospital, they were taken to Birmingham in automobiles sent by the Rev. Fred L. Shuttlesworth. FBI agents later arrested nine local residents, who were brought to trial, but some were acquitted and charges against the others were dropped. None were punished.

When the Trailways bus arrived an hour later, eight of the hoodlums boarded it. They forced all the CORE members to the rear, kicking and beating them. When veteran CORE activist Jim Peck and Walter Bergman, a retired college professor, remonstrated with their assailants they were knocked to the floor of the bus.

In two hours the bus pulled into the Birmingham terminal. Another mob of white men was waiting for them. Negro student Charles Person and his white teammate Jim Peck were the first to leave the bus. As soon as they entered the white wating room they were grabbed bodily and pushed into an alley, where five of them set upon Person and six began beating Peck. Police did not appear until both had been beaten unconscious. Person survived with a gash on the back of his head and a swollen face. Peck's face and head required fifty-three stitches at the hospital.

Plans to resume the ride the next day were thwarted by the refusal of bus drivers to take them. Rather than become embroiled in a prolonged campaign in Birmingham, they decided to fly to New Orleans since a rally had already been arranged for their arrival there.

The bus burning at Anniston and the savage beating of Jim Peck were widely reported, and newspapers throughout the

country took editorial note of the fact that unarmed men of ostensible good will had been attacked without striking back. Sidney Smyer, president of the Birmingham Chamber of Commerce, returning six weeks later from a tour of the Far East, said that his city had lost much prestige as a result of this violence.

In Nashville, a group of students from the sit-in movement resolved to carry on the freedom ride from Birmingham to New Orleans. They started out on May 18, the day after the CORE group landed in New Orleans. Although they were arrested by Alabama state police and returned to the Tennessee border, they went back, made their way to Birmingham and, after an all-night vigil at the bus terminal, succeeded in finding a driver who would transport them to Montgomery.

When they arrived, they were greeted by a surly mob numbering hundreds of people who had been called together by the Ku Klux Klan. The freedom riders were mauled, kicked and slugged as they left the bus. James Zwerg, a white member of the group, was cornered by sixteen Klansmen, beaten unconscious and left lying in the street for an hour before an ambulance took him to the hospital. Others were rescued by members of the Montgomery Improvement Association, whose cars were waiting for them. Police appeared belatedly but were unable to control the mob. In the ensuing riot, one Negro (not a freedom rider) was soaked with kerosene and set on fire. Finally the police resorted to tear gas to disperse the racists.

Sporadic violence continued through the day. In the evening the Federal Government stepped in when it became evident that the Governor of Alabama was unwilling to protect the freedom riders. Four hundred U.S. marshals were rushed to Montgomery, with another 266 following the next morning. Governor John Patterson, an arch-segregationist, insisted that they were not needed and even threatened to arrest them if they violated any local laws.

Even as he was saying this, local radio stations were broad-

casting the news that Montgomery Negroes led by Martin Luther King, who had returned from his new home in Atlanta, were planning a mass rally for the freedom riders at First Baptist Church. Carloads of white men from the rural areas began to converge on Montgomery, moving toward the church. Some 3,000 persons were besieged inside. The U.S. marshals attempted to turn back the mob, which succeeded in smashing some windows and injuring at least one person inside. Before the evening was over, Governor Patterson called out the National Guard and dispersed the mob.

Diane Nash, a Roman Catholic freedom rider, described the mood of the beleaguered Negroes:

In the dire danger in which we were that night, no one expressed anything except concern for freedom. . . . We stayed there until dawn and everyone was naturally tired, but no one said so. . . . I don't think I've ever seen a group of people band together as the crowd in the church did that night.[11]

The following morning, joined by three members of the first freedom ride and five New Orleans CORE members, the Nashville group resumed its journey. Before their departure, they ate together at the terminal restaurant without incident. There were now twenty-seven freedom riders in two buses, accompanied by a large escort of National Guard troops and highway patrolmen. They drove to Jackson, Mississippi, without making the usual rest stops. Instead of a mob, they were met by city police who arrested them as soon as they tried to integrate the terminal facilities. Brought quickly to trial and convicted of disturbing the peace, they chose to go to jail rather than pay fines.

The two initial freedom rides were soon followed by many more. The first was a group of ten men from colleges and seminaries in Connecticut, led by William Sloane Coffin Jr., chaplain of Yale University. When they arrived in Montgomery they spent an evening trying to persuade Justice Department

officials to arrange guarantees with state authorities that facilities would be integrated at the end of a "cooling-off period" called for by U.S. Attorney General Robert F. Kennedy. This cooling-off period meant, in effect, a temporary return to the segregated status quo, backed up with a court order barring the activities of freedom riders in Montgomery for ten days. "Why should Negroes always be asked to make the concessions?" asked the Connecticut group. "Why not allow free, unhampered travel during the moratorium period, allowing the white community to become accustomed to it? Or, if there are to be no freedom rides for a while, assure their right to resume freely at some mutually agreeable fixed date." [12]

Unable to obtain such assurances, the group proceeded to the bus terminal and were arrested at the lunch counter as they drank coffee with four Negro ministers.

Another freedom ride involved two Jewish rabbis and eight Negro and white Christian ministers, including Ralph Lord Roy and Robert McAfee Brown. This group went to Tallahassee under CORE auspices, while another which included officials of the United Auto Workers terminated in St. Petersburg and Ocala, Florida.

There were others as well, going to a variety of destinations, but the greatest number focused on Jackson, Mississippi. Most of them arrived by bus, but some came by air or rail. By mid-August over three hundred had been arrested. The last major event in the freedom ride chronicle was the arrest on September 13 of fifteen Episcopal priests who were on an interracial prayer pilgrimage from New Orleans to Chicago.

Nine days later the Interstate Commerce Commission issued new regulations to secure the right of integrated travel. Beginning on November 1, interstate buses were required to display a sign: "Seating aboard this vehicle without regard to race, color, creed or national origin, by order of the Interstate Commerce Commission." The same statement was printed on all interstate bus tickets the following year. Terminals servicing interstate buses were required to post similar signs.

CORE test teams found that compliance with the ICC regulations was widespread and included Birmingham and Anniston, though pockets of resistance continued elsewhere and were met with Federal Court injunctions or renewed freedom rides, not always successfully.

Unlike the sit-ins, the freedom rides exerted virtually no economic pressure. Indeed it is difficult to speak of strategy or tactics at all in a meaningful sense when participants only sit in waiting rooms or at lunch counters. The key fact of the freedom rides was what has been called "nonviolent insistence" —simple individual action undergirded by nonviolent conduct under provocation or attack. The pressure exerted was almost solely moral and indirect. The first freedom ride, building on the climate already created by the sit-ins, stung the consciences of others who formed subsequent freedom rides. The cumulative pressure of them all acted to compel the federal authorities to take the steps that followed. In all of this the involvement of well-known and respected church leaders was an intangible but relevant factor. In the Episcopal priests' pilgrimage were Malcolm Boyd, a writer and chaplain at Wayne State University, and Robert L. Pierson, assistant to the director of the American Church Union and son-in-law of Governor Nelson A. Rockefeller of New York. Regardless of their attitude toward the issue at stake, Federal officials did not want the embarrassment of appearing to condone the mistreatment of such men, once the latter showed that they would not be deterred by anything short of decisive action. In this respect, names may have compensated for lack of numbers.

This is not to deny the moral impact arising even when participants were "unknown." But it is a fact that the mere arrest of the Yale chaplain and the Governor's son-in-law had wide repercussions, while the brutal beating of James Zwerg went virtually unnoticed. In the press, the assault on Jim Peck, white, was dramatized and the fate of Charles Person, Negro, was barely mentioned. And a large part of the reason for dramatizing the Peck beating undoubtedly was the fact that it

was the first event of its kind. It was not enough, by itself, to bring about the ICC regulations, though it evidently was enough to swell the ranks of the freedom rides.

The testimony of John Maguire is relevant here. Born in Montgomery, he was professor of religion at Wesleyan University. He credited the freedom rides with accelerating the process of desegregation as well as his own move from benign neutrality to a positive, articulate position:

> For us who went on the freedom rides there has resulted an identification and empathy with Negroes that we never knew before, and the realization that just such a sense of identification by our national leaders will be necessary if they are to understand this group on the move, and sense the heart of this worldwide social revolution. The freedom rides have dramatized this need and profoundly affected the lives of everyone involved.[13]

Robert McAfee Brown, then professor of systematic theology at Union Theological Seminary, corroborated this view from his experience on the freedom ride to Tallahassee. He cited the rides generally as a "creative alternative to violence" which expressed solidarity with Negroes as well as strengthening the hand of white liberals in the South who, without necessarily expressing overt approval of this tactic, could "perhaps pick up and build upon whatever a freedom ride may have done to loosen segregation patterns in their own towns." [14]

One immediate outgrowth of the 1961 freedom rides was the 1962 Freedom Highways campaign launched by CORE to open Howard Johnson restaurants and other accommodations to interracial use. Again there were arrests and abuses such as the use of insecticides and ammonia against the nonviolent cadres, but by the end of the year all but eighteen out of 297 company-operated Howard Johnson restaurants were desegregated by negotiations without court action. This success in turn led to a new strategy, the "freedom task force" of CORE field workers and trained volunteers, concentrating on public accommodations in a number of cities, beginning in

1963 with communities located near the major highways where CORE had been working.

Other organizations such as SCLC, SNCC and the NAACP took a similar turn, often coupling such campaigns with drives to secure the right to vote for disfranchised Negroes, particularly in Mississippi, Alabama and Georgia. Although civil-rights activities increased in the Upper South and spread to the North and West, the most significant development was the onset of numerous campaigns in the Deep South. Rather than attempt a survey, two major contrasting campaigns have been chosen for detailed scrutiny, partly because of their historic importance for the over-all struggle in the United States but also because the detailed information that is available can compensate somewhat for the more general accounts presented elsewhere in this CASEBOOK. It is simply not feasible to do for, say, Debrecen in 1859, what we can do in the studies that follow.

The Albany Movement of 1962

Albany is a city in southwest Georgia. About a third of its 56,000 inhabitants are Negroes. It is the birthplace of the noted composer, Wallingford Riegger, and the site of Albany State College for Negroes, with a student enrollment of 650. Like many Deep South towns, it had maintained rigid patterns of white domination since the post-Reconstruction period, typified in the derogatory reporting of news of the Negro community in James Gray's daily *Albany Herald*.

For years, local Negroes endured the situation, but with the advent of the sit-ins there were stirrings of discontent. In January 1961 a group of Negro ministers wrote to the editor of the *Herald*, politely requesting that he stop degrading them in print. They were told in an editorial to mind their own business. As if to underline the point, white hoodlums threw stones at the homes of three of the ministers. Police did nothing to

apprehend them, and subsequent appeals to Mayor Asa D. Kelley went unheeded.

In July, SNCC field secretaries arrived to scout the possibility of a voter-education project for Albany and the surrounding rural areas, sponsored by the Field Foundation, SCLC and the American Missionary Association, an instrumentality of the United Church of Christ. By October the project was begun, but the SNCC workers did not confine their efforts to it. Two of them tested integration at the bus terminal when the ICC regulations went into effect on November 1, and were ordered to leave.

Soon afterward, one of the Negro community's leading citizens, Dr. William G. Anderson, brought together a number of local organizations to form the Albany Movement for a concerted campaign to improve the status of the city's Negroes. Founded on November 17, the Movement embraced the Ministerial Alliance, the Federation of Women's Clubs, the Negro Voter League, SNCC, the local NAACP branch and NAACP Youth Council and the Criterion Club, one of the South's oldest organizations of professional men. Again, requests for talks with the mayor were denied.

Its first direct-action project came on November 25, when three youths and two adults sought service at the bus station dining room. They were arrested. Moreover, there was an upsurge of sporadic incidents. Negro college girls were molested, and there were cases of arson and vandalism.

It was in this atmosphere, on December 10, that eight freedom riders arrived by train from Atlanta and were joined by Albany Negroes and SNCC workers at the station. They were jailed. When they were brought to trial two days later, 400 Negro high-school and college students marched in protest and were arrested when they refused to disperse. For two more days, with dwindling numbers, the marches continued, and the total number of those arrested rose to 560, of whom 300 chose to remain in jail, hoping thereby to exert further pres-

sure by encumbering the city officials with the problem of logistics which this would involve.

It seemed momentarily that a victory had been won. Police released 118 juvenile prisoners, and the mayor set up a biracial commission which had been requested by the ministers' group and again by the Albany Movement. The Movement suspended further demonstrations as negotiations began, late on December 14. The talks quickly reached an impasse and were broken off. Martin Luther King arrived the next day, and he and Dr. Anderson led a protest march in which they and 250 others were arrested. Negotiations were resumed and the city commission finally agreed to desegregate bus and train terminals and to hear the Negro community's grievances. A truce was established pending the election of a new commission on January 11, and the Movement agreed to abstain from mass demonstrations until after that date.

The Movement did not wait before initiating other types of nonviolent action. Marion S. Page, the Movement's executive secretary, made a special trip to Columbus to do his family's Christmas shopping, and many others followed suit. In January an organized selective-buying campaign was begun to persuade merchants to hire Negro sales clerks and open lunch counters, and indirectly to exert pressure on city officials to abolish segregation laws. No serious attempt was made to confer with businessmen either before or during this campaign. Ranging from fifty per cent to seventy-five per cent effectiveness, its effect was negligible since Negroes did not comprise a sizable market, and retailers did not figure importantly in the political power structure.

It was easier to get effectiveness in a boycott of the city buses, since ninety per cent of the passengers were Negroes. By the end of December the bus company agreed to desegregate and to hire at least one Negro driver, but the Movement held out for a written guarantee from the city commissioners promising not to hinder these moves. When this was refused, the Movement rejected the bus company's offer. The continued

boycott led to cessation of the company's operations early in February.

January 11 came and there was no change. Instead of resuming mass action, the Movement concentrated on its selective-buying campaign and SNCC workers devoted their efforts to voter education. In February, Martin Luther King and the others, including Ralph D. Abernathy, were convicted for their part in the December protest, but they were not sentenced until July 10. Thus nearly seven months passed without mass demonstrations and without significant progress.

Sentenced to forty-five days at hard labor, King and Abernathy decided not to appeal but to serve their sentences as a form of moral protest. This gesture brought new demonstrations. On July 11, thirty-six Negroes were arrested for marching or picketing. The next day, King and Abernathy were released when, according to the police, "an unidentified, well-dressed Negro" paid their fines.

For the next few days there were mass meetings, attended by more than a thousand Negroes each evening. King and the Albany leaders insisted that negotiations be reopened. Mayor Kelley replied that he would not negotiate with "lawbreakers." Throughout the week, singly or in small groups, Negroes tested parks, libraries and other facilities, seeking service but avoiding arrest by leaving when ordered to do so. As preparations were being made for mass action, the city officials sought to forestall it by obtaining an injunction by a Federal district judge prohibiting boycotts, picketing and speeches promoting racial demonstrations. Instead of halting the Movement, however, this triggered a series of three public demonstrations on July 21 in which 161 persons were arrested, while Movement lawyers went into court to obtain a stay of the injunction, which was granted on July 23.

Many Negroes took this to mean that there would be no arrests. They were infuriated when forty members of a prayer pilgrimage to city hall were arrested the next day. A crowd of 2,000 massed in the Negro district and when 170 police moved

in to disperse them, bottles and rocks were thrown, injuring two officers. Despite the wish of many Movement leaders to press forward, Martin Luther King stepped in and called a halt to further demonstrations, declaring a "Day of Penitence" on which nonviolent cadres visited Negro poolrooms, taverns and restaurants, preaching the need for discipline in the struggle. For the rest of the week, action was confined to prayer vigils of ten to thirty persons. Anderson and King led the first one and were arrested, as were the groups that followed. Toward the end of the week, a new tactic was introduced. When arrested, cadres "went limp," refusing to walk or stand, compelling the police to carry them bodily to jail.

During this period, Albany's police chief, Laurie Pritchett, had found an answer to the tactic of filling the jails, sending arrested Negroes to the jails in surrounding counties. Conditions there were worse than in Albany. In Terrell County, for example, Negroes outnumbered whites two to one, but whites held onto political power with a voting strength that outnumbered the Negroes fifty-eight to one—dangerous territory for integrationists. There were many incidents of violence against SNCC workers in the area as well as against those whom Pritchett exported. On July 23 the wife of real-estate agent Slater King, vice-president of the Albany Movement, was knocked down and kicked while attempting to deliver packages to prisoners in the Mitchell County jail at Leesburg. Mrs. King was five months pregnant and later had a miscarriage. Her brother-in-law, attorney C. B. King, was struck with a cane by D. C. Campbell, sheriff of Dougherty County, when he went to arrange medical care for William Hansen, a white SNCC field secretary who was badly beaten by fellow prisoners when police told them he was a "nigger-lover."

These and other incidents of violence, together with the repeated jailing of Martin Luther King, impelled a group of Negro and white ministers and rabbis in the North to plan a motorcade to Washington to seek White House intervention. At the same time a bipartisan group of ten U.S. Senators urged

the Department of Justice to take "all possible steps" on behalf of those arrested in Albany. On August 1, President John F. Kennedy said publicly that he could not understand the unwillingness of Albany officials to negotiate.

When the prayer-vigil trial of Martin Luther King and his associates was held on August 10, a group of thirty-five Northern ministers and rabbis was present in the courtroom. One of them wrote: "The trial was a farce. The judge had his opinion and judgment written out when he came into the court." [15] King and the others were given suspended sentences. Upon their release, small-scale testing tactics were used. Small bi-racial teams went to three public parks and two libraries. Instead of arresting them, officials closed these facilities. The pools remained closed until months later, when one of them was sold to James Gray and reopened for whites only. Seats were removed from the libraries and the checkout desk was opened on a desegregated basis.

Election time was drawing near, and the Movement gave new emphasis to voter registration. In the rural areas, SNCC workers encountered increased harassment as they labored to enroll Negro voters. Their meetings in country churches were invaded by white officials. They were threatened or beaten and local Negroes were intimidated. White-supremacy candidates openly encouraged these acts. At dawn on August 15, Shady Grove Baptist Church in Leesburg was dynamited by terrorists.

On the same day the Albany City Commission met and promptly adjourned after refusing to consider proposals made by the Movement. The Northern ministers and rabbis left the day after, taking with them a vivid impression of conditions in southwest Georgia. Before they departed, they were asked to organize another and larger pilgrimage. This they did. In ten days eighty men and women from Chicago and the Northeast arrived in Albany. After a briefing session at Bethel A.M.E. Church, seventy-five of them agreed to risk arrest. Going in groups of five, they assembled before the city hall for a two-

hour prayer vigil. After brief scripture readings, they were ordered to disperse and then hauled off to jail, where some of them fasted for thirty-six hours. Most of them then posted bail and returned to their homes. A few remained in jail for a week.

The pilgrimage focused national attention on Albany once more and stimulated sympathy within the religious bodies to which the pilgrims belonged. The ten rabbis in the group were given scrolls by the American Jewish Congress for their "courage, devotion to liberty and fulfillment of the teachings of our prophets." Their gesture of solidarity heartened the Negroes of Albany, but it had no discernible positive effect on the whites. Even as they were ending their fast, night riders in Lee County fired volleys of rifle bullets into the homes of four Negro families. And soon after the last of them left on September 3, there were more outrages. In Terrell County a white SNCC worker was wounded in the arm by a night rider's shotgun blast. In little more than a week, three more Negro Baptist churches were destroyed. One of them was rebuilt by the white citizens of Terrell County. Funds were collected by several agencies to enable SCLC to rebuild the others, including Shady Grove, but white vandals with a bulldozer knocked down the walls of one of them a year later, before it was even completed.

With the departure of the Northern clergymen, the Albany Movement declined. It had little to show for its efforts except bruises. Although it continued to stage demonstrations from time to time, it made no headway the following year. The pathos of the situation is suggested by the events of May 1963. In three weeks, May 7-27, some 120 people were arrested, sixteen of whom vowed to fast "until there is some indication of a total solution to the racial problem here in Albany." This gesture had no effect but to exhibit a capacity for bluffing. Unable to muster more than a hundred demonstrators, Dr. Anderson announced on May 10 that Martin Luther King had been asked to come. "Then the sparks will begin to fly—in a nonviolent way, of course." But King did not come. A month later, Anderson moved to Detroit to begin a residency in surgery,

turning over the presidency of the Movement to Slater King.

The Albany Movement, said one observer, "was successful only if the goal was to go to jail." In part, its failure was due to the skill of Police Chief Pritchett, who won fame as an expert in quelling "racial disturbances," and to the stubbornness of city officials. The inaction of Federal authorities was also a factor. But of greater concern to us is the strategic failure of the Movement itself.

One episode not already mentioned is the attempt at school integration. On September 3, Dr. Anderson announced at a mass meeting that an attempt would be made to integrate the schools. The next day, he took his fourteen-year-old daughter and thirteen others to Albany Senior High School, while four children were taken to two junior high schools in the same manner. After talking with the principals, who refused to register the students, the Negro parents applied to the superintendent of schools, also without result. Dr. Anderson thereupon threatened to sue. Seven months later, on April 8, 1963, the suit was filed, bringing a Federal Court order in July for the county school board to submit a desegregation plan.

Most of the Albany Movement's actions were hastily conceived, shortsighted, overambitious. The Movement relied too much on the inspiration of the moment. It had no definite plan or advance schedule, no provision for alternative moves. No serious attempt was made to evaluate different actions or to synchronize them. Each time a major thrust was made, it was pinned to the same blind hope that it would bring a sweeping solution. The bus boycott is an excellent example of the kind of error to which the Movement was prone. Here was the weakest point in the opponent's system, and the bus company's offer provided an opportunity for nonviolent direct action—boarding the buses on an integrated basis and either scoring an immediate victory or, if police intervened, attacking the segregation ordinances in the courts. This opportunity was simply thrown away, probably because the Albany leaders were trying

to do, and surpass, what they thought had been done in Montgomery.

Virtually no approaches were made to white leaders or masses except at the least accessible point—the mayor and police chief.

Professor Howard Zinn of Spelman College in Atlanta concisely summed up the Movement's defects in a valuable study for the Southern Regional Council:

Sometimes there has been a tendency simply to repeat old actions under new circumstances. The movement delayed legal action, for instance, which might have been initiated last winter [1961-62], and continued to depend mainly on demonstrations, instead of linking the two. There has been a failure to create and handle skillfully a set of differentiated tactics for different situations. The problem of desegregating Albany facilities involves various parties: some situations call for action by the city commission; some for decision by the Federal Courts; some for agreement with private businessmen. Moreover, there are advantages to singling out a particular goal and concentrating on it. This is an approach not only tactically sound for Negro protest but also creates a climate favorable to a negotiated solution. The community is presented with a specific, concrete demand rather than a quilt of grievances and demands which smothers the always limited ability of societies to think rationally about their faults.[16]

Rectifying such faults is not easy for a movement that has squandered its potential. After a series of defeats it is, for example, hard to persuade members of teenage gangs to give up their knives, and the use of those knives under stress will sabotage the efforts of the few nonviolent cadres that can be counted on. In Albany, defeat brought division and apathy concerning nonviolence and the Movement, while at the same time whetting the Negro community's bitterness and frustration, conjuring up new goals even farther-reaching than the old. As one observer stated, "If anything, the Negroes' ambitions have grown in ratio to the decline of their hopes."[17]

Birmingham 1963

To a great extent, what was learned from the failure in Albany was used in scoring an important victory in Birmingham, a city ten times larger and ranking among the ugliest in its racial attitudes. Unsolved bombings of Negro homes were not uncommon, nor was unprovoked police brutality under the administration of Eugene "Bull" Connor, commissioner of public safety. It seemed hardly a promising location for a breakthrough, but Martin Luther King was determined to achieve gains here that would recoup prestige lost at Albany.

Birmingham's own nonviolent movement began in 1956 when the Rev. Fred L. Shuttlesworth launched a bus boycott on the Montgomery pattern and founded the Alabama Christian Movement for Human Rights. Although the boycott did not reach mass proportions, it led to a suit that integrated the Birmingham bus lines. In subsequent years, Shuttlesworth made repeated forays against segregation. At one time in July 1961 he was under indictment in six criminal cases for breaking Jim Crow laws and was involved in a dozen civil cases.

In March 1962, Shuttlesworth launched a campaign to end segregation in hiring practices and at lunch counters of downtown Birmingham stores. There were brief demonstrations and a continuous boycott which inflicted serious economic losses on merchants. In September, when he announced an imminent renewal of demonstrations, white businessmen agreed to negotiate. As a first step toward meeting the Negroes' demands, they even removed the "white" and "colored" signs from drinking fountains and rest rooms. But as a result of pressure from city hall they reneged and suspended the talks.

In November a referendum was held which abolished the commission form of government and called for the election of a mayor and city council. Partly at the urging of white moderates, Shuttlesworth and his movement deferred further demonstrations until after the final run-off election on April 2, 1963, when moderate Albert Boutwell defeated Bull Connor

in the contest for the mayoralty. Seven weeks were to pass, however, before Boutwell could take office, pending a court ruling, since Connor filed suit to retain the old system until 1965, the end of the term for which he and his colleagues had been elected.

After the run-off, Shuttlesworth saw no reason for further delay. Boutwell gave no assurance of change, and the businessmen took no steps to integrate. SCLC leaders were called on for help, and on April 3 picketing and sit-ins began, involving some thirty Negroes. Twenty of them were arrested at Britt's Department Store. Others at Woolworth's, Loveman's and elsewhere found the lunch counters closed when they appeared.

Martin Luther King arrived and addressed a rally of 500 Negroes that evening: "We are heading for freedom land and nothing is going to stop us. We are going to make Birmingham the center of antidiscrimination activity in the nation. I have come to stay until something is done."

As sit-ins continued, a new tactic was added on April 6, a protest march to city hall led by Shuttlesworth, in which forty-two Negroes were arrested. The next day the Rev. John T. Porter and the Rev. A. D. King, Martin's brother, led a contingent of twenty-six to kneel in prayer there. They refused to disperse and were taken to jail as some 500 Negro bystanders looked on. Some of the policemen had police dogs on leashes and did not hesitate to torment bystanders with them. When one of the latter slashed at a dog with a knife, six policemen pounced on him and disarmed him. Only the efforts of SCLC staff members kept a riot from breaking out.

On Good Friday, April 12, Shuttlesworth, King and Abernathy led a group of fifty hymn-singing Negroes out of Sixth Avenue Baptist Church toward city hall. Five police vans awaited them en route, and they were hustled into them and driven to jail. It was Dr. King's thirteenth arrest. When he was jailed in 1960 during a sit-in at Rich's Department Store in Atlanta, presidential candidate John F. Kennedy had interceded for him. Again in 1962 President Kennedy told Justice

Department officials to keep him informed of King's well-being in the Albany jail. Now the President alerted Assistant Attorney General Burke Marshall to keep an eye on the Birmingham situation.

On Easter Sunday, small groups of Negroes sought admittance to six white churches. At First Baptist and First Presbyterian they were cordially received. At First Christian, two women were denied entry but were escorted to the parish house by four elders, who tried to explain their situation and prayed with them. Elsewhere, Negroes were turned away. At Sixth Avenue Presbyterian, SCLC Youth Secretary Bernard Lee walked halfway up the steps with two women. An usher blocked the door and said: "Go to the colored church. White people built this church and white people worship here."

Later in the day at Thurgood C.M.E. Church, after a worship service, the Rev. A. D. King emerged in his pulpit robe, Bible in hand, leading a procession of twenty-eight Negroes. They intended to march to the city jail and pray for his imprisoned brother and some 150 other cadres now being held. They did not get far before they were arrested. As they waited for the police vans, a crowd of about 2,000 Negroes gathered, protesting angrily against the arrests. After the prisoners were taken away, police seized a jeering woman and wrestled with her as she resisted arrest. A number of rocks were thrown from the rear ranks of the throng, smashing a police car's windshield. SCLC leaders remonstrated with the people in the crowd, imploring them to be nonviolent. Policemen moved in and one of them broke his nightstick on a young Negro's head. For ten minutes a serious riot threatened. Police reinforcements arrived and many of the Negroes drifted away as others followed SCLC cadres into Thurgood Church for another long service.

These incidents began to provoke responses, both locally and nationally. A group of eight Birmingham clergymen, including the two who had admitted Negro visitors at Easter, issued a statement characterizing the campaign as "unwise and

untimely," and commending the police for their restraint in keeping order. To this, Martin Luther King replied in a long letter from his jail cell. Widely reprinted, it stated in part:

I don't believe you would have so warmly commended the police force if you had seen its angry violent dogs literally biting six unarmed, nonviolent Negroes. I don't believe you would so quickly commend the policemen if you would observe their ugly and inhuman treatment of Negroes here in the city jail . . . if you would observe them, as they did on two occasions, refuse to give us food because we wanted to sing our grace together.[18]

Soon after the arrest of Abernathy and King, telegrams were sent to the President and the Attorney General, especially deploring the use of police dogs. Among the signers were prominent churchmen, literary figures, labor leaders and actors. Behind the scenes in Birmingham, small groups of Negro and white ministers began meeting. Through them, contact was established between representatives of SCLC, the Alabama Council on Human Relations, local merchants and Mayor-elect Boutwell. Together they began to sketch a program to meet the Negroes' demands, but the store owners hesitated to implement it without clear support from the larger business community, including Birmingham's industrialists.

On April 20, as daily arrests continued in the face of a sweeping injunction against demonstrations, King and Abernathy had themselves released from jail in $300 cash bonds in order to consult with their strategy committee. It was decided to organize Birmingham's Negro school children for a massive nonviolent assault on segregation, a tactic that had earlier been used in Statesville and Durham, North Carolina.

For over a week, SCLC cadres visited classrooms and school libraries, recruiting students. When principals called police, the cadres left and returned when the police were gone. The response was overwhelming; students flocked in large numbers to pledge themselves to nonviolence and receive training for action, which was conducted in a number of Negro churches. By Thursday, May 2, some 6,000 children were organized and

ready to march, and detailed arrangements were made to feed them at the churches where they assembled.

Shortly after noon, King and other leaders at Sixteenth Street Baptist Church addressed the first group of 300 children, ranging from six to sixteen years old. They divided into smaller groups and, joining hands and singing "We Shall Overcome," the first thirty-eight marched forth as a throng of some 400 Negro spectators cheered. They were arrested two blocks from the church. For four hours thereafter, successive waves of children marched out to be arrested, and others arrived at the church to wait their turn.

Three groups managed to reach the downtown shopping area and one was arrested only fifteen feet from the city hall steps. Marchers were given directions by older youths with walkie-talkies. Excellent discipline was maintained; when police approached, the youngsters fell to their knees and started to pray. In all, 959 children and ten adults, including A. D. King, were arrested on this day.

Another 250 were arrested on Friday. Although a thousand jammed the Sixteenth Street Church, only half of them got out before police barred the exits. Fire hoses, which had been held ready on Thursday, were now turned on with a pressure of fifty to one hundred pounds. Torrents of water knocked many of the children to the ground and literally ripped the T-shirt from one youth's back as he sprawled on the pavement. The dogs were also brought out and released into the crowds. Five Negroes were bitten and many more were savagely menaced. "The police made no effort to restrain them," said the Rev. Andrew J. Young, leader of SCLC's action workshop. "It was almost as if they were trying to incite a riot."

Despite these provocations, the Negro bystanders, few of whom had received training in nonviolent conduct, remained unusually well disciplined until a state police investigator deliberately swerved his car into the crowd. This brought a shower of rocks and bottles from a cluster of Negroes on a nearby rooftop, which injured a news photographer and two firemen man-

ning hoses. In retaliation the hoses were turned on the crowd.

Alarmed by these events, Burke Marshall arrived in Birmingham on Saturday to confer with both Martin Luther King and the white businessmen. Demonstrations continued and for half an hour unruly elements in the crowd hurled rocks and bottles at the firemen when the hoses were turned on. James Bevel, an SCLC secretary, borrowed a policeman's bull-horn amplifier and called to the crowd: "Everybody get off this corner. If you're not going to demonstrate in a nonviolent manner, then leave." Soon after the crowd cleared, further demonstrations were called off until Monday. Bevel saw a number of knives and pistols in the hands of Negro spectators and feared that bloodshed might occur.

On Sunday, small groups of Negroes again sought admittance to white churches. They gained entry to four and were turned away from seventeen others. Late in the afternoon a mass meeting was held at New Pilgrim Baptist Church. Lined up outside were fifty policemen and a fire truck with water pressure cranked up to 700 pounds. A little before sunset the crowd of about two thousand Negroes came out and faced the police. They knelt in silence as one of the ministers prayed solemnly: "Let them turn their water on. Let them use their dogs. We are not leaving. Forgive them, O Lord."

Perhaps for a moment this touched something in Bull Connor, for he let the Negroes cross the police line and spend fifteen minutes in a small park near the city jail, where they prayed and sang hymns within hearing of the hundreds of demonstrators inside. Afterward, they returned to the church, where it was announced that the children would definitely march on Monday.

At 1:00 P.M., May 6, comedian Dick Gregory led the first contingent of nineteen marchers from Sixteenth Street Baptist Church. They were quickly arrested. Then, as on Thursday, wave after wave of them went out. The last group, a little over an hour later, was led by Barbara Deming, a writer for *The Nation*. More than 200 others drifted rather than marched to

the downtown area, where they assembled and began picketing the stores. About a thousand Negroes were arrested, half of them adults. Fire hoses were present but not used, and again SCLC cadres remonstrated with a large crowd to remain calm. Only one incident occurred. When police attempted to force a woman off the sidewalk, she resisted. Five policemen wrestled her to the pavement and one of them pinned her down with his knee in her neck. An angered Negro man ripped the shirt of one of the officers and tried to slip his revolver from its holster. Both of the Negroes were arrested. At this moment a riot could have erupted but for the cadres' exhortations.

Since his arrival on Saturday, Burke Marshall met repeatedly with Negro and white leaders, while from Washington Attorney General Robert F. Kennedy, Secretary of the Treasury Douglas Dillon and Defense Secretary Robert McNamara made dozens of telephone calls to businessmen and industrialists, pressing for a speedy settlement. Believing that not enough was being done, Dean Eugene V. Rostow of Yale Law School volunteered his services by phoning Roger Blough, chairman of the board of United States Steel. A graduate of the law school, Blough agreed to call his associates in Birmingham and impress them with the national importance of reaching an agreement. By Tuesday morning, Marshall was strongly urging the Birmingham businessmen to accede to the Negroes' demands, and they were listening to him.

The jails by now were overflowing. According to the *Birmingham News,* the children were treated gently. But the reports that came to SCLC told a different story. All the girls were examined for venereal disease, like common criminals. Those who requested aspirin were given laxatives. When they complained to newspapermen, their complaints went unreported and they were made to scrub the halls with toothbrushes and steel wool as punishment. One day 800 children under sixteen were kept in the jail yard for four hours in pouring rain. Those who protested were placed in solitary confinement. Dick Gregory was beaten three times, and he was not the only one.

Yet none of them showed fear. Many, after being released on bail, marched and were jailed again.

Partly because of the congested conditions of the jails, police resorted to new tactics on Tuesday. When 500 children began marching from the church at noon, police broke up their formations and dispersed them without making arrests. Inside the church, the Rev. James Bevel said: "If they're not going to arrest our marchers, we'll charge downtown, right in the face of the white people." They streamed out by the hundreds, heading toward the business district by different zigzag routes, joined by others on the streets as they went, until more than 3,000 of them converged on the downtown area. Groups of them trooped in and out of stores, singing "Ain't gonna let nobody turn me 'round" and "I'm on my way to freedom land." After this brief foray—the first "sing-in"—they dispersed, returned to the church, regrouped and again streamed downtown. According to one SCLC staff member, this had a considerable effect on the white businessmen.

When they returned a second time, city police augmented by fifty sheriff's officers in steel helmets with guns and nightsticks cordoned off an eight-block area to bar a third raid. Many demonstrators were herded into the park across from the church, where together with bystanders they formed a crowd of about 2,000. Contrary to nonviolent discipline, they taunted the police: "Bring on the dogs! Bring on the water!" Jets of water smashed into the crowd, forcing them back. Neon signs and shop windows were shattered by the force of the blasts. Fred Shuttlesworth was knocked flat and taken away in an ambulance. Negroes broke up paving blocks and hurled them at the police. For an hour and a half they fought, as SCLC cadres pleaded with the Negroes to abandon violence. The final skirmish, ironically, was fought on the church steps, where retreating Negroes threw their last rocks and the hoses cracked stained-glass windows and flooded the basement. In the lull that followed, Negro leaders reiterated their pleas: "Go home. You are not helping our cause." Finally the remnant of the crowd

dissolved. Some forty Negroes were arrested. At least a dozen people were injured, including three policemen.

This episode played into Bull Connor's hands. At his request the Governor ordered 250 state troopers sent into the city. Given their reputation for racist brutality and given the rising Negro temper, the stage was being set for a bloodbath. The negotiators became anxious to reach agreement before it came, and they worked far into the night, deciding at last on a tentative accord. A one-day truce was to be called while details were worked out.

During the truce, downtown Birmingham bristled like an armed camp, with some 750 city, county and state police, firemen with hoses, an armored car with tear-gas guns, and the police dogs. Several thousand Negroes massed in churches near the downtown area, ready to march if the truce was broken.

They were ready again on Thursday morning in even greater force. There were 1,200 law officers at Kelly Ingram Park and ominous reports of increased activity by the Ku Klux Klan and other racist organizations. That morning, May 9, the agreement was confirmed and the truce extended. A Negro and a white lawyer worked out the exact terms that night.

The next morning, all of the 790 prisoners who remained in jail were released on bail. A total of $237,000 for this purpose was contributed by the United Auto Workers, the National Maritime Union and other groups. In the afternoon, Martin Luther King announced the four-point settlement. It provided for: 1) desegregation of lunch counters, rest rooms, fitting rooms and drinking fountains in all downtown stores within ninety days; 2) placement of Negroes in previously all-white clerical and sales positions, through upgrading or hiring, within sixty days; 3) release of prisoners, which by now had been accomplished; and 4) firm establishment of permanent communication between white and Negro leaders. "This is the most significant victory for justice we've ever seen in the Deep South," said King, beaming. But he added a sober note:

This is the time that we must evince calm, dignity and wise restraint. Emotion must not run wild. Violence must not come from any of us. . . . As we stand on the verge of using public facilities heretofore closed to us, we must not be overbearing and haughty in spirit. We must move now from protest to reconciliation.

Though less enthusiastic, Sidney W. Smyer, chairman of the white merchants' negotiating committee, called upon all of Birmingham's people to be calm and accept the pact. When white extremists urged that he encourage new violence as a pretext for repudiating the agreement, he publicly voiced "unalterable opposition" to this viewpoint. The thirst for revenge did not die so quickly, however. On Saturday night, after a Ku Klux Klan rally on the outskirts of town, a dynamite blast ripped the front part of A. D. King's home in suburban Ensley, and half an hour later another explosion tore a hole in the side of the A. G. Gaston Motel, which served as SCLC headquarters in the city.

Large crowds of Negroes milled about both places. Fortunately A. D. King was at home and unhurt. Although a few hotheads threw rocks and let the air out of the tires of police cars that had arrived, King quickly calmed and dispersed the gathering.

Near the motel the atmosphere was more volatile. Men flocked there from saloons in the nearby Negro slum area, some of them shouting angrily: "Let's get Bull Connor!" Police, firemen and members of a Negro civil-defense unit were also on the scene. SCLC executive secretary Wyatt Walker pleaded with the crowd: "Please, please move back. Throwing rocks won't help. This is no good. Please go home. It does no good to lose your heads."

"Tell it to Bull Connor," they roared. "This is what nonviolence gets you."

The rioting had begun to subside when, at 1:10 A.M., Colonel Al Lingo and his state troopers arrived. They piled out of their cars with machine guns, shotguns and unsheathed bayonets, and began to club and jab Negroes indiscriminately.

Walker's wife was struck in the head with a gun butt and taken to the hospital. Birmingham Police Chief Jamie Moore quickly intervened: "Wait, wait a minute now, you're going to get somebody killed with those guns."

"I damn sure will if I have to," Lingo retorted. But after further urging, he and his troopers got back into their cars, where they sat and watched the fighting.

The mob smashed police-car windows and slashed the tires. They set fire to a motorcycle and tried in vain to overturn a patrol wagon. In the melee, city police acted with restraint. One patrolman was knifed and others were punched, as were the Negro civil-defense men, but they did not resort to shooting. At one point, Chief Inspector William J. Haley was struck in the forehead with a brick, and an infuriated policeman started toward the crowd with a shotgun, knocking A. D. King out of the way with the butt as he went. But a police lieutenant grabbed him and ordered him back.

Enraged Negroes broke into three white-owned grocery stores, looted them and set them on fire, then stoned firemen who attempted to extinguish the blaze. Unchecked, the flames spread to adjoining Negro homes. Half an hour later, Negro civil-defense worker Sylvester Norris drove a fire truck through the barrage of stones, enabling the firemen to go into action.

By 3:40 A.M. the combined forces of white police and firemen and Negro CD workers and SCLC cadres brought the riot to an end. The pivotal event was perhaps an encounter between A. D. King and the drunken leader of the mob. King tried to talk to the man, who was cursing him as an Uncle Tom, when someone whispered to the man and he said: "You Dr. King? You been to jail? Your home got bombed?" King said he was, and the man turned to the crowd. "This is our leader," he told them. "He say you go home, you go home." Although obviously drunk, said King, the man's control over the crowd was amazing.

After the drunken mob dispersed, the state troopers went after Negroes who had taken no part in the riot, clubbing

old men and women sitting on their porches and forcing them indoors.

When daybreak came it was Sunday, Mother's Day. In the night's rioting an estimated fifty persons had been injured. Miraculously, no one was killed. Property damage was conservatively assessed at $41,775. In Washington, President Kennedy issued a statement in which he said:

The Birmingham agreement was and is a fair and just accord. . . . It was a tribute to the process of peaceful negotiation and to the good faith of both parties. The Federal Government will not permit it to be sabotaged. . . .

I call upon all the citizens of Birmingham . . . to realize that violence only breeds more violence. . . . There must be no repetition of last night's incidents by any group.

Martin Luther King was in Atlanta during the riot. He returned to Birmingham and on Monday set out on a pilgrimage of the Negro pool halls, accompanied by several aides. They entered the first one. Playing stopped and a number of others came in from the street to listen. King spoke of Saturday night's ravages and Abernathy asked them to pledge themselves to nonviolence, then led them in singing "We Shall Overcome," using a pool cue as a baton. They moved to another pool hall and did likewise. As they left, one of the players nodded toward the state troopers in the street and muttered: "I ain't gonna take none of that damn stuff." Others tagged along as the SCLC leaders headed for another pool hall. The procession now numbered about 100. They did not get far, however, before state troopers with carbines compelled them to disperse, ordered onlookers back into stores and houses and made King's group return to the Gaston Motel. With 700 state troopers in the city, it was as if martial law had been imposed. Police Chief Moore was privately known to be unhappy about their presence, fearing that they might provoke a new riot.

After a few tense days marked by minor, scattered incidents, Birmingham began to settle down. On May 23, scarcely two

weeks after the riot, the Alabama Supreme Court unanimously upheld Mayor Boutwell's election, and five days later the new city council authorized the formation of a biracial Committee on Community Affairs, in accordance with the pact. Waiting for tensions to ease, the resolution was not publicized for six weeks, when invitations were sent out. Only three persons declined, and on July 16 some 200 leading citizens, Negro and white, made their way through clusters of protesting Klansmen to enter city hall and register as members of the committee. By the following month, each of the provisions of the May agreement had been implemented. As a further gesture of good faith, the city opened its golf courses on an integrated basis, although they were not included in the pact.

Racist Counterattack: The Church Bombing

The Birmingham campaign was not perfect. It did not usher in a golden age, nor did it even initiate an upswing of unbroken progress. Bull Connor, Governor Wallace, the Ku Klux Klan and other die-hards were not suddenly converted to integration. Scarcely four months after the bombing of the Gaston Motel, four Negro children were killed and twenty injured in the first of a new series of terroristic acts. The children were attending a Bible class at Sixteenth Street Baptist Church, the very bastion of nonviolent action in the May campaign. It was not the first bombing, nor would it be the last in Birmingham. There had been some fifty unsolved bombings prior to 1963, and in the wake of the church bombing there were more, as well as shootings, arson and other depradations.

The church bombing followed the first steps in integrating the city's schools. It occurred as demagogues, including the Governor, urged defiance of the Federal Courts which had ordered these steps. It is outside our purpose here to detail all the facts. It is sufficient to note the impact of the tragedy, which posed a crisis for nonviolence. The instantaneous reaction of hundreds of Birmingham Negroes was understand-

able. They vented their panic and frustration by spilling into the streets and pelting police and firemen with rocks until the church's pastor, the Rev. J. H. Cross, pleaded with them to disperse. It was a blind lashing out at those who for many years had symbolized that same enemy from whose ranks the bombers undoubtedly came. At the same time, the attitude of city officials, though not repentant, was at least regretful. Mayor Boutwell offered his cooperation to Federal investigators, but he did so without conferring with Negro leaders. One noted Birmingham attorney, Charles Morgan, in an impassioned speech to the Young Men's Business Association, excoriated the mayor, the police and white ministers as well as the white population of the city: "Every person in this community who has in any way contributed during the past several years to the popularity of hatred is at least as guilty as, or more than, the demented fool who threw that bomb."

Some good might eventuate from such soul-searching—and from the shock felt by many complacent citizens in the South and throughout the nation. But of more concern here is the reaction of many Negro leaders, typified in this statement by Dr. Gardner Taylor, an influential figure in the Progressive Baptist Convention: "That incredible act forces a re-examination by serious Christians of the entire doctrine of nonviolence except as a tactical approach in selected situations." Writer John O. Killens said more pointedly that he doubted that nonviolence offered the way out in the civil-rights struggle and asserted the right of Negroes to defend themselves with weapons. "As a tactic, nonviolence has been successful, but as a philosophy we need to get rid of it."

Louis E. Lomax, author of *The Negro Revolt,* was present at a memorial service for the four dead children when Killens spoke. "The time is coming," Lomax said, "when the Negro must arm himself to defend his home." Also present was Christopher McNair, whose only child was one of those killed. With the authority of experience, he said: "Such an effort

would be fruitless. I'm not for that. What good would Denise have done with a machine gun in her hands?"

Nonviolence, it must be admitted, has no solution for bombs set off by unknown persons. Neither do pistols or shotguns in citizens' homes. And certainly the way to deal with a frenzied, rock-throwing mob, however righteous its anger, is not to urge more lethal weapons upon it—especially when their victims are sure to be indiscriminately chosen. What is required is neither a blind acceptance of nonviolence as a cure-all, nor the exasperated abandonment of nonviolence because it does not always work miracles, but a clear-sighted understanding of its possibilities and limitations in each situation. It is a hard fact, unaltered by all the bombings, riots and shootings, that in May nonviolence achieved stated objectives in a very brief span of time, objectives that were probably unattainable in any other way, certainly not by mob violence. Undoubtedly the capacity for violence, glimpsed in the incipient riots at the height of the May demonstrations, played a part in expediting a settlement. But any display of this potential could be effective only as it also showed the power of the SCLC leaders to curb it. The lesson is clear. Nonviolence can be effective when it is used skillfully. It does not require perfection, nor does it produce perfection. It does call for discipline, courage and restraint in the face of adversity, as well as good strategy. And in the pivotal Birmingham campaign of May 1963 it had all these attributes, winning out against fire hoses, police dogs and ingrained racist attitudes.

REFERENCES IN CHAPTER 20

1   Martin Luther King Jr.: *Stride Toward Freedom* (New York: Harper & Brothers, 1958), p. 58.
2   Carl T. Rowan: *Go South to Sorrow* (New York: Random House, 1957), p. 119.
3   L. D. Reddick: *Crusader Without Violence* (New York: Harper & Brothers, 1959), p. 178.

4 Glenford E. Mitchell: "College Students Take Over" in Mitchell and Peace, eds.: *The Angry Black South* (New York: Corinth Books, Inc., 1962), p. 79f. See also Louis E. Lomax: *The Negro Revolt* (New York: Harper & Brothers, 1962), pp. 121-146.

5 *Ibid.*, p. 80f.

6 Thomas Gaither: news report in *Community* (Chicago), June 1960, p. 4.

7 Jameson Jones: "Issues in the Sit-Ins" in *Motive* (Nashville), May 1960.

8 Merrill Proudfoot: *Diary of a Sit-In* (Chapel Hill: University of North Carolina Press, 1962), p. 94.

9 Mitchell, *op. cit.*, p. 87f.

10 Proudfoot, *op. cit.*, p. 185.

11 Diane Nash: "Inside the Sit-Ins and Freedom Rides" in Mathew H. Ahmann, ed.: *The New Negro* (Notre Dame: Fides Publishers, Inc., 1961), p. 55.

12 John David Maguire: "When Moderation Demands Taking Sides" in *Christianity and Crisis,* June 26, 1961, p. 115.

13 *Ibid.*, p. 116.

14 Robert McAfee Brown in *Presbyterian Life,* August 1, 1961.

15 Ralph Lord Roy: "Albany Diary" in *The New York Amsterdam News,* September 8, 1962.

16 Howard Zinn: *Albany* (Atlanta: Southern Regional Council, 1962), p. 19. See also Wyatt Tee Walker: "Achievement in Albany" in *New South* (Atlanta), June 1963.

17 Reese Cleghorn: "Epilogue in Albany" in *The New Republic* (Washington), July 20, 1963, p. 17.

18 Martin Luther King Jr.: *Letter from Birmingham City Jail* (Valley Forge, Pa.: American Baptist Convention, 1963), p. 13.

21

Episodes of Spontaneous
Nonviolence

Throughout history from earliest times, man has shown his capacity for revolt and resistance, frequently reckless and bloody. Sometimes he has also shown a capacity for restraint that has enabled him to voice his protest through direct action short of violence, actually refraining from bloodshed in circumstances that made it difficult to do so, yet without any guiding principle or plan of nonviolence.

In the Russian Revolution

In his monumental *History of the Russian Revolution,* Leon Trotsky tells of a remarkable encounter between a crowd of 2,500 striking industrial workers and a troop of Cossacks, the most ruthless and reliable of the tsarist armed forces for conducting anti-Semitic pogroms, quelling peasant uprisings and breaking strikes. The date is February 24, 1917, the second of the five days of mass demonstrations that preceded the seizure of power by the revolutionists. On this day, some 90,000 workers were out on strike, marching in the streets. Trotsky's source of information was Kayurov, a strike leader who participated in the incident described here.

The mass of 2,500 workers from the Erikson mill in the Vyborg district of Petrograd had marched to Sampsonevsky Prospekt, where they encountered the Cossacks. First the officers streamed through the crowd. Normally, the rank-and-file

345

horsemen would have galloped after them, fanning out and wielding their knouts or sabers as they came.

But the horsemen, cautiously, in a long ribbon, rode through the corridor just made by the officers. "Some of them smiled," Kayurov recalls, "and one of them gave the workers a good wink." This wink was not without meaning. The workers were emboldened with a friendly, not hostile, kind of assurance, and slightly infected the Cossacks with it. The one who winked found imitators. In spite of renewed efforts from the officers, the Cossacks, without openly breaking discipline, failed to force the crowd to disperse, but flowed through it in streams. This was repeated three or four times and brought the two sides even closer together. Individual Cossacks began to reply to the workers' questions and even to enter into momentary conversation with them. Of discipline there remained but a thin transparent shell that threatened to break through any second. The officers hastened to separate their patrol from the workers and, abandoning the idea of dispersing them, lined the Cossacks out across the street as a barrier to prevent the demonstrators from getting to the center. But even this did not help: standing stock-still in perfect discipline, the Cossacks did not hinder the workers from "diving" under their horses. The revolution does not choose its paths: it made its first steps toward victory under the belly of a Cossack's horse.[1]

This incident was not typical. Kayurov's group was unarmed and made no attempt to provoke violence, though elsewhere in the city twenty-eight policemen were beaten by workers on the same day and the day before. And the next day, with the ranks of the strikers swollen to 240,000, shooting began. Perhaps even more remarkable than the episode above was another in which Kayurov appealed to the Cossacks to defend the workers against the mounted police. Cap in hand, he turned to them: "Brothers—Cossacks, help the workers in a struggle for their peaceable demands." [2]

"The Cossacks glanced at each other in some special way," Kayurov continues, "and we were hardly out of the way before they rushed into the fight." And a few minutes later, near the station gate, the

NONVIOLENCE: A CHRISTIAN INTERPRETATION   347

crowd were tossing in their arms a Cossack who, before their eyes, had slaughtered a police inspector with his saber.[3]

Women strikers went up to infantrymen, boldly taking hold of their rifles and pleading: "Put down your bayonets—join us." On many occasions they did so, or at least broke ranks to permit the workers to pass.

Trotsky holds no brief for nonviolence, certainly, and he calls these episodes "more symptomatic than substantial," forming a prelude to a decisive clash of armed force, but nevertheless of key importance for winning support on the side of the insurgents.

It is not properly within the scope of nonviolence, of course, to encourage anyone to kill on our behalf. What is to the point is that, within history, it has happened repeatedly that unarmed men such as Kayurov—not a pacifist but a Bolshevik—have succeeded in appealing to their enemies, getting them either to stand aside neutrally or to defect to the other side, throwing down their weapons or handing them over or using them against the oppressor. As Trotsky, the great revolutionary theorist, points out, "The whole history of street fights and revolutionary victories swarms with such improvisations. But they are drowned without a trace in the abyss of great events."[4] In fact, few historians trouble to record these incidents in many cases. Of the Petrograd events, for example, Sukhanov says only that "fugitive meetings were held in the main streets and were dispersed by Cossacks and mounted police—but without any energy or zeal and after lengthy delays."[5] Trotsky, for his own reasons, stands alone among the major historians of the Russian Revolution in giving more than this cursory account.

Other Episodes: Hungary 1849, France 1871, Algeria 1962

If it was important to Trotsky to record these minor episodes as symptoms of the revolutionary situation, it was of

interest to Arthur Griffith as a proponent of passive resistance in the early days of the Sinn Fein resistance organization in Ireland to ferret out a similar episode that occurred during the Hungarian Revolution of 1849.[6]

A mob had lynched the Austrian Lord Lieutenant on his arrival in Budapest, and Lajos Kossuth was installed as president. To quell the revolt, the Austrian Grenadier Guards were sent from Vienna, but they refused to march. The Kaiser ordered the National Guard to fire on the recalcitrant Grenadiers, but they refused to do so and joined the latter in mutiny against the crown, cheering for Kossuth and for liberty. This was only a brief interlude, easily forgotten in the subsequent history of the Austrian and Hungarian revolutions and eclipsed by the military and political struggles that ensued.

Much the same occurred in Paris on March 18, 1871, when troops sent to suppress demonstrations in Montmartre refused to fire and fraternized with the insurgents—a prelude to the short-lived Paris Commune.

On August 31, 1962, a crowd of 20,000 workers thronged the streets of Algiers to forestall a threatened civil war between rival Algerian government factions, soon after the end of a bloody and bitter seven-year war for independence from France. Fighting had already begun and many persons had been killed, when the General Union of Algerian Workers threatened a general strike. In one district, union leaders declared:

Go out into the streets and shout your anger in front of the tanks and the armored cars. In front of the machine guns you will stand up, armed with your courage alone, to stop those who want to unleash civil war. Seven years of bloodshed is enough.[7]

On the border between two rival districts (*willayas*), reported the *Manchester Guardian,*

The soldiers of the two Willayas faced one another; but . . . on the insistence of the local villagers first the men, then the officers shook hands and laid aside their arms.[8]

At Boghari and elsewhere, the populace formed a human barrier against the troops, shouting: "No more bloodshed!" As a result the rival factions quickly declared a cease-fire which led to a political settlement.

A fact of key importance in the Algerian episode is that it occurred after the end of a long and exhausting war in which both of the now rival factions and the intervening peacemakers were all united against the French *colons*. In a different way, war weariness also helped to bring together the rank-and-file Cossacks and the Petrograd workers. This did not forestall bloodshed, but it contributed to a weighting of the workers' side of the scales which made the democratic February insurrection swift and successful. It is a moot question whether, without the dramatic and spontaneously nonviolent appeal for "no more bloodshed," the strife between the Algerian factions might have developed into a devastating civil war such as that which ravaged Russia after the Bolshevik seizure of power, some nine months after the brief democratic revolution. In any case this is not the place to examine the complexities of Russian history. But in evaluating the Algerian situation it is well to remember its parallel in Asia: the protracted struggle against the French in Indo-China, which was followed by years of guerrilla warfare in Vietnam and Laos, independent states that were carved out of the former French Indo-China.

The East German Revolt of 1953

June 17, 1953, is a memorable date in the annals of man's struggle for freedom. It is also a date that figures, if somewhat ambiguously, in the history of nonviolent direct action. This was the date on which workers throughout Soviet-occupied East Germany rose up and very nearly overthrew the totalitarian regime under which they lived. "The very fact that this great uprising could and did take place," said West Berlin's Mayor Ernst Reuter, "proves to the world that the totalitarian machine is not infallible or omnipotent, that it has its weak-

nesses, and that if the free world only had the political imagination to match the human courage which the enslaved world is ready to show, then the days of the Iron Curtain in Central Europe would be numbered." [9]

The people who revolted had lived under totalitarian rule for twenty years—twelve under Hitler and eight under Stalin and Ulbricht. One analyst, referring to those whose peaceful strike triggered the revolt, has stated:

The building workers of Berlin and the steel workers of Hennigsdorf were known for their support of revolutionary actions during the pre-Nazi era, 1918-1933. They were strongholds of the Communist movement in Berlin during that period. Under the Nazis they defied the regime whenever possible.[10]

Many of the other leaders of the strikes that spread throughout East Germany were former members of the banned Social Democratic Party, who maintained ties with their party in West Germany, in effect operating in the East Zone as an underground. M. S. Handler of *The New York Times* called the uprising "a masterpiece of direct action. . . . The rapidity and simultaneity of the strikes throughout East Germany indicated the extent of the ramifications of the underground organization." [11] In less than a week the revolt spread to 350 towns and villages, involving millions of people estimated at half the entire working population and including people of all social strata. According to Stefan Brant:

Irrespective of origin, character, sex, social and professional ties or age, millions of individuals acted as one, obeying the same signals, striving to reach the same goal and formulating the same program. . . .[12]

As Melvin J. Lasky, editor of *Der Monat,* pointed out, this was "an objective revolutionary situation" right out of the Marxist lexicon. "The notion of the general strike sprang to the minds of millions with a spontaneity that went beyond Sorel's fondest hopes." [13]

Georges Sorel, proponent of violent revolt, was not the East

Germans' only ideologue, however. Rainer Hildebrandt says that Gerald Wagner, a radio editor who managed to help spread the word of the uprising from the RIAS transmitter in West Berlin, "believed with Gandhi that the most moral resistance was the most demoralizing to the adversary." [14] However imperfect or indirect, this was a motif widely attested by observers and reporters, as epitomized in this sample by Norbert Muhlen:

Often the demonstrators went first to the prisons to ask for the release of political prisoners; only when their requests were refused did they storm the prisons and free the inmates. . . .

Yet in every case they refrained from taking the weapons of the disarmed guards and police for themselves. In the first place, they wanted to avoid bloodshed—a revolutionary pacifism unheard of in history. In the second place, they assumed . . . that if order were maintained, the Soviet occupying power would stand by neutrally.[15]

Naïve as the latter assumption may seem, it was not without some substance. Lasky, for example, saw East Berliners haul down the red flag on top of the Brandenburg Gate and destroy the Soviet bookshop on the Alexanderplatz while Soviet troops looked on indifferently.[16] Hildebrandt tells of two Soviet Army lieutenants who cast their lot with the struggle for liberty. One of them, a Lieutenant Gregoriev, fled to West Berlin after the revolt collapsed; the other, Lieutenant Rakit Kastanov, was executed.[17] Both expected, as did many others, that the revolt would succeed and spread to the USSR. Exact information in detail is hard to find, but by June 28 at least thirty-two men had been executed by Red Army firing squads for siding with the revolt, and these included Volkspolizei (East German militia or "people's police") who had been sent to help suppress the revolt and had instead torn off their uniforms and turned over their weapons to the insurgent workers. So widespread were the defections of German troops that the Soviet authorities moved to demobilize the East German Army (Bereitschaften) and reorganize it. Hundreds of its officers, reported C. L. Sulzberger, were "reduced in rank or court-

martialed." [18] In Goerlitz, on the Polish border, thousands of German demonstrators greeted Polish tanks that were sent in to disperse them. An Associated Press correspondent who witnessed the encounter reported:

The senior Polish officer stepped out of his tank, faced the Germans —and saluted. "I don't fire on German workers," he said. The Germans returned his salute.

When the Russians saw the Poles were not going to resist the Germans, they ordered the Polish troops back across the border and sent in Russian tanks.[19]

Throughout East Germany, efforts were made by revolt leaders to restrain their followers from resorting to violence, even under provocation, or at least not to initiate violence. The case of Friedrich Schorn, leader of the insurgents at East Germany's largest chemical plant, the Leunawerke near Leipzig, is indicative. Addressing the workers, Schorn, an accountant at the plant, said: "This isn't a matter of just Leuna. It's a matter of every German in the Soviet Zone. Everything is at stake. But violence isn't the answer. If we overrun the plant and wreck the machinery, we'll only have to rebuild it later. Let's keep order." [20] When factory guards handed over their weapons, Schorn gave orders that they were not to be used but locked in a storeroom.

From the plant, the workers marched to Merseburg. When Volkspolizei tried to block their path, the workers laughed and shouted: "Out of the way! Stand aside or join us!" Two or three of them doffed their caps and tunics and joined the ranks of the marchers.

They arrived at the Uhlandsplatz in Merseburg, where Schorn addressed a crowd of some 70,000 or more strikers from factories in the vicinity, together with their wives and children. When Soviet troops advanced on the square, Schorn asked the crowd to remain calm, telling them once more that violence would get them nowhere. At first they heeded him, but soon long pent-up emotions got the upper hand. As Schorn told Joseph Wechsberg,

Some began to shout abuse at the Russians and a few spat on their trucks. I knew that things would get out of hand if we stayed there much longer. I stepped back to talk the matter over with the other strike leaders, and they agreed that we had better break it up.[21]

Turning to the crowd again, he told the strikers to return to their factories but not to resume work. "The people reacted well," reports Wechsberg. "They formed columns and marched off in perfect discipline." [22]

Upon arrival at the Leunawerke, Schorn found Soviet troops in charge. The next night, strike leaders were arrested in their homes, but Schorn had not gone home and thus was able to flee to West Berlin. Even with a heavy Soviet guard and without leaders, however, the Leuna workers continued sitdown strikes for weeks.

As late as February 6, 1954, there continued to be widespread resistance, punctuated with outbursts of vocal protest demanding free elections, from workers throughout East Germany. At the Leunawerke, for example, at a compulsory Communist propaganda meeting to promote the Molotov proposal for German reunification, the workers shouted in unison: "We want free elections first!" In Brandenburg, high-school students were given the Molotov plan as their discussion topic for the day, but they refused to discuss it. There were similar actions in all the major centers of the June revolt, resulting in the formation of a special auxiliary police force made up of picked Communist party members.

As recently as August 1962 the West German newspaper *Bild Zeitung* quoted refugees as saying that there was "deep unrest" in East Germany. In several towns placards appeared, lettered "We want more to eat and we have not forgotten June 17." In Mühlhausen, Soviet tanks were again brought in when metalworkers went on strike to protest food shortages and high work norms. In Eisenach someone painted a rope around the neck of Walter Ulbricht in a huge public portrait. Thus the spirit of resistance continued to flicker long after actual revolt had died out.

In the first two or three days of the 1953 revolt, the insurgents came within an ace of seizing control of the country. In a number of towns, the workers went so far as to take charge of the local administration. H. F. Stille argues persuasively that "without the last-minute intervention of the Russian tank division [on June 18], the workers would have seized party and government headquarters with little chance of escape for the SED [East German Communist] leaders." [23] So widespread was the uprising that the SED's central committee complained that large numbers of party members were doing nothing to suppress it. "Tens of thousands of them sit in their offices, write some papers or other and simply wait," it reported.[24]

Three factors appear to account for the failure of the revolt. First, the intervention of Soviet tanks. Second, the failure of the West to aid the East German workers (U.S. officials obstructed efforts by RIAS to broadcast a call for a general strike). Third, the failure of the insurgents either to obtain and use sufficient armed force to repulse the Soviet tanks or to maintain a nonviolent discipline that might have disarmed the Soviet tankmen.

It is the last of these points that of course concerns us in this study. We have already seen that it was possible in this Stalinist country to begin and to sustain a massive resistance. We have seen that it was possible to neutralize or win over armed opponents in the police and the army and even in the Polish and some Soviet forces. And we have seen that discipline was maintained and orders obeyed—up to a point. This point is where we begin to enter the area of clear-cut nonviolence. Despite generally good organization, the East German workers had no deep-going understanding or resolve to stay nonviolent. In many cases they displayed great courage. As Stille says: "The workers did not run away when the guns of the Russian tanks were turning against them. They faced them with desperate courage and iron discipline. Politically conscious workers advised their colleagues not to engage in an open and

unequal fight with the Russian forces." [25] But in all except a few instances this advice was not heeded.

Ella Sarre was an instructor in the Freie Deutsche Jugend, the Communist youth organization, who sided with the revolt. Her story is typical of many of the clashes:

A Russian officer stood atop one tank and amiably waved the crowd aside. A hail of stones answered him. Ella was unhappy; she spoke some Russian and would have liked to tell the officer that the workers did not hate him, only his tank—but no parley was possible in the roar of a battle that saw tanks fought with stones and crowbars.[26]

We may admire this reckless courage and audacity, but in realistic terms stones and crowbars and shouted abuse are no match for military armor. Stefan Brant says that "eighteen Soviet officers and men were executed after June 17 for refusing to obey orders." [27] He also observes that even among Soviet tank groups that were not in habitual contact with the Germans but completely isolated in Soviet bases, there were several instances in which the Russians "showed great reluctance to open fire on the strikers." [28] There is no way of estimating the total number of Russian soldiers who acted in ways favorable to the workers, for example, by firing as ordered but aiming to miss. Certainly the total must have been far more than the eighteen who were executed; more even than those like Lieutenant Gregoriev, who escaped, or others who presumably were imprisoned rather than shot. Considering all the factors militating against such defections—the isolation, the stones and crowbars—it is noteworthy that there were so many who acted in this way. And it is certainly cogent to assume that there would have been substantially more if the East German workers had been trained in nonviolence, ready to lose as many lives as they did lose, but as a price for establishing rapport with the majority of Soviet troops who evidently did not know what to think and were stoned instead of persuaded. There was a demonstrated potential, and it was thrown away each time a rock was cast.

If the nonviolent alternative had failed, as well it might have, the outcome could hardly have been worse than the disaster which history records.

Budapest 1956

A few days after the East German revolt began, leaders of the Hungarian Workers Party (Communist) were summoned to Moscow and warned that unless they adopted reforms they faced the prospect of a similar uprising. On their return, they installed Imre Nagy, a Communist moderate, as premier, only to unseat him and expel him from the party two years later.

In Poland, too, currents set in motion by the impact of the East German uprising led to a revolt centered on the city of Poznan—and to a wiser response from Moscow, which replaced Poland's Stalinist government with that of the popular moderate, Wladyslaw Gomulka. This in turn led a group of Hungarian Communist intellectuals to band together as the Petöfi Circle and press for Nagy's reinstatement.

On October 13, 1956, Nagy's party membership was restored, whereupon the Petöfi Circle stepped up its clamor for his return to the premiership, culminating on Monday, October 22, in "an unprecedented series of mass meetings in Budapest's colleges and universities" [29] and a silent demonstration outside the Polish embassy. The university students drew up a list of fourteen demands, including immediate evacuation of all Soviet armed forces, general elections "by universal, secret ballot" and "complete recognition of freedom of opinion and expression." [30] During the night, mimeographed leaflets stating these demands were posted throughout the city and a mass demonstration was set for 3:00 P.M. the next day.

At 12:53 P.M. on October 23 the Communist government broadcast a communiqué forbidding the demonstration, but backed down an hour later when the students refused to abandon their plans. The effect of the ban, while it was in force, was to spur the demonstrators on and add to their ranks thousands

of workers who had not earlier planned to join in, as well as 800 cadets from Petöfi Military Academy. Through the after-noon and early evening they covered a lot of ground, rallying at the Petöfi monument not far from the Radio Building, mov-ing across the Danube to the Jozsef Bem statue and back over to Lajos Kossuth Square, facing the Parliament Buildings. By this time the crowd numbered between 150,000 and 200,000 marchers. They called for Nagy, and after some delay he appeared and tried to calm them. Part of the crowd, which continued to grow, split off and marched to the Stalin Memorial where, with ropes, acetylene torches and tractors, they toppled the huge statue of the Soviet tyrant. Another group of students went to the Radio Building, seeking to have their Fourteen Demands broadcast. The door was barred to them, and when they tried to force their way in, tear gas was used against them by the Communist security police or AVH, who were on guard there.

It is not clear how the order to open fire came to be given, but on the evening of October 23 AVH men began shooting at demonstrators in several parts of the city. Almost immediately there were defections from the Hungarian Army. These and munitions workers passed arms to insurgents who formed themselves into units of Freedom Fighters. Shooting between AVH detachments and Freedom Fighters raged through the night and were to continue for a week.

It was in such an atmosphere, on the morning of October 24, that tens of thousands of students, factory workers and white-collar employees marched down the boulevards to the Parliament Buildings, resuming their demonstrations. Along the way, they were joined by Soviet tanks. "The throng showed no hostility toward the soldiers who manned them," says Meray. "On the contrary, they began to fraternize with them." [31] They explained their cause, their goal of liberty and independence, and the Soviet soldiers listened and smiled, and allowed the Hungarian youths to climb aboard the tanks and plant Hun-garian flags on them.

358 NONVIOLENCE: A CHRISTIAN INTERPRETATION

Peter Fryer, who went to Hungary as a correspondent for the London *Daily Worker* and returned as an anti-Communist, continues the narrative:

Entering Parliament Square they met another Soviet tank which had been sent to fire on them, and this tank, too, turned and joined the demonstration. In the Square were three more Soviet tanks and two armored cars. The crowd went right up to them and began to talk with the soldiers.[32]

These reports are corroborated by John MacCormac of *The New York Times,* who said that in front of the Astoria Hotel the Russian soldiers "shouted that they did not want to fire on unarmed Hungarian workers," [33] and by Endre Marton of the Associated Press, who observed that the fraternizing students and soldiers "were smiling uneasily." [34]

An AVH officer appeared and ordered the crowd to disperse. He threatened them, and the crowd responded with a torrent of abuse: "Pig! Assassin! Down with the AVH!"

These epithets may have been well-aimed, but were they well-timed? From the roof of the Ministry of Agriculture, across the street, the AVH troops opened fire on the crowd. Presumably some of the fraternizers were still sitting on Russian tanks. In any case, as Meray reports,

The Russians, not knowing who the men were who had fired into the square . . . thought they had been ambushed—that the fraternal appeals and embraces to which they had been subjected were aimed at disarming their vigilance and laying them open to a surprise attack at the moment when they least expected it. Accordingly, they fired mainly at the AVH, but also into the crowd of demonstrators.

The square was soon strewn with the dead and wounded. According to many witnesses, the dead alone must have numbered between 170 and 180.[35]

Consistently, the AVH forces comprised the mainstay of Hungarian Stalinism. In Budapest they were increasingly backed up by Soviet armor. But even here, under provocative and ambiguous conditions not calculated to encourage fraterni-

zation, the noted Italian orchestra conductor, Mario Rossi, who left Budapest on October 26, said: "All eye-witnesses agree absolutely that Russian troops as well as Hungarians joined the insurgents." [36] One such eye-witness, Andor Heller, reported this incident:

A few blocks from us there is a bridge. As I came by, several Freedom Fighters, together with some bystanders, were near one end of it. A Red Army tank was rumbling up, but instead of firing, the driver, a young Ukrainian, stuck his head out and waved. He stopped alongside our boys, jumped down and walked away. Three of the Freedom Fighters got in and moved off toward firing in the center of the city.[37]

This event and others like it were all the more remarkable since the Hungarians had no pretensions of nonviolence. In Budapest after October 24, few attempts at fraternization were made. More often, Hungarian youths approached tanks with Molotov cocktails or paving stones, seeking to disable the vehicle and kill its driver rather than to win both for the cause.

That side of the struggle is well-known—the savagery of the AVH, the heavy reliance of the Freedom Fighters on guerrilla tactics and the frequent excesses of the Soviet troops. But this pattern applied chiefly to Budapest and a few other places, such as Magyaróvár, where 5,000 unarmed demonstrators were the targets of machine guns and hand grenades wielded by AVH men, who killed eighty-five and wounded an unknown number of the townspeople. Although refraining from initiating violence, the people soon turned to the Hungarian Army barracks for weapons and stormed the AVH headquarters. AVH Lieutenant Jozsef Stefko, who had given the order to fire and had been wounded in the fighting, was tracked down in his hospital, brought out on a stretcher, and kicked and trampled to death.

Elsewhere there was little AVH strength, hence little provocation for incidents bringing Freedom Fighters and Soviet troops into conflict. In Györ, for example, on October 27

"there was a strong concentration of Soviet troops, who did not attack the insurgents, not even to defend themselves when demonstrators pelted them with stones." [38] A broadcast over Radio Vienna relayed information from the liberated city of Miskolc:

Radio Miskolc has called on the Hungarian authorities to grant political asylum to all Soviet soldiers who left their units during the last few days and sided with the Freedom Fighters, adding that there were many Soviet soldiers who would claim political asylum if granted it.[39]

By October 28, Soviet tanks commanded all key points in Budapest but the Freedom Fighters were in control in virtually all the rest of the country and with the accession of seven divisions that had held back until now, the Hungarian Army was clearly on their side. Political events were keeping pace, for Nagy had formed a government that included two non-Communists and now promised reforms, including dissolution of the AVH. Given the demonstrated unreliability of the Soviet garrisons outside the capital, the USSR deemed it wise to pull its forces out of Budapest. They began their withdrawal on October 29 and completed it on October 31.

Meanwhile, Nagy declared that the Freedom Fighters were to become the new national guard. Social Democratic, Smallholders and Peasant Party newspapers resumed publication for the first time since 1945 and Jozsef Cardinal Mindszenty was released from prison. For the next four days, Hungary was free. So definite was the fact that Free Petöfi Radio announced that "members of a Soviet battalion in the Gyongyos area have handed their arms over to the civilian population, stating that they do not wish to fight the Hungarian people." [40] Cardinal Mindszenty commented on the fact that "very many Russian soldiers" had been among those who fought against the old Stalinist regime.

The revolution appeared to be clearly victorious. Pending free elections, Nagy formed a new government made up of

three Communists, eight representatives of parties formerly banned, and one independent.

Then at dawn on Sunday, November 4, the Soviet Union invaded Hungary with 6,000 tanks and 200,000 troops that had reportedly been secretly shifted to the Hungarian border from Soviet Central Asia. They struck instantly into Budapest, where the free radio gave its last frantic SOS alarm at 8:00 A.M. and then fell silent, speaking again at 5:00 P.M., no longer free.

Throughout the country and in isolated strongholds within the capital, the Hungarians maintained a brave but hopeless battle against the invaders. On November 9 the last of the free radio stations was silenced, and with the collapse of the Csepel Island stronghold in Budapest, large-scale fighting was over. Untold thousands of Hungarian youths were deported to the USSR. General Pal Maleter, leader of the Freedom Fighters, was lured to a parley with Soviet generals and taken prisoner, to be executed along with other leaders of free Hungary. Nagy was abducted, spirited out of the country and held in Rumania until June 15, 1958, when he was executed after a purported secret trial which probably never occurred at all. Others met a similar fate.

Moscow did not seek to reimpose the severe Stalinist regime of Matyas Rakosi, however, but installed as its puppet the moderate Janos Kadar, who had been a member of Nagy's Communist cabinet and a man who had been jailed along with Nagy during the height of Stalinist oppression. To Kadar was given the task of doing what Nagy had been supposed to do—institute reforms while keeping Hungary firmly under Communist control.

With the collapse of armed resistance, Hungarian workers held fast for weeks to the general strike they had begun on October 24-25. In Budapest in early November, appeals framed in tricolored stripes appeared on walls. A typical text, written about November 10, was this one: "Because enemy action is mainly causing the civilian population to suffer, it is necessary to put an end to desperate armed resistance. It is

necessary to follow a course of passive, moral resistance." [41]

Such resistance was impossible to maintain for a protracted period on the economic plane. After five weeks, the workers' general strike ebbed to seventy per cent effectiveness, gradually declining to a sporadic level by the turn of the year. The Hungarian writers, who had sparked the revolt, maintained a silence that lasted for more than a year. In January, François Fejto wrote:

This strike still continues. One seeks in vain the signature of any reputed writer in all the official newspapers and periodicals. The voluminous Christmas issue of *Nepszabadsag* was published without a single article or poem or story by any known living writer. [42]

Eventually, most of the Petöfi Circle men who neither fled to the West nor were executed made their peace with the Kadar regime. Several who were imprisoned were released on parole in March 1960. Among them was Tibor Dery, who maintained his silence for six years and never recanted. His first story published since the uprising appeared in the fall of 1962. It described the last days of a Hungarian professor who decided to escape after the revolt of 1956 was crushed, but changed his mind within sight of the Austrian frontier. Tired, the professor sits down and freezes to death.

During August and September 1962 the Kadar government carried out a purge of Stalinists that included the expulsion from the Communist party of Rakosi, Gerö and others whom the 1956 revolt had unseated, and in 1963 Cardinal Mindszenty was enabled to step out of the U.S. Embassy, where he had taken refuge during the Soviet invasion. Thus, gradually, in six or seven years, Kadar moved to restore much of what had been won in as many days under Nagy.

Taking a shorter perspective on the Hungarian revolution, Professor Hugh Seton-Watson drew these lessons from it:

The Hungarians have showed us that a united nation can unseat a totalitarian regime in two days.

The second lesson is that the forces which led the revolution were

precisely those on which the regime had counted for support. . . .

The third factor of course is the Hungarian army . . . built since 1947. . . .

Intellectual youth, workers and army joined in the Hungarian revolution. The rest of the nation . . . were of course behind them. Only the security police were against, and they were quickly overcome.[43]

Conclusion, or Beginning?

What, if anything, is the relevance of nonviolent action to Hungary's struggle for freedom? First, as a matter of record, it is important to note with Seton-Watson that the unsuspected possibility was actualized of marshaling one-sixth of the population of the capital city in demonstrations that were initially peaceful. In addition, we have seen the extent to which, even amid confusion and gunfire or stone-throwing, occupation troops showed a potential for moral conversion either to solidarity with the insurgents or to effective neutrality. These facts alone are of sufficient weight to warrant the inclusion of this episode in our study.

From here on, we have no further answers but a number of speculations that might be fruitful. One thing seems certain: with training and discipline in nonviolent conduct, the Freedom Fighters could have won considerably more Soviet troops to their side. More problematical is the question of the justly hated AVH forces. It is hard to imagine their being won over. Yet it was in fact impossible to win them at all, or to neutralize them, by venting verbal hatred on them, let alone shooting. Probably the possibilities of success in this direction would have hinged in part on a slower tempo for the whole course of events and a more restricted range of immediate goals. Given the Soviet acceptance of Poznan and Gomulka, there is reason to think that the perfidious onslaught of November 4 could have been avoided if Nagy had been permitted to consolidate earlier gains before moving to the extreme of leaving the Soviet

bloc, with all that this implied, including the panic it must have induced in Moscow.

In short, it is a fact of history that the four days of freedom which Hungary obtained through a mixture of moral suasion and armed struggle were only part of a process that led through the Soviets' ruthless attack on November 4 to its culmination in the Kadar reforms of 1962, at great cost in human lives. Nonviolence could not have brought freedom—lasting freedom—in two days or in ten days any more than armed revolt. What was in fact accomplished might have been gained sooner and at less cost by consciously adhering, despite the AVH, to the peaceful demonstrations of October 22-23 and capitalizing on the losses suffered from the AVH, making a moral appeal to Nagy to call them to heel, or seeking support from the Soviet troops.

It is easy to speculate from the distant perspective of a six-year retrospect, when none of the options are open. Given all the many complex circumstances, none of the events that came to pass could have been anticipated and adequately provided for. This is true not only of Hungary but of all the historic episodes we have studied, in this and other categories. The past is past; let the dead bury their dead. It remains for us the living to extract from it the historical generalities of possibility and limitation to flesh out the bones of theory and thus equip ourselves as best we can to face the tasks that confront us in our own time and place. Among the conditions that will determine the history that we will make are these lessons from the past, and our assimilation of them.

REFERENCES IN CHAPTER 21

1   Leon Trotsky: *The History of the Russian Revolution* (New York: Simon and Schuster, Inc., 1932), Vol. 1, p. 105.
2   *Ibid.*, p. 108.
3   *Ibid.*
4   *Ibid.*

5 N. N. Sukhanov: *The Russian Revolution 1917* (London: Oxford, 1955), p. 6.
6 See Arthur Griffith: *The Resurrection of Hungary* (Dublin: Duffy and Co., 1904), p. 27.
7 Quoted in *Peace News* (London), September 7, 1962.
8 September 1, 1962.
9 Ernst Reuter: "The Berlin Revolt" in *The New Leader*, June 29, 1953, p. 2.
10 H. F. Stille: "The East German Workers' Revolt" in *The New International*, May-June 1953, p. 141.
11 *The New York Times*, June 20, 1953.
12 Stefan Brant: *The East German Rising* (London: Thames and Hudson, 1953), p. 193.
13 Melvin J. Lasky: "Germany's 'June Days'" in *The New Leader*, July 6, 1953, p. 7.
14 Rainer Hildebrandt: *The Explosion* (Boston: Little, Brown & Co., 1955), p. 50.
15 Norbert Muhlen: "The People Speak in a People's Democracy" in *The Reporter*, September 1, 1953, p. 14.
16 See Lasky, *op. cit.*, p. 7.
17 See Hildebrandt: *op. cit.*, pp. 139-145.
18 *The New York Times*, July 4, 1953.
19 Don Doane, Associated Press dispatch datelined Berlin, June 22, 1953.
20 Quoted in Joseph Wechsberg: "A Reporter in Germany" in *The New Yorker*, August 29, 1953, p. 38.
21 *Ibid.*, p. 49.
22 *Ibid.*, p. 50.
23 Stille, *op. cit.*, p. 141.
24 Quoted in Gaston Coblentz, dispatch from Berlin dated June 22, in *New York Herald Tribune*, June 23, 1953.
25 Stille, *op. cit.*, p. 141.
26 Hildebrandt, *op. cit.*, p. 103.
27 Brant, *op. cit.*, p. 151.
28 *Ibid.*
29 Tibor Meray: *Thirteen Days That Shook the Kremlin* (New York: Frederick A. Praeger, Inc., 1959), p. 65.
30 Full text in *ibid.*, p. 77.
31 *Ibid.*, p. 109f.
32 Peter Fryer: *Hungarian Tragedy* (London: Dobson, 1956), p. 46.
33 *The New York Times*, October 27, 1953.
34 Associated Press dispatch dated October 25, 1953.
35 Meray, *op. cit.*, p. 110f.
36 Dispatch from Torino, Italy, in *News Chronicle* (London), October 29, 1953. Quoted in Melvin J. Lasky, ed.: *The Hungarian Revolution* (New York: Frederick A. Praeger, Inc., 1957), p. 90.
37 Andor Heller: *No More Comrades* (Chicago: Henry Regnery Co., 1957), p. 70.
38 Dispatch from Nickelsdorf in *Neue Zürcher Zeitung*, October 29, 1956, quoted in Lasky, *op. cit.*, p. 102.
39 Quoted in Lasky, *op. cit.*, p. 102.
40 Quoted in *ibid.*, p. 223
41 Quoted by Viktor Woroszylski in *France Observateur*, January 3, 1957.

42 François Fejto in *France Observateur*, January 24, 1957. Quoted in Lasky, *op. cit.*, p. 304.

43 Hugh Seton-Watson: "Eruption in East Europe" in *Commentary*, December 1956, p. 521f. (Copyright is held by the American Jewish Committee.)

Glossary

Agapaic. From Greek verb *agapaon,* "to love"—adjectival coinage signifying *agapē* (q.v.).

Agapē. New Testament Greek word for "active love."

Ahimsa. Sanskrit word for Hindu concept of nonharm, translated by Gandhi as "nonviolence."

ANC. African National Congress.

Cadre. Person acting under a discipline, e.g., of nonviolent conduct.

Civil disobedience. Deliberate refusal to comply with laws considered unjust, or with laws enacted by an unjust government.

Civil resistance. Strategic application of civil disobedience.

CORE. Congress of Racial Equality.

CPP. Convention People's Party (Ghana).

Defiance campaign. South African application of civil disobedience.

Direct action. Social action exerting direct pressure as distinguished from political, legislative, judicial or other types of indirect action.

FOR. Fellowship of Reconciliation.

Force. Action, armed or otherwise, usually employing proportionate restraint under law.

NAACP. National Association for the Advancement of Colored People.

Noncooperation. A form of passive resistance.

Nonresistance. A type of nonviolence which does not overtly resist but combats evil with agapaic love.

Nonviolence. A generic category of actions and attitudes that deliberately abstain from using force and violence in situations to which they might be applied.

367

Nonviolent direct action. A type of nonviolence which usually operates assertively, by making incursions into disputed areas, as exemplified by the sit-in.

PAC. Pan-African Congress (South Africa).

Passive resistance. A type of nonviolence which acts by noncooperation, withdrawal, etc.

Positive action. Nkrumah's term for passive resistance.

Satyagraha. Gandhi's concept of nonviolent action, often translated as "soul force" or "the power of truth."

Satyagrahi. One who uses *satyagraha;* a Gandhian cadre.

Shanti sena. Peace army as conceived by Gandhi, Bhave and others.

SCLC. Southern Christian Leadership Conference.

SNCC. Student Nonviolent Coordinating Committee.

Unviolent. Term used to designate acts which do not happen to be violent, as contrasted with those that employ nonviolence.

Violence. Illegitimate or disproportionate harmful acts or attitudes.

Bibliography

The following is a brief, select list of books for further study.

Those included are largely theoretical, though some contain historical cases which have been omitted from this book. As noted, some of these books contain one or more chapters that are of interest; some may be read in their entirety. The immense Gandhian literature is represented by only a few titles; a more extensive list will be found in Mayer, listed below. For documentation of historical episodes presented in this book, see the chapter footnotes.

BALLOU, ADIN: *Christian Non-Resistance* (Philadelphia: McKim, 1846). The impact of Ballou's idea of "moral resistance" on Tolstoy and Gandhi did much to condition Twentieth-Century conceptions of nonviolence. Of scholarly historical interest—not for the general reader.

BONDURANT, JOAN V.: *Conquest of Violence* (Princeton University Press, 1958). A sympathetic and careful analysis of Gandhian *satyagraha,* with studies of five key Indian campaigns.

BONHOEFFER, DIETRICH: *The Cost of Discipleship* (New York: The Macmillan Co., 1960). The chapters on "Revenge" and "The Enemy" are highly pertinent to an understanding of nonviolent conduct for Christians.

CAPITINI, ALDO: *La Nonviolenza, Oggi* (Milano: Comunità, 1962). A general study along pacifist-Gandhian lines with appendixes documenting noncooperation under the Mussolini regime, Italian peace marches in 1960 and 1961, etc.

CASE, CLARENCE MARSH: *Non-Violent Coercion* (New York: Century Co., 1923). A pioneer sociological study that evaluates techniques of nonviolence and presents a useful brief history

of religious nonresistance, conscientious objection and Gandhi's early campaigns.

CORMAN, LOUIS: *La Non-Violence* (Paris: Stock, 1949). Of chief interest are the chapters on Gandhi and Christianity, nonviolence in daily life and in the education of children. By a noted psychologist.

GALTUNG, JOHAN: *Forsvar Uten Militærwesen* (Oslo, Folkereisning Mot Krig, c. 1959). A pacifist booklet which includes a useful chapter on nonviolent national defense. By a noted social scientist.

GANDHI, MOHANDAS K.: *Nonviolent Resistance* (New York: Schocken, Books, 1962). A collection of newspaper articles from *Young India* and *Harijan,* rooted in the Indian struggle, which represents the best of Gandhi's thinking on questions of theory. Also published in India under the title *Satyagraha*.

GREGG, RICHARD B.: *The Power of Nonviolence* (Nyack, N.Y.: Fellowship Publications, 1959). Second revised edition of a book that has had considerable influence since it first appeared in 1934. The chapter on "moral jiu-jitsu" is of particular interest.

HERSHBERGER, GUY F.: *War, Peace and Nonresistance* (Scottdale, Pa.: Herald Press, 1944). A cogent presentation of Christian nonresistance as distinguished from modern pacifism and nonviolent resistance.

KING, MARTIN LUTHER, JR.: *Strength to Love* (New York: Harper & Row, 1963). The autobiographical essay, "Pilgrimage to Nonviolence," and sermons on "Love in Action" and "Loving Your Enemies" are especially valuable but by no means the only chapters worth reading.

KUPER, LEO: *Passive Resistance in South Africa* (New Haven: Yale University Press, 1957). The chapter on "The Sociological Nature of Passive Resistance" is of primary importance for theory.

LAKEY, GEORGE RUSSELL: *The Sociological Mechanisms of Nonviolent Action* (Philadelphia: University of Pennsylvania, unpublished M.A. thesis, 1962). A study which builds on the work of Case and Gregg and adds much detail from subsequent scholarship.

LEWIS, JOHN: *The Case Against Pacifism* (London: Allen & Unwin, 1940). A Marxist critique which embodies a healthy corrective for sentimental interpretations of purportedly nonviolent historical episodes.

LIGT, BARTHÉLEMY DE: *The Conquest of Violence* (New York: E. P. Dutton & Co., Inc., 1938). Highly propagandistic and largely outdated, this book nevertheless includes a chapter on "Lessons of History" which can serve as a basis for research. Not all of his examples will withstand scrutiny.

MAYER, PETER, ed.: *The Nonviolent Tradition* (New York: Orion Press, 1964). An anthology of writings on peace rather than nonviolence, it nevertheless contains some interesting material and an extensive bibliography.

MAYR, KASPAR: *Der Andere Weg* (Nürnberg, Germany: Glock und Lutz, 1957). An exposition of Christian pacifism which includes insights about nonviolence.

MITCHELL, GLENFORD E., and PEACE, WILLIAM H., III, eds.: *The Angry Black South* (New York: Corinth Books, Inc., 1962). The chapter on "Nonviolence" by Robert Brookins Gore, a seasoned cadre, is well worth study.

MURTY, K. S., and BOUQUET, A. C.: *Studies in the Problems of Peace* (New York: Asia Books, 1960). The chapter on "The Philosophies of Ahimsa and Forgiveness" embodies useful information as well as a penetrating critique of nonviolence.

MUSTE, A. J.: *Nonviolence in an Aggressive World* (New York: Harper & Brothers, 1940). A discussion of the relevance of nonviolence to the political and economic situation of the United States before World War II, with emphasis on labor struggles.

NANDA, B. R.: *Mahatma Gandhi* (Boston: Beacon Press, Inc., 1958). Probably the best brief biography of Gandhi as a leader on the socio-political scene.

RAMSEY, PAUL: *Christian Ethics and the Sit-In* (New York: Association Press, 1961). A conservatively oriented brief critique of some of the principles of nonviolence, with special attention to civil disobedience.

RÉGAMEY, PIE: *Non-Violence et Conscience Chrétienne* (Paris: Cerf, 1958). An incisive theological study from a largely

Thomistic perspective, which includes a detailed and balanced inquiry into a variety of questions posed by nonviolence.

SHARP, GENE: *The Politics of Nonviolent Action* (unpublished book manuscript). A monumental study of the techniques and dynamics of nonviolence with particular reference to its relationship to political power. The author is a sociologist at Oxford University who has done important studies such as *Gandhi Wields the Weapon of Moral Power* and *Gandhi Faces the Storm* (Ahmedabad: Navajivan).

SIBLEY, MULFORD Q., ed.: *The Quiet Battle* (Garden City, N.Y.: Doubleday & Co., Anchor Books, 1963). An anthology of classic texts on nonviolence, including documentation of several historic episodes, chosen by a noted political scientist.

TENDULKAR, D. G.: *Mahatma* (Bombay: Jhaveri & Tendulkar, 1954). This eight-volume biography is the most comprehensive study of Gandhi's career and includes an extensive bibliography.

TROCMÉ, ANDRÉ: *Jésus-Christ et la Révolution Non Violente* (Geneva: Labor et Fides, 1961). A biblical study which examines the teachings of Jesus in their historical context, contrasting them with the way of the Zealots and other sects and arguing persuasively for the relevance of Christian nonviolence to social struggle. By a French Reformed pastor.

WEINBERG, ARTHUR and LILA, eds.: *Instead of Violence* (New York: Grossman, 1963). Although chiefly an anthology of writings on peace, this book also includes brief pieces on nonviolence, from Lao-tzu to Danilo Dolci.

WOLFF, OTTO: *Mahatma und Christus* (Berlin: Lettner, 1955). A thorough-going and generally critical study of Gandhi's life, character and teachings. By a German Evangelical theologian.

WRIGHT, QUINCY, et. al., eds.: *Preventing World War Three* (New York: Simon & Schuster, Inc., 1963). The chapter by Arne Naess on "Nonmilitary Defense" is highly relevant.

Index

Disciples of Christ, 210
discipline, 79, 155ff, 194
dual power, 87, 91, 93
Duckwitz, Georg Ferdinand, 253
dvoevlastie, 87

egotism, 186
empathy, 146, 158f, 165, 177
eros, 25
estrangement, 173, 185f, 188
evil, 158
existential psychology, 32
expediency, 62

fasting, 57, 148, 170, 174, 265
fearlessness, 171
Feit, Edward, 283
Fellowship of Reconciliation, 298, 301, 306
Ferré, Nels F. S., 195ff, 199
Finch, Roy, 120
Finland, 244-250
force, 34, 63, 165
  manual, 93, 107
forgiveness, 161
Francesco d'Assisi, 29, 197
Frank, Jerome D., 109f
Freedom Charter, 272
Freedom Fighters, 357-361, 363
Freedom Highways, 319
freedom rides, 313-319
freedom task force, 319
Fry, Anna Ruth, 219f
Fugitive Slave Law, 73

Galtung, Johan, 104ff, 172
Gandhi, Manilal, 270

Gandhi, Mohandas K., 17, 25, 29, 38, 46, 48, 54, 69, 79, 91f, 119, 139, 169ff, 174, 193, 197f, 262, 265, 291, 297, 301, 351
Gbedemah, K. A., 295f
Ghana, 85ff, 287-297
"going limp," 56, 65, 163
Gollancz, Victor, 220
Gottwald, Norman K., 110ff
Greensboro, N.C., 306, 312
Gregg, Richard B., 156ff, 198, 306
Gregory, Dick, 334
Griffith, Arthur, 230, 238, 348
Guardini, Romano, 160, 171, 178f, 196f
guilt, 158, 161, 186
Gunther, John, 272
gymnastics, 166

hate, 158, 161, 185, 199
Heller, Andor, 359
Hildebrandt, Rainer, 351
Hinduism, 25ff, 29f
Hitler, Adolf, 206, 258, 291, 297, 350
holism, 62f, 93, 121, 169f
holy, 178
hostility, 57, 161, 186
Hughan, Jessie Wallace, 114
Hungary, 84, 230-242, 348, 356-364
  Reformed Church of, 231

in-group attitude, 199
India, 85ff, 91f, 151
indifference, 185f

$$\frac{\begin{array}{r} 45^{00} \\ 20 \end{array}}{90.00}$$